American Education
An Introduction to Teaching

American Education
An Introduction to Teaching

Sixth Edition

John H. Johansen
Northern Illinois University

•

Harold W. Collins
Northern Illinois University

•

James A. Johnson
Northern Illinois University

Wm. C. Brown Publishers

Book Team

Editor *Chris Rogers*
Designer *Laurie J. Entringer*
Art Editor *Janice M. Roerig*
Production Editor *Diane S. Clemens*
Permissions Editor *Vicki Krug*
Visuals Processor *Vickie Werner*

WCB **Wm. C. Brown Publishers**

President *G. Franklin Lewis*
Vice President, Editor-in-Chief *George Wm. Bergquist*
Vice President, Director of Production *Beverly Kolz*
Vice President, National Sales Manager *Bob McLaughlin*
Director of Marketing *Thomas E. Doran*
Marketing Communications Manager *Edward Bartell*
Marketing Manager *Kathy Law Laube*
Manager of Visuals and Design *Faye M. Schilling*
Production Editorial Manager *Colleen A. Yonda*
Production Editorial Manager *Julie A. Kennedy*
Publishing Services Manager *Karen J. Slaght*

The credits section for this book begins on page 493, and is considered an extension of the copyright page.

Printed in the United States of America by Wm. C. Brown Publishers, 2460 Kerper Boulevard, Dubuque, IA 52001

10 9 8 7 6 5 4 3 2 1

93059

Contents

Section

1

Becoming a Teacher

Section

2

The Teaching Profession

Section

3

The Role of Education in the United States

Section

4

The Learning Process

Section

5

The Organization and Governance of Public Education in the United States

Point of View

Research Findings

Research Finding 1 Teachers who set and communicate high expectations to all their students obtain greater academic performance from those students than teachers who set low expectations. *Chapter 1   15*

Research Finding 2 Many children who are physically handicapped or have emotional or learning problems can be given an appropriate education in well-supported regular classes and schools. *Chapter 2   33*

Research Finding 3 Schools contribute to their students' academic achievement by establishing, communicating, and enforcing fair and consistent discipline policies. *Chapter 3   69*

Research Finding 4 The most important characteristics of effective schools are strong instructional leadership, a safe and orderly climate, school-wide emphasis on basic skills, high teacher expectations for student achievement, and continuous assessment of pupil progress. *Chapter 4   90*

Research Finding 5 How much time students are actively engaged in learning contributes strongly to their achievement. The amount of time available for learning is determined by the instructional and management skills of the teacher and the priorities set by the school administration. *Chapter 4   96*

Research Finding 6 Teachers welcome professional suggestions about improving their work, but they rarely receive them. *Chapter 6   142*

Research Finding 7 Belief in the value of hard work, the importance of personal responsibility, and the importance of education itself contributes to greater success in school. *Chapter 8   175*

Research Finding 8 A school staff that provides encouragement and personalized attention, and monitors daily attendance can reduce unexcused absences and class-cutting. *Chapter 9   207*

Research Finding 9 Skimpy requirements and declining enrollments in history classes are contributing to a decline in students' knowledge of the past. *Chapter 10   246*

Research Finding 10 Good character is encouraged by surrounding students with good adult examples and by building upon natural occasions for learning and practicing good character. Skillful educators know how to organize their schools, classrooms, and lessons to foster such examples. *Chapter 11   259*

Research Finding 11 Children's understanding of the relationship between being smart and hard work changes as they grow. *Chapter 12   281*

Research Finding 12 Handicapped high school students who seek jobs after graduation are more likely to find them when schools prepare them for careers and private sector businesses provide on-the-job training. *Chapter 13   310*

Research Finding 13 The use of libraries enhances reading skills and encourages independent learning. *Chapter 14   334*

Research Finding 14 Advancing gifted students at a faster pace results in their achieving more than similarly gifted students who are taught at a normal rate. *Chapter 16   392*

Research Finding 15 Successful principals establish policies that create an orderly environment and support effective instruction. *Chapter 17   431*

List of Figures

List of Tables

Preface

This book was first published in 1971. Since that time, society and the schools have changed. So has the book. The original intent of the book was to introduce the reader to the profession of teaching. That intent remains the same. The sixth edition (1990) of *American Education: An Introduction to Teaching* is a thorough and extensive revision of the previous edition. New features that have been added include: two new chapters, one dealing with effective teaching, the other with the use of computers in the classroom; substantial content about discipline in chapter 3; twelve appendixes; an enlarged glossary; a new introductory page for each of the eighteen chapters featuring a preview statement, chapter objectives, and recommended enrichment experiences; a new feature entitled "Research Findings"—fifteen new presentations throughout the book describing recent research which provides practical suggestions for classroom teachers; and a greater emphasis on teacher empowerment and school-based management— both of which were advocated by reform reports and provide teachers with greater opportunities to participate in decision-making at the local school level.

This book has five sections arranged in the following sequence: "Becoming a Teacher," "The Teaching Profession," "The Role of Education in the United States," "The Learning Process," "The Organization and Administration of Public Education in the United States." The material presented in the book is designed to help individuals decide whether teaching could be a satisfying career for them. We started this book with "Becoming a Teacher" and "The Teaching Profession" because the material presented in those sections and chapters is likely to be of immediate interest to those considering teaching as a career; they also provide a frame of reference for the sections that follow. The nature and organization of the book, however, is such that content can be presented in differing sequences to accommodate various course structures.

The first seven chapters are particularly pertinent to teaching as a career choice. Those chapters provide information about the importance of education and teaching, public attitudes toward public schools and teachers, why teachers become teachers and why they leave teaching, alternative careers in education, teacher preparation programs, alternative certification, the roles of teachers, maintaining classroom discipline, effective teaching and teachers, teacher employability, rewards and challenges of teaching, and teacher organizations.

Section 3, "The Role of Education in the United States," presents an overview of the past and present goals of education in our society, and the expectations of both society and individuals for education. It also addresses the critical social problems in today's schools; the history of education thought and the persistent issues of education as related to the contemporary scene; and the current attitudes toward schools with respect to both traditional and progressive beliefs about education.

Section 4, "The Learning Process," includes information about the nature of learners, the nature of curriculum, and the instructional resources available to teachers today. Topics such as individual differences, self-perception, variations in ability, maturation rate, child growth and development, motivation and learning are discussed from the teacher's point of view. A wide range of curriculum topics are also presented in this section of the book. The instructional resources that educators utilize are discussed, with emphasis placed on the most recent technology such as instructional television, laser videodiscs, and computers. In fact, an entirely new chapter is devoted to the use of computers in the classroom.

Section 5, "The Organization and Administration of Public Education in the United States," deals with the purposes of the various levels of education from preprimary programs through adult education, including home instruction and private education. The governance and legal basis of education at the federal, state, and local levels are discussed, along with the financial aspects of the public educational enterprise.

Pedagogical study aids in the textbook include: brief quotations that stimulate thinking and reinforce content which appear throughout the book; charts, graphs, tables, photos, and examples which help the reader identify with and better understand the content. The discussion in each chapter closes with a brief, pertinent article selected to stimulate thought. In some instances these articles provide more detailed information about a topic, and in other instances they introduce different perspectives to the topics discussed in their respective chapters. The articles reflect the views of college professors, practicing teachers and other professionals, and school board members. Bibliographic information and discussion questions conclude each chapter.

The textbook has a supplementary manual, *Instructor's Manual to Accompany American Education: An Introduction to Teaching*. A significant addition to the manual in this edition is the availability of computerized test questions which are made available free of charge. This computerized test pack features a wide variety of test questions covering all eighteen chapters of the book. An extended scoring and item analysis service is also available for a moderate price. The manual also contains instructional objectives for each chapter in the book, an outline presenting the major points and topics discussed, and transparency masters. The suggested teaching aids in the manual provide an additional resource for instructors using this textbook.

American Education: An Introduction to Teaching has been shaped by the authors' experiences as teachers and administrators at all levels of education. The contributions made by the readers of earlier editions, the opinions of colleagues and students, and the evaluations of many experienced reviewers have been incorporated into this edition. Sincere appreciation is expressed to all of these people and to the many authors and publishers who granted us permission to use their materials in this revision. Special recognition is given to Nita Collins for her role in editing and typing the manuscripts.

We gratefully acknowledge the following reviewers for their assistance with this edition:

- Franklin Parker
  Western Carolina University
- Ross Underwood
  Northeastern State University
- Melva Burke
  Pfeiffer College
- Raymond L. King
  Samford University
- Rosalyn Ruffner
  Kentucky Christian College
- Helen Overbo
  University of North Dakota
- James Washington
  South Carolina State College
- Donald Schmitz
  University of Wisconsin–Eau Claire

American Education
An Introduction to Teaching

Becoming a Teacher

The teaching profession and education, as it has operated in the past two decades, are undergoing change and will continue to do so in the next few years. The changes were triggered by the publication of more than thirty-five reports in 1983–1988 about the status of education in the United States. The report that had a strong and immediate impact was *A Nation at Risk: The Imperative for Educational Reform,* published in 1983 by the National Commission on Excellence in Education. That report proposed major reform recommendations, as did many others. Recommendations from the many reports are discussed throughout this book.

Teaching as a career is viewed more positively today than it was five years ago. The public attitudes toward education are upbeat with 64 percent of the public school parents awarding their local teachers with grades of A and B. Morale of teachers is high with 85 percent of the teachers indicating that they are satisfied with their jobs. Teaching has, in fact, been a satisfying career for many people and will continue to be for many people in the future. There are, however, some indicators of dissatisfaction. These include, among others, low salaries, poor working conditions, and the low standard of the profession. Higher salaries for teachers have been recommended in almost all the recent reports about education.

Chapter 1 aims to help individuals decide whether or not teaching may be a satisfying career for them.

What is teaching like? How can persons determine whether or not teaching would be a desirable and satisfying career for them? What do teacher training programs consist of? What do teachers do as they practice their chosen profession? What is effective teaching? How can discipline be maintained? What opportunities are available for work as an educator outside the traditional classroom setting in public and private schools? This section of the book attempts to provide direct answers to questions like these. It provides suggestions for ways in which prospective teachers can assess their interest in and qualifications for teaching. It encourages action, thinking, and reflection on teaching as a career.

Like many careers, teaching requires at least a minimum of four years of undergraduate work for the earning of an entry-level certificate. Some teacher education programs require five years including an internship before a permanent certificate will be granted.

The earlier individuals can determine whether or not teaching is for them, the easier it is to change career direction without setbacks. Teaching is not for everybody. It requires a commitment to become a teacher and dedication to remain one. Successful teaching requires enthusiasm. It is hoped that this section of the book can help you determine whether or not teaching is the career for you. If some determine that teaching is for them, and they become teachers, enjoying productive and satisfying careers, then they, their students, and society will all benefit. If others determine that teaching is not for them, then they, the students they might have worked with, and society are all better off.

Is Teaching a Career for You?

Objectives

After studying this chapter, you should be able to:

- Explain why education is important to society and an investment for society.

- Describe the public's attitudes about the success of education in the United States.

- Describe the public's attitudes and their satisfaction with teachers.

- List the reasons why teachers become teachers and why they leave teaching.

- Identify the characteristics of successful teachers.

- Recognize ways to verify an interest in teaching.

- List three recommendations that might improve the status of teaching as a profession.

- Identify alternative careers in education.

- Explain education as an economic investment.

- Articulate a personal assessment of teaching as a career.

- Describe the characteristics of a profession, and recommend changes for education and for teachers that could make teaching an authentic profession.

Enrichment Experiences

The following experiences will help you determine whether teaching is a career for you:

- Interview early childhood, elementary, secondary, or special education teachers to discuss how they feel about teaching as a career.

- Visit a classroom and after the visit record your feelings and questions about teaching. Discuss your comments and suggestions with your peers, professors, or former teachers.

- Inquire of practicing teachers how they feel about teaching as a career. Ask what they like and dislike about teaching.

- Be a helper in a church nursery or child care center, or a youth leader in the YMCA, YWCA, or other places for opportunities to work with children and young people.

- Invite a principal to your class to present her or his views on the characteristics needed for successful teaching.

- Become a member of the student associate affiliate of the teacher organization(s) at your college or university.

The purpose of this chapter is to help you determine if teaching is the career for you. It provides information relevant to the status of education in the United States and to the teaching profession. In this chapter you will learn about the importance of education and the importance of teaching; public attitudes toward the success of education, and their satisfaction with teachers; and why people become teachers and why they leave teaching. This chapter provides a perspective on teaching as a profession and presents information on alternative careers in education. ■

■ Importance of Education

Education is a high priority in the United States. Strong and solid educational programs are extremely important to individuals, to business and industry, to our government, to our collective and pluralistic society, and to our competitiveness in a global economy.

It is through education that people have the opportunity to advance their status in life and to become productive citizens. It is through education that skilled workers are provided for our businesses and industries to bolster the productivity of our economy. It is through education that citizens learn the significance of our democratic government, and that our citizens learn to live in our pluralistic society. Granted, other institutions also have an impact on people and society. Nevertheless, education provides the basis for developing our society. As a teacher you will be in a career that is very important. Teachers are the backbone of education, creating, maintaining, and providing excellent education for their students.

Since 1983 when *A Nation at Risk: The Imperative for Educational Reform* was published, education has been in the national spotlight. That report by the National Commission on Excellence in Education was highly critical of the status of education in the United States, and made many recommendations for educational reform. The report made it very clear that education is *extremely important* to the United States. The report began with the following statement:

Our Nation is at risk. Our once unchallenged preeminence in commerce, industry, science, and technological innovation is being overtaken by competitors throughout the world. This report is concerned with only one of many causes and dimensions of the problem, but it is the one that undergirds American prosperity, security, and civility. We report to the American people that while we can take justifiable pride in what our schools and colleges have historically accomplished and contributed to the United States and the well being of its people, the educational foundations of our society are presently being eroded by a rising tide of mediocrity that threatens our very future as a Nation and a people. What was unimaginable a generation ago has begun to occur—others are matching and surpassing our educational attainments.

Many of the reforms proposed in *A Nation at Risk,* along with reforms proposed by other groups, associations and individuals will be discussed throughout this book. The effectiveness of the reform proposals will also be addressed. The reform movement will continue to be challenging and exciting for educators over the next few years.

■ **Public's Attitudes toward Public Schools**

Question: Students are often given the grades A, B, C, D, and FAIL to denote the quality of their work. Suppose the public schools themselves, in this community, were graded in the same way. What grade would you give the public schools here—A, B, C, D, or FAIL?

■ **Table 1.1** Community Schools

	National Totals %	No Children In School %	Public School Parents %	Nonpublic School Parents %
A + B	43	39	56	25
A	12	9	19	7
B	31	30	37	18
C	30	29	30	45
D	9	9	9	15
FAIL	4	4	3	8
Don't know	14	19	2	7

© 1987, Phi Delta Kappan, Inc.

■ **Public's Attitudes toward Public Schools**

One way to measure the relative success of the education profession is to survey the opinions of the people about the public schools. The 19th Annual Phi Delta Kappa/Gallup Poll of the Public's Attitudes toward the Public Schools (1987) provides insight into the public's perceptions of the success of the public schools. Tables 1.1, 1.2, and 1.3 illustrate the opinions of the respondents. Table 1.1 indicates that 43 percent of the respondents awarded the public schools either an A or a B rating. Fifty-six percent of the public school parents awarded the public schools either an A or a B rating. The 43 percent rating is up 2 percent from 1986, and is the highest rating since 1975 and 1985. Table 1.2 provides a more comprehensive breakdown of the data. It is worthwhile to note that those respondents who are most likely to give the schools high grades are the best educated and those in the higher income categories (more than $30,000 a year). Those least likely to award the local public schools high marks

tend to be younger (under age 30), less affluent, residents of central cities and nonwhite.[1]

It is interesting to note that elementary schools received higher ratings than secondary schools. Forty percent of the respondents awarded As and Bs to public high schools. Correspondingly, they awarded 52 percent As and Bs to the public elementary schools.[2]

As contrasted with the A and B ratings of local schools (43 percent), the responses when the public was asked to grade the schools in the nation as a whole dropped to 26 percent A and B ratings (table 1.3).[3]

The 20th Annual Gallup Poll of the Public's Attitudes toward the Public Schools (1988) indicated that only 40 percent of the respondents awarded the public schools either an A or B rating; down from 43 percent in the previous year (1987). Fifty-one percent of the public school parents responding to the 20th Annual Gallup Poll in 1988 awarded the public schools either an A or B rating; down from 56 percent in the previous year.[4]

	A + B %	A %	B %	C %	D %	FAIL %	Don't Know %
Table 1.2 Community Schools							
National Totals	43	12	31	30	9	4	14
Sex							
Men	42	12	30	34	9	3	12
Women	43	11	32	27	10	5	15
Race							
White	43	11	32	30	9	4	14
Nonwhite	35	14	21	34	11	8	12
Age							
18–29 years	36	8	28	34	12	4	14
30–49 years	44	13	31	33	10	5	8
50 and over	46	13	33	25	6	4	19
Community Size							
1 million and over	35	10	25	29	13	7	16
500,000–999,999	42	12	30	37	7	3	11
50,000–499,999	44	12	32	34	7	4	11
2,500–49,999	45	15	30	26	7	3	19
Under 2,500	53	13	40	28	7	2	10
Central city	28	7	21	39	14	6	13
Education							
College	46	11	35	30	10	3	11
Graduate	49	12	37	26	11	3	11
Incomplete	42	9	33	33	10	4	11
High School	40	11	29	32	9	5	14
Graduate	43	12	31	33	10	3	11
Incomplete	35	9	25	30	7	8	20
Grade school	40	19	21	22	6	6	26
Income							
$40,000 and over	48	13	35	29	10	4	9
$30,000–$39,999	47	13	34	31	10	3	9
$20,000–$29,999	45	12	33	31	7	5	12
$10,000–$19,999	35	8	27	32	9	4	20
Under $10,000	45	16	29	24	10	3	18
Region							
East	39	11	28	29	11	6	15
Midwest	45	13	32	29	7	4	15
South	47	12	35	30	7	4	12
West	36	10	26	34	13	4	13

■ **Table 1.3**   Nation as a Whole

	National Totals %	No Children in School %	Public School Parents %	Nonpublic School Parents %
A + B	26	26	30	17
A	4	3	7	4
B	22	23	23	13
C	44	44	42	59
D	11	9	14	12
FAIL	2	2	2	3
Don't know	17	19	12	9

© 1987, Phi Delta Kappan, Inc.

■ **Table 1.4**   Public's Attitudes toward Teachers

Question: What grade would you give the teachers in the public schools in this community—A, B, C, D, or FAIL?

	National Totals %	No Children in School %	Public School Parents %	Nonpublic School Parents %
A + B	49	44	64	44
A	15	12	24	12
B	34	32	40	32
C	25	25	25	31
D	6	5	7	9
FAIL	3	3	2	5
Don't know	17	23	2	11

© 1987, Phi Delta Kappan, Inc.

A study commissioned by the Metropolitan Life Insurance Company used another approach to measure the success of education in the United States.[5] The study asked parents and teachers, "Is the education that children receive in school better today or worse today than was being given?" Figure 1.1 portrays the findings of the opinion survey. The survey results indicate that a strong majority of both parents and teachers believe that overall the education that children receive in school today is better than it was in the past. Nevertheless, approximately four out of ten parents and three out of ten teachers believe that the education children receive today is worse than what they received when they were in school.

■ **Public's Attitudes toward Teachers**

Public's attitudes toward teachers were also surveyed in the 19th Annual Phi Delta Kappa/Gallup Poll. Table 1.4 portrays the findings of that survey.

Question: Is the education that children receive in school better today or worse today than the education that was being given? (READ EACH ITEM.)

Parents Base: 2.011

	Better today	Worse today	Same, no difference (VOI . .)	Not sure
Three years ago	58	18	15	9
Ten years ago	62	26	5	7
When you yourself were in school	62	32	3	3

Teachers Base: 1.002

Three years ago	71	11	16	2
Ten years ago	71	21	5	4
When you yourself were in school	65	28	4	3

■ **Figure 1.1**

How parents and teachers compare education today with education in the past

Teachers in the local public schools received high grades; 49 percent of the public gave teachers a grade of A or B. Sixty-four percent of the public school parents gave them grades of A or B. Elementary school teachers were graded higher than secondary school teachers; 53 percent of the respondents gave them As or Bs as contrasted to 43 percent for high school teachers. The 20th Annual Gallup Poll did not survey the public attitudes toward teachers.

Why Teachers Become Teachers

Why do individuals choose teaching as a career? A recent study by the National Education Association reveals three major reasons: a desire to work with young people (65.6 percent), the value or significance of education in society (37.2 percent), and interest in a subject-matter field (37.1 percent).[6] Table 1.5 provides a more detailed list of reasons why teachers originally decided to become teachers.

A further analysis of respondents of the survey to the item "a desire to work with young people" revealed that teachers under thirty years of age gave this reason at a much higher frequency (76.6 percent) than did older teachers. Furthermore, more females (67.2 percent) than males (62.2 percent) gave this reason; and elementary teachers gave this reason more often (73.5 percent) than did middle and junior high or senior high school teachers (58.7 percent each).[7]

In respect to the item "the value or significance of education in society," (37.2 percent) teachers under the age of thirty and over the age of fifty were somewhat more likely to choose this reason (43.8 percent and 40.7 percent respectively) than were their colleagues between the ages of thirty and forty-nine (about 35 percent). A higher percentage of minority teachers (43.2 percent) selected this reason than did Caucasian teachers (36.5 percent).[8]

■ **Table 1.5**   Principal Reasons Selected by All Teachers for Originally Deciding to Become a Teacher, 1971–1986

Reason	1971	1976	1981	1986
Desire to work with young people	71.8%	71.4%	69.6%	65.6%
Interest in subject-matter field	34.5	38.3	44.1	37.1
Value or significance of education in society	37.1	34.3	40.2	37.2
Influence of a teacher in elementary or secondary school	17.9	20.6	25.4	25.4
Long summer vacation	14.4	19.1	21.5	21.3
Influence of family	20.5	18.4	21.5	22.9
Job security	16.2	17.4	20.6	19.4
Never really considered anything else	17.4	17.4	20.3	21.0
Opportunity for a lifetime of self-growth	21.4	17.4	13.1	9.7

From National Education Association, *National Education Association Response: Status of the American Public School Teacher 1985–1986*, 56, 1987. Copyright © 1987 National Education Association, Washington, DC.

The third major reason for becoming a teacher, "interest in a subject-matter field" (37.1 percent) revealed that middle or junior high school teachers and senior high teachers chose this reason with greater frequency (46.1 percent and 60.6 percent respectively) than did elementary school teachers (16.5 percent). A higher percentage of males (46.6 percent) than females (32.7 percent) chose this reason. Interest in a subject-matter field was chosen more frequently by teachers under age thirty (46.7 percent) than by teachers age thirty to forty-nine (38.3 percent) or by teachers aged fifty and over (27.8 percent).[9]

■ Why Teachers Continue to Be Teachers

The aforementioned National Education Association study identified four major reasons why teachers continue to teach: a desire to work with young people (62.6 percent), too much invested to leave now (36.5 percent), the long summer vacation, and the value or significance of education in society.[10] Table 1.6 provides other reasons that teachers continue to teach. The reason "too much invested to leave now" does not appear in Table 1.6; however, it is discussed in the narrative. The reason "a desire to work with young people" was cited by those persons deciding originally to become a teacher. Those continuing to be a teacher also cited this reason (62.6 percent).[11]

■ Table 1.6   Reasons Teachers Entered Teaching Compared With Reasons They Continue, 1981–1986

Reason	Initial		Present	
	1981	**1986**	**1981**	**1986**
Value or significance of education in society	40.2%	37.2%	37.6%	34.4%
Desire to work with young people	69.6	65.6	69.0	62.6
Interest in subject-matter field	44.1	37.1	39.3	26.2
Influence of a teacher in elementary or secondary school	25.4	25.4	5.9	4.2
Influence of family	21.5	22.9	4.4	3.8
Need for income after termination of marriage	1.1	0.9	2.7	3.1
Financial rewards	4.9	2.8	9.8	5.9
Long summer vacation	21.5	21.3	37.1	36.1
Job security	20.6	19.4	33.2	28.9
Need for second income in family	4.8	4.6	17.5	17.1
Never really considered anything else	20.3	21.0	10.9	8.3
One of the few professions open to me	. . .[a]	10.3	. . .[a]	5.2
Opportunity for self-growth	13.1	9.7	16.6	12.1
Sense of freedom in my own classroom	. . .[a]	7.5	. . .[a]	15.7

[a]Not asked in 1981.

From National Education Association, *National Education Association Response: Status of the American Public School Teacher 1985–1986,* 57, 1987. Copyright © 1987 National Education Association, Washington, DC.

As was indicated earlier, the reason "too much invested to leave now"(36.5 percent) does not appear in table 1.6. The narrative provided the following information. As could be expected, the likelihood that a teacher would select this reason for continuing to teach increased with age. The data indicated that 18 percent of those that chose that reason were thirty or under in age; 50.8 percent aged fifty years and older also chose that reason.[12]

Those persons who chose the reason "a long summer vacation" were largely females under forty years old. They are most likely to be responsible for their own young children during school vacations.[13]

The reason "the value or significance of education in society" (34.4 percent) was also cited by those persons deciding originally to become teachers. The data reported for continuing teaching is very similar to the data reported by those persons who cited this reason for entering teaching originally.[14]

The following list of reasons for choosing a teaching career have been consistent over fifteen years:[15]

- a desire to work with young people (responses ranging from 66% to 72%)
- interest in a subject matter field (responses ranging from 35% to 44%)
- the value or significance of education in society (responses ranging from 37% to 40%)
- the influence of family (responses ranging from 18% to 23%)
- job security (responses ranging from 16% to 21%)
- never really considered anything else (responses ranging from 17% to 21%)

■ Why Teachers Leave Teaching

Reasons why teachers leave teaching were identified by the study commissioned by the Metropolitan Life Insurance Company. The study surveyed former teachers about why they left teaching, and also surveyed current teachers as to why they were considering leaving teaching. The following paragraphs state the most important findings of the study.

The Reasons That Former Teachers Give

Inadequate salary and poor working conditions dominate the list of reasons that former teachers give for leaving. Sixty percent of former teachers cite inadequate salary as the main reason that caused them to leave. Working conditions rank as the second most important motivating factor, with 36% of former teachers citing as their main reason for leaving such conditions as too much paperwork, too many non-teaching duties, and especially lack of input into educational decision-making (14%).

Student-related factors rank next in importance; 30% of former teachers point to factors such as lack of student discipline and lack of student motivation. Discipline alone is cited by 15%. Administration-related reasons are just as important; 30% of current teachers cite reasons such as lack of administrative support (17%) and dissatisfaction with administrators (10%) as their main motivation.

Emotional aspects such as boredom, stress, frustration, and burnout are mentioned by 27% of former teachers. Lack of respect is mentioned by another 17% as their chief reason. Parent- and community-related factors are mentioned by 16% of former teachers. And many cite miscellaneous themes such as no chance for advancement (15%), or the availability of an opportunity to do something else (14%).

Reasons Cited by Current Teachers Considering Leaving

This litany of complaints is underscored by the testimony of those *current teachers* who were or are considering leaving teaching to go into a different occupation. As they explain the reasons that caused them to consider leaving teaching, current teachers cite the *same* major themes as do former teachers, and they cite them in quite similar proportions. Thus, over 6 in 10 cite low salary and over 4 in 10 cite difficult working conditions.[16] (These data were collected as part of the annual survey of teachers conducted by Louis Harris and Associates, Inc., for Metropolitan Life Insurance Company. Reprinted by permission.)

While the Metropolitan Life Insurance Company survey indicated that teachers were dissatisfied with some aspects of teaching, it also revealed that teacher morale rose significantly from 1986 to 1987. In 1986, 81 percent of the respondents reported that they were satisfied with their jobs, and in 1987, 85 percent of the respondents reported that they were satisfied. Furthermore, the number of teachers reporting that they are likely to give up teaching within the next five years declined from 27 percent in 1986 to 22 percent in 1987. A dramatic change in the percentage of teachers contemplating a career change was evident in those teachers with less than five years experience. In 1986, 39 percent of those teachers indicated their likelihood of leaving the profession; that percentage dropped to 20 percent in 1987. Between 1985 and 1987 the percentage of inner-city teachers contemplating leaving teaching declined from 36 percent to 25 percent.

■ Perspective on Teaching

Teaching, like any other career, has its advantages and disadvantages. Currently on the positive side it can be said that education is recognized as being crucial to the nation. Education provides the basis for developing our society. Teachers play the major role in education. As such, teachers are very important contributors to the health of our nation.

When one considers the challenges of public elementary and secondary school teachers and the commitment of the United States to provide education to *all* the children, it is remarkable how well teachers are perceived by the public. Of course, improvements can be made in education and in teaching. Improvements are underway, stimulated by the reform movement. For example, low salaries have been at the top of the list as the major disadvantage of teaching as a career for many years. The reform movement has called for higher salaries, and in some states salaries have increased. If the momentum of the educational reform can be sustained, it is likely that the outlook for teaching as a career will become increasingly positive. However, if the reforms and improvements achieved to date are not carried through, and if teachers who have the responsibility for implementing reforms are not given the opportunity to participate in shaping the reforms, the outlook for teaching as a career is likely to become increasingly negative.

■ Characteristics of Successful Teachers

Successful teachers have a solid understanding and command of the subjects they teach. They also have the abilities to communicate with students, parents, and other constituencies; motivate

Successful teachers have the abilities to communicate with students.

and inspire students; and maintain classroom discipline. Successful teachers have high expectations for their students and are enthusiastic and optimistic in their interactions with students. They provide a positive role model for their students.

Communicating includes understanding and relating. Teaching can be characterized as communicating, understanding, and relating. Successful teachers are those who communicate to students in a personalized way that they respect them, have confidence in them, believe in them,

feel that they are important, and have high expectations that they can and will learn. Successful teachers also know how to organize and communicate the knowledge that the students are expected to learn. Furthermore, they expect success for their students, and communicate that expectation to them. The likelihood of such messages being received by students is enhanced by teachers who do, in fact, believe sincerely that students should be respected, are important, and have confidence that each and every student can and will learn. Communication is further enhanced by understanding the nature of young

Research Finding

1

Teachers who set and communicate high expectations to all their students obtain greater academic performance from those students than teachers who set low expectations.

The expectations teachers have about what students can and cannot learn may become self-fulfilling prophecies. Students tend to learn as little—or as much—as their teachers expect.

Students from whom teachers expect less are treated differently. Such students typically:

are seated farther away from the teacher

receive less direct instruction

have fewer opportunities to learn new material

are asked to do less work

Teachers also call on these students less often and the questions they ask are more likely to be simple and basic than thought-provoking. Typically, such students are given less time to respond and less help when their answers are wrong. But when teachers give these same students the chance to answer more challenging questions, the students contribute more ideas and opinions to class discussions.

Brophy, J. E. (1981). "Teacher Praise: A Functional Analysis." *Review of Education Research*, Vol. 51, pp. 5–32.

Purkey, S., and Smith, M. (March 1983). "Effective Schools: A Review." *The Elementary School Journal*, Vol. 83, No. 4.

Good, T. L. (December 1982). "How Teachers' Expectations Affect Results." *American Education*, Vol. 18, No. 10, pp. 25–32.

Source: *What Works: Research About Teaching and Learning*. Washington, DC: U.S. Department of Education, 1987, page 35.

persons, and being understanding of them. Relating has its basis in communicating and understanding.

How do teachers communicate? Obviously they use words. They also send powerful messages nonverbally through facial expressions, shrugs, and other forms of body language. Nonverbal communication is an effective means of communication. Oftentimes though, the sender is unaware of the message being sent and how it is received. To say "I believe in you" to a student and at the same time have a student perceive your nonverbal cues and overt actions as otherwise is

in fact very ineffective verbal communication. Effectively communicating with and relating to colleagues and parents are also vital to being a successful teacher. Being perceived by them, as well as by students, as being sincere, interested, positive, and enthusiastic gives promise of success.

Last, if a teacher relates well, but does not know or communicate the knowledge and skills for which he or she is responsible, and students for that reason do not learn, failure of the teacher

A teacher affects eternity; he can never tell where his influence stops.

Henry Adams

is inevitable. The skills to transmit knowledge are largely technical and are learned in teacher education programs.

Good classroom discipline is extremely important for student achievement. Effective communication can be a strong factor in establishing and maintaining good discipline. Teachers that establish rules and regulations for student behavior and conduct, along with the penalties for violations of the rules and rewards for good behavior, are creating an atmosphere for good discipline. In effect they are letting students know that they are in charge of the classroom, and have high expectations for their behavior just as they have high expectations for their achievement. The sanctions for misbehavior or misconduct must be applied in a quick, firm, and fair fashion. The sanctions should also be consistent. Positive student behaviors should be rewarded.

Most schools have a code for student behavior. Teachers' classroom rules, regulations, and sanctions must be in harmony with the schools' code for behavior. Otherwise teachers should seek administrative approval of their rules that are not in harmony with the code. Implementing the techniques of effective teaching will also help in maintaining good classroom discipline (see chapter 4).

■ Verifying Interest in Teaching

The previous pages have provided information about teaching as a career including topics such as the importance of teaching; the public attitudes toward public schools and public school teachers; why teachers become teachers; why teachers leave teaching; and the characteristics of successful teachers. These topics are helpful in learning about education and the teaching profession, and may influence a person to have an interest in teaching as a career. However, it does not help in answering one crucial question, "Would you enjoy teaching?" A second question is, "How can individuals who consider teaching as a career verify their interest in, and their personal potential for, becoming a successful teacher?"

Teaching is one profession that many people feel they are knowledgeable about and understand. Why? Probably because they spent a number of years in school as students. They were affected by teachers, remember what they liked or disliked about them, and have ideas about what teaching behaviors they thought were effective or ineffective. Experiences as a student, however, are not the same as experiences as a teacher.

Earlier in this chapter it was pointed out that the major reason reported by practicing teachers for having chosen teaching as a career was that they desired to work with young people. The best way for the would-be teacher to verify such a desire is to work with young people. In effect, prospective teachers need to have encounters with children or adolescents in situations best described as instructional, both formal and informal. Time spent as a teacher aide in a classroom, as a helper to an athletic coach, as a helper in a church nursery or child care center, or as a youth leader in a YWCA or YMCA can be helpful in testing whether or not you truly desire to work with young people. Preferably you should test that desire with young people at varying age levels: preprimary, primary, early adolescent, and late adolescent. As a college student seeking to decide (1) if teaching is an appropriate career choice, and (2) what level or age

*A world whose schools are
unreformed is an unreformed world.*

H. G. Wells

group might be most satisfying to work with; your images of what tenth graders or first graders are like may or may not be reinforced by real encounters. Real encounters are undoubtedly the best way to decide whether or not you have a desire to work with young people. Furthermore, real encounters can help an individual decide whether or not one has the necessary personality attributes to cope and survive as a teacher in today's schools. Many teacher training programs today require such experiences early in the program to assist students in deciding about teaching as a career choice.

While actual direct experiences with children and young people are the most helpful ways to decide whether or not a person would enjoy a teaching career, there are also other activities that can be helpful in making that decision. Among them are:

- Interview early childhood, elementary, secondary, adult education, and special education teachers to discuss how they feel about teaching as a career. You can also gain insight as to what level of education you wish to teach.
- Visit classrooms, and after the visits record your feelings and/or questions about teaching. Discuss your comments and questions with your peers, professors, or former teachers.
- Inquire of practicing teachers how they feel about teaching as a career. Ask what they like and dislike about teaching.
- Invite a principal to your class to present her or his views on the characteristics needed for successful teaching.

Today most colleges of education require early field experiences at the freshman or sophomore levels. These early experiences in public and private elementary schools make it possible for students to change an academic major with little loss of applicable credits and time.

■ Importance of Teaching to Society

One reason practicing teachers reported that they chose teaching as a career was its value or significance to society. Educated individuals benefit both themselves and society. Further, education is also viewed as a vehicle for solving societal problems and thus changing the nature of our society. In the United States, public education is a service provided by various governmental levels to serve the nation and its people.

Educated individuals, for example, are less likely to become prison inmates, and less likely to become residents in mental hospitals. Educated individuals are more likely to earn higher incomes, and therefore are less likely to be unemployed or suffering in poverty. While it is not possible to document a perfect cause and effect relationship between the incidence of crime and education, mental health and education, and income and education, there is sufficient evidence to strongly suggest that education tends to reduce crime, reduce admissions to mental hospitals, and enhance personal income.

Schools are frequently selected to act directly as agents to improve or change society. One illustration of this function is the provision of monies by the federal government to local school districts to improve the educational experiences

These teachers and students communicate in a casual setting.

necessary to be an informed citizen (such as literacy), and the skills necessary for problem solving are developed and enhanced through education. The values of society, that is, the ways of life that we cherish, are transmitted in part through our educational system. While not particularly dramatic, these functions of teaching are perhaps the most important.

■ Education as an Investment

Education provides substantial economic returns for both society and individuals. At one time economists used a formula containing the elements of land, labor, and capital to estimate economic development. It soon became evident that another variable was exerting a significant influence. There is now agreement that education is that significant variable. Using gross national product as an economic index, it can be shown that there is a positive relationship between gross national product and educational development. While this type of analysis is beset with some difficulties, such as comparable data indices and the time lags associated with the contribution of education in terms of when the education was acquired and when its effects were realized, nevertheless the evidence does indicate the importance of education to economic development. Investment in education is an investment in the human resources of our society.

A second ecomonic benefit of education accrued to society is teaching individuals a skill. As the demand for unskilled labor decreases, a proportionate demand for skilled labor increases, thus leaving education to fulfill the need to give the unskilled a skill to meet our society's needs.

of children from low income families. A second illustration is the role the schools are expected to play in fostering an integrated society by desegregating schools. In both instances, schools are clearly viewed as agents of societal change, and teachers are viewed as important persons expected to foster the desired changes.

Last, but basic to the traditional purpose of education in America, is the premise that only with an educated citizenry can democracy be expected to survive. The major functions of teaching are to transmit knowledge and culture. The skills

I love to teach as a painter loves to paint, as a musician loves to play, as a singer loves to sing, as a strong man rejoices to run a race. Teaching is an art—an art so great and so difficult to master that a man or a woman can spend a long life at it, without realizing much more than his limitations and mistakes, and his distance from the ideal.

William Lyon Phelps

■ Alternative Careers in Education

Librarians and Learning Center Directors

A school librarian is, in one sense, really a teacher whose classroom is the library. Some people erroneously think of a school librarian as one who only takes care of books and periodicals. Much to the contrary, a good librarian can be one of the most effective teachers in an entire school. One of the major goals of American public education is to help each student become capable of learning on his or her own without the help of the classroom teacher. The library contains many of the resources necessary for independent study, and the task of the librarian is to help each student learn how to use these resources. To do this effectively, a librarian must be able to order, classify, catalog, and shelve books and also be able to work effectively with individuals and groups of students.

Almost all of the junior and senior high schools in this country have libraries, and therefore, librarians. Only recently have elementary schools begun to have libraries. The library has been expanded into "learning resource centers" where a wide range of learning materials such as books, periodicals, learning machines, computers, programmed self-teaching materials, film strips, single concept films, records, audiotapes, and dial access materials are made available for students to use. Schools of the future are destined to put a greater emphasis on learning centers, and with this emphasis will come an increased demand for well-trained librarians and directors of learning centers.

Media Specialists

A later chapter discusses the general topic of instructional resources that are available for use by teachers. More and more school systems are now employing specialists who have been trained in media, and whose sole job it is to help teachers create and utilize different kinds of media in their teaching. These media specialists must, of course, be familiar with all of the different kinds of audiovisual equipment available for use in schools. Such equipment includes, for example, movie projectors, film strip projectors, 35-mm slide projectors, opaque projectors, overhead projectors, computers, audiotape recorders, videotape recorders, record players, overhead transparency makers, photocopy machines, cameras—the list gets longer each year as more and more such hardware is developed and made available for use in schools.

The media specialist, in some schools, also does minor repair work on audiovisual equipment: however, the main function of the media specialist so far as media hardware is concerned is to advise the school system on what hardware to buy and help teachers use such equipment.

A media specialist should have prior teaching experience and a master's degree with a major in educational media.

Counselors

A school counselor works to a great extent in a one-to-one relationship with individual students. These students may need vocational or college information, help in selecting elective courses, someone to talk with concerning a girl- or boyfriend, help with peer or parental conflict, or assistance with any one of a variety of emotional and psychological problems. School counselors do not, however, attempt to provide therapy for students with severe problems, but rather refer such cases to appropriate specialists, such as a clinical psychologist or psychiatrist. The long-term goal of counselors is not to solve problems for the students, but rather to help students solve their own problems. To do this, counselors must themselves be well adjusted, have a good understanding of human psychology, be familiar with and proficient in using a wide variety of counseling techniques, respect the dignity and worth of individual students, and possess a sincere desire to understand and help others.

In most states, to be certified as a counselor requires that a person have some teaching experience and possess a master's degree with a major in school counseling. There are some states, however, that do not require prior teaching experience to be certified as a school counselor.

School Social Workers

An educational career closely related to the school counselor is that of school social worker, one distinction being that a social worker goes out into the community, and into the home to work with students and parents. For instance, if a school counselor, in working with an individual student, suspects that the student's problem may be caused by conditions in the home, he or she may then refer the case to the school social worker. The social worker will then visit the home and attempt to work closely with members of the family to bring about a solution to the problem.

Of course, not all schools have a school social worker on the staff. In some school systems, this function is carried on by a school counselor, and in other schools the teacher does whatever work in the home with parents that needs to be done.

An increasing number of school systems, however, are finding it advantageous to have a school social worker on the staff who is specifically trained to do this kind of work.

A school social worker typically possesses a master's degree with a major in school social work.

Education-Related Positions
Outside the Schools

In recent years many graduates of teacher education programs have found employment in a rather wide range of education-related positions outside the schools. Increasingly employers are finding that those graduates who have been trained as teachers possess unique skills that can be valuable in business, industry, military, government, institution, and agency settings. Examples of specific positions in these settings for which people trained as teachers are particularly well-suited are presented in table 1.7. Many employers feel that persons trained as teachers usually have a good understanding of human behavior, enjoy working with people, and possess excellent human relations skills. These qualities are extremely useful in nearly any position which involves working with people.

Beyond this are a number of education dimensions to nearly all business or agency endeavors. For instance, employees must be trained and retrained to properly and efficiently perform their jobs. Educators possess the unique skills and knowledge to design and carry out these training programs.

The increasing demand for educators in private sectors of our economy have caused some colleges and universities to create new training programs especially designed to prepare educators for such nonclassroom education-related careers.

■ Table 1.7   Employment of Educators Outside the Schools

1. U.S. Office of Education (administrator, consultant, director, researcher, teacher corps program developer)
2. U.S. Department of State (administrator, Peace Corps)
3. U.S. Department of Defense (military educator, staff development, foreign teacher)
4. U.S. Bureau of Indian Affairs (administrator, staff developer, program developer)
5. Most other U.S. Agencies (staff development, education specialist, program developer, researcher, editor, writer, media specialist, interpreter)
6. Foreign Countries (educator, education specialist, interpreter, tour director, consultant)
7. Professional Organizations (administrator, public relations, researcher, field worker, editor, writer, media specialist)
8. State Education Agencies (administrator, consultant, researcher, editor, writer, field worker, media specialist, staff developer)
9. Local Municipal Agencies (recreation director, playground supervisor, camp instructor or director, community education worker, community planning and development, educator in special community projects)
10. Private Foundations (administrator, researcher, program evaluator, human relations work, editor, writer)
11. Hospitals and Clinics (patient education, staff development, writer)
12. Religious Organizations (religious educator, instructional materials development, media specialist, writer, editor, youth worker)
13. Banking (staff development, writer, consultant, teller, administrator)
14. Retail Sales (customer relations, advertising, staff development)
15. Insurance (staff development, writer, human relations consultant)
16. Wholesaler (customer relations, writer, market research)
17. Manufacturing (educational product development, researcher, writer, marketing consultant)
18. Advertising (education consultant, writer, researcher, human psychology consultant)
19. Television and Radio (education consultant, TV or radio teacher, researcher, script writer)
20. Newspapers (education writer or editor, consultant, researcher)
21. Publishing (education editor, author, education materials sales, consultant)
22. Private Consultant (proposal writer, evaluator, speaker)
23. Museums (educational consultant, program developer, in-service trainer, public relations consultant, speaker)
24. Teaching in a variety of capacities in foreign countries

■ Summary

The purpose of this chapter was to help you determine if teaching is a career for you. In meeting that purpose, information was provided about a number of relevant topics. Among them were the importance of education, the public attitudes toward schools and teachers, why teachers become teachers and why they leave teaching, the characteristics of successful teachers, verifying an interest in teaching, alternative careers in education, and teaching as a profession.

Education is a high priority in the United States. It was noted that education undergirds American prosperity, security and civility. Teachers who interact with children and young people are on the frontline of education. Good, solid education of youth is a major factor in shaping productive citizens and developing and maintaining a desirable society and economy. Not only is education important, teachers and teaching are important.

The public attitudes toward education are upbeat with 56 percent of the public school parents awarding grades of A or B to their local schools.

Sixty-four percent of public school parents awarded their local teachers with grades of A or B. When one considers the challenges of public elementary and secondary school teachers and the commitment of the United States to provide education for *all* the children, it is remarkable how well schools and school teachers are perceived by the public. Morale of teachers is high with 85 percent of the teachers indicating that they are satisfied with their jobs, and only 22 percent indicating that they would be likely to give up teaching in the next five years. Corresponding percentages for 1986 were 81 percent and 39 percent. Part of the percentage changes is likely to be the result of the reform movement.

Over the last fifteen years, the three major reasons that teachers chose teaching for a career were a desire to work with young people, the value or significance of education in society, and interest in a subject matter field. Inadequate salaries and poor working conditions dominated the reasons that former teachers gave for leaving teaching.

Successful teachers have a solid understanding and a command of the knowledge of the subjects they teach. They also have the abilities to communicate with students, parents, and other constituencies; motivate and inspire students; and maintain classroom discipline. Successful teachers have high expectations for their students and are enthusiastic and optimistic in their interactions with students. They provide a positive role model for their students.

By far the best way to verify an interest in teaching is to work with young people. This can be done by volunteering to work in a church nursery or a child care center, the YMCA or YWCA, and other such agencies.

There are careers in education other than teaching. Some are school-related such as being a school librarian, media specialist, counselor, or social worker. Other education-related careers include those in business, industry, the military, government, and other institution and agency settings.

The reform movement has resulted in many recommendations to improve teachers and teaching, some of which will be discussed in detail in chapter 2. The question of whether or not teaching is a profession has been raised. The answer depends on how a profession is defined. Three characteristics of a profession are ability to control one's destiny, employ one's judgment, and accept responsibility for one's actions.

If you feel that you would like a career that is perceived as one that is important to and respected by society, you know from experience that you like to work with children and young people, and think that you can master the knowledge needed to teach along with the skills and abilities of successful teachers, then teaching could be a career for you. You should also be willing to accept relatively low salaries and poor working conditions, or have faith that the reform movement will result in higher salaries and better working conditions, both of which have been strongly recommended in a number of reform reports.

Point of View

Is teaching a profession? That is a question that is frequently debated. Most often the answer is that teaching is not a profession. The point of view for this chapter, "The Professionalizing of Teaching" points out the characteristics of a profession, and the changes that need to be made to make teaching a profession. A quote from the point of view article states, "If teaching is ever to be considered a true profession, major changes must occur not just in classrooms, schools, and communities, but in the minds of teachers themselves." It is possible that sometime in the near future, if changes are made, teaching could become an authentic profession.

The Professionalizing of Teaching

It is generally agreed that professionals do have certain characteristics in common: the ability to control one's destiny, to employ one's individual judgment, and accept accountability for one's actions. Traditionally, teaching, while being a profession in name, has not been considered a true profession by many, including teachers themselves. Certainly many of the conditions under which teachers operate raise questions about the degree of professionalism they enjoy.

The public often perceives teachers as 180-day-a-year employees who enjoy summers and vacations "off." Teachers' unions, based on an industrial model that appears to be more concerned with starting and ending times than with truly professional issues, have also often contributed to the perception. Unions claim they have been pushed into this factory approach by administrators and boards that have, for many years, been unwilling to accept teachers as participants in the decision making process in schools. It is obvious that both unions and school district management must change if public and self perceptions are to change.

■ Teaching in the Post-Industrial Age

The changes that need to occur will center around both the ways contracts are negotiated and what is included in them; however, probably the greatest changes must come in the day-to-day management and operation of schools. While recognizing that condition of employment issues such as salary and grievance procedures will continue to be part of the process, other ways for unions, administrators and boards to work together on subjects such as staff development and other professional topics need to be addressed. Schools must move away from the factory model to one that encourages participatory management by those involved. Teachers' unions can become more involved in issues dealing with teaching as a profession, for instance, by developing inservice programs, by heightening legislative awareness to the needs of the profession, and by policing their own members to insure that teachers are all highly qualified and capable and remain so throughout their tenure.

Teachers also need to be more directly involved in the decision making process, particularly in those areas that directly affect how they function in the classroom, such as curriculum, instructional activities, student concerns, and staff development activities. But it is essential that this involvement take place within a context of mutual trust that gives meaningful expression to the decision making process. This can be achieved by providing teachers with real opportunities to participate in activities designed to enhance the educational program. Committees of teachers with clearly established goals and objectives which identify advisory and decision making responsibilities in the overall mission are essential.

Accountability must then follow. Teachers have long recognized the need for accountability but have been understandably cautious about embracing it when they did not have control over how they function in schools. When this is achieved, teachers will welcome accountability.

■ New Roles for Administrators

This approach will also require that school administrators at all levels examine the ways in which they function. They must move away from what is often a totally autocratic style, sometimes accompanied by *pro forma* committees, to one in which they serve more as coordinators and facilitators. All agree that administrators are necessary and desirable. Research reveals, however, that a change in leadership style is necessary to enhance their performance and effectiveness.

Within school buildings an atmosphere must exist that allows for and encourages shared decision making about those issues which affect both the process and the product of education.

School district staff, also, must play a role in "opening up" education to the community and parents by encouraging partnerships and other methods of working together.

■ The Egg Crate Syndrome

Isolationism is yet another inhibitor of the professionalizing of teaching. Most teachers spend most of their time in their own classrooms either working directly with students, planning activities, or other similar tasks. Little opportunity is provided for teachers to work together, to confer, or to participate in mutually beneficial activities. Opportunities must be provided that diminish the feeling of isolation. Grade level meetings, peer coaching teams, conference and visitation days both in house and outside the district, attendance at local, regional, state, and even national conferences are some ways to assist teachers in achieving the collegiality necessary to the professional.

But teachers are not isolated only from each other. They are also walled off from the community of which they should be a very vital part. Greater communication with the business community, including curriculum development activities and speaking to groups about schools and their programs, must also be encouraged. Schools are very much a part of the community in which they are located and, as such, must be both responsive to community needs and looked to for leadership in directing what schooling should occur.

■ The Constant Need for Improvement

Teachers, like all true professionals, must be provided with opportunities, not only to maintain skills, but to grow and develop those necessary to a constantly changing career. As more is learned from educational research about what works and what doesn't work in the classroom, and as state mandates and curriculum requirements mount, teachers need increasing opportunities to learn if they are to maintain, much less improve, their

effectiveness. And teachers should have a primary role in directing these efforts.

But self improvement alone does not make a professional. True professionals have influence and control over the environment in which they work and opportunities to grow within that environment. Career paths must be established to provide educators opportunities to pursue a variety of activities designed to enhance the profession.

Those students entering teaching should begin the growth process by serving a paid internship under the direction of a mentor teacher. Both should be provided ample time to work together in order to insure that the intern experiences a full range of opportunities. A mentor teacher would be an individual with experience in the profession assigned to work with interns as they begin their careers. Experienced educators desiring to serve in this capacity should have not only the opportunity but also the time to do so. They should be relieved of some classroom responsibilities while mentoring but should resume them upon completion of the mentoring process. Thus, the position is not a rung on a separate career ladder but one that values the expert teacher in both the teaching and mentoring roles.

Another path which educators may choose is that of teacher trainer. These people work with teacher training institutions in preparing teachers. Among their activities are curriculum development, supervision of instruction using a clinical model, and other activities necessary to facilitate the teaching/learning process. Like mentor teachers, trainers would move back and forth between their classroom and training responsibilities.

■ The Paraprofessional

Another important characteristic of professionals is that they are freed from nonprofessional activities, thus making time available not only to concentrate on the professional act itself, whether filling a tooth or trying a case, but also for the preparation and renewal necessary to maintain growth in the profession. Teachers must be able to call upon paraprofessionals so that they are able to plan, to meet, to share, and to study, both collectively and individually. Support staff should be provided to free teachers from clerical duties, monitoring functions, and other non-teaching activities so that they may engage in more teacher/learner interactions, development activities, parent conferences, etc.

■ Becoming Professional

Literally for centuries, teachers have been thought of—and have thought of themselves—as providers of a service at best, "dishing out" instruction to their "customers" in classrooms much as a waiter goes from booth to booth. This perception has been fostered by communities and school boards who may think of "English teacher" or "third grade teacher" as a generic unit; administrators who may see these same people as five-fifths of an instructional unit; and by teachers themselves who may think of themselves as having been trained in their youth (for all time) and then doing much the same thing year after year, with only the students and the salary step changing. And this perception has been further strengthened by union/management focus of concern on salary and working conditions rather than on professional issues.

If teaching is ever to be considered a true profession, major changes must occur not just in classrooms, school, and communities, but in the minds of teachers themselves. Teachers must *behave* as professionals, both in and out of their classrooms, speaking positively and pridefully about teaching, the school, students and community.

Teaching still has a long way to go to achieve the status of a profession; however, there are definite signs that movement has begun in areas

such as those noted above. The term, "professional," may soon be an authentic one that teachers can claim with pride.

From "The Professionalizing of Teaching," *A View From the Inside: A Look at National Reports, A Report of the Select Seminar on Excellence in Education,* September 1987. Copyright © 1987 The Capital Area School Development Association, Albany, NY. Reprinted by permission.

■ Questions for Discussion

1. Of the many teachers you have had, which do you remember favorably and why? What qualities did they have that made them "good" teachers?

2. What experiences have you had that verify your interest in teaching? Why?

3. Why do you think teaching is important to society?

4. What do you as an individual see as the advantages and disadvantages of teaching as a career? Why?

5. At what level—preprimary, elementary, secondary, adult—do you wish to teach? Why? Do you wish to teach handicapped persons? Why?

6. Do you think that the common characteristics of professionals presented in the first paragraph of the Point of View article can be achieved by teachers? Why? Or why not?

■ Notes

1. Alec Gallup and David Clark, "The 19th Annual Phi Delta Kappa/Gallup Poll of Public Attitudes Toward the Public School," *Phi Delta Kappan* 69, no. 1 (September 1987):25.

2. Ibid., p. 25–26.

3. Ibid., p. 26.

4. Alec Gallup and Stanley Elam, "The 20th Annual Gallup Poll of the Public's Attitudes toward the Public Schools," *Phi Delta Kappan* 70, no. 1 (September 1988):36.

5. *The Metropolitan Life Survey of the American Teacher 1987: Strengthening Links Between Home and School*, a survey conducted for Metropolitan Life Insurance Company by Louis Harris and Associates, Inc. (New York: Metropolitan Life Insurance Company, June 1987), p. 22. Courtesy of Metropolitan Life Insurance Company, New York.

6. National Education Association, *National Education Association Response: Status of the American Public School Teacher 1985–86* (Washington, D.C.: National Education Association, 1987), p. 55.

7. Ibid.

8. Ibid.

9. Ibid.

10. Ibid., pp. 55–56.

11. Ibid., p. 55.

12. Ibid., p. 55.

13. Ibid., p. 56.

14. Ibid., p. 56.

15. Ibid., p. 57.

16. *The Metropolitan Life Survey of Former Teachers in America*, a survey conducted for the Metropolitan Life Insurance Company by Louis Harris and Associates, Inc. (New York: Metropolitan Life Insurance Company, June 1985), p. 17. Courtesy of Metropolitan Life Insurance Company, New York.

■ Selected References

Feistritzer, Emily C. *The Making of a Teacher: A Report on Teacher Education and Certification.* Washington, D.C.: National Center for Education Information, 1984.

Gallup, Alec, and Clark, David. "The 19th Annual Phi Delta Kappa Gallup Poll of Public's Attitudes Toward the Public Schools." *Phi Delta Kappan* 69, no. 1 (September 1987).

Gallup, Alec, and Elam, Stanley, "The 20th Annual Gallup Poll of the Public's Attitudes Toward the Public Schools" *Phi Delta Kappan 70,* no. 1 (September 1988):36.

Martin, Ralph E., Wood, George H., and Stevens, Edward W. Jr. *An Introduction to Teaching: A Question of Commitment.* Needham Heights, MA: Allyn and Bacon, Inc., 1988.

Metropolitan Life Insurance Company. *The Metropolitan Life Survey of the American Teacher 1987: Strengthening Links Between Home and School.* New York: Metropolitan Life Insurance Company, 1987.

National Education Association. *NEA Research/ Gallup Opinion Polls: Public and K–12 Teacher Members Spring 1986.* Washington, D.C.: National Education Association, 1987.

National Education Association. *Status of the American Public School Teacher 1985–1986,* Washington, D.C.: National Education Association, 1987.

Ryan, Kevin and Cooper, James M. *Those Who Can Teach.* Boston: Houghton Mifflin, 1988.

Travers, Paul D., and Rebore, Ronald W. *Foundations of Education: Becoming a Teacher.* Englewood Cliffs, NJ: Prentice Hall Inc., 1987.

Chapter 2

Teacher Education Today

Objectives

After studying this chapter you should be able to:

■ Describe the components of teacher education today.

■ List the general requirements of teacher education by states, the federal government, and accrediting agencies.

■ Speculate about what teacher education may be like in the near future.

■ Explain the reasons for competency testing and performance assessment.

■ Describe the highlights of the Holmes, Carnegie, and the Governors' Reports.

■ Identify the points of agreement and disagreement among the Holmes, Carnegie, and Governors' Reports.

■ Explain the importance of the need for minority teachers.

■ Identify the reason for certification and describe the certification process.

■ Contrast the elements of traditional certification with alternative certification.

■ Recognize the importance of continuing professional development.

■ Assess the status of the teacher education reform movement.

Enrichment Experiences

The following experiences will help you in learning more about becoming a teacher, and perhaps assist you in deciding what kind of teacher education program would be best for you.

■ Study selected college and university catalogues to compare teacher preparation programs and requirements in different educational institutions.

■ Discuss your concerns about teacher education with your advisor.

■ Visit another college or university to find out about their teacher education program.

■ Ask some of your professors their opinions about regular four-year teacher education programs as compared with five-year programs.

■ Contact the certification officer at your college or university or your State Department of Education to learn the certification requirements.

■ Ask some of your high school teachers what they think the components of a good teacher education program should include.

Teachers everywhere have as important a role to play as politicians and diplomats . . . One of the most important tasks of the teacher, as I understand it, is to bring to clear consciousness the common ideals for which men should live. These common ideals have a force which unites.

U Thant

The major purpose of this chapter is to help you understand the components of teacher education today (1989) and what is likely for teacher preparation programs in the next three to five years, dependent somewhat upon the recommendations made in the many recent educational reform reports, and the degree and speed of the implementation of the recommendations from those reports. In this chapter you will learn about the components of teacher education today; the requirements of teacher education that are mandated by states, the role of the federal government and accreditation agencies; competency testing and performance assessment; the reports of the Holmes Group, Carnegie Task Force on Teaching as a Profession, and the National Governors' Association and their common points of agreement and disagreement; traditional ways of certification and alternative certification; continuing professional development; and the growing consensus for teacher education reform. ■

In 1983 and 1984 there were more than thirty national reports published dealing with recommendations for improving American education. Between 1985 and 1989 many more reports were published. Since teachers are the most important factor in education, almost all the reports dealt with teacher preparation, urging more stringent admission requirements for teacher education, greater rigor in the teacher education curriculums, stricter retention requirements during the programs, and exit examinations. These recommendations, along with others, will be discussed later in this chapter.

Let us first examine the traditionally common components of all teacher preparation programs. Today most teacher education programs designed for entry-level positions are four-year programs. While there are some similarities in all programs, there are also differences, institution to institution and state to state.

■ Teacher Education Programs Today

Teacher education programs are offered by many colleges and universities to prepare a variety of types of teachers. There are some elements common to all programs, yet a program designed to prepare a nursery school teacher will be decidedly different from a program designed to prepare a chemistry teacher.

Colleges and universities have the responsibility for conceptualizing the various training programs. Basic guidelines used in the process include state teacher certification laws, and the guidelines of various national accrediting associations. Further, the process frequently involves not only college and university specialists in education and subject-matter disciplines, but also practicing teachers, administrators, personnel directors, counselors, and other practitioners in related areas such as social work; personnel from state certification agencies, and from national accrediting agencies; and students, both graduate and undergraduate. Programs so designed lead to certification in the state where the institution is located. It should be noted, however, that each state has its own certification laws and such laws do differ somewhat from state to state. Within a state there are likely to be slightly different programs, institution-to-institution, leading to the same certificate. More information about certification and accreditation is provided later in this chapter.

■ Common Components in Teacher Education Programs

All teacher education programs—elementary, secondary, and special education—contain three common components: general education, professional education including student teaching, and a specialization.

General Education Component

General education, or liberal education, most often makes up approximately 40 percent of a total four-year degree program in teacher education and includes study in the social sciences, the natural and physical sciences, and the humanities. The average general education requirements among the states for initial elementary certification is 40 percent (about 50–54 s.h.) of the semester hours required for a degree. For initial secondary certification, the average percentage was 38 percent (about 48–52 s.h.). The general education component has been discussed in some of the national reports in a number of ways. It is likely that in the next few years the percentage of the baccalaureate degrees in general education for those seeking elementary certification will increase, and that there will be greater consistency in that requirement among the states. Frequently, the general education requirements for a baccalaureate degree in any program as prescribed by a specific higher education institution will also be required for those pursuing teacher education programs and will meet the general education requirements for teacher certification. The rationale for the inclusion of general education within teacher education is basically to the effect that teachers have the responsibility for the general education of young Americans and therefore are expected to have a rich educational background themselves.

1. Achieve personal fulfillment.
   a. Attain optimum physical and mental health.
   b. Clarify moral and aesthetic values.
   c. Develop creative expression.
2. Develop understanding and skills in symbolics of information.
   a. The ability to speak, read, and write English fluently, accurately, and critically.
   b. Additional understanding and/or performance capability in at least one area of symbolics of information, such as mathematics, computer science, logic, linguistics, communications (verbal and nonverbal), or a foreign language.
3. Understand the natural and social environments.
   a. A basic understanding of how data, hypotheses, and laws are related within the framework of scientific method.
   b. An appreciation of the interrelatedness and complexity of the natural world, and of human dependence on the natural world, and of human dependence on the living and nonliving environment.
   c. A general understanding of the social forces which shape present and future societies.
   d. An understanding of the social system of the United States and of social systems which differ from our own.

■ **Figure 2.1**
Objectives of the general education component of teacher education

Teachers are also expected to be effective purveyors of culture. "They should have acquired the characteristics of a scholar, and reflect excitement about learning in many areas. They should be familiar with a broad continuum of ways of knowing. They should have developed skills to a high degree in both oral and written communication."[1] Figure 2.1 illustrates how one state has established objectives for the general education component of teacher education.

The objectives for general education presented in figure 2.1 are representative of a viewpoint on general education with which a majority of those concerned would agree. There will always be some debate as to how to achieve those objectives. Competency testing for teachers, which has been mandated in forty-eight states, includes testing on the information and skills learned in the general education component of teacher education.

Professional Education Component

While the general education component of teacher education programs is likely to be almost identical in all programs, the professional education component is likely to be somewhat different. In general, the professional education component includes courses related to the teaching profession, and to teaching and learning. Those courses dealing with the teaching profession include courses in the history and philosophy of education, and the nature of schools. Those dealing with teaching and learning include psychology, human growth and development, learning theory, tests and measurements, methods of teaching, and student teaching. Differences in the professional component are related to the types of students the teacher education candidate is preparing to teach. For example, students preparing to teach at the elementary school level will take child psychology, while those preparing to teach at the secondary level will take adolescent psychology. Candidates preparing to teach handicapped children will take specific courses related to a specific type of handicap, such as learning disabled or hearing impaired. Methods courses will also

differ, with the individual preparing to teach elementary school children usually taking a series of methods courses in reading and language arts, social studies, mathematics, science, music, art, and physical education; while the candidate preparing to teach secondary school students usually takes a methods course in teaching a specific discipline such as English, mathematics, or art. Those planning to teach the handicapped will take methods courses related to the nature of a specific handicap.

In effect, the professional component of programs designed to prepare elementary school teachers prepares candidates to teach children a variety of courses. The professional component of special education programs prepares candidates to teach handicapped persons either a variety of courses or a specific course area. The professional component of secondary school teacher programs prepares candidates to teach adolescent age youngsters a specific body of knowledge.

Early Clinical Experiences

Early clinical experiences can be defined as interactions or encounters prior to student teaching with students of the age and/or type that the prospective teacher eventually plans to work with. Two major objectives for such experiences are: to help prospective teachers determine whether or not teaching is in fact a desirable career choice for them; and to facilitate learning, particularly in respect to relating theory to practice. Teacher education candidates are likely to be expected to participate in a prescribed number of clock hours of early experiences planned to occur throughout the preparation period, usually beginning in the sophomore year. The early experiences are sequenced, generally proceeding from observation through various levels of participation (in the public or private school classrooms) in activities ordinarily carried on in the classroom with students and by the teacher. The experiences are structured in the sense that the prospective teachers are expected to participate in prescribed activities and achieve specific competencies. The prospective teachers are evaluated throughout the experience and given feedback information on their individual level of performance. It is reasoned that such experiences will, in fact, help prospective teachers in making the decision as to whether or not teaching is a desirable career choice for them. Further, such experiences will provide better preparation for student teaching, enhancing the quality of the student teaching experience, and therefore the eventual quality of the teacher.

Microteaching

Some teacher education programs require microteaching. This involves teaching a minilesson in a microteaching laboratory, for a few minutes to a few students, demonstrating one or more specific teaching skills. The performance is videotaped, played back, and critiqued by the prospective teacher, the instructor, and occasionally the peers of the prospective teacher. Most often microteaching is done concurrently with methods classes. Microteaching laboratories frequently utilize materials that are designed to assist the candidate in achieving specific teaching skills. Candidates are expected to demonstrate competency in these skills as a part of the teacher training program. Videotaping teacher candidates teaching in a regular classroom setting is also used as a technique to refine teaching skills.

Student Teaching

Student teaching, the capstone of the professional sequence, is designed to gradually introduce prospective teachers to the full responsibilities of teaching. It is done under the guidance of an experienced teacher and a university supervisor. Currently, it is most often done in off-campus school settings. However, student teaching in some instances can be done on-campus in a laboratory school. The trend today is toward a full semester or quarter of full-time student teaching.

Teacher Induction Programs

Teacher induction programs are designed to provide support services to their graduates when they become teachers. Teacher induction programs were stimulated in part by the National Council for Accreditation of Teacher Education (NCATE), a voluntary national teacher education accreditation association. One of their criteria for compliance for accreditation states that "the institution has developed arrangements with school districts in the area to provide professional development services to its graduates as an extension of the professional education program."[2] The induction programs include providing mentors who work with beginning teachers helping them with one-to-one assistance; offering special clinics for beginning teachers to attend; conducting follow-up studies; and having a teacher hot line. Some programs offer two years of induction support services.

Specialization Component

The third common component in all teacher education programs is a specialization, usually taken concurrently with general education and the

Student teaching is an important aspect of teacher education programs.

professional education components. The term *specialization* as used here is synonymous with *major* as used in college catalogs. Students preparing to teach at the secondary level take a major in a discipline such as art, music, English, mathematics, or physical education. Students preparing to teach at the elementary level specialize or take a major in elementary education, while those preparing to teach handicapped persons major in special education.

Multicultural Education

In addition to the three common components of teacher education programs, that is, general education, professional education including student teaching, and a specialization, students in many states are required to have instruction and experiences in multicultural education either because of state mandates or accreditation agencies. For example, NCATE has a criterion for compliance to one of their five standards that specifies

Research Finding

2

Many children who are physically handicapped or have emotional or learning problems can be given an appropriate education in well-supported regular classes and schools.

In the past, educators often assumed that some children needed "special" education that could be provided only in special places—such as resource rooms, special classes, or special schools. In some cases, handicapped children were removed from their own homes and local schools and placed in special residential schools. Now more of them are learning well in regular classes and schools.

Regular teachers can support each other by meeting to discuss children's problems, provide instructional suggestions and support, and increase teacher skills and comfort in dealing with children with special needs. Such meetings provide a forum where teachers can use their creativity and problem-solving abilities, share their skills and knowledge, and help each other cope with classroom problems.

Wang, M. C., Reynolds, M. C., and Walberg, H. J. (Eds.) (in press). *The Handbook of Special Education: Research and Practice*, Oxford, England. Pergamon Press.
Source: *What Works: Research About Teaching and Learning.* Washington, DC: U.S. Department of Education, 1987, page 69.

"that each program area . . . includes study and experience related to culturally diverse and exceptional populations," and that "all programs incorporate multicultural and global perspectives."[3] NCATE further defines a multicultural perspective as " . . . a recognition of (1) the social, political, and economic realities that individuals experience in culturally diverse and complex human encounters, and (2) the importance of culture, race, sex and gender, ethnicity, religion, socioeconomic status, and exceptionalities in the education process."[4] A global perspective is defined as "the recognition of the interdependence of nations and peoples and the intertwined political, economic, and social problems of a transnational and global character."[5]

Mainstreaming

A more technical term for mainstreaming is "the least restrictive alternative program" for handicapped children. For some handicapped children a regular classroom with children who are not handicapped is the least restrictive environment. In essence, mainstreaming means moving handicapped children from their segregated status in special education classes and integrating them with nonhandicapped children in regular classrooms. Mainstreaming is not new, but it has received a new impetus from the passage of PL94-142, Education of the Handicapped Act, federal legislation hailed as a "Bill of Rights for the Handicapped." While the legislation has many provisions, a significant portion of it reads:

> Handicapped and nonhandicapped children will be educated together to the maximum extent appropriate, and the former will be placed in special classes or separate schools "only when the nature of the severity of the handicap is such that education in regular classes," even if they are provided supplementary aids and services, "cannot be achieved satisfactorily."

Under PL94-142 all teacher education programs for the preparation of teachers of non-handicapped children must include some preparation in special education for all teachers to enable them to provide effective instruction for all students in mainstreamed classrooms.

■ Recent Initiatives in Teacher Education Reform

There were four major initiatives in the last few years that received strong attention. They were: the teacher competency testing movement; the Holmes Group Report, *Tomorrow's Teachers,* the Carnegie Task Force, *A Nation Prepared,* and the National Governors' Association Reports, *Time for Results in Education: 1987.* Each of these initiatives will be discussed on the following pages.

Competency Testing. The competency testing movement in teacher education was in a large part a result of the student competency movement. It was observed that "If the public, alarmed by reports of barely literate students graduating from high schools by the thousands, had inspired some sort of mandated minimal competency tests for students, why not do the same for teachers?"[6]

R. W. Cole, in an editorial in the December 1979 *Phi Delta Kappan,* wrote:

> Should teachers be required to pass a state examination to prove their knowledge in the subjects they will teach when hired? Can we no longer trust teacher preparation institutions—approved by state, regional, and national accrediting agencies—to weed out weak teachers? Can we not rely on the screening that takes place when a district hires new teachers? Should teachers be retested every few years to see if they are keeping up-to-date? In the most recent *Gallup Poll of the Public's Attitudes Toward Public Schools* (1979), 85 percent of those polled said yes, teachers should be required to pass an exam in their subject and they should be continually retested.[7]

Table 2.1 indicates the extent of the testing movement and its growth and the year in which the tests were or will be implemented.

There are at least two potential disadvantages to quantitative standards for teacher education program admissions and certification: (1) policies that restrict entrance to the profession may contribute to a teacher shortage, and (2) a disproportionate number of minority students fail to gain entry into the teaching field due to low pass rates on these tests.[8] The failure rate of entrance to the profession for minority students is often as high as 60 to 70 percent. This fact is distressing when minority enrollment in the public schools is increasing and our nation needs more minority educators.

There are questions concerning teacher testing that have not yet been answered.

- Does the ability to perform on an admission, certification, or recertification test relate significantly to classroom performance?

■ Table 2.1 State Teacher Testing Programs by Year Mandated and by Year Implemented

State	Year of Mandate								Year of Implementation									
	<1980	1980	1981	1982	1983	1984	1985	1986	<1980	1980	1981	1982	1983	1984	1985	1986	1987	1988
Alabama		E									X							
Arizona		L									X							
Arkansas	L												X					
California			L										X					
Colorado			L										X					
Connecticut				E									X					
Delaware				E									X					
Florida	L									X								
Georgia	E								X									
Hawaii						E										X		
Idaho								E								X		
Illinois							L								X			
Indiana						L										X		
Kansas						L							X					
Kentucky				L					X									
Louisiana	L																	
Maine						L												X
Maryland								E									X	
Massachusetts	E											X						
Michigan								L										
Minnesota							L											X
Mississippi				E												X		
Missouri			E												X			
Montana							E									X		
Nebraska						L										X		
Nevada						E									X			
New Hampshire						E									X			
New Jersey						E												
New Mexico			L											X				
New York						E						X						
No. Carolina	E											X						
North Dakota								E										
Ohio							E										X	
Oklahoma		L										X						
Oregon				E											X			
Pennsylvania						E											X	
Rhode Island				E												X		
So. Carolina	L												X					
South Dakota							E									X		
Tennessee	E								X									
Texas			L											X				
Utah	E									X								
Virginia		L										X						
Vermont		E													X			
Washington	E												X					
West Virginia				E											X			
Wisconsin								E										
Wyoming				E									X					
Totals	10	5	5	8	0	10	5	5	3	2	2	5	9	2	7	8	3	2

L denotes testing was mandated by the state legislature, E denotes testing was mandated by the state board of education, X denotes first year of scheduled or actual implementation.

Note—Alaska and Iowa have not adopted and are not in the process of adopting some form of teacher testing program as of April 1987.

Source: J. T. Sandefur, "Historical Perspectives," *What's Happening in Teacher Testing: An Analysis of State Teacher Testing Practices.* Washington, DC: Office of Educational Research and Improvement, Department of Education, August 1987, p. 13.

If you become a teacher, by your pupils you'll be taught.

Anna

- Do teacher testing programs actually yield improved public confidence?
- Do existing observation instruments accurately indicate everyday classroom behaviors?
- Which other modes of assessment beyond paper and pencil tests can be used for improved teacher testing?
- What are the lower limits of knowledge and skill necessary to teach different ages and different subjects effectively?[9]

It is clear that those persons who choose to become teachers will be required to take a number of tests as a part of their teacher education program. Those tests, depending on the various state requirements, may include an admission test, test in subject matter, and a certification test. Testing is one way to judge the knowledge of an individual—a teacher or a prospective teacher. An assessment of the quality of a teacher, however, involves more than testing; for example, observations of performance or behavior of teachers that cannot be measured on a paper-pencil test. Nevertheless, testing is valuable, as it does provide information about the knowledge level of prospective teachers.

Performance Assessment   There is a relatively recent trend among the states to require an internship as a part of a beginning teacher assessment program. While the internship programs vary somewhat from state to state, they usually occur after the successful completion of an approved teacher preparation program including student teaching. The interns are expected to successfully master a list of state designated competencies before receiving their regular certification. During the internship in the elementary or secondary schools, they are observed and evaluated by an experienced teacher, an administrator, and a faculty member from a college of education. That group is expected to provide assistance to the intern throughout the internship year. At the end of the year, they make a recommendation to the State Board of Education whether the intern is to be certified.

As of 1987, there were seven states with existing internship programs using classroom observation instruments (Florida, Georgia, Kentucky, North Carolina, Oklahoma, South Carolina, and Virginia). As would be expected, not all of these programs are identical. Thirty-two other states are considering some type of internship programs. It is clear that those who choose teaching as a career are increasingly likely to be expected to successfully demonstrate their competencies in a classroom setting. (See appendix A for the Virginia Beginning Teacher Assessment Program.)

Tomorrow's Teachers: The Holmes Group.   The Holmes Group released its report *Tomorrow's Teachers* in 1986. The Holmes Group is a group of about 100 college of education deans from major research universities in the United States. There are about 1200 colleges and universities in the United States that have teacher education programs, with approximately 550 having NCATE accreditation. While the number of members that belong to the Holmes Group is relatively small, they represent prestigious institutions and their Report has had a powerful impact, receiving much attention from the teacher education community. The basic reform goals of the Holmes Group are presented in figure 2.2. A theme that permeates the Holmes Report is that of improving the professional status of teachers and teaching. The goals of the Holmes Group indicate quite clearly the components they believe will provide an improved professional status.

1. To make the education of teachers intellectually more solid.
2. To recognize differences in teachers' knowledge, skill, and commitment, in their education, certification, and work.
3. To create standards of entry to the profession—examinations and educational requirements—that are professionally relevant and intellectually defensible.
4. To connect our own institutions to schools.
5. To make schools better places for teachers to work and to learn.

Drafts of Specific Goals

The Institutional Environment for Teacher Education

1. The university honors its commitment to the nation's elementary and secondary schools through multiple investments in teachers and teaching.
2. The university works with selected school districts to create exemplary school sites for student and faculty learning about teaching excellence.
3. The university fosters an interdisciplinary climate in teacher education that reflects the importance of disciplinary diversity, depth, and relatedness to teaching.
4. The university expects an ethos of inquiry to permeate its teacher education programs at the university.
5. The university creates significant opportunities for teacher education students to develop collegial and professional norms.
6. The university assures equitable rights and responsibilities to the academic unit accountable for teacher education.
7. The university supports regular improvement of teacher education and participation in a national consortium for ongoing research, development, and program improvement.

Faculty in Teacher Education

1. The faculty responsible for preparing teachers is drawn from competent and committed teachers.
2. The faculty responsible for educating teachers includes both university-based and school-based faculty members.
3. The academic faculty members responsible for teacher education contribute regularly to better knowlege and understanding of teaching and schooling.
4. The teacher education faculty members who demonstrate competence as strong teacher-scholars are recognized for this unique and important combination of abilities.

Students in Teacher Education

1. Students passing through the various phases of study required for career professionals are academically talented and committed to teaching.
2. Students recruited and accepted into teacher education reflect our nation's obligation to a multicultural society.
3. Students evidence mastery of requisite content knowledge through written examination at various stages of their development.
4. Students, as judged by professionals, evidence appropriate ethical commitments and teaching capabilities prior to successful completion of their internship.

Curriculum in Teacher Education

1. The curriculum for prospective career teachers does not permit a major in education during the baccalaureate years—instead, undergraduates pursue more serious general/liberal study and a standard academic subject normally taught in schools.
2. The curriculum for prospective career teachers requires a master's degree in education and a successful year of well-supervised internship.
3. The curriculum for elementary career teachers requires study in multiple areas of concentration (each equivalent to a minor) in the subject fields for which teachers assume general teaching authority and responsibility.
4. The curriculum for secondary career teachers includes significant graduate study in their major teaching field and area concentrations in all other subjects they would teach.
5. The curriculum for all prospective career teachers includes substantial knowledge and work designed to develop skill regarding appropriate policy and practice in teaching students with special needs—advanced graduate study would be required for career professional roles in special education.
6. The curriculum required for teacher attainment of career professional status requires advanced study appropriate for specialized work in education with other adult professionals.

■ **Figure 2.2**
Holmes group goals

The Holmes Report has engendered some controversy just as other reports have. The major controversy centers around items one and two of the Holmes Group Goals under the heading *Curriculum in Teacher Education*. Those two recommendations imply a six-year teacher education program. The elimination of the undergraduate major in education to be replaced with more serious general/liberal study along with a standard academic subject normally taught in schools has been criticized, primarily by those institutions that are not Holmes Group members. In general those institutions feel that the Holmes goal "to make the education of teachers more solid" can be accomplished in a four-year baccalaureate program that includes pedagogy. The Holmes Group also feels strongly about the need for graduate study (primarily pedagogy) and clinical experiences (supervised and supported work in elementary and secondary schools). There are other programs in the United States that merge pedagogy and clinical experiences in a fifth-year graduate program that are less controversial. The Holmes Report, while controversial, is provocative and may stimulate some changes that could advance the professional status of teachers teaching.

A Nation Prepared: Teachers for the 21st Century (1986) is a report prepared by the Carnegie Task Force on Teaching as a Profession. The Report calls for the following reforms in teacher education:[10]

1. Make teachers' salaries and career opportunities competitive with those in other professions.
2. Require a bachelor's degree in the arts and sciences as a prerequisite for the professional study of teaching.
3. Relate incentives for teachers to schoolwide student performance, and provide schools with technology, services, and staff essential to teacher productivity.
4. Develop a new professional curriculum in graduate schools of education leading to a Master in Teaching degree, based on systematic knowledge of teaching and including internships and residencies in the schools.
5. Create a National Board for Professional Teaching Standards, organized with a regional and state membership structure, to establish high standards for what teachers need to know and be able to do, and to certify teachers who meet those standards.
6. Restructure schools to provide a professional environment for teaching, freeing them to decide how best to meet state and local goals for children while holding them accountable for student progress.
7. Restructure the teaching force and introduce a new category of lead teachers with the proven ability to provide active leadership in redesigning the schools and in helping their colleagues to uphold high standards of learning and teaching.
8. Mobilize the nation's resources to prepare minority youngsters for teaching careers.

The Carnegie Report differs from the other major reports in that it recommended the creation of a National Board for Professional Teaching Standards, organized with a regional and state membership structure, to establish high standards for what teachers need to know and be able to do, and to certify teachers who meet those standards. The Board members are divided into two categories: teaching professional members, and public and other educator members. Two-thirds of the Board will be composed of teaching professionals who have the kind of skills, knowledge, and competence valued by the Board, and who regularly draw on that skill, knowledge, and competence in the conduct of their professional activities. Other Board members, making up one-third of the Board will be made up of public and other educators including members such as governors, state legislators, chief state school officers, school board members, principals, superintendents, university presidents, college deans and faculty members, parents, advocates for minority-student rights, and business and industrial leaders.[11] The Board started with an initial group of thirty-three members and will not exceed sixty-three members. Mary Futrell, president of the National Education Association (NEA) and Albert Shanker, president of the American Federation of Teachers (AFT), were among the initial members of the Board, and are likely to continue as members. The NEA and the AFT, two powerful teacher groups, are very likely to have their presidents as members of the National Board for Professional Teacher Standards. The full implementation of the National Board is still a few years away; many decisions dealing with how it will function, and what its role will eventually be need to be made.

The Carnegie Report, *A Nation Prepared: Teachers for the 21st Century,* recognized the importance of the need for minority teachers. It has been estimated that around the year 2000, about one out of three Americans will be a member of a racial minority. Minorities constitute about 25 percent of the elementary and secondary students, yet the percentage of minority teachers is currently small, estimated at 7 percent or lower. At this stage in history, and in our pluralistic society, it is extremely important for minority students and our nation that there be more minority teachers in our schools. Minority teachers, like non-minority teachers, provide positive role models for students, raising students' aspirations for success in school and in future careers. An issue today is how to produce enough minority candidates who can meet the higher admission standards. Many prospective teachers from minority groups fail to meet high standards, not for lack of ability, but because the schools have failed to provide and demand what was needed for success.[12]

Results in Education: 1987   This report, published by the National Governors' Association in 1987, is a progress report reflecting back to their original report *Time for Results: The Governors' 1991 Report on Education* (1986). In the 1986 Governors' Report they defined seven major issues that will require the *continuing* attention of governors and other state education leaders. Those issues were:[13]

1. Creating a more highly professional teaching force
2. Strengthening school leadership and management
3. Promoting greater parent involvement and choice in their youngsters' education
4. Helping at-risk children and youth meet higher educational standards
5. Making better and more effective use of new technologies in education
6. Making better use of the resources invested in school facilities
7. Strengthening the mission and effectiveness of colleges and universities

In the 1987 Governors' Report, *Results in Education: 1987*, it is proposed that the states take the following steps to assure progress in school reform.[14] Some of the steps presented here have been abbreviated.

1. States will have to assume larger responsibilities for setting educational goals and defining outcome standards.

2. States will need to develop more appropriate and realistic sanctions for failure to meet goals and for consistently poor performance by schools or districts.

3. State education agencies will need to stimulate local inventiveness. For example, both the improvement of educational productivity and the professionalization of teaching will require new school structures that allow more varied instructional arrangements, greater collegial interaction among teachers, and greater teacher involvement in decision making.

4. States will have to examine carefully existing regulations to determine which interfere with local autonomy regarding educational practices, and which serve other purposes.

5. States will need to develop more useful and sophisticated assessment systems. . . . Deregulating educational practices and holding educators accountable for results requires the capacity to accurately measure the results we want.

6. The demands for improved outcomes for elementary and secondary education parallel the demands upon higher education institutions. Therefore, states will need to strengthen coordination between their K–12 and higher education systems.

7. State officials will have to work hard to maintain the broad constituency for education quality.

It is clear that the governors of the states have a role in educational reform, and that they can be powerful and influential. Governors do, however, have to gain the support of their respective legislature to pass laws that foster the development of strong and comprehensive education. Those same legislatures must also authorize expenditures to pay the school reforms. There are quite a few states where reforms were approved but not funded, or had reduced funding.

Agreements among Recent Reports   A study of recent reports conducted by the Education Commission of the States sought to look for points of agreement among nine reports.[15] The reports analyzed were:

1. *Who Will Teach Our Children?*, California Commission on the Teaching Profession.

2. *What Works: Research about Teaching and Learning*, U.S. Department of Education.

3. *Tomorrow's Teachers: A Report of the Holmes Group*, the Holmes Group.

4. *A Nation Prepared: Teachers for the 21st Century*, Carnegie Forum on Education and the Economy.

5. *What Next: More Leverage for Teachers*, Education Commission of the States.

6. *Transforming the State Role in Undergraduate Education*, Education Commission of the States.

7. *Time for Results: The Governors' 1991 Report on Education*, National Governors' Association.

8. *First Lessons: A Report on Elementary Education in America,* William J. Bennett.

9. *College: The Undergraduate Experience in America,* Ernest L. Boyer.

The common points of agreement and disagreement found from the study were:[16]

1. Progress has been made in improving education, but a second round of reforms is needed to better prepare students for a changing society and to address omissions in initial reform reports.

2. Teaching should become a profession, or at least more like a profession.

3. Education policy must enable learning to occur by improving the conditions for learning and teaching.

4. There is cause for optimism that education can be improved because educators know what needs to be done.

5. Other things—attitude, climate, relationships, community support—are as important as money.

6. Real reform is local, because the act of learning is ultimately an individual act.

7. More collaboration is needed, both within the education establishment and beyond to include parents, legislators, governors, and the community as a whole.

8. Education must take new steps to address the needs of minorities.

The reports left several points unresolved, pointing to areas where agreement is difficult to obtain.

1. Many of the reform studies call for more confidence in teachers, principals, schools and districts, but recommended that states be ready to intervene when efforts miss the mark.

2. Educators need assistance in doing things in new ways that take time to show results, the reports acknowledge; but at the same time, they call for immediate assessment and fail to delineate who should judge results or how and when they should be measured.

3. Calls for leadership by governors, boards, legislators, or others create questions of who should do what and conflict with the desire for more collaboration among education constituents and groups outside education.

■ Certification

The ultimate goal of individuals pursuing a program of teacher preparation is to achieve certification, which is in effect their license to teach.

Certification is a function of each of the respective states. It has its legal authority in actions of the respective state legislatures, and is most often implemented through a state office of education. Certification is established to protect state interests. Hopkins has provided a rationale for the relationship between state and public interests and a system of certification.

. . . the right and responsibility of the State to certify teachers is a legitimate, moral and rational use of the political power of the State, only to the extent that teacher certification protects and promotes some demonstrably legitimate public interest of the people for whose welfare and benefit State accredited schools are established. Statutes, policies, and procedures which together constitute teacher certification are not authorized to protect private interests, such as the desires of aspiring teachers for some official State acceptance of previous training and experience. Just as the State does not examine and license physicians in order to assist the graduate of a medical school in pursuing his special private interest of setting up a practice and making money, so the proper purpose of State procedures for teacher certification is not to assist the graduate of a school of education in pursuing his legitimate private goal of getting a job.[17]

Teacher education students seeking information in respect to certification requirements in a specific state should write to the state office of education in the state in which they wish to be certified. This is crucial since requirements are changing rapidly, state by state, throughout the nation. The state office of education is usually located in the capital city of the state and its specific address can be obtained from a directory found in most libraries.

The Certification Process

There are two basic ways in which teachers are certified in the United States today, (1) individual assessment or transcript evaluation, and (2) institutional assessment or program approval. In effect, under transcript evaluation applicants submit their transcript or transcripts to the state agency of education, where they are compared with the state requirements for a specific certificate. If the applicant is judged as meeting the requirements, the appropriate certificate is then issued. Under program approval, the programs of a teacher education institution are evaluated, and either accredited or not accredited by the respective state agency. Students completing accredited programs are granted certification by the state upon recommendation of the institution.

In some states both processes are available, while in other states only one of the two ways is available. Increasing importance and recognition, however, are being placed on program approval. Its major advantages are seen as (1) fixing the responsibility for assessing and recommending individuals on a teacher-preparing institution, and (2) permitting the development of preparation programs that are not straightjacketed by a set of department and credit hour rules.[18] Its weaknesses are (1) reliance on standards that have no empirically established relationship to the performance of those recommended for certification, (2) reliance on human testimony provided by visitation team members, and (3) reliance on the same institution and ultimately the same personnel both to prepare an individual and to determine whether the same individual should be certified.[19] Nevertheless, it is seen by many as superior to the piecemeal, rule-laden interpretation of transcripts. "In short, even under the best of circumstances, transcript evaluation as a means of certificating is on the one hand too rigid and on the other too abstract to enable one to argue that the resultant certificate is directly related to the promotion or protection of state interests.[20] Increasingly, state reciprocity in certification is based on the completion of a teacher training program approved by a state educational agency.

Teacher Alternative Certification Programs[21]

There are at least eighteen states that allow alternative routes to teacher certification. Alternative programs are designed to tap the pool of *college-educated,* non-education majors for the teaching profession.

The typical alternative certification program includes a formal instruction component, some type of intensive field experience, and close supervision of the participant by local school and/or institution of higher education personnel.

In the more traditionally structured programs, participants are full-time students at a college or university for the first semester and combine student teaching and academic course work during the second semester. Programs which depart from the pattern feature full- or part-time classroom teaching responsibility for a school year. In these programs, formal instruction occurs during after-school hours and sometimes on Saturdays. Some programs require coursework and/or classroom observation during the summer as well.

Much of the formal instruction presented to participants in alternative certification programs resembles the content of traditional undergraduate teacher education: philosophical, historical, and sociological foundations of American education; and methods courses, a rubric that covers instructional strategies, classroom organization, organization and management skills, diagnostic and evaluation techniques, and topics specific to the level or subject to be taught. As was indicated earlier, alternative programs do not include subject matter preparation. Participants are selected because they have already mastered a discipline.

Field experiences are rigorous; in some programs the participants teach everyday and then attend late afternoon or evening classes. The field experiences are supervised by a mentor. Generally, participants in alternative certification programs receive more supervision than the average student or first-year teacher.

Designers of alternative certification programs have used different strategies to create a teacher preparation curriculum that: meets state requirements for certification; takes into account the post-graduate status and the maturity of the persons being recruited; and in most cases synthesizes and compresses the material to be covered in a shorter time frame than traditional programs.

■ Continuing Professional Development

The completion of a baccalaureate level teacher preparation program, and the securing of initial certification prepares one to start a teaching career. It does not, however, signal the end of professional development. Practicing professionals, for a variety of reasons, continue to study and improve themselves. Education beyond the initial preparation of teachers is commonly referred to as in-service training.

There are a number of reasons that teachers participate in in-service training. Among them are: (1) upgrading skills because of the changing needs and aspirations of students; (2) developing new skills resulting from new state and federal mandates; (3) responding to dramatic changes in society, and in turn schools, which require changes in role definition; (4) securing a permanent or different credential; and (5) seeking extrinsic rewards such as advancements in salary. There are undoubtedly many other reasons.

A major concern among practicing teachers today centers around who determines or controls in-service teacher education. This is a complicated issue. Obviously in some instances it is the

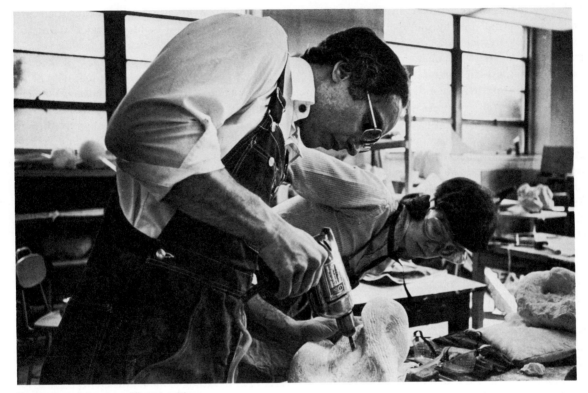

Teachers work in many different settings.

individual self-motivated teacher seeking to improve her or his own performance or advancement. In other instances it is a local board of education that decides that the total staff of teachers or selected teachers need retraining or additional training. Still in other instances it may be the state or federal government that mandates curricular changes that require in-service education for large numbers of teachers. In instances other than self-motivation, teachers feel strongly,

and rightfully so, that they should be involved in the decision making. They seek a voice in determining the nature or content of in-service programs whenever possible; mandated programs by state or federal legislation permit only limited choices. Locally determined programs, however, permit many options and choices. Teachers seek a strong voice in how the training will be conducted, and who shall actually provide the training. In some school districts, such items have become a part of the negotiated professional agreement between the local board of education and the local teachers' association. There is little question that teachers, through their local, state, and national organizations, have gained much ground in their quest to control not only the elements of initial certification, but also the nature of in-service training.

■ A Look to the Future

Predicting the future of teacher education is a tenuous undertaking at best; nevertheless, some inferences can be made based on existing trends. Teacher organizations (AFT and NEA, for example) are likely to continue striving to gain more strength and power at all three levels, local, state, and national. The number of collective bargaining agreements will probably continue to increase, as will the scope of the existing agreements. While in the past many of the benefits gained dealt with teacher welfare, the future is likely to see more agreements giving teachers more control over the curriculum, in-service training, and teacher evaluation. Teachers' organizations at the state and national levels will continue to support candidates for office and sponsor legislation. The membership of teachers on boards of education has increased fivefold in the last decade. In many states, teachers serve on certification boards, having gained that privilege legislatively. They also serve on evaluation teams for the accreditation of teacher education programs. The trend of teachers to gain further control of their profession is likely to continue.

Once almost solely the function of college and university personnel, the education of teachers will increasingly be shared with practicing professionals. Closer relationships between colleges, universities, and public schools will be established. As these relationships strengthen, benefits will accrue to teacher education students, practicing teachers, college and university personnel, and to children and young adults. Teacher education and education in general should benefit as a result.

There is likely to be an increase in teacher-parent contacts and relationships, and perhaps an increasingly important role played by teachers in the community as relationships between schools and communities become more solid.

As the general trend toward individualized instruction intensifies, it is likely that more paraprofessionals, along with more instructional hardware and software, will be used in classrooms. The teacher will become more like a manager—managing the learning process, interacting directly with some students and indirectly with others, and also interacting with students' parents in their homes, and in other community facilities.

The level of professionalism will increase. Trends that point toward this include: the increasing quality of teacher education in the areas of preservice and in-service, the changing roles of the teacher as mentioned previously, and the increase in teacher-parent interactions.

■ Summary

The major purpose of this chapter was to describe the components of teacher preparation programs today (1989); and to look at what teacher preparation programs may be like three to five years from now, dependent somewhat upon the recommendations made in the many recent reports, and the degree and speed of the implementation of the recommendations from those reports.

The vast majority of teacher preparation programs today are four-year programs with general educational, professional, and specialization (academic major) components. In addition, there are state and federal mandates, including instruction in multicultural education and mainstreaming, that must be accommodated. A relatively new activity stimulated by NCATE is the concept of teacher induction. Teacher induction programs provide a variety of support services from colleges and universities and cooperative school districts to first year teachers and sometimes to second year teachers.

Recent initiatives in teacher education reform that were discussed were the testing movement, and the Holmes, Carnegie and National Governors' reports. The testing movement is well underway and in most states prospective teachers must pass an admissions test; and, in some states, a certification test and a test of subject matter knowledge. Seven states now require performance tests, and in seventeen states performance tests are now under study. Essentially, a performance test means that individuals have to exhibit in a classroom or other setting her/his ability to demonstrate mastery of a variety of selected teacher competencies.

The reports of the Holmes Group, the Carnegie Task Force, and the National Governors' Association were discussed. The common points of agreement and disagreement from nine reports were presented. The relatively strong agreement on common points bodes toward optimism for educational reform. As long as reform is closely linked to economic development, the pressure for making changes in education will continue—it is not likely to go away—another factor that bodes toward optimism. Certification in the traditional way, along with alternative ways of securing certification was also presented.

As a prospective teacher, you can expect that you will have to pass an admission test and perhaps other tests in your teacher preparation program. It is possible that you may have a five-year teacher education program, depending upon what college or university you choose to attend. You may also have the opportunity to accept the challenge of a new, different, and exciting teacher preparation program.

Point of View

The point of view article written by Robert D. Barr is entitled "Reform of Teacher Education and the Problem of Quality Assurance." The article provides supplemental information to the issues discussed in Chapter 2. Questions asked and answered are: What form will the changes in teacher education take, and will the changes made improve the quality of public education? The teacher education reform proposals are reviewed and assessed in regard to their acceptance, their controversial nature, and their likely effectiveness.

Reform of Teacher Education and the Problem of Quality Assurance
Robert D. Barr

After more than three decades of harsh and sometimes bitter criticism, the field of teacher education is once again the focus of debate for education reformers. And this time, the field that has so remarkably resisted change may be on the verge of a major transformation. Teacher education is suddenly alive with ferment, both from within and without, and the chance for lasting change seems very real. The questions, of course, are: What form will the change take? And, will the change improve the quality of public education?

The current concern for reforming teacher education has been fueled by a flurry of new recommendations spawned by the politically-charged *Nation At Risk* report. Reformers have shifted the focus of concern from K–12 public schools to higher education. They have cranked up their sights, and while they have leveled their barrage against the entire undergraduate curriculum, their target is clearly teacher education.

Most significant is the fact that this reform effort is not simply the product of some concerned group of social scientists; this time the reform movement has been championed by almost every component of the educational establishment. Even the Deans of Education of elite research universities are actively involved. The movement has attracted an assortment of strange bedfellows that includes prominent southern governors, prestigious state legislators, the Carnegie Foundation, and even Texas millionaire Ross Perot.

This effort at reforming teacher education involves professional associations, accreditation groups, state certification agencies, both the AFT and NEA and their state affiliates, state systems of higher education, AACTE and NCATE. Reform of teacher education has also moved into the State houses and legislatures of the land and been swept into the intense arena of state and local politics. Never has the field of teacher education been charged with such interest.

For a field that has often been criticized for having few new ideas, suddenly teacher education is dealing with "fast tracks," "front loading," competency testing, career ladders, induction programs, basic skills testing, and debates over whether or not teacher education should abandon the undergraduate degree. Controversies are raging over whether or not teacher education should be a one year-fifth year graduate program, or an extended five-year program with both undergraduate and graduate components. There also is serious talk of national standards and a "bar" exam for teachers.

Perhaps most provocative have been a number of controversial, often obscure developments that hold promise for revolution in the field. These developments have raised the most fundamental questions of all regarding teacher education:

- Do teachers need any pedagogical training?
- Should teacher education occur in the context of higher education?
- Should teachers be evaluated solely on the basis of their ability to foster student learning?
- Can teacher effectiveness be predicted?
- Should teacher education be deregulated?

Terms such as "educational productivity," "teacher warranties," and "quality assurance" have entered the discussion of teacher education. These concepts could prove to be the basis for profound change in the field. They could also come and go as yet another passing fad or the newest educational gimmickry. Regardless of the long term impact, these concepts and questions have slipped into the reform debate and already are having an impact on the way teacher education is viewed.

◘ Reform Consensus

While controversies abound in the reform arena, there is an emerging consensus shaping the discussions of the future of teacher education. This consensus is being built through the parallel and often overlapping interests of the major forces working for reform. One such force is the Holmes Group, organized by a group of Deans of Education from major research universities and now composed of more than 100 of the nation's leading schools and colleges of education. The second major force is clearly the *Report of the Task Force on Teaching as a Profession*, prepared by the prestigious Carnegie Forum on Education and the Economy. The third and, in some ways, the most powerful force, is the dramatic and largely independent action of a growing number of governors and the National Governors' Association, legislatures, and state regulatory agencies. Overlapping all of these efforts are those of the AACTE and NCATE. The work of these forces and groups is shaping an emerging consensus for reform of teacher education.

Hiring High Quality Teachers

Most agree on the need to ensure that individuals who teach the nation's youth are intelligent and able. This has led to a number of developments: more vigorous recruitment efforts; enhanced admission standards for teacher education; and teacher testing for competence in basic skills.

While few developments have been more controversial than the testing of classroom teachers, the use of required basic skills testing of preservice teachers is quickly becoming accepted nationwide (Smith, 1986). Unfortunately these tests are eliminating a high percentage of minority students interested in careers in teaching (Hrabowski, 1986).

Requiring Academic Baccalaureate Degrees

There is increasing agreement that all teachers should be required to hold an undergraduate academic degree prior to pursuing teacher certification, though the type of academic degree that would best serve elementary teachers and some areas in vocational and technical education has yet to be determined. Areas such as business education and industrial education pose especially difficult problems.

Mandating Graduate Education Degrees for Teachers

Perhaps most controversial is the growing interest in moving teacher education to a fifth-year program that culminates in a Master's degree, or a Master of Arts in Teaching. The primary controversy revolves around whether or not teacher education would be completely restricted to a one year-fifth year graduate program, or if teacher education would be an extended program with both an undergraduate and a graduate component. Just as two decades ago states throughout the country required bachelor's degrees of all public school teachers, now another shift toward graduate education for beginning teachers seems to be occurring.

Developing National Standards and National Teacher Exams

Equally controversial, but clearly an issue that is gaining acceptance, is the interest in developing national teacher standards and teacher examinations similar to those required of attorneys and nurses. Regardless of opinions within the professional arena, more and more states are requiring the testing of preservice teachers over the content areas in which they plan to teach and in the area of pedagogy. Far more controversial will be the development of national standards and a possible national teacher test. The Carnegie Foundation already has funded Stanford University to begin preliminary research development in this area.

Improving Conditions for Teachers

Conditions in the nation's classrooms also are being related to teacher education. Recommendations are now encouraging career ladders, mentor teachers, higher salaries, and more autonomy for teachers. There is consensus that the induction process during the first years of teaching is an essential element of teacher education.

■ Reform Disappointments

While the reform consensus has stimulated an energetic retooling of teacher education in all parts of the country, there is a disappointing side effect to the reform furor. There is no real assurance that the reform efforts now being considered will improve the quality of public education in America (Soder, 1986). The same research universities that are now calling for the transition of teacher education to the graduate fifth year have conducted little or no research to indicate that such programs will prepare better teachers or improve the quality of our schools. Indiana University, long recognized for high quality teacher education, has flatly refused to replace its undergraduate program with a fifth year program without better data supporting such a move (Mehlinger, 1986). And because the fifth-year model has been tried on numerous occasions—most notably in California— without documented improvement in public education, there are many who are reluctant to support this recommendation.

A fifth year teacher education program could also represent a significant ''detraining'' of beginning teachers when compared to existing undergraduate programs, or when compared to the extended (4 plus 1) teacher education program at Florida State University and the University of Kansas. There is also a fear that existing undergraduate teacher education programs will simply be moved to the fifth year and "inflated" into a second class advanced degree providing higher cost teachers to local public schools without the noticeable benefit of improved teacher effectiveness or "productivity."

Requiring teachers to hold academic baccalaureate degrees represents less of a step forward than it would appear. Such a development is based in misconceptions of existing high quality teacher education programs, perhaps even a mythology regarding teacher education. An informal assessment (conducted by the author) of a few major schools of education revealed that approximately 20% of the teacher education students are now entering programs as post baccalaureates following graduation with a BS or BA degree in an academic area. Another 30% of teacher education students, typically secondary education majors, pursue double undergraduate majors, or a major in an academic area while pursuing teacher certification. The other half of the teacher education students are elementary education majors. Academic majors may not serve the nation's schools any better than an existing undergraduate teacher education program. And there is real question about whether an elementary teacher can be adequately prepared in a one-year program.

Little evidence exists to suggest that further study in academic areas or demonstration of knowledge in academic areas as measured by the National Teacher Examination will improve classroom teaching effectiveness (Murray, 1986). In fact, few teachers are ever evaluated as being ineffective because of a lack of subject matter knowledge. The vast majority of teachers who are judged to be ineffective have difficulties with

classroom management, discipline, and planning—not subject matter. And while no one would argue that teachers should have minimum basic skills in reading, writing, and mathematics there is no assurance that classroom teaching will be improved by reaching a particular cutoff score on a basic skills examination.

Further, will the reforms attract better, higher qualified students who are interested in teacher education programs and teaching? Certainly, there is some anxiety that the brighter, more able students might not wish to spend a year beyond their baccalaureate degree and subject themselves to the somewhat humiliating experience of being tested for basic skills and content knowledge in order to enter a profession with salaries far below those of an attorney, a nurse, or even an accountant. Higher standards and longer programs could lead to a significant reduction in the number of teachers being prepared. This reduction is in addition to that already occurring from the impact of testing on the number of minority teachers entering our nation's schools. From this point of view, it may not be true that the more things change, the more they stay the same; a growing fear is that the more things change, the worse things may become (Cornbleth, 1986).

With the exception of the issues that relate teacher education to the work place (i.e., career ladders, mentor teachers, induction programs for beginning teachers, and higher salaries), the consensus reforms have very traditional, academic characteristics. They focus on degrees, academic majors, length of programs, grade point averages, test scores, program level in higher education, and a variety of academic issues largely divorced from the realities of the nation's classrooms. Unfortunately, they also tend to be divorced from research in the field. There are, however, a number of intriguing developments which have emerged to focus attention on performance rather than knowledge.

■ Reforms Focusing on Performance

While the mainstream reform of teacher education is alive with controversy, there are a variety of independent but conceptually interrelated developments that can only be viewed as potentially revolutionary for the field. Some of these developments have been dictated by the educational marketplace, others are the result of a "consumer revolt" which has demanded more and more accountability from the educational establishment, and a number of them come from unique educational research and development projects. Taken together, these developments may profoundly affect the future of teacher education in America.

Far from dealing with the traditional, academic components of teacher education, these developments take teacher education into very new and different directions. The developments can be clustered in two broad categories: (a) the growing interest in deregulating teacher education and (b) the issues surrounding quality assurance in teacher education.

Deregulation of Teacher Education

Since the mid-1950's, teacher education in the United States has been carefully and thoroughly regulated—both by State teacher certification agencies and by the National Council for the Accreditation of Teacher Education. Most of these regulations function through the establishment of standards that are then translated into program requirements by teacher education institutions. State certification agencies review programs of teacher education institutions, and then, if they meet the established standards, they are sanctioned. This "approved program" approach to teacher education has become the status quo; teacher education is, as a consequence, regulated through program and course requirements (Behling, 1986). To determine if an individual is qualified for certification, transcripts are reviewed to determine if all course requirements have been met. Over time, the requirements of approved programs have steadily increased to include special education, multicultural education, specified subject matter content, issues dealing with discrimination, state and local government, consumer finance, career education, and sometimes even Red Cross training. Recent public concerns regarding substance abuse, child abuse, and even AIDS may well lead to additional requirements in approved programs.

Until very recently, it was assumed that students were prepared if they had completed the course requirements of approved programs. Now this assumption is being questioned, as well as the companion assumption that the knowledge gained through approved programs actually relates to teaching effectiveness in school classrooms. In recent years, recognition of grade inflation in education programs, the tremendous variation in quality of the more than 1000 institutions preparing teachers in America, and the fact that teacher education majors may well be the weakest students in higher education, has led to a demand for testing of teacher candidates.

Fast Track into Teaching

The most dramatic development, and potentially most damaging to traditional teacher education programs, is the notion of "fast tracks" into teaching that allow college graduates to enter the public school classrooms with little or no professional education and none of the traditional requirements for teacher certification. Rather than being required to meet established teacher education requirements, these fast track teachers are evaluated on their effectiveness as classroom teachers. Initiated in a number of states as a response to teacher shortages, most notably in New Jersey and California, the fast track focuses interest on performance rather than course/program requirements. Even the traditionally conservative state of Oregon has established a highly regulated fast track program for selected teacher shortage areas. The concept is simple: When qualified teachers are not available, school districts are permitted to seek college graduates with degrees in needed content areas. When hired, these individuals are provided interim certification and a professional development program designed to improve their pedagogical skills. Their teaching effectiveness is then evaluated. After a period of time with successful evaluations, teachers earn regular certification.

While most states provide individual exceptions to approved programs, either through temporary or emergency certification to meet specific local school needs, the fast track concept could revolutionize teacher education in America—especially if a teacher shortage emerges. The impact could be even greater if the evaluation of these fast track teachers proves positive; that is, if nontrained teachers are "apparently" as effective as trained teachers.

School-Based Teacher Education

Directly related to the fast track into teaching is the associated development of moving the responsibility for teacher education from colleges and universities to local school districts. The Los Angeles Public Schools now clearly constitutes a major teacher education institution. The school district prepares more new teachers than any college or university in California. Such developments render the discussion of degree requirements and approved programs largely irrelevant.

Certification through Teacher Testing

Almost every state has established requirements for testing the basic skills of reading, writing, and mathematics. There is also an increase in the use of subject matter content tests and tests of pedagogy. In spite of strong disclaimers by the

Education Testing Service (and others) that there is no direct relationship between the National Teachers Examination and teaching effectiveness, the National Teacher Examinations have typically been used as the assessment instruments for both content and pedagogy (Galambos, 1986). The next step may be national standards, including a national examination for teachers.

As these tests have been required by institutions and states, their use has been accompanied by a growing conviction that standardized tests may gauge a person's preparation to teach better than a college transcript or a student's cumulative grade point average. In keeping with other states, Oregon already has established new standards that permit certified teachers to add new teaching endorsement areas by performing satisfactorily on the appropriate NTE content exam, rather than by completing the course requirements of an approved program.

Unfortunately, most of the content exams currently in use measure only "minimum basic knowledge" in a particular subject matter area. There is no doubt that teacher testing combined with performance evaluation during on-the-job teaching provide a powerful alternative to the approved program approach to teacher education. For now, few states have been willing to consider the wholesale abandonment of the approved program, but an increasing number are considering some combination of approved program requirements with mandated testing programs. The next step will likely be the emergence of teacher education programs that employ assessment of both knowledge and teaching performance in a classroom setting.

Oregon is one of the states currently wrestling with the need to deregulate teacher certification. An Interim Legislative Committee recently issued a report calling for the State Certification Agency, the

Oregon Teacher Standards and Practices Commission, to consider new certification requirements. The report says:

Some believe that this "program approval" function should be eliminated, so that each institution would be completely free to design programs as they [sic] pleased. The certification of teachers would then be solely based on performance on various certification tests. After much discussion, however, the committee agreed that total "deregulation" of teacher education is unwarranted at this time.

Instead, the Teacher Standards and Practices Commission, the State's certification agency, should substantially reorient its existing process of "program approval." Rather than rely largely on "input" measures such as the number of course hours required in various areas, TSPC should begin to put its primary emphasis on such "output" measures as the success of graduates on various licensure exams and in actual classroom teaching. (Teaching As A Profession, 1986, page 15.)

Quality Assurance for Teacher Education

The concern for developing "Quality Assurance Teacher Education" (QATE) has not only involved interest in knowledge assessment and teaching performance, it has focused on the concept of "educational productivity" as the primary component to be used to assess teacher performance. The QATE has engendered the possibility of predicting teacher effectiveness. The only development that brought these issues together was the announcement by a few colleges and universities of a warranty for beginning teachers (Barr, 1984). And while some institutions may have initiated teacher warranties as a media gimmick, the power of the concept soon became apparent. It seems to have special merit with regard to the design of an induction phase for teacher education. The concept is also reflected in certain sections of the new NCATE Accreditation Standards (Barr, 1985).

Teacher Warranties

During the last three years, more than a dozen schools and departments of education have created warranty programs that assure the quality of their teacher education graduates. These programs have been initiated at several major universities (Oregon State University-Western Oregon State College, Purdue University, University of Virginia, University of Nebraska, University of Northern Colorado, North Texas State University, and Montana State University), a few medium-sized universities (Emporia State University, Eastern Washington University), several small colleges (Doane College, Adelphi, Concordia of Seward, etc.), and two predominantly black institutions (Grambling State University and University of Arkansas at Pine Bluff). Federal legislation also has been passed requiring the U.S. Department of Education to develop criteria for a model warranty program.

While each of the warranty programs described is distinctive, there are a number of features that all seem to have in common:

- Teacher warranty programs are a form of quality assurance for employers.
- Teacher warranty programs are a form of institutional commitment to graduates.
- Teacher warranty programs are a means of providing assistance to beginning teachers.

Each warranty program emphasizes the careful evaluation of teachers during their first year in the classroom and involves a commitment to provide a wide variety of support services (Barr, 1985). The services typically include: "Hot-line" telephone consultation; onsite observation, consultation, and support; funds for substitute teachers to allow beginning teachers to participate in professional development activities; and special workshop opportunities for beginning teachers to return to campus for additional coursework, which is tuition free.

At a recent Wingspread Conference on Quality Assurance in Teacher Education, representatives from AACTE, NCATE, and the Holmes Group met with teacher educators who had initiated warranty programs. Many participants arrived as interested skeptics, but most left the conference agreeing on the primary advantages of warranty programs:

1. The warranty programs provide an exciting new avenue for working with public schools. Even those public school educators who never had occasion to use the warranty felt it was good to know it was there. The warranty clearly helped to strengthen relationships between public schools and SCDEs.

2. The warranty provides a legitimate process for college and university professors to act as ombudsmen or advocates for the beginning teachers. Through experience with warranty programs, it was discovered that approximately half of the beginning teachers who were experiencing difficulty were placed in situations that made effective teaching nearly impossible. Many beginning teachers were "misassigned" to areas outside their certification areas, or were assigned multiple, often five or more, teaching preparations. Often the beginning teachers were assigned the worst students in the worst schools.

3. The warranty confronts SCDE faculty members with their responsibilities for preparing teachers, not for just teaching courses. It has caused teacher educators to increase program admission standards, to develop more rigorous programs, and to screen students more closely as they matriculate through programs.

4. The warranty provides teacher educators with an opportunity to work with former students after they enter their own classrooms.

Educational Productivity and Teacher Evaluation

There has always been interest in assessing the educational productivity of schools. No other factor has motivated education reform quite so much as the declining SAT scores of high school seniors. Almost every state in the country has established mandatory achievement testing programs, and many states have established final "barrier exams" as a prerequisite to graduation. The State of Washington has recently required all college and university sophomores to pass a competency exam before they progress to upper division courses. In recent years educators have also seen the development of the National Assessment of Educational Progress (NAEP) and interest in utilizing the testing program of NAEP to develop comparative "report cards" for each of the nation's fifty states. Some states are already developing school profiles based on standardized achievement tests to compare schools and school districts.

The concept of educational productivity also has been encouraged by the body of research referred to as the "Effective Teaching and Effective Schools Research." This research relates enhanced student learning to a number of interrelated teaching variables. Extrapolations from this research have become the single most powerful force for improving the content of teacher education programs.

The politically charged question that is now being raised is whether teacher productivity (i.e., the degree to which a teacher fosters student learning) can be used as the key indicator of teacher effectiveness.

The issue, of course, is complex. Teachers and their unions have always resisted using student learning as an element in the evaluation of teaching effectiveness; there are simply too many variables affecting learning that are beyond the teachers' control: socioeconomic level of students, parental support, family mobility, student motivation, class size, curriculum. There is also the very real concern about using standardized achievement tests as the primary, or even sole basis for assessing student learning. Yet the public and the legislatures are now demanding to know what children have learned and what they have not learned. They are not satisfied that a student has spent a year in the third grade, or finished elementary school, or graduated from high school. Increasingly, if students have not learned, the public is demanding to know just why this has been allowed to occur.

Interest in educational productivity has stimulated cost analysis of education programs. Highly complex formulae are being developed to compare financial costs of various approaches and programs to educational outcomes (Hanushek, 1986). Some superintendents are demanding that investments in professional staff development show discernible student achievement results. Teacher inservice for elementary teachers in the areas of mathematics and science have been accompanied in some districts with expectations for improved student achievement in these areas. Even the Carnegie Forum concluded that a better understanding of educational productivity could lead to long-range reductions in educational costs. Productivity data regarding computer assisted learning, autotutorial learning labs, and other types of individual or programmed learning, are increasingly providing new ways of learning and better educational accountability (Ellson, 1986). And, researchers are increasingly identifying key variables that affect both student learning and teacher effectiveness (Schalock, 1977; Resnick and Resnick, 1985).

In the end, an interest in deregulating teacher education, or developing realistic quality assurance must focus on developing better techniques of evaluating teacher effectiveness. Those working with warranty programs have discovered a wide variety of teacher evaluation systems being used in local schools which have helped to dramatize how poorly this important function is being carried out. However, none of the systems, many of which are highly sophisticated for analyzing classroom interactions, deal with the ultimate question: Are the teachers who are being evaluated able to foster or enhance a district's goals for learning among the students they teach? Even the most recent publication on teacher evaluation, published cooperatively by three national school administrators' professional associations and the NEA, carefully avoids any mention of this difficult topic (Duke and Stiggins, 1986). In the end, regardless of the difficulties associated with the task, this is precisely what the educational enterprise is all about, and it seems ever more apparent that this is exactly what parents, citizens, and legislatures will be demanding. Unfortunately, research on this topic is all too rare.

In a little known development project in Oregon, 10 small school districts have been involved for more than a decade with the Oregon Department of Education in developing goal-based educational programs. The 10 districts have agreed upon basic learning goals for the elementary grades and have developed assessment procedures that permit teachers and administrators to monitor student progress toward goal attainment. Related analysis procedures have been developed that permit student learning to be analyzed for individual teachers as well as across teachers at each grade level and school.

This assessment capability has permitted the districts involved to identify teachers who are able to foster learning across all subject areas and all students, and obviously, other teachers who are unable to do so in one or more subject areas. Teachers have been identified who are able to foster learning with gifted students, but not with "at risk" youth, other teachers have just the opposite pattern (for a fuller discussion of these data, see the article in this issue of the *Journal* by Mark Schalock). The culmination of this work has led educators to believe that with current technology, teaching effectiveness can be linked to student achievement and that staff development programs can be targeted to enhance student achievement.

In a related development, the OSUWOSC School of Education has developed a Teacher Productivity Evaluation System for use in its teacher education program. This system, which is being field tested for the first time this year, evaluates the success of student teachers on the basis of their ability to identify learning goals and to develop an assessment program to measure the success of their students in achieving the goals. The evaluation of the student teacher will include a detailed profile of his or her ability to foster student learning with respect to these goals. The profiles will be available to potential employers. While this work is just beginning, demonstrable results seem to occur when students fully understand that their success as student teachers depends on their ability to show that their students learn what they are being taught. This requirement seems to help students focus their energies, and address with real purpose the important responsibility of teaching.

The Prediction of Teacher Effectiveness

The final question for teacher educators, of course, is not just whether a student teacher's ability to foster student learning can be assessed, but whether or not the ability to foster learning as a first- or second-year teacher can be predicted from that person's performance as a student teacher or intern. Only when such predictions can be made will a true warranty program be possible. Already, a few colleges and universities which have established warranty programs are pursuing just this line of work (see the article in this issue of the *Journal* by Del Schalock).

The approach being taken in the merged Oregon State University-Western Oregon State College School of Education takes the form of collecting detailed assessment information during a student's teacher education program—information regarding basic skills levels, knowledge levels in content and pedagogy, and a cumulative record of the ability to foster student learning in short term controlled settings, including student teaching or a graduate practicum or internship—and using this information to make targeted predictions of teacher success during his or her first teaching job. Work also is underway in Oregon to combine predictions of success for first-year teachers with teacher evaluation during the first three years of teaching. The aim of this work is to improve the "million dollar" decision that is made by a district each time it tenures a teacher, a decision that is fundamentally a prediction as to the long-term effectiveness and productivity of the teacher being tenured (Barr and Schalock, 1986).

Predictions in the realm of teaching are recognized as an area fraught with problems. Graduates trained in one type of setting with one type of student may ultimately find jobs in a setting dramatically different from their training experience. Few believe that predictions would be possible across the wide gamut of school settings, but predictions for particular types of settings might, nonetheless, prove helpful. Certainly predictions of effectiveness made during on-the-job evaluations should prove invaluable.

■ Conclusion

While public and professional attention will certainly continue to be focused on the academically based, consensus reforms described earlier, it is possible that developments around the assessment of teacher performance will find their way into teacher education in a more substantial manner. A beginning can be found in the new NCATE Standards, in the programs of a few major colleges and universities, and in a few research and development activities. Further, the concept certainly can be found in sections of the Carnegie Forum report. If, however, performance assessment is to have an impact, it must build on the research of the past regarding quality control and the teacher competency movement. It must also become the focus of research efforts to explore the many obscure facets of the problem. If this does not occur, teacher effectiveness will continue to be evaluated on a superficial, subjective basis that will fail to distinguish the effective teachers from those who are ineffective.

From Robert D. Barr, "Reform of Teacher Education and the Problem of Quality Assurance," *The Journal of Teacher Education*, XXXVIII (5): 45–51, September/October 1987. Copyright © 1987 American Association of Colleges for Teacher Education, Washington, DC. Reprinted by permission.

■ Questions for Discussion

1. What are the strengths and weaknesses of teacher testing and performance assessment?

2. What is your reaction to the recommendations of *Tomorrow's Teachers, A Nation Prepared,* and *Time for Results?*

3. Will the recommendations made in the aforementioned three reports improve the status or prestige of the teaching profession? Why? Why not?

4. Why has training in multicultural education become a requirement for teacher certification in many states?

5. What is the legal basis for teacher certification?

■ Notes

1. Division of Teacher Education and Certification, Kentucky Department of Education, *Kentucky Teacher Preparation and Certification Handbook* (Frankfort, KY: Superintendent of Public Instruction, 1976), pp. 37–38.

2. National Council for Accreditation of Teacher Education, "Standards, Procedures and Policies for the Accreditation of Professional Teacher Education Units" (Washington, D.C.: October, 1986), p. 32.

3. Ibid., p. 47.

4. Ibid.

5. Ibid., p. 46.

6. J. T. Sandefur, "Historical Perspective," *What's Happening in Teacher Testing: An Analysis of State Teacher Testing Practices* (Washington, D.C.: Office of Educational Research and Improvement, Department of Education, August, 1987), p. 11.

7. R. W. Cole, *Phi Delta Kappan* editorial (December 1979):233.

8. J. T. Sandefur, "Standards for Admission to Teacher Education Programs," an issue paper prepared for the Minnesota Higher Education Coordinating Board (August 1984).

9. Lawrence M. Rudner, "Questions and Answers Concerning Teacher Testing," *What's Happening in Teacher Testing: An Analysis of State Teacher Testing Programs* (Washington, D.C.: Office of Educational Research and Improvement, Department of Education, August 1984), p. 7.

10. Text of Carnegie Report excerpted from *Education Week,* vol. v, no. 35, May 21, 1986, pp. 11–18.

11. Lynn Olson, "Carnegie Unveils Makeup of National Teacher Board," *Education Week,* vol. vi, no. 34, May 20, 1987, pp. 1, 14, 15.

12. Lynn Olson, "Carnegie Teaching Panel Charts 'New Framework' ", *Education Week,* vol. v, no. 35, May 21, 1986, p. 14.

13. "Introduction," *Results in Education 1987* (Washington, D.C. National Governors' Association, 1987), p. 1.

14. "Introduction," *Results in Education 1987* (Washington, D.C.: National Governors' Association, 1987), pp. 3–4.

15. Joslyn Green, *The Next Wave: A Synopsis of Recent Education Reform Reports.* (Denver, CO: Education Commission of the States, 1987), p. 40.

16. Joslyn Green, "Summary of Common Points," *The Next Wave: A Synopsis of Recent Reports* (Denver, CO: Education Commission of the States, 1987), p. 1–2.

17. John Hopkins, *Basic Legal Issues in New York State on Teacher Certification* (Lincoln, NE: Study Commission, 1973), p. 4.

18. Larry Freeman, "State Interest, Certification, and Teacher Education Program Approval," *Legal Issues in Teacher Preparation and Certification* (Washington, DC: ERIC Clearinghouse on Teacher Education, Suite 616, One DuPont Circle, NW 20036, June 1977), p. 82.

19. Ibid.

20. Ibid.

21. Excerpted from N. E. Adelman, "An Examination of Alternative Certification Programs," *What's Happening in Teacher Testing: An Analysis of State Teacher Testing Practices* (Washington, DC: Office of Educational Research and Improvement, Department of Education, August 1984), pp. 131–134.

■ Selected References

American Association of Colleges for Teacher Education. *Minority Teacher Recruitment and Retention: A Call for Action.* Washington, D.C.: American Association of Colleges for Teacher Education, 1987.

American Association of Colleges for Teacher Education. *Teaching Teachers: Facts and Figures.* Washington, D.C.: American Association of Colleges for Teacher Education, 1987.

Carnegie Forum on Education and the Economy. *A Nation Prepared: Teachers for the 21st Century.* Washington, D.C.: Carnegie Forum on Education and the Economy, 1986.

Green, Joslyn. *The Next Wave: A Synopsis of Recent Education Reforms.* Denver, CO: Education Commission of the States, 1987.

The Holmes Group. *Tomorrow's Teachers: A Report of the Holmes Group.* Lansing, MI: The Holmes Group, 1986.

National Council for Accreditation of Teacher Education. "Standards, Procedures and Policies for Accreditation of Professional Teacher Education Units. Washington, D.C.: National Council for the Accreditation of Teacher Education, 1986.

National Governors' Association Center for Policy Research and Analysis. *Time for Results: The Governors' 1991 Report on Education.* Washington, D.C.: National Governors' Association, 1986.

National School Boards Association. *Good Teachers: An Unblinking Look at Supply and Preparedness.* Alexandria, VA: National School Boards Association, 1987.

Office of Educational Research and Improvement. *What's Happening in Teacher Testing: An Analysis of State Teacher Testing Practices.* Washington, D.C.: Office of Educational Research and Improvement, Department of Education, 1987.

Romanish, Bruce. "A Skeptical View of Educational Reform." *Journal of Teacher Education* 38, no. 5 (May-June 1987):9–12.

Chapter 3

The Teacher's Changing Role

Objectives

After studying this chapter, you should be able to:

- Describe the day-by-day work routine of the teacher.

- Contrast the work of contemporary educators with that of their historical counterparts.

- Illustrate that teachers are better prepared and increasingly competent as professional educators.

- Understand the concept that the most effective learning takes place when the teacher serves as a ''learning facilitator'' rather than as a ''dispenser of knowledge.''

- Articulate the importance of the ''planning'' a teacher must do if effective learning is to take place.

- Describe the diagnostic and evaluation functions an educator must fulfill.

- Discuss the implications of ''mainstreaming'' for the regular classroom teacher.

- Describe the role of the teacher as a manager of the instructional team.

- Understand various approaches to maintaining classroom control.

Enrichment Experiences

The following activities will help you learn more about some of the important topics in this chapter:

- Plan a hypothetical lesson using the suggestions presented in this chapter.

- Analyze the pupil's cumulative record presented in figure 3.6. What does this record tell you?

- Interview a teacher concerning his or her role as an educator.

- Talk to a variety of parents about their expectations of teachers.

- Study the report card in figure 3.7. What does it tell you about Sue Stone? How could this type of report card form be improved?

- Role-play several situations in which a teacher displays poor human relations skills. Also role-play some situations in which a teacher exhibits good human relations skills.

- Visit with a local school administrator about discipline problems in schools today.

The purpose of this chapter is to help you understand how the role of the teacher has changed considerably over time. The role of today's teacher is complex and includes such dimensions as attending to classroom detail, designing learning experiences, deciding learning objectives, helping students to learn in a wide variety of ways, maintaining a good classroom environment, providing students with a positive learning environment, working with mainstreamed handicapped students, providing multicultural education, assessing learning outcomes, providing feedback to pupils and parents, managing the instructional team, understanding and getting along with people, and becoming a self-renewing professional. Particular emphasis is placed on the subject of maintaining good classroom discipline because this turns out to be one of the more difficult tasks for student teachers and beginning teachers. The topics discussed in this chapter are of particular significance and extremely practical for the new teacher. ■

A teacher wears many hats in the course of a school day, a school week, and a school year. For example, every teacher must be a lesson planner, purveyor of knowledge, motivator, disciplinarian, counselor, confidant, mediator, curriculum planner, worker for a professional teacher's organization, human relations expert, and record keeper. Truly, a teacher must have a multitude of talents and be competent in many different roles in order to be successful. In this chapter we will examine some of the more specific tasks included in the role of the teacher.

■ Attending to Classroom Details

One of the tasks that has historically consumed much of a teacher's time is traditionally called *keeping school*. School-keeping involves such "chores" as ordering supplies, keeping the classroom tidy and clean (even though most schools now hire competent custodians to do all the major cleaning, a teacher still has a good deal of minor housecleaning chores to perform), keeping attendance records, checking books in and out, collecting lunch money, putting up bulletin boards and displays of various sorts, and filling out forms and reports that the school may require. While school-keeping chores such as these are important and must be done, they have historically consumed too much of a teacher's valuable time—time better spent working with students. Fortunately, in recent years schools have found ways to relieve the teacher of many of these chores. Many schools have developed simplified methods of record keeping that require very little time on the part of the teachers. Also, some schools now employ "paraprofessional" help to do these school-keeping chores, thereby freeing the teacher for spending more time working with students.

■ Designing Learning Experiences

One of the most important roles that a teacher plays is that of "planner." A teacher is given a great deal of freedom and autonomy in planning what will take place in the classroom. This is as it should be, because today's teacher is a highly trained, competent professional who is the best qualified to determine what each student needs in the classroom. In some instances, a teacher will be given a broad planning document such as a curriculum guide that may originate at the state,

Education is a painful, continual and difficult work to be done by kindness, by watching, by warning, by precept, and by praise, but above all—by example.

John Ruskin

county, or school district level. Such documents, however, are only general guidelines, and each individual teacher must still plan the specific day-to-day program. An increasing amount of the planning task is being done cooperatively by groups of teachers in conjunction with team teaching, or in summer efforts to prepare various types of units and other curricular materials. More and more, school districts are realizing the value that can accrue from hiring teachers during the summer to do such cooperative planning.

The success of a school program for a given student will be dependent, in large measure, upon the quality of planning that went into that student's program. By the same token, the success of the educational program of an entire school system will be determined by the planning that goes into that program. The same thing is true, incidentally, for the entire American educational system.

There are a number of different levels of planning a teacher must do. These levels are shown in figure 3.1, wherein a teacher begins with a general long-range yearly lesson plan for each subject taught. This yearly lesson plan must be flexible so that changes can be made in the plan during the year as the need arises. Figure 3.1 also shows that a teacher must make semester plans as well (or quarter plans, depending upon how the school year may be divided). Like the yearly plan, these semester plans must be general and flexible. One of the many values of these long-range plans is that they permit the teacher to gather more and better instructional materials (some of which may be difficult to obtain) by the time they are needed. Long-range planning also permits teachers to think through what they really want the students to learn over a long period of time.

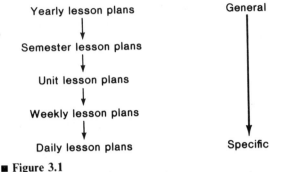

■ Figure 3.1
Levels of lesson planning

Perhaps the single most important and valuable type of planning that a teacher does is what is commonly known as the unit lesson plan. The unit plan is one that is done for a rather discrete segment of the year's work in a given subject. Units can vary greatly in size; however, most of them range between a week and a month in length. Units can also vary greatly in scope, depending upon the grade level and subject. Examples of typical units are: finger painting in first grade art, the Native American in third grade social studies, poetry in fifth grade English, the digestive system in seventh grade science, squares and square roots in tenth grade mathematics, forms of mental illness in twelfth grade psychology, or the role of the teacher in a college introduction-to-teaching course.

A unit may be defined as an organization of learning activities and experiences around a central theme developed cooperatively by a group of pupils under a teacher's leadership. The essential features implied by this definition are that (1) learning takes place through many types of experiences rather than through a single activity such as reading and reciting; (2) the activities are

No nation can remain free which does not recognize the importance of education. Our public schools are the backbone of American life and character. We must recognize their importance and stand firmly against any groups which oppose popular education.

Liberty can never flourish in any nation where there is no popular education.

Samuel M. Lindsay

unified around a central theme, problem, or purpose; (3) the unit provides opportunities for socialization of pupils by means of cooperative group planning; and (4) the role of the teacher is that of leader rather than that of taskmaster.

There are a variety of different approaches that a teacher can take in planning a unit. For instance, a teacher can plan what is essentially a "subject matter unit," a selection of materials and educative experiences centering upon those materials, which are arranged around a central core found within the subject matter itself. The core may be a generalization, a concept, a topic, or a theme. The unit is to be studied by pupils for the purpose of achieving learning outcomes derivable from experiences with subject matter.

A teacher may also plan what is essentially an "experience unit." This is a series of educative experiences organized around a pupil purpose, problem, or need, utilizing socially useful subject matter and materials, resulting in the achievement of the purpose, and in the achievement of learning outcomes inherent in the process.

In actuality all units use both experience and subject matter. The difference is primarily one of emphasis. It should be understood that in actual practice the terminology used is not the important consideration. What is important is that the teacher must be concerned with providing rich and varied learning experiences for each student.

A third type of unit plan is commonly referred to as a "resource unit," which is not ordinarily planned as a single teaching unit. It is usually developed by a committee of teachers with little or no pupil assistance. Hence it becomes a "resource *of* units." Frequently they are not developed with any particular group of children in mind; in fact, the materials may be used in several grades; they cover broad areas of content and always contain more information and many more suggestions than could be used with any one class. A resource unit on conservation might include materials to be used in teaching several units on recreation, public health, lumbering, fishing, mining, and flood control.

In preparing a unit plan, it is recommended that a teacher:

a. State clearly the purposes (*objectives* or *goals,* as they are often called) of teaching the unit. In other words, what changes does the teacher want to make in the child in terms of knowledge, skills, habits, attitudes, and appreciations? These stated purposes of the unit should be expressed in "behavioral" terms, or, in other words, in terms of student behavior that will be exhibited when the purposes of the unit have been accomplished. When stated this way, a teacher can measure the success of the unit.

b. Look up references on the subject, read them, and write a content outline of the material, listing references.

c. List the materials to be used in the unit. This will include such items as pictures, slides, movies, models, and construction materials.

d. List the ways in which the teacher will lead the children into the unit of work; these are called *possible approaches.*

e. List the activities that will help the children attain the purposes or outcomes of the unit.

f. List the means by which the teacher will evaluate the unit. If a written test is considered, at least a rough draft of the test should be included in the unit.

Many schools ask teachers to make very brief weekly lesson plans so that in the event a regular teacher becomes ill, a substitute teacher would have an idea of what was planned each day for each class. These weekly lesson plans are usually extremely brief—frequently written on special forms prepared for this purpose.

A teacher's most specific planning is that done for a specific lesson on a given day. Daily lesson planning is relatively simple, providing the teacher has already made adequate unit lesson plans. Excellent unit plans will have permitted the teacher to gather all of the necessary learning resources ahead of time and to have clearly thought through the general objectives for the unit. The final detail and specific objectives necessary in a daily lesson plan flow naturally and quite easily out of a well done unit lesson plan. The lesson plan is designed simply as a means to good instruction. It has no magic value in and of itself, and cannot be justified as an elaborate masterpiece. The lesson plan is simply a means to an end—a device to help the teacher be well prepared to teach.

Lesson plans may take numerous forms. There is no one best way to prepare lesson plans; however, most teachers find it desirable to follow some structured format and to do much of this planning on paper. One lesson plan format that has been found useful by many educators is that found in figure 3.2. This format can serve for all the levels of planning that a teacher must do, whether they be yearly plans, semester plans, unit plans, weekly plans, or daily plans. As the figure shows, the first task that a teacher has in planning is to determine the plan's objectives. Objectives become the road map of the lesson—they

A. Objectives
B. Materials needed
C. Procedure
   1. Teacher activity
   2. Student activity
D. Provisions for measuring extent to which stated objectives were achieved

■ **Figure 3.2**
A suggested lesson plan format

indicate the purposes of the lesson and the desired learning outcomes for the students. As has already been suggested, educational objectives should always be stated in terms of student behavior that can be measured. This is necessary so that after the lesson is completed, the teacher can determine whether or not each student has achieved the desired outcomes. Objectives thus stated are frequently called *behavioral objectives.*

The figure also shows that in planning a lesson, a teacher must determine what materials will be needed for that lesson. As will be indicated in chapter 14, a wealth of instruction materials is now available to educators. A teacher must be familiar with these teaching materials and must also know which is the most effective material to use in a given situation.

Figure 3.2 further indicates that teachers must thoroughly plan the procedure for each lesson. To effectively do this, they must have a thorough understanding of the nature of the learner—a topic discussed in chapter 12. They must also be familiar with a wide variety of teaching techniques.

Lastly, the figure shows that a teacher must make provisions for measuring the extent to which the stated objectives for each lesson are achieved.

This provides the teacher with a measure of the overall success of the lesson and also helps in determining which students have learned the contents of the lesson and which need additional instruction.

One last important point concerning the planning role of a teacher deals with the need to individualize the learning experiences for each student insofar as it is humanly possible to do so. Unfortunately, since a typical elementary school teacher has between 20 and 30 students, and a typical secondary teacher may have as many as 150 students each day, it is just not possible for a teacher to make a specific lesson plan for each student. At best, a teacher can hope to modify a single lesson plan to fit the individual needs of each specific student. There is an indication that some of the newer innovations in education, such as individually prescribed instruction, modular scheduling, computer-assisted instruction, independent study, team teaching, and a differentiated teaching staff—all of which are discussed in some detail elsewhere in this book—will make it possible for teachers to do a much better job of tailoring an educational program for each individual student.

◘ Helping Students to Learn

Historically, the role of the teacher has been viewed mainly as that of a "dispenser of knowledge." Today's teacher can better be characterized as one who "helps students to learn." This new "helping" role of the contemporary teacher is exemplified by a teacher assisting a group of students as they plan a small group project; circulating in a science laboratory giving help to individual students; listening to an individual student who has a reading problem read aloud; or counseling with a student who has a personal problem. The following factors have helped to bring about this new relationship that the teacher has with the student:

- Whereas colonial school teachers had very few tools to use, except a few poorly written textbooks and their own knowledge of the subject matter they were attempting to teach, contemporary educators have a wealth of teaching aids at their disposal. These instructional devices now make it possible for teachers to help students learn much more efficiently and effectively than was possible when teachers had to "dispense" whatever knowledge the students were to learn.

- An increased understanding of the learning process has also helped educators to assume their present "helping" relationship with students. Since the turn of the century, thanks to the pioneering efforts of the child study movement, and the continued refinement of the discipline of educational psychology, an ever-increasing knowledge of the manner in which learning takes place has been made available to teachers. One of the tasks of teachers is to mold this knowledge of the learning act into excellent learning experiences for each of their students. Colonial school teachers had very little knowledge of the learning act at their disposal, and consequently cannot be blamed for their ignorance of the fact that students tend to quickly forget rotely-memorized facts, learn best from firsthand experiences rather than being lectured to, and learn more quickly and permanently that which they are highly motivated to learn—all of which are examples of important principles of learning that have grown from an increased understanding of those learning processes that guide the work of contemporary educators.

- Another factor that has contributed to the view that teachers should help students learn rather than dispense knowledge has been the changes that have taken place in educational philosophy down through the ages. There was a time, for instance, when children were viewed by the church, most parents, and most teachers to be basically bad and full of original sin which somehow must be beaten from them. And "beat," literally, many schoolteachers did, in their misguided efforts to teach and discipline their students. Fortunately, most contemporary educators agree with Jean-Jacques Rousseau (1712–78)—the great French philosopher who deserves at least part of the credit for bringing about this change in the way the young are viewed—that children are born basically good and become bad only in the hands of man. This change in the philosophical view of the nature of a child has had a profound influence on the relationship between teacher and student.

- Another change that has contributed to the idea that teachers should help children learn rather than dispense knowledge has

been the gradual infusion and acceptance of the concept of democracy into many education philosophies. Most American educators strongly believe that the relationship between a teacher and students should be a democratic one; that is, one in which students have a voice and are respected as individuals. Students who participate in such a classroom are likely to enjoy school more, learn more, and become better citizens in our democratic society.

■ Discipline in American Schools

A recent survey found that nearly one-half of the teachers in the public schools believe that students are more disruptive today than they have been in the past.[1] This same survey asks teachers to indicate the extent to which student misbehavior interfered with their teaching. Figure 3.3 shows the results of that question. As you can see, most teachers indicated that student misbehavior did to varying degrees interfere with their teaching. Almost one-third (29 percent) of all public school teachers indicated that they had seriously considered leaving teaching because of student misbehavior, and 17 percent reported they had seriously considered leaving in the last twelve months. This study asked teachers to evaluate the extent to which student behavior interfered with their own teaching and also with effective learning. Most teachers reported that student behavior interfered with their teaching to a small

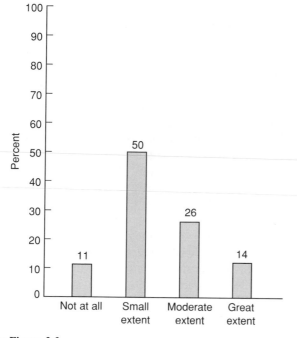

■ Figure 3.3

Extent to which student behavior interferes with teaching

Source: Office of Educational Research and Improvement Bulletin, U.S. Department of Education, Center for Education Statistics, October 1987, page 3.

of teachers stated that student behavior greatly interfered with their teaching, 27 percent stated that student behavior greatly interfered with effective learning. Teachers were also asked about interference from drug or alcohol use. Eight percent of senior high teachers and 3 percent of junior high teachers indicated that drug or alcohol use interfered with learning to a great extent; 24 percent of senior high and 8 percent of junior high teachers indicated it interfered to a moderate extent.

On a weekly average, teachers reported: 17.3 instances of disruptive whispering or note passing, 5.3 instances of a student being late, 2.9 instances of a student talking back, 1.9 instances of a student throwing something, and 1.6 instances of a student being absent without permission. Considered nationally, these numbers total per week to: 33.3 million instances of whispering or note passing, 10.2 million instances of students being late for class, 5.6 million instances of students talking back, 3.7 million instances of students throwing something, and 3.4 million instances of students being absent without permission. To put these numbers in perspective, about 40 million students are enrolled in public elementary and secondary schools.

Although the rank order frequency of instances of the different types of minor infractions was the same across school levels, several infractions occurred more frequently at the junior and senior high levels. For example, unexcused absenteeism occurred most frequently in senior high schools where teachers reported an average of 3.6 absences without permission per week, compared

extent (50 percent) or a moderate extent (26 percent). Only 11 percent indicated that it did not interfere at all, and 14 percent indicated that it interfered to a great extent. Teachers in urban schools more frequently reported that student behavior interfered with their teaching to a great extent (24 percent) than did teachers in rural schools (8 percent).

A number of teachers distinguished between the impact of student behavior on their teaching and its impact on learning. While only 14 percent

*I have never let my schooling
interfere with my education.*

Mark Twain

*Historically, students have generally been treated badly in
schools. A variety of frightening and ingenious
punishments have been devised by teachers in the past.
This illustration of a German school during the late
nineteenth century shows examples of punishment then
employed. These included the hanging of various marks of
disapproval around the offender's neck, wearing of a
dunce cap, hanging of a boy in a basket to the ceiling,
tying a boy to a stationary ring, and frequent whippings.*

with 1.1 in junior high schools and .4 in elementary schools. Teachers in urban schools more frequently observed, or had reported to them, physical fights between students than did teachers in suburban or rural schools. An average of 2.1 fights per month were reported by urban teachers compared with 1.1 for rural and 1.0 for suburban teachers.

Teachers were also asked whether they had ever been threatened by a student and whether they had ever been physically attacked by a student in their school. Almost 20 percent of teachers indicated that they had been threatened at some time, and 8 percent had been threatened in the last twelve months. Eight percent indicated that they had been physically attacked by students in their schools at some time, and 2 percent had been attacked in the last twelve months. It should be noted that the types of behaviors included under physical attack may range widely, from being kicked in anger by a first grader to more serious physical attacks by students.

Overall, teachers reported that about 7 percent of the students they taught were habitual behavior problems. Estimates did not vary significantly by school level; however, estimates for urban teachers (8.1 percent) were slightly higher than those of rural teachers (6.1 percent).

Figure 3.4 shows the results when principals and teachers were asked to evaluate how productive specified actions would be in improving discipline in their school. The actions included student, parent, school, principal, and teacher-related actions. Those actions rated as "very productive" in improving school discipline by a majority of respondents were: increased student self-discipline developed at home (74 percent), smaller classes (63 percent), and increased parental support (62 percent). Other actions, such as the principal making discipline a higher priority, increased use of positive reinforcement, and stricter enforcement of rules were rated "very productive" by about 40 to 45 percent of the teachers. Teachers in elementary schools more frequently than those in senior high schools rated positive reinforcement as very productive (50 percent elementary, and 34 percent senior). Increased teacher autonomy and easier procedures for suspension or expulsion (27 percent) were least frequently rated as "very productive."

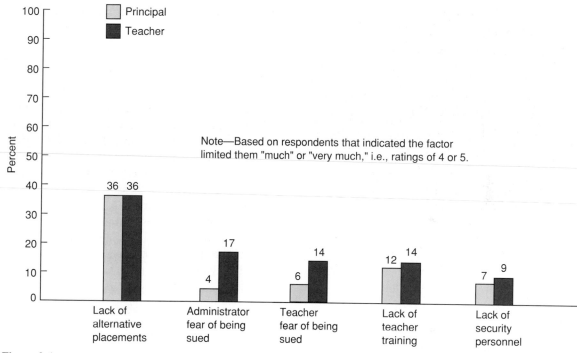

■ Figure 3.4

Percent of respondents rating each factor as greatly limiting the ability to maintain order in their school: comparison of secondary school principals and teachers

Source: "Public School Teacher Perspectives on School Discipline," *OERI Bulletin*, U.S. Department of Education, October 1987, page 6.

This national survey shows that discipline is a serious problem in schools throughout the country. All teachers, to be successful, absolutely must develop the ability to control a classroom of students. It is difficult to give advice to teachers about how to do so, because each teacher must utilize his/her own skills to solicit cooperation from students.

■ Assertive Discipline

One approach to establishing and maintaining good discipline that has received considerable support is that created by Lee Canter and labeled "Assertive Discipline." He suggests that teachers are in charge of a classroom and must be assertive in bringing about good classroom behavior. Mr. Canter thinks that concerning discipline, teachers fall into three basic categories—assertive, nonassertive, and hostile. He believes that nonassertive and/or hostile teachers are quite likely not to be successful in their discipline efforts.

Assertive teachers take the following positions regarding discipline in their classrooms:

- They tolerate no student preventing them from teaching.
- They will not tolerate any student preventing other students from learning.
- They will not tolerate students engaging in any behavior that is not in the student's best interest or in the best interest of other students in the classroom.
- Lastly, they insist that whenever a student chooses to behave appropriately, they immediately recognize and reinforce such good behavior.

An example of an appropriate action that an assertive teacher might take when a student begins to talk and disrupts others is to walk up to the student, look him/her in the eye, and say, "You must stop talking and get to work."

By way of contrast, the nonassertive teacher may ignore the misbehavior altogether and when it eventually gets worse, simply say "I don't know what to do with you." The hostile teacher, on the other hand, would probably yell at the student and say something extremely derogatory about the student's being stupid or having a big mouth. Sometimes hostile teachers even physically abuse the students. While that type of behavior on the

part of the teacher may scare the students into behaving, it is also likely to destroy their interest in learning.

By the same token, an assertive teacher always remembers to compliment a student for good behavior. Such an example might be simply telling the student, with a smile on your face, "That's great work!" By contrast, a nonassertive teacher would probably ignore a student's good behavior rather than reinforce it. Likewise a hostile teacher would probably either ignore good behavior or recognize it by saying something negative like "It's about time."

Mr. Canter believes that many teachers who have difficulty with classroom control are laboring under common misconceptions about student behavior. Some of these misconceptions include:

- The student who misbehaves in school has an emotional problem.
- The misbehaving student comes from a home in which the parents do not make the student behave.
- The child who misbehaves in school is usually from a low socioeconomic background.
- Students from racial and economic minority groups are most likely to misbehave in the classroom.
- Misbehaving students are educationally handicapped and should be expected to misbehave.

Our most effective teachers realize that these misconceptions are not true. Rather, all students will misbehave from time to time if the teacher allows them to do so. Teachers who have well behaved classrooms realize it's their responsibility

Research Finding

3

Schools contribute to their students' academic achievement by establishing, communicating, and enforcing fair and consistent discipline policies.

For 16 of the last 17 years, the public has identified discipline as the most serious problem facing its schools. Effective discipline policies contribute to the academic atmosphere by emphasizing the importance of regular attendance, promptness, respect for teachers and academic work, and good conduct.

The discipline policies of most successful schools share these traits:

- Discipline policies are aimed at actual problems, not rumors.
- All members of the school community arc involved in creating a policy that reflects community values and is adapted to the needs of the school.

- Misbehavior is defined. Because not everyone agrees on what behavior is undesirable, defining problems is the first step in solving them. Students must know what kinds of behavior are acceptable and what kinds are not.
- Discipline policies are consistently enforced. Students must know the consequences of misbehavior, and they must believe they will be treated fairly.

Brodinsky, B. (1980). "Student Discipline: Problems and Solutions." AASA Critical Issues Report. Arlington, VA: American Association of School Administrators, ERIC Document No. ED 198206.

DiPrete, T. A. (1981). *Discipline, Order, and Student Behavior in American High Schools.* Chicago: National Opinion Research Center. ERIC Document No. ED 224137.

Duke, D. L., and Jones, V. F. (1983). "Assessing Recent Efforts to Reduce Student Behavior Problems." Paper presented at Annual Meeting of the American Educational Research Association, Montreal, Canada. ERIC Document No. ED 233440.

Source: *What Works: Research About Teaching and Learning.* Washington, DC: U.S. Department of Education, 1987, page 61.

to cultivate a classroom atmosphere in which students are allowed to productively learn and not be denied this opportunity by a poor classroom climate. Teachers who are having difficulty with classroom control must first of all recognize that they have an obligation to bring about good classroom discipline. A good first step is to think through precisely what kind of behavior you want your students to exhibit at all times. Most teachers want their students to follow directions, stay in their seats, raise their hand when they want to speak, come to class on time, not disrupt other students, not swear at or tease other students, bring the necessary supplies with them, etc. The teacher must communicate clearly these expectations to the students, and reinforce them frequently until students do them automatically.

Assertive teachers must also set limits of behavior for students. They must also explain the consequences for students who do not function within these limits. Teachers might think of these consequences as the "discipline plan" for each particular classroom. When students violate classroom rules, they must be reminded of their action and they must suffer the consequences that the teacher has explained in advance. This does not mean that a teacher should use "overkill" for minor infractions. On the other hand, if minor infractions are always ignored, classroom discipline will be sure to degenerate over a period of time. Each teacher must decide what they believe are appropriate consequences for classroom misbehavior. Typically, these consequences will range from writing the student's name on the board as a warning, to loss of privileges, to more severe consequences such as contacting the principal and/or parent. Of course, sooner or later, all teachers have students who exhibit severe behavior problems. Such students require more time and effort on the part of the teacher to correct these severe behavior problems.

One key to creating a good classroom climate is for the teacher to systematically apply the classroom rules to all students at all times. This is especially important during the beginning of each class and at the beginning of the school year. If teachers systematically apply their discipline plan, students will quickly come to realize what is expected and usually conform to the classroom behavior expected by the teacher.

It is equally important for the assertive teacher to systematically reinforce good behavior. This eventually becomes an automatic part of the teacher's actions. Our most effective teachers develop the ability to constantly praise students and reward them with smiles and nonverbal behavior such as little pats on the back or a wink. Research has shown that most students basically wish to please the teacher and receive the teacher's acknowledgement for good work and good behavior. The old adage, "An ounce of prevention is worth a pound of cure" is especially appropriate when it comes to establishing good classroom climate and preventing student misbehavior. Sending positive notes home to parents who, in turn, praise their students for good school work and behavior is another way to reinforce and recognize good student behavior.

In the final analysis, teachers must realize that they are the boss in their classroom and have the responsibility for creating and maintaining a positive learning environment. Teachers have the right to teach and students have the right to learn in a well-disciplined climate.

Teacher education students should use every opportunity during their college years to learn and practice as much as they can about classroom discipline. This can be done by reading a wide variety of material related to this topic and taking every opportunity to work with children and try various techniques for soliciting their cooperation.

■ Encouraging Self-Discipline

The goal of all teachers should be to help all students exercise self-discipline. Self-discipline has the goal of causing each student to behave of their own volition, rather than when they are told by someone else to behave. An excellent publication on self-discipline, by the American Association of School Administrators, suggests the following differences between discipline and self-discipline:[2]

Discipline vs. Self-Discipline: What's the Difference?

There's a big difference between the way people define discipline and self-discipline.

1. **Discipline,** as most people refer to it, is imposed from the *outside*. **Self-discipline,** on the other hand, grows from the inside. It involves good judgment, courage, ethical conduct, and a sense of personal responsibility. For example: **Discipline**—a rule enforced by a coach—requires all team members to report to practice on time. But only **self-discipline**—decisions made by individual players—can induce the athletes to stay *after* practice and spend more time perfecting their skills.

2. **Discipline** often involves training people to obey rules. But **self-discipline** means more than just following orders. **Self-disciplined** individuals follow rules of behavior because they have accepted those rules for themselves.

3. **Discipline** can help schools provide quiet study times during the school day. But students need **self-discipline** to turn off the television set long enough to concentrate on their schoolwork at home.

4. **Discipline** often involves *conforming* to certain accepted standards of behavior. But truly **self-disciplined** individuals may *not* always conform to their peers, especially when doing so would violate their own codes of conduct or values.

5. **Discipline** can make young people obey rules prohibiting the use of alcohol or drugs on the school grounds. But only **self-discipline** will enable students to decide for themselves that they will not abuse drugs or alcohol *away* from school—even if their friends are experimenting.

Self-discipline involves the ability to weigh short-term interests against long-term goals. The well-known educational researcher, Benjamin Bloom, spent several years studying young people who had achieved outstanding success in a variety of fields—from concert pianists to Olympic swimmers to scientific researchers. He found that during adolescence, these high achievers typically spent 20 or more hours a week perfecting their talent. Dr. Bloom noted that, on average, American teenagers spend that much time watching television.

Perhaps the most important thing to remember about self-discipline is that it grows from and, yes, enhances self-esteem. Thus, self-discipline involves more than "just saying no." The truth is, helping students develop self-discipline involves helping them to say "yes"— accepting goals for appropriate behavior and deciding to act responsibly to meet those goals. (From "Discipline vs. Self-Discipline: What's the Difference?" *Self-Discipline: Helping Students Succeed,* 4–5. Copyright © American Association of School Administrators, Arlington, VA. Reprinted by permission.)

■ The Use of Corporal Punishment

Corporal punishment can be defined as the use of physical force on the part of the teacher or administrator to discipline a student. The most common form of corporal punishment might be a paddling.

Corporal punishment is still legal in 41 states. According to a recent survey by the Temple University National Center for the Study of Corporal Punishment and Alternatives in the Schools, at least 2,000,000 U.S. school children are physically punished each year. Figure 3.5 shows a

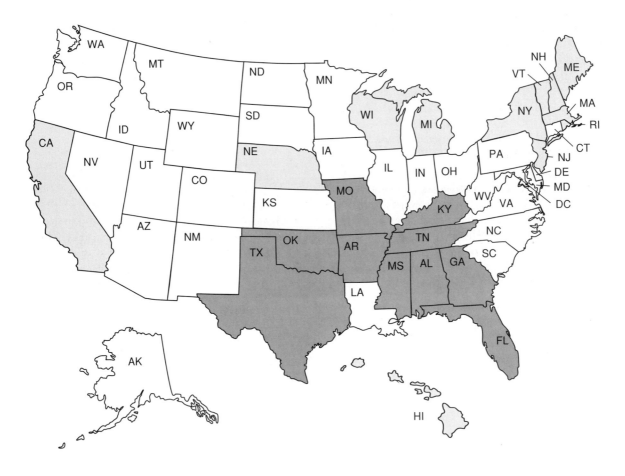

The 10 states where schools use corporal punishment most frequently

The 12 states that have abolished corporal punishment in the schools

 Figure 3.5
States where schools use corporal punishment most frequently and states that have abolished corporal punishment in the schools

number of interesting facts about corporal punishment. It shows that nine states have thus far abolished corporal punishment in the schools. This figure also shows the ten states where schools use corporal punishment most frequently.

It is interesting to note that the use of reasonable corporal punishment in schools has generally been upheld by our court systems. The Supreme Court ruled in Ingrahm vs. Wright that the use of corporal punishment does not necessarily constitute cruel and unusual punishment and thereby violate the Fourth Amendment. There have been individual court decisions, however, that should warn teachers against using unusually harsh forms of corporal punishment. For instance, a Fifth Circuit Court of Appeals ruled that the parents of an eight-year-old girl who had been tied to a chair much of the school day had the right to sue the teacher, the principal, and the school district. A Georgia court found a teacher guilty of criminal assault charges for severely paddling a student. A Louisiana special education teacher was convicted of cruelty to a juvenile and sentenced to one and one-half years of hard labor for using excessive corporal punishment. A Missouri court upheld the dismissal charges of a teacher for slapping a student. These are but a few examples of the growing number of cases in which the courts have determined that educators cannot use unusually harsh corporal punishment methods.

Educators who use corporal punishment should use the following guidelines:

1. Make sure that you follow your school's policies on corporal punishment.
2. If you utilize corporal punishment, have an adult witness who will be able to corroborate testimony concerning the event.
3. Never use excessive force or administer more than several moderate blows.
4. Only administer corporal punishment to the buttocks. Never slap, punch, or shove a student.
5. Do not use corporal punishment for minor student misbehavior.

Of course, educators can use reasonable force to restrain a student who poses an immediate threat to others. Even when restraining a student, however, educators should be careful not to injure the student.

While it is legal in many states to use corporal punishment, and while the courts have generally upheld a teacher's right to use reasonable corporal punishment, most educators and authorities believe that it is best never to do so. The National Education Association has adopted a resolution opposing the use of corporal punishment in schools. The American Medical Association, the American Academy of Pediatrics, and the National PTA have also advocated the abolishment of all forms of corporal punishment in our schools. The authors of this book believe that, in the long run, corporal punishment doesn't teach better behavior, but rather, usually causes the students to become more aggressive. Furthermore, corporal punishment may cause long-lasting psychological problems for the students. We believe that creative and effective teachers can develop much more positive ways to elicit desirable student behavior. The use of corporal punishment more often than not creates a barrier that prohibits a positive learning climate in the classroom. All of this, plus the fact that corporal punishment can lead to lawsuits and even teacher dismissal, strongly suggest that teachers should avoid the use of corporal punishment.

■ Working with the Mainstreamed Student

There has been a recent movement to put the special education student back into the regular classroom. This concept has become known as *mainstreaming*. This movement has placed another set of demands on the regular classroom teacher. The teacher must now be able to work effectively with students who have a wide range of physical, mental, and emotional handicaps. For instance, it is now quite possible for a teacher to have a class that not only includes the usual range of individual differences found among so-called "normal" students, but also a blind or partially sighted child, a deaf or hard-of-hearing child, a physically handicapped child, a mentally retarded child, an emotionally disturbed child and/or a child with some type of learning disability.

Teachers must develop new diagnostic skills so they can identify the particular learning problems these students have. Teachers must also develop a wider range of teaching skills and strategies to provide for the unique needs of the mainstreamed exceptional student. In fact, given the recent advances in the field of special education, it is a considerable challenge for the classroom teacher to simply become familiar with the terminology now used in special education circles. Terms such as Public Law 94–142, dyslexia, orthopedically handicapped, psychomotor dysfunction, neurological impairment, hyperkinetic behavior—to name a few—become important to teachers who have mainstreamed children in their classrooms.

Much controversy surrounds the mainstreaming movement. Many overburdened teachers feel that it is simply impossible to do a good job with handicapped students who are mainstreamed in their classes. This viewpoint is typified by Jeanne Latcham, a counselor in the Detroit School System, who says:

> Mainstreaming is ludicrous. We have children whose needs are complicated: a child in the third grade who has already been in 16 schools, children who need love and attention and disrupt the classroom to get it. Ten percent of the students in Detroit's classrooms can't conform and can't learn. These children need a disproportionate amount of the teacher's time. It's a teacher's nightmare—she can't help them, but she never forgets them.[3]

Of course, not all teachers would agree with this viewpoint—however, very likely all teachers would agree that having mainstreamed students in their classrooms is additional work and makes teaching more difficult.

■ Providing Multicultural Education

Teachers have recently been given yet another responsibility by society; that of providing multicultural education. As our society has become more complex, and as the concept of cultural pluralism has gained in popularity, our schools have been asked to add this area to an already crowded curriculum. The goal of this movement is to help children become aware and more accepting of cultural differences in the United States and, in fact, throughout the world. Surely one cannot disagree with the desirability of this goal; however, many educators feel that given their present class size and work load, they are not able to do justice to this assignment.

Evaluation, as contrasted with measurement, embraces a wider range of technique and evidence.

Paul L. Dressel
Lewis B. Mayhew

■ Assessing Learning Outcomes

In addition to school-keeping, planning, and helping students to learn, a teacher must also be an evaluator. For it is through a well-planned program of evaluation that a teacher is able to determine the abilities and achievements of each student. This knowledge is essential for the teacher to plan an appropriate program for each student. In his role as an "evaluator," the teacher is continually assessing each student's abilities, interests, accomplishments, and needs. To help him gather data to accomplish evaluation, an educator employs standardized tests, teacher-made tests, and subjective observations.

A standardized test is one that has been constructed with the employment of carefully prescribed techniques; and one for which norms have been established. There are literally hundreds of commercially prepared standardized tests available for teacher use to measure different dimensions of student aptitude, achievement, and interest. Most school districts now have rather well-developed standardized testing programs that supply teachers with a wide variety of data to use in their role as evaluator.

Recently, the use of standardized tests has received a good deal of attention and debate. Millions of dollars are spent each year on these tests, and some people question not only their value, but also their validity. Some of the specific questions now being debated are:

1. Should standardized tests be used to measure student achievement?
2. Would a moratorium on standardized testing serve a useful purpose?
3. Are standardized tests inherently culturally biased?
4. How can tests be used to promote learning?
5. What kind of tests should be used to guide college admissions?
6. Do criticisms of mental tests reflect flaws or abuses?
7. Can standardized test scores contribute to the individualization of instruction?
8. To what extent are tests themselves responsible for the lower scores that minorities tend to make on them?[4]

Teacher-made tests, as the name implies, are those which teachers themselves construct. These tests are usually designed to measure student achievement in the various subjects. Constructing good teacher-made tests is a time-consuming task, and requires a thorough knowledge of the principles of test construction on the part of the teacher.

In addition to the data obtained from standardized tests and teacher-made tests, a teacher can obtain useful evaluation information by simply observing students. The skilled educator can learn a good deal about a student's abilities, achievements, interests, and needs through careful observation.

A record of the evaluative data accumulated on each student is usually kept by a school district. It becomes part of a so-called *cumulative record,* and contains standardized test scores, grades, health information, and other background information about the student. A sample cumulative record card for a pupil is shown in figure 3.6.

```
           Homewood-Flossmoor High School        31-May-88      02:29 PM

    Student Master
    ------------

    Frame  4    Attendance and Permanent Record

    Student  ID    049389    Last              First
                                     Middle

    Birthdate  691113    Sex  F    Counselor  05     Grad Yr  87

    ++ Attendance Area ++                    ++ Permanent Record ++


            Enr  Att        Rank    9 of  588 as of 870626    UP10 %

    Qtr A
    Qtr B                   SEM - SPCs  Att       Earn
    Qtr C                   SEM - GPA
    Qtr D
    Y-T-D
         ++ Cumulative ++
                    SPCs       272.50
                    GPA        13.840
                    4 Pt GPA    3.600

                         ++    Flags    ++
                    Ill Con - P    US Con - P    Driver Ed - P
```

■ **Figure 3.6**
A sample cumulative record

■ Providing Feedback to Pupils and Parents

A role of the teacher that is closely connected with evaluating is that of "reporting," which basically involves making known to the parents their child's progress in school. This is usually accomplished in two ways: in writing, on one of the many different forms that have been created by schools for this purpose, and in person, during a conference.

There is a large variety of forms used by various schools in their efforts to report to parents. In fact, most schools create their own report card forms. An example of such a form is shown in figure 3.7.

The role of "reporter" requires that a teacher possess not only a thorough knowledge of the progress of each student, but also the communication and human relations skills necessary to effectively pass this information along to parents.

■ Managing the Instructional Team

A relatively new teacher role emerging in many schools has to do with the managing of a larger group of people who, in one way or another, contribute to the instruction program, and may be thought of as members of the "instructional team." Such people include peer student aides, parent volunteer workers, a range of different

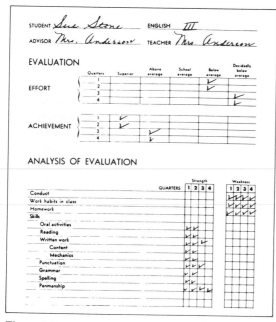

STUDENT *Sue Stone*   ENGLISH *III*

ADVISOR *Mrs. Anderson*   TEACHER *Mrs. Anderson*

EVALUATION

Quarters	Superior	Above average	School average	Below average	Decidedly below average
EFFORT 1				✓	
2				✓	
3					✓
4					✓
ACHIEVEMENT 1	✓				
2	✓				
3			✓		
4			✓		

ANALYSIS OF EVALUATION

QUARTERS	Strength 1	2	3	4	Weakness 1	2	3	4
Conduct					✓	✓	✓	✓
Work habits in class					✓	✓	✓	✓
Homework					✓	✓	✓	
Skills								
Oral activities	✓	✓						
Reading	✓	✓						
Written work	✓	✓	✓					
Content	✓	✓						
Mechanics	✓	✓						
Punctuation	✓	✓						
Grammar	✓	✓						
Spelling	✓	✓						
Penmanship	✓	✓	✓	✓				

■ **Figure 3.7**
A sample report card

types of paid paraprofessionals, teacher education students engaged in some type of early clinical experience, student teachers, interns, and junior members of team teaching. In fact, in a real sense other professionals in the school, such as learning center directors, reading specialists, librarians, audiovisual specialists, and even guidance counselors and administrators are at times members of the instructional team, and must be "managed" by the classroom teacher.

The extent to which such persons become involved in the instructional team varies considerably from school to school. Unfortunately, in many schools, regular classroom teachers work completely by themselves, and so each is the "only"

member of the instructional team. Increasingly, however, many schools are effectively adding a variety of people to the instructional team. Some schools have even developed rather elaborate differentiated staffing systems that include a wide variety of people with different roles on the instructional team. This practice seems likely to increase, conceivably to that point at which nearly all teachers will require the skills needed to manage a larger group of individuals who assist with the instructional program.

■ Understanding and Getting Along with People

One of the most important general tasks common to all teachers is that of understanding and getting along with the many different people with which each must deal. The teacher must possess good human relations skills and, in a sense, must be a public relations expert. One who is not able to successfully fulfill this role is destined to failure.

There are many different groups of people with whom the teacher must relate. Obviously, the people that the teacher spends the most time with are the students. It may seem redundant to suggest that a teacher must be able to understand and get along with students; however, there are a number of teachers who do have difficulty in these areas. For instance, the teacher who continually has classroom discipline problems quite likely does not understand students and obviously can't get along very well with them.

Parents constitute another group with which a teacher must get along. Most parents are extremely interested in and often emotional about their child's progress in school. Furthermore, it is difficult for many parents to be objective about

The teacher, like the artist, like the philosopher, and the man of letters, can only perform his work adequately if he feels himself to be an individual directed by an inner creative impulse not dominated or filtered by an outside authority.

Bertrand Russell

their child's success and/or behavior in school. It requires a good deal of understanding and human relations skill on the part of the teacher, for instance, to tell a mother and father that their child has been behaving badly, and/or is not achieving academically.

Lastly, a teacher must understand and get along with fellow teachers, supervisors, and administrators—colleagues all. This is more true today than it has ever been before due to the fact that education is now a very complex undertaking and teachers often work in teams, do joint planning, have the help of specialists and paraprofessionals, and generally work together more closely than has traditionally been the case (the one-room country school teacher had no colleagues). Some teachers understand and get along with students but find it difficult to relate to their colleagues. The teacher in this situation is doomed to failure just as surely as the one who cannot relate to students.

In order to understand people, teachers must develop insight into human motivations, needs, fears, hopes, weaknesses, prejudices, and desires. Teachers' ability to get along with people is largely dependent upon their own personality, attitudes, and values, as well as the extent to which each basically likes and respects people in spite of the fact that they may be different and may possess weaknesses. Individuals who are considering entering the teaching profession should carefully assess their human relations skills and decide whether or not their personality, attitudes, and values are such as to enable them to get along effectively with the many people with whom they will have to deal as teachers.

■ Becoming a Self-Renewing Professional

American education, both the task and the teacher, are rapidly changing. Teachers must not only keep pace with these changes, but must actually bring some of them about through devising improved teaching methods, developing educational innovations, and helping to expand the body of knowledge within their disciplines. This means that teachers must keep up to date on all aspects of their work—advances in knowledge in the subject matter, improved teaching techniques (including discovering some of one's own), changes in our social system, changes in our youth, and changes on the national and international political scene. Then, too, teachers must keep up on research findings in education and put into practice those findings that are of use in their own particular work. In fact, in order to be most effective, teachers must become students of teaching, constantly studying and experimenting with learning, and constantly improving their work as educators.

This means that a teacher must spend a good deal of time reading professional literature; attend professional conventions, conferences, and workshops; take an active part in in-service training programs; go back to a college or university and take graduate courses, and possibly work on an advanced degree; and, in general, seek out ways of keeping up to date. The recent "teacher-center" movement initiated by the federal government and strongly supported by national teacher associations represents one innovative attempt to help teachers become self-renewing professionals.

The good news is that most teachers in the United States are doing a good job of self-renewal. A recent study found that just over one-half of all public school teachers have now earned a graduate degree.

■ Professional Growth Activities for Teachers

A recent survey of the National Education Association shows that it is very common for today's teachers to participate in a wide variety of professional growth activities.[5] This survey shows that 73 percent of our teachers participate in workshops sponsored by their school districts during the school year. Thirty-four percent serve on various committees in the school or community in an effort to improve education, 31 percent work on curriculum committees within the school districts, 32 percent work in activities sponsored by their teachers' organizations during the school year, and 21 percent enroll in college courses during the school year. Another 15 percent participate in summer workshops sponsored by their school districts, etc. These data support the assertion that today's educator must constantly strive to improve professional performance.

■ The Teacher of the Future

The college student who is currently enrolled in a teacher education program will probably still be teaching in the year 2010. This fact makes it tempting to speculate about what a teacher's job might be like during the early part of the twenty-first century. It seems relatively safe to predict that the teacher's role will become more complex and, in a sense, more demanding. If one believes

Teachers participate regularly in professional growth activities.

that society itself will continue to become more complex, and that the rate of change will continue to accelerate in our society, then it seems logical to believe that our schools and the role of the teacher will likewise become more complex.

It also seems likely that the "knowledge explosion" will continue and probably even accelerate into the next century. This will mean that schools and teachers will have even more content to teach than is now the case. Parenthetically, it is interesting to note that contemporary teachers claim they cannot possibly teach all the material that should be taught now.

■ Summary

This chapter has pointed out that a teacher's work is demanding, complex, and constantly changing. Our society expects a great deal from our teachers. A teacher must be able to plan lessons that will provide for the wide range of abilities and levels of motivation found among the students in each classroom. The teacher must also be able to diagnose the educational needs of students and to creatively serve as a learning facilitator for each student. Teachers must be able to measure and evaluate what students learn—a task that requires a keen understanding of current educational measurement techniques. Since handicapped students are now mainstreamed into all regular classrooms, each teacher must also understand the wide range of handicapping conditions, to be able to serve visually handicapped students, deaf and hard-of-hearing students, physically handicapped students, learning disabled students, etc.

This chapter has devoted considerable space to the subject of discipline, which many teachers identify as their number one problem. The authors advocate "assertive discipline" as a very effective approach to classroom control. The chapter further points out that even though corporal punishment is legal in many states, it is legally dangerous and not recommended by most authorities. Of course, a teacher's ultimate goal should be to help students develop "self-discipline" wherein they behave in an acceptable manner of their own accord.

There are many important implications in this chapter for a person who is considering a teaching career. For instance, the role of the teacher outlined is complex. It has been suggested that the successful teacher must be extremely dedicated, willing to work long and hard hours, and be a bit of a custodian. On top of that, a teacher must be dedicated to helping students, able to wisely plan a learning program for each student, and be able to motivate each student. The teacher must furthermore be capable of assessing student progress and designing remedial learning experiences where required. The teacher must be a "human relations expert" capable of understanding, communicating with, and getting along well with a wide variety of people—students, parents, voters, colleagues, administrators. Above all, teachers must keep up with the knowledge explosion, and constantly improve their teaching skills, and, in a sense, be continuing "students of teaching." Teaching is a demanding profession. By the same token, teaching is an exciting and rewarding experience for those who possess the right skills, attitudes, and personalities.

Point of View

The following point of view is offered by Adam Urbanski, a teacher, president of the Rochester Teachers Association and a Vice President of the American Federation of Teachers. He advocates radical changes be made in the teaching profession, if we are to bring about improvements in our schools. Some of these needed changes are being pioneered in the Rochester, New York, "Careers in Teaching" plan. This plan gives teachers a more important decision-making role in the school system, and provides substantial pay raises—as high as $70,000 for lead teachers. It also provides a mentoring system whereby teachers help one another to become more effective educators. The Rochester plan is an excellent example of the way school districts and teachers are creatively attempting to improve our schools.

Restructuring the Teaching Profession
Adam Urbanski

For too many students in the United States—and especially for those from economically and educationally disadvantaged backgrounds—schools are failing.

To improve the learning opportunities for all students, we must first improve the teaching occupation. By taking risks and abandoning traditional postures, we can restructure the profession in ways that promise more productive schooling.

It's not so much that teachers *are* the problem; it's that teachers *have* problems that impede effective teaching and learning.

Stultifying and archaic school structures, along with the disincentives now built into the teaching occupation, are yielding us a teacher shortage of unprecedented proportions. The following statistics suggest the extent of the problem:

- One in 13 American teachers is not certified.
- One in 6 has taught a grade or a subject in which he or she received no preparation.
- Twenty-four percent of America's teachers say that, if they could start over again, they would not teach.
- There are more school districts in the United States than there are physics teachers.

How do school districts cope with the problem of teacher shortage? Nineteen percent of districts simply increase class size; 35 percent eliminate or reduce courses; 39 percent permit out-of-license teaching; and 41 percent issue temporary or emergency teaching certificates.

Now, who ever heard of "emergency surgeons" or "temporary attorneys"? Why should standards be so flagrantly disregarded in teaching? While we'll always be able to find enough adults willing to face students, we should insist on debunking the myth that "all you have to do to be a good teacher is love kids." That's about as smart as saying that all you have to do to be a good surgeon is love patients.

If we were to design a "profession" that would virtually guarantee isolation from one's colleagues and lack not only intrinsic rewards but also most of

the characteristics of a real profession, we could hardly find a better model than the current lot of teachers.

Not simply a step in the drive to transform the teaching occupation into a genuine profession, Rochester's Career in Teaching plan also incorporates a feature that directly attacks a major obstacle to student learning: the frequent failure of schools to match "at risk" students—the toughest teaching assignments—with those teachers who are best equipped to accept them, the experienced and expert lead teachers.

Under the current structure, the most difficult students often fall, by default, to the least experienced and most vulnerable teachers. With the help of negotiated seniority rules, veteran teachers can choose to avoid such assignments. This dynamic probably contributes to the decision of 7 out of every 10 teachers to leave the classroom before their 10th year of teaching.

It makes sense to match the most challenging students with the most experienced, expert practitioners. Certainly success with these students shouldn't be expected of first-year teachers, who have enough to do just to learn the job. Rookie teachers' taking on the toughest assignments would be tantamount in the medical profession to interns' performing open-heart surgery while master surgeons treat skin abrasions.

The Rochester pact also calls for shared governance through a school-based planning process. Playing a major role in shaping the instructional program and other school dynamics, teachers will even participate in decisions about filling vacancies for staff positions in their schools.

No longer will strict seniority be the determinant for voluntary interschool transfers. Moves will occur instead in the context of a districtwide "schools of choice" system.

The notion of giving parents a choice of public schools is predicated on two pillars of the American system: equal opportunity and open-market competition. Schools that have to compete for students are less likely to become complacent and are more apt to adjust and improve what they have to offer. Not surprisingly, schools that don't have to compete exhibit many of the characteristics of monopolies.

Lack of choice limits the ability of parents and students to affect the school, heightens their sense of frustration, and often leads to resignation and apathy. This cycle can and should be broken.

Chosen schools should be more productive for students and professional staff. Research supports the notion that selection of a school contributes to a positive attitude toward learning. Teachers are likely to gain interest in the effectiveness and attractiveness of their schools if the stakes are retention of programs and "saleability" to consumers. Accountable for their failure, unsuccessful schools would be compelled to change.

Schools that must compete also are more likely to develop a sense of specialness and shared purpose. Such an ethos of teamwork would create an appropriate context for collegiality and shared governance, and would dovetail with the teacher-empowerment movement. It would be unthinkable, for example, to put schools on a competitive basis while retaining the dictatorial, top-down management that now characterizes most schools. With the school's very survival at stake, teachers couldn't afford to leave all major decisions to the principal.

- Learning—or failing to learn—their trade by their own devices, new teachers serve no internship and receive little help. As much is expected of them their first day on the job as is expected of a 30-year veteran.
- Teachers cannot be promoted except out of teaching. Consequently, a teacher's status, pay, and responsibilities are not substantially different on retirement than on the day that teacher was hired.

- Pedagogical decisions are made by nonpractitioners. The farther they escape from the classroom, it seems, the more authority they have to dictate to those left behind.
- Teachers are evaluated and "assisted" by nonpractitioners who can see that the window shades are all evenly drawn but can rarely assess the teacher's competence or knowledge of subject matter.
- Teachers who lack competence are neither assisted nor removed. Administrators are unwilling or unable to use the evaluation process to ensure quality teaching.

Various study groups in recent years have identified factors such as these that limit the effectiveness of teachers. But can nationwide reform rhetoric be translated into practical local improvements?

In Rochester, N.Y., we have begun to restructure the teaching profession. Last year we negotiated and implemented the Peer Assistance and Review (PAR) Program, which involves teachers in monitoring quality within their own ranks by providing mentors to inexperienced teachers and offering assistance to experienced teachers whose performance should be improved.

Building on the PAR Program, we have now developed a career path that, while retaining them as practitioners, would allow teachers to assume leadership in matters relating to instruction and to the profession. This "Career in Teaching" program consists of four levels: intern teacher, resident teacher, professional teacher, and lead teacher.

The incorporation of peer review and the provision of additional professional options for qualified teachers distinguish our plan from merit-pay schemes that purport to be "career ladder" programs. Lead teachers would achieve higher status and pay in exchange for accepting more responsibilities and working a longer school day or year. To ensure that they wouldn't be perceived by fellow teachers as angling for administrative jobs, lead teachers would make themselves ineligible for administrative appointments for the duration of their tenure as lead teachers and for two years thereafter.

The new agreement in Rochester also establishes significant pay raises for teachers; top pay for lead teachers will be nearly $70,000 in the third year of the contract.

Even more important than the provisions of the Rochester contract is the spirit of the settlement. Achieved through a process best described as "principled negotiations," the agreement is based on trust, mutual respect, and labor-management collaboration. Union and management share a joint commitment to the notion that excellence without equity is not worth pursuing; that unionism and professionalism are complementary, not mutually exclusive; that there is no reason not to use the collective-bargaining process to build a genuine profession for teachers; and that teacher empowerment must be accompanied by teacher accountability.

If accountability means assuming responsibility for the decisions and choices that one makes, then teachers, to be held accountable, must not be locked out of the decision-making process. And the measure of accountability should be productivity, i.e., student outcomes. Specific criteria might include such factors as dropout rates, suspensions, course-selection choices, failure rates, aggregate test scores, and attendance rates.

The education-reform movement has heightened teachers' aspirations. Since the most powerful revolution is the revolution of rising expectations, it will be impossible to unring the bell. With a willingness to take risks, we will dwell more on potential solutions than on past problems. The risks are worth taking because so much is at stake.

I have learned that in this nation the real division is not so much between the economic haves and have-nots as between those who have hope and those who have none. Public education is still the best hope for millions of young people in our country—especially those from educationally and economically disadvantaged backgrounds.

At this pivotal juncture, we face a critical choice: Do we constrain ourselves to merely tinkering with the status quo, or are we willing to significantly restructure our schools? If we choose the former, we'll continue to get the dismal results that prompted the cry for reform. The latter can offer hope for a much-improved milieu for teaching and learning. Only then would the motto "All children can learn and we should choose to educate all children" not only sound good but also be good and sound.

From Adam Urbanski "Restructuring the Teaching Profession," *Education Week*, October 28, 1987, 32, 25. Copyright © 1987 Editorial Projects in Education, Washington, DC.

■ Questions for Discussion

1. How did the role of the teacher in colonial America differ from that of contemporary educators?

2. In what ways might "school-keeping" chores be minimized so that teachers might spend more time working with students?

3. What factors have helped to bring about the idea that teachers, rather than dispensing knowledge, should help students to learn?

4. What qualities must a teacher possess in order to have good human relations skills?

5. What are your views about maintaining good discipline in today's schools?

■ Notes

1. "Public School Teacher Perspectives on School Discipline," *OERI Bulletin,* U.S. Department of Education, October 1987, pp. 3–8.

2. "Discipline vs. Self-Discipline: What's the Difference?" *Self-Discipline: Helping Students Succeed* (Arlington, VA: American Association of School Administrators), pp. 4–5.

3. "Help! Teacher Can't Teach!" *Time,* June 16, 1980, p. 54.

4. Robert L. Ebel, "Critical Issues in Standardized Testing," *Thresholds in Education 6,* no. 1 (1980), pp. 9–10.

5. *Status of the American Public School Teacher 1985–86* (Washington, DC: National Education Association), p. 49.

■ Selected References

Charles, C. M. *Elementary Classroom Management.* New York: Longman, 1983.

Cronlund, Norman E. *Measurement and Evaluation in Teaching.* New York: Macmillan, 1985.

Dembo, Myron H. *Teaching for Learning: Applying Educational Psychology in the Classroom.* Santa Monica, CA: Goodyear Publishing, 1977.

Ebel, Robert L. "Critical Issues in Standardized Testing." *Thresholds in Education 6,* no. 1 (1980):9–10.

Heavilin, Barbara Anne. "Confusion Worse Confounded: Incompetence Among Public School Teachers." *The Teacher Educator 16,* no. 2 (Autumn 1980):11–20.

Joyce, Bruce and Weil, Marsha. *Models of Teaching.* Englewood Cliffs: Prentice-Hall, 1986.

Lay-Dopyera, M. and Dopyera, J. *Becoming a Teacher of Younger Children.* New York: Random House, 1987.

Patterson, Arlene H. "Professional Malpractice: Small Cloud, but Growing Bigger." *Phi Delta Kappan 62,* no. 3 (November 1980):193–96.

Schwartz, William. "Education in the Classroom." *Journal of Higher Education 51,* no. 3 (May 1980):235–54.

Spillman, Carolyn V. "Classroom Management: Mystery or Mastery." *Education 101,* no. 1 (Fall 1980):41–45.

Chapter 4

Effective Teaching

Objectives

After studying this chapter, you should be able to:

- Discern the classroom management techniques that are most effective.

- Explain how a teacher's self-concept is related to effective teaching.

- Analyze the relationship between what a teacher expects of students and how students perform.

- Discern between effective and ineffective teaching strategies.

- Discuss how a teacher can create and maintain a positive attitude about students.

- Discuss the elements that create a democratic classroom.

- Explore the value of an excellent understanding of subject matter for the teacher.

- Explore systems for analyzing classroom activity.

- Explain the limitations of the Effective Schools formula.

Enrichment Experiences

The following suggestions will help you delve more deeply into some of the important topics discussed in this chapter.

- Visit with several teachers to see what they consider to be effective teaching strategies.

- Critically review a research report found in a professional education journal about effective schools.

- Select one of the effective teaching strategies contained in this chapter, and do additional library research on that topic.

- Do a critical analysis of the work of one of the researchers connected with the Effective Schools movement.

- Make a list of all the effective teaching strategies that have been verified by research.

- For the next year, watch for and read articles that appear in professional journals about effective teaching research and practices.

This chapter will enable you to briefly examine an exciting development in the field of education. This excitement is caused by the results of a large number of research projects generally referred to as "Effective Schools Research." When synthesized, this growing body of research has convinced an increasing group of educators that they can now apply a teaching formula shown to be effective. The Effective Schools formula will undoubtedly continue to change and evolve over the next thirty years; however, teacher education students who are preparing for teaching careers absolutely must become familiar with the current research dealing with effective schools. This chapter is designed to help you get started on this task. ∎

For many, many years, educational researchers have expended a great deal of time and energy in an effort to find the "best" or most effective way to teach. This effort was based on an assumption that there was a "best" way to teach, and if we could only discover it, then teachers would know how to be effective. Answers to this question were illusive. In fact, researchers found the relationship between teacher behavior and learning outcomes to be extremely complex.

It has been only during the past decade that encouraging results have begun to emerge from this massive research effort. A growing number of researchers believe that we have made great strides in recent years toward understanding the relationship between what teachers do and what students learn.

In this chapter, we will briefly review what this growing body of research has revealed about effective teaching variables. As a generalization, research has shown that effective teachers are good managers, use systematic instruction techniques, expect much of their students and themselves, have confidence in themselves, use many teaching strategies, do not label students, prevent discipline problems, care about students, are democratic, are task-oriented, teach for perceptual meanings, are comfortable with students, know their subject matter, are readily accessible to students, teach to student needs, and are flexible, enthusiastic, and imaginative.[1]

This is not to say that every good teacher exhibits all of these qualities nor that poor teachers exhibit none of these qualities. However, as a rule, our best teachers tend to fit this description better than do poor teachers. The remainder of this chapter will briefly discuss each of the variables that many researchers believe are generally associated with effective teachers.

∎ Good Classroom Management

It is perhaps trite to remind people that classrooms must be well organized and teachers must be good managers. Nevertheless, the fact remains that not all classrooms are well organized and not all teachers are good managers. A beginning teacher needs to spend time thinking seriously about organizing the classrooom in such a way that students will understand exactly what they are expected to do and be able to find the necessary learning materials as they go about their work.

In recent years, a number of research studies have indicated that our very best teachers tend to be very good managers. That is to say, they organize all aspects of their classrooms, learning experiences for students, teaching materials, and the day's schedule in a manner so that things happen by design, and not by chance. A well-organized classroom minimizes the amount of time that is wasted by students and the teacher. This allows a maximum amount of time to be spent on actual learning experiences. Research such as that of Brophy, Fisher, and others has shown that a well-managed classroom increases student learning.

Teachers who are good managers find a way to get the school year off to a very good start by being well organized and knowing what they intend to accomplish and how they intend to operate their classrooms. These teachers have a well-organized classroom where everything has its proper place and where students understand what aids are available to them in their studies. Things that at first may seem minor take on considerable importance in a well-organized classroom. For instance, students need to be able to move easily and freely throughout the classroom and to be able to use chalkboards and other learning aids in an organized manner. A well-managed classroom has logical, well-understood routines and procedures so that students do not waste time and end up getting in trouble with the teacher because they did not understand how the classroom was organized, what constituted acceptable behavior, and what they were to be doing at all times.

Well-organized teachers have a businesslike way of quickly dispatching with all the housekeeping duties that must be done within the typical classroom. This means that a minimal amount of time will be spent on such duties and maximum time on actual learning experiences.

Teachers who use systematic instructional techniques help their students learn more.

■ Using Systematic Instruction Techniques

Another characteristic of effective teachers is that they teach by design rather than by accident and that they utilize preplanned specific instructional strategies. To do so requires that teachers be very well prepared for each lesson they teach. Obviously, if teachers do not know what they intend to teach and how they intend to teach it before the beginning of a lesson, they will have to rely on whatever thoughts pop into their minds at the moment to teach that lesson. Such an unplanned lesson also prevents the teacher from having decided in advance which instructional techniques would work best for this particular lesson.

Fortunately, the typical teachers today have available at their disposal a wide variety of instructional materials and techniques. These techniques usually include some type of audiovisual

One must learn by doing the thing;
for though you think you know it you
have no certainty, until you try.

Sophocles

material (overhead projectors, videotapes, computers, etc.) as well as a wide variety of excellent print material. It is understandable then that to systematically use all of these materials requires advance planning. Recent research has shown that teachers who use systematic instructional techniques help their students learn more. Appendix E lists and describes teaching functions which are research-based and are representative of teachers who use systematic instructional techniques.

■ Teacher Expectations

Ever since a piece of research published in 1968, "Pygmalion in the Classroom," educators have become increasingly interested in the degree to which a teacher's expectations affect the result of student learning in the classroom. This study indicated that students tend to learn according to the way teachers expect them to learn. To the degree that this is true, it is very important that teachers treat all students as though they have the ability to learn and to really expect all students to learn. Teachers who expect their students to learn produce higher learning results in their students than do teachers who, for instance, basically do not care what their students learn. It may seem difficult to believe that some teachers operate in a manner which seems to reflect an opinion that they basically do not care how much their students learn; however, studies have shown that not all teachers actually have high expectations of their students. Some research has suggested that students tend to learn the way their teachers expect them to learn.[2]

Teachers with high expectations for their students generally feel guilty if their students are not learning, and such teachers continue to search for new and more effective teaching techniques.

Teachers with high expectations tend not to blame students for poor learning, but rather, feel that they are responsible for bringing about effective learning in their students.[3]

Teachers with high expectations assign meaningful homework to their students. Such teachers also hold students accountable for homework assignments and for other learning responsibilities.[4] Effective teachers communicate their expectations to the students in the form of objectives. These teachers then teach very directly to their objectives. Effective teachers also provide logical excellent learning opportunities for their students. Teachers with high expectations tend to make themselves readily available to their students outside of class hours. Lastly, teachers with high expectations really believe that their students can learn well and reach their potential[5] and treat each student accordingly.

■ Use of Teaching Strategies

Researchers have found that our best teachers inevitably use a wide variety of instructional techniques and have an uncanny ability to use the right teaching technique at the right time. It has been said that there are an infinite number of teaching techniques that a teacher might use at any one moment in time. These techniques could range from lecturing on the one hand to direct purposeful student experiences (such as dissecting a frog) on the other hand. Effective teachers use simulation, role playing, laboratory work, field trips, movies, videotapes, overhead transparencies, slides, small group instruction, large group discussion, independent study, homework, creative assignments, print materials, etc. throughout the school year. All of these strategies have their place in the schools, and it is perhaps more difficult for a teacher to decide when to use a particular strategy than it is to develop the ability to use the strategy in the first place.

Yet another way to put it is that our most effective teachers are innovative when it comes to utilizing instructional techniques. These outstanding teachers also have an ability to demonstrate the use of various teaching strategies in a way that provides a systematic set of learning experiences for their students. These teachers also utilize instructional techniques to insure "over learning" so that students have adequate opportunity to review each concept to the point at which it will be retained.[6]

■ Preventing Discipline Problems

Effective teachers do not wait for students to misbehave before they attend to discipline; rather, they prevent discipline problems from occurring in the first place. The old adage, "An ounce of prevention is worth a pound of cure," is particularly true when it comes to maintaining good classroom control. Research has shown that if students are kept highly motivated and productively busy, they will tend to not misbehave in the classroom.

Teachers who are constantly able to monitor classroom activity can change teaching strategies when necessary to prevent classroom disruptions.[7]

Effective teachers seem to develop the ability to do many things at the same time. An example of this might be the teacher who is working in one part of the room with one group of students but is still able to sense what is happening throughout the rest of the classroom. The teacher who develops this ability keeps his/her "finger on the pulse" of all the students in the room and is able to monitor the total classroom activity at all times.

Yet another principle for maintaining good classroom control is to be be very well prepared for the instruction that is taking place. Teachers must have all the teaching materials ready in advance and waiting at their fingertips. They must also have contingency plans to fall back on when the situation calls for it. Our best teachers also develop subtle techniques for letting the students know that they are being communicated with and watched at all times. An example of this might be maintaining eye contact with each student periodically and calling upon students to respond to questions or actively participate in the class throughout the day. These same excellent teachers develop techniques for dealing with disruptive or inattentive students without bringing too much attention to the problem. In other words, they do not make a "big deal" out of the minor discipline problems that inevitably occur in every classroom.

Our better teachers experiment with different classroom control techniques and search out those that tend to be positive and nonpunitive. An example might be the use of behavior modification techniques from time to time. Another example might be employing the "reality therapy" techniques developed by Dr. William Glasser when more serious discipline problems occur.

Research has shown that teachers list classroom control as one of their major problems. Beginning teachers must realize that it is not easy to get students to behave and work productively in the classroom, and that effective teachers simply must develop this ability. Research has also shown that inability to control students is one of the major reasons that teachers fail and leave the

Research Finding

4

The most important characteristics of effective schools are strong instructional leadership, a safe and orderly climate, school-wide emphasis on basic skills, high teacher expectations for student achievement, and continuous assessment of pupil progress.

One of the most important achievements of education research in the last 20 years has been identifying the factors that characterize effective schools, in particular the schools that have been especially successful in teaching basic skills to children from low-income families. Analysts first uncovered these characteristics when comparing the achievement levels of students from different urban schools. They labeled the schools with the highest achievement as "effective schools."

Schools with high student achievement and morale show certain characteristics:

- vigorous instructional leadership
- a principal who makes clear, consistent, and fair decisions
- an emphasis on discipline and a safe, orderly environment
- instructional practices that focus on basic skills and academic achievement
- collegiality among teachers in support of student achievement
- teachers with high expectations that all their students can and will learn
- frequent review of student progress

Doyle, W. (May 1985). "Effective Secondary School Practices," in R. Kyle (Ed.) *Reaching for Excellence: An Effective Schools Sourcebook*, (pp. 55–70). Washington, DC: U.S. Government Printing Office.

Edmonds, R. (1982). "Programs of School Improvement." *Educational Leadership*, Vol. 10, No. 3, pp. 4–11.

Finn, C. E., Jr. (April 1984). "Toward Strategic Independence: Nine Commandments for Enhancing School Effectiveness," *Phi Delta Kappan*, Vol. 65, No. 8, pp. 513–524.

Source: *What Works: Research About Teaching and Learning*. Washington, DC: U.S. Department of Education, 1987, page 57.

classroom. Developing the ability to maintain good classroom control is an essential for the career teacher. Our most effective teachers manage to accomplish this task. The secret is usually to prevent the discipline problem from occurring in the first place. The subject of classroom control is discussed more fully in chapter 3.

■ Teachers' Self-Concept

Good teachers tend to have more self-confidence about their teaching ability than do poor teachers. It would be logical to presume that this self-confidence grows, at least in part, out of successes that a good teacher enjoys. There's an old saying that suggests "success breeds success," which is likely to be especially true for teachers. It is probably the case that beginning teachers and student

The sine qua non *of innovative policy is controversy.*

Richard Neustadt

teachers who work hard, are well-organized, and exhibit other effective teaching characteristics, will have more success which in turn improves self-confidence and leads to greater success "ad infinitum."

■ Maintaining a Positive Attitude about Students

It is the case that, by the time we become teachers, we have developed our personal characteristics to the point where they are very difficult to change. This means that the person who already tends to be cold and aloof is unlikely to become a warm and caring teacher. The implication of this is obvious—people who do not possess the personal characteristics that are likely to be important as teachers should probably not become teachers in the first place. College students who are contemplating teaching careers would profit from thinking about their own personal characteristics and how well suited they are to the work that a teacher does.

Our best teachers tend to be very fair in the way they treat students.[8] These teachers treat all students equally and do not prejudge students. They tend to realize that there is "a lot of good and a little bad" in all students. In other words, students differ from one another by degree and not by kind. These excellent teachers seem to respect students as human beings and treat them accordingly.

Effective teachers tend to be good listeners[9] and have a sincere interest in understanding what each student attempts to communicate to them. These teachers have a good sense of humor and an innate ability to communicate with students on a one-to-one basis. Good teachers tend to be empathetic and receptive to their students. By the

same token, our best teachers have a strong commitment to their work, to serving their students,[10] and they seem to derive a great deal of personal enjoyment from helping students learn.

Effective teachers tend to be more interested in helping their students than they are in their subject matter. They accept the fact that not all students are as interested in the curricular content as is the teacher, and that the students must be nurtured individually if they are to develop more interest in the subject matter.

One might say our best teachers are student-centered rather than subject-centered. These teachers are careful not to stereotype students, utilize good human relations skills in dealing with their students, present a model of understanding and warmth, and allow their students a good deal of involvement and input into classroom activity.

■ A Democratic Classroom

Teachers who are not dictatorial, but rather approach teaching in a democratic manner, are more effective. Such teachers involve students in the planning of the activities that will take place in the classroom. These teachers constantly seek student input into the learning and evaluation process. In this way, students have a feeling that they are involved and not simply being told exactly what to do with no explanation.

Democratic teachers also seek out opportunities to participate, along with other staff members, in planning the school curriculum and solving any other school problems that exist. This takes additional time on the part of the democratic teacher but pays off in a feeling that one is helping to organize, plan, and conduct the total school program.

Democratic teachers also involve parents in planning and sometimes even in carrying out the instructional program. For instance, parents who understand and have had a hand in planning their child's education will very likely feel better about the school program and work harder to support it. Informed and involved parents are also more likely to help their children with homework and to encourage them to excel in school.

■ Task-Oriented Teachers

Our most effective teachers have a "game plan" and work very hard to accomplish what they set out to do. In a sense, our best teachers are driven by an insatiable desire to provide a good education for their students. These teachers are not happy with mediocre results on the part of the students, but rather, stick to the task of expecting and requiring their students to obtain a good education.

Being task-oriented requires first that a teacher be well organized and well prepared for each instructional session. Obviously, teachers cannot be task-oriented if they aren't even sure what their task is.

■ Teaching for Perceptual Meanings

Research has shown repeatedly that students tend to forget many specific facts that they have rotely memorized. On the other hand, research has shown that if students can acquire the overall meaning of a concept, they are more likely to retain such learning. Today's effective teachers understand this truism and strive to help all their students learn the perceptual meaning of concepts rather than simply memorize facts and events. This is not to say that effective teachers do not teach facts; however, they are not content when students are able to regurgitate facts on a test. Rather, they realize that to teach perceptual meanings is more difficult than to teach facts. To do this, teachers must go beyond facts and events and strive to help students develop a deeper understanding of the implications of individual bits of information. To do so takes additional time and effort on the part of the teacher. Such effort pays off, however, in helping the students to develop insights about overall concepts that they are more likely to retain.

■ Good Teachers Are Comfortable with Students

It has already been pointed out that our most effective teachers like students and enjoy interacting with them. It is important to realize that our most effective teachers are comfortable in their role interacting with students. In a sense, these teachers feel comfortable trusting students to take an active role in planning their learning experiences. Effective teachers seem to be able to develop a relationship with students which is not stressful, and which is family-like in the sense that students and the teacher easily and freely communicate and work together.

This is not to say that such teachers expect less of students or are not very demanding of their students. In fact, it is usually quite the opposite, wherein our best teachers expect a great deal of their students. However, effective teachers are able to require more work of their students without causing the students to be resentful.

■ Knowing the Subject Matter

Our very best teachers know a great deal about the subjects they teach. Knowledgeable teachers constantly strive to learn more about their subject so they can pass this information on to their students. All teachers realize that we live in an era when knowledge expands at a phenomenal rate. This makes it very difficult for career teachers to remain current on their subject matter and also on the most recent teaching strategies. Nevertheless, our most effective teachers find a way to do so by constantly reading journals, attending conferences, and returning to graduate school frequently.

This is not to say that our most effective teachers always know all the subject matter they need to know. In fact, our best teachers are quick to admit it when they do not have the answer to a student's question. It is not necessary that a teacher always know the answer to a question a student may raise in class. It is perfectly acceptable for teachers to simply say, "I don't know the answer to that, but let's try to find out the answer together."

■ Accessibility to Students

Effective teachers make themselves available to students outside of class. To be sure, this is a time consuming commitment; however, students simply must have access to the teacher if they are to learn. This means that teachers must be extremely well organized and manage their time efficiently so that they will be able to spend time with individual students outside of class. Each teacher must decide how much time he/she is willing to devote to students.

Effective teachers make themselves available to students outside of class.

Some teachers find it useful to create a club related to the subject matter of the class for highly motivated students. For instance, a science teacher might create a science club which would meet periodically and give students a chance to spend additional time with the teacher through this club. Other effective teachers may simply designate the thirty minutes before school each morning and/or the thirty minutes after school as time when students may drop in for individual help or simply to visit with the teacher. Those teachers lucky enough to have a free period often let students know that they are available at that time for individual consultation. The point is that effective teachers must find a way to be available to students outside of class. Research has shown that our most effective teachers do so more than our less effective teachers.

It is a fear of the future that makes the future fearful.

Jan Christian Smuts

■ Teaching to Student Needs

Effective teachers realize that individual students have their own best learning styles and that each student must be presented a program of learning that meets her or his needs. Likewise, each class or group of students, given their individual abilities and interests, will respond best to particular instructional strategies. Effective teachers seem to have the ability to sense rather quickly the individual needs of students and to be able to adjust their teaching styles to these needs.

Of course, even our best teachers must compromise between what they would ideally like to do on the one hand, and what the realities of the teaching world will allow on the other hand. For instance, there are only so many hours in each teaching day and teachers must make value judgments about how to use this limited amount of time to accomplish the greatest learning possible on behalf of their students.

■ Analyzing Classroom Activity

Good teachers do not depend totally upon their intuition to understand what is taking place in their classrooms. Rather, they analyze what the teacher and students are actually doing. Figure 4.1 is an example of an observation sheet which might be useful to a teacher who wants to better understand the interacting taking place between the teacher and each student. By having a colleague fill out this form during a lesson, the teacher could then analyze these data and, hopefully, better understand classroom interaction.

Different data-gathering devices can be used to collect and analyze information on a wide variety of different types of classroom activities. The point is that our best teachers constantly strive to better understand and analyze their classroom activity.

■ Flexible, Enthusiastic, and Imaginative Teachers

By way of summary, research has shown that our very best teachers are flexible in their approach to students and teaching. In other words, they are constantly adjusting their teaching to meet the needs of the moment. This does not mean that they are not well prepared and have clearly enunciated objectives. Rather, it is a matter of the teacher constantly monitoring the needs of their students and adjusting their teaching strategies to meet these needs.

Yet another difference between our very best teachers and their less effective colleagues is the amount of enthusiasm that teachers exhibit for their work. Our best teachers are excited and enthusiastic about teaching. Enthusiasm seems to cause our best teachers to grow professionally and remain "alive" as educators.

Our best teachers can also be characterized as imaginative concerning their work. By way of contrast, some teachers seem to get stuck in a rut after their first few years of teaching and never seem to be able to creatively grow as educators. Our best teachers are constantly growing and changing. These teachers experiment with new and imaginative approaches and seem to thrive on a dynamic teaching philosophy.

Teacher's Name _____

Observer's Name _____

Date _____

Each time the teacher interacts with a student (during recitation or seatwork), place the appropriate symbol in that student's box.

(Front of room)

Row 1	Row 2	Row 3	Row 4	Row 5	Row 6	Row 7

"Everyone Responds" Tally

- Academic:
- Non-academic:

Symbols

✔ = Opportunity to respond/interact. Teacher gives student a chance to answer questions, read aloud, give a report, receive help from the teacher. (These are student or teacher initiated interactions about academic and non-academic matters.)

+ = Praise

− = Desist: Short request/demand to stop a behavior

★———★ = Teacher movement (put a star when he/she moves 2 ft. or more)

Activities (You may wish to provide a brief description of each activity—when it occurred, who was involved, etc.)

Time   Teacher Activity   Student Activity

■ **Figure 4.1**

Interaction observation form

Research Finding

5

How much time students are actively engaged in learning contributes strongly to their achievement. The amount of time available for learning is determined by the instructional and management skills of the teacher and the priorities set by the school administration.

Effective time managers in the classroom do not waste valuable minutes on unimportant activities; they keep their students continuously and actively engaged. Good managers perform the following time-conserving functions:

- *Planning Class Work:* choosing the content to be studied, scheduling time for presentation and study, and choosing those instructional activities (such as grouping, seatwork, or recitation) best suited to learning the material at hand;

- *Communicating Goals:* setting and conveying expectations so students know what they are to do, what it will take to get a passing grade, and what the consequences of failure will be;

- *Regulating Learning Activities:* sequencing course content so knowledge builds on itself, pacing instruction so students are prepared for the next step, monitoring success rates so all students stay productively engaged regardless of how quickly they learn, and running an orderly, academically focused classroom that keeps wasted time and misbehavior to a minimum.

Berliner, D. (September 1983). "The Executive Functions of Teaching." *The Instructor,* Vol. 93, No. 2, pp. 28–40.

Brophy, J. (1979). "Teacher Behavior and Its Effects." *Journal of Educational Psychology,* Vol. 71, No. 6, pp. 733–750.

Hawley, W., and Rosenholtz, S. with Goodstein, H., and Hasselbring, T. (Summer 1984). "Good Schools: What Research Says About Improving Student Achievement." *Peabody Journal of Education,* Vol. 61, No. 4.

Source: *What Works: Research About Teaching and Learning.* Washington, DC: U.S. Department of Education, 1987, page 39.

■ Limitations of the Effective Teaching Movement

It should be noted that not all authorities believe that the effective schools formula is a good one. Lawrence Stedman, writing in a recent issue of a respected school publication, typifies those who are hesitant, if not downright critical, of the effective schools movement.[11]

Stedman indicates that the effective schools formula has been hastily adopted, particularly by large cities throughout the United States. He believes that the evidence cited to support this movement is weak and inconclusive. He points out, for instance, that most of the effective schools research has been done on minority children in large-city schools, and may not be generalizable to students in other settings. He also points out that, even in large urban schools, the evidence cited from the effective schools research, in his opinion, is very weak.

Stedman also believes that the results of effective schools practices have not been impressive. For instance, the research that is usually cited actually showed very minor learning gains on the part of students. It might be that similar small improvements in learning would have been achieved by using virtually any new teaching strategies.

Yet another possible problem with the effective schools movement, in Stedman's opinion, is that many pieces of research actually contradict the findings of the studies upon which the effective schools formula has been built. It has been very difficult to synthesize the research on effective schools. People who analyze this body of research do not always come out with the same formula for effective teaching. Stedman, for instance, believes that effective schools research has indicated that we should concentrate our efforts to improve schools on the following nine broad categories:

- ethnic and racial pluralism
- parent participation
- shared governance with teachers and parents
- academically rich programs
- skilled use and training of teachers
- personal attention to students
- student responsibility for school affairs
- an accepting and supportive environment
- teaching aimed at preventing academic problems[12]

Furthermore, Stedman believes that we should think of these nine factors as highly interrelated items which are dependent in large part upon one another. For instance, if one finds a way to more effectively use and train highly skilled teachers, it will likely bring about improvements in the other eight factors.

It is the case that the effective schools formula, at this point in time, is not conclusive. Most authorities, however, feel that the research upon which this formula is based is sufficiently convincing that educators should draw from it in their quest for more effective schools. To be sure, we need to continue to refine this research and to generally continue a massive research effort to find ways to improve our schools. In the final analysis, each teacher must decide which research results are worthy of implementation in his/her classroom. To do so, of course, a teacher must be very familiar with the research literature related to the field of education.

■ Summary

This chapter has briefly reviewed the effective schools movement in the United States. It has pointed out that a growing body of research suggests that teachers who utilize particular teaching strategies bring about more effective learning on the part of their students. Some of these strategies deal with: good classroom management, using systematic instructional techniques, developing a healthy self concept on the part of the teacher, the dangers of labeling students, the importance of high student expectations on the part of the teacher, the essentialness of using a wide variety of good instructional techniques, the importance of preventing discipline problems, the need for teachers to maintain a positive attitude about their students, the advantages of a democratic classroom, the importance of being well organized and task oriented on the part of the teacher, the advantages of teaching for perceptual meaning, why teachers must develop a good comfortable relationship with their students, the importance of teachers having a very good understanding of their subject matter, why teachers need to find a way to be accessible to their students outside of the classroom, why teachers must gear their teaching specifically to each student's needs, the importance of teachers being flexible and enthusiastic and imaginative, etc. Each of these factors have grown out of research studies that show their importance for effective teaching and learning. Lastly, this chapter has raised caution about relying totally on the effective schools research at this point in time. This research is inconclusive and incomplete at the moment. Teachers will need to monitor educational research throughout their careers so that they may employ the best research outcomes in their classrooms at all times.

Point of View

Much of the school effectiveness movement is based on a belief that factors related to the quality of education can be accurately measured. Not everyone subscribes to this belief. The following point of view, offered by Eva L. Baker, questions our current ability to fairly measure the quality of education. It should be of considerable interest to future teachers, since the effectiveness of their work will be frequently measured and since they constantly attempt to measure student learning.

Can We Fairly Measure the Quality of Education?

Eva L. Baker

American political attention has turned with increasing intensity to the matter of educational quality. From the reports of commissions and panels to debates by presidential candidates, the focus on students, teachers, and schools grows sharper every day. At the center of concern is a deceptively simple question: How well do our schools prepare our students?

Whether the language emphasizes excellence, subject matter understanding, productivity, or competitiveness, the meaning of the debate is clear: Can we describe, judge, and improve the effectiveness of public schools?

Over the years, significant investments have been made in trying to answer these questions. Standardized achievement tests, educational program evaluations, teacher testing, and minimum competency tests for students are all thought to provide useful information to help make judgments about the effects of educational services on students.

Many of these options have roots in the mid-1960s enactment of federal legislation to assist educationally disadvantaged students. This new legislation required that the federal government evaluate the effects of its efforts to provide compensatory resources for students. The legislation was directly responsible for the rapid development and growth of the evaluation field and for many scientific developments in the measurement of human performance.

Through the ensuing decades, one or another particular version of evaluation or measurement was selected as the new solution for understanding school effectiveness—the options coming, it seemed, in overlapping waves. Remember?

Different solutions included setting objectives and measuring student performance, local standardized student testing, program evaluation, analysis of Scholastic Aptitude Test (SAT) score decline, state minimum competency examinations, teacher testing, state assessment, and "The Wall Chart," a national comparison of state educational systems promoted by the U.S. Department of Education.

None of these approaches were found to be wholly satisfactory, but, after the initial blaze of interest died down, none were retired either. Instead, our attempts to understand educational quality have created an ever-increasing set of measures and approaches designed to shed some light on the issue. But do they? Imagine that we could start over, fresh and unsullied by our prior measurement experience. What would be fair measures of the effectiveness of our educational programs?

To answer this question, we must first decide what level of information we want. The public seems equally interested in the concrete accomplishments of local schools and the general descriptions of the educational system at large. Making a judgment about all of American education and assessing the effectiveness of First Street School in your hometown, however, require different levels of information. When taking a nationwide view, we look for common features of schools and curriculums on which to base our judgment. When looking at a particular school, we can be much more attentive to the community characteristics, the kinds of students attending the school, the particular goals of the school, and other special conditions. In both cases, we simply want to know the following:

- What are the students learning?
- How well do the teachers teach?
- What is the quality of our schools?

The answers to these questions should not simply describe the state of performance for students, teachers, and school administrators, but should permit us to devise actions to make things better. We want information for more than curiosity's sake; we want it to help us improve education. This desire to face and fix what's wrong requires that the information we collect give us more than categorical "good" or "poor" labels. We need enough detail to guide our policies and practices.

Traditionally, student learning has been measured by achievement tests. When the measurement is for purposes of public accountability, teacher-made tests have never been regarded as sufficient. Rather, because accountability implies some sort of comparison, school districts have used tests that have standard content and rather general applicability. After two decades of concerns about standardized testing, a few issues remain salient:

- Standardized tests allow comparisons among schools and regions. They may, however, be somewhat insensitive to curricular and instructional variations. Because they are designed to be of widest utility, standardized tests may omit areas of particular emphasis for particular schools. Further, they provide information on only a narrow slice of school activities.

- Standardized tests most often ask children to answer questions given in a multiple-choice format. I believe this format greatly underestimates student performance.

- For technical reasons of test design, very small absolute differences (for instance, one more test item correct) might mean an improvement of a grade level or so. Inferences about educational quality based on such differences are shaky at best.

Test performance still is, in that unfortunate phrase, the "bottom line" for many who would assess the effectiveness of the schools. At this time, many policymakers regard standardized tests as credible and objective. Achievement testing will not go away, and for good reason. Schools must be held accountable for teaching students and for attempting to measure what they have learned. Many people think standardized tests are the best approach we have.

But these tests can be greatly improved. At the Center for Research on Evaluation, Standards, and Student Testing (CRESST), sponsored by the U.S. Office of Educational Research and Improvement, we are in the midst of a five-year research program to improve the quality of testing for use in the schools.

The precepts of our program, and the way we believe testing ought to be improved, fix on a small set of critical issues, all related to validity—the quality of the information the test provides us and the degree to which we can believe it.

Validity of achievement measures has a number of components. One that is critical is the degree to which the way performance is measured matches the mode in which learning best occurs. With the advances in cognitive science, we believe we can design measures that more productively represent the richness of learning. For example, we're interested in assuring that in mathematics, science, and history, students be given different ways to demonstrate their competence, perhaps in multiple-choice tests, perhaps in other paper-and-pencil formats, perhaps using computer dynamic displays, perhaps in writing.

■ Student Learning

Many testing formats in current use developed because they were convenient to administer and score rather than because they were the best ways to assess complex human understanding.

Standardized tests often force students to give the first, quick response, rather than a thoughtful, reasoned answer. The balance between conserving the time spent on testing and providing enough opportunity for adequate thought is still unsettled. Perhaps a more diverse menu of testing approaches will increase the overall validity of our measures and allow testing approaches better to match student propensities.

A second validity concern relates to the content or subject matter of what is to be tested. One of the sadder outcomes of the behavioral objective movement and the inquiry approaches of the early 1970's was the attention paid to process *at the expense* of the content to which a process applied. We have seen the pendulum swing widely on this issue during the last two decades. Given the popularity of books like E. D. Hirsch's *Cultural Literacy* and the scandalous blanks and misunderstandings in our students' knowledge, we are on the verge of another swing towards content. Thus it's tempting to devise tests that can pinpoint content errors.

This time, however, we want to make sure that we go well beyond identification or recognition of specific facts and concepts. We intend to integrate measurement approaches that wed content with sophisticated approaches to demonstrating understanding, such as complex essays. We at UCLA are developing the technology to score such essays reliably and relatively inexpensively.

Third, we are interested in measures that can be related directly to instructional options. We should be measuring performance that schools can affect. This means that, where possible, we should be collecting information about teaching practices, student familiarity with content, and so on, at the same time that we measure student performance.

Fourth, our measures must be valid when individual and group differences are considered. Whether a test is fair is a psychological as well as an empirical issue. We particularly want to ensure that our measures validly assess strengths and weaknesses of our pluralistic student body in a way that contributes to their motivation to continue learning.

Even when student achievement is measured validly, the way the findings are interpreted makes a difference. Interpretation involves relating findings to those yielded by similar measures of performance, comparing findings to the performance of similar groups of students or schools, analyzing findings in the light of previous performance to see the development of trends over time, or looking at performance in terms of some predetermined standard. Comparison to other student groups is the most common interpretation strategy. This comparison is the basis of "norms"— averages provided for many nationally standardized tests. Some state assessments compare the performance of students in schools of similar size and community location. More recently, the federal government has reported the comparison of student performance on the SAT state by state, a specific approach to be discussed later.

A central issue of interpretation is what is being compared. Are tests of individual students used to make comparisons among schools? What other information needs to be collected if such use of information is to be sensible?

The first question for these sorts of comparisons is: Is the comparison fair? One shouldn't compare a small, stable suburban school with a central city school that has a high mobility rate. Given the increasing diversity of our students, comparisons now must take into account factors such as language in the home and length of time in the school in addition to the more usual socioeconomic measures.

Another option has been international comparison. While this might be useful in setting goals for our students, the inference persists that we should adopt practices embedded in other cultures or in other, more centralized arrangements for educational policymaking. Such an inference is probably unwarranted.

Moreover, the bane of most normative comparisons is that half of the group is always below average, a status unacceptable to most educational policymakers. No one yet has figured out how all students can perform "above the average."

To sum up, what should we want in student achievement measurement:

- More than one measure of a single phenomenon, such as reading comprehension, to allow for corroboration from different sources—but with no expectation that all students need to take all measures.
- More than one kind of testing format, such as multiple-choice and written answers.
- Tests that give students adequate time to perform serious cognitive tasks.
- Tests that measure both the content (what) and the process (how) that students use to solve complex problems of understanding.
- Tests that can be analyzed to guide instructional planning.
- Test results that are understandable, timely, and useful for teachers in instruction and planning.
- Reports of test results that are fair to students, teachers, and schools.

■ Quality of Teaching

A second enduring concern in education is the quality of teaching. This interest is obvious; when we think of schools we think of teachers. Given the instructional and economic dominance of teachers in schooling, it's natural to want to judge the effectiveness of educational investments in part by looking at teaching. The problems begin when one tries actually to measure the quality of teaching and confuses the measure with the ''quality'' of teachers.

Just as in assessing student achievement, the principal trouble spot in measuring quality of teaching is validity. There is little real agreement on what good teaching is. When good results occur, we can attempt to infer which teaching practices were responsible. Principles such as providing students with opportunity to learn, clear task directions, and feedback, undoubtedly apply—on the average. Our problem is that we are often interested not in teaching on the average, but in a particular teacher's competency, perhaps to determine eligibility for merit pay or other forms of advancement. When the individual teacher is our focus, we must take special care to allow for differences in pedagogical style, since for various topics, objectives, grade levels, personalities, settings, and student groups, no ''best'' pedagogical approach has been identified.

The Carnegie Foundation is supporting development of new approaches to the assessment of teaching competencies. Although designed to permit special certification of teachers rather than assess educational effects, this effort may have some positive influence on the measurement of teaching capability.

Because teaching quality itself has been hard to measure, many have supported the measurement, instead, of prerequisites that good teachers are presumed to need. Such prerequisites include mastery of subject matter; mastery of basic knowledge about teaching, student development, and learning; and mastery of basic skills. Tests— some with associated sanctions—have been devised to assess teachers in many of these areas.

Although the right of the state or school district to set standards of this sort is not in dispute, conflicts have developed on a number of points. In a 1987 paper written for the Office for Educational Research and Improvement, L. M. Rudner and associates point out that the standards for many of these tests have been set very low. Two studies from the UCLA Center for the Study of Evaluation elaborate on the strains in the testing process. In *A Case Study of the Texas Teacher Test* (1987), Lorrie Shepard describes how it might be possible to pass a teacher test by being testwise rather than by being skilled in the area the test was assessing. M. C. Ellwien and G. V. Glass infer from their *Case Studies on Education Standards* (1986) that teacher testing is mostly symbolic and has very little to do with actually identifying deficiencies and improving instruction. Many of the analyses of teacher testing involve the question of when it should occur (preservice? preteacher education program?) and to whom the sanctions should apply (the teacher? the degree-granting institution? the teacher training institution?).

Student achievement also can be used to estimate teaching effectiveness. It seems like a reasonable tactic; after all, teachers ought to help students learn. The use of such measures to assess teachers unfortunately adds new complexity to existing concerns about the validity of student testing. Minimally, these comparisons may necessitate complex tracking of students who enter particular teachers' classes.

Statistically equating students who have different entry competencies is sure to be an unsatisfactory way to compare teachers' relative merit in promoting achievement. While it's harder to teach students who have inadequate backgrounds, it's also difficult to show real improvement when a student group comes in with very strong achievement levels because of the way tests are typically developed. In either case, the achievement tests will probably misrepresent the nature of the teacher's effort. Fortunately, recent assessment systems for teachers are attempting to represent more broadly the nature of teachers' efforts.

■ Quality of Schools

Who wants to know? The desire to find out how schools are doing is clearly legitimate, and educators, policymakers, and researchers continue to propose alternative sources of information. One of the problems we face is providing the right information to the right people. Congressional policymakers want to know whether the schools are working. At different times, their concern may be focused on the quality of what is learned (as in the post-Sputnik period) or on who is learning (when equity concerns are central on the educational agenda). Their needs are to assess the impact of resources they have invested and to target continuing or new needs. They need relatively unambiguous, clear information.

To an even greater extent, state-level policymakers are concerned with the effects of specific financing, curriculum, and certification policies—their efforts to reform schools in their states. Local school boards and administrations need information on the quality of their policy implementation and on progress toward discretionary goals, given the particular characteristics of their community.

Each set of policymakers needs different levels of detail and has different opportunities to influence the reality of classroom practice. The hodgepodge of conflicting information from local, state, and national evaluations doesn't make evaluation of educational effectiveness any easier. Some new approaches may offer some relief.

The federal government is now considering a funding proposal to transform the measurement practices of the National Assessment of Educational Progress (NAEP) so that state-by-state comparisons will be possible. NAEP has been periodically measuring U.S. students in reading comprehension, writing, and mathematics. The administration of these measures presently allows for interpretation by broad geographical region, rather than by state. The proposal calls for administering these measures so that a representative sample of students in each state would be tested and described in NAEP reports. The proposal also expands the number of subjects assessed.

If accepted, this approach could focus the evaluation of schooling on the NAEP achievement measures. Is this a good thing? There is a clear division of opinion. Proponents argue that:

- A common basis for understanding student achievement would be systematically available if NAEP were expanded.
- The quality of measures would continue to improve because of the salience of the new measures.
- States could use such information for their own policy assessment to check their progress.
- Interpretation for policy purposes would be simplified.
- States would be able to compare themselves to subsets of other similar states.
Critics contend that:
- NAEP may turn into a national achievement test, and a national curriculum may follow.
- NAEP would not be sufficiently responsive to local or regional differences in curriculums, students, or economic factors to permit legitimate comparisons.
- NAEP would drive out state and local tests, which are more responsive to local curriculums.
- Pressure for school district comparisons will follow state comparisons.

• Because NAEP's strength is in making comparisons over time, the pressure to keep NAEP measures the same would inhibit development of new goals for the curriculum and new approaches to measurement.

• A single set of measures can be wrong. Given the state of understanding of achievement measurement, investing in different assessment approaches is the most prudent way to collect information that's relevant to policy.

For each of these points, both positive and negative, there are counter arguments, and counter-counter arguments. If the problem were simple, it would already be solved. What's significant is that the attractiveness of a clearly understood, single set of measures of American education is strong, even when the validity of the measures for assessing local and state educational policies is questioned. The state-by-state NAEP approach needs to be understood as an attempt to catch hold of what our schools are doing.

Another tack is the quality indicators movement. The goal of this effort is to identify and systematically collect information that can give a picture of the overall quality of American education, not just achievement test scores. Work in this area has been conducted by the Rand Corporation, the Center for Policy Research in Education at Rutgers, our own Center for Research on Evaluation, Standards, and Student Testing (CRESST) at UCLA, and numerous other institutions and scholars. Part of its impetus comes from the realm of economic indicators, where seemingly simple numbers like the Gross National Product, unemployment figures, and the Dow Jones average efficiently communicate the economic health of the country.

The Center for Education Statistics (a division of the U.S. Office of Educational Research and Improvement) has been working on indicators of educational quality. These indicators include figures such as dropout rates, per capita student funding, student-teacher class ratios, enrollment figures, and the like. The problems the researchers encountered include the vastly different ways of reporting even such seemingly simple phenomena as dropout rates. Different districts and states count dropouts at different intervals, count them at different ages or grades, use different base rates, track student mobility differently, and so on. Getting everyone to agree on a single reporting approach, even for such an "easily understood" concept, is a Herculean task.

Even so, outcomes like achievement test scores, college admission rates, or dropout figures represent the easiest indicators to collect. Quality indicators should also take into account input variables and measures of process.

Suppose we wanted a "quality indicator" related to some intermediate process, such as student coursework (in fact, UCLA and the Rand Corporation are collaborating to develop such indicators). We'd have to consider how to determine "quality" in a valid and comprehensive way, how to collect such information accurately and comfortably in schools, and how to report the findings so that the effects of educational reform can be tracked. If we (or others) can solve such a problem, educational achievement tests can be relieved of the perhaps excessive burden they carry as measures of the effects of different policies.

Changes such as adding coursework requirements, strengthening the content of the curriculum in a particular area, or requiring textbooks to exhibit certain content standards are all elements that policymakers hypothesize will help schools. Developing indicators of the extent to which these suggestions are followed is a first step;

studying the relationship of the level of their use to resultant levels of student achievement is a second critical link.

Yet the indicator movement must be cautious about identifying a single magic index or number to stand for complex educational processes. As Leigh Burstein of UCLA points out, the context in which such data are reported, understood, and interpreted is central to the success of this effort.

■ Summary

The search for approaches to assess schools, their teachers, and students, will continue. This discussion has touched lightly on a number of complex issues. Controversies also will continue, and we can be sure that almost any decision will be rethought sometime in the future. Our interest as members of the research community is to keep a few issues in front of the public and the decisionmakers in this area.

First, we believe that the validity of any measure or indicator should be paramount, whether it is a measure of outcomes, like student achievement; of input, like teacher knowledge; or of processes, like student coursework. These measures should be designed so as to offer multiple or flexible ways to demonstrate success for different students. They should help us to pinpoint and fix weaknesses in policy and practice. Finally, these measures first must serve the interests of students and improve their schools. We must overcome our habit of preparing measures for the convenience of test developers, administrators, legislators, or even teachers. Rather, we need to consider the impact that our approaches to assessing educational effectiveness will have on our current and future students.

■ Questions for Discussion

1. What is a good definition of effective teaching? Effective learning? Effective school research? Effective schools formula?

2. What are the major components of the effective teaching formula?

3. Which of the effective teaching strategies discussed in this chapter are most important? Least important? Why?

4. What are some of the things a teacher can do to acquire and maintain a healthy positive attitude about students and about teaching?

5. What are your major criticisms and the limitations of the effective school movement?

■ Notes

1. *Effective Teaching Observations from Research.* (Arlington, VA: American Association of School Administrators, 1986), p. 4.

2. Steven M. Cahn, "The Art of Teaching." *American Educator* (Fall 1982).

3. Jere Brophy, "Classroom Organization and Management." *Elementary School Journal* (March 1983).

4. Barak V. Rosenshine, "Content, Time and Direct Instruction." *Research on Teaching: Concepts, Findings and Implications.* Edited by Penelope Peterson and Herbert J. Walberg. (Berkeley, CA: McCutchan, 1979).

5. Stewart Purkey and Marshall S. Smith, "Too Soon to Cheer? Synthesis of Research on Effective Schools." *Educational Leadership* (December 1982):64–69.

6. L. Anderson, C. Evertson, and J. Brophy, "An Experimental Study of Effective Teaching in First Grade Reading Groups." *The Elementary School Journal* 79 (1979):193–222.

7. Jacob S. Kounin, *Discipline and Group Management in Classrooms*. (New York: Holt, Rinehart & Winston, 1970).

8. Lovely H. Billups and Marilyn Rauth, "The New Research: How Effective Teachers Teach." *American Educator* (Summer 1984):39.

9. Thomas L. Good, *Teachers Make a Difference* (New York: Holt, Rinehart & Winston, 1975).

10. John L. Goodlad, *A Place Called School* (New York: McGraw-Hill, 1984).

11. Lawrence C. Stedman, "It's Time We Changed the Effective Schools Formula," *Phi Delta Kappan* (Bloomington, IN: November 1987), pp. 215–224.

12. Ibid., p. 218.

■ Selected References

Brandt, R. "On Improving Teacher Effectiveness: A Conversation with David Berliner." *Educational Leadership* (October 1982):12–15.

Brophy, J. "Classroom Management and Learning." *American Education* (March 1982):20–23.

Brophy, J. "Classroom Organization and Management." *Elementary School Journal* (March 1983):266–285.

Brophy, J., and Good, T. *Teacher-Student Relationships: Causes and Consequences.* New York: Holt, Rinehart & Winston, 1974.

Cooper, H. "Pygmalion Grown Up: A Model for Teacher Expectation, Communication and Performance Influence.: *Review of Educational Research* 49 (1979):389–410.

Cooper, H., and Good, T. *Pygmalion Grows Up: Studies in the Expectation Communication Process.* New York: Longman, 1983.

Cummings, C. *Teaching Makes a Difference.* Available from TEACHING, 331 8th Ave. So., Edmonds, WA 98020.

Dillon-Peterson, B., editor. *Staff Development/ Organization Development.* Alexandria, VA: ASCD, 1981.

Duke, D., editor. *Helping Teachers Manage Classrooms.* Alexandria, VA: ASCD, 1982.

Educational Leadership (December 1982): Issue on "Toward More Effective Schools."

Emmer, E.; Evertson, C.; and Anderson, L. "Effective Classroom Management at the Beginning of the School Year." *Elementary School Journal* (1980):219–231.

Emmer, E., et al. *Organizing and Managing the Junior High Classroom.* R&D Report 6151, R&DCTE, University of Texas, Austin.

Evertson, C., et al. *Organizing and Managing the Elementary School Classroom.* R&DCTE, University of Texas, Austin.

Gage, N. *The Scientific Basis of the Art of Teaching.* New York: Teacher's College Press, 1978.

Good, T. "Teacher Expectations and Student Perceptions: A Decade of Research." *Educational Leadership* (February 1981):415–421.

Good, T., and Brophy, J. *Looking in Classrooms.* New York: Harper and Row, 1973.

Joyce, B., and Showers, B. "The Coaching of Teaching." *Educational Leadership* (October 1982):4–11.

Levin, T. and Long, R. *Effective Instruction.* Alexandria, VA: ASCD, 1981.

Mohlman, G.; Kierstead, J.; and Gundlach, M. "A Research-Based Inservice Model for Secondary Teachers." *Educational Leadership* (October 1982):16–19.

Rosenshine, B. "Teaching Functions in Instructional Programs." *Elementary School Journal* (March 1983):335–351.

Sergiovanni, T., editor. *Supervision of Teaching.* Alexandria, VA: ASCD, 1982.

Slavin, R. "Synthesis of Research on Cooperative Learning." *Educational Leadership* (May 1981):655–660.

Sparks, G. "Synthesis of Research on Staff Development for Effective Teaching." *Educational Leadership* (November 1983):65–72.

Squires, D.; Huitt, W.; and Segars, J. *Effective Schools and Classrooms: A Research-Based Perspective.* Alexandria, VA: ASCD, 1983.

Wallace, D., editor. *Developing Basic Skills Programs in Secondary Schools.* Alexandria, VA: ASCD, 1982.

Section 2

The Teaching Profession

The chapters of this section have been developed to provide an overview of the nature of the work, problems, rewards, and challenges of the teaching profession. Chapter 5 considers the employment prospects for new teachers, chapter 6 outlines the rewards and challenges of teaching, and chapter 7 presents information relevant to membership in teacher organizations.

The employment prospects for new teachers are improving. Supply and demand of teachers has more overall balance for the 1990s than 1980s. Yet, several factors continue to impinge upon the demand for teachers. The supply and demand picture for new teachers has changed drastically over the last two decades, from a shortage of teachers in the 1950s and early 1960s, to an oversupply in the late 1960s and early 1970s. The general oversupply of teachers continued in the late 1970s with signs of modest shortages of teachers in certain academic areas. As a consequence of continued declining birthrates, subsequent enrollment declines, and taxpayer attitudes toward the rising costs of education, the production of new teachers was greatly curtailed.

The latest data indicate that public school enrollments are increasing. While the enrollments in teacher education programs are also increasing, a shortage of teachers is still anticipated. It has been projected that by 1992 colleges and universities will be only able to supply 63.7 percent of the demand for additional teachers through their supply of teacher graduates. Other reasons for the shortage of teachers include the number of teachers leaving the profession for retirement or other jobs, the lack of appeal for the teaching profession among young adults, and the lack of taxpayer support for the school systems which prevents schools from hiring all the teachers they need.

Most people give attention to economic aspects when seeking a career. Considerable salary data from various sectors of the United States is provided in chapter 6. A portion of salary gains is attributable to the strong call for higher salaries for teachers in the educational reform reports. Fringe benefits are provided by most school districts. The benefits may include paid insurance programs, sick leave, and annuities.

Teachers rate their profession as above average (67%) in terms of personal satisfaction derived from work. That satisfaction comes from helping students learn, and observing their progress as they become productive citizens.

The challenges of teachers are many and various in nature. Inspiring students who are not motivated, providing individualized instruction, maintaining classroom discipline, communicating to parents, and dealing with the school bureaucracy and its paperwork are among the challenges.

Most communities are aware of recent teacher militancy. Teacher strikes, or threats of them, have aroused emotions within the teaching profession and the entire educational community. Teacher organizations are commonly viewed as unions by the lay public. Chapter 7 provides considerable information about membership, organizational structure, and the objectives of both major teacher organizations, the American Federation of Teachers (AFT) and the National Education Association (NEA). In addition, selected activities and merger trends at the national, state, and local levels are reviewed.

Chapter 5

Employment Prospects for New Teachers

Objectives

After studying this chapter, you should be able to:

■ Supply information relative to the number of new teacher graduates in the United States.

■ Give data about the total number of teachers needed for both public and private schools through 1990.

■ List conditions which have an influence on the decreasing supply of qualified teachers.

■ Report on birthrates in the United States, 1940–1990.

■ Formulate a picture of enrollment trends in elementary and secondary education.

■ Note that the employment prospects for prospective teachers will improve throughout the 1990s.

■ Hypothesize about the needs for special education teachers.

■ Suggest some of the important aspects of seeking and obtaining a teaching position.

Enrichment Experiences

The following activities will help you learn more about some of the important topics discussed in this chapter:

■ Study a report about the supply and demand of teachers and report on those fields which are least crowded and most overcrowded.

■ Invite a school administrator to your class to discuss what he/she looks for when hiring new teachers.

■ Visit with ten of your fellow students to get their views on teaching as a career.

■ Visit a variety of different schools—nursery, elementary, middle, secondary, trade and/or community college. Try to arrange informal discussions with teachers and administrators regarding teaching as a career choice.

■ Prepare a checklist you might use to evaluate a school system in which you are considering employment.

■ Do an analysis of enrollment trends in different sections of the country.

*T*his chapter will help you realize that there is good news for teacher education students today. This good news is that the prospects for a job are excellent. In fact, many experts predict that the growing shortage of teachers in the United States will become critical in the next few years. This chapter explores a variety of factors related to the supply and demand for teachers throughout the United States. Topics discussed in this chapter include teacher production, increasing birthrates, school enrollment trends, pupil-teacher ratios, the demand for teachers, why teachers leave the classroom, teacher shortage by subject areas, teacher supply/demand by geographical regions, the acute shortage of teachers in our large urban school districts, and employment opportunities in private schools. There are many things that college students can do to make themselves more employable as teachers when they graduate. These variables are also presented in the upcoming chapter. ■

Many factors determine the supply/demand conditions for teachers. People preparing for teaching careers should study these factors carefully to decide what the future holds by way of employment prospects and what the rewards and frustrations of a teacher will be. In this chapter, we will explore the employment prospects for new teachers by examining a number of the factors that influence this picture. The next chapter in this book will present information about the rewards and challenges of teaching.

■ Teacher Production

Today a much lower percentage of our college students are anticipating careers as teachers than has traditionally been the case. For one thing, historically, teaching was viewed by young women as one of their best career options. This is no longer the case, since virtually all careers have now been opened to bright young women. This disconcerting decline on the part of college freshmen expressing an interest in a teaching career has decreased from almost 20 percent in 1970 to just over 6 percent in 1985. Clearly, this means that we are producing far fewer teachers in our colleges today than has traditionally been the case. It helps to explain why experts are now predicting a very large shortage of teachers throughout the United States. This means students who are now preparing for teaching careers will very likely have excellent job opportunities upon graduation.

Table 5.1 projects the supply of new teacher graduates throughout the United States in the next few years. As you can see, it is anticipated that we will be supplying fewer teachers over this time period.

■ Table 5.1   Projected Supply of New Teacher Graduates

Fall of Year	Supply of New Teacher Graduates
1986	144,000
1987	142,000
1988	139,000
1989	139,000
1990	139,000
1991	138,000
1992	137,000

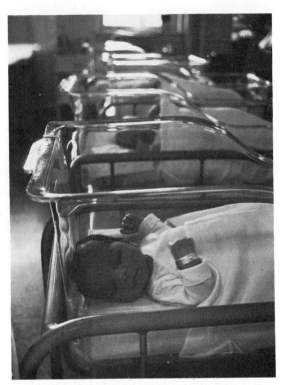

As birthrates continue to increase in the United States, so too does the demand for teachers.

Not everyone believes that we will experience a shortage of teachers in the near future. Emily Feistritzer recently wrote in *Teacher Crisis: Myth or Reality?* that she believes there will be an adequate supply of teachers available. She claims that the law of supply and demand will produce the number of teachers that we need in the United States. She acknowledges that there may be shortages in certain geographical areas and in certain fields such as special education and science. However, she argues that, generally speaking, an adequate supply of people will enter the teaching field as jobs become available. Daniel Hecher, of the U.S. Department of Labor, Bureau of Labor Statistics, agrees. He claims in *Occupational Outlook Quarterly* that higher pay will more than likely lure sufficient numbers of new people into the teaching profession to fill our classrooms with qualified teachers. These viewpoints seem to be in the minority, with most experts predicting a very serious shortage of teachers in the near future.

Table 5.2 lists several conditions reported by thirty-six states as having an unusual influence on decreasing the supply of qualified teachers. It

■ **Table 5.2**   Conditions Having an Unusual Influence on Decreasing the Supply of Qualified Teachers

Condition Contributing to a Smaller Supply in 1979	Number of States (36) Reporting Condition Contributed		
	To a Small Extent	To a Moderate Extent	To a Great Extent
Better opportunities in other types of employment	6	14	14
Location of vacancies not attractive	7	13	13
Fewer persons completing preparation	2	20	12
Salaries and benefits not attractive to beginning teachers	7	13	8
Fewer QUALIFIED persons completing preparation	6	14	7
Salaries and benefits not attractive to experienced teachers	9	12	7
Working conditions less attractive in teaching	12	9	7
Fewer former teachers applying to reenter active employment	12	11	4
Fewer teachers moving into state	9	7	0

From National Education Association *Teacher Supply and Demand in Public Schools, Research Memo*, 1979. Copyright © 1979 National Education Association, Washington, DC. Reprinted by permission.

should be noted that, in addition to the fewer number of persons completing teacher preparation programs, the better opportunities in other fields of employment, and the unattractiveness of the location of teaching vacancies were factors that have lowered the supply of qualified teachers. If salaries continue to improve, and if teaching jobs become plentiful, more and more college students will choose teaching as a career.

■ Increasing Birthrates

School enrollment is, of course, influenced by birthrates. Figure 5.1 shows the number of live births in the United States from 1940 to 1990. That number peaked in 1960 at an all-time high of 4.25 million. With the exception of slight increases during the late 1960s, birthrates declined through the mid-1970s. As the number of annual

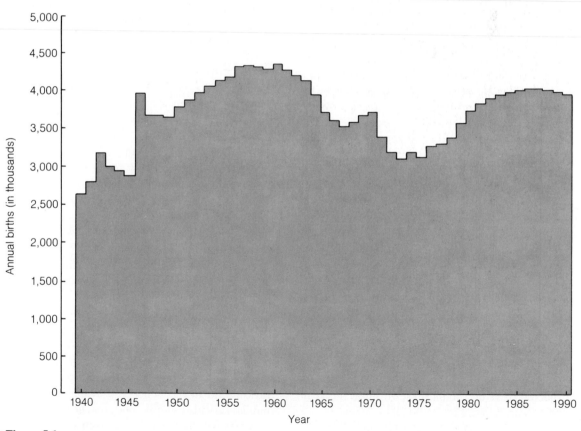

■ Figure 5.1

Number of annual births: 50 states and D.C., 1940–1990

Source: *Projections of Education Statistics to 1990–1991*. Washington, DC: National Center for Education Statistics, page 9.

births increase, the number of school-age children increases, resulting in the need for more teachers.

■ School Enrollment Trends

All school enrollment projections are based on projections of school-age population. Figure 5.2 shows our government's projections of school-age populations until the year 2000. By studying these figures, it can be seen that the projected number of elementary-age children will increase until 1995 and then level off until the year 2000. Secondary-age children are projected to increase gradually from 1990 until 2000. College-age students will decrease until 1995 and then begin to increase steadily until the year 2000. The generalization that can be reached from these projections is that the number of school-age people in the United States will increase over the next decade.

Public school enrollment by grade level is shown in figure 5.3 for the time period between 1965 and the year 2000. This figure shows steady increases in public school enrollment at all grade levels. Public enrollment in grades K–8 decreased from 32.6 million in 1969 when it peaked, to a low of 26.9 million in 1985. Public enrollment in K–8 is projected to rise steadily until 1996 when it is projected to level off until the year 2000. Public school enrollment in grades 9–12 peaked in 1976 at about 14.3 million students. Enrollment then declined to 12.4 million students in 1986. Enrollment in our public high schools is projected to be on the increase through the year 2000.

It has been pointed out that school enrollment in recent years has started to increase. Of course this increase is taking place in certain geographical parts of the United States. The largest

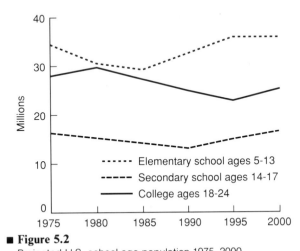

■ Figure 5.2

Projected U.S. school age population 1975–2000

Source: U.S. House of Representatives, Select Committee on Population. *Domestic Consequences of United States Population Change,* 95th Congress, 2d Session, 1978, page 45.

increases in school enrollment are taking place in the South and Southwest as well as in the state of Washington and certain states in New England. Some states are not experiencing a growth in enrollment in their public schools at all. Some of the upper midwestern states, along with Oregon, Montana, Wyoming, New York, Pennsylvania, Kentucky, Tennessee, and North Carolina have had modest decreases in school enrollments in recent years.

■ Pupil-Teacher Ratios

Yet another factor which influences the demand for teachers is that related to the pupil-teacher ratio found in our schools. Obviously, the more pupils served by any one teacher, the fewer teachers will be needed in a given school. Figure 5.4 shows the history of the pupil-teacher ratio in public schools from 1960 to 1985. This figure

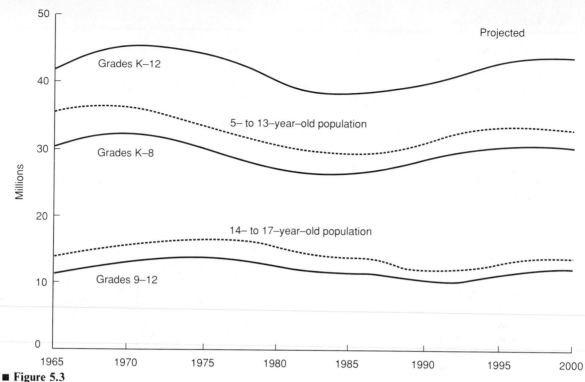

■ **Figure 5.3**

Public elementary and secondary enrollments: Outlook to the year 2000

Source: U.S. Department of Education, March 1987.

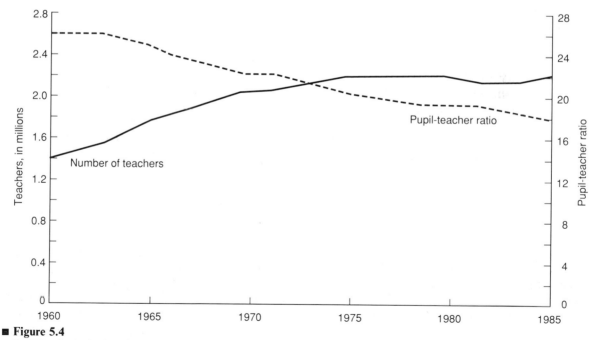

■ **Figure 5.4**

Pupil-teacher ratios in public schools

Source: *Digest of Education Statistics*, U.S. Department of Education, 1987.

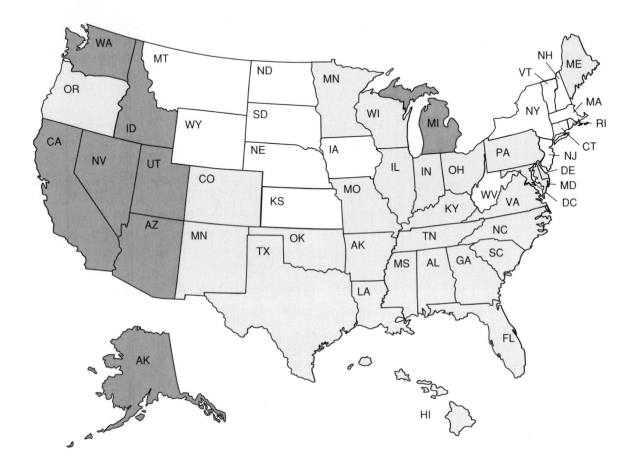

Pupil-teacher ratio of 20-to-1 or higher

Pupil-teacher ratio from 19-to-1 to 16-to-1

Pupil-teacher ratio less than 16-to-1

■ **Figure 5.5**
Pupil-teacher ratio averages by state

shows that the pupil-teacher ratio has declined over this time period from approximately twenty-six pupils per teacher in 1960 to approximately eighteen pupils per teacher in 1985.

Figure 5.5 shows the pupil-teacher ratio by state. The average pupil-teacher ratio in the United States is 17.8 to 1. Obviously, the pupil-teacher ratios vary considerably from school to school and state to state. It ranges from 1 to 13.45 in Wyoming to 1 to 24 in Utah. If this trend continues to decrease the number of pupils served by each teacher, it will require more teachers to serve the students in classrooms throughout the United States.

■ The Demand for Teachers

As has been stated earlier, there is a growing demand for additional teachers in our classrooms. Table 5.3 shows the projected supply of new teacher graduates compared to projected demand for additional teachers until 1992. This figure points out that by 1992 we will only be able to supply 63.7 percent of the demand for additional teachers through the supply of new teacher graduates. In other words, we will not be producing enough teachers to meet the demand for additional teachers.

There are many factors which contribute to the teacher supply picture, including the following:

1. The number of teachers leaving the profession for retirement or for other jobs.
2. The lack of appeal for the teaching profession among our young adults.
3. A mobile population which contributes to increasing demand for teachers in certain geographical parts of the country.

■ Table 5.3	Projected Supply of New Teacher Graduates Compared to Projected Demand for Additional Teachers		
Fall of Year	Projected Supply of New Teacher Graduates	Projected Demand for Additional Teachers	Supply as Percent of Demand
1988	139,000	162,000	85.8
1989	139,000	177,000	78.5
1990	139,000	188,000	73.9
1991	138,000	204,000	67.6
1992	137,000	215,000	63.7

Because of the lack of data, the table and graph in this report do not account for:
- new teacher graduates who do not seek teaching jobs;
- former teacher graduates not currently in the labor force who seek teaching jobs;
- unemployed teachers; and
- former teacher graduates employed in other occupations who are seeking teaching jobs.

Condition of Education, 1985 Edition. National Center for Education Statistics, U.S. Department of Education.

4. A shifting demand among subject areas which causes certain subjects to require more teachers than are available.
5. Lack of taxpayer support for the school systems which prevents schools from hiring all the teachers they need.

Taxpayer attitude greatly influences teacher demand. Insofar as people are willing to pay higher taxes to support education, more teachers can be hired. Some authorities have even suggested that we now have an "underemployment of teachers" brought about by the taxpayers' unwillingness to pay higher taxes to support education. Most educators feel that we always need more teachers than the schools can afford to hire.

Countless other factors influence the demand for teachers in various ways and to different extents; however, the two main factors that will determine the future employment prospects for new

■ **Table 5.4** Instructors Needed to Educate the Handicapped

Area of Handicapped	Estimated Children of Elementary and Secondary School Age	Number of Additional Teachers and Specialists Needed
Speech Handicapped	1,833,230	12,733
Emotionally Disturbed	1,047,560	121,791
Mental Retardation	1,204,694	58,406
Specific Learning Disabilities	523,780	22,564
Hard of Hearing	261,890	12,100
Crippled and Other Health Disorders	261,890	5,674
Visually Handicapped	52,378	2,877
Deaf	39,283	823
TOTAL	5,224,705	236,968

From Council for Exceptional Children, National Education Association, Washington, DC.

teachers will be the number of new teachers produced and the number of students enrolled in our schools.

The conditions discussed to this point in the chapter have combined to produce a shortage of teachers in the United States. There are several recent indicators suggesting that this shortage of teachers may become more severe in the near future. The total demand for elementary and secondary school teachers includes those needed to allow for increased enrollment, additional staff required for lowering pupil-teacher ratios, and those needed for replacement of teachers leaving the profession.

Another aspect of the rising teacher demand is related to the subject-matter area. The main subjects taught by departmentalized elementary teachers and secondary teachers are English,

mathematics, and the natural sciences, which could be a reflection of curriculum interests in our schools as well as areas of high demand for prospective teachers. These areas provide the best employment opportunities.

Table 5.4 gives an indication of the employment opportunities in special education. This table clearly points to a need for many qualified teachers and specialists in the area of special education. Recent state and federal laws provide funds for hiring trained special education teachers for the schools.

Another factor that could lead to a brighter employment picture for beginning teachers is earlier teacher retirement. Since there seems to be a trend toward earlier retirement in all fields of work, it is not inconceivable that a similar trend may occur in the teaching profession. If, for example, more states would pass legislation making

Increasing numbers of children are being served in programs for the handicapped.

it possible for teachers to retire with full retirement benefits at age fifty-five, the demand for new teachers would sharply increase.

The advent of compulsory early childhood education is another factor that has created many new teaching jobs. More states have mandated compulsory early childhood education programs, resulting in a need to hire a great number of teachers to staff those programs.

The message in the current teacher supply-and-demand picture for students considering a career in teaching is that schooling will continue to be one of the nation's largest enterprises. Teacher education graduates with good credentials who are willing to accept teaching positions where they occur are going to continue to get jobs. The employment prospects for prospective teachers appear to be improving considerably.

■ Variables Affecting Teacher Supply and Demand

A recent publication by the U.S. Department of Education[1] reveals some interesting facts that help to determine the supply and demand of teachers for our classrooms. Some of these data are as follows:

- In the fall of 1985 public elementary and secondary school enrollments increased for the first time since 1971.

- In contrast to the declining elementary and secondary school enrollments during the 1970s and early 1980s, there was substantial enrollment growth in preprimary education. Between 1970 and 1980, preprimary enrollment rose by 19 percent. From 1980 to 1985, preprimary enrollment increased another

20 percent. Another important aspect of the increasing participation of young children in preprimary schools is the rising proportion in full-day programs. In 1985 about 37 percent of the children attended school all day compared to 17 percent in 1970.

- Despite drops in enrollment during the late 1970s and early 1980s, increasing numbers of children were served in programs for the handicapped. In 1976–77, about 8 percent of children were served in programs for the handicapped compared to 11 percent in 1984–85. Most of this increase may be attributed to the proportion of children who were identified as learning disabled, which rose from 2 percent of all children in 1976–77 to 5 percent of all children in 1984–85.

- While public schools enrollments were decreasing during the 1970s and early 1980s, the number of teachers was generally rising. In consequence, the pupil-teacher ratio declined markedly. Between 1970 and 1985, the pupil-teacher ratio for public schools fell from 22 to 18.

- The average salary for teachers has grown rapidly in recent years, reaching $25,313 in 1985–86. After adjustment for inflation, teacher's salaries rose 14 percent between 1980–81 and 1985–86, recouping much of the loss in purchasing power suffered during the 1970s.

- Comparisons of the number of high school graduates and the 17-year-old population suggest that an increasing proportion of young people are graduating from high school. In 1968–69, there were 77 graduates for every 100 persons 17 years of age. This ratio

generally declined throughout the 1970s, falling to a low point of 71 percent in 1979–80. Since 1980, the graduation ratio has been rising, reaching 75 percent in 1984–85. (Source: *Digest of Education Statistics,* 1987. U.S. Department of Education.)

■ Teachers Leaving the Classroom

Recent estimates by the National Education Association tell us that a high percentage of our current teaching force will leave the classroom by 1990–1995. For instance, between 30 and 50 percent of our current teachers will retire by that time. Other studies have shown that a surprising number of teachers leave the classroom prior to retirement for a wide variety of reasons. One of the major reasons is higher salaries which are available for well-trained teachers outside the classrooms. Then too, many teachers who leave the classroom cite poor working conditions as their main motivation for seeking other employment. A recent study by Metropolitan Life showed that a surprising number of teachers leave the classroom after only a few years of teaching. Other studies have shown that teachers of certain subjects, such as mathematics and science, leave the classroom more frequently because attractive jobs are readily available to them in the private sector of the economy.

Whatever the reason that teachers leave our schools, it is important to remember that many people who are qualified to be teachers choose not to spend a long career in the classroom. This contributes significantly to the supply/demand picture for educators in the United States.

The freedom to choose one's area of study and one's vocation, allowing for personal talents, interests, and market opportunities, is perhaps the most sacred of all freedoms. If students are willing to give their time and effort and to forego income for education, society should do no less than provide the institutional setting and facilities.

Howard R. Bowen

■ **Table 5.5** Relative Demand by Teaching Area 1988 Report	

Based upon a survey of teacher placement officers

Areas with considerable teacher shortages (5.00–4.25):

Bilingual Education	4.35
Special Education—ED/PSA	4.33
Special Education—LD	4.26
Special Education—Multi. Handi.	4.26

Areas with some teacher shortage (4.24–3.45):

Special Education—MR	4.15
Science—Physics	4.01
Mathematics	4.00
Speech Pathology/Audio.	4.00
Science—Chemistry	3.96
Special Education—Deaf	3.91
Computer Science	3.79
Special Education—Gifted	3.74
Data Processing	3.59
Language, Mod.—Spanish	3.59
Psychologist (school)	3.57
Library Science	3.56
Science—Earth	3.52

Areas with balanced supply and demand (3.44–2.65):

Special—Reading	3.43
Language, Mod.—French	3.43
Science—General	3.42
Science—Biology	3.37
Language, Mod.—German	3.34
Counselor—Elementary	3.12
English	3.11
Industrial Arts	3.07
Counselor—Secondary	3.03
Social Worker (school)	3.01
Music—Instrumental	3.00
Journalism	2.91
Speech	2.91
Business	2.90
Music—Vocal	2.89
Agriculture	2.88
Elementary—Intermediate	2.72
Elementary—Primary	2.71
Driver Education	2.70

Key: 5 = Greatest Demand, 1 = Least Demand

Source: 1989 Ascus Annual Job Search Handbook for Educations, Association for School, College and University Staffing, Inc. (301 S. Swift Rd., Addison, IL 60101) p. 8.

■ Teacher Shortages by Subject Areas

Many subject areas are experiencing severe teacher shortages throughout the United States. Table 5.5 shows the relative teacher demand by subject areas throughout the United States in 1988. This table shows that the subject areas of mathematics, science, bilingual and special education all have considerable teacher shortages. Other shortage areas include computer science, speech pathology, and modern language. A recent study by the Rand Corporation indicates that by the year 1995 an additional 300,000 mathematics and science teachers will be needed by our nation's schools.

■ Teacher Supply-and-Demand by Geographical Region

It is important to realize that the information presented in this table is generalized to the entire United States and may not apply to given school districts. In fact, many school districts would have a completely different list of teacher shortage areas than that shown in table 5.5.

Certain geographical parts of the United States have their own unique teacher supply-and-demand figures. Appendix B found in the back of this book shows a detailed analysis of this phenomena. People preparing for teaching careers and anticipating settling in one or another particular region of the country may be interested in studying the teacher supply-and-demand phenomena currently operating for those particular parts of the country.

■ **Table 5.6** Private School Enrollment Trends: 1970 to 1985

October of year	K–12 enrollment (In thousands)			Private school enrollment as a percentage of total K–12 enrollment
	Total	Public	Private	
1970	51,848	46,193	5,655	10.9
1975	49,522	44,521	5,001	10.1
1981	45,598	40,897	4,701	10.3
1985	44,660	39,788	4,872	10.9

Source: U.S. Department of Commerce, Bureau of the Census, *School Enrollment—Social and Economic Characteristics of Students*, October 1984.

■ Lack of Teachers in Large Urban School Districts

Our largest school systems found in our largest cities are experiencing great difficulty in attracting sufficient teachers to fill their vacancies. These shortages are most severe in California, Texas, and Florida, all of which are experiencing significant population growth spurts. The National Education Association conducted a survey of our large urban schools and found that most of them are experiencing a signficant shortage of teachers. These teacher shortages in our largest school districts are expected to grow in the near future.

■ Employment Opportunities in Private Schools

Private schools are an important form of education in America and they employ thousands of teachers each year. Working in a private school is a viable option for teacher education students when they complete their certification requirements. There is not a convenient way to gather information on private schools in America. For that reason, statistics that are reported about private schools do not always agree with one another.

Table 5.6 shows private enrollment trends in the United States for the fifteen-year period between 1970 and 1985. This table shows that enrollment in private K–12 schools has remained between 10 and 11 percent of all of the K–12 students in the United States over this fifteen-year period. It also shows that approximately five million students enroll in private K–12 schools each year.

The vast majority of students who attend private schools do so because of a desire to be enrolled at a school with religious affiliations. It is estimated that about 86 percent of all the private school students in grades K–12 are in church-related schools. One exception to this rule is at the preschool level where many young children attend nonreligious preschool programs, presumably because their mothers are employed.

Teacher salaries in private schools tend to be somewhat lower than those in the public school system. Even so, approximately 10 percent of all the K–12 teachers in the United States work in private schools.

It is estimated that there are approximately 350,000 private school teachers in the United States today. Of these, approximately 260,000 teach elementary schools while 95,000 teach secondary schools. There are an additional 207,000 private college and university teachers in America. This means that approximately 561,000 private school teachers teach at all levels. Private schools obviously constitute another viable employment option for teachers.

■ Summary

An attempt has been made in this chapter to analyze the current teacher supply-and-demand picture in the United States. Topics such as birthrate trends, teacher production, and school enrollment projections have been discussed in an effort to help the reader understand employment prospects for new teachers.

Predicting the future is, of course, a very difficult task. While one can, as has been attempted in this chapter, analyze different variables and apply logic to a prediction, all predictions must be based on assumptions. If the assumptions do not prove to be accurate, the predictions will be wrong. It therefore behooves you to critically analyze the data and assumptions set forth in this chapter and arrive at your own conclusions concerning the employment prospects for beginning teachers.

Prospective teachers are encouraged to study the job market, especially with regard to geography and academic study areas. Since teachers will be in shortest supply in those locations where the population is expanding you should seriously weigh the pros and cons of moving to those places to begin your career. Likewise, many teacher preparation programs provide flexibility for certification to teach in more than one subject and more than one level. Even if your preference is for teaching at the secondary level, you will have a distinct advantage in obtaining your first position if you are also qualified to teach at the elementary level, since the greatest demand in the late 1980s will be there. You might also consider expanding your undergraduate majors so as to be qualified to teach in those areas of greatest secondary demand, such as the sciences and mathematics. The addition of a few courses could make you a stronger entry level candidate. General employment prospects for new teachers are good. The best prospects await those of you who are willing to locate where the need is greatest and those who are prepared to teach different grade levels and/or to teach in those academic areas in greatest demand.

Point of View

For those trying to decide whether to pursue teaching as a career, and those nearing the completion of a teacher education program, considerations about obtaining a teaching position are of utmost importance. The following discussion by William Roe and Rose Verdi contains excellent and relevant suggestions about selecting a teaching career direction and obtaining a teaching position.

Selecting the First Teaching Position
William H. Roe and Rose M. Verdi

The first basic decision you must make which definitely affects how you go about selecting a teaching position is determined by looking inward. Considering you—yourself—honestly, dispassionately, objectively, you ask yourself the question, "Am I looking for a position where there is the greatest need for help, where I can do the greatest good for society, where my abilities will be challenged to the utmost by difficult situations or am I looking for a position which will be most beneficial to me—gives me the greatest opportunity to travel, pays the highest salary, contains the pleasantest environment, commands the strongest resources, and includes the most stylish and compatible faculty?'' Your choice is a very personal one and to be happy and successful in your first professional experience it must be fought through with yourself honestly and dispassionately for the good of your own mental health and the goodness of society. Dedicated, superior teachers are needed desperately in the slums, ghettos, in poverty-stricken outlying areas and in developing countries—but what we don't need is more frustrated, unhappy, and inept teachers who may do more harm than good. Nor do we need the ''do-gooder'' who is impervious and unconscious to the real problem.

You must face yourself honestly in regard to this question and not feel guilty for the direction you choose. There are many legitimate reasons why you should not seek out trouble in your first experience. One important consideration is that in the safe sanctity of the suburb you may find opportunity to gain needed experience before facing more difficult teaching experiences.

Now that you have faced the more personal and philosophical question of how far you are ready to go in helping society, the next step of decision-making is simpler in terms of establishing an objective list of pros and cons.

Selecting implies choosing, making comparisons, evaluating and carefully arriving at a final decision. While you can make this next phase of the selection process quite simple and mechanical, it does take time. You should not relegate it to a last-minute activity during your senior year. The task is too crucial. Do not think you are just choosing a job for one year but rather you are beginning a career.

To keep the choice of the first teaching position from becoming a near-perfunctory one you might ask significant questions such as the following:

- What do I look for in the school system with which I wish to be associated?
- How important are working conditions?

- What are the opportunities for professional growth?
- What are the positions for orientation and induction of new teachers?
- Can I make a contribution to this school and community?
- Is recognition given to staff achievement and contributions?
- How will I be evaluated?

Many of the answers to questions like these can be secured by early and persistent investigation of numerous and various sources of information available to you. Talk with teachers already employed in school systems in which you are interested. Talk with your college and university instructors and the people in the placement bureaus about the local schools or schools in another state. Even more valuable would be visits to these schools during semester breaks. These visits would permit you to see and appraise firsthand the physical facilities, variety of instructional materials and methods, and also sense the climate of the school and community.

If you are interested in teaching in another state, you can secure additional information about the schools and communities by writing to the state departments of education, the superintendents of the various school systems or to the chambers of commerce. State educational associations and state departments of education very often publish comparative fact sheets about the schools of their states which would assist you in analyzing a school system. Most school systems publish brochures, pamphlets or handbooks containing information on the school program, salary schedules and prerequisites, teaching and special services staff, policies pertaining to supervision and tenure, opportunities for professional growth, professional associations, and the history of the community. Some schools publish separate and special materials for new teachers which include very detailed orientation information on daily teaching schedule, classroom discipline, policies regarding homework, procedures for fire drills, location and distribution of instructional materials and resources, samples of forms for reporting pupil progress, checklists of duties and suggested teaching plans for the first few days of school.

A critical examination of all the information you receive through informal discussions or printed materials will enable you to eliminate from future consideration those teaching situations which are least promising or attractive to you. The personal visits that you make to schools and communities recommended by teachers in service or by college staff will reveal whether you can adjust to the situation, and, more important, be stimulated to grow as a member of the profession. Analysis of the content of the printed materials you receive can also help you in selecting the most promising teaching situation. These materials often contain statements about "meeting the needs of pupils of varying interests and abilities" or "providing for the gifted, the mentally retarded and the emotionally disturbed." Are there supportive statements regarding special services personnel, flexibility in the educational program and descriptions of special programs? Take a careful look at the sample report card or reporting form which the school system uses in communicating to parents the growth of the progress of the child. Many educators agree that the pupil reporting forms reflect the operating philosophy of the school, the curriculum and the organizational pattern. Does the report form set forth a list of subject matter areas and a letter or numerical grade for each area? Can this type of reporting be reconciled with statements about "full partnership in evaluating each child's growth," "attainment and uniqueness of each child" or "learning is personal, unique, unstandardized"? Examine the statements concerning supervision and evaluation of probationary teachers. Who is involved in evaluation? Are written records kept? Are these records available to you? What new

media or procedures are being used for appraising performance? What support, cooperation and assistance will be given during your beginning years of service? Those school systems which you feel are presenting the most positive or desirable practices in these areas should be included on the list of school systems to which you would apply for your first teaching position.

The personnel in the placement office in your college or university can give you much help in obtaining a teaching position. There are many forms to be completed and records to be filed. Great care should be given to the preparation of these materials. You will also need to write a letter of application. It, too, should be carefully written. Specific suggestions about the form and content of these letters are usually presented by the college director or coordinator of student teaching. Sample letters may be found in publications such as student teacher handbooks or professional texts dealing with the student teaching program. Your letter should include a statement regarding arrangements for an interview.

For most students the interview is a strained one. They often report that they were tense, nervous, and uncomfortable. However, if you devoted the necessary time and thought in visiting and inquiring about many schools, and applied only in selected schools, your interview should be an exhilarating experience. The background of information that you will already have about the school system will not only allow you to ask pertinent and meaningful questions but will also facilitate communicating your own dedication to teaching and your sincere interest in the particular teaching position. It will also permit you to respond to questions with confidence and clarity, and serve you well in decisions you will have to make.

The decision regarding the particular position to accept is often a troublesome one, especially when accompanied by a deadline date for acceptance. However, your preliminary research should make your decision an easy one. Since you have applied only in selected systems, any offer should be immediately desirable to you.

When you have signed the contract, you should inform your college placement office that you have accepted a position. It is also in good taste to notify at least the school systems which interviewed you and include some expression of gratitude or appreciation for any consideration they may have given to your application.

From William H. Roe and Rose M. Verdi, "Selecting the First Teaching Position," *Teaching Opportunities for You.* 1969, 19–20. Copyright © 1969 Association for School, College and University Staffing, Addison, IL.

■ Questions for Discussion

1. Since the early 1980s, the number of students preparing to teach has been stable, but enrollments are predicted to increase through 1990. What will be the effect on the supply-and-demand situation for beginning teachers? Explain.

2. How does taxpayer attitude influence the demand for teachers? What other factors influence teacher demand?

3. School enrollment is, of course, influenced by birthrates. From the enrollment projections provided in this chapter, when will the respective elementary and secondary job markets for teachers change? What kind of changes can be predicted on enrollment projections?

4. Many administrators place great emphasis on the personal interview when hiring new teachers. How do you feel a candidate should act during an interview to make a favorable impression?

5. If you were an administrator, what would you look for when hiring a new teacher?

■ Note

1. *Digest of Education Statistics,* 1987. U.S. Department of Education.

■ Selected References

Akin, James N. *Tenth Annual Teacher Supply/ Demand 1986: A Report Based upon an Opinion Survey of Teacher Placement Officers.* Association for School, College and University Staffing, 1986.

Carlson, Robert V. and Matthes, William. "Teacher Recruitment and Retention: A Rural School Need," *The Rural and Small School Principalship,* December 1985.

Darling-Hammond, Linda. *Beyond the Commission Reports: The Coming Crisis in Teaching.* The Rand Corporation, July 1984.

Feistritzer, C. Emily. *The American Teacher.* Washington, D.C.: Feistritzer Publications, 1983.

Feistritzer, C. Emily. *Teacher Crisis: Myth or Reality?* National Center for Education Information, 1986.

Gosman, Erica J., *Classrooms without Teachers? Supply and Demand in the West.* Western Interstate Commission on Higher Education, July 1986.

Haberman, Martin. "Licensing Teachers: Lessons from Other Professions," *Phi Delta Kappan,* June 1986.

Jensen, Mary Cihak, *Recruiting and Selecting the Most Capable Teachers.* Oregon School Study Council, May 1986.

A Job Search Handbook for Educators. Madison, WI, The ASCUS Annual Report 1985, Association for School, College and University Staffing, 1984.

The Metropolitan Life Survey of the American Teacher 1985: Strengthening the Profession, conducted for Metropolitan Life Insurance Company by Louis Harris and Associates, Inc., 1985.

National Education Association, Survey of 100 of the Nation's Largest School Districts, Summer 1986.

A Nation Prepared: Teachers for the 21st Century. The Report of the Task Force on Teaching as a Profession of the Carnegie Forum on Education and the Economy, May 1986.

Olson, Lynn and Rodman, Blake, "Growing Need, Fewer Teachers: Everybody is Out There Bidding." *Education Week,* June 18, 1986.

Chapter 6

Rewards and Challenges of Teaching

Objectives

After studying this chapter, you should be able to:

■ Describe the public's and teachers' opinions in regard to the complexity of teaching, increased difficulty of teaching, the image of teaching, personal satisfaction of teaching, and dissatisfaction with salaries.

■ Describe the current status of teachers' salaries.

■ Identify the reasons supporting merit pay and career ladders.

■ Explain the concepts of merit pay and career ladders.

■ Identify the two major issues that hamper teacher acceptance of performance-based pay programs.

■ List the common fringe benefits that teachers are likely to receive.

■ List the helping and hindering conditions for teaching.

■ Identify and explain three trends that indicate the likelihood of higher salaries.

■ List three challenges to the teaching profession.

■ Explain a traditional salary schedule, and how the schedule can be adjusted and restructured.

Enrichment Experiences

The following experiences will help you decide whether you can accept or be comfortable with the rewards and challenges of teaching:

■ Obtain a teacher salary schedule from a school district. Present and discuss the advantages and disadvantages with your class.

■ Organize a debate on the favorable and unfavorable aspects of merit pay.

■ Conduct a similar debate on career ladders.

■ Conduct interviews with teachers for the purpose of discussing the tangible and intangible rewards and problems of teaching.

■ Ask student teachers or the supervisor(s) of student teachers about what student teachers think are the helping and hindering conditions of teaching.

■ Interview teachers about whether they would choose teaching as a career again. Why or why not?

The direction in which education starts a man will determine his future life.

Plato

*T*his chapter is written to help you gain information in regard to the rewards and challenges of teaching. One of the major rewards of teaching is the personal satisfaction that teachers receive from their work. One of the major challenges of the teaching profession is to continue to work toward higher salaries. This chapter includes the opinions of the general public and members of the National Education Association about various aspects of the teaching profession; information about teacher salaries, merit pay, career ladders, and fringe benefits for teachers; intangible rewards of teaching; helping and hindering conditions for teaching; challenges of teaching; and willingness to teach again. ■

Prospective teachers are urged to carefully weigh both the rewards and challenges of classroom teaching when considering the school as a place of employment. Teaching, while rewarding in many ways, is hardly a profession free of frustrations. The most attractive professions are those which provide challenges to problems, and a proportionate balance of tangible rewards to the professional who satisfactorily meets those challenges. Teaching as a vocation is an attractive profession, and has the potential of becoming increasingly more attractive.

Historically, the rewards of teaching focused on community status, the love of working with learners, satisfaction associated with helping students prepare for life, and job satisfaction. While these rewards of teaching are affirmed by many, teachers generally continue to become more militant about changing the focus to increasing the economic benefits of teaching. Various educational reform reports and studies highlighted the need to increase teacher salaries as a means for improving education; and, in fact, many states have raised salaries between 1982–83 (the beginning of educational reform) and 1986–87. Salaries for teachers must continue upward in order to keep good teachers in the classrooms and to attract top quality new teachers to the profession.

The following quotation is from a recent publication of the National Education Association (NEA). It is the result of a survey conducted for the NEA by the Gallup Organization, and presents the opinions of the general public and NEA teacher members about various aspects of the teaching profession.[1]

> The general public and teacher members view teaching as a complex, demanding, and socially beneficial profession, yet one that fails to provide adequate compensation to those engaged in it. Almost all teacher members (96%) and more than three-fourths of the general public (78%) rate teaching a '3' or '4' on a 4-point scale measuring the complexity of the work—that is, the degree to which it requires using judgment to make decisions in unpredictable situations. Of other professions tested, only airline pilots were ranked by the public significantly above school teachers in terms of job complexity. Teacher members rated their profession as similar in complexity to airline piloting.

> The length of a teacher's workday is seen by many (45%) in the public as above average when compared with other professions requiring similar levels of formal education. Only 11% rate teaching below average in this area. Similarly, 42% of the public rate the demands of a teacher's daily workload as above average, while only 9% rate the workload as below

average. These results would not suggest that length of school day is an issue in the public's mind in evaluating the teaching profession.

The public and teacher members solidly feel (89%) that the job of teaching has become more difficult over the past ten years. Despite much recent publicity that the people going into teaching today may not measure up in ability to past teachers, the public expresses a great deal of confidence in new teachers. Three-fourths (76%) say today's new teachers are at least as qualified as those who entered teaching ten years ago, including 27% who rate today's new teachers as better qualified. One more indication of the profession's positive image among the public is the extent to which people feel teachers should be represented on boards certifying new teachers. More than eight in ten (84%) feel at least half of these boards should be composed of practicing teachers.

Another factor that underscores both the public's positive image of teaching and teacher members' feelings of self-worth is how highly they rate the profession's contribution to society. Fully 62% of the public rate teaching a '4' on a 4-point scale measuring the profession's overall benefits to society. Consistent with past survey data, this places the teaching profession well above most other occupations in the public ratings on this factor. Eight in ten teacher members rate the profession at this level. Teacher members rated their own profession above that of newspaper editors, computer systems analysts, hospital administrators, airline pilots, and accountants—all occupations with higher pay and, in many cases, higher status in the community.

Aside from the personal satisfaction teachers may receive from their work, the rewards of teaching are seen by the public as not measuring up to the job's worth and difficulty.

Half of those interviewed (50%) rate the salary level for teachers as below average relative to jobs requiring similar education, making this the characteristic that most often distinguishes teaching from other occupations. In terms of fringe benefits, time off, decision-making, and status in the community, teaching typically gets an average rating. Opportunities for career growth or advancement are seen as average (43%) or below average (37%). . . . Teachers overwhelmingly see the profession as offering lower than average salaries (87%), but rate it above average (67%) in terms of personal satisfaction derived from the work. In fact, other than the internal rewards they get out of teaching, no other aspect of the profession rates above average in the view of teachers. For example, the majority of teacher members feel teaching is an occupation with lower than average status in the community (56%); two-thirds rate teaching below average in terms of opportunities for advancement and career growth.

■ Teachers' Salaries

As was indicated earlier, teachers' salaries have increased over the past few years. Table 6.1, Average Teacher Salary Trends, presents data showing the average salary for 1982–83, average salary for 1986–87, the percentage of gain over those two periods, state rank by the percentage of increase, and state rank for 1985–86 by salary. In the years between 1982 and 1986 average teacher salaries raised 21.5 percent. Every state in the nation raised teacher salaries between 1984–85 and 1985–86, for a national average increase in that year of 7.2 percent.[2]

■ Table 6.1. Average Teacher Salary Trends—1982 to 1986

State	Average Salary 1982–83*	Average Salary 1986–87**	% Increase 1982–86	Rank by % Increase	Rank by 1985–86 Salary
Alabama	$17,900	$22,934	28.1%	9	27
Alaska	35,297	41,480	17.5	38	1
Arizona	18,843	24,640	30.8	5	24
Arkansas	15,029	19,538	30.0	6	49
California	23,935	29,132	21.7	27	6
Colorado	21,470	25,892	20.6	28	16
Connecticut	20,795	26,610	28.0	11	13
Delaware	20,625	24,624	19.4	33	22
D.C.	26,740	33,990	27.1	13	2
Florida	18,275	22,250	21.8	25	33
Georgia	17,412	22,080	26.8	14	34
Hawaii	25,308	25,845	2.1	51	18
Idaho	17,573	20,969	19.3	34	40
Illinois	22,611	27,170	20.2	31	10
Indiana	20,145	24,274	20.5	29	25
Iowa	18,990	21,690	14.2	43	37
Kansas	18,231	22,644	24.2	18	29
Kentucky	18,384	20,940	13.9	45	41
Louisiana	18,400	20,460	11.2	47	45
Maine	16,248	19,583	20.5	29	48
Maryland	22,786	27,186	19.3	34	9
Massachusetts	20,240	26,800	32.4	2	12
Michigan	24,304	30,168	24.1	19	4
Minnesota	22,875	27,360	19.6	32	7
Mississippi	14,320	18,443	28.8	7	50
Missouri	17,521	21,974	25.4	17	35
Montana	19,702	22,482	14.1	44	31
Nebraska	17,187	20,939	21.8	25	42
Nevada	22,067	25,610	16.1	40	20
New Hampshire	15,360	20,263	32.0	3	47
New Jersey	21,535	27,170	26.2	15	10
New Mexico	20,465	22,644	10.6	50	29
New York	25,000	30,678	22.7	22	3
North Carolina	17,801	22,795	28.1	9	28
North Dakota	18,774	20,816	10.9	49	43
Ohio	20,004	24,500	22.5	23	23
Oklahoma	18,270	21,419	17.2	39	39
Oregon	21,746	25,788	18.5	37	19
Pennsylvania	21,178	25,853	22.1	24	17
Rhode Island	23,175	29,470	27.2	12	5
South Carolina	16,430	21,570	31.3	4	38
South Dakota	15,592	18,095	16.1	40	51
Tennessee	17,697	21,800	23.2	21	36
Texas	19,545	25,160	28.0	21	21
Utah	19,859	22,341	12.5	46	32
Vermont	15,328	20,325	32.6	1	46
Virginia	18,535	23,382	26.2	15	26
Washington	23,413	26,015	11.1	48	15
West Virginia	17,322	20,627	19.1	36	44
Wisconsin	21,496	26,525	23.4	20	14
Wyoming	23,822	27,224	14.3	42	8

*SOURCE: American Federation of Teachers.
**SOURCE: National Education Association, and ''Rewarding Excellence: Teacher Compensation and Incentive Plans,'' National School Boards Association, September 1987, Alexandria, VA.

■ Table 6.2. Average Salary of Teachers Compared to Annual Earnings in the Private Sector, 1986

Rank	State	Annual Earnings		Ratio of Teachers to Private Sector
		Teachers	Private Sector	
1	Rhode Island	$29,470	$16,644	1.77
2	Hawaii	26,038	16,845	1.55
3	Wisconsin	26,720	17,565	1.52
4	Alaska	41,647	28,489	1.46
5	Montana	22,482	15,526	1.45
6	Maryland	26,580	18,546	1.43
7	Nevada	25,606	17,922	1.43
8	Wyoming	27,461	19,255	1.43
9	Minnesota	27,360	19,256	1.42
10	Oregon	25,664	18,154	1.41
11	Washington	26,182	18,810	1.39
12	California	29,258	21,324	1.37
13	Pennsylvania	26,006	19,041	1.37
14	South Carolina	21,428	15,762	1.36
15	Massachusetts	26,800	19,764	1.36
16	Colorado	25,892	19,133	1.35
17	New York	30,490	22,536	1.35
18	North Dakota	20,815	15,409	1.35
19	Florida	22,250	16,491	1.35
20	Nebraska	20,834	15,470	1.35
21	North Carolina	22,476	16,770	1.34
22	New Mexico	22,526	16,835	1.34
23	Kansas	22,644	16,980	1.33
24	Iowa	21,802	16,406	1.33
25	D.C.	32,067	24,247	1.32
26	Arizona	23,931	18,121	1.32
27	South Dakota	18,095	13,702	1.32
28	Illinois	27,172	20,702	1.31
29	Alabama	22,934	17,496	1.31
30	New Jersey	28,000	21,368	1.31
31	Michigan	29,461	22,748	1.30
32	Virginia	23,388	18,091	1.29
33	Tennessee	21,800	17,021	1.28
34	Idaho	20,971	16,546	1.27
35	Georgia	23,046	18,247	1.26
36	Delaware	24,625	19,529	1.26
37	Utah	22,229	17,685	1.26
38	Ohio	24,988	19,881	1.26
39	Vermont	20,379	16,239	1.25
40	Arkansas	19,926	15,918	1.25
41	Indiana	24,248	19,382	1.25
42	Oklahoma	22,444	17,967	1.25
43	Mississippi	18,472	14,939	1.24
44	Connecticut	26,898	21,857	1.23
45	Maine	19,583	15,922	1.23
46	Kentucky	20,948	17,572	1.19
47	Texas	24,419	20,490	1.19
48	New Hampshire	20,163	17,530	1.16
49	Missouri	21,974	19,208	1.14
50	West Virginia	20,625	18,591	1.11
51	Louisiana	20,460	18,687	1.09

From *Survey and Analysis of Salary Trends*, 1986. Used by permission of the American Federation of Teachers, Washington, DC.

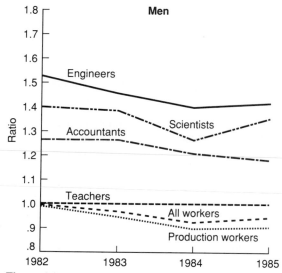
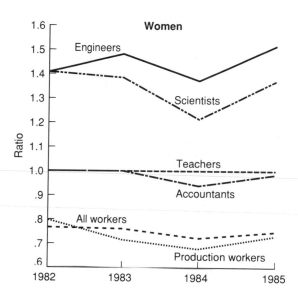

■ **Figure 6.1**

Ratio of earnings of other workers to teacher earnings, by
selected occupation: 1982–1985

Source: Bureau of the Census, *Current Population Reports.*

Table 6.2 shows the average salary of teachers
compared to annual earnings in the private sector,
1986. According to data collected by the American Federation of Teachers (AFT), the average
salary for teachers in 1986 was higher than the
mean average salary for all workers in the private
sector. The AFT showed an average salary for
teachers in 1986 was $25,240 compared to the
average annual earnings of $19,488 for the pri-
vate sector. A study by the New York School
Boards Association in 1987 compared teacher
salaries adjusted to reflect a twelve-month work
year with other professions. The association found
that the median teachers' salary ($37,053) in New
York state was in the midrange of salary distribution for eight professions, including attorneys,
engineers, accountants, and system analysts.[3]

Figure 6.1 portrays a ratio of earnings of
other workers to teacher earnings by selected occupations: 1982–1985. It should be noted that
teacher earnings are for twelve months, and it is
not known to what extent earnings for teachers
who normally work under nine- or ten-month
contracts have been augmented by earnings from
part-time or summer jobs. *Total* teacher earnings are based on data obtained from the Bureau
of Census, Current Population Reports.[4] It is interesting to note (1) for male workers, earnings
of engineers, scientists, and accountants exceeded those of teachers, while earnings of full-
time workers and production workers were below
those of teachers, and (2) for female workers,
earnings of engineers and scientists exceeded

those of teachers, while earnings of all full-time workers and production workers were below those of teachers. It is also worth noting that the ratios of females, with the exception of teachers with ratios of 1.0 for both males and females, are all below the ratios of males. The data in figure 6.1 is based on twelve months of earnings. It is quite possible that teachers do not have summer earnings. Under that circumstance, the ratios of earnings of other workers from selected occupations to teacher earnings would be higher, thus indicating that teachers' earnings are substantially lower, with the possible exception of all workers and production workers, than other professions.

In summary, teachers' salaries have increased over the last few years in all of the states. Many of the educational reform reports have recommended that teacher salaries be increased. However, the data indicate that teachers' salaries do not compare to salaries in the private sector except at the *all* workers or *production* workers level. The AFT study mentioned earlier has pointed out that

> A large portion of the recent gain in average teacher salaries is attributable to layoffs of young, low-paid teachers in the 1970s and minimal hiring of beginning teachers over the past decade. While the average teacher salary rose approximately $3,900 (in 1987 dollars) between 1975–76 and 1986–87, the pay level for a teacher with a BA and eleven years of experience declined by $2,600 over the same period.[5]

With the qualifications of teachers, that is college degrees, and the importance of their work and its associated responsibilities, they deserve higher salaries.

The National School Board Association makes the following recommendations about teacher compensation.[6]

> In assessing teacher salaries and their effect on local school budgets, school district leaders should:
>
> • Consider strategies for building public awareness and support for raising and maintaining teacher salaries at competitive levels.
> • Let local taxpayers know what steps the district is taking to ensure the quality of instruction.
> • Consider ways of cooperating with state policymakers to find additional sources of state revenues to support local salary initiatives.
> • Consider what can—and cannot—be expected from salary increases.
>
> Typically, across-the-board pay raises do not lead to sustained productivity increases for teachers already in the profession.

What teachers earn across the United States varies from city to city, district to district and state to state, and region to region. Generally school districts in the cities and the suburbs pay higher salaries than rural districts. A major factor in the level of salaries paid is the level of wealth of the school district. Teacher salary increases in most districts are based on the number of years of teaching in the system and advanced degrees.

The average beginning salary in 1987 was $17,800. Alaska, California, Connecticut, New York, New Jersey, and Texas have starting salaries in excess of $19,000, while only Nebraska, Vermont, South Dakota, Idaho, Iowa, Maine, and Mississippi reported average starting salaries

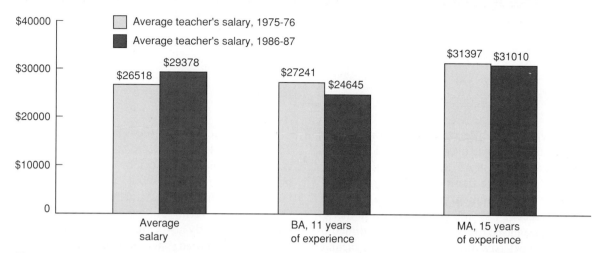

*Average salary data correspond to AFT's largest locals in 1985-86. Other 1975-76 data correspond to the 70 largest school districts in 1975-76. Other 1986-87 data correspond to school districts serving the 170 largest cities in the U.S.

■ **Figure 6.2**

Trends in teacher salaries by education and experience for the nation's largest school districts* (1987 dollars)

below $15,000.[7] Figure 6.2 shows the trends in teacher salaries by education and experience for the nation's largest school districts.

A study done by the National Education Association has estimated that the national average teacher salary for 1987–88 will be $28,031, up 5.5 percent over the 1986–87 average of $26,554. Table 6.3 provides information on estimated average salaries in 1987–88 for each state.[8]

■ **Merit Pay**

As was indicated earlier, most school systems utilize teacher salary schedules which increase salaries on the basis of years of experience and levels of preparation in the teaching field. For example, for teachers with the same years of experience, master's degree teachers are paid more than bachelor's degree teachers. These kinds of salary schedules for teachers make no provisions for teacher excellence. Rather, all teachers who are at the same levels on the salary schedules are paid the same yearly salary. A wide range of salary schedule reforms have been proposed, one of

■ **Table 6.3.** Average Teacher Salary

U.S.	$28,031	Missouri	$24,703
Alabama	23,320	Montana	23,798
Alaska	40,424	Nebraska	23,246
Arizona	27,388	Nevada	27,600
Arkansas	20,340	New Hampshire	24,019
California	33,092	New Jersey	30,778
Colorado	28,651	New Mexico	24,351
Connecticut	33,515	New York	33,600
Delaware	29,575	North Carolina	25,073
District of		North Dakota	21,660
Columbia	36,465	Ohio	28,778
Florida	25,382	Oklahoma	22,006
Georgia	26,177	Oregon	27,750
Hawaii	28,785	Pennsylvania	28,961
Idaho	22,783	Rhode Island	32,858
Illinois	29,735	South Carolina	24,241
Indiana	27,386	South Dakota	19,750
Iowa	24,867	Tennessee	23,785
Kansas	24,364	Texas	25,655
Kentucky	24,274	Utah	23,882
Louisiana	20,885	Vermont	23,397
Maine	23,425	Virginia	27,436
Maryland	30,829	Washington	27,960
Massachusetts	30,019	West Virginia	21,736
Michigan	32,926	Wisconsin	29,206
Minnesota	29,620	Wyoming	29,378
Mississippi	20,669		

From "Average Teacher Salary is Now $28,031," *NEA Today* 6 (10):8, May/June 1988. Copyright © 1988 National Education Association, Washington, DC. Reprinted by permission.

which is merit pay. Merit pay is not a new concept. It actually began in the 1920s, and has been popular off and on up to the present time. The major difficulty with merit pay has been in measuring and determining the various levels of teacher effectiveness. Many approaches to merit pay have been used to the extent that it is difficult to define merit pay. In general terms, it means rewarding teachers for outstanding performance, either through a permanent raise or a bonus which is not permanent.

The acceptance of the merit pay concept has led the nation's two teacher unions, the National Education Association (NEA) and the American Federation of Teachers (AFT), to relax their long-standing opposition to it. In some places, the unions are working closely with politicians and school officials in drawing up such plans. The unions agree that outstanding teachers should receive additional remuneration, thus not categorically opposing merit pay. The opposition has centered on the belief that merit pay systems typically were developed to pay a few people more so the other teachers could be paid less. So long as the problem of raising the low salaries paid to all teachers is also considered, additional incentives for outstanding teachers (merit pay) is of great interest to teachers, as well as to the general public.

■ Career Ladders

The concept of career ladders is similar to the "merit pay" concept in that they both use performance-based pay. The concepts are different in that the career-ladders concept designates different categories of teachers, for example, beginning teachers, senior teachers, and master teachers, while the "merit pay" concept most often designates only one category for all teachers. *A Nation at Risk,* the first education reform report, endorsed a master teacher plan, therein recommending two categories of teachers—regular and master teachers.

Former Governor of Tennessee Lamar Alexander was an early advocate of career ladders. In 1983, he proposed that the uniform salary schedule for the state's teachers be replaced with one that provides more pay for better instructors. In addition to a category for beginning teachers, two additional categories would be created. Twenty-five percent of the teachers would be classified as "senior teachers" and paid as much as $4,000 more a year. Fifteen percent would be placed in the highest category, "master teacher," and paid as much as $7,000 more a year. Master and senior teachers would be expected to work longer than the nine-month academic year. They would be assigned to work with student teachers and beginning teachers in the summer months. Under the Tennessee plan, committees of fellow teachers, not administrators, would determine who was suited to be elevated in rank. After reaching an agreement with the Tennessee Education Association, an affiliate of the National Education Association, legislation was passed by the Tennessee legislature, and a modified and refined version of the original proposal was implemented.

In 1986, Missouri, Tennessee, Texas, and Utah each had full implementation of a state program of career ladders. Four states, Alabama, Florida, Nebraska, and West Virginia, had state career ladder programs under development. Other states had career ladder pilot projects underway. Seven states were still in the discussion stage about the overall concept of performance-based pay plans.[9]

Career ladders and other methods for paying teachers based on performance are undergoing extensive scrutiny, and in some cases, revisions. Florida, Tennessee, and Texas are considering changes or have made changes in their programs. Their programs are likely to be revamped at the urging of both teachers and administrators. There have been political battles over statewide career ladders, and the enthusiasm for career ladders and the speed of their implementation has diminished.[10]

There appears to be a trend toward decentralization which would allow local districts to design their own teacher incentive plans under broad state guidelines. The state would supply the funding for the local plans.[11]

Albert Shanker, president of the American Federation of Teachers, made the following statement: "I think state-imposed career ladders are not going to be very popular, because basically people have gotten a lot smarter. They know that you can't bring about improvements by imposing them from the top." Shanker noted that "in many places school boards and teachers are now working together to develop district-based career ladders."[12]

The major issue in performance-based pay programs, including career ladders, is the lack of adequate evaluation systems to determine teacher effectiveness, and therefore, the ability to choose those teachers most deserving of rewards.

An NEA spokesman, Harold Carroll, has stated:

> The problem with pay incentive programs is that we're caught up in semantics. The bottom line is that if teachers are involved in the beginning, at the outset, on any one of these pay plans—regardless of what you call them—and it meets with their satisfaction, then it's fine.[13]

There is little question that the early-on participation of teachers in the development of incentive plans, and other plans for that matter, is more likely to ensure effective implementation of the plans than if they are not participants in the planning.

■ Fringe Benefits for Teachers

Fringe benefits accrue to teachers in the forms of paid insurance premiums, sick leave, emergency or personal leave, and sabbatical leave. In addition to examining the salary provisions, beginning teachers would be wise to investigate the nature of the fringe benefit program in the district wherein they are seeking employment. Districts vary greatly in this regard, with fringe benefits often worth considerable amounts.

Due to the rapidly escalating costs of fringe benefits, more and more school districts are attempting to reduce benefits as a means of reducing the overall school budget. In addition, the Internal Revenue Service is taxing certain fringe benefits as ordinary income. Such efforts are serving to minimize the value of the fringe benefits offered to teachers. Teacher organizations work diligently to protect teacher benefits which have been gained over the years.

■ Intangible Rewards of Teaching

While a slight majority (56 percent) of teachers feel that teaching is an occupation with lower than average status in the community, they rate the teaching profession above average in terms of the personal satisfaction they have derived from their work. Teachers benefit from assorted intangibles associated with working with youth. A kind of

There are many intangible rewards received from teaching.

what you are doing as a teacher is productive. Because of this aspect of teaching, the ego gratification afforded teachers through their job is at a minimum.

Thus, the rewards and challenges of teaching are both tangible and intangible. Certainly, there are times when an individual teacher might feel that the problems of teaching outweigh the rewards. However, the overall attractiveness of the teaching profession steadily improves. Tangible rewards are increasing while tangible problems are being solved. The intangible rewards continue to provide teachers with drives for professional improvement. Teaching as a career offers much to those who enter the profession well prepared in their chosen area of specialty. Further, prospective teachers who orient their preparation toward those specific areas of teacher shortage can be assured of finding employment opportunities throughout the United States.

pride is generated within teachers from feelings that they are contributing to the future of their nation through helping to educate the young. Only in the United States has universality of educational opportunity come to be a part of the national tradition. Whatever the tangible problems and rewards, certain intangibles of teaching as a career are well worth considering.

All the intangibles of teaching are not so positively idealistic. Teachers are often hard pressed to produce evidence of their accomplishments. The accomplishments of teachers are not readily given to visual assessment. Therefore, teaching is accompanied by a kind of personal mental anxiety brought on by the lack of knowledge that

■ Helping Conditions for Teaching

In a recent survey,[14] teachers identified the types of conditions that helped them in their service as teachers. Those factors which were identified as helping conditions were (1) interest in children and teaching (23.6 percent), (2) training, education, and knowledge of subject matter (15.4 percent), (3) cooperative and competent teacher colleagues (12.6 percent), (4) help from administrators and specialists (12.3 percent), (5) school environment and freedom to teach (11.3 percent), and (6) good materials, resources, and facilities (7.9 percent).

Over the last 10 years, interest in children and teaching has moved from third place (1976) to first (1981 and 1986). Training, education, and knowledge of subject matter moved from first

■ Table 6.4	Ranking of Helping and Hindering Conditions for Teaching 1986		
Rank	**Helping Condition**	**Rank**	**Hindering Condition**
1	Interest in children and teaching (23.6%)	1	Heavy workload (17.6%)
2	Training, education, and knowledge of subject matter (15.4%)	2	Incompetent and uncooperative administrators (15.9%)
3	Cooperative and competent colleagues (12.6%)	3	Discipline and negative attitudes of students (14.2%)
4	Help from administrators and specialists (12.3%)	4	Negative attitudes of the public and parents (9.2%)
5	School environment and freedom to teach (11.3%)	5	Lack of funds and decent salaries (8.9%)
6	Good materials, resources, and facilities (7.9%)	6	Class size (8.1%)

From National Education Association, "Attitudes Toward the Profession," *Status of the American Public School Teacher 1985–86*, 1987, 61–63. Copyright © 1987 National Education Association, Washington, DC. Reprinted by permission.

place in 1976 to sixth in 1981 and back to second in 1986. A new interest in school environment and freedom to teach crept in: as "independence in the classroom," it was ranked sixth in 1976, and it moved to fifth place in the surveys of 1981 and 1986.

■ Hindering Conditions for Teaching

Conditions that teachers reported as hindering their efforts at teaching were (1) heavy workload and extra responsibilities (17.6 percent), (2) incompetent and uncooperative administrators (15.9 percent), (3) discipline and negative attitudes of students (14.2 percent), (4) negative attitude of the public and parents (9.2 percent), (5) lack of funds and decent salaries (8.9 percent), and (6) class size (8.1 percent).

The lists of hindrances that teachers named in 1981 and 1986 were very similar. In both years, heavy workload and extra responsibilities constituted their major complaint. The attitudes of students and problems with administrators took second and third places both years, although not necessarily in that order. In both years, negative attitudes on the part of the public and parents came in fourth, and lack of funds and decent salaries ranked fifth. Table 6.4, Ranking of Helping and Hindering Conditions for Teaching 1986 portrays these conditions.

■ Challenges of Teaching

Teachers may often feel frustrated in their work. Much of this frustration comes about from the very nature of teaching. Many teachers enter the profession filled with a high degree of idealism, eager to do a socially important job. Such idealism would probably survive if each of the teachers' classes consisted of one, or at most, a very small number of pupils. However, the problem of large class size and other problems might demoralize the teacher almost from the start. The challenge of teaching requires exceptional dedication to assure that one's efforts are effectively related to desirable classroom objectives.

Good teachers use challenges as driving forces to come up with fresh solutions to the problems they encounter.

Teaching is also accompanied by a sense of isolation. When faced with problems in the classroom, it seems logical that a teacher would seek assistance from peer professionals. More often than not, such assistance is not meaningful to the teacher's situation; often outside assistance is not available at all. Teachers are constantly challenged to demonstrate flexible teaching strategies to solve their unique classroom problems.

Evaluation of teaching effectiveness is a somewhat loosely arranged endeavor. Building administrators, department chairpersons, and teaching colleagues are reluctant to attempt to evaluate teacher effectiveness, since the criteria for evaluation are nebulous. Consequently, a teacher has little feedback regarding effectiveness and is, therefore, disturbed by this vague aspect of teaching. Most of us like to know when we are effective in our work, and our jobs are less frustrating when we realize that our work is effective. Those who take the frustrations as continuing challenges of the profession often use them as the driving forces for improvement in their teaching skills. For those whose personality disposition requires constant reinforcement through feeling that their work is effective, the frustrations are often cause enough for leaving the teaching profession.

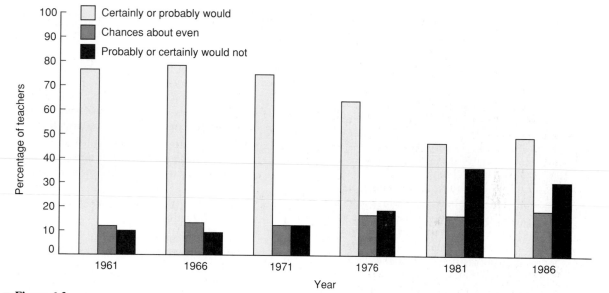

■ **Figure 6.3**
Teachers' willingness to enter teaching again, by year

■ Job Satisfaction: Willingness to Teach Again

Since 1961, surveys have included a question requesting respondents to select from a range of five options related to willingness to become teachers if they had to make the choice again. Specifically the options were: certainly would, probably would, chances about even, probably would not, and certainly would not as to whether they would become teachers again.[15] Figure 6.3 displays the responses over the years to teachers' willingness to enter teaching again.

In 1986, 22.7 percent replied they certainly would, 26.3 percent said they probably would, 19.8 percent said the chances are about even, 22 percent said they probably would not, and 9.3 percent said they certainly would not.

The trends in figure 6.3 reveal that the percentages of those who "certainly or probably would" enter teaching again declined from about 77 percent in 1961 to 49 percent in 1986; those respondents indicating that they "probably or certainly would not" enter teaching again rose from about 10.5 percent in 1961 to 31 percent in 1986. As is indicated in the aforementioned sentence, 1986 data show that 49 percent of the teachers certainly would or probably would enter teaching again, while 31 percent of the teachers indicated that they probably or certainly would not enter the profession again.[16] The reasons for the trends are likely to include low salaries, poor working conditions, relatively low status of the profession, and "the perceived increasing difficulty of teaching today as compared with ten years ago."[17]

Research Finding

6

Teachers welcome professional suggestions about improving their work, but they rarely receive them.

When supervisors comment constructively on teachers' specific skills, they help teachers become more effective and improve teachers' morale. Yet, typically, a supervisor visits a teacher's classroom only once a year and makes only general comments about the teacher's performance. This relative lack of specific supervision contributes to low morale, teacher absenteeism, and high faculty turnover.

Supervision that strengthens instruction and improves teachers' morale has these elements:

- agreement between supervisor and teacher on the specific skills and practices that characterize effective teaching

- frequent observation by the supervisor to see if the teacher is using these skills and practices
- a meeting between supervisor and teacher to discuss the supervisor's impressions
- agreement by the supervisor and teacher on areas for improvement
- a specific plan for improvement, jointly constructed by teacher and supervisor

Bird, T., and Little, J. W. (1985). "Instructional Leadership in Eight Secondary Schools." Final Report to the National Institute of Education. Boulder, CO: Center for Action Research. ERIC Document No. ED 263694.

Fielding, G. D., and Schalock, H. D., (1985). *Promoting the Professional Development of Teachers and Administrators.* Eugene, OR: ERIC Clearinghouse on Educational Management.

Natriello, G. (1984). "Teacher's Perceptions of the Frequency of Evaluation and Assessments of Their Effort and Effectiveness." *American Educational Research Journal,* Vol. 21, No. 3, pp. 579–595.

Source: *What Works: Research About Teaching and Learning.* Washington, DC: U.S. Department of Education, 1987, p. 68.

■ Summary

The purpose of this chapter was to help prospective teachers learn about the rewards and challenges of teaching. The major reward of teaching is the personal satisfaction that teachers receive from their work. In a recent survey, no other internal reward was rated by teachers as above average. One of the major challenges of the profession is to continue to work toward higher salaries.

Average salaries have increased in every state ranging from 32.6 percent in Vermont to 2.1 percent in Hawaii. A portion of the salary gains is attributable to the strong call for higher salaries for teachers in the educational reform reports. Another portion of the gains is attributed to the layoffs of young low-paid teachers in the 1970s (student decline), and the minimal hiring of beginning teachers over the past decade.

Generally the education reform reports expressed dissatisfaction with traditional salary schedules because they do not provide opportunities to reward excellent teachers. In other words, a good teacher receives the same salary as a teacher whose performance borders on incompetency. The traditional salary schedule is based on the level of education and years of experience of a teacher. Teachers with the same degree and the same years of experience receive the same salary regardless of their level of competency.

As a result of the dissatisfaction expressed with the traditional salary schedule, the concept of merit pay which has been used off and on over the years is now being reconsidered, and a new concept, career ladders, has been introduced and implemented in a few states. Both merit pay and career ladders are based on teacher performance—the better the performance, the better the pay the teacher receives. The major difference between merit pay and career ladders is that merit pay rewards a teacher or teachers for outstanding performance(s) either through a permanent raise or a bonus which is not a permanent raise, and most often designates only one category of teachers. The concept of career ladders designates different categories of teachers, such as beginning teachers, senior teachers and master teachers. The salary that a teacher is paid is based in part on the category in which the teacher is placed—a beginner receives less salary than a senior teacher and a senior teacher receives less than a master teacher. Teachers are placed in a category based on their performance, and frequently are assigned more and different responsibilities.

The major issue in performance-based pay, including career ladders, is the lack of adequate evaluation systems to determine teacher effectiveness, and therefore the ability to choose those teachers most deserving of rewards.

The top three helping conditions expressed by teachers were: interest in children and teaching; training, education, and knowledge of subject matter; and cooperative and competent colleagues. The top three hindering conditions expressed were: heavy workload and extra responsibilities; incompetent and uncooperative administrators; and the discipline and negative attitudes of students.

The percentage of teachers that have indicated that they "certainly or probably would" enter teaching again declined from 77 percent in 1961 to 49 percent in 1986. The percentage of teachers that have indicated that they "probably or certainly would not" enter teaching again increased from 10.5 percent in 1961 to 31 percent in 1986. It is likely that the reasons for two corresponding trends include low salaries, poor working conditions, relatively low status of the profession, and the perceived increasing difficulty of teaching today as compared with ten years ago.

Prospective teachers who have a desire to work with young people, have an interest in a subject matter field, value the significance of education to society, and can accept low salaries, poor working conditions, and low status, or are willing to work hard to improve salaries, working conditions and the low status of the profession *should seriously* consider being a teacher. It is likely that you would enjoy your work, and feel the personal satisfaction that many teachers cherish.

Point of View

Much of this chapter dealt with teacher salaries. This point of view article written by Nancy Needham, "Better Salaries: On Schedule" is very practical in its approach to teacher salaries. It highlights how some local association affiliates of the National Education Association have negotiated higher salaries by adjusting their salary schedules. It also provides information about how poorer districts were able to raise salaries. The article is an excellent source for prospective teachers to learn to understand salary schedules.

Better Salaries: On Schedule

Nancy R. Needham

Finally some teachers are being paid salaries that could be called "professional"—like $45,000. A few individuals even make over $50,000—but not very many, and not just anywhere.

If you wanted to move to one of the handful of districts that paid teachers at least $40,000 on average in 1986–87, you'd find the best pickings among the high school districts in the North Shore suburbs of Chicago or the K–12 districts in the wealthier suburbs of New York City.

But not everybody wants to—or can—work near the Big Apple or the Second City. For most teachers the more likely question is, How can I make sure the district I'm already in pays well?

Four trends—economic recovery, school reform, teacher demographics, and Association political action—are propelling school boards in some places to pay teachers truly professional salaries. This year and next, NEA is building on these trends by giving each state Association $20,000 to plan long-range projects that can help each state affiliate reach its specific compensation goals—for teachers, for support personnel, and for higher education faculty—within five years. Special grants will fuel intensive campaigns in five to 10 key states where success will exert upward pressure on salaries nationwide.

Already, at the local level, Associations are managing not only to raise their salary schedules but to restructure them into engines of income production for members, now and throughout their careers.

The most common strategies:

- Raising the base, that is, the B.A. starting salary.

- Reducing the number of steps on the schedule.

- Identifying the "career rate," that is, the maximum salary most teachers will attain (typically the maximum on the M.A., M.A. +30, or M.A. +60 lane) and linking it to the base. This might mean setting the maximum at twice the base after 15—or even 10—years of experience.

The Indiana State Teachers Association has neatly wrapped its salary goals into the slogan "10-25-50-90." Which translates: "by 19*90*, starting salary will be *$25*,000 and the MA maximum will top out at *$50*,000 on step *10*."

An early proponent of reducing the number of steps in the salary schedule—also called *compacting* or *compressing* the schedule—was David Helfman, a research staffer with the Pennsylvania State Education Association.

"Throughout the 1970s," Helfman explains, "many districts added steps to their schedules. They provided decent increases to those at the top but moved the beginning rate farther and farther away from the professional salary at the top of the scale."

The 1980s have seen the rise of the opposite notion: reducing the number of steps, in order to "get more money to more people more quickly," as New Jersey Education Association President Dennis Giordano puts it.

That's what the Union Township Education Association (UTEA) in northern New Jersey did in the three-year contract it negotiated earlier this year for teachers and support personnel.

Explains UTEA President Michael Cohan, "We got our teacher members an increase of 30.1 percent over three years and reduced the number of years it takes to get to the maximum from 21 to 15.

"But not every teacher liked the contract," Cohan notes. "There were teachers, mostly at the maximum, who got a smaller percentage increase—25 percent—than average.

"Other locals that want to reduce steps should realize that when people from two or three adjacent steps on one schedule all move onto the same step in the new schedule," Cohan warns, "their percentage increases can't be the same. Of course, I understand how these teachers feel. It's all in the luck of the draw—depending on which step you happened to be on under the old contract. But I think everyone is benefiting handsomely from our contract in dolllar terms, and we're pleased with the impact the schedule's new structure will have on career earnings."

What factors made the increases possible? "New state aid for beginning salaries and a stable local tax base that includes lots of commercial property," Cohan says. "It helps that there are teachers from other districts on our school board."

"The district hopes to reduce its future salary costs," Cohan adds, "by offering retirement incentives—such as $75 a day for unused sick leave—to the large numbers of teachers on the top steps who are near retirement after 30 to 35 years of service."

The experiences of two Illinois locals in negotiating new contracts are instructive because a different combination of factors is at work in each case.

The Naperville Unit district lies a few miles beyond the first generation of suburbs southwest of Chicago. Dianne McGuire, president of the Naperville Unit Education Association, characterizes the area as "the Silicon Valley of the Midwest."

"The district has a growing tax base and no debt," she explains, "and political action by our Association has produced a school board that includes ex-teachers and is open to the Association's ideas."

NUEA's new contract "condensed 34 steps to 19 over three years," McGuire reports. "We used to have one teacher at career salary (M.A. +42). Now we have nearly 100! And in fall 1989 the M.A. +42 maximum will move to $51,728—two-and-a-third times the BA base at $22,000."

Oswego, a small district with 2,300 students and some 225 teachers, lies about five miles west of Naperville.

Oswego Education Association chief negotiator Paul McDowell reports that a new three-year contract will take the B.A. salary from $15,300 to $20,000 and the career salary (M.A. +47) from $35,000 to $44,600.

"Nearby districts are going over $50,000," McDowell observes, "but here you can still get a house for under $100,000 and there you can't."

The Oswego district has been able to finance three-year pay increases of more than 25 percent, McDowell says, because the local economy has recovered from recession and become more diversified. As a result, after four or five failures, the voters finally passed a referendum in 1986 to increase tax rates for the education fund.

"We've been active politically, too, and recently we were able to shift from an adversarial to a cooperative relationship with the board and superintendent," McDowell notes.

Community relations are often crucial to salary increases even when taxpayers don't have an opportunity to vote directly on school budgets.

In negotiations over the past two years, Maryland's Montgomery County Education Association, in a high-income suburb of Washington, D.C., condensed its salary schedule and won significant increases—25 percent over three years.

"But we couldn't have gotten the salary increases," says MCEA president Mark Simon, "if we hadn't established credibility in the community on other issues, such as class size, planning time for elementary teachers, and tuition reimbursement.

"We trained 70 MCEA members to go out to groups like Kiwanis, the NAACP, and the PTA to lead discussions about school problems," Simon explains. "Our members presented the teachers' solutions—more planning time, professional development—and presented collective bargaining as a device for solving such problems."

Poorer districts typically don't have the money to make substantial increases in the base, the middle, and the maximum all at once.

With state legislatures and local school boards focusing on raising the base, Associations in low-revenue districts often negotiate higher starting pay and reduce steps in the schedule—thus setting the stage for future increases in top-of-the-schedule salaries.

Until last year, Wolcott, Conn., had the lowest starting salary in the state, according to Gloria Brown, president of the Wolcott Education Association.

"The district had to use the new state salary 'enhancement' money to raise the base salary from $13,600 to $22,500 over three years," Brown explains. "But the contract has also condensed the number of steps from 17 to 10. In the second and third years the contract shifts relatively more money into the maximum salary. So by the third year, 1988–89, the M.A. +30 maximum will have reached $42,500, which is not quite double the new higher base."

Similarly, in the farm country of south-central Iowa, the tiny Moulton-Udell school district (27 teachers, 335 students) got new state salary money, but in a one-year contract used it mainly to raise starting salaries and restore budget cuts.

Bruce Jensen of Moulton-Udell, a former president of the UniServ unit, explains, "We got a raise for everyone and raised the base from $14,165 to $18,000. We also condensed the number of steps from 17 to 11. In an area where land values have dropped more than 80 percent in a few years, that's all we could do in one year. We raised the maximum salary, but we want to do much more in future negotiations."

Michigan's Redford Union Education Association, part of Wayne County's eight-district Multiple Association Bargaining Organization, took a different tack to keep salaries at a professional level when faced with depression in the automotive industry eight years ago.

This fall teachers at the M.A. maximum are earning more than $42,000, reports Elaine Miller, a past president of RUEA.

"Several factors—including the fact that the community taxes itself at nearly the top millage level allowed—account for our relatively high salaries," she explains. "Most important was the position we took on district spending in the early '80s. We said that the administration could make decisions about cuts—including programs and teachers—but that the teachers who were left would be paid decently.

"In effect," Miller adds, "we forced the district to set priorities, to stop subsidizing programs by underpaying teachers. We made the district decide what programs it wanted to pay for at the going rate. Which was a more honest decision, I think, than if the district had offered a greater number of underfunded programs taught by underpaid teachers."

With enrollments falling as well, Miller points out, "we're a leaner district—with 265 teachers now as opposed to 450 a few years ago. And now that the economy is turning up, the district is receiving more state equalization money, and using it to reinstate some of the programs—and people—that were cut."

What does a local association do for an encore after it has achieved its current career salary goals? Is there a perfect schedule structure that can float with only cost-of-living increases?

Not very likely. As Maryland's Mark Simon says, "The salary schedule is like an accordion. You remove steps or add them according to which strategy better increases member earnings."

After the base and career salary are taken care of—at least for the time being—a local might want to index steps off the base—that is, set the base at 1.00 and the annual increments as multiples of 1.00 (1.20, 1.30, etc.) that are equi-distant from each other.

Or a local Association might want to shorten the time it takes members to go from the base to the career salary from, say, 15 steps to 10—or 7. Or increase the number of lanes horizontally.

In fact, local leaders see the salary schedule as a highly malleable device that can accomplish different ends at different times—but always to the benefit of members and education.

From Nancy R. Needham, "Better Salaries: On Schedule," *NEA Today*, 6:(1):10–1, September 1987. Copyright © 1987 National Education Association, Washington, DC. Reprinted by permission.

■ Questions for Discussion

1. How does the public view the various aspects of teaching?

2. What are the pros and cons of merit pay and career ladders?

3. What are the similarities and differences between merit pay and career ladders?

4. What factors have influenced the increase in teacher salaries in the last few years?

5. What do you consider to be the three most important problems related to inadequate teaching conditions? Why?

■ Notes

1. National Education Association, *NEA Research/Gallup Opinion Polls: Public and K–12 Teacher Members* (Washington, D.C.: National Education Association, 1987), pp. 6–7.

2. National School Boards Association, *Rewarding Excellence: Teacher Compensation and Incentive Programs* (Alexandria, VA: National School Boards Association, 1987), p. 11.

3. Ibid., pp. 13, 14, 16.

4. Joyce D. Stern and Marjorie O. Chandler, *The Condition of Education, 1987* (Washington, D.C.: Center for Education Statistics, 1987), pp. 52–53.

5. The Research Department of the American Federation of Teachers, *Survey and Analysis of Salary Trends 1987* (Washington, D.C.: American Federation of Teachers, AFL–CIO, 1987), p. 2.

6. National School Boards Association, *Rewarding Excellence: Teacher Compensation and Incentive Plans, Executive Summary* (Alexandria, VA: National School Boards Association, 1987), pp. 1–2.

7. The Research Department of the American Federation of Teachers, *Salary and Analysis of Salary Trends, 1987*, p. 3.

8. National Education Association, "Average Teacher Salary Is Now $28,031," *NEA Today* 6 no. 10 (May–June 1988):8.

9. Lynn Olson, "Performance-Based Pay Systems for Teachers Are Being Re-Examined," *Education Week* Vol. VI, No. 29, April 15, 1987, p. 17.

10. Ibid., pp. 1, 16.

11. Ibid., p. 16.

12. Ibid.

13. Ibid., p. 17.

14. National Education Association, "Attitudes Toward the Profession," *Status of the American Public School Teacher 1985–86* (Washington, D.C.: National Education Association, 1987). Excerpted from *Helps and Hindrances to Teachers*, pp. 61–63.

15. National Education Association, "Attitudes Toward the Profession," p. 58.

16. Ibid.

17. National Education Association, *NEA Research/Gallup Opinion Polls: Public and K–12 Teacher Members*, p. 22.

■ Selected References

Boyer, Ernest. *High School.* New York: Carnegie Foundation, 1983.

Gallup, Alec and Clark, David L. "The 19th Annual Kappa/Gallup Poll of the Public Attitudes Toward the Public Schools," *Phi Delta Kappan* Vol. 69, no. 1 (September 1987):17–30.

Goodlad, John I. *A Place Called School.* New York: McGraw-Hill, 1983.

Johnson, Charles E.; Ellet, Chad; and Capie, William. *An Introduction to Teacher Performance Instruments: Their Uses and Limitations.* Athens, GA: College of Education, University of Georgia, 1980.

National Association of Elementary Principals, National Association of Secondary School Principals, and American Association of School Administrators. *Teacher Incentives: A Tool for Effective Management.* Reston, VA: National Association of Elementary Principals, National Association of Secondary Principals and the American Association of School Administrators, 1984.

National Education Association. "Issues '88," *NEA Today Special Edition* Vol. 6, no. 6 (January 1988).

National Education Association, *NEA Research/ Gallup Opinion Polls: Public and K–12 Teacher Members, Spring 1986 Annual Public Polls.* Washington, D.C.: National Education Association, 1987.

National Education Association. *Status of the American Public School Teacher 1985–86.* Washington, D.C.: National Education Association, 1987.

National School Board Association. *Rewarding Excellence: Teacher Compensation and Incentive Plans.* Alexandria, VA: National School Board Association, 1987.

The Research Department of the American Federation of Teachers. *Research Report: Survey and Analysis of Salary Trends 1987.* Washington, D.C.: American Federation of Teachers, AFL–CIO, 1987.

Chapter 7

Teacher Organizations

Objectives

After studying this chapter, you should be able to:

■ Describe the size, type of membership, history, and governance structure of the NEA and AFT.

■ Identify the differences between the NEA and the AFT on the previously mentioned characteristics.

■ Point out the differences between the goals of the NEA and the objectives of the AFT.

■ Speculate on the likelihood of a merger of the NEA and AFT.

■ Explain the relationship that each organization has with its state and local affiliates.

■ Describe the types of support services each organization provides to their respective memberships.

■ Report on the status of strikes.

■ Cite possible reasons why there has been a decline in the number of strikes in the last few years.

■ Recognize and express the importance of the rights of teachers as presented in the documents in this chapter.

■ Identify and explain the changes in labor relations.

Enrichment Experiences

The following experiences will help you gain perspectives about the roles, functions, and importance of teacher organizations in American education and society.

■ Invite representatives of the state affiliates of the NEA and the AFT to class sessions to discuss their respective organizations.

■ Conduct a debate in your classroom using volunteers with one group aligned with the NEA, the other with the AFT.

■ Interview the officers of a local teacher association regarding their relationships with their board of education.

■ Invite a negotiator for school boards to your class to discuss her or his views regarding the role of teacher organizations in negotiations.

■ Invite an elected political figure to a class to discuss his or her views regarding the role of teacher organizations.

■ In your own terms, list the factors that are similar and those that are different in a comparison of the Bill of Teacher Rights (NEA) with the Bill of Rights (AFT).

*T*he purpose of this chapter is to introduce you to the two major teacher organizations: the American Federation of Teachers (AFT) and the National Education Association (NEA). The chapter provides information about the size, type of membership, history, and the governance structure of both organizations; compares the goals of the National Education Association with the objectives of the American Federation of Teachers; explains the relationship that each organization has with their respective state and local affiliates; describes their support services to their respective memberships; updates information about strikes; and includes the Bill of Teacher Rights (NEA) and the Bill of Rights (AFT); and mentions the availability of other teacher organizations. ■

Teacher organizations give teachers a collective voice.

Membership in teacher organizations may be considered an important determinant of social success, and even physical survival in certain situations. Organizations are prized by some members in terms of what the organization can do for them. Often the pressures of special interest groups, such as teacher organizations, have a significant influence on the operations of school government. In this way teacher organizations are effective agents in dealing with teacher concerns.

Teachers are solicited for membership in numerous types of organizations. The most popular types of organizations are those which bring members of an occupational group together for the advancement of their mutual purposes. The two major teacher organizations are the (1) American Federation of Teachers (AFT), a union affiliated with the American Federation of Labor and Congress of Industrial Organizations (AFL–CIO), and (2) the National Education Association (NEA). The NEA membership population is 1.8 million, and consists of teachers in large city schools, suburban schools, and rural schools throughout the United States. The AFT members number more than one-half million (660,000), and are drawn mostly from teachers in large city schools. Since the social milieu of the city teachers is similar to that of lower level employees of mass industry, the union identification of the AFT with the AFL–CIO is perceived by city teachers as the best means of attaining their goals. In the last decade, as the NEA has become more and more unionistic in identification, additional members have been attracted from the large city school systems. At the same time, the NEA has kept a professional association image which helps to sustain membership among teachers outside the large metropolitan centers. While there are other organizations for teachers in the private schools, independent city organizations, and other local teacher groups, the National Education Association (NEA), and the American Federation of Teachers (AFT) are the two largest and most powerful teacher organizations. Chances are very good that most beginning teachers will be solicited to join either the NEA or the AFT during their first year of teaching.

■ National Education Association (NEA)

The NEA was originally founded in 1857 as the National Teachers Association. In 1870 the National Association of School Superintendents and the American Normal School Association merged to form the National Education Association (NEA). The two purposes stated in the charter are "to elevate the character and advance the interests of the profession of teaching, and to promote the cause of education in the United States."

In 1966, black and white educators demonstrated their concern for the unity and integrity of the teaching profession by arranging a merger of the National Education Association with the American Teachers Association. The merger of NEA and ATA paved the way for merger agreements between black and white associations in state and local affiliates throughout the South. It also signaled NEA's great leap forward in terms of promoting civil and human rights of educators and children. For decades the ATA had sought to eliminate discrimination in education; to eradicate racism in American society; to improve the education of children; and to strengthen the educational systems of communities.

Today, the NEA is governed by the annual Representative Assembly composed of 8,046 delegates from affiliated state and local associations. This body develops policy resolutions which are interpreted by a Board of Directors, which consists of one director for each state affiliate plus an additional director for each 20,000 active NEA members within that state affiliate, and the Executive Committee, made up of the three executive officers and six members elected at large by the Representative Assembly.

Tied into the NEA are a number of standing committees and special committees. While a part of the parent NEA, these committees often represent the major organizational affiliation for the teachers. These committees are self-governing groups within the profession, with some serving general interests. The standing committees facilitate operations and advise NEA's governing bodies in various program areas. Special committees are established to accomplish specific

Local and state teacher delegates vote to determine national policies and programs.

tasks. The organization chart of the NEA, as outlined in figure 7.1, shows the various standing committees of the representative assembly, standing committees relating to programs, and special committees within the NEA.

The income of the Association is derived almost entirely from membership dues, with a small amount returning from the sale of publications.

Headed by the Executive Director, who is chosen by the Executive Committee, a staff of several hundred individuals serves in the NEA Center (1201 Sixteenth St. N.W., Washington, D.C. 20036), and in six regional offices. The Association is an affiliate of the World Confederation of Organizations of the Teaching Profession (WCOTP), which includes national teacher organizations in practically every country of the free world.

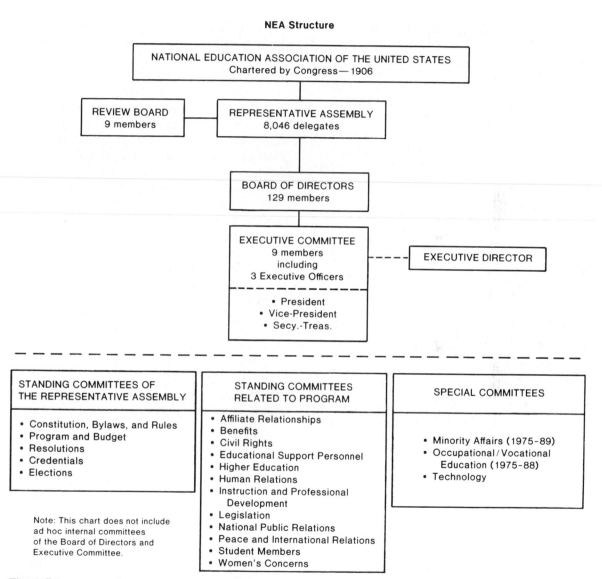

NEA Structure

NATIONAL EDUCATION ASSOCIATION OF THE UNITED STATES
Chartered by Congress—1906

REVIEW BOARD
9 members

REPRESENTATIVE ASSEMBLY
8,046 delegates

BOARD OF DIRECTORS
129 members

EXECUTIVE COMMITTEE
9 members
including
3 Executive Officers

• President
• Vice-President
• Secy.-Treas.

EXECUTIVE DIRECTOR

STANDING COMMITTEES OF
THE REPRESENTATIVE ASSEMBLY

• Constitution, Bylaws, and Rules
• Program and Budget
• Resolutions
• Credentials
• Elections

Note: This chart does not include
ad hoc internal committees
of the Board of Directors and
Executive Committee.

STANDING COMMITTEES
RELATED TO PROGRAM

• Affiliate Relationships
• Benefits
• Civil Rights
• Educational Support Personnel
• Higher Education
• Human Relations
• Instruction and Professional
  Development
• Legislation
• National Public Relations
• Peace and International Relations
• Student Members
• Women's Concerns

SPECIAL COMMITTEES

• Minority Affairs (1975–89)
• Occupational / Vocational
  Education (1975–88)
• Technology

■ **Figure 7.1**
Organization chart of the National Education Association

■ American Federation of Teachers (AFT)

The American Federation of Teachers is not a new organization. It was formed on April 15, 1916, affiliated with the American Federation of Labor May 9, 1916, and has grown in membership and influence every year since. While the AFT is the largest teachers' union in the United States, the general membership of approximately 660,000 is small compared with that of the NEA. However, the AFT functions as the dominant teachers' organization in some of our largest cities.

In the fall of 1961, an election was held among New York City teachers to elect an agent to bargain with the Board of Education. In the election, the United Federation of Teachers (AFL–CIO) defeated the Teacher's Bargaining Organization which was supported by the National Education Association. This election has been referred to as the opening skirmish of what has grown to be a noisy battle for the loyalties of American teachers. The New York election is cited as a major factor in the rise of the AFT to a position of national prominence.

The general offices include those of the president, secretary-treasurer, administrative staff, and the following departments: organizational, colleges and universities, editorial, legislation, international education, human rights and community relations, public relations, AFT-Cope, convention/travel, research, and educational issues.

The annual convention functions as the AFT's governing body. Delegates to this convention are elected by local union members.

The interim governing and administrative body is the Executive Council of 34 vice-presidents, the secretary-treasurer, and the president, who is a full-time officer. The president, secretary-treasurer, and vice-presidents are subject to election every two years. Vice-presidents, who are assigned to specific geographical areas, serve without remuneration (see figure 7.2).

Organized labor was a major driving force in establishing our system of free public schools and has actively backed every practical public school improvement at local, state, and national levels. The objectives of the American Federation of Teachers coincide with labor philosophy on the importance of public education.

Labor affiliation gives the AFT and its members the support of about 15 million members of unions in the AFL–CIO. Local and state teachers' federations can rely on the support of state and local central labor bodies. AFT local unions have often won better salaries and other benefits for teachers with the aid and support of local labor trades and labor councils, after teachers' organizations outside the labor movement failed to accomplish these objectives.

In 1986 the AFT revised its constitution in respect to its rules for membership. Article III (membership), Section II, second paragraph states:

> Nothing contained in this article shall permit locals to admit into or retain in membership any nonteaching person who holds the position of principal or any higher position. This provision shall not be applicable to holders of such positions who held membership in any local prior to the adoption of this article.

Labor affiliation does not impose any obligations on union teachers that would deter them from the best professional service they can render and the highest professional ethics they can command. Labor affiliation, by emphasizing the dignity of the teaching profession, makes it easier for teachers to act, on the job, as the professionals

Table of Organization

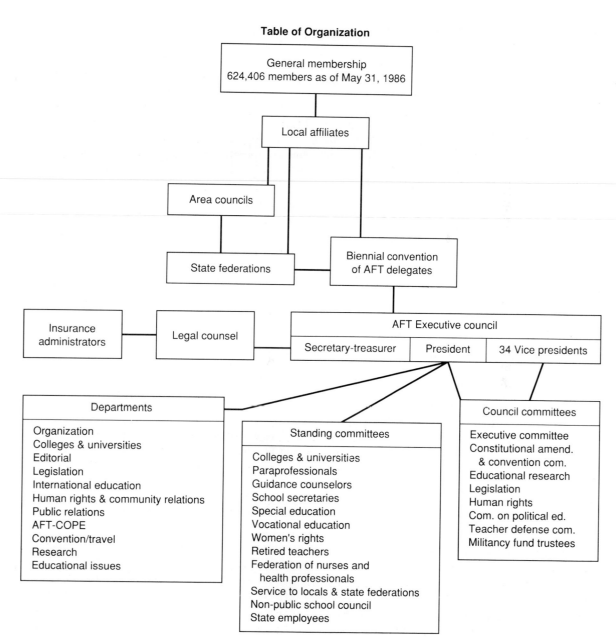

General membership
624,406 members as of May 31, 1986

Local affiliates

Area councils

State federations

Biennial convention
of AFT delegates

Insurance
administrators

Legal counsel

AFT Executive council

| Secretary-treasurer | President | 34 Vice presidents |

Departments

Organization
Colleges & universities
Editorial
Legislation
International education
Human rights & community relations
Public relations
AFT-COPE
Convention/travel
Research
Educational issues

Standing committees

Colleges & universities
Paraprofessionals
Guidance counselors
School secretaries
Special education
Vocational education
Women's rights
Retired teachers
Federation of nurses and
 health professionals
Service to locals & state federations
Non-public school council
State employees

Council committees

Executive committee
Constitutional amend.
 & convention com.
Educational research
Legislation
Human rights
Com. on political ed.
Teacher defense com.
Militancy fund trustees

■ **Figure 7.2**
Organization chart of the American Federation of Teachers

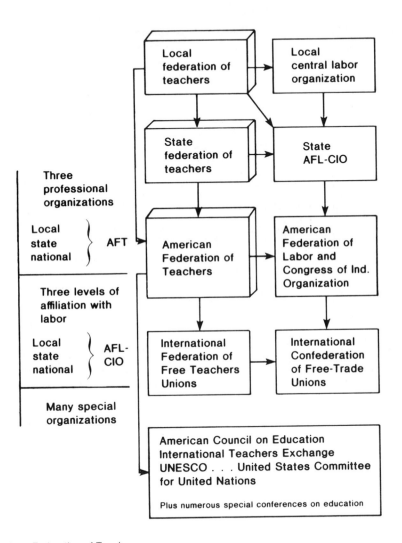

■ Figure 7.3
Relationship of American Federation of Teachers
to AFL–CIO

*He who governs well, leads the
ignorant; he who teaches well, trains
them to govern themselves in justice,
mercy, and peace.*

Alexander G. Ruthven

they are. Figure 7.3 outlines the relationship of the American Federation of Teachers to the AFL–CIO. As with the NEA, a Student Federation of Teachers may be chartered in any college or university under the auspices of the parent AFT.

The AFT boasts that John Dewey held Membership Card Number 1 in the American Federation of Teachers. Dr. Dewey, who died in 1952 at the age of 93, was professor of philosophy at Teachers College, Columbia University. In an address published in the *American Teacher,* a publication of the AFT, in January, 1982, he said:

> The very existence of teachers' unions does a great deal more than protect and aid those who are members of it; and that, by the way, is one reason the teachers' union is not larger. It is because there are so many teachers outside of it who rely and depend upon the protection and support which the existence and the activities of the union give them, that they are willing to shelter behind the organization without coming forward and taking an active part in it.
>
> And if there are teachers . . . who are not members of the union, I should like to beg them to surrender the, shall I call it, cowardly position, and come forward and actively unite themselves with those who are doing this great and important work for the profession and teaching.

Total membership in the AFT at the time of Dr. Dewey's address (1928) was approximately 5,000. The steady rise in membership had reached approximately 60,000 at the time of the 1961 New York City teacher election won by the United Federation of Teachers supported by the AFL–CIO labor union. From May 1, 1968, to May 1, 1979, the membership in the teachers' unions affiliated with AFL–CIO rose to 519,279,

which represented a gain of approximately 356,000 during a five-year span. While the rivalry for membership between the NEA and the AFT continues strong, the total membership of the two organizations combined represents about 60 percent of all teachers. Obviously, then, many teachers elect to join local teacher groups or do not join any teacher organizations.

■ Goals and Objectives: NEA versus AFT

During the past decade, the tactics and behaviors of the AFT have greatly influenced the tactics and behaviors of the NEA, and vice versa. While the two organizations have differences, these are becoming less and less obvious. Appendixes C and D illustrate that so far as stated objectives of the AFT and the NEA are concerned, the two organizations are not in basic conflict. In view of the general similarities of purposes which continue to evolve, considerable speculation also evolves regarding the possible merger of the AFT and NEA to form a single, more representative organization for all teachers in the United States.

Over the years, there has been off and on speculation regarding a merger of the NEA and AFT. Local officers of each organization are typically less vocal against a merger than the national leaders of the respective organizations. The major difference between the NEA and AFT is the AFT's affiliation with organized labor, which it claims provides its members with a broad base of support and labor's financial resources. The NEA claims its larger membership and professionalism provides superior ability to represent American teachers.

Recently (1988), the California affiliate of the NEA presented its AFT counterpart with a written proposal for melding the two state groups into one organization. The NEA has indicated support for the idea of establishing one united organization for teachers at either the state or national level; its leaders have made it clear, however, that all of its members would have to belong solely to the NEA.[1] Mr. Shanker (AFT) said his organization might support a state merger where all members of the united organization would belong to both nationals or have the option of choosing which national they want to belong to. He commented that "If you really want to unite teachers, you have to work out a compromise that is acceptable to both sides."[2] It is not likely that the NEA and AFT will merge in the next few years.

Appendixes C and D display the twelve objectives of the AFT as expressed in their Constitution (1986), and the ten goals of the NEA, as expressed in the Preamble of their Constitution as it appears in the *NEA Handbook* (1987–88). The NEA has a list of resolutions directly related to each of the ten goals. The resolutions state the position of the NEA on specific topics.

When the AFT objectives and the NEA goals are compared, they are relatively similar. They differ in that the AFT, in Sections 5 and 9, deals with standards for nurses and other allied health professions, and with promoting the welfare of the health care consumer. The NEA has the topic of nursing home standards in its current legislative program, but its documents do not as yet provide the emphasis to the health professions and to the health care consumers that the AFT documents provide.

In other matters common to both organizations such as bargaining rights, teacher rights, human and civil rights, child health and welfare, educational standards, democracy, member benefits, working with their state and local affiliates, and each seeking to be the leader of the nation's educators, the objectives of the AFT and the goals of the NEA overall are quite similar. That is logical in that they essentially deal with teachers and educational and societal issues. They differ in style, and often in the emphasis they place on specific issues. They also differ in their positions they take on a specific issue. That also is to be expected.

■ National, State, and Local Affiliation

In the early years of the sixties decade, the NEA was viewed philosophically and operationally as the national organization that served as an umbrella under which the state and local associations were sheltered. Each of the three levels of affiliation could remain as autonomous as desired by their respective memberships. Individual teachers could pay membership dues for local membership only, for both state and local membership, or for national, state, and local membership. This mutually autonomous organizational structure and membership dues arrangement was espoused as a desirable feature in membership recruitment announcements by the NEA and state affiliates. During the mid-sixties teacher militancy increased sharply, lending to the concept of teacher power. Concomitant with the expansion of teacher power was a new need for unification of the three levels of affiliation. Local associations sought increased support from state associations, and state associations sought

Education is an admirable thing, but it is well to remember from time to time that nothing that is worth knowing can be taught.

increased national unity. The need for unity across state and local levels of membership to build teacher power prompted an alteration in the NEA point of view regarding the independent organizational and dues structures. The later years of the sixties found the NEA espousing the desirability of a unified dues approach in which members would pay a single membership fee to cover all three levels of association affiliation. Several state associations have taken direct unification steps by amending their bylaws so that their dues include membership fees for both the state and national associations. The National Education Association has taken indirect steps toward unified membership by requiring both state and national association membership as criteria for eligibility for various fringe benefit programs, such as insurance programs, which are NEA sponsored.

The AFT has always had a single dues arrangement whereby AFT members were automatically members at the local, state, and national levels. Under the NEA unified dues approach, a teacher in a given association would pay set yearly dues which would cover national, state, and local costs. As indicated earlier, the AFT has always had a unified dues arrangement.

A recent decision by the U.S. Supreme Court restricting the ways unions may use fees collected from nonunion members is likely to result in a modest reduction in the income of teachers' unions. Over half of the states have collective bargaining laws that require teachers and other public employees who choose not to belong to unions but who benefit from their presence to pay dues—commonly called agency fees—to them. In *Ellis v. Railway Clerks* (1984), in an 8-to-1 decision the Court ruled that unions cannot spend dues collected from nonunion members on union

organizing or on union litigation that is not connected with the bargaining unit. The justices said in their opinion that unions should either set up interest-bearing escrow accounts for nonmembers who charge a union with misspending their dues or reduce the nonmembers' dues.

In 1986, the U.S. Supreme Court held that procedural safeguards are necessary to protect nonunion members from being compelled to subsidize political or ideological activities not germane to the collective bargaining process.[3]

■ Teacher Strikes

Teacher strikes occur when negotiations between a local teachers' organization and the local board of education do not produce acceptable resolutions to the teachers' demands. The use of the strike by teachers became the vehicle of teacher power in the latter part of the sixties decade. A summary of teacher strikes for the 1967–68 school year showed that a total of 114 work stoppages (strikes) occurred, which was considered a veritable explosion in teacher strikes. These 114 strikes accounted for over one-third of the number of teacher strikes in the twenty-seven years since 1940. Following the record number of 194 teacher strikes in 1975–76, there seemed to be a trend for fewer strikes in the late 1970s. However, in September 1981, teacher contract disputes in several large cities and smaller districts once again threatened massive strikes throughout the United States. While boards of education are tightening control, teachers apparently are not willing to settle for less than what they desire.

As the 1984–85 school year began, the low number of strikes in progress had union representatives and school officials across the nation predicting a relatively quiet year. School and union officials attributed the decline in teacher strikes to the nation's economic recovery, the influence of the school-reform movement, and maturing labor relations between unions and school boards.

The number of strikes in 1986–1988 have also been relatively minimal compared with the past. Reasons for fewer strikes may be that (1) recommendations in education reform reports called for more teacher participation in decision making at the school district and school levels (teacher empowerment), (2) teacher empowerment has been implemented in some schools, and is being considered in others, (3) up until the present, there has been a surplus of teachers. A shortage of teachers combined with a healthy economy could lead to an increase in strikes in an effort to increase salaries.

■ Organizational Support Programs

The NEA and the AFT differ in degree in their approaches to specific benefits or programs, but in general terms each organization strives to offer similar benefits to its members. Figure 7.4 illustrates the kinds of fringe benefits and support programs that are of mutual concern to both organizations.

Affiliate publications come to the members of the teacher associations. These usually consist of national journals and state journals, newsletters, handbooks, research studies, and various booklets and reports.

The benefits of research services come to members in the form of reports, such as salary studies, estimates of school statistics, negotia-

■ Figure 7.4
Mutual concerns of the AFT and the NEA

tions information, summaries of court decisions, leaves of absence, and fringe benefit programs that exist.

Each of the parent associations have legislative committees at both the state and national levels. These legislative committees work on improving certification standards and improving the laws that relate to teaching.

Teacher welfare is an area of prime importance to the parent associations. Many kinds of programs that focus on advancing and protecting the welfare of members are sponsored by the parent organizations.

The AFT is steadily increasing research services, publications, printed materials, insurance programs, and consultant services for their members. Among the state educational association teacher welfare programs are: teacher placement services, investment programs, retirement benefits, insurance programs, liability protection, auto leasing programs, and regional service centers. Similar programs are sponsored by the NEA, but to be eligible for their programs the teacher must also belong to the state association. The requirement of state membership is consistent with the unified dues emphasis of the NEA, and prevents the teacher from paying only the national dues in order to profit from the nationally sponsored NEA welfare programs.

■ Bill of Teacher Rights—Bill of Rights

The philosophical statements of the two major national teacher associations are expressed in the form of the Bill of Teacher Rights (NEA) and the Bill of Rights (AFT). The two statements are included here in their entirety.

Bill of Teacher Rights

National Education Association

Preamble

We, the teachers of the United States of America, aware that a free society is dependent upon the education afforded its citizens, affirm the right to freely pursue truth and knowledge.

As an individual, the teacher is entitled to such fundamental rights as dignity, privacy, and respect.

As a citizen, the teacher is entitled to such basic constitutional rights as freedom of religion, speech, assembly, association and political action, and equal protection of the law.

National Education Association, Washington, D.C. Reprinted by permission.

In order to develop and preserve respect for the worth and dignity of man, to provide a climate in which actions develop as a consequence of rational thought, and to insure intellectual freedom, we further affirm that teachers must be free to contribute fully to an educational environment which secures the freedom to teach and the freedom to learn.

Believing that certain rights of teachers derived from these fundamental freedoms must be universally recognized and respected, we proclaim this Bill of Teacher Rights.

Article I Rights as a Professional

As a member of the teaching profession, the individual teacher has the right:

Section 1. To be licensed under professional and ethical standards established, maintained, and enforced by the profession.
Section 2. To maintain and improve professional competence.
Section 3. To exercise professional judgment in presenting, interpreting, and criticizing information and ideas, including controversial issues.
Section 4. To influence effectively the formulation of policies and procedures which affect one's professional services, including curriculum, teaching materials, methods of instruction, and school-community relations.
Section 5. To exercise professional judgment in the use of teaching methods and materials appropriate to the needs, interests, capacities, and the linguistic and cultural background of each student.
Section 6. To safeguard information obtained in the course of professional service.
Section 7. To work in an atmosphere conducive to learning, including the use of reasonable means to preserve the learning environment and to protect the health and safety of students, oneself, and others.

Section 8. To express publicly views on matters affecting education.

Section 9. To attend and address a governing body and be afforded access to its minutes when official action may affect one's professional concerns.

Article II Rights as an Employee

As an employee, the individual teacher has the right:

Section 1. To seek and be fairly considered for any position commensurate with one's qualifications.

Section 2. To retain employment following entrance into the profession in the absence of a showing of just cause for dismissal or nonrenewal through fair and impartial proceedings.

Section 3. To be fully informed, in writing, of rules, regulations, terms, and conditions affecting one's employment.

Section 4. To have conditions of employment in which health, security, and property are adequately protected.

Section 5. To influence effectively the development and application of evaluation procedures.

Section 6. To have access to written evaluations, to have documents placed in one's personnel file to rebut derogatory information and to have removed false or unfair material through a clearly defined process.

Section 7. To be free from arbitrary, capricious, or discriminatory actions affecting the terms and conditions of employment.

Section 8. To be advised promptly in writing of the specific reasons for any actions which might affect one's employment.

Section 9. To be afforded due process through the fair and impartial hearing of grievances, including binding arbitration as a means of resolving disputes.

Section 10. To be free from interference to form, join, or assist employee organizations, to negotiate collectively through representatives of one's own choosing, and to engage in other concerted activities for the purpose of professional negotiations or other mutual aid or protection.

Section 11. To withdraw services collectively when reasonable procedures to resolve impasse have been exhausted.

Article III Rights in an Organization

As an individual member of an employee organization, the teacher has the right:

Section 1. To acquire membership in employee organizations based upon reasonable standards equally applied.

Section 2. To have equal opportunity to participate freely in the affairs and governance of the organization.

Section 3. To have freedom of expression, both within and outside the organization.

Section 4. To vote for organization officers, either directly or through delegate bodies, in fair elections.

Section 5. To stand for and hold office subject only to fair qualifications uniformly applied.

Section 6. To be fairly represented by the organization in all matters.

Section 7. To be provided periodic reports of the affairs and conduct of business of the organization.

Section 8. To be provided detailed and accurate financial records, audited and reported at least annually.

Section 9. To be free from arbitrary disciplinary action or threat of such action by the organization.

Section 10. To be afforded due process by the organization in a disciplinary action.

Bill of Rights

American Federation of Teachers

The teacher is entitled to a life of dignity equal to the high standard of service that is justly demanded of that profession. Therefore, we hold these truths to be self-evident:

I

Teachers have the right to think freely and to express themselves openly and without fear. This includes the right to hold views contrary to the majority.

II

They shall be entitled to the free exercise of their religion. No restraint shall be put upon them in the manner, time or place of their worship.

III

They shall have the right to take part in social, civil, and political affairs. They shall have the right, outside the classroom, to participate in political campaigns and to hold office. They may assemble peaceably and may petition any government agency, including their employers, for a redress of grievances. They shall have the same freedom in all things as other citizens.

IV

The right of teachers to live in places of their own choosing, to be free of restraints in their mode of living and the use of their leisure time shall not be abridged.

V

Teaching is a profession, the right to practice which is not subject to the surrender of other human rights. No one shall be deprived of professional status, or the right to practice it, or the practice thereof in any particular position, without due process of law.

American Federation of Teachers AFL–CIO. Reprinted by permission.

VI

The right of teachers to be secure in their jobs, free from political influence or public clamor, shall be established by law. The right to teach after qualification in the manner prescribed by law, is a property right, based upon the inalienable rights of life, liberty, and the pursuit of happiness.

VII

In all cases affecting the teacher's employment or professional status a full hearing by an impartial tribunal shall be afforded with the right to full judicial review. No teacher shall be deprived of employment or professional status but for specific causes established by law having a clear relation to the competence or qualification to teach proved by the weight of the evidence. In all such cases the teacher shall enjoy the right to a speedy and public trial, to be informed of the nature and cause of the accusation; to be confronted with the accusing witnesses, to subpoena witnesses and papers, and the assistance of counsel. No teacher shall be called upon to answer any charge affecting his employment or professional status but upon probable cause, supported by oath or affirmation.

VIII

It shall be the duty of the employer to provide culturally adequate salaries, security in illness and adequate retirement income. The teacher has the right to such a salary as will: a) Afford a family standard of living comparable to that enjoyed by other professional people in the community b) To make possible freely chosen professional study c) Afford the opportunity for leisure and recreation common to our heritage.

IX

No teacher shall be required under penalty of reduction of salary to pursue studies beyond those required to obtain professional status. After serving a reasonable probationary period a teacher shall be entitled to permanent tenure terminable only for just cause. They shall be free as in other professions in the use of their own time. They shall not be required to perform extracurricular work against their will or without added compensation.

X

To equip people for modern life requires the most advanced educational methods. Therefore, the teacher is entitled to good classrooms, adequate teaching materials, teachable class size and administrative protection and assistance in maintaining discipline.

XI

These rights are based upon the proposition that the culture of a people can rise only as its teachers improve. A teaching force accorded the highest possible professional dignity is the surest guarantee that blessings of liberty will be served. Therefore, the possession of these rights imposes the challenge to be worthy of their enjoyment.

XII

Since teachers must be free in order to teach freedom, the right to be members of organizations of their own choosing must be guaranteed. In all matters pertaining to their salaries and working conditions they shall be entitled to bargain collectively through representatives of their own choosing. They are entitled to have the schools administered by superintendents, boards or committees which function in a democratic manner.[4]

■ Other Teacher Organizations

As mentioned earlier, the total membership of the NEA and AFT combined represents about 60 percent of all teachers. Teachers also belong to other organizations which are dedicated to the improvement of teachers and instructions. Many of these organizations produce professional journals which keep teachers and administrators informed of trends in subject fields, new curriculum materials, and new management strategies. Several other teacher organizations that have a subject matter orientation, skill orientation, and honorary educational associations are:

- American Association for Health, Physical Education, and Recreation
- American Educational Research Association
- Association for Childhood Education International
- International Reading Association
- National Catholic Education Association
- National Council for Geographic Education
- National Council for the Social Studies
- National Council of Teachers of English
- National Council of the Teachers of Mathematics
- National Parent Teacher Association
- National Science Foundation
- National Science Teachers Association
- National Society for the Study of Education
- Phi Delta Kappa
- Religious Education Associations
- State Reading Associations

■ Summary

The purpose of this chapter was to introduce you to the two major teacher organizations: the American Federation of Teachers (AFT) and the National Education Association (NEA). The NEA has a membership of about 1.8 million. Its membership consists of teachers in rural, suburban, and city schools. The AFT has a membership of about 660,000 teachers. The early membership of the AFT was primarily from large cities. In the last few years, they have maintained their city membership and have gained membership in suburban, small city, and rural schools.

An early basic difference between the AFT and the NEA essentially dealt with collective bargaining. The AFT believed that teachers must have their own voices and that the teachers' interest could not be adequately represented through the voices of administrators. In its early days, the NEA had many administrators as members. The NEA was opposed to collective bargaining, viewing it as "unionistic." They depended upon the administrators to see to it that teachers would receive adequate compensation and fair treatment. The NEA teachers expressed their desires to their administrators, and in some instances, particularly in wealthy districts, they gained better salaries than did the AFT. Over the years, the NEA adopted and implemented collective bargaining. The NEA today is frequently labeled as a union and recognized as a powerful union.

The two unions, AFT and NEA, have common and similar goals that they both support. Those goals include bargaining rights, teacher rights, human and civil rights, child health and welfare, educational standards, democracy member benefits, working with state and local affiliates, and each seeks to be the leader of the nation's educators. They differ in style, and often in the emphasis they place on specific issues. They also differ in the positions they take on a specific issue. It is expected that they would take different approaches in support of a similar goal. It is also expected that their debate would be focused on specific points of a similar goal.

On occasion, there have been discussions about a possible merger of the AFT and the NEA. From the evidence currently available, it appears unlikely that the two organizations (AFT and NEA) will merge in the next few years.

The Bill of Teacher Rights of the NEA and the Bill of Rights of the AFT were included in this chapter. They provide information that is very important to those persons considering teaching as a career.

As a new teacher, you are likely to be recruited to join a teacher organization. Most local classroom teacher associations are affiliated with the NEA or AFT. It is not urgent that you join a teachers' union immediately. However, if the school district in which you are teaching has a strong local union, it would be wise and prudent to join the union. You might also consider joining other professional education organizations that are related to your teaching responsibility or are of interest to you. Some of those organizations are mentioned in this chapter.

Point of View

Historically unions and school boards have approached one another as adversaries. From that posture, they negotiated items such as salaries, working conditions, and grievance procedures. The final contract reached during negotiations became the document that specifically defined the relationship of the union and the school district.

In recent years, administrators and union teachers are talking about a new approach to labor relations, centered around educational policy. It is strongly implied that teachers and management should work together in joint planning, goal setting, and the redefinition of teacher roles. In part, the new approach was a result of recommendations of educational reform reports to involve teachers in significant decision making. The point of view article "A 'New Generation' of Teacher Unionism" authored by Charles T. Kerchner cites illustrations of the implementation of the new teachers-management-shared decision making concept of labor relations. Tomorrow's teachers and administrators may function differently than those of the past in regard to their respective roles in labor relations.

A 'New Generation' of Teacher Unions
Charles T. Kerchner

The signs all around us indicate that a new generation of teacher unionism is emerging. Ongoing changes in the practices of administrators and teachers suggest a shifting of ideologies and the coming of a new approach to labor relations, with educational policy as its center. At issue is the willingness of organized teachers to assume part of the responsibility for winning increased respect for public education, improving the effectiveness of schools, and making teaching a profession.

Administrators and teachers are engaging in labor-relations practices that would be considered heresies under conventional belief systems: peer review, differentiation among teachers, standards setting, problem solving, and self-management. Following years of party-line solidarity, the memberships of union, management, and school-board organizations are vigorously debating what constitutes good labor relations. And, after years of relative quiet, the subject of teachers' unions is attracting renewed public interest.

Among the heretical practices, we find unionized teachers starting to take seriously the idea that teachers should evaluate other teachers. Under conventional ideology, the idea that one member of a bargaining unit would evaluate another is a traitorous violation of the "solidarity" norm.

But since 1981 teachers in Toledo, Ohio, have actively engaged in peer evaluation for new teachers and in an intervention program for experienced teachers who are not performing adequately. Though this agreement remains controversial in many quarters, provisions for similar undertakings have found their way into statute in Ohio, and peer-review plans are under study by unions and managements as far away as Lompoc, Calif. In the new thinking, teacher solidarity means self-policing as well as self-protection.

According to the conventional ideology, responsibility for fixing school problems belongs to management. Decisions are management's prerogative; the less involvement with the union, the better, management believes. Labor accepts this turf division. From its standpoint, an offer to make decisions is sucker bait, an invitation to take the heat because management is too weak to make tough decisions. Besides, decisions are complex and messy, and getting teachers involved is a tough job that union officials would rather duck.

Now, in 27 school sites represented by the National Education Association, managers and teachers are engaged in joint planning, goal setting, and redefinition of teacher roles. In Hammond, Ind., members of the American Federation of Teachers bargaining unit are involved in a school-site management plan, and in New York City teachers have negotiated a contract allowing teachers and site administrators to waive work-rule restrictions in the citywide contract in order to restructure their schools.

In conventional labor ideology, the contract encompasses the relationship between union and school district. Although teachers' unions have always engaged in professional development through publications and workshops for members, their official relationship with the school district hinges on the union's standing as the legitimate representative of teacher self-interest through collective bargaining. While the onset of collective bargaining legitimated teacher self-interest and signaled the end to the suffering-servant mentality, the ideology of good-faith bargaining hardened opposition to teacher participation in educational policy.

However, in the emerging belief system, teachers' unions also have a right and a responsibility to speak for the public good. In Pittsburgh and Miami, unions are engaged in practices that "go beyond collective bargaining" into school improvement. In Petaluma and four other California districts, the union and management are establishing a new type of written contract, called a "policy trust agreement," in addition to their regular relationship.

These changes underscore the importance of ideology to labor relations and the extent to which change in unionism is driven by conflict over competing ideas of what unions should do. Labor and management belief systems have progressed through two distinct historical and organizational realities: the first centered around meet-and-confer relationships and the second around good-faith collective bargaining. My research, along with the evidence of recent events, suggests that a third generation of labor relations, with educational policy as its focus, is arriving now.

Because the battles are not simply tugs-of-war about who gets more or less, but ideological struggles over what is good and proper, periods of change between labor-relations generations are particularly tumultuous. The internal tension frequently experienced by national unions and management organizations are reflected in school districts as "radicals" of either the left or the right vie for attention and loyalty with the conventional wisdom. Conflict often becomes public, and in its settlement new leaders emerge: School-board members lose elections, superintendents are sacked, and union officers face defeat at the hands of the members they thought they understood.

It is easy to recall the organizing wars of the 1960's and 1970's as the ideological emphasis of teacher organization changed from participation and consultation through various meet-and-confer mechanisms to self-representation through collective bargaining resulting in written, enforceable contracts. Pitched battles were fought

within the NEA over whether collective bargaining was a legitimate undertaking for teachers. The old guard said it would cheapen the profession, and the Young Turks of the NEA Urban Project countered that the current process was a failure. While the AFT had no historic problems with explicit unionism, it had to resolve the battle between its revolutionary and pragmatic wings.

And in thousands of school districts across the country, teachers went through the process of acting out the then-radical notion that they had the right to speak for themselves.

The events we are witnessing now can be seen in this mirror of history. Representatives of the two national unions debate the wisdom and meaning of recent contractual changes, such as the Rochester career-stage plan. The National School Boards Association appoints a commission to study ways of promoting productive, harmonious relationships, but does so in language so provocative that the result is likely to be a clash of wills over unionism itself. U.S. Secretary of Education William J. Bennett castigates the NEA for footdragging on reform issues, to which the NEA replies that Secretary Bennett's idea isn't what it had in mind. Internally, the NEA and the AFT consider radically restructuring. In all these cases, the question being asked is not whether teachers have the right to an economic interest in their jobs, but how the energy and commitment of organized teachers can be brought to bear on problems of school reform.

Although the battle lines have not yet hardened, the struggle for teacher unionism in the 1990's is taking shape around three important issues in public education:

- How does public education retain popular support?
- How can union activity aid school effectiveness?
- How can teachers become employed professionals?

As public education's best-financed and organized interest group, unions play a pivotal role in developing support for public education. The NEA, in particular, is a lobbying nonpareil; its members are politically active in virtually every Congressional district in the country. But interest-group representation does not subsume educational politics. The larger perception that public schools are incapable of solving their problems breeds reform movements that either attempt remote control of the schools by close-order certification and testing or seek to disinvest in them by proposing vouchers and other mechanisms that would structurally alter the institution of education in the United States. Unions are hard pressed to come up with credible alternatives.

The next generation of labor relations also faces the problem of making schools effective places for learning. This means that labor, management, and the public must come to terms with a vastly broadened scope of interaction between organized teachers and their employers. Part of the compact that surrounds existing collective bargaining is an assertion that it is possible to cleave between the teachers' legitimate interests in their salaries and working conditions on the one hand and the educational policies of the school district on the other. Elaborate restrictions in the scope of bargaining were supposed to segregate bargaining from school policy.

Of course, nothing of the kind happened. Even in the most restrictive scope of bargaining, establishing the wage-and-salary schedule, transfer policy, and class size for a school district effectively accounts for the allocation of as much as 90 percent of the school's operating budget.

Savvy administrators and union leaders recognized this fact and developed side agreements. Some actually helped one another. But the explicit involvement of unions in school management, and the expectation that such involvement was a central role of unions, not a social service they performed for their members, was not publicly recognized until recently.

Finally, unions face the problem of redefining teaching as a profession. The next decade represents a unique opportunity that the grand hope that a teaching profession can be created will triumph over the grand illusion that one already exists. This decade's teaching-reform movement presages the organizational reform movement of the next. Moreover, it is now recognized that professionals can be employed for wages. Lawyers and physicians more and more commonly belong to large firms that face analogous problems in the clash between professional and bureaucratic authority systems.

For unions, solving the professionalism question means more than muscling control over state teacher-certification boards or winning a chair at the table where the national examination will be drafted. It requires that unions look seriously at the set of policies and practices that define teaching work within school districts. How is employed professionalism defined in school sites? What responsibility are teachers willing to take to define and enforce their own standards? What relationship does the union have to the behavior of teachers in the workplace?

The responses of the unions and management to these issues will significantly influence the shape of teaching in the next decade. As it is currently emerging, the increased involvement of unions in the determination of educational policy will place teachers in roles of greater responsibility: for the public's perception of their status, for the redefinition of their own work, and for the worth of their schools.

From Charles T. Kerchner, ''A 'New Generation' of Teacher Unions,'' *Education Week*, VII (17):36, 30, January 20, 1988. Copyright © 1988 Editorial Projects in Education, Washington, DC.

■ Questions for Discussion

1. What are the major differences between the NEA and the AFT?
2. What are some of the benefits of union membership? Why?
3. Why has there been a decline in the number of strikes in the last few years?
4. What are some of the reasons that have brought about the recent changes in the approaches used in labor relations by teachers and administrators?
5. Would a merger of the NEA and the AFT be advantageous to teachers? Would it be advantageous to society?

■ Notes

1. Blake Rodman, "NEA, AFT Affiliates Pondering Merger in California," *Education Week* Vol. VII, No. 17, January 20, 1988, p. 5.
2. Ibid.
3. Chicago Teachers Union, *Local No. 1 v. Hudson* (1986).
4. American Federation of Teachers, *Bill of Rights* (Washington, D.C.: American Federation of Teachers).

■ Selected References

American Association of School Administrators. *Challenges for School Leaders*. Arlington, VA: American Association of School Administrators, 1988.

American Federation of Teachers. *Constitution of the American Federation of Teachers, AFL–CIO 1986*. Washington, D.C.: American Federation of Teachers.

American Federation of Teachers. *The AFT vs. the NEA*. Washington, D.C.: American Federation of Teachers.

Kerchner, Charles T. "Teacher Professionalism through Labor Relations," *Policy Briefs*. San Francisco, CA: Far West Laboratory for Educational Research and Development, 1986.

Kirst, Michael M. *Who Controls Our Schools?* Stanford, CA: Stanford Alumni Association, 1984.

Kirst, Michael W. "Who Should Control Our Schools?" *NEA Today Special Edition* Vol. 6, no. 6 (January 1988):74–79.

Mitchell, Douglas E. "A New Approach to Collective Bargaining," *Policy Briefs*. San Francisco, CA: Far West Laboratory for Educational Research and Development, 1985.

National Education Association. *NEA Handbook 87–88*. Washington, D.C.: National Education Association, 1987.

Ornstein, Allan and Levine, Daniel U. *An Introduction to the Foundations of Education*. Boston: Houghton Mifflin Company, 1985.

Travers, Paul D. and Rebore, Ronald W. *Foundations of Education: Becoming a Teacher*. Englewood Cliffs, NJ: Prentice-Hall Inc., 1987.

Section 3

The Role of Education in the United States

The recent series of national reports dealing with education, including *The Nation at Risk,* have once again helped initiate a reexamination of the role of education in the United States. This section of the book explores education's role from sociological, historical, and philosophical points of view.

American society is a reflection of our representative form of government, and as such, it professes the ideal precepts of a democracy. The basis of these ideals is freedom: freedom of expression, freedom of opportunity, and the freedom of the people to determine their own destinies. A high premium is placed on the worth of the individual and his or her opportunities for education. A major function of education in a democracy is to develop individuals to their fullest capacities so that they in turn may contribute to the achievement of a democratic society's ideals.

Society's expectations for education are numerous, but among them two readily recognized goals come to the fore: the perpetuation of certain knowledge elements of our culture, and the refinement of our actual ways of living to cause them to become more congruent with our ideals. The second of these gives rise to expectations for the schools to be instrumental in resolving some of our social problems.

Individual expectations for education are also numerous. All Americans, in their own individual ways, have ideas of what they want the schools to do for them and for their children. Their expression of these expectations is reflected by our school programs. Individual voices join to form societal choruses to be heard by those who are charged with directing education. While the size and complexities of our society make it increasingly difficult for the individual to be heard, our form of government and our educational systems are committed to the protection of the right of individuals to be heard.

One aspect of sociology discussed in chapter 9 deals with the social problems which impact our schools. Students bring these social problems with them into our classrooms. Teachers must understand problems such as poverty, violence, drug abuse, teenage pregnancy, child abuse, AIDS, illiteracy, and prejudice if our students are to be well served.

Historically, expectations for education have changed as our nation has evolved. Generally, our educational system has responded to the demands of individuals and to the demands of society, but, in the future, the needs of individuals and of society are not likely to be met by schools that take merely a reflective or responsive posture. The schools must assume a leadership stance.

Individuals from all walks of life hold beliefs about education. Philosophers, scholars, professional educators, and lay citizens in either a very formal or informal way function from a set of beliefs about the basic purposes of education, including what should be taught and the methodologies of instruction. These beliefs have had a powerful influence on education and will continue to do so in the future. The last chapter in this section provides a brief introduction to the relationship of beliefs, or philosophies, to American education.

Chapter 8

Education's Purpose in Our Society

Objectives

After studying this chapter, you should be able to:

- List a variety of expectations that Americans hold for their schools.

- Explain the nature of culture, subcultures, and the concept of cultural pluralism.

- Discuss values, and raise questions about the values that schools should transmit.

- List and critique the relationships of many activities that have been relegated to the schools over the years.

- Analyze the question of whether our schools should transmit, respond, or lead in our society.

- Discuss goals and priorities of American education.

- Analyze the status of public confidence in our schools and discuss ways to restore this confidence.

Enrichment Experiences

The following activities will help you learn more about some of the important topics discussed in this chapter:

- Gather and analyze demographic and sociological data in the area of the institution that you attend, looking specifically for cultural diversity.

- Devise a questionnaire designed to secure societal expectations for schools and use it to interview individuals selected in a random fashion.

- Think about what purposes you believe our schools should serve in our society.

- Invite persons of differing cultural backgrounds and different socioeconomic group levels to your class to gain their perceptions of American education.

- Visit a vocational school in your geographical area to better understand the work done there.

- Study and evaluate any recent national report on education.

O ur schools are expected to serve our society. Therefore, teachers should clearly understand what our society expects of our school system. Since you are considering a teaching career, this chapter will help you begin to explore education's purpose in our society. General topics discussed in this chapter include transmission of culture, education for democracy, pluralism and values, social class structure, increasing demands on our schools, parental and pupil expectations, our schools' attempt to increase public confidence in our educational system, the importance of education to our industrial complex, education for citizenship, our schools' responsibility in Americanizing immigrants, education for personal growth, as well as a philosophical discussion about the roles the schools might play in our society. This chapter concludes with a thought-provoking point of view entitled "Schools and Democratic Values." We sincerely believe and hope that you will find this chapter useful in your study of the American school system. ∎

Each American has her/his own individual expectations of our school system. Collectively, Americans expect many things from schools. Most of these, however, can be grouped into two major categories: (1) the transmission of culture, and (2) helping to solve our social problems.

■ Transmission of Culture

Culture may be defined as the ways of living that societies have developed as their members have encountered and interacted with themselves and their environment. As such it includes knowledge, beliefs, arts, morals, values, laws, languages, tools, institutions, and ideas. Every individual is cultured—has a way of living; however, rarely, if ever, would one know the complete culture of one's own society. For example, while most citizens of the United States enjoy and use plumbing facilities, they do not have the specialized knowledge of plumbers. Nor do most citizens have a complete knowledge of medicine, yet they benefit from its advanced state in our culture. Individuals learn the culture of their societies beginning at infancy; much of it they gain from imitation and by osmosis. With maturity, individuals consciously or unconsciously choose for their purposes that which they value from the dominant culture.

The United States, because of its multiethnic origins, contains many subcultures. Most large cities have neighborhoods which reflect immigrant cultures. These neighborhoods feature the foods, arts, and handicrafts of the ancestoral backgrounds of the inhabitants.

Frequently, the neighborhood residents sponsor festivals featuring facets of their ethnic culture. Cultural elements with a distinct uniqueness also develop in geographic regions of our nation, and in the rural, suburban, and urban demographic groups. From these fertile milieus, which have been accumulating, admixing, and altering for the past three and one-half centuries, Americans seek to identify the uniqueness of their total culture.

Culture is a human production, and man differs from animals because he creates culture, and because he transmits what he has learned and what he has created from one generation to the next.

Robert J. Havighurst

Learning to read is a necessary early step toward inculturation.

Schools in our society have been given the responsibility of transmitting culture. They are expected by the citizenry to accomplish this task. What shall they transmit? While a clear and specific answer to this question cannot be given, history has provided some guidelines.

There is little question that the schools are expected to transmit knowledge. Historically, in our early colonies, this meant to teach the young to read, write, and cipher, using the Bible as the basic textbook. As the colonies grew and became a nation and the westward movement began, knowledge came to include vocational skills necessary for our growth. During these periods, the secondary schools came into existence, partly in recognition of the added knowledge necessary to foster the development of our growing nation. Today, one need look only at the curriculum of a modern secondary school to realize that *knowledge* has become an increasingly comprehensive term. It still represents reading, writing, and ciphering, but it also represents social studies, biological and physical science, agriculture, home economics, industrial education, languages, business, art, and a multitude of other specialties ranging from automobile body repair to contract bridge.

The "knowledge explosion" has caused many educators to seriously consider what knowledge the school should transmit. It is obvious that in the amount of time customarily dedicated to formal schooling, only a small portion of the total knowledge that humanity now possesses can be passed on to the student. If one could conceptualize knowledge as being of a material nature, such as books, and then try to imagine the size of the mountain it would make, the immensity of the task can be partly realized. Selectivity is necessary as decisions are made regarding which portions of the total knowledge available are to be transmitted by the schools. Americans seem to have said: first of all, let us make certain that each individual is required to learn what knowledge is necessary for one's survival in our society; secondly, let us permit individuals to determine what they want to learn that will assist themselves and perhaps, incidentally, advance our society; and thirdly, let us plan and hope that in the process, skills will be mastered to foster and enhance the development of more knowledge to the betterment of our way of life. So certain parts of

Research Finding

7

Belief in the value of hard work, the importance of personal responsibility, and the importance of education itself contributes to greater success in school.

The ideals that children hold have important implications for their school experiences. Children who believe in the value of hard work and responsibility and who attach importance to education are likely to have higher academic achievement and fewer disciplinary problems than those who do not have these ideals. They are also less likely to drop out of school. Such children are more likely to use their out-of-school time in ways that reinforce learning. For example, high school students who believe in hard work, responsibility, and the value of education spend about 3 more hours a week on homework than do other students. This is a

significant difference since the average student spends only about 5 hours a week doing homework.

Parents can improve their children's chances for success by emphasizing the importance of education, hard work, and responsibility, and by encouraging their children's friendships with peers who have similar values.

Ginsburg, A., and Hanson, S. (1985). *Values and Educational Success Among Disadvantaged Students.* Final Report to the U.S. Department of Education, Washington, D.C.

Hanson, S., and Ginsburg, A. (1985). *Gaining Ground: Values and High School Success.* Final Report to the U.S. Department of Education, Washington, D.C.

Stevenson, H. W., Lee, S., and Stigler, J. W. (February 1986). "Mathematics Achievement of Chinese, Japanese, and American Children." *Science,* Vol. 231, pp. 293–699.

Source: *What Works: Research About Teaching and Learning.* Washington, DC: U.S. Department of Education, 1987, page 15.

the "mountain" are parcelled out to all young people, after which they can select some more if they want to, while the mountain gets larger and larger simultaneously.

Knowledge transmission, through the American school system, has undoubtedly contributed to the relatively high leadership position of the United States in materialistic manifestations of cultural accomplishments. Our standard of living is closely related to the United States' commitment of knowledge for all citizens through public education. Level of education is definitely a fourth variable in the land, labor, and capital economic formula.

A second traditionally accepted responsibility of the schools in terms of cultural transmission is that of citizenship education. The schools are expected to, and do, make efforts to enable children to appreciate and understand our system of government. An educated citizenry is one that not only has knowledge, but one that is composed of individuals who will use this knowledge to foster an effective scheme of government, of, by, and for the people. In addition to formal instruction in our schools, youngsters also learn about good citizenship by participating in various forms of student government simulating our local,

Because our schools help shape the mind and character of our youth, the strength or weakness of our educational system today will go far to determine the strength or weakness of our national wisdom and our national morality tomorrow. That is why it is essential to our nation that we have good schools. And their quality depends on all of us.

Dwight D. Eisenhower

state, and national systems. Student councils, mock elections, and student government days are examples of these activities. While specific societal expectations for citizenship education will vary, perhaps from blind indoctrination to the advocacy of laissez-faire behavior, the most common position of the schools has been that of enabling mature students to critically analyze, and then to participate in improving our system.

Our overall society has prescribed democratic ideals—ideals toward which our society is striving, and which the schools are expected to exemplify, practice, and teach. A democratic society places a high premium on the worth of the individual.

In citizenship education, the schools are expected to bring about a congruency between American ideals and real life circumstances. Some of the dissension apparent in young people today can be attributed to this lack of congruency. Students seem to be saying, "Your actions speak so loudly that I can't hear your words." They have accused the older generations of professing peace and practicing war, espousing equality of opportunity and perpetuating inequality, and advocating participation in political and school decision making while at the same time castigating those who would dare raise a dissenting voice. Some persons seem to have lost faith in the American system, advocating its destruction, while still others strive to work from within to improve it. Schools today, particularly at the levels of secondary and higher education, in response to student dissent and protest, are changing their traditional ways of participatory student citizenship education.

While American society in general recognizes the necessity of, and subscribes rather unanimously to, the transmission of knowledge and training for citizenship in our schools, the unanimity begins to fragment as subcultural elements are considered. The influence of community subcultures can be observed as local schools decide what they shall teach. The increase of Afro-American studies in many urban schools is indicative of this phenomenon.

■ Education for Democracy

Many Americans are concerned that our young people are not learning enough about our democratic values. They fear that we have come to take democracy for granted and that, unless the schools devote more attention to instruction in democratic ideals, our society will suffer. The American Federation of Teachers recently sponsored a project involving a wide range of organizations, to improve our schools' curriculum concerning democracy. According to this project, fewer than twenty states require high school students to study history and our government in order to graduate. This document states "the basic ideas of liberty, equality, and justice, of civil, political, and economic rights and obligations are all assertions of right and wrong, or moral values." The document goes on to state "it is absurd to argue that the state or its schools cannot be concerned with citizens' ability to discern between right and wrong."

The final report which grew out of this project is entitled "Education for Democracy" and specifically recommends:[1]

• A more "substantial, engaging, and demanding" social studies curriculum that includes the history of the United States and democratic civilization, and the in-depth study of world geography and at least one non-Western society.

- School curricula with history and geography at their core.
- More history, chronologically taught, with the central theme being "the dramatic struggle" of people to obtain their freedom.
- More attention to world studies, particularly the "realistic and unsentimental" study of both democratic and nondemocratic nations.
- Broader and deeper instruction in the humanities, particularly in literature, biography, and ideas.

■ Pluralism and Values

As has been indicated, America is a pluralistic society consisting of many different subsocieties. This is a result not only of our multiethnic origin, but also of our emphasis on the protection and enhancement of individual freedoms, as specified in the United States Constitution and as practiced in our daily life. Thus, the democratic form of government fosters pluralism. Gans has suggested that American democracy needs to be modernized so as to accommodate itself to pluralism.

> I believe that the time has come to modernize American democracy and adapt it to the needs of a pluralistic society; in short, to create a pluralistic democracy. A pluralistic form of democracy would not do away with majority rule, but would require systems of proposing and disposing which take the needs of minorities into consideration, so that when majority rule has serious negative consequences, outvoted minorities would be able to achieve their most important demands, and not be forced to accept tokenism, or resort to despair or disruption.

Pluralistic democracy would allow the innumerable minorities of which America is made up to live together and share the country's resources more equitably, with full recognition of their various diversities. Legislation and appropriations would be based on the principle of "live and let live" with different programs of action for different groups whenever consensus is impossible. Groups of minorities could still coalesce into a majority, but other minorities would be able to choose their own ways of using public power and funds without being punished for it by a majority.[2]

The National Coalition for Cultural Pluralism, a newly formed group, has issued the following statement calling for action to help bring about a truly multicultural society:

> America has long been a country whose uniqueness and vitality have resulted in large part from its human diversity. However, among all the resources formerly and currently used to insure physical and social progress for this nation, the human resource with its myriad ethnic, cultural, and racial varieties has not been used to its fullest advantage. As a result, the American image that has been delineated by its governmental, corporate, and social structures has not truly reflected the cultural diversity of its people.
>
> There should be no doubt in anyone's mind that America is now engaged in an internal social revolution that will thoroughly test her national policies and attitudes regarding human differences. This revolution manifests itself in many ways, through many movements. Blacks, Spanish Americans, women, college students, elderly people, etc., are all finding themselves victimized by technological and social systems which look upon significant differences among people as unhealthy and inefficient. But,

whether the society likes it or not, many individuals and groups will never be able to "melt" into the American "pot." And it is these groups who are now gearing themselves up to be more self-determining about their own destinies. For them it is a simple matter of survival in America.

In the future, surviving in America will of necessity be the major concern of every citizen, regardless of his wealth, heritage, race, sex, or age. This has already been made abundantly clear by the developing crisis in ecology. The national concern over pollution, overpopulation, etc., will probably be solved through our technological expertise. But the social crisis facing this country will require a different solution concept, one which will provide unity with diversity where the emphasis is on a shared concern for creating and maintaining a multicultural environment.

The concept of cultural pluralism, therefore, must be the perspective used by the different social groups in their attempt to survive as independent, yet interdependent, segments of this society. Pluralism lifts up the necessary and creative tension between similarity and difference. It strongly endorses standards of variety, authentic options, diverse centers of power, and self-direction.

It is the institutions of our society which provide the supports for some individual and group attitudes, values, and standards which, when applied, are clearly discriminatory against others. It is these same institutions which can reverse many of the current social trends by establishing supports for a culturally pluralistic society—where everyone recognizes that no single set of values and standards is sufficient to inspire the full range of human possibilities.

The creation of a truly multicultural society will not happen automatically. There must be established a plan of action, a leadership, and a

cadre of supporters that will effectively implement the concept of cultural pluralism throughout the length and breadth of every community in America. Institutions, groups, and individuals must be actively engaged in working toward at least three goals, which are:

• The elimination of all structural supports for oppressive and racist practices by individuals, groups, and institutions.
• The dispersal of "power" among groups and within institutions on the basis of cultural, social, racial, sexual, and economic parity.
• The establishment and promotion of collaboration as the best mechanism for enabling culturally independent groups to function cooperatively within a multicultural environment.

The accomplishment of these and other goals can be facilitated only through a national effort. Therefore, the emergence of the National Coalition for Cultural Pluralism is an important first step in the right direction. . . .[3] (From Madelon D. Stent, William R. Hazard, and Harry N. Rivlin, *Cultural Pluralism in Education.* Copyright © 1973 Fordham University. Reprinted by permission of Prentice-Hall, Inc., Englewood Cliffs, NJ.)

The fostering of pluralism encourages the perpetuation and development of many different value systems. What are values? Phenix has recognized two distinct meanings of the term *values:* ". . . a value is anything which a person or persons actually approve, desire, affirm, or expect themselves to obtain, preserve, or assist. According to the second meaning, a value is anything which *ought to be* approved, desired, and so forth, whether or not any given person or persons in fact do adopt these positive attitudes

Of all the work that is done or that can be done for our country, the greatest is that of educating the body, the mind, and above all the character, giving spiritual and moral training to those who in a few years are themselves to decide the destinies of the nation.

Theodore Roosevelt

toward it."[4] Schools must be concerned with both definitions—they operate in "what is" and are expected to create "what ought to be," and have some difficulty being certain of the values in either case. The United States Constitution has set forth some values, and a body of case law seeks to define them. What of issues not so clearly defined? What, for example, are the value preferences of different groups of people regarding honesty, cleanliness, manners, loyalty, sexual morality, and punctuality? As one reflects upon this problem, it becomes clear that people cherish different viewpoints. Whose viewpoints should be perpetuated? When must individual freedom be sacrificed to the needs of society? Are there absolute values that must be accepted and adhered to by all for the success and vitality of our society? Or, are values relative in nature depending upon circumstances?

Absolutists believe that there are time-honored *truths,* upon which value systems can be based. These truths are generally thought of as being derived from either God or Nature.

The search for universal values continues while the trend is currently toward relativism. Sorokin has said:

> We live in an age in which no value, from God to private property, is universally accepted. There is no norm, from the Ten Commandments, to contractual rules and those of etiquette, that is universally binding. . . . What one person or group affirms, another denies: what one pressure group extols, another vilifies. . . . Hence the mental, moral, religious, social, economic and political anarchy that pervades our life and culture. . . .[5]

Yet, it seems that if we are to survive in a pluralistic society some agreement on major or superordinate values must be reached. Further,

these values must then be learned by children of that society. Such a system would certainly not preclude the holding of different values so long as they did not conflict with the overall values.

The task of the schools in doing their part in educating youth for citizenship in pluralistic urban America is both complex and immense.

■ Our Shrinking Middle Class

Not many years ago, most Americans belonged to the middle class. There were relatively few very rich people and by the same token not very many extremely poor people in our society. In recent years, this picture has changed considerably. We are rapidly becoming a society made up of either very rich or very poor people.

One statistic to substantiate this claim is that the wealthiest 40 percent of the American families earn almost 70 percent of the national income. By the same token, the poorest 40 percent of Americans earn only 16 percent of the income. The middle 20 percent of Americans earn only 17 percent of our national income. An increasing number of American families are earning very large incomes. The number of millionaires in America is rising very rapidly. This is due in part to the fact that the executive group of Americans is expanding rapidly and providing an increasing number of our citizens with very high salaries.

Unfortunately, other statistics show that an ever increasing percentage of our citizens are living in poverty. Already an estimated 20 percent of our children live below the poverty line. Also, the high divorce rate has caused formerly middle class women to lose considerable income and slip into the lower class. A divorced woman typically loses 73 percent of her disposable income.

Greeting his pupils, the master asked: "What would you learn of me? And the reply came: How shall we care for our bodies? How shall we rear our children? How shall we work together? How shall we live with our fellowmen? How shall we play? For what ends shall we live?" . . . And the teacher pondered these words, and sorrow was in his heart, for his own learning touched not these things.

Chapman and Counts

Yet another indication of this changing phenomena is the realization that not many years ago the typical teacher would be placed in the middle or even upper middle socioeconomic class. Today, the typical teacher is placed in the lower middle class or, in some instances, even the lower class of our society.

■ Increasing Demands on Our Schools

Nearly half a century has passed since Chapman and Counts submitted the above dialogue, which illustrates individual learning needs and desires for other than book learning. How well have we done in meeting such individual learning needs? Daily newspapers yield indications that these learning needs have not as yet been satisfactorily met. During the decade of the sixties, the criticism of irrelevance was leveled against existing operations of the schools. The eighties have shown the American experiment struggling for survival in an era marked by misplaced loyalties in the political realm, by deprivation and material scarcities, by high crime rates, and by a myriad of other urgent human problems. It seems likely that today's pupils would respond to the master's question in much the same way that pupils responded half a century ago.

One challenge for today's teachers assisting their pupils in finding individual answers to such questions lies in keeping abreast of the times. Pupils prefer those teachers who possess current knowledge, who have an outlook on life that goes beyond the knowledge domain, and who demonstrate attitudes that are flexible to the stresses of the times. Consider just one of the pupils' questions—How shall we rear our children? During the last half century the answers to that question

have been dealt with primarily within the home. Since the family unit served as the general environment within which to raise children, the schools were not expected to be deeply involved with the question of rearing children.

It has been suggested that recent social changes—including more women in the work force, fewer of relatives living in the household, and greater geographic mobility of families—have combined to make the family a less effective environment within which to raise children.[6] These changes in the family are directly related to changes in the ways children are raised today. However, many teachers obtained their knowledge and attitudes regarding the rearing of children within the traditional family setting. Therefore, some teachers are still likely to feel that the family should be the agent for providing child-rearing knowledge. But, *if* the family setting today is truly a less effective agent in rearing children than when our teachers were raised, then such teachers are likely to have difficulty accepting contemporary attitudes regarding the basic question—How shall we rear our children?

During the past half century the schools have adjusted in many ways to the shift of many former family responsibilities onto the school. Teachers have inherited many of the responsibilities formerly reserved for the home. Today's schools and teachers are very much expected to be involved with various responsibilities related to rearing children. A significant aspect of the operations of the schools deals with pupil personnel services, including health and dental care, sex education, guidance, discipline, manners, and codes of dress. Increasing emphasis is being placed on early childhood education. Some programs propose parental involvement extended as far back as prenatal care. At the same time, much attention is

Democratic nations care little for what has been, but are haunted by visions of what will be; in this direction their unbound imagination grows and dilates beyond all measure. . . . Democracy, which shuts the past against the poet, opens the future before him.

Alexis de Tocqueville

being directed toward the adult and continuing education aspect which stresses education as a lifelong process.

Educators are now questioning—Where does all this end? Who decides what the limits are? What are or should be the actual responsibilities of the teacher in this regard? Our schools have made valiant strides in attempting to meet the various student needs that were formerly within the province of the family household. *By high school age, many of today's pupils are sophisticated enough to be able to determine their own unique needs, and the schools should be flexible enough to meet individual needs regarding things other than subject matter.* Perhaps the most relevant questions are those that ask individuals what it is that *they* desire or need assistance with as related to their own individual health, sex education, guidance, or manners.

Many other persistent needs exist that pupils expect their education to satisfy, whatever the societal setting. The task of the teacher becomes that of constantly examining the ways in which individual expectations can be satisfied within the framework of the school system that has been typically group oriented (primary attention given to societal needs). The current acceptance of the interaction of societal and individual needs is a recent development that has generated new excitement within the school setting as related to individual needs. The general axiom that new teachers tend to teach as they have been taught needs careful examination in light of increased emphasis on individual expectations with regard to education. Teachers, particularly new teachers, must find the appropriate means for directing knowledge and understanding gained from their own educational experiences toward the individual expectations their pupils have regarding their own education.

■ Parental and Pupil Expectations

Both parents and pupils expect the schools to satisfy a wide variety of individual needs. When parents and pupils are asked "What are the most important reasons for going to school?" their responses concur, for the most part, with the major societal expectations of the schools as previously discussed. For example, pupils of all ages are quick to suggest that intellectual development is the highest expectation within their educational experiences. Likewise, individuals expect the schools to provide meaningful school experiences with regard to citizenship, personality, vocational training, recreation, and health.

■ Reduced Public Confidence

Parents have historically felt that the public schools provided their children with the essential ingredients for a successful life. Unfortunately, this public confidence in our schools has gradually dwindled in recent years.

This change is reflected in the 1987 Gallup Poll of the Public Attitudes Toward the Public Schools, which asked:

> Students are often given the grades A, B, C, D, and FAIL to denote the quality of their work. Suppose the *public* schools, themselves, in this community, were graded in the same way. What grade would you give the public schools here— A, B, C, D, or FAIL?[7]

In 1974, 18 percent awarded the schools an A, but in 1987, only 12 percent did so. By the same token, in 1974 only 6 percent gave the schools a D, but the percentage offering this grade rose to 9 in 1987.

. . . Democracy is always weakened from within. Only its own feebleness or complacency destroys it. We in Europe see more clearly than you that democracy dies from lack of discipline, unwillingness to compromise, group pressure, corruption, usurpation of public power because the public is greedy or indifferent. It dies unless it draws life from every citizen. . . . .

A statement from Czechoslovakia published in the New York Times, September 25, 1937.

■ Attempts to Improve Public Confidence

Educators and others who place a high value on education are naturally concerned about public confidence in our schools. Indeed, the future of our public schools is dependent upon public confidence. The public is not likely to be willing to financially support a school system in which it does not have confidence.

The critical question for those who believe in our public school system then becomes: How can public confidence in our public education system be improved? Some argue this can best be done by raising standards; others suggest improving efficiency and thus reducing costs; still others argue for better teachers; others insist on a clarification of national educational goals. Many educators hope that the attention focused on education by *A Nation at Risk* and other similar reports will produce changes that will help restore public confidence in our educational system.

Actually, no one has yet demonstrated just how public confidence in our schools can be improved. While many are concerned about the problem, and many are attempting to do something about it, only time will answer this difficult question.

■ Industry's Interest in Education

Increasingly, large industries are making business decisions based, at least in part, on the quality of schools. The idea is that corporations wish to locate their factories in areas that are served by good educational facilities. Corporate leaders see education as a very important cornerstone to the foundations necessary for business success. The workers in a factory are more inclined to be available and happy if good schools are nearby to serve their children. Also, industry likes to draw their work force from a well-educated population so that they will not have to spend their own resources remediating the results of poor education. Corporations spend literally tens of billions of dollars on training programs for their employees and they realize that a poor educational system adds to those industrial costs.

A recent survey of the factors that influence business decisions was conducted by the accounting firm of Grant Thornton. They determined that the quality of education available in the area is a very important factor in corporate business decisions. It ranked, for instance, ahead of energy costs, taxes, cost of living, and health care costs in importance. Only wages, unionization, and availability of work force ranked higher than the importance of education when it comes to corporate business location decisions.

Communities and states should work hard to provide excellent education if they are interested in attracting business development in their geographical areas.

■ Education for Citizenship

One of the functions ascribed to the public schools has been that of helping students become "good citizens." Parents, board of education members, school administrators, teachers, and legislators have given much attention to citizenship as a dimension of an individual's education. Most states have laws which direct the schools to engage in specific teaching tasks aimed at developing citizenship behavior in students. For example, an Illinois law states that every public school teacher shall teach the pupils honesty, kindness, justice, and moral courage for the purpose of lessening crime and raising the standard of good citizenship. Implied in this law is that honesty, kindness, justice, and moral courage are criteria for lessening crime and, therefore, contribute to the promotion of good citizenship. Terms such as honesty, kindness, justice, and moral courage are not only difficult to define, but are also difficult to teach within the school setting. In spite of such difficulties, schools (that is, teachers) are expected to accept the challenge of providing individual pupils with learning experiences which will help each of them to develop alternatives for solving the moral problems of life. The schools are also expected to help enable youth to understand the desirability of being kind and just individuals even if some adults they know are unkind and unjust. Individual moral courage, while an admirable attribute of character, and important to citizenship, is difficult to teach in a formalized school setting.

Teaching as related to these aspects of good citizenship draws heavily from an idealistic premise that charges teachers to serve as models in their manner of participation as citizens. Likewise, this idealistic approach draws heavily upon the character analysis of great citizens past and present.

Since the early 1930s the American public schools have also been charged with the responsibility for developing other aspects of citizenship. American patriotism, the principles of representative government as enunciated in the American Declaration of Independence, and the Constitution of the United States of America have been emphasized in citizenship training. For many years, teachers have taught that all citizens should demonstrate their patriotism by serving their country in peace as well as in war, by respecting the United States flag, and by voting in elections. A kind of nationalistic idealism was assumed when good citizenship was taught in this manner. This form of idealism seemingly held true in an era when our society was closer knit, less complex, and agrarian oriented. Many living Americans coming from this heritage continue to operate from such a basis of idealism, not cognizant of the conflicts resulting from the impersonal, complex, and multigroup influences of the contemporary, urban, pluralistic, machine-oriented society. Our younger people tend to utilize bold dramatic methods in their desire to be heard, whereas older people believe the way to be heard is through more traditional procedures. In the reality of today, when one pursues the traditional channels of expression, that person is frequently overwhelmed by the massiveness and complexity of our contemporary society. With all of our technological sophistication, communication problems are still manifest among us. A small voice is practically unheard, and a letter to an elected governmental representative is likely to be of minor importance in and of itself. Thus, an increasing number of young people seem to find it necessary to pool their efforts for the purposes of being heard.

One's attitudinal development is considerably influenced by the person's environment, including the influences of various societal institutions. In turn, an individual's attitudes and values influence that person's behavior. Each individual is ultimately privately responsible for determining what his or her citizenship behavior shall be. The individual elects to vote or not, to violently protest or not, to accept normative standards or not. Notwithstanding these many influences upon an individual, as a participatory citizen, that individual eventually stands alone and practices the act of citizenship in his or her own unique way.

■ Americanizing Recent Immigrants

America is known as the land of immigrants. Almost all of us had ancestors who immigrated to this new land. Many people do not realize that immigrants continue to move to the United States in huge numbers. Figure 8.1 provides a great deal of information about the wave of recent immigrants who have come to the United States. This figure shows that there have been three great waves of immigration. The first was during the middle 1800s when approximately five million Europeans moved to our new land. The second wave took place from about 1901 to 1921, during which time over 15 million people, mostly Europeans, came to the United States.

Between 1970 and today, approximately 9.5 million legal immigrants as well as an estimated

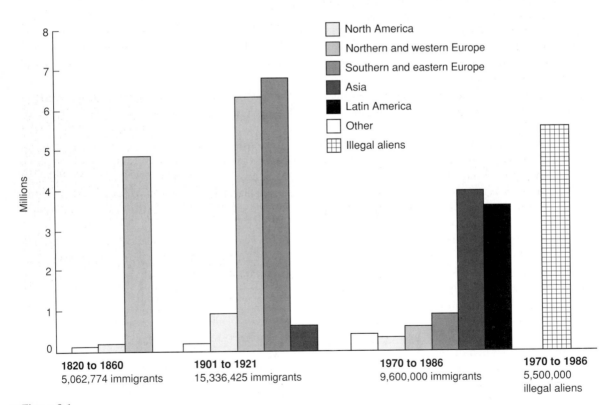

■ **Figure 8.1**

Waves of immigration

Sources: Population Reference Bureau, Bureau of the Census, and Immigration and Naturalization Service.

All youth need to develop salable skills and those understandings and attitudes that make the worker an intelligent and productive participant in economic life.

Education Policies Commission
Education for All American Youth
(Washington, D.C.: National
Education Association, 1944), p. 26.

5.5 million illegal aliens have moved to our country. This recent group of immigrants, however, for the most part have come from Asia and Latin America. These most recent immigrants have settled in our large cities and in the southwestern parts of the United States. Like their earlier counterparts, they have come seeking a better life and more freedom. Some are very well educated, particularly those from Asia. Often their parents have made great sacrifices so that their children could obtain a good education. Some of these immigrants are in a position to be rather quickly assimilated into our culture, and to become self-supporting, productive citizens over a short period of time.

Unfortunately, many have recently come with very little formal education and no English language skills. Our society looks to our schools to help Americanize this recent wave of immigrants. These students present an enormous challenge to our public school system.

Another unusual feature is the fact that many recent immigrants are in our country illegally. Figure 8.1 shows this number to be estimated at 5.5 million people. The bulk of these illegal aliens have come from Latin America, most notably Mexico. The United States government recently passed an amnesty law which allows many illegal immigrants to become legal citizens over a period of time. Our courts have determined that our schools must also serve the children of illegal immigrants.

Experts believe that this recent wave of immigrants is changing the face of America in a permanent way. Our schools, these experts believe, will face a major challenge in helping to inculcate this flood of new immigrants into the American society.

■ Education for Personal Growth

Individuals are unique with regard to personality. In fact, no two personalities are exactly alike. One's *personality* is considered to be the habitual patterns and qualities of behavior as expressed by physical and mental activities and attitudes, and also the distinctive individual qualities of a person considered collectively.

Many differing experiences affect the personality development of an individual. Since the experiences of life vary among individuals, it follows that personalities also differ among individuals. Behavioral scientists have observed that, in

Children bring many different values and cultural heritages with them to school.

addition to the influences of heredity, similar personality characteristics in individuals are related to the similarities of life experiences of the individuals. In essence, this line of reasoning assumes that personality characteristics are learned from experience. Thus, particularly with peers, school experiences do in fact contribute to the development of one's personality. One's peer group identity and experiences with the peer group are strong influences on that individual's personality development. Therefore, it appears to be a reasonable expectation of parents that schools should provide experiences that will enhance the personality development of their children. As pupils mature, they become increasingly aware of many dimensions of their own personality and often select activities and courses that they believe will help develop their personality.

Such biological qualities as age, sex, stature, and pigmentation also influence one's personality. Various ethnic and racial groups influence the behavior patterns of their young through the sharing of similar experiences. Characteristics of an individual's personality are in part reflections of the individual's age group, sex group, and racial group. One's behavior is partially adjusted to the forces of these impinging biological qualities.

An individual's behavior is affected by the total impact of that person's life experiences. Heredity and environment interact to make each individual a distinct and unique person.

■ Should the Schools Transmit, Respond or Lead?

What should be the posture of the school in American society? Historically, and into the present, schools have been responsible for the transmission of culture. In this role, as has been indicated, they have assumed a passive and reflective posture. What society deemed as being the "good" of the past and that which is worth preserving, even if not utilitarian or relevant, was presented to children in school for their use and for posterity. In many schools today, transmission is still the primary goal. However, schools have also added another role, a different posture: that of *responding*. As society changes, and needs are recognized in society that can be fulfilled by the school, the school responds or adjusts to these needs. For example, as computers were developed and operators were needed, the schools began to train the specialists necessary. Much of the schools' reactions to social problems fall into the response posture. As poverty was recognized as a problem, and children came to school hungry, the schools fed them. A third posture is possible—that of *leading*. In this posture, the schools would strive to achieve the ideal society as it has been envisioned. In this role, the school would act as the agent of change for society, attempting to mold and shape it to desired ends. While schools have not served as initiator, they have been placed in a position of leadership in building an integrated society. It appears that they may be increasingly called upon to take the leadership role. Schools assume all three postures (transmit, respond, lead) in their various responsibilities. The blend of these postures changes as societal expectations change.

■ Summary

That our society expects many things from our schools was illustrated by the content of this chapter. Furthermore, different citizens expect different things from our schools. It is extremely important that teachers understand these many and often conflicting demands that parents and their children place on our schools. Even though a teacher (and likewise a school) cannot possibly fulfill all expectations of all the citizens, it is important for prospective teachers to understand what society thinks about the role of education in the United States.

The overall expectations that society has for our schools include elements related to the transmission of our culture, to preparing future citizens for an active role in our democratic society, to value and respect cultural pluralism, to understand and fulfill an acceptable role in our social class structure, to educate a citizenry capable of functioning in our increasingly industrial society, to Americanize immigrants, to provide an education that will maximize personal growth, etc. In addition to these global national goals, each local community has its own unique demands upon local school systems. Educators must be responsive to societal expectations if they are to succeed.

Point of View

The following point of view by Ann Bastian is entitled, "Educating for Democracy: Raising Expectations." It offers some thought-provoking ideas about education's purpose in our society.

Teachers often make the mistake of thinking too little about the overall role that our schools are expected to play in our society. While not every citizen has the same expectations for our schools, nevertheless there are fairly clear overall societal expectations that teachers must accommodate. The following point of view should help teachers contemplate the role that schools play in the perpetuation of democratic values.

Educating for Democracy: Raising Expectations

Ann Bastian

When we ask today's teachers to have high expectations for every child, we are asking for more than effective pedagogy. We are asking teachers to fulfill a basic democratic promise of public education. We are asking teachers to act on the principle that every child can learn, every person can contribute to society, every citizen can be empowered by knowledge. High expectations say that everyone has potential, everyone can succeed, everyone counts.

The problem is that teachers and students aren't alone in setting expectations. Teachers aren't the only ones communicating to children what their potentials, choices, and destinies may be. Nor are children the only ones who influence teachers' perceptions about how well they're likely to learn or how far they're likely to go in school.

Messages come from the family, community, and society surrounding the school—and these messages can make it hard for students and teachers to sustain high hopes on their own.

Today, people are paying considerable attention to the impact of home and community inputs—the socialization process—in advancing or retarding school achievement. In fact, an estimated 30 to 50 percent of American children are entering school with levels of deprivation that put them at risk of school failure. The impulse is to look at how we can improve parenting skills, early childhood enrichment programs, and community support systems to reverse these trends. On the whole, this impulse is well-motivated and may generate an infusion of urgently needed resources.

But it is simply not enough to say that cultures of poverty in the inner city—or changing family structures and shifting social values in the suburbs—are responsible for the levels of underachievement that beset our educational system.

Family stress, social alienation, and cultural dislocation do exist across this country. They erode children's aspirations and they challenge the capacity of schools to motivate achievement, *but they do not exist in a vacuum.*

We need to look at the economic context of education as well as family influences and the school experience itself if we are to accurately assess the problem of expectations, to understand the full challenge facing educators, and to appreciate the high stakes for democracy. To put it another way, expectations are determined not only by personal inputs but by probable outcomes.

The growing gap between school and work— between educational aspirations and employment realities—is a crucial influence lowering expectations, achievement, and democratic values in public education today.

Observers across the political spectrum acknowledge that we are experiencing a profound restructuring of the American economy and the labor market that serves it. Some see a new economic miracle emerging from high-tech and high-finance wizardry, despite recent events on Wall Street. Others of us see a different and disquieting picture. The outlook particularly changes if we turn our sights away from the Silicon Valleys and the lifestyles of the rich and famous.

■ **School-to-Work Gap**

When we look at the country as a whole, we cannot miss the startling deterioration of our industrial base, of the urban centers and now aging suburbs. We can't escape the nationwide farm crisis and the disintegration of rural communities. A great many youngsters live in economic environments that will not sustain their futures.

When we look at America's socio-economic ladder, we see rapid mobility at the top, particularly for highly skilled professional-technical employees. At the bottom of the ladder, the incidence of poverty has risen by one-third in the 1980s. Both the yuppies and the homeless are hallmarks of this decade.

In between, in the great American middle class, we find mounting insecurity and stagnation. The economic middle is besieged by multiple pressures: global competition, the export of investment capital, de-industrialization, automation, the repeal of union standards, and the return of "laissez-faire" approaches to government.

When we look to job trends, we find some frightening statistics:

- Job growth is occurring, but largely in the low-skill, low-wage sectors of service and trade. In *The Great American Job Machine,* Barry Bluestone and Bennett Harrison point out that 58 percent of all new jobs created between 1979 and 1984 paid less than $7,000 a year, well below the poverty line.

- Forty percent of the approximately 11.5 million industrial workers displaced by plant closings between 1979 and 1984 have not found new jobs, and of those who have, two-thirds are working at substantially lower wages, according to the U.S. Office of Technology.

- One out of every five jobs in this country is temporary, without basic employee benefits, reports the U.S. Bureau of Labor Statistics (BLS).

- In July 1987, with the nation officially at a 6 percent jobless rate, there were 7.2 million unemployed, 1 million discouraged workers who'd given up the job search, and 5.5 million workers involuntarily working short hours, according to the BLS. Among the jobless, fewer than 30 percent were receiving unemployment compensation.

While specific areas of labor shortage exist, due in part to population cycles, these shortages haven't dramatically altered the dead-end nature of job expansion or significantly raised wages and benefits. If anything, shortages will accelerate the drive for automation or overseas production.

Nor can we count on high-tech industries to bail us out. As Rumberger and Levin point out in their analysis for the Center for Educational Research at Stanford University, high-tech firms will provide only 3 to 8 percent of job growth in the next decade, and high-tech occupations will amount to only 6 percent of all new jobs.

To put it simply, we live in an economic hourglass—a time when the rich are getting richer, the poor are getting poorer, and the middle class is getting squeezed.

Youth are particular victims of these polarizing trends, because they are entering the labor market just as the middle rungs of the ladder are dropping out. Youth unemployment rates are three times the national average. In the inner cities and many rural areas, youth unemployment exceeds 50 percent. The statistics represent millions of low-income and minority youth who will be marginal to the labor force their entire lives. They are victims of both the overall shrinkage of economic opportunity and ongoing patterns of racial discrimination and gender segregation.

Prospects are also dimming for the sons and daughters of working class families. Bluestone and Harrison note that working class youth are moving into the dead-end job sectors at very high rates, while their entry rates into middle and high status employment are declining. Even college-educated youth face tougher odds—over 50 percent of new graduates will enter nonprofessional jobs outside their fields of study. The vast majority of working young adults will not match the comfortable life-styles their parents achieved in an era of U.S. economic supremacy and expansion.

Beyond the barriers to employment and the declining material rewards of work, there is also evidence that many jobs are becoming more de-skilled and alienating. New technology creates an initial increase in skill requirements for some jobs, but it can also produce a reduction in skill requirements for others, especially as mechanization proceeds.

■ Job Alienation

This effect is well-illustrated by the fate of the computer programmer, an occupation that has gone from the glamorous front lines of high technology to the tedious backrooms in 10 short years. In many more cases, computerization and electronic communication will be used to increase the specialization, repetition, and isolation of job duties, rather than expanding job variety, initiative, and interaction.

Moreover, young people may accurately perceive the world of work as personally hostile and de-humanizing. Workplaces are not democratic organizations concerned primarily with human potentials and the inalienable right to the pursuit of happiness. Workplaces are governed by the bottom line of material productivity, usually measured by profit rates or production quotas (even test scores). The overwhelming majority of workplaces operate under a command structure, with hierarchical levels of authority, autonomy, and status, where the Bill of Rights gets about as far as the parking lot.

Of course, unions, where they function to give workers a voice, can promote greater measures of economic democracy. But unions represent less than 20 percent of today's workforce, and they're weakest in the sectors that are most rapidly expanding. And, truth be told, American unions have in too many instances grown hide-bound and defensive. Beset by global competition, employer assault, government hostility, and a changing workforce, the American labor movement has not yet found effective ways of fighting back or of capturing the spirit of a new generation of workers.

Things are not so different on the management side of the fence. Despite a lot of fanfare on the MBA circuit, very few companies have embraced the "quality of work life" (QWL) approach to management, emphasizing worker input and job satisfaction. And very few QWL experiments have gone beyond cosmetic changes in the traditionally autocratic style of American corporate management. Indeed, a number of QWL plans have functioned primarily as union-busting attempts.

What does this picture of the employment future tell American educators? Obviously, a lot of the news is bad, and some of it's going to get worse. On the other hand, the clearer we are about the realities we're up against, the more strategically we can direct our responses.

Reality #1: The polarization of job futures, and the increasingly alienated forms of labor awaiting most students, ostensibly gives lie to the democratic ideals of opportunity and equality we have vested in education.

■ The Squeeze on Schools

We're caught in the bind that education means more for a few, but means less for many in terms of standards of living, meaningful work, social influence, and self-determination. The message that millions of students are getting from the world of work is: learn for what?

Reality #2: The unavoidable result is that, outside of upwardly mobile communities, schools are increasingly hard-pressed to motivate any large portion of their students through career aspiration or the work ethic. The school-to-work gap is growing.

Reality #3: Schools don't have to mirror existing socio-economic conditions; schools don't have to be driven by market imperatives. This is fortunate in light of the first two realities. It's true that schools are never immune from economic influences and never escape the pressure to serve the competitive demands of a stratified economic structure. It's also true that in stressful or uncertain economic times, there will inevitably be a struggle for the soul of schooling—a battle over making education more elitist or more democratic to meet the challenges of the future.

■ Schools and Change

But it's equally true, and important to remember in such times, that our schools are public institutions, supported in the public interest and open to public governance. If we fight to uphold the democratic mission of public education, in the face of anti-democratic economic trends, schools can be countervailing institutions and even springboards for social progress. Schools can provide models of democratic experience that alter our expectations —not only of children's potentials, but of society's potentials as well.

Many of these models are already at hand: in school systems that have successfully integrated, in schools that produce high rates of achievement despite high rates of disadvantage, in schools that bring parents and community members together with teachers to diminish the risks and pressures afflicting youth. The Comer Process, a collaborative effort to re-design the inner-city schools of New Haven, is one outstanding example of how schools can begin to deliver equity with excellence—and transform aspiration along the way. The Committee for Economic Development's *Children in Need* includes case studies of the Comer Process and similar efforts to transform public schools.

We know that democratic schooling can transcend elitist barriers—the real questions are, how do we spread the lessons? Clearly, some of the answers have to come through the political process, from the national agendas we advocate and the kind of leadership we choose. But some of the answers will come from the school reform movement—from inside local schools.

In *Choosing Equality: The Case for Democratic Schooling,* my co-authors and I identified three levels of school improvement that relate educating for democracy to educating for the world of work. These levels could be called: coping with realities, challenging realities, and defining new realities.

At each level there is the underlying premise that we can raise expectations for all students, and for all teachers, if the bottom-line for schooling is empowerment, not employment. As we enter the 21st century, schools should not be training children for a given occupation or a single skill. They should be preparing children to apply knowledge, to solve problems, to make choices, and to participate in setting priorities.

These are the generic skills and disciplines young people need to lead productive lives—as self-directed individuals, as family members and role models, as neighbors and as citizens—regardless of their job status. Not coincidentally, these are also the skills young people need to survive in the world of work, to influence the terms of employment, and to reassess our nation's economic policies.

Response #1: One urgent task for public education is to insure universal literacy, which is the minimal condition for participation in tomorrow's labor market. This means getting resources to illiterate parents as well as to children at risk. It should be clear, however, that basic skills for today's labor market include much more than functional literacy, simple computation, or narrow job training.

Most young people now entering the workforce will have a number of different jobs across their working lives. Technologies will change at an accelerating pace, opportunities will shift across economic sectors, and most specific skills training will occur on the job.

■ Survival Skills

To maximize their chances for survival in a rapidly shifting and diversified job market, students need learning approaches that enhance intellectual as well as vocational flexibility. Students need schooling that emphasizes critical thinking and reasoning capacities, and the ability to interact with peers and teachers in tackling unfamiliar material. Meaningful work experience or vocational preparation programs should be continuously integrated with an academic program. Counseling needs to be holistic too, encouraging personal as well as career development.

This approach may seem like common sense, as the National Commission on Secondary Vocational Education suggests. However, it is not common practice. The rule is to promote narrow vocational training, increasingly in trades or technologies that are obsolete. We have also widely succumbed to early tracking based on presumed labor market destinies, to test-driven and quantifiable curriculums, and to the mastery of highly segmented and specific skills. School counseling, which is chronically under-staffed, offers too little, too late, in too many separate pieces.

Most importantly, we should not forget that the foundation for a decent school-to-work transition is a decent school culture—not just an extra program or a saleable skill. An alien or hostile classroom environment, or an attitude of benign neglect, can be far more destructive than the absence of a computer science program, although computer science is needed too.

Recently, the Council for Economic Development has done outstanding work at the national level to link issues of job readiness with broader school improvement strategies, including teacher empowerment. Opportunities for educators to argue this case will multiply at the state level and should be seized.

The essential point here is that we can raise children's expectations for the future by giving them more than the tools for a specific job. Schools can give students the tools to adapt and advance in the job market, along with the confidence they need to succeed.

■ Economic Literacy

Response #2: I'm an unabashed advocate for totally overhauling the ways we introduce students to the world of work. We need a program for economic literacy built into the social studies core curriculum. The exploration of work should start in the primary grades, when children are fascinated by the mysterious claims of work on the adults around them and understand the intrinsic dignity of all kinds of occupations, apart from salary and status.

By middle school and high school, as students themselves encounter the vocational sorting process, they should be learning how the labor market functions. What determines supply and demand? How are wages and benefits set? What barriers are posed by discrimination, segregation, and stereotyping? How has it changed over the years? Why has it changed?

Students should be learning about options across the entire career cycle, particularly about family–career choices and pressures. Students need first-hand exposure to corporate organization, management techniques, and personnel practices. Students need first-hand exposure to labor rights, union organization, collective bargaining, government regulation, protective legislation, workplace health and safety standards.

The world of work is a world of many conflicts—particularly conflicts over the inequities of wealth, power, health, and security—that accompany our market system. Some of the most important conditions affecting students, their families, and communities have to do with plant closings, farm foreclosures, pay equity and comparable worth, job tenure, workplace hazards and toxic waste disposal, maternity leave and child care. Even NFL idols go on strike.

These are the kitchen table topics that children learn about at home, but often without a sense of how broad the problems are, or where they come from, or how they can be resolved. Schools shy away from these issues because they are genuine conflicts: they're always controversial, often divisive, and never value-free.

On the other hand, schools do tackle controversial and value-laden issues when the crisis is intense enough, when the public interest is at stake. When we're confronted by teen suicides or drug abuse, by teen pregnancy or the AIDS epidemic, we turn to the public schools and live with the tensions that ensue.

Let me suggest that the school-to-work breakdown presents just as critical an assault on the well-being of youth and the condition of society. If we want to prepare students for the real world of work, we have to help them investigate its real problems. My own experience in tackling these controversies in the classroom suggests two approaches.

First, social studies curriculums need to include labor history and the role of social movements in shaping economic standards. History provides crucial reference points for understanding current workplace and economic conflicts, and for understanding how social progress is achieved. Distance and hindsight can also make the lessons fuller and sharper. Oral history projects are an especially fertile way to engage labor and social history, and they can connect students to the work experience of family and community members.

Second, we need to revitalize the study of current events, including labor events, from a local strike to the most recent unemployment statistics to the emissions from a nearby chemical plant. Topical discussions about what students see happening in front of them can point to the underlying public issues of job creation, labor rights, and economic vitality. Here too, classroom activity can be combined with field investigation, such as on-site interviews or public hearings.

If the teaching profession can claim more creative time and classroom autonomy, as many school reform experts are urging, it could do much to reshape the messages students receive from the labor market and workplace. Not all those messages will be pleasant or encouraging, but they can be relevant and interesting. Students need tools for understanding employment obstacles as well as opportunities. They need tools for understanding how injustice is challenged and how progress is negotiated.

High expectations can't be sustained unless they're also realistic expectations. The trick we need to teach is that realities change and people can change them.

■ Educating for Citizenship

Response #3: The essence of my argument is that schools can best counteract economic polarization and workplace hierarchy by educating students for citizenship. There is, of course, a certain Catch-22 in this proposition.

Students who see themselves as powerless, alienated, and cynical in the world of work also feel that way in a political process dominated by money and in a mass culture dominated by conspicuous consumption and commercial relationships. It's not any easier to motivate learning through the model of the good citizen than it is through the model of the productive worker when both models are visibly contradicted by events.

There are, nonetheless, large and small steps schools can take to convey the potentials for personal and social empowerment that lie in the democratic process. The most important way to teach democratic values in the face of negative examples, political or economic, is for schools to function democratically themselves—to offer children both positive example and first-hand experience.

In my view, the schools that best convey democratic values are organized as communities rather than as factories. Their school cultures put a

premium on interaction, participation, initiative, and collaboration—not only between teachers and students, but among teachers and students. They measure success by mastery and individual progress, not by competition based on winners and losers. They broaden the mainstream to include the full spectrum of needs children bring to school. They respect diversity and explore it. Teachers have the central role in a collegial governance system, and parents are an active element in setting and implementing school goals.

But however one imagines the ideal school culture, the underlying point is that schools send messages about the value of democracy through the relationships they establish, quite apart from the formal democratic values they espouse. As we debate the directions for school reform in the next decade, including professional reform, we can't ignore these qualitative issues.

It's also time to take a long look at civics education, which has pervasively become the lowest form of life in the social studies curriculum. We need to find hands-on ways that students can learn that the democratic process offers more than passive choices of ratification or periodic choices of representation. Democracy is also about participation, it's about taking collective action and setting new agendas, it's about making choices from the bottom up as well as from the top down.

I think the most important single advance we can make in civics education—and in rebuilding the connection between school, community, and work—is to establish public service programs that place high school and even middle school students in helping roles outside the school. Youth today, affluent or poor, need the experience of service, of using their labor and their judgment to make a difference to others. They need the sense of mastery that comes from initiative and intervention. They need the social awareness and sense of possibility that comes from personal involvement and commitment.

Educating for citizenship, by example and by practice, means that children can raise their expectations for a democratic future in at least three ways: they perceive that realities change, they learn that they can contribute to change, and they begin to envision what new realities can be. As this generation of youth enters the world of work, it will sorely need a new vision for economic development and a belief in its capacity to restructure the terms and conditions of employment.

■ Schools Can't Do It All

Reality #4: I have argued that schools can make a difference in filling the school-to-work gaps: the gaps in expectations, the gaps in gratification, the gaps in democratic values. I've also asserted that schools would make a bigger difference if we had different schools, if we built our models for reform on schools that have best fulfilled their democratic mission, and if we matched our professed concern with adequate and equitable resources.

Having said all this, I must add that schools can't succeed, for *all* students, unless some other priorities change as well. This society needs to invest in its youth beyond the schoolhouse. We need to invest in the wellness and security of children before they reach school. We need to invest in decent jobs, in healthy communities, and in students' cultural enrichment after they graduate as young adults.

Educators need to take responsibility for what schools can do; indeed, we need to overload the system with success. But we also need to demand accountability for the other variables, the elements of social and economic justice that fulfill high expectations, reward personal achievement, and produce more equitable outcomes. In economic as well as in educational spheres, we need to embrace John Dewey's precept: the solution to the problems of democracy is more democracy.

■ For Further Reading

For an overview of the tension between democratic and economic missions of schooling:

Choosing Equality: The Case for Democratic Schooling. Ann Bastian, Norm Fruchter, Marilyn Gittell, Colin Greer, and Kenneth Haskins, Temple University Press, 1986.

Schooling and Work in the Democratic State. Martin Carnoy and Henry M. Levin. Stanford University Press, 1985.

For an understanding of current employment and technological trends:

"Educational Requirements for New Technologies." Henry M. Levin and Russell W. Rumberger, The Center for Educational Research at Stanford University, 1986.

"Forecasting the Impact of New Technologies on the Future Job Market." Russell W. Rumberger and Henry M. Levin, The Center for Educational Research at Stanford University, 1984.

"The Great American Job Machine." Barry Bluestone and Bennett Harrison. Report of the Joint Economic Committee of the U.S. Congress, December 1986.

For recommendations on school improvement strategies and instructional issues addressing the school-to-work connection:

Investing in Our Children: Business and the Public Schools. Committee for Economic Development, Research and Policy Committee, 477 Madison Ave., New York, NY 10022, Sept. 1985.

Children in Need: Investment Strategies for the Educationally Disadvantaged. Committee for Economic Development, Research and Policy Committee, Sept. 1987.

The Unfinished Agenda. National Commission on Secondary Vocational Education, Washington, D.C., December 1984.

For innovative curriculum resources on labor history and labor in the economy:

The American Social History Project, Graduate Center of the City University of New York, 33 W. 42nd St., New York, NY 10036: A seven-part series of videotape presentations portraying working men and women, slave and free, in landmark American labor struggles of the 19th century.

The American Labor Education Center, 1835 Kilbourne Pl., N.W., Washington, DC 20010: An elementary school curriculum exploring contemporary occupations and the dignity of work.

■ Questions for Discussion

1. What should be done to improve the public confidence in our schools?
2. What values should the school transmit as being representative of our culture?
3. Should the schools be used as agents of planned social change?
4. What provisions, if any, should be made for the schools to transmit the cultural elements of local ethnic subgroups?
5. How valuable is vocational education today? Why?

■ Notes

1. "Education for Democracy," *Education Week*, (May 27, 1987):5.
2. Herbert J. Gans, "We Won't End the Crisis Until We End 'Majority Rule,'" from *More Equality*. Copyright Pantheon Books, 1973.
3. Madelon D. Stent, William R. Hazard, and Harry N. Rivlin, *Cultural Pluralism in Education*, pp. 149–50. Copyright 1973 by Fordham University.
4. Philip O. Phenix, "Values in the Emerging American Civilization," *Teachers' College Record* 61 (1960): 356.
5. Pitirim Sorokin, *The Reconstruction of Humanity* (Boston: Beacon Press, 1948), p. 104.
6. James S. Coleman, "Social Change," *Bulletin of National Association of Secondary Principals* 49, pp. 11–18.
7. Alec M. Gallup and David Clark, "The 19th Annual Gallup Poll of the Public's Attitudes Toward the Public Schools," *Phi Delta Kappan*, September 1977, p. 25.

■ Selected References

Brodzinsky, David M., Gormly, Anne V. and Ambron, Sueann R. *Lifespan Human Development*. New York: Holt, Rinehart & Winston, 1986.

Brown, B. Frank. "A Study of the School Needs of Children from One-Parent Families." *Phi Delta Kappan* (April 1980):537–40.

Gallup, Alec M. "The 17th Annual Gallup Poll of the Public's Attitudes Toward the Public Schools." *Phi Delta Kappan* (September 1985):36.

Lapointe, Archie E. "The Good News About American Education." *Phi Delta Kappan* (June 1984):663–68.

A Nation at Risk: The Imperative for Educational Reform. A report to the nation by the National Commission on Excellence in Education, 1983.

Orlosky, Donald. *Introduction to Education*. Columbus, Ohio: Charles E. Merrill, 1982.

Persell, Caroline H. *Understanding Society*. New York: Harper & Row, 1987.

Rich, John Martin. *Innovations in Education: Reformers and Their Critics*. Boston: Allyn and Bacon, 1985.

Chapter 9

Critical Social Problems in Our Schools

Objectives

After studying this chapter, you should be able to:

- Discuss the relationship between our schools and our society.

- Explore the problems of race relationships in America.

- Examine the topic of sexism in education.

- Present information on the problems of poor people.

- Discuss school truancy.

- Analyze unemployment and its implications for education.

- Present information on crime and violence in America.

- Understand student use of drugs, alcohol, and tobacco.

Enrichment Experiences

The following activities will help you learn more about some of the important topics discussed in this chapter:

- Poll some public school teachers regarding the kinds of competencies teachers must have to assist students in meeting the needs suggested in this chapter. Formulate a list of these competencies in collaboration with your classmates.

- Survey your community's social services. In what ways could the schools and these agencies cooperate to better provide for the needs of youth?

- Obtain copies of available documents on social problems that affect our youth today. Analyze and critically appraise one or more of these documents.

- Invite authorities from various social service agencies in your area to discuss what they perceive the functions of schools to be in relation to the social problems with which they are concerned.

- Arrange for interviews with practicing front-line school social workers, both those who work in cities and in rural areas, to gain their perceptions of the role that schools can play in solving social problems.

This chapter will help you realize that our society expects a great deal from our school system. For one thing, our schools are expected to help solve some of our most critical social problems. We will now look at a variety of topics related to critical social problems that affect the lives of teachers in our school system. We will discuss topics such as the public's view of school problems, the widening poverty gap, our society's hidden poor, welfare dependency, unemployment and underemployment, crime and violence in our society, drug abuse in our schools, student use of alcohol and tobacco, school truancy, school dropouts, teenage pregnancy, sexism in our schools, child abuse, the frightening problem of suicidal students, AIDS, the importance of good school health programs, single-parent children, literacy, and school racial integration problems. Future teachers should seize the opportunity to learn as much as possible about social problems because teachers are expected to deal with them. ■

Our society has come to expect our schools to help solve social problems. This expectation has led to considerable debate, with some people arguing that schools should be concerned only with teaching, and others claiming that our schools are the only institutions capable of solving many of our social problems. While this debate continues, the fact remains that students bring their social problems with them to school. At the very least, teachers must have a basic understanding of the social problems that impinge upon the lives of students. This chapter provides a brief glimpse of some of these.

■ The Public's View of School Problems

Each year a Gallup poll on the public's attitude about our public schools is conducted and receives considerable national attention. Table 9.1 shows the results of this annual survey from 1970 to 1988. In 1988, this table shows that, according to the general public, the number one problem in our public schools was the use of drugs. The second biggest problem cited was discipline. Discipline has always been at or near the top of the list of problems cited by the public in this annual poll since 1970. On the other hand, drugs have increased from 11 percent in 1970 to 32 percent in 1988. This shows that the general public is much more concerned about the use of drugs in our public schools today than they have been historically. Parenthetically, it is also interesting to note that the general public does not feel that teachers' lack of interest, curriculum standards, racial integration, or class size are very big problems.

■ **Table 9.1.**   Items Most Frequently Cited by the General Public as the Chief Problems Facing the Local Public Schools: 1970 to 1988

Problems	Percent					
	1970	**1975**	**1980**	**1985**	**1987**	**1988**
Discipline	18	23	26	25	22	19
Integration	17	15	10	4	4	4
Finances	17	14	10	9	14	12
Getting good teachers	12	11	6	10	9	11
Drugs	11	9	14	18	30	32
Size of school/classes	—	11	7	5	8	6
Curriculum/standards	—	—	11	11	8	11
Teachers' lack of interest	—	—	—	4	5	3

—Data not available

■ The Widening Poverty Gap

A serious social problem that is ultimately related to education is poverty. While the United States is one of the richest nations on earth in terms of material wealth, some of its people suffer from extreme poverty. Many individuals and families in the United States fall below the poverty level. In fact, over 32 million Americans now live in poverty. A far greater percentage of nonwhite than white people live in poverty—approximately 20 percent of nonwhite and 7 percent of white families in our country. While there is a higher percentage of nonwhite families living in poverty, numerically there are many more impoverished white families. Nonwhites have historically had, and still have to this day, significantly shorter life expectancies at birth than do whites. This fact is attributed to poorer nutrition and health care, both of which in turn are related to poverty as well as poorer education.

Many more statistics could be cited to further delineate the problem. Let it suffice to say that poverty in America is an extremely serious problem; that, while poverty affects both whites and nonwhites, the problem in percentage is much more serious for nonwhites; that it is widely distributed throughout both metropolitan and rural areas; and that, with the exception of the suburban areas, approximately one of every four children is being reared under conditions of poverty.

How does the poverty problem relate to education? Children of poverty, sometimes inaccurately labeled as "culturally deprived" or "disadvantaged," simply do not possess at the time of entrance into school as many of the skills needed for academic success as those children who have not been impoverished. This is caused by combinations of many factors, among them physical debilitation, lack of intellectual stimulation, different cultural background, negative self-concept, and many other factors related to their environmental background. Further, and perhaps more significantly, many schools have not developed the kinds of programs necessary to enable these students to succeed. As a result, their poverty background is reinforced by failure in school. Many teachers, either having been of the middle class originally, or having become a part of the middle class due to upward social mobility, have difficulty in relating to, and therefore teaching impoverished children. The schools then have the task of adjusting their programs, changing their techniques, and doing their very best to enable their students to obtain the skills necessary to compete favorably in our society. The federal government has recognized this task and is endeavoring to help. Title I, in particular, of the Elementary and Secondary Act of 1965, provided funds to state education agencies specifically for the purpose of improving education programs for the poor. Under Title I, local school districts design programs, ranging from those providing physical necessities such as eyeglasses and shoes to those providing counselors and remedial reading specialists to supplement their existing programs. Funds are allocated on the basis of the number of poor families in a school district. Other federal programs such as Head Start, National Teacher Corps, and Upward Bound are aimed at improving the opportunities of the poor.

Jencks and Bane, in their controversial essay "The Schools and Equal Opportunity," challenged the assumption that the primary reason poor children cannot escape from poverty is that they do not acquire basic cognitive skills. Other evidence points out the fact that there is almost as much economic inequality among those who score high on standardized tests as there is in the general population. Jencks concludes:

> In America, as elsewhere, the long-term drift over the past 200 years has been toward equality. In America, however, the contribution of public policy to this drift has been slight. As long as egalitarians assume that public policy cannot contribute to equality directly but must proceed by ingenious manipulations of marginal institutions like the schools, this pattern will continue. If we want to move beyond this tradition, we must establish political control over the economic institutions that shape our society. What we will need, in short, is what other countries call socialism. Anything less will end in the same disappointment as the reforms of the 1960s.[1]

Interesting recent statistics help us to better understand the fact that the number of people living in poverty in America is not only increasing, but includes many people that we typically do not think are affected by poverty. Consider the following facts:

1. There are now over 32 million poor Americans who are living under the poverty level established by the federal government.
2. Thirty percent of the poor live in rural areas.
3. Forty percent of the poor live in large central cities.
4. Only 7 percent of the poor live in ghettos. Welfare programs serve only 30 percent of the poor. Many of the people living in poverty in America have jobs.

There is nothing more difficult to take in hand, more perilous to conduct, or more uncertain in its success than to take the lead in introducing a new order of things.

Niccolo Machiavelli

5. Over two million children live in families that have income below the poverty level even though at least one parent is employed full time.

6. Two-thirds of the poor are white people despite the common assumption that poverty is a black problem. Two-thirds of all homeless Americans fall outside the category of mentally or emotionally handicapped.

Most authorities believe that the only long-range solution to poverty is to provide better education and job training so that poor people can improve their position in our society.

■ Our Hidden Poor

It may come as a surprise to many readers to realize that many of the poor people in America do not live in large city ghettos, are not receiving welfare, and are not necessarily members of a minority group. In fact, many poor people in America are scattered throughout all sections of the country and are employed or underemployed white workers. A number of these people are divorced white women who must support themselves, and frequently dependent children.

Figure 9.1 shows the rapid growth of people who are employed but poor adults. In fact, in recent years this group has increased by approximately 50 percent whereas the number of poor people who are already receiving welfare has increased by only 14 percent. Approximately 60 percent of all able-bodied adults now work. The problem is that often this work is seasonal or part time and does not pay very well. This makes it extremely difficult for many Americans to earn

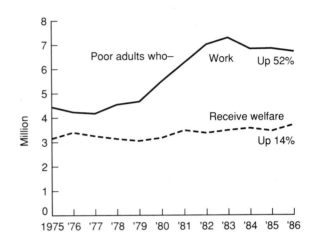

■ Figure 9.1

The poor aren't who you think they are
Note: Figures for working adults are for those age 22 to 64. 1986 figure for adults on welfare is *USN&WR* estimate.

Sources: U.S. Census Bureau and the Social Security Administration.

enough money to support themselves and their families. Inflation has wreaked havoc with the purchasing power of many working Americans. It is possible for a person to be fully employed at minimum wage and still not earn enough money to rise above the poverty level in a given year. Over the period from 1978 to 1986, the number of poor adults who averaged thirty or more weeks of work per year and who still fell below the poverty line rose by 52 percent. There are now nearly seven million Americans in this category.

Once again, our society has asked our school systems to help solve this perplexing problem. Many schools are offering adult programs to help raise the skills of our unemployed or underemployed, in hopes that they will be able to earn sufficient money to support themselves and their families.

■ Welfare Dependency

A growing number of Americans are disenchanted with our national and state welfare systems. This is largely due to the fact that in spite of huge amounts of money spent to solve the problem, the number of people in poverty continues to grow. For instance, our current poverty rate of over 15 percent is higher than the poverty rate twenty years ago when the war on poverty started. Somewhat more than $400 billion is now spent annually on social welfare programs by all levels of government. Ironically, this amounts to more than $11,000 per person in poverty (or more than $33,000 per family of three).

Americans ask why more people than ever are poor after so much has been spent to get rid of poverty. Of course, there is no easy answer to this question. Critics of our current welfare policy would undoubtedly point out that we are currently paying (encouraging) people to be poor. Other critics would suggest that we need to spend much more of our welfare dollars on education for the poor (basic skills, job training, etc.). In any event, it seems inevitable that our national approach to welfare will need to be reevaluated.

■ Unemployment and Underemployment

Closely related to problems of poverty are the problems of unemployment and underemployment (that is, individuals working at jobs who are qualified for better jobs). It has been estimated that today there are about 10 million underemployed, 6.5 million of whom work full time and earn less than the annual poverty wage. Approximately 500,000 of the unemployed are "hard-core" unemployed who lack the basic education necessary to secure and hold a job. While unemployment statistics such as these vary considerably from month to month (due to seasonal work), and from year to year (due to general economic conditions), even in the best of times many Americans are unemployed or underemployed.

High percentages of those who are unemployed or underemployed are nonwhite. This fact helps to explain, at least in part, the difference in annual income between white and nonwhite Americans. There is a relationship between unemployment rates and years of school completed. While the relationship is not perfect, undoubtedly because of other variables, the positive correlation between increased level of education and reduced unemployment rate is evident. Also, the unemployment rates for women tend to be higher than those for men. Recognizing that relationships are not indicative of "cause and effect," one possible explanation of the data in respect to nonwhites and women could be discrimination.

Do the schools have a role in solving the problem of unemployment and underemployment? They certainly do, from basic reading and writing skills to vocational and technical training programs for adults. Efforts are being made in these directions in high schools through day and night programs, technical and trade schools, and community colleges. Further, schools must continue to urge equal opportunity for education and employment in society. Again though, the schools cannot completely resolve the problem; they can, however, as one agency of society, make a major contribution.

School drug prevention programs are essential.

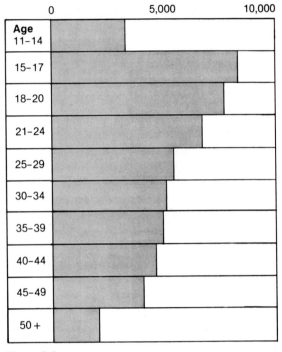

■ Figure 9.2
Arrest rate per 100,000 population, by age

■ Crime and Violence in Our Society

The extent of the current crime and violence problem in our country is shockingly revealed in the following data:

- Serious crime rose by a record 17 percent in the United States in one recent year.
- Youth under eighteen years of age now account for over one-fifth of our total arrests.

It is a sad reality that, in one way or another, crime and violence touch the lives of all our students and all our schools. Figure 9.2 points out this fact vividly by showing the arrest rate per 100,000 population by age.

This national crime and violence also spills into our schools with frightening consequences. Former President Ronald Reagan addressed this problem by pointing out that:

- Each month, approximately 2½ million students are victims of robberies and thefts.

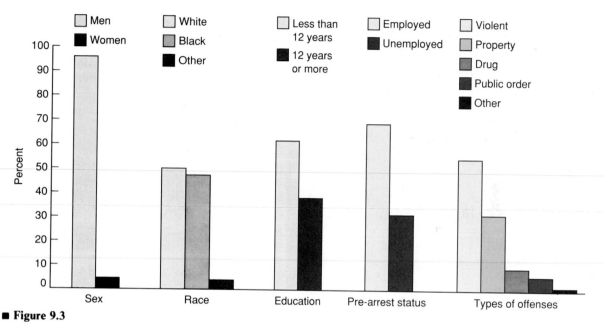

■ Figure 9.3

Prisoner profiles in the United States

Source: Bureau of Justice Statistics.

- An estimated 250,000 students are physically attacked in our schools each month.
- About 6,000 teachers are robbed in our schools each month.
- Approximately 125,000 teachers are physically threatened by students each month; at least 1,000 teachers are assaulted by students so severely they require medical attention.

Educators must take the initiative in making school a safe, violence-free environment where students can concentrate on learning and need not fear for their safety. All Americans and many other agencies have an obligation to help our schools accomplish this difficult task.

■ Prisoner Profiles in the U.S.A.

A very high percentage (95 percent) of men and women who are currently in prisons throughout the United States have been previously convicted of crimes or have been convicted of first-time violent crimes. A profile of nearly one-half million Americans now incarcerated in our state prisons is presented in figure 9.3. This figure shows that the vast majority of our prison inmates are men, have had previous arrests, have been convicted of violent crimes or crimes against property. This figure also shows that over 60 percent of the inmates did not finish the public schools. These data should provide an additional incentive for our nation to work hard on our school dropout problem and on other education-related solutions to our crime problem.

■ **Table 9.2.**   Trends in Drug Use Among High School Seniors, by Type and Frequency of Drug Use, United States, 1975 and 1985.

Type of Drug and Frequency of Use	Class of 1975	Class of 1985
Percent Reporting Having Ever Used Drugs		
Alcohol	90.4	92.2
Any illicit drug abuse	55.2	60.6
Marijuana only	19.0	20.9
Any illicit drug other than marijuana	36.2	39.7
Use of selected drugs		
Cocaine	9.0	17.3
Heroin	2.2	1.2
LSD	11.3	7.5
Marijuana/hashish	47.3	54.2
PCP	——	4.9
Percent Reporting Use of Drugs in the Past 30 Days		
Alcohol	68.2	65.9
Any illicit drug abuse	30.7	29.7
Marijuana only	15.3	14.8
Any illicit drug other than marijuana	15.4	14.9
Use of selected drugs		
Cocaine	1.9	6.7
Heroin	0.4	0.3
LSD	2.3	1.6
Marijuana/hashish	27.1	25.7
PCP	——	1.6

Source: U.S. Department of Health and Human Services, Alcohol, Drug Abuse, and Mental Health Administration, *Drug Abuse Among American High School Students and Other Young Adults: National Trends Through 1985.*

■ Drug Abuse in Our Schools

It is difficult to generalize about student use of drugs throughout the United States. Obviously, in certain schools in certain locations, drugs are more commonly used than in others. The federal government conducts an annual survey in an attempt to find out how extensively various types of drugs are used in our senior high schools. Table 9.2 shows the results of these surveys in 1975 and again in 1985. High school seniors were asked what type of drugs they used and how frequently they used them. The table shows that alcohol consumption has remained relatively stable over this ten-year period and is the most frequently used drug by high school seniors. Marijuana use and other drug form uses have increased slightly over this ten-year period.

Senator Harold W. Hughes, chairman of the Senate subcommittee on alcoholism and narcotics, in referring to drug abuse said: "The truth is that we have a cancerous problem that has the capability of destroying our society. By and large, we have not begun to awaken to its magnitude."[2]

For the most part, schools have not made sufficient effort to solve the student drug problem. Furthermore, the few schools that have made a concerted attack on the drug problem have not been successful. Clearly, our schools need better drug-education programs. Such programs clearly need teachers who are extremely well informed about the drug problem.

■ Student Use of Alcohol and Tobacco

Statistics show that mortality from lung cancer (largely attributed to smoking) continues to skyrocket—to an estimated 100,000 in 1988.[3] While there has been a slight decrease in the number of adult smokers in recent years, there has been a disappointing increase in the number of student smokers. The percentage of girls who smoke is increasing much faster than that of boys. Many schools have initiated vigorous smoking-education programs in an effort to stem the rising tide of student smokers. A good example of such a program is one in New York State initiated by McRae and Nelson.[4] This particular program was based on the assumptions that the bulk of students smoke because their friends smoke and that students wish to be independent and develop their own life-style. The program depended on youth-to-youth communication and was designed and carried out by a teenage youth committee. Students in seventy-five schools participated in the program. The plan also involved corresponding units of instruction in certain classes on topics such as cancer.

A recent Department of Health, Education, and Welfare task force found that teenage drinking is commonplace in our country—93 percent of our high school senior boys and 87 percent of the girls use alcohol in varying amounts.

Dr. Morris E. Chafety, director of the National Institute on Alcohol Abuse and Alcoholism, recently stated that half the tenth graders drink in cars at night, 60 percent of our traffic fatalities among youth involve alcohol, and the number of high school students who have ever used alcohol was up 90 percent in a recent three-year period. A recent study in New York shows that almost 10 percent of the city's junior and senior high school students are already or are potentially alcoholics. A Houston "drying out" program for teenage drinkers has increased its clientele from 6 to 1,200 in three years.

These statistics vividly point out the problems that our schools and our society face regarding student use of alcohol and tobacco. Most authorities believe that our schools alone will not be able to solve the problem, so both our schools and our society will have to devote more attention to these areas in the future.

■ School Truancy

Students are "skipping school" more frequently and in increasing numbers. Richard Benedetto captures the essence of this problem when he writes:

> When a high school student is absent in Tallahassee, Fla., a parent has 48 hours to call the school with an excuse.
>
> "They used to have them write notes," says teacher Pat Faircloth, "but too many kids were forging the notes."
>
> In another room in the same school, teacher Ionia Smith holds up a book saturated with red marks, "Those are for the tardies and unexcused absences for this semester alone," she says.

In Sacramento, the police have become truant officers. If a teenager is seen out of school without a written excuse, he or she is picked up and released only to a parent or school official.

In Charlotte, N.C., high school principal Richard Cansler says he's ready to drop the perfect attendance award because nobody ever wins it. His school's average daily attendance is 85 percent. Ten years ago it was 96 percent.

As one New York City school official put it: "It's tough enough to teach these kids how to read and write. You can't teach them if they're not in school."

Average attendance in New York's 1,000 public schools is about 84 percent. That means that 160,000 are absent every day.

School officials can tick off a long list of reasons why children don't show up. They include lack of parental concern, the need to take care of younger children in the family, teenage pregnancy, emotional and economic problems, boredom, failure to achieve and a growing belief that school isn't a key to success.

Urban school districts throughout the country report similar trends, and it now appears the disease is spreading to the suburbs and beyond.

At White Oak Junior High in the suburbs of Cincinnati, parents of absent students receive a phone call to determine whether the absence is legitimate. If there is no answer at home, a parent is called at work.

Terry Byrne, the White Oak principal, says the call-a-parent program has been used for five years "because it's effective." The school's average attendance is 93 to 94 percent.

At Schoharie Central High School in rural upstate New York "there was a lot of cutting going on, so we had to start taking attendance in every class," says principal Edward Reid. "It's like an hourly bed check."

Reid says his attendance rate is about 93 percent, but on Fridays and Mondays it drops below 90 percent when there are farm chores to be done.

"Nobody's afraid of the truant officer anymore," says Tim Wendt, assistant to the deputy chancellor of the New York City schools who is working on an attendance improvement program there.

He noted that New York has attractions like Yankee Stadium, Coney Island and Times Square where students gather when they skip school. The schools have set up satellite centers in those areas where truants picked up by police are taken. The schools are then notified, and the students are sent back. "But many don't come back," says Wendt.

One attendance aide called a mother to find out why her daughter hadn't been in school for a week. "I haven't seen her in a month," the mother replied.

Sarah Pearlmutter, a teacher at Louis Brandeis High School in Manhattan, said she has improved attendance by posting pictures of students who show the greatest attendance improvement. "These children just like to know someone cares," she said.[5] (Copyright 1980, Gannett News Service. Reprinted with permission.)

Unfortunately, many of today's truants are tomorrow's school dropouts. Educators must work hard to combat the school truancy problem.

Research Finding

8

A school staff that provides encouragement and personalized attention, and monitors daily attendance can reduce unexcused absences and class-cutting.

Absences are a major problem at all levels of school. Too many missed opportunities to learn can result in failure, dropping out, or both.

The school climate set by teachers, counselors, and administrators can significantly affect student attendance. Teachers who establish and communicate clear goals and high standards for performance and behavior, maintain discipline, allow as much learning time as possible, and consistently show support for their students have fewer attendance problems.

A school with an effective system for monitoring both daily and class attendance can identify potential dropouts early and then provide appropriate service to them.

Good attendance in school is another example of the connection of time and learning. Just as homework amplifies learning, regular attendance exposes students to a greater amount of academic content and instruction. Students, of course, must concentrate on their lessons in order to benefit from attendance.

Brodinsky, B. (1980). "Student Discipline: Problems and Solutions." *AASA Critical Issues Report.* Arlington, VA: American Association of School Administrators. ERIC Document No. ED 198206.

Byrne, R. (1981). "Capturing the Elusive Student: Putting Accountability Theory into Attendance Practice." *NASSP Bulletin,* Vol. 65, No. 445, pages 29–33.

Collins, C. H., Moles, O., and Cross, M. (1982). *The Home-School Connection: Selected Partnership Programs in Large Cities.* Boston: Institute for Responsive Education.

Source: *What Works: Research About Teaching and Learning.* Washington, DC: U.S. Department of Education, 1987, page 63.

■ Our Growing Educational Underclass

Each year school doors close for about two million students who drop out and join the ranks of the growing number of students who do not receive sufficient education to prepare them for employment and life as a full citizen in the United States. While approximately one in four high school students in the United States never graduate at all, a problem discussed elsewhere in this chapter, it is less well understood that nearly a million of our high school students who graduate each year are not able to read and write at a sufficient level. More frightening is the prediction that by the year 2000 our high school dropout rate will have increased from its current 25 percent to an anticipated 40 percent. A disproportionate number of these dropouts and poorly educated graduates come from the ranks of the poor and are black or Hispanic. It is this group of students that is frequently referred to as America's educational underclass. Typically these students enter high school with many strikes against them. Many of them have been raised in difficult environments by a single parent and have lacked the family support which helps children complete our public school system successfully. Many of these children have received inadequate nutrition and health care. Many of these students suffer from drug abuse, and many of these girls become pregnant before completing their education. Is it any wonder that this educational underclass has such a difficult time completing a public school education?

These statistics are frightening:

1. About 60 percent of all high school dropouts come from families with incomes of less than $15,000 per year.
2. One-half of all minority students drop out of high school before graduation, compared with 20 percent of white high school students.
3. Over 40 percent of black high school dropouts are unemployed compared to only 22 percent of white high school dropouts.
4. Thirty-seven percent of black high school dropouts live below the poverty line compared with only 22 percent of black high school graduates. The comparable figures for white students suggests that 16 percent of white high school dropouts are unemployed compared to only 8 percent of white high school graduates.

This represents yet another enormous challenge to our public school systems in the United States—particularly those found in our large cities where many of our minority students are found. Our society simply must be made to understand that not providing high school programs that will keep minority students in school is a very costly mistake. It is estimated that it costs our society approximately $75 billion a year to pay the cost of our school dropouts. This cost consists of lost tax revenues from potential earnings, crime and crime prevention costs, unemployment, and welfare. This $75 billion amounts to a per capita cost of $800 each year for every taxpayer in the United States. It would be far less expensive to provide improved education in the first place than to pay the consequences later.

■ Levels of Education Completed by Americans

Figure 9.4 shows that adults in America have achieved higher and higher educational levels over the last thirty-five years. For instance, in 1950 approximately 8 percent of our adults 25 years or older had completed four or more years of college; whereas in 1985 this figure had risen to 20 percent. By the same token, in 1950 approximately 35 percent had completed at least twelve years of school whereas in 1985 this figure had risen to 75 percent.

While these data would not apply to all subgroups in our American society, they nevertheless indicate a tremendous accomplishment of the American school systems which have managed to educate masses of Americans.

Unfortunately, this chart also shows that appalling numbers of Americans still do not manage to complete high school. As our society becomes

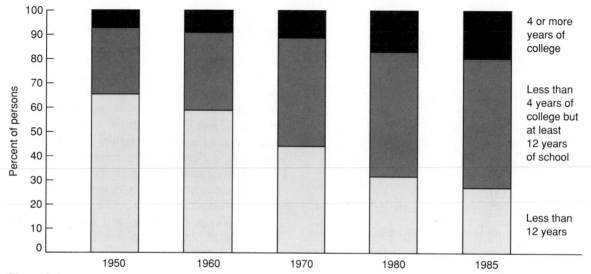

■ Figure 9.4

Years of school completed by persons 25 years and over:
1950–1985

Source: *Digest of Education Statistics, 1987.* U.S. Department of Education.

more technically advanced, so must our citizens become more educationally advanced. Increasingly, people who do not complete at least a high school education will have difficulty living in our society.

■ Teenage Pregnancy

Increasing numbers of teenage girls are becoming pregnant. The following national statistics illustrate the extent of this problem:[6]

- More than 200,000 young women under 18 give birth each year.
- One in four black babies are born to teenage mothers, compared with one in seven white babies.
- There are more than one million teenage mothers in America.
- Ninety-six percent of teenage mothers keep their babies.
- Women and children make up 80 percent of all Americans in poverty.
- Families headed by young mothers are seven times more likely to be poor.

Historically, pregnant students were usually expelled from our schools. Fortunately, school officials now realize that pregnant students need to complete their education fully as much as any student. More and more schools are developing special programs for pregnant students and students' parents.

■ Sexism in Our Schools

Yet another pressing social problem of a slightly different nature that currently affects our schools is sexism. This problem is far-reaching in its implications, touching on such things as equal educational opportunity for females, federal legislation such as Title IX (discussed elsewhere in this book), equal employment opportunities for women, sex stereotyping, and, in fact, the civil rights and quality of life of American females. Space permits only a brief discussion of one aspect of this larger problem—that of sexism in our schools.

Some authorities feel that we would take a large step toward solving this problem if we could find a way to provide true sex equality or neutrality in our language. They argue that language is the key element in human interaction and that any language which is oriented in favor of one sex will inevitably result in that sex having a dominant role in the society.

One need not ponder long to determine that common language usage in America is male-oriented and filled with sex stereotyping. Authors commonly use "he" when referring to people in general; we call the person in charge of a meeting a "chairman" even if it happens to be a female; and we address unknown persons as "Dear Sir" in correspondence. In our school books, doctors, lawyers, merchants, police, soldiers, and people in charge such as the school principal are usually male; while nurses, waitresses, elementary school teachers, and persons who clean, cook, sew, and generally do lower level and lower paying work are female. Also, males are often depicted as tough, smart, and aggressive while females are assigned roles that are weak, docile, and subservient.

Even though most people today fully realize that females are as capable and competent as males and also believe that females should have equal opportunities in all aspects of life, they don't realize the subtle influence and damage that language can do to the young. Most people also do not realize that our sex-oriented language is probably just as damaging to boys as it is to girls.

Developing sex equity in our language will probably take a good deal of time and will certainly take the concerted hard work of a great many people (including educators) in our society. Helping people become aware of the problem is undoubtedly one of the early necessary steps in this process. Figure 9.5 entitled "Practical Suggestions for Fairness in Language," represents yet another kind of step that must be taken to eventually resolve this problem.

Fortunately, considerable progress has recently been made on this social problem. Dr. Cecelia H. Foxley lists the following gains which have been made in providing sex equality in education:[7]

1. Virtually all courses at all educational levels are now open to students of both sexes.
2. Extracurricular programs and athletics are now more equally available to females and males.
3. Publishers and authors have made a considerable effort to eliminate sexist and stereotypic elements in publications and other educational materials.
4. Admission standards and requirements are the same for men and women.
5. Women are earning an increasing percentage of college degrees at all levels.

After assumptions have been clarified and new perspectives considered, many people still have a problem with sex bias in language: How can I speak and write fairly and clearly, without tripping over myself?

The following examples offer alternatives to traditional forms. Each is intended to be inclusive, convenient, and clear. These resources can suggest further possibilities for bias-free language; a great many inventive solutions remain to be explored.

Avoid a choice of gender

1. By plural forms
   Instead of: A student can choose his adviser as late as his senior year.
   Try: Students can choose their advisers as late as their senior year.
2. By rephrasing to omit pronouns or the necessity to choose a male or female noun
   Instead of: When a youth gets a part-time job, he is likely to face increased stress.
   Try: When getting a part-time job, you are likely to face increased stress.
3. By using labels that show the activity, not the gender of the actor
   Instead of: mailman, stewardess, lineman, housemother
   Try: mail carrier, flight attendant, line worker, house parent
4. By using common gender "they" in writing as well as in oral communication
   Instead of: Everyone who wants to play should bring his instrument to tonight's informal concert.
   Try: Everyone who wants to play should bring their instruments to tonight's informal concert.

Choose inclusive forms

1. By using "he or she," "she or he," "s/he," or "he/she"
   These forms work best when used in combination with the suggestions above. A large number of "he or she" forms in a short passage will be less smooth to read or hear than one such form in the context of a variety of nouns and noun phrases.
   Try: A student can choose an activity as late as his or her senior year.
2. Alternating female and male pronouns
   This strategy can help raise the awareness of others when customary sex role references are avoided.
   Try: A professor . . . she; the housekeeper . . . he; the attorney . . . she.
3. By using as examples persons of both sexes
   Try: Researchers such as Margaret Mead and Franz Boas have revealed how people live in widely varying cultures around the world.

Try to avoid these things

1. Stating that you mean "he" generically and continuing to use only "he" to refer to unspecified persons.
   Problem: Whatever you say, listeners are still more likely to receive images of males.
2. Saying inclusive pronouns with long pauses or heightened vocal emphasis.
   Problem: Some listeners will interpret these behaviors as antagonistic toward women or feminism. Others will simply lose your train of thought.

When in doubt

1. Ask people what they prefer to be called.
2. Assume that people are human beings first and that women and men are presumed worthy of respect in whatever they are choosing to do.

Last lines about letters

Several methods for beginning a letter can avoid sex-biased wording
    Dear Barbara Bates: Dear Director of Education:
    Dear people: Dear *Village Voice* Staff:

All of these suggestions for practical fairness in language are based on a single belief. The belief is that language can affect human experience both positively and negatively. Words can limit, confuse, and stereotype. But words can also communicate the encouraging conviction that what is possible for any human being is possible for oneself as well.

■ **Figure 9.5**
Practical suggestions for fairness in language

6. A higher proportion of elementary school teachers are males.
7. More and more educators, parents, and students are aware of the detrimental effects of sexism and sex-role stereotyping.

(From Cecelia H. Foxley, "Sex Equity in Education: Some Gains, Problems and Future Needs," *Journal of Teacher Education*, 33(5):6–9. September/October 1984. Copyright © 1984 American Association of Colleges for Teacher Education, Washington, DC. Reprinted by permission.)

■ Increasing Child Abuse

Reports of child abuse have increased in the United States in recent years. For instance, there were a total of 1,211,323 reported child abuse cases in the United States in 1981. Four years later, there was a 55 percent increase to 1,876,564 cases. Experts point out that this increase is due, at least in part, to improved reporting opportunities. Schools now are asked to help identify abused children and to make reports about such children to the appropriate authorities. In some states, the increase in reported child abuse cases has been particularly dramatic. An example would be the state of Arizona which experienced a 445 percent increase in reported child abuse cases between 1981 and 1985. Oregon experienced a 367 percent increase, Utah a 210 percent increase and many states, including Wisconsin, West Virginia, Vermont, New Mexico, and Mississippi, experienced well over 100 percent increases.

The National Education Association has published an excellent book entitled "Child Abuse and Neglect: A Teacher's Handbook for Detection, Reporting and Classroom Management." Joy Byers, of the National Committee for Prevention of Child Abuse, has helped to prepare another excellent booklet for educators on the subject of child abuse.[8]

Authorities recognize child abuse as one of the most difficult problems because of the traditional powers given to parents and the difficulty of using young children as witnesses in our courts. Fortunately, the problem is now receiving a great deal of attention. A recent report by a Justice Department task force on family violence recommends:[9]

- Police should make it a priority to arrest offenders rather than allow them to stay in the home.
- Congress should pass a law requiring background checks for criminal records on volunteers and employees of agencies that receive federal funds for the care and training of the young.
- Courts should encourage procedures that "lessen the victim's trauma," such as allowing children to testify by videotape.
- Local authorities should place tighter limits on an offender's access to victims, especially in sexual-abuse and battering cases.
- Cities should establish a system of safe-home networks in which citizens can provide temporary shelter to victims of abuse.
- The government should give victims of family violence priority for federally supported housing.
- States should include sex abuse and other family crimes in victim-compensation programs.

In addition, our schools and teachers must help provide the basic education that is required to help solve this perplexing problem that turns life into a nightmare for so many innocent children.

■ Suicidal Students

More young people are committing suicide than ever before. As life becomes more complex, pressures mount on youth—pressures with which some of our students cannot deal. Consider these data:

- Each year, approximately 400,000 teenagers attempt suicide.
- Of these, approximately 15,000 youth take their own lives, according to National Institute of Mental Health estimates.
- The teen suicide rate has tripled in the last thirty years.
- Among teenagers 15 to 19 years of age, suicide is now the second leading cause of death.

Once again our schools, administrators, counselors, and teachers have been asked to play a key role in combating this problem. Educators should be aware of the distress signals listed in figure 9.6 that students contemplating suicide often exhibit.

■ Acquired Immune Deficiency Syndrome

One of the frightening recent sexual-related diseases is that commonly called AIDS. In 1981, there were only 336 diagnosed cases of AIDS in the United States. Today this number has grown to approximately 150,000. It is estimated that by 1991 there will be nearly 300,000 active cases of AIDS diagnosed in the United States. There is no known prevention or cure for AIDS. People with active AIDS cases eventually die from that disease. The nation has turned to our school system to help educate students about this killer

- Direct statements (e.g., "You won't have to put up with me much longer") that are all easily—and too often—dismissed. *Take them seriously.*
- Withdrawal from close friends.
- Sudden decline *or sudden improvement* in academic performance.
- Sleeplessness or excessive oversleeping.
- Abrupt changes in eating habits.
- New interest or involvement in high-risk activities, with little or no regard for the caution that common sense dictates.
- Uncharacteristic hostility, disruptive behavior, violent outbursts.
- Alcohol or drug abuse.
- "Sign-off" behavior, such as giving away valued possessions

Should a student exhibit any of these symptoms, heed the succinct advice of Dr. Kurt Glaser, staff psychiatrist at the Sheppard and Enoch Pratt Hospital's Child and Adolescent Care Division in Baltimore, Md.: *"The one thing not to do is to do nothing."*

■ Figure 9.6
Suicide distress signals

disease. It is essential that all teachers be knowledgeable about the disease so that they, in turn, can help their students understand the great danger of this disease.

Experts believe that it will take many years to develop preventive vaccines for AIDS. They believe that, in the meantime, the only effective weapon against this fearful disease is an understanding of how the virus is spread. Teachers are probably in the best position to help provide this understanding. AIDS is caused by a virus that attacks the white blood cells that protect the body from infections. Once a person has an active case

■ **Table 9.3.**   Race and Ethnicity of Persons with AIDS (U.S.)

Percentages are by row; some rows don't total 100% due to incomplete statistics on ethnicity.

	White	Black	Hispanic
Men who have sex with men	75%	15%	10%
IV drug users	19	51	30
Both of the above	65	22	13
Heterosexual cases	14	72	13
Blood clotting disorders	86	5	7
Transfusion recipients	77	14	7
Undetermined	37	42	19
Children with AIDS	20	55	24

"The Facts About AIDS: A Special Guide for NEA Members," The Health Information Network, 1987, page 6. Copyright © 1987 National Education Association, Washington, DC. Reprinted by permission.

■ **Table 9.4.**   Gender of Persons with AIDS (U.S.)

	Male	Female
Men who have sex with men	100%	0%
IV drug users	79	21
Both of the above	100	0
Heterosexual cases	48	52
Blood clotting disorders	98	2
Transfusion recipients	64	36
Undetermined	78	22
Children with AIDS	55	45

"The Facts About AIDS: A Special Guide for NEA Members," The Health Information Network, 1987, page 6. Copyright © 1987 National Education Association, Washington, DC. Reprinted by permission.

The U.S. average is 13 cases per 100,000 people. Excluding these metropolitan areas, the rate is 5 per 100,000.

Note: Figures are cumulative from June, 1981, to Dec., 1986, for metropolitan areas reporting at least 300 cases.

AIDS cases per 100,000 people

■ **Figure 9.7**
AIDS hot spots

Source: Centers for Disease Control, U.S. Department of Health and Human Services.

of AIDS, it prevents the immune system from functioning normally to ward off illnesses that otherwise would not necessarily be serious. Research shows the AIDS virus is transmitted by sexual contact or through blood. Table 9.3 shows the distribution of AIDS by race and ethnicity within the United States. This table shows that intravenous drug users and homosexuals constitute two high-risk groups. Table 9.4 shows the gender of persons with AIDS in the United States. As this table shows, men who have sex with men and IV drug users who are males have a very high risk of acquiring AIDS. Figure 9.7 shows those cities which have the highest incidence of AIDS per 100,000 population. Since homosexuals and IV drug users tend to be found in large cities, it would be expected that our largest cities would show the greatest incidence of this frightening disease.

Obviously, all teachers need to be knowledgeable about AIDS. Fortunately, there is a great deal of good information and resources available to help teachers with this task. For instance, the National Education Association has recently published an excellent resource booklet entitled "The Facts About AIDS."[10] Other excellent sources of accurate information about AIDS are available from the Department of Public Health. Appendix E provides answers to some of the commonly asked questions about AIDS.

■ The Importance of Good School Health Programs

Health education has been considered a fundamental and essential component of good educational programs for a long time. Today's students face many serious health problems, including the following:[11]

- At least one-third—and perhaps as many as 60 percent—of American youth already exhibit at least one of the prime risk factors for heart disease, the nation's leading killer.

- In the past 20 years, the incidence of obesity among teenagers has increased 39 percent.

- In that same period of time, the incidence of anorexia nervosa has doubled.

- In a 1983–84 test of basic physical fitness, only 36 percent of American young people aged 6 to 17 met the standard for "average fitness."

- Suicide is the second leading cause of death among 15- to 24-year-olds.

- Of the 29 million adolescents over age 12, about 12 million are sexually active.

- Seventy-five percent of all sexually transmitted diseases are found in the 15 to 24 age group.

- Each day, 3,000 girls in the United States become pregnant. Four out of 10 teenagers will become pregnant sometime before they reach the age of 20. Fifty percent of teenage mothers drop out of school.

- Nearly one quarter of young people between the ages of 12 and 17 have a serious drinking problem. More than half of all teenage deaths are related to the use of alcohol or other drugs.

- The leading causes of death among Americans—including heart disease, high blood pressure, and cancer—are at least partly related to factors that individuals can learn to control, such as smoking, diet, weight, and stress.

- The American Medical Association found that two-thirds of all students have used an illegal drug before they leave high school; 1 in 16 uses alcohol daily.

- Both drug use and sexual activity place adolescents at greater risk for developing AIDS and other sexually transmitted diseases.

(From *Why School Health,* 1987, 1–2. Copyright © 1987 American Association of School Administrators, Arlington, VA. Reprinted by permission.)

All of these serious health problems dictate that our schools develop and maintain good health education programs. In fact, if students are to be successful in our schools, they must be basically healthy. Any health problems make it difficult for students to concentrate on school work and to be educationally successful.

Poor health costs Americans a great deal of resources each year. For instance, total health expenditures in the United States have skyrocketed to the point at which the average American today spends over $1,000 per person on health care costs. Some health care costs stagger the imagination. Each year, for instance, it costs our nation over $16 billion for aid to families of dependent children to pay for teenaged childbearing costs alone.

Some of the goals of a good health education program in our schools should include the following objectives:[12]

- Reduce illness and time away from school.
- Reduce the number of accidents.
- Reduce the incidence of teenage pregnancy.
- Adopt health-promoting behaviors.
- Increase physical and mental fitness.
- Reduce smoking.
- Reduce the incidence of drug and alcohol abuse.

A good program should provide instruction in:

- Disease prevention and control
- Mental health
- Nutrition
- Personal growth and hygiene
- Safety and first aid
- Tobacco, alcohol, and drugs
- Consumer health
- Environmental health
- Personal and family survival
- Physical education
- Parenthood and family relationships

Parents play a leading role in seeing that their sons and daughters:

- Eat nutritious foods
- Get enough sleep and exercise
- Receive proper medical, eye, and dental care (AASA, 1987)

College students who are preparing for educational careers should learn all they can about good school health programs. Such information will be useful to them when they become teachers.

■ Children from Single-Parent Homes

Educators have become aware of the fact that single-parent children often bring special problems to our schools. There are more single-parent children in our schools than ever before. In fact, one child in five is living with a single parent. It is estimated that approximately one-half of the children born this year will eventually live in single-parent homes. Most single-parent households are headed by women (only 10 percent of single-parent children live with their fathers).

Mr. Robert D. Allers, an authority on this subject, offers the following suggestions to teachers of children living with one parent:[13]

- Notice when a child shows signs of stress, such as daydreaming, acting out, moodiness, depression, withdrawal, truancy, declining grades. Try to determine where the stress is coming from: The source may be a parent's death or a divorce. Then, whatever the source, try to help the child.
- Be a friend. People's value systems often govern the way they approach others. Children from one-parent homes can suffer because adults around them disapprove of their family structure. Let your actions show that the child is OK regardless of family status.
- Gear programs around the child's needs. If a student's parent has died, obtain books and other materials dealing with death that can help all the children accept what has happened.
- Recognize that the school needs as much information about each child as possible, such as the names and phone numbers of noncustodial parents. Parents may be very helpful in devising forms which will elicit this information without confusion or offense.

• Be attuned to comments and assignments that may negatively affect the child. When a teacher asks students to question their fathers about their jobs, a child who has no father may feel very uncomfortable. When a teacher tells a child to have his or her mother sign a note and the child does not see a mother during the week, the child may be in a quandary about what to do.

To avoid discomforting such children, speak in general terms when possible. Ask the children to interview "a parent or friend" and suggest that "an adult in your family" sign the note.

• Do not restrict any child's involvement in school activities by setting up events unsuited to the child's family situation. Hold suppers and events for parents and child, or adult and child, not father and son or father and daughter.

• Encourage noncustodial as well as custodial parents to attend conferences and become active in their child's education. Include stepparents, even grandparents. The more adults who are involved in and concerned about the child's education, the better the child will usually feel and perform.

• Urge school authorities to schedule conferences in the evening—and provide baby-sitting services. For many parents, it is difficult to find and pay for babysitters while meeting with the teacher. Recruit volunteer high school students (perhaps from a class that includes instruction in child care) to set up a room where parents can leave their small children while attending conferences.

• Help set up low-cost after-school day care for latchkey children, preferably at the school. Such programs now in existence appear very promising, but many more will be needed as more mothers go out to work and governments reduce their support for day-care centers.

• Prepare for unexpected events such as cancellation or early closing of school in bad weather by providing a caretaker for children who have no parent at home.

• Request in-service education that will give greater insight into the experiences and needs of children from one-parent homes.

• Ask the school psychologist, social worker, or counselor to set up support groups for these children. Support groups are highly effective in helping children deal with their changing world.

(Allers, 1983)

■ Levels of Literacy

Most Americans believe that we have one of the best education systems in the world, and because of this our citizenry in general is literate and well educated. It comes as a shock to most of us to hear the following facts:

1. It is estimated that one in five adults lacks the reading and writing skills needed for daily living.

2. About 13 percent of our high school graduates have only sixth grade reading and writing skills.

3. Over one-third of our adults have not completed high school.

4. Our country is receiving an increasing number of immigrants who have practically no English skills.

5. It is estimated that we spend more than 6 billion dollars each year to keep 750,000 illiterates in jail, pointing out a direct correlation between crime and illiteracy and between unemployment and illiteracy.

6. It is estimated that as much as 6 billion dollars are spent each year on welfare and unemployment due to illiteracy.

7. Literacy Volunteers of America estimate that an additional 200+ billion dollars a year in unrealized earnings are lost by people who lack basic learning.

Currently many different definitions of illiteracy seem to be used by various people when discussing the problem in the United States. For instance, it is not uncommon to find politicians claiming that an appalling number of Americans are "computer illiterate" or "economically illiterate," and "mathematically illiterate." Other experts point out that many of our citizens are "geographically illiterate" because they do not know enough about world geography.

Actually, the most common definition of illiteracy deals only with a person's inability to read and write. If one uses that definition, then relatively few of our citizens today are technically illiterate. The Census Bureau has published information that suggests 20 percent of our country's adults were illiterate in 1870, 10.7 percent in 1900, 3.2 percent in 1950, and fewer than 1 percent are illiterate today. While the Census Bureau does not use precisely the same definition of illiteracy over this period of time, it is nevertheless obvious that relatively few normal American adults today cannot read and write on at least a basic level.

Yet another definition that is commonly used today is "functional illiterates." Some people define functional illiteracy as the inability to read and write below a sixth grade level. Others use the eighth grade level or twelfth grade level to define functional illiteracy. Recent estimates of functional illiterates in the United States, depending upon which definition one uses, range from 27 million all the way to 72 million people.

Obviously, if the nation is to study, understand, and remediate illiteracy in our country, we must be careful in our definitions of illiteracy. Currently it is difficult to understand the facts regarding the problem of illiteracy because of our lack of precision when discussing the topic.

■ Large Problems in Our Large Schools

Some of the most severe social problems in American education are found in our largest city schools. Table 9.5 summarizes some of these problems. For instance, this table shows that dropout rates exceed 30 percent in all of the schools listed. It also shows that there are a large number of reported assault cases in these large schools each year. And sadly, this table shows that the case load for counselors in our large city schools is huge; so large, in fact, that it would be impossible for counselors to provide very much individual help for students. This table provides yet additional factual data which help explain the magnitude of some of the problems our large city schools are facing.

■ Decline in Minorities Going to College

There has been an alarming decline in the percentage of minority students in the United States who go on to college in recent years. Figure 9.8 presents data related to this increasing problem.

■ Table 9.5.

SCHOOL PROFILES City (Number of students in thousands)	Minorities % of students that are black and Hispanic	Dropouts % who enter ninth grade but left before 4 years*	Assaults Number of cases reported last year	Counselors Ratio to high school students
Boston (56)	63%	46%	410	1/313
Chicago (431)	83%	45%	698	1/398
Houston (192)	81%	41%	128**	1/500
Los Angeles (592)	75%	45%	493	1/298
Miami (255)	75%	NA	909 ('86)	1/420
New York (939)	72%	34%	1,606	1/623
St. Louis (47)	76%	30%	NA	1/390

*Cities compute rate in different ways; figures include students who moved   NA — Not available   **Arrests

Copyright 1988 Time, Inc. Reprinted by permission.

This chart shows a decline over the past ten years for Hispanic and black students that should be of concern to all educators. Ten years ago approximately 34 percent of all black high school graduates between the ages of 18 and 24 were in college. Today that figure has declined to just over 25 percent. There has also been a considerable decrease in the number of Hispanic students going on to college.

Our nation must find ways to make it possible for this trend to be reversed. Experts speculate that the major cause of this decline in minority students attending college deals with their inability to finance a college education. One possible solution would be to increase the availability of scholarships to minority students.

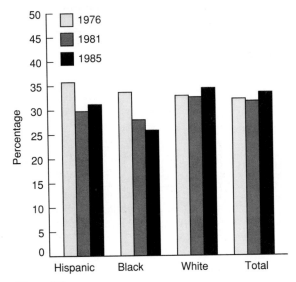

■ Figure 9.8

Proportion of 18-to-24-year-old high school graduates in college

■ Summary

In summary, our teachers are asked to help solve the social problems that students bring into our schools. These problems include the use of drugs, poverty, unemployment, crime, truancy, school dropouts, pregnancy, sexism, child abuse, suicide, AIDS, single-parent homes, illiteracy, and racism.

We have briefly touched on only a few of the social problems that affect the lives of our nation's youth and our schools. These are pressing problems that our schools and society at large must join hands to solve if our youth are to be served. Teachers must understand these social problems in order to understand today's students and to design learning experiences which will help solve these social problems. Of course, schools and teachers alone cannot solve these problems. Solutions will require the concerted effort of many of our institutions and all levels of our government.

The courts instituted racial integration in the public schools.

Point of View

■

Teenage pregnancy has become an enormous problem in our society, especially in our large cities. The following point of view regarding this growing problem is offered by James Buie who has conducted research on the impact that teen pregnancy has on our schools. In this article entitled "Teen Pregnancy: It's Time for the Schools to Tackle the Problem," Dr. Buie suggests that schools should more vigorously attack this serious problem. He offers a number of suggestions for doing so.

Teen Pregnancy: It's Time for the Schools to Tackle the Problem

James Buie

The topic is hot. The time is ripe. While the national media and U.S. parents are focusing their attention on the problems of teen pregnancy and teen parenting, school administrators need to act— carefully but courageously—to establish innovative programs to deal with these problems in their own communities.

A recent survey by the Education Research Group (ERG) suggests that school administrators already know what needs to be done. More than half of the 716 administrators surveyed favored providing students with "birth control" as part of comprehensive school-based services. Thirty percent said that birth control should be provided only with parents' permission, while 27% said that birth control should be provided without a provision for parental permission.

Yet 96% of U.S. school districts do not provide birth control, according to the survey. The vast majority have not begun to develop comprehensive plans to deal with the problems of teen pregnancy or teen parenting.

Why the discrepancy? The most obvious answer is that school administrators—by nature, a cautious lot—do not want to broach a subject with such potential to inflame. Several administrators interviewed by ERG admitted as much. "I've got lots of other problems without opening that can of worms," said one. "We don't advertise a sex education course," said another. "We're trying to avoid controversy."

Bringing up such an emotional subject as birth control has obvious risks. But national statistics and anecdotal information from the local level compel action. Among the disturbing statistics:

- More than 20% of administrators surveyed by ERG say that teen pregnancy is among the top five problems their school systems face.
- More than one million teenage girls in the U.S. become pregnant every year.
- Some 400,000 teenagers have abortions each year, and 470,000 others—the majority of whom are unmarried—give birth.

Several states and localities have developed programs to deal with these problems that could serve as models for the nation. No single approach is a panacea; administrators must choose programs that fit their communities and tailor those programs to local needs. But some things are clear.

Traditional sex education is not enough. Research has repeatedly shown little correlation between participation in a unit on sex education and level of sexual activity. Simply incorporating a unit on sex education into other course-work may increase students' knowledge, but it rarely changes their behavior. Sex education must be expanded beyond a one- or two-week session in high school to become, instead, part of a 12-year learning program with a broader agenda that includes encouraging young people to set long-term goals and to think beyond the present.

The Life Planning Education Program, developed by the Center for Population Options, is a good start in this direction. It approaches sex education from a purely practical point of view, teaching students "the impact pregnancy can have on their education, their careers, and their wallets."

To effectively attack teen pregnancy medically, school-based medical clinics or special schools for pregnant and parenting teens are necessities in some areas. In communities with especially high rates of teen pregnancy and large numbers of teen parents, administrators must dare to push for school-based clinics or special schools for pregnant and parenting teens that offer child care and comprehensive health services, including birth control information and referral. About 100 school-based clinics were operating in 1986, primarily in economically deprived urban areas. Most of these clinics distributed birth control information and methods or provided referrals for them. Initially, parents may have opposed such services, but over time they have come to accept them.

Consider, for example, the success of the School-Age Parenting Program in Fresno, California. When the program began, some members of the Fresno community snidely referred to it as "the baby factory" and suggested that pregnant teens and teen parents should receive no special attention or special services. "They made their beds. Now they should lie in them," was a frequently expressed attitude, according to Janice Klemm, program director. Most of the complaints died down after a few years, Klemm added, as people began to realize how cost-effective the program was.

"The long-range cost to the taxpayers for welfare and aid to families with dependent children runs much higher," Klemm said. If the schools can intervene early enough in a child's life to see that basic needs are met, the child's chances of living a normal, productive life are enhanced, she added.

The Fresno program "takes the romanticism out of having a baby," Klemm said, by exposing students to the full responsibilities of parenthood.

The program provides child care from 7:30 A.M. to 4 P.M. each weekday. Three registered nurses care for the children, maintain their health records, and offer parenting tips to the mothers. The program provides diapers, formula, and solid foods for the babies while their mothers are attending classes. The program also provides child-development activities and classes in parenting skills. Last year the program served 300 Fresno teenagers and their babies in centers on seven high school campuses.

The program takes a balanced approach to the issue of abortion. When adolescents seek counseling regarding a pregnancy, the nurses who work in the program are required to offer referrals to three different types of clinics: one that encourages abortion, one that does not approve of abortion, and a third that takes a middle-of-the-road stance.

Programs must be imaginatively geared to individual and community needs. No single approach to teen pregnancy and teen parenting will substantially reduce these problems. It takes creative community involvement to promote the right mindset in students. For example, the Teen Theater Troupe, a part of the New Orleans Center for Creative Arts, uses the performing arts to help high school students make responsible decisions about sexuality and other issues.

Other pregnancy-prevention programs focus on enhancing students' self-esteem. Seventh- and eighth-graders in San Marcos, California, study a four-pronged curriculum intended to help them develop the necessary self-confidence to abstain from sex. The curriculum includes a six-week course for seventh-graders aimed at developing study skills, a six-week course for seventh-graders aimed at developing self-esteem and values, a six-week course for eighth-graders on "Sexuality, Commitment, and Family," and 10-minute lessons each day for classes at most grade levels in most schools on "How to Be Successful." These daily lessons emphasize goal-oriented behavior.

Although mainstreaming pregnant teens and teen parents is increasingly popular (favored by more than 80% of the administrators in the ERG study), it is not necessarily the best approach. Under some circumstances, mainstreaming can be crueler than isolating teen parents in special programs. "When you're eight months pregnant, and you can't fit into your desk, and everybody laughs at you, it takes toughness to survive," noted Anne Rogers, project manager for TAPP (Teenage Alternative Pregnancy Program) in Eatontown, New Jersey. TAPP operates on a separate campus from the regular high school, and instruction is geared to the individual needs and learning styles of the students. The program combines academic courses, pre- and postnatal instruction, home economics, consumer education, instruction on money and time management, and the development of employment skills. The students have access to individual and group counseling and to classes designed to prepare them for childbirth, child development, child care, and parenting. Clearly, to be effective for pregnant and parenting teens, mainstreaming must be combined with individualized programs and services. Just as clearly, few mainstream schools can offer as many services as TAPP does.

Parents, churches, and other community groups must be involved early in the decision-making process. Over and over, administrators told ERG researchers that the single most important factor in designing effective programs for pregnant teens and teen parents is community involvement.

Groups that oppose school-based programs must be challenged to offer their own solutions to the problems of pregnant teens and teen parents. It is not enough to just preach at teenagers, to threaten to punish them, or to slap the vague label of "secular humanism" on school-based approaches. Strong religious values may indeed inhibit some students from irresponsible sexual behavior; however, giving lip service to these values without backing them up with practical solutions can actually make the problems of teen pregnancy and teen parenting worse.

Much of the ideological opposition to sex education and to special programs for pregnant teens and teen parents can be defused by involving parents and community leaders in developing positive approaches to these problems. In the ERG study, many school officials who believed that their systems were effectively dealing with the problem of teen pregnancy had consciously cultivated the support of their communities, allowing parents to express their views during the program-development stage.

In the suburban community of Selma, California, for example, Superintendent Steven Bojorguez pointed out that the drive for sex education had begun in the community, not in the schools. A group of parents started a sex education program for adolescents, and they established enough credibility to garner school support.

In designing a school policy on teen pregnancy, school officials in Show Low, Arizona, first surveyed students and published the results in the local newspaper. This approach dramatized the issue and marshaled public opinion in favor of a special program for pregnant teens, according to Thomas Neel, superintendent of the Show Low school district. "We have had lots of community involvement from the start," Neel said.

Following heated debate within the community and a one-vote mandate from the school board, DuSable High School in Chicago opened a school-based clinic—and then strengthened support for that venture by instituting an open-door policy encouraging parents to visit the clinic at any time. A staff member keeps parents up-to-date on clinic policies and procedures. Before students can avail themselves of clinic services, their parents must visit the clinic with them and sign a consent form. Before students can receive contraceptives, they must attend a counseling session in which they are advised, among other things, to refrain from sex.

Making the sex education curriculum a topic for community discussion in Fremont, Iowa, helped to establish a consensus on what should be taught, according to Superintendent Catherine Tibbett. Mental health and medical personnel offered helpful suggestions, as did many of the parents. However, Tibbett acknowledged that encouraging such discussion involves risks. "As an administrator, you've got to be willing to take the heat for a little while, until the program is started," she said.

U.S. teens under age 15 are 15 times more likely to give birth than their peers in any other western nation. That shameful statistic alone should spur U.S. educators, politicians, and parents to work together to give adolescents the direction and the guidance they need.

Good programs and creative ideas are multiplying quickly. What better time than now to implement them?

Reprinted with permission from Capitol Publications, 1101 King St., Alexandria, VA 22314, (703) 683–4100.

■ Questions for Discussion

1. How, and to what degree, have the schools you attended helped you to deal with the social problems you have faced?

2. What do you believe are our country's major social problems, and how do you feel our schools might help to solve these problems?

3. How do you believe our schools should attack the problem of providing equal educational opportunity for all students?

4. Discuss the pros and cons of school busing to accomplish racial integration.

5. What are some viable plans that schools could use to reduce student use of drugs, alcohol, and tobacco?

■ Notes

1. Christopher Jencks and Mary Jo Bane, "The Schools and Equal Opportunity," *Saturday Review,* September 16, 1972, pp. 37–42.

2. National School Public Relations Association, *Drug Crisis: Schools Fight Back with Innovative Programs* (Arlington, Va.: National School Public Relations Association, 1971), p. 3.

3. R. L. Neeman and N. Neeman, "Complexities of Smoking Education," *The Journal of School Health* 45, no. 1 (January 1975):17–23.

4. C. F. McRae and D. Nelson, "Youth to Youth Communication on Smoking and Health," *The Journal of School Health* 41 (1971):445–47.

5. Richard Benedetto, "Truancy: A Disease That's Now an Epidemic," *Special Report on American Education in the 1980s* (Washington, D.C.: Gannett News Service, 1980).

6. Margaret C. Dunkle and Susan M. Bailey, "Schools Must Ease the Impact of Teenage Pregnancy and Parenthood," *Education Week* 4, no. 8 (October 28, 1984):24.

7. Cecelia H. Foxley, "Sex Equity in Education: Some Gains, Problems and Future Needs," *Journal of Teacher Education* 33, no. 5 (September/October 1984):6–9.

8. "Child Abuse and Neglect: What to Watch for, What to Do," *Education Week,* November 25, 1987, p. 9.

9. *U.S. News & World Report,* October 1, 1984, p. 74.

10. *The Facts About AIDS: A Special Guide for NEA Members* (Washington, D.C.: National Education Association, 1987).

11. *Why School Health* (Arlington, VA: American Association of School Administrators, 1987), pp. 1, 2.

12. Ibid., pp. 4, 5, 6, 9.

13. Robert D. Allers, "Children from Single-Parent Homes," *Today's Education* 1982–83 Annual, National Education Association, pp. 68–70.

■ Selected References

Banks, James A. "Multiethnic Education as the Crossroads." *Phi Delta Kappan* 64, no. 8 (April 1983):559.

Chaze, William L. "Now, Nationwide Drive to Curb Child Abuse." *U.S. News & World Report,* October 1, 1984, pp. 73–74.

Dunkle, Margaret C., and Bailey, Susan M. "Schools Must Ease the Impact of Teenage Pregnancy and Parenthood." *Education Week,* October 24, 1984, p. 24.

Eshelman, J. Ross. *The Family: An Introduction.* Boston: Allyn and Bacon, Inc., 1985.

Gist, Ted; Skrzycki, Cindy; Solorzano, Lucia; and Thornton, Jeannye. "War on Alcohol Abuse Spreads to New Fronts." *U.S. News & World Report,* December 24, 1984, pp. 63–64.

Grant, Carl A. "The Impact of Social Issues on Schooling." In *Bringing Teaching to Life.* Boston: Allyn and Bacon, 1982, pp. 69–80.

Kniker, Charles R., and Naylor, Natalie A. "Implementing Equal Educational Opportunity." In *Teaching Today and Tomorrow.* Columbus, Ohio: Charles E. Merrill, 1981, pp. 317–42.

Persell, Caroline H. *Understanding Society: An Introduction to Sociology.* New York: Harper & Row, 1987.

Sadker, Myra Pollack, and Sadker, David Miller. *Teachers Make the Difference, An Introduction to Education.* New York: Harper & Row, 1980.

Spring, Joel. "The School and the Social Structure." In *American Education.* New York: Longman, 1982, pp. 1–120.

Steinberg, Laurence. *Adolescence.* New York: Alfred A. Knopf, 1985.

Williams, Jeffrey W. "Characteristics of Households with Children Enrolled in Elementary and Secondary Schools." *National Center for Education Statistics Bulletin.* Washington, D.C.: U.S. Department of Education, September 1984.

Wissot, Jan. "Motivating the Alienated Student." *Humanist Educator* 18, no. 3 (March 1980):144–52.

Chapter 10

Historical Influences on Education

Objectives

After studying this chapter, you should be able to:

■ Provide a chronicle of the historical development of our educational system.

■ Point out the various periods in the development of the American educational system.

■ Conceptualize the historical support that Americans have provided for education.

■ Understand the concept that education has played a key role in the growth of our American society.

■ Trace the evolution of the elementary and secondary school.

■ Highlight the historical development of our teacher training programs.

■ Explain the dependency of a democratic society on its educational system to produce an informed citizenry.

■ Discuss the educational history of minority groups in America.

■ Explain the important contributions women have made to education.

Enrichment Experiences

The following suggestions will help you learn more about some of the important topics discussed in this chapter:

■ Develop a creative project centered around some aspect of the history of American education. (Examples: a one-act drama, a history of education game, or a multimedia presentation.)

■ Write a paper on the contributions to education of Horace Mann, Henry Barnard, Samuel Hall, Catherine Beecher, or Maria Montessori.

■ Invite an elderly person to your class to informally discuss "education in the good old days."

■ Interview a retired teacher about the nature of his or her teacher training, and also about his or her first teaching position. You may wish to tape record the interview.

■ Locate some artifact related to the history of education (an old textbook, slate, teaching aid, or school records) and, using library references, write a paper about the artifact.

■ Locate and read some library resources on the contributions of minority educators.

T his chapter will help you realize that education has contributed immensely to the development of our society and to the improvement of humankind down through history. In fact, without education, there would be no human progress. This chapter should help you realize that the teaching profession has a long and proud heritage. It will point out that, like all professions, teaching has evolved from very humble beginnings to its current advanced stage. All of this progress can be attributed to dedicated individuals who devoted their lives to teaching. This chapter will point out that our early educational practices were transplanted from Europe by our early colonial settlers. From that time, over three and one-half centuries, our educational system has grown rapidly and changed dramatically. Topics contained in this chapter include educational expectations in colonial America, early school laws, our first colleges, Latin grammar schools, the American Academy, the educational needs of our new nation, the development of the common school, the growth of the public high school, the historical development of education of blacks, the importance of women in education, and the history of teacher education. ■

History permits us to climb to a high place and look back over the road that we have traveled. Once we can see this road clearly, we can avoid some of the mistakes we made before. By the same token, we can capitalize on the successes in our educational past. Moreover, a knowledge of the history of education permits a teacher to appreciate the proud heritage that American educators possess. Let us proceed then with a brief look at the history of American education.

■ Great Teachers of the Past

History is replete with educators who have made great contributions to mankind. Only a few of the more notable ones will be mentioned here.

Socrates (470–399 B.C.) is often mentioned as one of the world's first truly great teachers. This man, who lived in the Greek city-state of Athens, devoted his life to teaching students who followed him wherever he went. His main method of teaching consisted of asking leading questions which helped the students discover the answer for themselves. In fact, this technique has been so closely identified with Socrates that it has come to be known as the "Socratic Method" of teaching. Socrates was eventually put to death for inciting the people against the government in his relentless search for truth. His dedication to teaching, knowledge, and truth inspired many of his students to become renowned educators in their own right. Plato became one of Socrates' most famous students.

Another famous teacher of his day was Quintilian (A.D. 35–95), a Roman educator. Quintilian, also a prolific educational writer, exhibited a perceptive understanding of students far in advance of his time when he wrote:

> I am by no means in favor of whipping boys, though I know it to be a general practice. In the first place, whipping is unseemly, and if you suppose the boys to be somewhat grown up, it is an affront in the highest degree. In the next

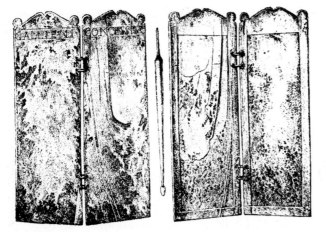

Dipticha, or Roman wax tablet with stylus—found on the Esquiline Hill, Rome, and preserved in the local museum. The tablets were covered with wax and were used for accounting or in schools by writing on the wax with the stylus. The name on the upper end of the left illustration, Galleri Concessi, shows its owner to have been a man of some importance.

place, if a boy's ability is so poor as to be proof against reproach he will, like a worthless slave, become insensible to blows. Lastly, if a teacher is assiduous and careful, there is no need to use force. I shall observe further that while a boy is under the rod he experiences pain and fear. The shame of this experience dejects and discourages many pupils, makes them shun being seen, and may even weary them of their lives.

One of the most famous teachers of the Dark Ages was an Englishman by the name of Alcuin. Alcuin became Charlemagne's educational advisor and established the Palace School at Frankland, which Charlemagne himself frequently attended.

There were many famous educators during the Renaissance and Reformation periods, including Erasmus (1466–1536), Melanchthon (1497–1560), Ignatius of Loyola (1491–1556), Jean Baptiste de la Salle (1651–1719) and Johann Amos Comenius (1592–1670). Comenius authored a great number of textbooks, and his textbooks were some of the first to contain pictures. Comenius was also among the first to recommend that a series of schools be established. Concerning this point he wrote, "There should be a maternal school in each family; an elementary school in each district; a gymnasium in each city; an academy in each kingdom, or even in each considerable province."[1]

There were countless numbers of great educators during the eighteenth and nineteenth centuries. Some of the famous American educators from this period, such as Benjamin Franklin, Horace Mann, Henry Barnard, and Samuel Hall, are discussed in more detail later in this chapter. There were also a number of famous European educators during this time whose work greatly influenced American education. These included, among others, Jean Jacques Rousseau (1712–1778), Johann Friedrich Herbart (1776–1841), Friedrich Froebel (1782–1852), and Johann Heinrich Pestalozzi (1746–1827). Of these, Pestalozzi, a Swiss educator, stands out as one who gained a great deal of fame as the founder of two schools—one at Burgdorf (1800–1804), and another at Yverdun (1805–1825).

It was at these schools that Pestalozzi put into practice his educational beliefs that children should be treated with love, respect, understanding, and patience (a belief that was in contradiction to the prevailing, religiously inspired

1. The lower schoolroom of Eton College, founded in 1440. The wood from which these benches were made, as well as the wainscoting and timbers in the room, was taken from the wrecked vessels of the Spanish Armada. This was one of the means by which patriotic ideals were instilled in the English boys.

2. The library of the University of Leyden in the sixteenth century. By this time, the library had become an important part of the university. The books are chained to the shelves so they could not be stolen—an indication of their scarcity and value. Leyden was founded in 1575 and for over a century was the center of advanced thought and instruction.

3. Pestalozzi's first teaching experience was at Stans in 1798. There he took charge of a group of children orphaned by one of the massacres of the French Revolution. There were no teaching aids, so Pestalozzi taught by using objects. This illustration is from an early nineteenth century woodcut.

4. Pestalozzi eventually moved to Yverdun where, at this castle, he conducted an experimental school for twenty years. Educators came from all around the world to visit and study the teaching methods and materials he developed here.

A colonial hornbook from which children learned the ABC's. It consisted of a heavy sheet of paper tacked to a piece of wood and covered with a thin sheet of cow's horn.

view that children were born full of sin and inherently bad). Pestalozzi reflected his beliefs when he wrote:

> I was convinced that my heart would change the condition of my children just as promptly as the sun of spring would reanimate the earth benumbed by the winter. . . . It was necessary that my children should observe, from dawn to evening, at every moment of the day, upon my brow and on my lips, that my affections were fixed on them, that their happiness was my happiness, and that their pleasures were my pleasures. . . .

> I was everything to my children. I was alone with them from morning till night. . . . Their hands were in my hands. Their eyes were fixed on my eyes.[2]

Pestalozzi also believed that teachers should use objects and games to help students learn. In fact, he developed a series of teaching materials which were very advanced for their time. A number of American educators visited Pestalozzi's schools and brought many of his ideas back to the United States where they were put into practice.

■ Educational Expectations in Colonial America

When the colonists arrived at Jamestown in 1607, they brought with them their ideas concerning education. Earlier in this book, it was pointed out that Americans today have various expectations of the public schools. Just as contemporary Americans have certain expectations of the present-day educational systems, so were there certain educational expectations in colonial America. Colonial America was divided roughly into three geographical areas—the northern colonies in the New England area, the middle colonies centered in New York, and the southern colonies located in the Virginia area. The colonists in each of these three areas had somewhat different expectations of the schools that existed in their respective areas. A New England Puritan, expressing his or her expectations in contemporary language, might have said:

> I expect two things from our schools here in the northern colonies. First, my children must learn to read so they can understand the Bible. Secondly, the schools must teach my boys Latin and Greek so that if they wish to go on to college they will be qualified to do so.

*Religion, morality, and knowledge
being necessary to good government
and the happiness of mankind,
schools and the means of education
shall forever be encouraged.*

Northwest Ordinance of 1787

This interest in education in the northern colonies coupled with the fact that most of the colonists in that area were of similar religious convictions led to the early establishment of public schools in that area. In fact, by 1635, only fifteen years after Boston had been settled, a Latin Grammar School was established in that area. Grammar schools had existed in Europe for many years prior to their appearance in colonial America. As their name implies, the Latin Grammar Schools included instruction in the classical languages of Latin and Greek. Such instruction was considered to be absolutely essential for the very few colonial boys who went on to a university. The schoolboys—for only boys were admitted—who attended the Latin Grammar School spent most of their time memorizing and then reciting what they had learned to the schoolmaster. Recalling his experiences as a Latin Grammar School student, one graduate recalled:

> At ten years of age I committed to memory many rules of syntax, the meaning of which I had no notion of, although I could apply them in a mechanical way. The rule for the ablative absolute, for instance—"A noun and a participle are put in the ablative, called absolute, to denote the time, cause or concomitant of an action, or the condition on which it depends"—I could rattle off whenever I encountered a sample of that construction, but it was several years after I learnt the rule that I arrived at even the faintest conception of what it meant. The learning by heart of the grammar then preceded rather than accompanied, as now, exercises in translation and composition.

The educational expectations of a typical colonist from the middle colonies can be illustrated by the following statement that could have been made by a parent living in that area at that time:

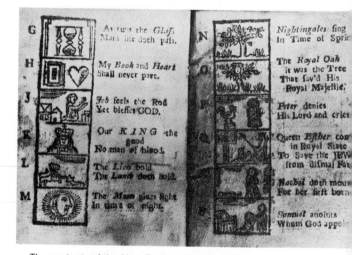

The contents of the New England Primer reflected the religious emphasis of education in colonial America.

Since there are many different religions represented here in the middle colonies, I want my children to attend a parochial school where they will not only learn to read and write, but also where they will receive instruction in my particular religion.

These middle colonies are sometimes referred to as the "colonial melting pot" because they were settled by people of many different nationalities and religions. These divergent backgrounds made it difficult for the middle colonists to agree upon the curriculum for a public school system, and therefore each religious group established its own parochial school system. It is interesting to note that many of these same educational problems that were found in colonial America still exist today. For instance, there are still many divergent groups in the American society, so that we may still be considered a melting pot (or if you prefer to use more recent popular terminology, a vegetable stew).

Yet another example of an educational problem that has persisted since colonial times is that dealing with parochial education. Just as the middle colonists did, a number of religious groups still feel the need to maintain their own parochial school systems.

The southern colonies consisted of large plantations and relatively few towns. This meant that two rather distinct classes of people—a few wealthy plantation owners, and a mass of poor black slaves and white indentured servants who worked on the plantations—lived in the southern colonies. This also meant that people lived far apart in the southern colonies. If we could turn back the clock to colonial days, we would probably hear a southern plantation owner explain his educational expectations something like this:

> Let me say first of all that we don't really need a public school system here in the southern colonies because, in the first place, the plantation workers do not need any education at all, and in the second place, the children of plantation owners live so far apart that it would be impractical to have a central public school for all of them to attend. For these reasons, we do not have and do not need a public school system. I hire a tutor to live here on my plantation and teach my children. When my boys get old enough I'll send them back to Europe to attend a university.

The only education available to the poorer people in the southern colonies was that provided by individual parents for their children and that provided by certain missionary groups interested in teaching young people to read the Bible. A boy from a poor family who wished to learn a trade would receive his practical education by serving an apprenticeship with a master craftsman who was already in that line of work.

The earliest known illustration of a secondary school in America. This is the Boston Latin Grammar School founded in 1635. This illustration comes from an old pictorial map of Boston made about 1748, just before this school building was torn down. This was probably not the original building which housed the Boston Latin Grammar School.

■ Early School Laws

The first law passed in colonial America dealing with education was passed in Massachusetts in 1642. This law, requiring parents to educate their children, reads as follows:

> This Court, taking into consideration the great neglect of many parents and masters in training up their children in learning, and labor, and other implyments which may be profitable to the common wealth, do hereupon order and decree, that in every towne ye chosen men appointed for managing prudentiall affaires of the same shall henceforth stand charged with the care of the redresse of this evil, so as they shalbee sufficiently punished by fines for the neglect

thereof, upon presentment of the grand jury, or other information on complaint in any Court within this jurisdiction. And for this end they, or the greater number of them, shall have power to take account from time to time of all parents and masters, and of their children, concerning their calling and implyment of their children, especially of their ability to read and understand the principles of religion and the capitall lawes of this country, and to impose fines upon such as shall refuse to render such account to them when they shall be required: and they shall have power, with consent of any Court or the magistrate, to put forth apprentices the children of such as they shall [find] not to be able and fitt to imploy and bring them up.

In 1647, yet another law dealing with education was passed in Massachusetts. This law, which has come to be known as the "Old Deluder Act," required towns of certain size to establish schools. This law stated:

It being one chiefe project of that old deluder, Satan, to keepe men from the knowledge of the Scriptures, as in former times by keeping them in an unknown tongue, so in these latter times by persuading from the use of tongues, that so at least the true sence and meaning of the originall might be clouded by false glosses of saint seeming deceivers, that learning may not be buried in the grave of our fathers in church and commonwealth, the Lord assisting our endeavors,—

It is therefore ordered that every township in this jurisdiction, after the Lord hath increased their number of 50 householders, shall then forthwith appoint one within their towne to teach all such children as shall resort to him to write and reade, whose wages shall be paid either by the parents or masters of such children, or by the inhabitants in general, . . .

and it is further ordered that where any towne shall increase to the number of 100 families or householders they shall set up a grammar schoole, the Master thereof being able to instruct youth so farr as they shall be fitted for the University, provided that if any town neglect the performance hereof above one year, that every such town shall pay five pounds to the next school till they shall perform this order.

In addition to the passage of these laws, further proof of the colonists' early interest in education can be found in the following agreement signed by a number of the citizens living in Roxbury in 1645:

Whereas, the Inhabitantes of Roxburie, in consideration of their relligeous care of posteritie, have taken into consideration how necessarie the education of theire children in Literature will be to fitt them for public service, both in Churche and Commonwealth, in succeeding ages. They therefore unanimously have consented and agreed to erect a free schoole in the said town of Roxburie, and to allow twenty pounds per annum to the schoolmaster, to bee raised out of the messuages and part of the lands of the severall donors (Inhabitantes of said Towne) in several proportions as hereafter followeth under their hands. And for the well ordering thereof they have chosen and elected some Feoffees who shall have power to putt in or remove the Schoolemaster, to see to the well ordering of the schoole and schollars, to receive and pay the said twenty pounds per annum to the Schoolemaster and to dispose of any other gifte or giftes which hereafter may or shall be given for the advancement of learning and education of children. . . .

◼ Our First Colleges

In 1636, only sixteen years after the settlement of Boston, the first college was established in colonial America. This school was named Harvard College after the man who helped to finance the school's humble beginning. The conditions surrounding the establishment of Harvard, and the school's philosophy and curriculum, are explained in the following document, written in 1643 and entitled *New England's First Fruits,* which is partially reproduced here:

Harvard College building constructed in 1675, 1699, and 1720. These buildings were dormitories. Most of the instruction took place in the homes or offices of the president and tutors.

> In Respect of the Colledge, and the Proceedings of "Learning" Therein: 1. After God had carried us safe to New England, and wee had builded our houses, provided necessaries for our livelihood, rear'd convenient places for God's worship, and setled the Civil Government: One of the next things we longed for, and looked after was to advance Learning and perpetuate it to Posterity; dreading to leave an illiterate Ministery to the Churches, when our present Ministers shall lie in the Dust. And as wee were thinking and consulting how to effect this great Work; it pleased God to stir up the heart of one Mr. Harvard (a godly Gentleman, and a lover of Learning, there living amongst us) to give the onehalfe of his Estate (it being in all about 1700.1.) towards the erecting of a Colledge: and all his Library: after him another gave 300.1. others after them cast in more, and the publique hand of the State added the rest: the Colledge was, by common consent, appointed to be at Cambridge, (a place very pleasant and accomodate) and is called (according to the name of the first founder) Harvard Colledge.
>
> The Edifice is very faire and comely within and without, having in it a spacious Hall; (where they daily meet at Commons, Lectures and Exercises), and a large Library with some Bookes to it, the gifts of diverse of our friends, their Chambers and studies also fitted for, and possessed by the Students, and all other roomes of Office necessary and convenient, with all needfull Offices thereto belonging: And by the side of the Nolledge a faire Grammer Schoole, for the training up of young Schollars, and fitting them for Academicall Learning, that still as they are judged ripe, they may be received into the Colledge of this Schoole. Master Corlet is the Mr., who hath very well approved himselfe for his abilities, dexterity and painfulness in teaching and education of the youth under him.
>
> Over the Colledge is master Dunster placed, as President, a learned conscionable and industrious man, who hath so trained up his

Pupils in the tongues and Arts, and so seasoned them with the principles of Divinity and Christianity, that we have to our great comfort, (and in truth) beyond our hopes, beheld this progresse in Learning and godliness also; the former of these hath appeared in their publique declamations in Latine and Greeke, and Disputations Logicall and Philosophicall, which they have wonted (besides their ordinary Exercises in the Colledge-Hall) in the audience of the Magistrates, Ministers, and other Schollars, for the probation of their growth in Learning, upon set dayes, constantly once every moneth to make and uphold: The latter hath been manifested in sundry of them, by the savoury breathings of their Spirits in their godly conversation. Insomuch that we are confident, if these early blossomes may be cherished and warmed with the influence of the friends of Learning, and lovers of this pious worke, they will by the help of God, come to happy maturity in a short time.

Over the Colledge are twelve Overseers chosen by the generall Court, six of them are of the Magistrates, the other six of the Ministers, who are to promote the best good of it and (having a power of influence into all persons in it) are to see that every one be diligent and proficient in his proper place.

Further insight into the nature of Harvard College may be found in the following entrance requirements published in 1642:

When any scholar is able to read Tully, or such like classical Latine author *extempore,* and make a speak true Latin in Verse and Prose, and decline perfectly the paradigms of nounes and verbes in the Greek tongue, then may he be admitted into the college, nor shall any claim admission before such qualifications.

Harvard was the only colonial college for nearly sixty years until William and Mary was established in 1693. Other colleges which were established early in our history included Yale (1701), Princeton (1746), King's College (1754), College of Philadelphia (1755), Brown (1764), Dartmouth (1769), and Queen's College (1770).

■ Latin Grammar Schools

The Latin Grammar School was the only form of secondary school found in the colonies until the early 1700s, at which time a few private secondary schools were established. These schools were created out of a need for a more practical form of secondary education than the existing Latin Grammar Schools provided. Insight into the nature of these early private secondary schools can be gained from the following newspaper ad, which was published in the October–November 1723 edition of the *American Weekly Mercury* of Philadelphia:

There is a school in New York, in the Broad Street, near the Exchange where Mr. John Walton, late of Yale-Colledge, teacheth Reading, Writing, Arethmatick, whole Numbers and Fractions, Vulgar and Decimal, the Mariners Art, Plain and Mercators Way; also Geometry, Surveying, the Latin tongue, and Greek and Hebrew Grammers, Ethicks, Retorick, Logick, Natural Philosophy and Metaphysicks, all or any of them for a Reasonable Price. The School from the first of October till the first of March will be tended in the Evening. If any Gentleman in the Country are disposed to send their sons to the said School, if they apply themselves to the Master

A picture of the academy and charitable school of Philadelphia founded by Benjamin Franklin in 1751. It is the first institution in America, so far as the present records show, to bear the title of academy. Later on it developed into the University of Pennsylvania.

he will immediately procure suitable Entertainment for them, very cheap. Also if any Young Gentleman of the City will Please to come in the evening and make some Tryal of the Liberal Arts, they may have opportunity of Learning the same things which are commonly taught in Colledges.

■ The Academy

In 1751, Benjamin Franklin opened a secondary school in Philadelphia which he called an academy. The curriculum in Franklin's Academy included practical training in areas such as surveying, navigation, and printing, as well as courses in English, geography, history, logic, rhetoric, Latin, and Greek.

Franklin's Academy served a real need as the colonies developed a greater need for technically trained citizens. Other academies were quickly established, and this type of school flourished for approximately one hundred years. These academies were private schools, and many of them admitted girls as well as boys.

■ The New Nation and Its Educational Needs

One of the great problems facing the United States, after winning her independence from England, was that of welding her people, who had come from many diverse political and religious convictions, into a nation of informed voters. This meant that all citizens should be able to read so that they could keep informed on the issues the country faced. This interest in education found in the new nation was manifested in a number of different ways; for instance, groups of citizens created petitions for better schools. An example of such a petition is the following, which was submitted in 1799 to the General Assembly of Rhode Island:

A PETITION FOR FREE SCHOOL. *To the Honorable General Assembly of the State of Rhode Island and Providence Plantations, to be holden at Greenwich, on the last Monday of February,* A.D. *1799:*
The Memorial and Petition of the Providence Association of Mechanics and Manufacturers respectfully presents—

That the means of education which are enjoyed in this state are very inadequate to a purpose so highly important . . . we at the same time solicit this Honorable Assembly to make legal provision for the establishment of free schools sufficient to educate all the children in the several towns throughout the state. . . .

Another indication of the new national need for and interest in education is the following comment made by Thomas Jefferson in 1816:

If a nation expects to be ignorant and free in a state of civilization, it expects what never was and never will be. . . . There is no safe deposit but with the people themselves; nor can they be safe with them without information.

What indeed is the good teacher if not a well-informed lover? . . . To teach is to love. And in the final analysis we learn only from those whom we love . . . the most important of all qualities in the world. . . . This is because the most important of all desires of a human being is the desire to be loved, and at the same time to love others.

Ashley Montagu

Despite this new interest in education, the school of the early 1800s was very humble and inadequate. An excellent description of an 1810 New England school is contained in the following reflection of a teacher who taught in this school.

(A) The school building: The School house stood near the center of the district, at the junction of four roads, so near the usual track of carriages that a large stone was set up at the end of the building to defend it from injury. Except in the dry season the ground was wet, and the soil by no means firm. The spot was particularly exposed to the bleak winds of winter: nor were there any shade trees to shelter the children from the scorching rays of the summer's sun, as they were cut down many years ago. Neither was there any such thing as an outhouse of any kind, not even a wooden shed.

The size of the building was 22 × 20 feet. From the floor to the ceiling it was 7 feet. The chimney and entry took up about four feet at one end, leaving the schoolroom itself 18 × 20 feet. Around these sides of the room were connected desks, arranged so that when the pupils were sitting at them their faces were towards the instructor and their backs toward the wall. Attached to the sides of the desks nearest to the instructor were benches for small pupils. The instructor's desk and chair occupied the center. On this desk were stationed a rod, or ferule: sometimes both. These, with books, writings, inkstands, rules, and plummets, with a fire shovel, and a pair of tongs (often broken), were the principal furniture.

The windows were five in number, of twelve panes each. They were situated so low in the walls as to give full opportunity to the pupils to see every traveller as he passed; and to be easily seen. The places of the broken panes were usually supplied with hats, during school hours.

A depression in the chimney, on one side of the entry, furnished a place of deposit for about half of the hats, and the spare clothes of the boys: the rest were left on the floor, often to be trampled upon. The girls generally carried their bonnets, etc., into the schoolroom. The floor and ceiling were level, and the walls were plastered.

The room was warmed by a large and deep fire place. So large was it, and so efficacious in warming the room otherwise, that I have seen about one-eighth of a cord of good wood burning in it at a time. In severe weather it was estimated that the amount usually consumed was not far from a cord a week. . . .

The school was not infrequently broken up for a day or two for want of wood. The instructor or pupils were sometimes, however, compelled to cut or saw it to prevent the closing of the school. The wood was left in the road near the house, so that it often was buried in the snow, or wet with rain. At the best, it was usually burnt green. The fires were to be kindled about half an hour before the time of beginning the school. Often, the scholar, whose lot it was, neglected to build it. In consequence of this, the house was frequently cold and uncomfortable about half of the forenoon, when, the fire being very large, the excess of heat became equally distressing. Frequently, too, we were annoyed by smoke. The greatest amount of suffering, however, arose from excessive heat, particularly at the close of the day. The pupils being in a free perspiration when they left, were very liable to take cold.

The ventilation of the schoolroom was as much neglected as its temperature: and its cleanliness, more perhaps than either. There were no arrangements for cleaning feet at the door, or for washing floors, windows, etc. In the summer the floor was washed, perhaps once in two or three weeks.

(B) The Instructors: The winter school usually opened about the first week of December, and continued from twelve to sixteen weeks. The summer term commenced about the first of May. Formerly this was also continued about three or four months, but within ten years the term has been lengthened usually to twenty weeks. Males have been uniformly employed in winter, and females in summer.

The instructors have usually been changed every season, but sometimes they have been continued two successive summers or winters. A strong prejudice has always existed against employing the same instructor more than once or twice in the same district. This prejudice has yielded in one instance, so far that an instructor who had taught two successive winters, twenty-five years before, was employed another season. I have not been able to ascertain the number of instructors who have been engaged in the school during the last thirty years, but I can distinctly recollect thirty-seven. Many of them, both males and females, were from sixteen to eighteen years of age, and a few, over twenty-one.

Good moral character, and a thorough knowledge of the common branches, formerly were considered as indispensable qualifications in an instructor. The instructors were chiefly selected from the most respectable families in town. But for fifteen or twenty years, these things have not been so much regarded. They have indeed been deemed desirable; but the most common method now seems to be to ascertain, as near as possible, the dividend for that season from the public treasury, and then fix upon a teacher who will take charge of the school, three or four months, for this money. He must indeed be able to obtain a license from the Board of Visitors; but this has become nearly a

The town and church schools of the early colonial period were supplemented by the dame school. In fact, it was a common requirement for that period that children know how to read before entering a town school. Hence, the necessity of these dame schools, which taught the children the alphabet, and possibly the catechism and the rudiments of reading.

matter of course, provided he can spell, read, and write. In general, the candidate is some favorite or relative of the District Committee. It gives me great pleasure, however, to say that the moral character of almost every instructor, so far as I know, has been unexceptional.

Instructors have usually boarded in the families of the pupils. Their compensation has varied from seven to eleven dollars a month for males; and from sixty-two and a half cents to one dollar a week for females. Within the past ten years, however, the price of instruction has rarely been less than nine dollars in the former case, and seventy-five cents in the latter. In the few instances in which instructors have furnished their own board the compensation has been about the same, it being assumed that they could work at some employment of their own enough to pay their board, especially the females.

(C) The Instruction: Two of the Board of Visitors usually visit the winter schools twice during the term. In the summer, their visits are often omitted. These visits usually occupy from one hour to an hour and a half. They are spent merely in hearing a few hurried lessons, and in making some remarks, generally in their character. Formerly, it was customary to examine the pupils in some approved Catechism, but this practice has been omitted for twenty years.

The parents seldom visit the school, except by special invitation. The greater number pay very little attention to it at all. There are, however, a few who are gradually awakening to the importance of good instruction; but there are also a few who oppose everything which is suggested as, at the least, useless, and are scarcely willing their children should be governed in the school.

The school books have been about the same for thirty years. Webster's Spelling Book, the American Preceptor, and the New Testament, have been the principal books used. Before the appearance of the American Preceptor, Dwight's Geography was used as a reading book. A few of the Introduction to the American Orator were introduced about twelve years since, and, more recently, Jack Halyard.

Until within a few years, no studies have been permitted in the day school but spelling, reading, and writing. Arithmetic was taught by a few instructors, one or two evenings in a week, but, in spite of the most determined opposition, arithmetic is now permitted in the day school, and a few pupils study geography.

A portrait of Horace Mann—the father of the common school.

■ The Development of the Common School

The national interest in education during the late eighteenth and early nineteenth centuries culminated in a movement to establish free public schools—or common schools, as they were then called—for all children. The man who led this fight for common schools was Horace Mann (1796–1859). Horace Mann became the first secretary (a position we now call the state superintendent of schools) of the Massachusetts state board of education in 1837. In that position, Mann was able to do a good deal to promote the common school cause. Each year, Mann wrote an annual report of his work as the secretary of the state

Laws for the liberal education of youth, especially of the lower class of people, are so extremely wise and useful, that, to a humane and generous mind, no expense for this purpose would be thought extravagant.

President John Adams

board of education. His twelfth annual report included the following statement about the importance of the common school:

> Without undervaluing any other human agency, it may be safely affirmed that the common school, improved and energized as it can easily be, may become the most effective and benignant of all the forces of civilization. Two reasons sustain this position. In the first place, there is a universality in its operations, which can be affirmed of no other institution whatever. If administered in the spirit of justice and conciliation, all the rising generation may be brought within the circle of its reformatory and elevating influences. And, in the second place, the materials upon which it operates are so pliant and ductile as to be susceptible of assuming a greater variety of forms than any other earthly work of the Creator. The inflexibility and ruggedness of the oak, when compared with the lithe sapling or the tender germ, are but feeble emblems to typify the docility of childhood when contrasted with the obduracy and intractableness of man. It is these inherent advantages of the common school, which, in our own state, have produced results so striking, from a system so imperfect, and an administration so feeble. In teaching the blind and the deaf and dumb, in kindling the latent spark of intelligence that lurks in an idiot's mind, and in the more holy work of reforming abandoned and outcast children, education has proved what it can do by glorious experiments. These wonders it has done in its infancy, and with the lights of a limited experience: but when its faculties shall be fully developed, when it shall be trained to wield its mighty energies for the protection of society against the giant vices

which now invade and torment it—against intemperance, avarice, war, slavery, bigotry, the woes of want, and the wickedness of waste,—then there will not be a height to which these enemies of the race can escape which it will not scale.

Through his work as secretary to the Massachusetts state board of education, his speaking, and his writing—including his annual reports such as the one just quoted—Horace Mann deserves much of the credit for helping to establish the common school system in the United States. So much so, in fact, that he is now remembered as the "father of the common school."

Another of the many men who did much to help promote education in the United States during the midnineteenth century was Henry Barnard (1811–1900). Barnard served as the secretary of the state board of education in Connecticut and then in Rhode Island. Barnard was a prolific writer and his writings were very influential in helping to sell the need for better education. He edited and published the *American Journal of Education* which represented a gigantic compilation of information about education. In 1867, Henry Barnard became the first United States Commissioner of Education.

The work of Horace Mann, Henry Barnard, and others who saw the value of a common education for all citizens did much to establish elementary schools throughout the United States. Massachusetts, the state that led the way in many facets of education, passed the first compulsory school attendance law in 1852. Other states eventually passed similar laws so that by 1900, thirty-two states required compulsory school attendance.

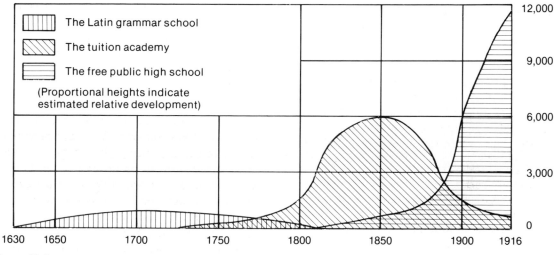

■ **Figure 10.1**
The historical development of secondary schools in the
United States

■ The Development of the Public High Schools

It was mentioned earlier in this chapter that the
Latin Grammar School was the first form of sec-
ondary school that existed in this country. The
academy eventually replaced the Latin Grammar
School as the dominant secondary school in the
United States.

In 1821, a new form of secondary school,
one unique to the United States, was established
in Boston, Massachusetts. This new secondary
school was called the "English Classical School"
but three years later its name was changed to the
"English High School."

The curriculum of this new English High
School emphasized mathematics, social studies,
science, and English. The first high schools were
for boys between the ages of twelve and fifteen,
but later on girls were also admitted.

At about 1900, the high school replaced the
academy as the dominant type of secondary school
in this country, and, needless to say, remains so
today. Figure 10.1 shows, in graphic form, the
historical development of secondary schools in the
United States.

■ Education for Minorities

Historically, education was for the most part reserved for white well-to-do boys. With a few notable exceptions, black children, Indian children, children of Spanish descent, and poor white children received very little, if any, formal education. Likewise, most girls—even many from wealthy families—received little formal education.

Slave owners commonly felt that education and slavery were incompatible. Frederick Douglass, one of the few slaves who managed to educate himself and become a prominent black leader, relates that his master characterized this viewpoint when he said in his own words:

> If you give a nigger an inch, he will take an ell. A nigger should know nothing but to obey his master—to do as he is told to do. Learning would spoil the best nigger in the world. Now if you teach that nigger how to read, there would be no keeping him. It would forever unfit him to be a slave. He would at once become unmanageable, and of no value to his master. As to himself, it could do him no good, but a great deal of harm. It would make him discontent and unhappy.[3]

Douglass goes on to point out how he came to realize that education was the "pathway from slavery to freedom." It was not until after the Civil War that any serious attempt was made to provide education for blacks. Even then, many of these efforts were left up to religious groups—whose motive was to teach blacks to read the Bible and gain salvation.

The Freedmen's Bureau was created by congress in 1865 in an attempt to provide basic education to blacks in hopes of helping them to become self-sufficient after receiving freedom from slavery. While many blacks learned to read and write through the efforts of the Freedmen's Bureau, it did little to improve their lot in life. A few black colleges, such as Tuskegee Institute founded by Booker T. Washington, were established prior to 1900, but important as they were, they did little for the masses of black people in America during their early years.

Throughout American history, providing formal schooling and eventual equal educational opportunities for blacks has been an uphill struggle. Some significant dates and events in this uphill struggle are presented in appendix F. Recent developments in black education are discussed in greater detail elsewhere in this book.

For the Native American, education had very little utility during the colonial period. The Native American's major concern was retaining the land and eventually simply surviving against the ever increasing encroachment of the whites. A few missionary groups such as the Quakers and the Society for the Propagation of the Gospel attempted to teach some Native Americans to read and write; however, it was not until late in the 1800s that any serious national effort was made to provide education for Native Americans. This happened when the federal government finally provided money as part of its land treaties for educational efforts in the various tribes. This system of federally operated schools for Native Americans has existed right up to the present.

The same basic story just told about blacks and Native Americans can be told about the educational history, or more accurately the lack of it, for other minority groups in America. The Mexican Americans, Puerto Ricans, Japanese Americans, Chinese Americans, and other minority groups simply were not afforded equal educational opportunity in the historical development of America.

Most recently, attention has been brought to the fact that in many respects American women represent yet another group who have not received equal educational opportunity down through American history.

■ The Importance of Women in Education

Women have played a key role in the historical development of our schools, but unfortunately, have received little credit for it. Actually, women have almost exclusively taught America's elementary school children from the early colonial dame school held in some kindly housewife's log cabin down through the ages to our present elementary schools. Furthermore, many of our country's innovators and educational leaders have been women. Figure 10.2 lists but a few of these women who made important educational contributions.

■ The Development of Teacher Education

As the United States developed a need for better schools and better education, it was inevitable that the subject of better-trained teachers should also receive attention. Citizens of the United States were slow to realize that good education required good teachers. Until the mid-1800s teachers had, for the most part, been very poorly prepared for their work. A teacher's job was not considered very important, and commanded very little prestige. In fact, advertisements that appeared in a Philadelphia newspaper during colonial times show that even indentured servants were sold as schoolteachers.

Since education had a strong religious motive in the colonies, the schools were often conducted

Catherine Beecher established Hartford seminary for girls, recruited female teachers for the western frontier, and wrote about the need to improve schools.

Emma Willard established Troy Seminary for women in 1821.

Mary Lyon opened Mount Holyoke Seminary for girls in 1836.

Marietta Johnson experimented with and adapted the ideas of Rousseau in her Fairhope, Alabama school.

Jane Addams campaigned for better educational opportunities for girls.

Susan Anthony taught school as a young woman and supported the concept of female education throughout her life as a public figure.

Mrs. Carl Schurz established the first kindergarten in the United States at Oshkosh, Wisconsin.

Maria Montessori developed a new system of elementary education which is still used throughout the world today.

Mary McLeod Bethune, whose parents were slaves, served as an early president of the American Teachers Association and later founded a college.

◘ Figure 10.2
Examples of important women in education.

in the church by the minister. When the job got too big for the minister to handle by himself, a layperson would be hired to teach at the school. Oftentimes, in addition to teaching the school, the teacher would be required "to act as court messenger, to serve summonses, to conduct certain ceremonial services at the church, to lead the Sunday choir, to ring the bell for public worship, to dig the graves, and to perform other occasional duties."

Some boys became teachers by serving as an apprentice to a schoolmaster. This method of learning the art of teaching was quite logical since the apprenticeship was a well-established way of learning trades in that day. The following record of such an apprenticeship agreement was recorded in the courts of New York City in 1772:

> This Indenture witnesseth that John Campbel Son of Robert Campbel of the City of New York with the Consent of his father and mother hath put himself and by these presents doth Voluntarily put and bind himself Apprentice to George Brownell of the Same City Schoolmaster to learn the Art Trade or Mystery—for and during the term of ten years. . . . And the said George Brownell Doth hereby Convenent and Promise to teach and Instruct or Cause the said Apprentice to be taught and Instructed in the Art Trade or Calling of a Schoolmaster by the best way or means he or his wife may or can.

Benjamin Franklin, in proposing the establishment of his academy, claimed that

> a number of the poorer sort [of academy graduates] will be hereby qualified to act as School masters in the Country, to teach children Reading, Writing, Arithmetic, and the Grammar of their Mother Tongue, and being of good morals and known character, may be recommended from the Academy to Country Schools for that purpose; the Country suffering at present very much for want of good Schoolmasters, and obliged frequently to employ in their Schools, vicious imported Servants, or concealed Papists, who by their bad Examples and Instructions often deprave the Morals and corrupt the Principles of the children under their Care.

It is interesting to note that Franklin suggested that the "poorer" graduates of his academy would make good teachers. This wording indicates again the low esteem of teachers at that time.

The first formal teacher-training institution in the United States was a private normal school established in 1823 at Concord, Vermont. This school was established by the Rev. Samuel Hall, and was called the Columbian School. Some insight into the nature of Hall's school can be obtained from the following advertisement, which appeared in the May 20, 1823, edition of the *North Star* newspaper:

> COLUMBIAN SCHOOL, CONCORD, VT. The second term will commence on the third Tuesday (17th day) of June next. The School will be under the direction, and will be principally instructed by the Rev. Mr. Hall.
>
> Books used in the school must be uniform. Hence, arrangements are made so that they may be obtained at either of the stores in town. Branches taught, if required, are the following: Reading, Spelling, Defining, Geography (ancient and modern), History, Grammar, Rhetoric, Composition, Arithmetic, Construction of Maps, Theoretical Surveying, Astronomy, Natural Philosophy, Chemistry (without experiments), Logic, Moral Philosophy, Mental Philosophy, and General Criticism.
>
> It is wished to have the languages excluded.— This will not, however, be strictly adhered to.
>
> TERMS: For Common School studies, $2. per term of 12 weeks. Other branches from $2.50 to $4.
>
> It is intended to have instruction particularly thorough, and hence an additional instructor will be employed, when the School amounts to more than 20. Board obtained near the School room, on reasonable terms.
>
> Application may be made to Mr. Lyman F. Dewey, Mr. John Barnet, or Mr. Hall.
>
> *Concord, Vt. May 14, 1823.*

What can only be taught by the rod and with blows will not lead to much good; they will not remain pious longer than the rod is behind them.

Martin Luther

To Be DISPOSED of,

A Likely Servant Mans Time for 4 Years who is very well Qualified for a Clerk or to teach a School, he Reads, Writes, underſtands Arithmetick and Accompts very well, Enquire of the Printer hereof.

Lately improted from Antigua *and to be Sold by* Edward Jones *in* Iſacc Norris's *Alley.*

A PARCEL of likely Ne-groWomen &Girls from thirteen to one and twenty Years of age, and have all had the Small-Pox.

To Be SOLD,

TWO verly likely Negroe Boys, Enquire of Capt. *Benjamin Chriſ-tian,* at his Houſe in *Arch-Street.* Alſo a Quantity of very good Lime-juice to be Sold cheap.

An advertisement in a 1735 issue of the Pennsylvania Gazette showing an indentured servant for sale as a schoolmaster. The lower two ads show Negro slaves for sale.

The first high school in the United States, established in 1821 at Boston. This was the counterpart of the Latin Grammar School. The term high school was not applied to it until the school had existed for several years. It was first called an English Classical School.

This ad points out that the curriculum in Hall's normal school included "Mental Philosophy," which was the forerunner of educational psychology, and "General Criticism" (presumably of the student's practice teaching).

The first public tax-supported teacher-training school in this country was the Lexington Normal School located in Lexington, Massachusetts. This school was opened in 1839. Horace Mann, as secretary of the state board of education, was very influential in the establishment of this state normal school. The curriculum in the Lexington Normal School, and other similar state normal schools which were quickly established,

was patterned after similar schools that had existed in Europe since the late 1600s. These early normal schools offered a two-year program designed to prepare their students, many of whom had not attended a secondary school, to teach elementary school. The normal schools eventually developed four-year programs and, during the 1920s, changed their names to "state teachers' colleges." Then later, during the 1950s, many of these institutions expanded their curricula to include liberal arts, and changed their names to "state colleges." During the last several decades, many of these same institutions that started as

Research Finding

9

Skimpy requirements and declining enrollments in history classes are contributing to a decline in students' knowledge of the past.

Earlier generations of American students commonly learned the history of American institutions, politics, and systems of government, as well as some of the history of Greece, Rome, Europe, and the rest of the world. Today, most States require the study of only American history and other course work in social studies. Indications are that students now know and understand less about history.

In most State requirements for high school graduation, a choice is offered between history on the one hand and courses in social science and contemporary social issues on the other. Most high school students, even those in the academic track, take only one history course.

Students enroll in honors courses in history at less than half the rate they enroll for honors courses in English and science. Typically, requirements have also declined for writing essays, producing research-based papers, and reading original sources. Similar declines are reported in the requirements for such reasoning skills as evaluating sources of information, drawing conclusions, and constructing logical arguments.

Fitzgerald, F. (1979). *America Revised: History School Books in the Twentieth Century.* Boston: Atlantic Little-Brown.

Owings, J. A. (1985). "History Credits Earned by 1980 High School Sophomores Who Graduated in 1982." *High School and Beyond Tabulation.* Washington, DC: National Center for Education Statistics.

Thernstrom, S. (1985). "The Humanities and Our Cultural Challenge." In C. E. Finn, D. Ravitch, and P. Roberts (Eds.), *Challenges to the Humanities.* New York: Holmes and Meier.

Source: *What Works: Research About Teaching and Learning.* Washington, DC: U.S. Department of Education, 1987, page 77.

two-year normal schools have begun offering graduate work, including doctoral programs, and have changed their names to "state universities."

It was not until about 1900 that states began passing teacher certification laws which regulated the amount and type of training that a person must have to become a teacher. Prior to the passage of these laws, anyone could legally teach school.

In summary, this chapter has pointed out a number of important concepts concerning the history of education in the United States. These concepts include the following:

- The educational program in colonial America was largely transplanted from Europe.
- The colonists attempted to make educational provisions almost as soon as they set foot on the new world.

- The motive for providing education in colonial America was almost entirely religious in nature.
- Education has played an increasingly important role in the development of the United States, from 1607 when the first colonists settled at Jamestown to the present.
- Many of the educational problems of colonial America have persisted to the present time.
- The role of education in the United States has increased in importance down through time, so that today education has a larger and more important role to play in our country than ever before.

A chronology of some of the highlights of the history of American education is presented in appendix G.

◘ Summary

The chapter has highlighted the historical development of the American educational system. Within this general framework, the concept that education has played a key role, perhaps even *the* key role, in the development of America has been articulated. The well-accepted notion that a democratic society such as ours is totally dependent upon its schools' ability to produce an informed electorate has been developed.

This chapter has also dealt with topics such as educational expectations in colonial America, presented some of the first school laws ever created in our country, reviewed the establishment of Harvard, our first colonial college, explained the development of Latin Grammar Schools which were our first form of secondary education, told the story of the creation of the American Academy by

Benjamin Franklin, the development of education after we won our independence from England, the evolution of the elementary school which was referred to as the common school, the development of our public high schools, the education (or lack of education) for minorities and women, the important roles that females played in the development of elementary schools in our country, and the evolution of teacher education.

A basic understanding of the history of education is of practical value to today's teacher. Such knowledge helps a teacher appreciate the key role that education has played in the development of our country, and to develop a pride in the teaching profession.

Point of View

The following interesting point of view is a set of regulations governing a very early 1645 grammar school in New England. How is it similar to and how is it different from today's school regulations? What insights does it provide into the educational expectations of that time? What does it tell us about the life and work of teachers in early colonial America? How was school discipline viewed at that time? What, in general, does this set of regulations tell us about these very early beginnings of our current public schools?

Regulations Adopted by Dorchester, Massachusetts for the Town Grammar School (1645)

Upon a general and lawful warning of all the inhabitants, the 14th of the 1st month 1645, these rules and orders presented to the town concerning the school of Dorchester are confirmed by the major part of the inhabitants then present.

First . . . three able and sufficient men of the plantation shall be chosen to be wardens or overseers of the school abovementioned, who shall have the charge, oversight, and ordering thereof and of all things concerning the same . . . and shall continue in their office and place for term of their lives respectively, unless by reason of any of them removing his habitation out of the town, or for any other weighty reason, the inhabitants shall see cause to elect or choose others in their room.

Secondly, the said wardens shall have full power to dispose of the school stock, whether the same be in land or otherwise, both such as is already in being and such as may by any good means hereafter be added, and shall collect and receive the rents, issues, and profits arising and growing of and from the said stock . . .

Thirdly, the said wardens shall take care, and do their utmost, and best endeavor, that the said school may from time to time be supplied with an able and sufficient schoolmaster, who nevertheless is not to be admitted into the place of schoolmaster without the general consent of the inhabitants or the major part of them.

Fourthly, so often as the said school shall be supplied with a schoolmaster . . . the wardens shall from time to time pay or cause to be paid unto the said schoolmaster such wages . . . as shall of right come due to be paid.

Fifthly, the said wardens shall from time to time see that the schoolhouse be kept in good and sufficient repair . . .

Sixthly, the said wardens shall take care that every year, at or before the end of [December], there be brought to the schoolhouse twelve sufficient cart- or wainloads of wood for fuel, to be for the use of the schoolmaster and the scholars in winter . . .

Lastly, the said wardens shall take care that the schoolmaster for the time being do faithfully perform his duty in his place, as schoolmasters ought to do, as well as in other things as in these which are hereafter expressed, viz.:

First, that the schoolmaster shall diligently attend his school and do his utmost endeavor for benefiting his scholars according to his best discretion without unnecessarily absenting himself to the prejudice of his scholars and hindering their learning.

Secondly, that from the beginning of [March], until the end of [September], he shall every day begin to teach at seven of the clock in the morning and dismiss his scholars at five in the afternoon. And for the other five months, that is from the beginning of [October], until the end of [February], it shall every day begin at eight of the clock in the morning and end at four in the afternoon.

Thirdly, every day in the year the usual time of dismissing at noon shall be at eleven, and to begin again at one, . . .

Fourthly, every second day in the week he shall call his scholars together between twelve and one of the clock to examine them what they have learned on the Sabbath day preceding, at which time also he shall take notice of any misdemeanor or disorder that any of his scholars shall have committed on the Sabbath, to the end that at some convenient time due admonition and correction may be administered by him according as the nature and quality of the offense shall require; at which said examination any of the elders or other inhabitants that please may be present to behold his religious care herein and to give their countenance and approbation of the same.

Fifthly, he shall equally and impartially receive and instruct such as shall be sent and committed to him for that end, whether their parents be poor or rich, not refusing any who have right and interest in the school.

Sixthly, such as shall be committed to him he shall diligently instruct as they shall be able to learn, both in humane learning and good literature, and likewise in point of good manners and dutiful behavior towards all, especially their superiors, as they shall have occasion to be in their presence whether by meeting them in the street or otherwise.

Seventhly, every sixth day of the week at two of the clock in the afternoon he shall catechize his scholars in the principles of Christian religion, either in some catechism which the wardens shall provide and present, or in defect thereof, in some other.

Eighthly, and because all man's endeavors without the blessing of God must needs be fruitless and unsuccessful, therefore, it is to be a chief part of the schoolmaster's religious care to commend his scholars and his labors amongst them unto God by prayer, morning and evening, taking care that his scholars do reverently attend during the same.

Ninthly, and because the rod of correction is an ordinance of God necessary sometimes to be dispensed unto children, but such as may easily be abused by overmuch severity and rigor on the one hand, or by overmuch indulgence and lenity on the other, it is therefore ordered and agreed that the schoolmaster, for the time being, shall have full power to minister correction to all or any of his scholars without respect of persons, according as the nature and quality of the offense shall require whereto. All his scholars must be duly subject and no parent or other of the inhabitants shall hinder or go about to hinder the master therein. Nevertheless, if any parent or others shall think there is a just cause of complaint against the master for too much severity, such shall have liberty, friendlily and lovingly, to expostulate with the master about the same; and if they shall not attain to satisfaction, the matter is then to be referred to the wardens who shall inpartially judge betwixt the master and such complainants . . .

And because it is difficult, if not impossible, to give particular rules that shall reach all cases which may fall out, therefore, for a conclusion, it is ordered and agreed in general, that where particular rules are wanting, there it shall be a part of the office and duty of the wardens to order and dispose of all things that concern the school, in such sort as in their wisdom and discretion they shall judge most conducible for the glory of God and the training up of the children of the town in religion, learning, and civility. . . .

Source: "Regulations Adopted by Dorchester, Massachusetts for the Town Grammar School (1645)" from *Fourth Report of the Boston Record Commissioners* (Boston, 1880), pages 54–57.

■ Questions for Discussion

1. Trace briefly the history of elementary education in the United States, mentioning only the highlights.
2. What were the basic differences in the early educational programs that developed in the northern colonies, middle colonies, and southern colonies?
3. Briefly describe the function and curriculum of the Latin Grammar School.
4. Trace the historical development of secondary education in the United States.
5. What basic changes have taken place in teacher education in the history of the United States?

■ Notes

1. G. Compayre, *History of Pedagogy,* trans. W. H. Payne (Boston: D. C. Heath, 1885), p. 128.
2. Ibid., p. 425.
3. Frederick Douglass, *Narrative of the Life of Frederick Douglass* (Boston: Published by the Anti-Slavery Office, 1845), p. 43.

◼ Selected References

Butts, R. Freeman. *Public Education in the United States: From Revolution to Reform.* New York: Holt, Rinehart & Winston, 1978.

Butts, R. Freeman, and Cremin, Lawrence A. *A History of Education in American Culture.* New York: Holt, Rinehart & Winston, 1953.

Cohen, Sheldon S. *A History of Colonial Education.* Studies in the History of American Education. New York: John Wiley & Sons, 1974.

Conant, James B. *Thomas Jefferson and the Development of American Public Education.* Berkeley and Los Angeles: University of California Press, 1962.

Cordasco, Francesco; Alloway, David N.; and Friedman, Marjorie Scilken. *The History of American Education: A Guide to Information Sources.* Education Information Guide Series, vol. 7. Detroit: Gale Research Co., 1979.

Cremin, Lawrence A. *American Education: The Colonial Experience, 1607–1783.* New York: Harper & Row, 1970.

————. *The Transformation of the School.* New York: Knopf, 1961.

Cuban, Larry. *How Teachers Taught.* New York: Longman, 1984.

Dewey, John. *Democracy and Education.* New York: Macmillan, 1916 (chapters 11, 12).

Freeman, Ruth S. *Yesterday's Schools: A Looking Glass for Teachers of Today.* Watkins Glen, N.Y.: Century House, 1962.

Greer, Colin. *The Great School Legend: A Revisionist Interpretation of American Public Education.* New York: Basic Books, 1972.

Gulliford, Andrew. *America's Country Schools.* Washington, D.C.: The Preservation Press, 1984.

Historical Highlights in the Education of Black Americans. Washington, D.C.: National Education Association.

Hufstedler, Shirley. "America's Historic Commitment," *American Education.* May 1980, pp. 6–7.

Karier, Clarence. *Shaping the American Education State, 1900 to the Present.* New York: Free Press, 1975.

Kaufman, Polly Welts. *Women Teachers on the Frontier.* New Haven and London: Yale University Press, 1984.

Matthews, Barbara. "Women, Education and History." *Theory Into Practice* 15, no. 1 (February 1976): 47–53.

Mayer, Frederick. *A History of Educational Thoughts.* 3d ed. Columbus, Ohio: Charles E. Merrill, 1974.

Morris, Robert. *Reading, Riting and Reconstruction: The Education of Freedmen in the South 1861–1870.* Chicago: The University of Chicago Press, 1981.

Our Educational History in Five Thousand Slides. Creative Educational Materials, Box 244, DeKalb, IL 60115.

Pendergast, Sister M. Richard. "On Inkwells, Hickory Sticks, and Other Memories," *School and Society* 59 (January 1974): 19–20.

Pulliam, John D. *History of Education in America.* Columbus, Ohio: Charles E. Merrill, 1987.

Ravitch, Diane. *The Troubled Crusade American Education 1945–1980.* New York: Basic Books, 1983.

Spring, Joel. *The American School 1642–1985.* New York: Longman, 1986.

Video Tapes on History of Education. Learning Center, Gabel Hall, Northern Illinois University, DeKalb, IL 60115.

Chapter 11

Beliefs about Education

Objectives

After studying this chapter, you should be able to:

- Identify the aspects of cultural pluralism in U.S. society.

- Relate the nature of cultural pluralism to philosophical issues facing the schools today.

- Compare the current discord regarding the education of our young to similar controversies in the past.

- Identify central criticisms of American education.

- List characteristics of the traditional view of education from the perspective of student, teacher, curriculum, and method of teaching.

- List characteristics of the progressive view of education from the perspective of student, teacher, curriculum, and method of teaching.

- Comment on the current adult preference for moral instruction in the public schools.

- Defend the alternative education concept as an appropriate educational option for students, parents, and teachers.

- Explain the need to refocus the fragmented identity of our schools.

Enrichment Experiences

The following experiences will help you gain a perspective on educational philosophies and their relationship to society and teaching.

- Ask a sociologist with a specialty in demographics to address your class in regard to background and nature of cultural pluralism.

- Collect data on the demographics of the area in which you are located.

- Invite a teacher from an elementary school, one from a middle school or junior high school, and one from a high school to your class to discuss the traditional and progressive philosophies of education as related to their jobs. Summarize the teachers' views in terms of educational philosophy.

- Do a survey in your immediate area to determine the attitudes of the public toward the teaching of morals in the public schools.

- Invite a teacher or administrator of an alternative school, including private schools and home instruction schools, to your class to explain what he/she feels in regard to the benefits of his/her school as contrasted to traditional schools.

- Reflect upon your own schooling and analyze it in relation to the philosophical bases of education explained in this chapter.

The principles of American political freedom embody a liberal and dynamic educational philosophy.

E. Edgar Fuller

The primary purpose of this chapter is to help you clarify your views and beliefs about education and teaching. Specific topics related to the purpose include: the pluralistic nature of our nation; the confusion today about what and how the selected content should be taught; the traditional and progressive views about the appropriate subject matter to be taught and the methodology that should be used; the teaching of morals in the public schools; and alternative education. ■

Prospective teachers should actively seek to clarify their views and beliefs about education and teaching. Too often the word *philosophy* conjures up notions of names, long words, and dense reading. Developing one's beliefs about education—educational philosophy—need not be laborious and dull, but indeed does require some thinking and effort. Educators commonly agree that teachers need more than a knowledge of subject matter and practice teaching experience before they enter the classroom. They also need a synthesized view of cultural pluralism in our society; attitudes and expectations of parents and students about their schools; and the several views of traditional and progressive theories of education—all of which will firm up their own set of beliefs about education.

■ Cultural Pluralism

The early American immigrants were essentially poor, oppressed people who brought with them different languages, religions, racial backgrounds, and political beliefs. Most of the initial 30 million immigrants were from Europe. The early American culture was predicated upon white, Anglo-Saxon Protestant norms which also became the dominant norms of the colonial school culture. While our early schools helped assimilate millions of immigrants into the Anglo-dominated culture of colonial America, millions of others, including Native Americans, black Americans, Hispanics and most recently Asians, have not been assimilated. Nonetheless, the early American thrust toward assimilating the many subcultures into a new, perhaps forced, single larger culture came to be spoken of as the "melting-pot" concept. The growth of the comprehensive American system of education has obviously been aligned with the growth of the American way of life which in turn has been identified with this melting-pot notion. Only within the last twenty-five years have the injustices brought upon those not assimilated served to help us gain a new appreciation of cultural pluralism.

Even though our schools are slow in coming to advocate cultural pluralism as the new ideal which would more readily permit the retention of diverse cultural heritages, selected overall functions will continue to be considered as basic components associated with American mass education.

Regardless of race, color, or creed, the importance of education to freedom, patriotism, and national security will continue to be the theme of writers, orators, and legislators. If we possessed an infallible means of knowing the way of government and the way of our social life for the years ahead, we would be able to look to the contents, objectives, and values stressed in our present-day schools for the purpose of meaningful evaluation.

Those things which would be deemed worthwhile in the future life of a person, and of a nation, would be taught in the schools. Even though we do not have the infallible means for predicting the future, it has been generally approved as a fundamental principle in public education throughout the world that schools should help the student acquire worthwhile knowledge, feelings, and skills deemed important for the student's future life. Lingering questions among legislators, parents, students, and teachers are: what types of knowledge, feelings, and skills are worthwhile to possess? what is the best way to teach those things? what should the school provide? what should other agencies, including home and church, provide? In response to such questions as these, varying beliefs about education surface. Such beliefs vary by race, ethnic character, nationality, economic status, geographical area, and a host of other criteria. It is practically impossible to pinpoint the root cause(s) of one's own educational beliefs. But, each of us as student, parent, or teacher does indeed have convictions about the methods and substance of education. One of the main purposes identified with the study of philosophy of education is to provide prospective teachers with a foundation for isolating and analyzing their individual philosophy of education.

■ Confusion about Education

Present-day educators are definitely not in accord regarding the education of our young. When one views the magnitude of the educational enterprise requiring compulsory education, the confusion regarding the process of teaching (educating) appears distressing. History reminds us, however, that confusion about education is not unusual. In the time of the famous early Greeks,

Aristotle (and his contemporaries) could not agree upon the method of educating the young because social conditions were in a state of rapid change. In addition, the political institutions were undergoing change, the economy of Greece was burgeoning, there were international conflicts, problems with foreign trade, and problems resulting from times of war. It was obvious that these several concerns and problems had considerable influence on teaching.

Seemingly, the problems regarding education in the twentieth century have similar tones. One of the most noticeable effects of the advance of contemporary science and technology is the constant doubling and redoubling of information and knowledge. The notion that a person may be possessed of almost all knowledge has long been vanquished. Today, the matter of choice boils down to one of deciding in which small area to specialize. Given that specialization decision, subsequent decisions must be made regarding method of study and choice of schools. Through the high school years, the choice of schools is limited, but even that dimension is undergoing change. Beyond high school, the school choice is often very much related to teaching methodology and curriculum approaches. It is small wonder that people today, as twenty-five hundred years ago, are raising the age-old questions about how to educate their children to face the dynamic social conditions in which they live. Faced with this continuing conflict regarding educational practice, beginning teachers are likely to find themselves inconsistent with their classroom tactics and mentally anguished by the lack of direction among their experienced colleagues. Typically, and oftentimes slowly, teachers tend to settle their thinking toward the "traditional" approach, on the one hand, or toward the "progressive" approach, on the other. Beliefs regarding educating from the traditional stance to meet the demands of changing times focus on a program of studies selected for their enduring value. Literature, history, mathematics, sciences, languages, logic, and doctrine provide the basis of subject matter content. The more progressive view stresses content that aims at the reconstruction of experience. Subject matter of social experiences are emphasized through social studies, projects, and problem-solving exercises. The major point of this chapter is to call the attention of prospective teachers to this traditional-progressive schism in pedagogical practice. The matter of fashionable advocacy of one approach over the other is of little importance. One often hears that most of our teacher-preparation programs are too progressive-oriented. Whether that be the case or not, beginning teachers, once in the classroom, are just as inclined to traditional as to progressive pedagogy. Since it is almost always difficult to believe one way and practice another way, prospective teachers would do well to begin to think about, to examine, and to pull together their particular beliefs about education. Surely, the pedagogical practice of any one teacher which is consistent with known and verified beliefs about the education of young minds will be the most effective practice that that teacher can provide.

■ Criticism of American Education

Honest and responsible criticism is considered essential to the preservation of our democratic society and, therefore, to the preservation of our schools. At the same time, exaggerated criticism contributes little to educational progress. The gamut of criticisms of education typically span the subject-centered/pupil-centered continuum in a sometimes astonishingly changing thrust. Professional educators, authors, military and government personnel, and politicians, along with lay citizens, union leaders, workers of all kinds, and cause-oriented group leaders search for the most visible vehicles for expressing their criticisms of education.

In some instances, the positions advocated by some critics of education are in harmony with the public mood. For example, the current popularity of the suggestion to "devote more attention to teaching of basic skills" is consistent with the critics who argued following the Sputnik era of 1957 that schools ought to concentrate on cognitive learning in order to "catch up" with the Russians' space technology. On the other hand, "the romantic critics argued that undue emphasis on subject matter and academic rigor destroys the intrinsic adventure of learning by crippling natural interest and curiosity in learners.[1] In these instances, the critics of education are in contradiction with the public mood. Practicing teachers can profit from these wide-ranging educational criticisms by using such criticisms to more clearly focus upon the specific teaching problems confronted by the teacher, and then follow with approaches aimed at solving the teaching problems.

Traditional View

Two American educational philosophies form the foundation for what is here considered as the traditional view. William C. Bagley defined Essentialism as a clearly delineated educational philosophy in 1938. Essentialism suggests that emphasis on subject matter provides the essential components of education. The learner is expected

■ Table 11.1   Traditional View of Education

	Traditional View
Student	Reasoning is learned through mental exercise. Student can learn through conditioning. Mind is capable of integrating pieces of learning. Mental calisthenics are important to develop the mind.
Teacher	Model of study, scholarliness, expert stance. Demonstration of content and knowledge. Mental disciplinarian, spiritual leader. Curator of knowledge and tradition.
Curriculum	Literature and history as subjects of symbol. Mathematics and science as physical world subjects. Languages and logic as subjects of the intellect. Great books and doctrine as subject matter of spirit.
Method	Mastering facts and information. Stress on rote and memorization. Assigned reading and homework. Study as a means of intellectual discipline.

to master facts in order to learn through observation and nature. Discipline, required reading, memorization, repetition, and examinations are considered important to learning.

Perennialism, sometimes suggested as the parent philosophy of Essentialism, is a significant part of the traditional view. The early work of Thomas Aquinas is recognized as the cornerstone of Perennialism. Thomism placed much emphasis on the discipline of the mind. In this respect, the study of subject matter is considered important for disciplining the mind. Attention to Perennialism in America has been associated with the works of Robert M. Hutchins and Mortimer Adler. Hutchins and Adler advocated study of the great books as a desired means to education. The processes of both Essentialism and Perennialism are strongly subject-centered and authoritarian in that subjects of study are prescribed. Advocates argue that the educated person must be firmly drilled in content in order to possess the tools required for rational thinking. This traditional view toward education is probably still the most common approach throughout the international scene.

Table 11.1 outlines a few considerations of the student, the teacher, the curriculum, and the method of education as associated with the traditional view of education. The traditional approach places emphasis on the discipline of the mind as the primary means for gaining knowledge. Also, the rapid development of experimental sciences during the first half of the twentieth century has been a strong factor in the growth of the school testing movement and in the development of educational psychology. The traditional conservatism of the American heritage is strongly present in education as we know it today. The current emphasis on the "return to basics" in American education is suggestive of the popularity of the traditional approach among many parents in the United States.

Progressive View

As previously indicated, Progressivism as an educational view is uniquely American, and was established in the 1920s. The early pragmatism of Charles S. Pierce and William James serves as the origin of Progressivism, while the writings of

■ **Table 11.2** Progressive View of Education

	Progressive View
Student	Learner is an experiencing person. Learner has freedom of choice. Student awareness and acceptance highly esteemed. Human experiences important as related to change. Learning through experiences.
Teacher	Research project director. Teacher serves as guide for learner activities. Teacher is never obstrusive, always respecting rights of all. Motivator.
Curriculum	Content should not be compartmentalized. Interest of pupils may demand what is to be studied. Group learning and field trips are valuable. Subject matter of social experience.
Method	Maximum of self-expression and choice. Formal instruction minimized in favor of areas of learning that appeal to the student. Problem solving. Teach how to manage change.

John Dewey provide the principles of Progressivism as an educational philosophy. Dewey opposed the thesis that schools should be concerned exclusively with the development of the mind. His pragmatic antithesis held that schools should provide for the growth of the whole child. In his view, subject matter of social experience is deemed highly important. This experimental method is held to be one of the best methods of achieving the continuity of unity of subject matter and method. The pragmatic thought of Dewey and his followers has greatly influenced teaching at the elementary level. While teaching at the secondary and college levels has been less affected by the progressive approach, the American teacher-preparation institutions have been greatly influenced toward advocacy of the pragmatic leadership of John Dewey. While the last quarter of the century has unfolded with much criticism of educational Progressivism, the basic tenets of the progressive view still remain as alternatives to traditional approaches.

Another dimension of the progressive view concerning education stems from the influence of Existentialism as a newer mode of thought. Existentialism is not considered as a single school of philosophy since it encompasses many variations and opposing views. It is accepted as a movement that touches upon the field of philosophy and human thought with implications for educational practice. With Existentialism, most considerations begin with the individual person. The reality of personal existence makes possible freedom and choice. Other significant concepts that can be identified as existentially oriented relate to human personality as a foundation for education and the goals of education expressed in terms of awareness, acceptance, commitment, and affirmation.

Table 11.2 outlines a few considerations of the student, the teacher, the curriculum, and the method of education as associated with the progressive view of education. Most of the polarity regarding views of education in the United States is represented by the concepts outlined in tables 11.1 and 11.2. Obviously, this overly simplistic schism does not allow for the extended degree of differences when examined through educational research and teaching experiences. Many education and philosophy texts further expand on the so-called traditional and progressive strategies for learning (and teaching).

Energetic group activities provide learning experience.

■ Moral Instruction

The general success of Republican candidates in the 1980, 1984, and 1988 elections provided new impetus for such expressions as a new wave of conservatism, moral majority, swing to the right, demise of liberalism, and others, all of which have extended implications for the public schools. Generally, the more conservative thinking citizens are strongest in criticizing the schools for betraying the public trust by straying from the basics in the curriculum, in drifting away from discipline, and in disregarding moral instruction in the schools. It is therefore implied, at least, that the back to basics movement also includes back to discipline and back to morals concepts. In the early years of public school education, the teaching of morals was regarded as an integral part of the educational program. Early textbooks considered the teaching of morals as important as the teaching of reading. One self-identified educational critic on the Far Right states: "At one time schools supported and promoted traditional values, but today it's a different story. Students are encouraged to adopt only those values that suit them."[2]

Examination of current literature yields a host of approaches such as Values Clarification, Moral Development, Ethics Instruction, Values Analysis, Public Issues Approach, and Cognitive Development Approach. Whether or not classroom teachers are qualified to teach values, prospective teachers may obtain some guidance from the following suggestion:

In all teaching and learning, the character of teachers and administrators is a critical factor: *who* teachers and administrators are and what they *do* make a decisive difference. Schools cannot develop character and integrity in students unless there are teachers with integrity and character in the classroom with them.

The young will take seriously what they see taken seriously by others whom they have come to trust. The most important teaching of morality is done by living example. Students learn about how to treat others through the ways in which they themselves are treated. . . .

The human aspect of education minimizes the current emphasis on technology.

If education is to serve ideals of morality, teachers and administrators must embody those ideals in their treatment of students and each other. Minimally, this means that teachers and administrators should understand and aspire to be reasonable people of good will, and that they must be willing to tell students what they think and why.[3]

Some persons feel that many of the past concerns related to the separation of church and state controversy will again surface as calls for moral instruction in the schools increase. Prayer in the public schools is once again a hotly debated issue. The least support for prayer in the public schools is found among the best educated citizens and among the youngest adult age group, and these two groups will play the greatest role in determining future trends in public attitudes.

■ Alternative Education

An outgrowth of the traditional versus progressive approach controversy has been the involvement of the alternative education concept. This concept suggests that the appropriate options for students, parents, and teachers can best be obtained through public schools of choice. In this fashion, an entire school district would not be committed to either the traditionally oriented approach or to the progressively oriented approach. Obviously, this does not resolve what has been a generally long-standing schism within education. However, this approach does permit equally good educational programs to exist within the same school system regardless of the divergent beliefs among alternative programs. One of the early advocates of alternative education was Mario Fantini who suggested:

> A system of choice maximizes variation in both the substance and personnel of education. For example, consumers who select a school program based on a Montessori model will have important substantive differences from those who select a classical school. Choice does legitimize new programs, each of which carries with it new curriculum and new personnel.

Research Finding

10

Good character is encouraged by surrounding students with good adult examples and by building upon natural occasions for learning and practicing good character. Skillful educators know how to organize their schools, classrooms, and lessons to foster such examples.

The home, the school, and the community all contribute to a child's character development. Children learn character traits such as honesty, courtesy, diligence, and respect for others in part from examples set by their parents, teachers, peers, and the community as a whole.

Schools can reinforce good character by how they organize and present themselves, how the adults conduct themselves, and how standards for behavior and integrity are set and enforced. Positive character traits are reinforced through school activities that identify worthwhile achievements and exemplary behavior of students.

Educators become good role models through their professionalism, courtesy, cooperation, and by demanding top performance from their students. They maintain fair and consistent discipline policies, including matters of attendance, punctuality, and meeting assignment deadlines.

Parr, S. R. (1982). *The Moral of the Story: Literature, Values, and American Education.* New York: Teachers College Press.

Rutter, M., et al. (1979). *Fifteen Thousand Hours: Secondary Schools and Their Effects on Children.* Cambridge, MA: Harvard University Press.

U.S. Department of Education, *Japanese Education Today.* (1987). Washington, DC: U.S. Government Printing Office.

Wynne, E. A. (1980). *Looking at Schools: Good, Bad, and Indifferent.* Lexington, MA: Lexington Books, D.C. Heath and Company.

Source: *What Works: Research About Teaching and Learning.* Washington, DC: U.S. Department of Education, 1987, page 59.

Certainly, professionals who are attracted to a Summerhill-like school are different from those who prefer a classical school environment.

The point is that a public school system that maximizes consumer choice legitimizes new as well as old educational approaches to common objectives. The new educational approach will be made operational by public consent. Moreover, *educators* will also be able to choose from among these educational alternatives, possibly enhancing their sense of professional satisfaction.

This choice model, therefore, tends to minimize conflict among interest groups because *each* individual is making *direct* decisions in educational affairs. Furthermore, as a supply and demand model, the choice system has a self-revitalizing capability. As the options prove successful, they will increase in popularity, thereby increasing the flow of successful programs into the public schools and generating a renewal process for public education.

Under the present system, new programs are introduced into the public schools largely through professional channels, with parents, students, and teachers having little say. However, parents, students, and teachers can actually veto any new program. Some programs, such as sex education, become controversial, especially if they are superimposed by the administration.

School systems are currently structured to present only one model or pattern of education to a student and his parents. If economic factors or religious beliefs preclude nonpublic schools as an alternative, the parent and student have no choice but to submit to the kind and quality of public education in their community. With the exception that one or two schools may be viewed as "better" or "worse" by parents and students (generally because of "better teachers" or because "more" graduates go to college or because the school is in a "good neighborhood"), the way materials are presented and "school work" is done is esssentially the same in all schools on the same level. It should be possible to develop within one school or cluster of schools within a neighborhood, district, or system several different models that would offer real choices to all those involved in the educative process.[4]

In school districts where alternative education programs have been provided, the primary thrust has dealt with the elementary level. It is administratively and programmatically more feasible to work within the elementary schools when considering the size of the pupil group being served, the clustering of faculty who share common beliefs, and compatible building administrative leadership. Alternative education models at the middle school/junior high school and high school levels are less likely to be found operable to any great degree.

Hopefully, in this chapter some consideration for the importance of identifying and pulling together one's specific view of educational practice has been highlighted. The study of classical philosophy is rigorous and demanding. Our suggestion for prospective teachers is that time and effort invested in philosophical study may be most worthwhile in helping to refine your individual beliefs about education. The most successful classroom practices appear to be those based upon a system of beliefs that is best suited to the particular teacher—whether traditional or progressive in nature.

■ Summary

The primary purpose of this chapter was to help prospective teachers to clarify their views and beliefs about education and teaching. Developing your beliefs about education—educational philosophy—need not be laborious and dull but indeed does require thinking and effort.

Beliefs of all kinds are abundant in various cultures. The original culture in the land now known as the United States was that of the Native Americans, often referred to as American Indians. As the United States was created and developed, many people representative of many countries emigrated to the United States bringing their various cultures and beliefs with them. Many of the immigrants were assimilated into the dominant Anglo-Saxon culture—accepting its values. Others were not assimilated for a variety of reasons, among which was discrimination against persons because of their race or religion. Discrimination still persists in the United States. The United States today is referred to as being culturally pluralistic, wherein there are various cultures with different beliefs. It is in this context that education in the United States operates, seeking values and beliefs that are common and necessary to our society and at the same time allowing the retention of diverse cultural heritages and recognizing the enrichment such heritages provide in our nation.

Nevertheless, questions related to beliefs about education continue to prevail. What kind of knowledge, attitudes, and skills should be taught in our schools? How should they be taught? What beliefs should be taught and nurtured in school? What should other agencies, including the church, provide? One of the important purposes of studying philosophy (beliefs) is to provide prospective teachers with a foundation for analyzing their individual philosophies of education.

Traditional and progressive views were presented, contrasting the two views on their philosophical positions in regard to students, teachers, the curriculum, and teaching methodology. In general, the traditional view focuses on a curriculum selected for its enduring value. Literature, history, mathematics, sciences, languages, and logic provide the basis of the subject matter content. The progressive view believes that content should not be compartmentalized. The interest of pupils may demand what should be studied. Subject matter emphasis is on social experience. Very seldom do individuals, including teachers, identify with a pure educational philosophy; they are more likely to pick and choose components from different philosophic views in shaping their own philosophies of education.

In the last few years, there has been a strong effort urging the teaching of morals and values in the public schools. Less than one-half of the respondents to a survey indicated that public schools should teach values and ethics; a little over one-third of the respondents indicated that the teaching of values and ethics should be left to parents and teachers. That evidence does not indicate strong support for the teaching of values and ethics in the public schools. Perhaps if the survey had asked about the public schools teaching "democratic values," the respondents may have indicated more support than they did for the teaching of values and ethics.

Alternative schools within public school districts provide an option for divergent beliefs about education and teaching. Private schools provide another option as does home instruction.

The study of the philosophy of education can help prospective teachers clarify their views and beliefs about education and teaching. The most successful classroom practices appear to be those based upon a system of beliefs that is best suited to the particular teacher—whether traditional or progressive in nature. Prospective teachers are urged to try to sort out those classroom practices which best suit their beliefs and use those practices consistently on a day-to-day basis as they begin their teaching careers. When experience suggests that other approaches may prove more effective, adjustments in teaching philosophy can be made. Successful teachers are those who have learned how and when to effectively use several classroom strategies.

Point of View

The point of view article, "Refocusing the Identity of Schooling: Education for a Democracy of the Intellect," authored by J. Amos Hatch and John M. Conrath, is an excellent supplement to chapter 11. It reviews the historic connections of the schools and society, addresses social change and the corresponding loss of identity of the schools, and proposes a concept for the future—educating for a democracy of intellect. Educating for a democracy of the intellect is dependent upon each person's responsible participation in the decisions that shape our future as a nation. To be responsible in decision making, people must be knowledgeable of the issues under consideration. The article implies that our current society with a fragmentation of goals and values must establish, through wide participation of knowledge and informed people, purposes, goals and values for the schools. Once that is done, schools are likely to regain their identity.

Refocusing the Identity of Schooling: Education for a Democracy of the Intellect

J. Amos Hatch and John M. Conrath

At the birth of our nation, Thomas Jefferson noted the importance of literate populace to the survival of our democracy. Recently, the authors had the privilege of hearing Ralph Tyler speak on educational change. Dr. Tyler was articulate and persuasive as he recounted the evolution of education in the United States. A major theme of his address was the impact education has had on the development of literacy since Jefferson's time. Even in the face of some apparently alarming statistics,[1] Tyler asserted that educators have done a good job of bringing literacy to a complex and dynamic society. He stressed that no other nation has taken on the task of educating *every* individual while facing the problems of educating large numbers of people for whom the mainstream language is not the first language and the mainstream culture is not the native culture.

Dr. Tyler's insights led us to ask: "Why, if we have done a respectable job as educators, are we mired in such a state of negative perceptions?" It occurred to us that one way of understanding the success or failure of U.S. education is to reexamine what functions schools serve in relation to "the survival of our democracy." In this article, we will argue that historically there have been clear connections between our democratic society and U.S. education, a condition which gave schools a sense of purpose and identity. We believe that contemporary conditions in society and schools have blurred perceptions concerning what schools ought to be about and left them without a recognizable identity. We will offer the notion of educating for a democracy of the intellect as a purpose which gives identity back to schools and restores connections with society.

■ Schools' Historic Connections to Society

Beginning with the colonial period, the functions of schools in relation to society were clear. During our country's early history, society's concerns were centered around the desire to preserve a religious heritage and the need for a disciplined citizenry.[2] The schools stressed Bible reading and promoted the Puritan ethic. With the colonies' separation from Europe and their embarkation into democratic government came calls for an education designed to prepare individuals to participate in their own governance. The notion that education had an important connection to society's well-being was firmly established. In Thomas Jefferson's words, "The people themselves therefore, are [the government's] only safe depositories. And to render even them safe, their minds must be improved to a certain degree."[3] Jefferson called for schools that would prepare individuals to "perform their duties and protect their rights as citizens."[4] Formal schooling of the time was restricted to a select few but their education was focused on beliefs and knowledge tied directly to the perceived social needs of the day.

During the 1800's the "common school" movement took hold.[5] Cities were growing rapidly and immigration from Europe was increasing. The idea that free public education ought to be universal was widely accepted. Following the Civil War, public school systems were organized and attendance made compulsory in many states.[6] This period also marked the beginnings of the transition from an agricultural to an industrial economy. More and more children were enrolling in school and it became society's expectation that experiences in classrooms would replace "on the job training" practices of the past.[7] The purposes of schooling were again clear and evident to all: schools were to provide for the "Americanization" of all chlidren and begin to prepare individuals to work in a society rushing toward industrialization.

During the first half of this century, society and our economy continued to become more diverse. Immigration, industrialization, urbanization, occupational specialization, two world wars, a major depression, and a "cold war" brought dramatic changes to society. Educators responded with "scientific" approaches to education. They studied what skills, knowledge, and attitudes were needed in the workplace, then systematically included these in the curriculum.[8] U.S. involvement in international conflicts created the need for intense feelings of nationalism among America's young people. Later, the arms and space race with the U.S.S.R. gave Americans a new sense of anxiety and a renewed sense of competition. The purposes of schools were, again, well understood: to prepare workers for an increasingly complex industrialized economy and to promote a spirit of unity and nationalism.

▣ Social Change and the Loss of Identity for Schools

During the past twenty-five or so years these historic connections between society's needs and the purposes of schools have been blurred beyond recognition. Fundamental social changes in three important areas have occurred during this time frame, changes that have left schools without clear purposes or identity. These areas are: the explosive growth of knowledge and technology; the proliferation of special interest groups and subsequent fragmentation of national priorities; and the emergence of a "me first" approach to individual ethical decision making.

The rapidity with which the knowledge base in every field of inquiry has grown is staggering. This growth in concert with parallel technological advances has pushed us from an industrial society into what Naisbitt and others have called an "information society."[9]

Traditional models of delivering instruction and organizing curriculum are insufficient to keep us with the explosive growth of our information society.

Educators are beseiged by calls for "futures" currriculum emphases but many have turned a deaf ear.[10] Schools continue to masquerade as places wherein one generation passes along its accumulated knowledge to the next while virtually all the participants in schooling activity know that such a goal is no longer achievable. This awareness promotes not a sense of purpose or identity, but growing feelings of alienation and loss of identity among educators.

A second important contemporary change has been the growth of special interest groups. As Toffler characterizes the present and the onrushing future, he describes a "de-massification" of society. He documents the rising level of diversity in our society and notes the reduction of emphasis on the society as a whole. In his words,

The forces that made mass society have suddenly been thrown into reverse. Nationalism in the high-technology context becomes regionalism instead. The pressures of the melting pot are replaced by the new ethnicity. The media, instead of creating a mass culture, de-massify it.[11]

In the past, society has been bound together with common goals and values. Today we see a fragmentation of goals and values as individuals join together into a multitude of special interest groups. Promoting the good of the nation or the society has been replaced by promoting sub-groups which often have very different aims. We have seen the emergence of advocacy for minority rights, women's rights, gay rights, children's rights, older citizens' rights, fundamentalists' rights, consumers' rights, handicapped citizens' rights, and on and on.

Schools are not equipped to *act* in the present de-massified cultural climate. Schools have been forced to react as various advocacy groups have taken center stage in the political area; for example, accommodations for handicapped students were mandated by federal law. As schools react, they end up responding piecemeal to a multitude of divergent forces and, as a consequence, lose their focus and fragment their purpose. Schools frequently respond using traditional means that are no longer effective. It is no wonder that the back-to-the-basics movement would present itself as we run for cover in the refuge of our past.

The third social change to affect schooling is the development of what Yankelovich calls a "duty-to-self ethic." Yankelovich argues that seeking self-fulfillment has replaced sacrificing for others as the ethical norm that guides individual behavior in our society.[12] This "me-focused" morality has had profound effects on traditional institutions, especially the family and schools. Parents who are seeking to fulfill themselves behave differently toward their children than parents whose primary goal was to make life for their children better than what they experienced. Parents who believe in a situational morality that maximizes the expression of self teach their children different lessons than parents who believe in established standards of behavior and following rules. The schools, again, have been forced to *react* to a generation of students nurtured by "duty-to-self" oriented parents and have been unable to meet the challenge. The result is disharmony between the expectations of the institution and its clients and a sense of meaninglessness growing from both directions.[13]

In sum, we believe a large measure of school problems are due to lost connections between society and its schools. Society is undergoing dramatic change, becoming more complex, fragmented, and self-oriented. Schooling is addressing these changes in a reactive mode and often with only another "special program" or an additional layer of bureaucracy.[14] We believe that within the multitude of reform proposals ought to be a concern for re-establishing connections between schools and society and regenerating a sense of identity and purpose in the schools.

■ Educating for a Democracy of the Intellect

Bronowski concluded *The Ascent of Man,* his classic description of the evolution of our culture, by warning that if western civilization is to survive, a "democracy of the intellect" is essential.[15] He argues that our cultural survival is dependent on each person's responsible participation in the decisions that shape our future. Such participation requires "informed integrity," which means that every individual must take responsibility for the integrity of what we are as a people, and knowing what our world is like and how it works is essential to informed participation in the decisions that will determine our destiny. Bronowski is pessimistic about our culture's survival chances because of what he calls a "retreat from knowledge" into a world run by specialists (an aristocracy of intellect). He believes that knowledge is the destiny of our civilization and that taking knowledge out of the hands of the citizens spells the end of civilization as we know it. In his words,

We must not perish by the distance between people and government, between people and power, by which Babylon and Egypt and Rome failed. And that distance can only be conflated, can only be closed, if knowledge sits in the homes and heads of people with no ambition to control others, and not up in the isolated seats of power.[16]

We find Bronowski's arguments compelling and believe educating for a democracy of the intellect is a worthy purpose for schools, one that addresses directly the needs of contemporary society. The question then becomes: What ought schools to be doing to help develop individuals who possess the knowledge and integrity necessary to be active participants in the direction of our culture's future? We see "aims of education" proposed by Webb as conceptual tools that schools can use to redirect the focus of what they do and what they ask children to do.[17] Webb's aims are built on beliefs that are parallel to Bronowski's.

Webb argues that education should be aimed at enhancing creative intelligence, encouraging cooperation, and developing self-respect. In the discussion to follow, we will show how these three strands offer ways for schools to work toward a democratization of the intellect.

Webb relies heavily on Dewey as he describes creative intelligence. Intelligence is not thought of as a score on an I.Q. test or as a discrete set of measurable "thinking skills." Intelligent action is response to problematic situations based on ordered and thoughtful inquiry. Dewey believed that a healthy democratic society depends on a common commitment to intelligence as a way of recognizing and solving problems. In his view, societies are more than collections of individuals; democracies actively involve individuals in the construction and continual reconstruction of societal values and purposes.[18] Intelligence is not taken to be a native capacity but as:

a habit of mind which must be learned in interaction with others. Intelligence involves powers of observation that allow individuals to recognize and define problems. It involves reasoning and judgment. It demands that we learn from experience and put what is learned in our stock of knowledge where it can be called on when needed in the future. Most importantly, intelligence allows us to examine our habits and social customs to determine if they still serve useful purposes. When they do not, intelligence gives us a means for changing them. However, when habit and custom do prove worthwhile, intelligence gives us reason to support them.[19]

Creative intelligence prepares citizens who are neither blind conformists accepting the status quo without question nor rebellious radicals rejecting established norms and values for the sake of rejection.[20] Schools today fail to develop creative intelligence because they over-emphasize memorization, skill mastery, and conformity, while devaluing or ignoring children's divergent production and problem solving capacities.

Encouraging cooperation is Webb's second aim. He recognizes that competition is highly valued in our society and in schools but cites evidence that cooperation can be developed through varying the organization and implementation of classroom activities.[21] We see the schools' role in this area as critical. Yankelovich argues that an "ethic of commitment" will emerge in our society to replace the current ethic of self-fulfillment.[22] Individuals operating within an ethic of commitment would make moral decisions based on the effects of their decisions on others and on society. Such commitment requires a sense of connectedness to others that can and ought to be addressed in school.

Self-respect is Webb's third aim. He argues that for many students, self-respect is hard to come by. Self-respect comes when students are engaged in activities that they see as important and that are recognized by others as important.[23] We have argued above that the purposes of students and schools do not match. Students are unwilling to invest their energies in school tasks they see as meaningless and are becoming less willing to pretend to be involved in order to get by. We agree with Webb that self-respect comes when students value their school tasks and value the feedback they receive from others.

In summary, we believe the development of creative intelligence, cooperation, and self-respect are tied to educating for a democracy of the intellect. If our democratic society is to continue and grow it must have active, informed participation by its citizens. In order for them to participate effectively, citizens need intelligence that gives them the power to analyze problematic situations, explore alternatives and consequences, make decisions, and learn from the results. These processes can be fostered in school. In order for our society to continue, it must move from a self-centered, "me-first" orientation toward a new sense of connectedness to others and to the whole. This connectedness can be encouraged by developing cooperative approaches in classrooms. Finally, if our society is to survive, a sense that "I can make a difference" has to be re-generated. So long as individuals feel a sense of powerlessness, they will not participate in democratic decision making, and the demise of Western civilization anticipated by Bronowski will be at hand.

Implementing educational aims for a democracy of the intellect is not an easy task and results might not be evident immediately. It is important to note that the human processes involved in establishing aims that bring meaning back to education have value in and of themselves. Working toward aims that connect society and schools can regenerate a sense of integrity among educators and refocus the fragmented identity of our schools.

■ Footnotes

1. The U.S. Department of Education estimates that 17–20 million adults in the U.S. cannot read, while University of Texas researchers report that fully half of the U.S. populace may be on the borderline of illiteracy. See "Losing the War of Letters," *Time Magazine*, 127, (1986), 68.

2. William H. Lucio, *Readings in American Education*, (Chicago: Scott Foresman and Company, 1963).

3. From Jefferson's "Notes on the State of Virginia," quoted in R. Freeman Butts, *The Revival of Civic Learning*, (Bloomington, Ind.: Phil Delta Kappa Educational Foundation, 1980), p. 55.

4. L. Jennings Wagoner Jr., *Thomas Jefferson and the Education of a New Nation*, (Bloomington, Ind.: Phi Delta Kappa Fastback #73, 1976), p. 25.

5. M. S. Katz. *A History of Compulsory Education Laws*, (Bloomington, Ind.: Phi Delta Kappa Fastback #75, 1976).

6. Ibid.

7. Butts, *The Revival of Civic Learning*.

8. Two seminal works of this type are Franklin Bobbitt, *The Curriculum*, (Boston: Houghton Mifflin Company, 1918), and W. W. Charters, *Curriculum Construction* (New York: The Macmillan Company, 1923).

9. John Naisbitt, *Megatrends*, (New York: Warner Books, 1982), p. 12.

10. See Alice Meil, "Making Room for the Future in the Curriculum," *The RECORD*, 21, (Fall, 1984), 14–16; and Paul Dickson, "Education Tomorrow," *Creative Living*, 14, (Autumn, 1985), 9–14.

11. Alvin Toffler, *The Third Wave*, (New York: William Morrow and Company, 1980), p. 250.

12. Daniel Yankelovich, *New Rules: Searching for Self-Fulfillment in a World Turned Upside Down*, (New York: Random House, 1981), p. 240.

13. Teachers' estrangement from their work is documented in Aston, Patricia T., and Rodman B. Webb, *Making a Difference: Teachers' Sense of Efficacy and Student Achievement*, (New York: Longman Inc., 1986). The alienation of students is discussed in Charles Silberman, *Crisis in the Classroom*, (New York: Random House, 1970).

14. For a discussion of the proliferation of educational technologies and bureaucracies, see J. Amos Hatch, "Technology and the Devaluation of Human Processes," *The Educational Forum*, 48, (Winter, 1984), 243–252.

15. J. Bronowski, *The Ascent of Man*, (Little, Brown and Company, 1973), p. 434.

16. Ibid., p. 435.

17. Rodman B. Webb, *Schooling and Society*, (New York: Macmillan Publishing Co., Inc., 1981), pp. 290–310.

18. See John Dewey, *Human Nature and Conduct*, (New York: Random House, Inc., 1930); and *Democracy and Education*, (New York: The Free Press, 1966).

19. Webb, *Schooling and Society*, p. 29.

20. On this point, Webb cites W. I. Thomas, "Social Personality: Organization of Attitudes," in *W. I. Thomas on Social Organization and Personality*, ed. Morris Janowitz, (Chicago: University of Chicago Press, 1966).

21. See for example, David W. Johnson, and Robert T. Johnson, *Learning Together and Alone*, (Englewood Cliffs, N. J.: Prentice-Hall, Inc., 1975).

22. Yankelovich, *New Rules*.

23. See John Rawls, *A Theory of Justice*, (Cambridge, Mass.: Harvard University Press, 1971).

From J. Amos Hatch and John M. Conrath, "Refocusing the Identity of Schooling: Education for a Democracy of the Intellect," *Kappa Delta Pi Record*, 24(2):41–45, Winter 1988. Copyright © 1988 Kappa Delta Pi Honor Society in Education, West Lafayette, IN. Reprinted by permission.

■ Questions for Discussion

1. What effects have cultural pluralism had on American education?

2. Alternative schools are popular notions that offer alternatives to what has been going on in the schools. Why is this notion so popular? How would you defend the education you have received thus far?

3. How might a decision to teach or not to teach in the public schools be related to one's philosophy of education? Which educational view seems most satisfactory for you? Why?

4. What differences would exist in the ways in which a traditional teacher and a progressive teacher would direct the classroom? What discipline techniques would be used?

5. Do you think that educating for a democracy of the intellect is essential to the survival of our nation? Why? Why not?

■ Notes

1. Richard Wynn et al., *American Education,* 8th ed. (New York: McGraw-Hill, 1977), p. 2.
2. Barbara M. Morris, "The Real Issues in Education as Seen by a Journalist on the Far Right," *Phi Delta Kappan,* May 1980, p. 613.
3. William J. Bennett and Edwin J. Dellattre, "A Moral Education," *American Educator,* Winter 1979, pp. 6–7.
4. Mario Fantini, "Options for Students, Parents, and Teachers: Public Schools of Choice," *Phi Delta Kappan,* May 1971, pp. 541–43.

■ Selected References

Bagley, William C. "An Essentialist's Platform for the Advancement of American Education." *Educational Administration and Supervision* 24, April 1938, pp. 241–56.

Dewey, John. "Challenge of Democracy to Education." *Progressive Education,* February 1937, pp. 79–85.

Dewey, John. *Democracy and Education.* New York: Macmillan, 1916.

Hutchins, Robert M. "The Schools Must Stay," *The Center Magazine* 6 (January–February 1973):12–23.

Knight, George R. *Issues and Alternatives in Educational Philosophy.* Berrien Springs, MI: Andrews University Press, 1982.

Morris, Van Cleve. *Introduction to Education.* Columbus, OH: Charles E. Merrill, 1982, pp. 63–88.

Morris, Van Cleve and Pai, Young. *Philosophy and the American School.* Boston: Houghton Mifflin Company, 1976.

"Our Future as Teachers Will Be Profoundly Influenced by Which Philosophy Finally Prevails." Item #31. Washington, D.C.: American Federation of Teachers.

Rich, John Martin. *Innovations in Education: Reformers and Their Critics.* Boston: Allyn and Bacon, Inc., 1987. (See chapter 17 "Cognitive Moral Development," pp. 262–73.)

Torrance, E. Paul. "Creativity and Futurism in Education: Retooling." *Education* (Summer 1980):298–311.

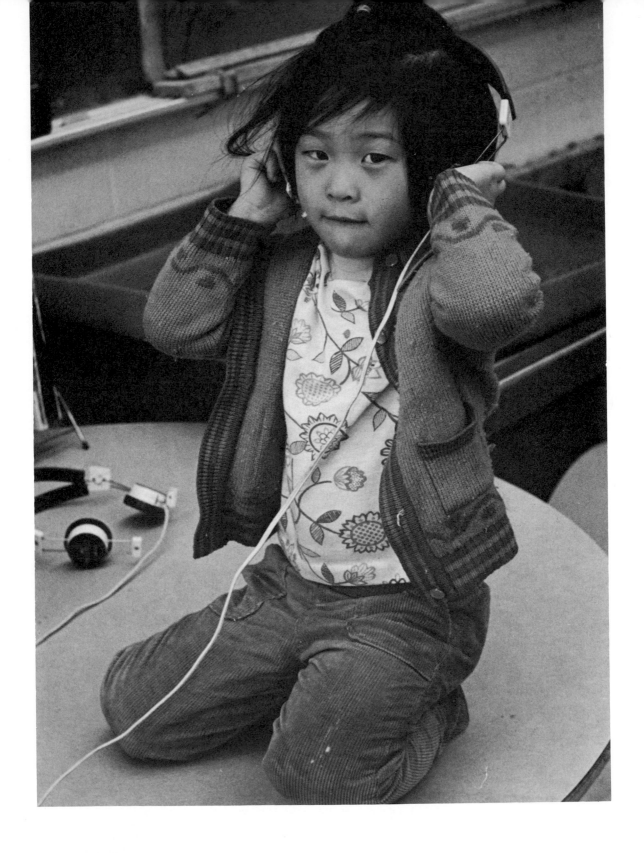

Section 4

The Learning Process

Earlier chapters provided overviews for such aspects of American public education as the career of teaching, the teacher's changing role, selected topics related to the teaching profession, and the role of education including purposes, social problems, historical influences, and philosophical beliefs. Section 4 is concerned with the nature of learners and learning, the nature of curriculum, and the instructional resources available for meeting the needs of students—with special emphasis on the use of computers in the classroom.

The operations of the systems of schools, public and private, that serve the educational needs of youth are geared to bringing groups of learners together with one teacher for all or part of each of the learner's days in school. Yet, no matter how the schools group learners, the obviousness of meeting the individual needs of learners is apparent at the outset. The most effective teachers meet the educational expectations for the group while maintaining the individuality of each learner within the group.

Contemporary teachers have vast resources of information about human differences and the learning process, child growth and development, emotional and social development, and motivation for learning to serve them in helping teach their pupils. Ultimately, effective teachers are those who use their motivational skills to develop a positive climate that nurtures the educational growth of children.

Another dimension of the learning process is the curriculum. Expectations of people at the national, state, and local levels are a major source for the curriculums of our schools. In most basic terminology, the curriculum consists of "what is taught, or perhaps, what is learned." While experts might disagree on the technical definitions of curriculum, for purposes of this book, it is defined as consisting of three parts: (1) *goals,* or what students should learn, (2) *methodology,* or how they are going to learn it, and (3) *evaluation,* or how well they have learned. The teacher as a front-line person interacting daily with students can be a valuable resource person in developing curriculum.

In the past decade, tremendous strides have been made in the development of instructional resources. Multimedia resources, while frequently used by one teacher or one learner, are also often used with paraprofessional help. The rapid development of the microcomputer has changed our entire outlook on computer use in education. Future instructional technology will include cost efficient programs utilizing the telecommunication potential of space satellites. Many of the instructional resources are not only helpful in working with classes of learners, but are especially useful in individualizing instruction to meet the unique needs of learners.

Computers and television are two relatively new instuctional devices now available to teachers. Both of these forms of technology hold great potential as teaching devices and are explored in some detail in this part of the book.

The learning process is both fascinating and challenging. When learning occurs, teaching can be a most gratifying profession. When learning does not occur, teaching can be challenging. Teachers, curriculum, and instructional resources all exist to facilitate the learning process among students.

Chapter 12

The Nature of Learners

Objectives

After studying this chapter, you should be able to:

- Establish the need to meet individual differences among learners as a starting point.

- Consider the importance of self-perception and variations in abilities as central to the study of human growth and development.

- Cite the work of Jean Piaget, which coincides with the current dominant environmentalist explanation of intellectual development.

- Draw attention to differences in maturity levels and differences in rate of maturation among youth.

- Recognize variations in societal demands as impacting upon the programs of our schools.

- Devote attention to the collection of data about and definition of child growth and development terminology.

- Distinguish motivation as being a complex rather than a simple phenomenon.

Enrichment Experiences

The following suggestions will help you learn more about some of the important topics discussed in this chapter:

- Recent attention has been given to the educational needs of our adults. Discuss the role of the public school in the education of adults.

- Visit a special education class. List the techniques used by the teacher to motivate his/her pupils. Discuss the effects of those techniques.

- Read and report on the findings of a research study related to self-concept and learning.

- Visit an open classroom and state its advantages and disadvantages. Visit a private school and indicate its strengths and weaknesses.

- Engage the members of your class in a discussion for the purpose of identifying and listing the competencies for teaching that the content of this chapter suggests.

- Visit with experienced teachers about how students think, behave, and learn in today's schools.

NEA / AFT

"The teacher unions: how the
NEA and AFT sabotage
reform and hold students..."

Myron

Myron, Lieberman

wife might give her husband
ren, who were reckoned hers.
t degrade her to slavery
r if she had borne her
e Code did not allow the
not, he could do so. The
ne rank; the first wife
ree woman, was often dowered
ate. She could only be
If a wife became a
maintain her in the home
ed to take her dowry and
free to remarry. In all
nd legal heirs.
a man having children by a
ny case, and their mother
dged, and she was free on
e legitimized by their
and were often adopted. They
r's estate, but if not
ook first choice.
ve children, yet they could
that such a wife would
might marry slaves and
were free, and at the
half what she and her
nd children; the master

till their marriage. He had
r keep. He might hire
hem for debt, even sell them
he absence of the father;
dead. A father had no claim
hey retained a right to

This chapter will help you learn that the operations of the systems of schools, public and private, that serve the educational needs of youth are geared to bringing groups of learners together with one teacher for all or part of each of the learner's days in school. This does not mean to imply that teachers and learners shall not have the opportunity to interact on a one-on-one basis. However, the simple economics of the business of education does mandate that the learner/teacher ratio be approximately twenty to one (or higher) for most school systems. Yet, no matter how the schools group learners, the obviousness of meeting the individual needs of learners is apparent at the outset. So in preparation for becoming a teacher, each person needs the opportunity to learn about ways in which teaching can be facilitated through both group processes and through individualization. Seemingly, the mere learning by teachers about group processes and individualization has the potential for being classified as meaningless unless the teachers first learn about the ways in which learners differ from each other. Further, the more heterogeneous the learner group, i.e., the more representative of the entire learner population, the greater the need for understanding learner differences. ■

For most of our educational history, schools have brought students together in groups with a teacher for the purpose of studying (learning) various selected and elected subjects. This so-called traditional arrangement has been the subject of criticism from progressive educators who suggest that the approach to learning should be more student-centered than subject-centered. Further extension of this thinking suggests that, in a freer approach to education, the learners will seek what they need to know when they want to do so. Implied is the notion that the student's motives for learning will be intrinsic with a greater degree of persistence associated with what is learned.

While most educators are quick to express the need for greater attention to the individual needs of the learner, most do not sanction undirected chaos in the learning environment. Most students seem to desire direction and consider initiating structure to be important. Likewise, students seem to need some means of knowing that they have accomplished something. The task for the beginning teacher is to experiment with the various techniques available for meeting the needs of individuals within the framework of their school system.

Teachers sometimes tend to minimize the fact that learning is natural. Children do not have to be forced to learn; they have to be forcibly restrained to prevent them from learning something. But this does not mean that they will learn what we want them to learn. Teaching may be generally defined as the process by which one person helps others achieve new skills, knowledge, and attitudes. While teaching involves both the teacher and the learner, learning is an activity of the learner. Guidance for the learner is provided by good teachers who help create conditions that direct learning toward that which the teachers want learned. New research shows that what teachers expect of their pupils is usually what they get from them. The influence of teachers' expectations on students' performances is a popular research area because of its potential implications for classroom application.[1]

CHILDREN LEARN WHAT THEY LIVE
If a child lives with criticism,
    He learns to condemn.
If a child lives with hostility,
    He learns to fight.
If a child lives with ridicule,
    He learns to be shy.

If a child lives with shame,
    He learns to feel guilty.
If a child lives with tolerance,
    He learns to be patient.
If a child lives with encouragement,
    He learns confidence.

Teachers at all levels need mastery of their subject matter specialization. However, mastery of subject matter areas is not enough. In most states, before the teaching certificate is issued, prospective teachers are required to include in their study professional education courses that include educational psychology. A basic intent of educational psychology is to assist teachers in using the principles of psychology (behavior) to help students learn. For example, schools can do a great deal to develop in children desirable attitudes toward their classmates—attitudes of fair play, friendliness, and cooperation—which make their lives and the lives of those around them more agreeable. Schools can also do a great deal to develop in children desirable attitudes toward their studies, toward their teachers, and toward the whole educational process. In this task, educational psychologists can often help.

Psychology is the science that studies human and animal behavior. Psychologists are interested in understanding the needs and motives of people, their thought processes, their feelings and emotions, and how people learn. Psychology is usually classed with biology, sociology, and anthropology as one of the behavioral sciences. The modern psychologist is concerned with behavior rather than skills, knowledge, and attitudes. Therefore, psychologists generally agree that learning refers to changes in performance (behavior) arising from experience.

■ Individual Differences

There is a wide range of differences among individuals. At the approximate age of puberty, individual differences in physical size among youngsters are particularly evident, including such differences as height, weight, physical fitness, and motor coordination. As children grow and mature, sex differences become pronounced with regard to size and strength, aptitude and motivation. Age differences, socioeconomic differences, and intellectual and academic differences also exist. These many differences among individuals play a great part in the patterns of adjustment pupils make with regard to the typical school setting.

Twenty-five years ago, children were considered and treated as young adults. The teacher's task was to see that the child gained knowledge necessary to enter and function in the adult world. Emphasis was placed on group instruction with less attention to meeting the needs of individuals within the group. Current thinking recognizes that as children develop they take on characteristics which are common to other children who are at the same stage of development.[2] The work of several psychologists has contributed much to the realm of child development theory. Teachers now allow for the fact that children of the same age develop socially, psychologically, cognitively, and physically at varying rates. While age is considered a major factor related to a given stage of development, the range of characteristics for an age group varies considerably. These developmental theorists emphasize the continuous study of behaviors when considering aspects of human growth and development from preschool age to adulthood. The point here is that school personnel must constantly be reminded that the school setting in itself does not adequately deal with the wide range of differences among individual pupils.

Schools have responded in one way to individual differences by providing programs centered on ability groups, ranging from gifted children to retarded children to many others.

If a child lives with praise,
  He learns to appreciate.
If a child lives with fairness,
  He learns justice.
If a child lives with security,
  He learns to have faith.

If a child lives with approval,
  He learns to like himself.
If a child lives with acceptance and
friendship,
  He learns to find love in the world.

  Dorothy Law Nolte

Generally, such attempts by our schools for dealing with individual differences have not been glowingly successful. Classroom teachers are, and have been, somewhat adept at providing for individual differences within our schools. This aspect of the teaching task is becoming increasingly more difficult, since increasing numbers of children of varied abilities and backgrounds are in attendance. The contemporary teacher comes into daily contact with much larger numbers of pupils than ever before. Further, the impact of science and technology on teaching can result in increasing impersonality in the teaching process. Yet teachers are constantly and continually called upon to be skilled at providing for individual differences. In the future, teachers who will be the most competent at providing for individual differences will be those who continue to learn about learners. This will enable them to know how to better provide for human variability and learning within the group framework of our American public schools.

Human Differences and Learning

Any discussion regarding human differences and learning brings out several theoretical assumptions that are charged with controversy. Hardly a statement can be made regarding human differences and learning that some psychologist or educational psychologist will not take exception to as being oversimplified, incomplete, or irrelevant. Nonetheless, most successful educators agree that the thorough understanding of learners is basic to the task of teaching. When the schools (teachers) are aware of and understand the nature of individual differences among students but fail to serve individual needs, the students' natural zest for learning is dulled. It behooves the classroom teacher, especially, to allow for such human differences as self-perception, intelligence, and rate of maturation. In addition, variations in societal demands are often significant for more thoroughly understanding the nature of learners.

Given these several human differences among the students, different methods of directing the learning activities are necessary. Teachers must spend much time in preparing materials for assignments if they understand that individuals learn differently.

Self-Perception

The most important form of perception is self-perception. Whom does the individual perceive himself or herself to be? Teachers often find that some of their pupils associate prospects of failure with themselves rather than ambitious self-expectations for success. Whether or not such expectations evolved from previous school experiences that involved both their parents and teachers, the self-perception of mediocrity is a major determinant in subsequent behavior of the learner in new classroom settings. If pupils hold low expectations for themselves, it is unlikely that they will perform beyond those low expectations.

Another dimension of differences in perception as related to learning, which teachers often overlook, is the fact that people usually behave in accordance with what *they* perceive to be the related conditions rather than what others might wish them to believe the conditions to be. Most of us can quickly recall certain teachers and their "pet" subjects that they taught us to love. For example, one music teacher was sure that each of her pupils would demonstrate appreciation of the musical classics by recognizing various music themes for the rest of their lives, whether the selection was heard in total or as part of a popular tune, or whatever. The outcomes, in terms of the students' feelings, may be far different from the objectives. In the case of at least one pupil, some musical themes have indeed been recalled (from memory). But in this instance there is no pleasure, love, or appreciative feeling associated with such recall. Rather, what is recalled is the painful experience of being hit with a ruler across the knuckles for talking during music appreciation class, or of being shouted at, or of the intense dissatisfaction that accompanied compulsory attendance for that activity. In these instances, the teacher perceives the objectives of the teacher-learning experience differently than the student does. Indeed, in terms of the students' feelings, it could be readily envisioned that some of the learners would come to dislike classical music very much as a result.

With regard to academic self-concept, it has been demonstrated that successful learning experiences enhance positive academic self-concept, whereas unsuccessful school experiences enhance negative academic self-concept. Benjamin S. Bloom, Distinguished Service Professor of Education at the University of Chicago, is a renowned researcher in the field of outcomes of school learning. Citing the relevant research on this topic, Bloom reports that "for the students at the extreme limits of academic achievement (top and bottom fifths), the relation between academic self-concept and school achievement is very strong, with little overlap in academic self-concept between these extreme groups."[3] Bloom also provides figure 12.1 to support his findings.

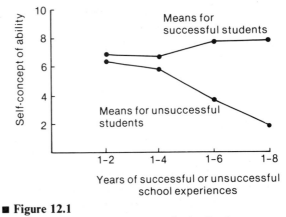

■ **Figure 12.1**

Self-concept of ability over years of schooling for successful and unsuccessful students

Source: Edward Kifer, "The Effect of School Achievement on the Affective Traits of the Learner." Unpublished dissertation, 1973.

■ Variations in Abilities

Intelligence and ability have many varying dimensions among children. It should be obvious to educators that the school population represents cross sections of varying levels of ability and intelligence. Some argue over the causes of these differences, while others hold that the schools cannot provide totally adequate learning environments needed to rule out such differences among pupils. Some suggest that the curriculum provisions must be formulated from the premise that "all learners are equal" with equal potential for learning. The adult population provides information which suggests that differences are obvious and continuous. Many adults do not read or compute well, and probably never will. From this, our conceptions of achievement and success must recognize the fact that there are many people who

Every person born into this world represents something new, something that never existed before, something original and unique. . . . Every person's foremost task is the actualization of his or her unique, unprecedented and never recurring potentialities, and not the repetition of something that another, and be it even the greatest, has already achieved.

Martin Buber

are successful in areas unrelated to the utilization of reading and computation skills. If the assumption is valid that each learner has equal potential for learning, then motivational factors are absolutely necessary to overcome certain limited learning rates among pupils for effective learning to occur.

Psychologists have not questioned that factors of both heredity and environment are important influences in explaining individual differences. One of the most comprehensive theories of cognitive growth and development was formulated by Swiss psychologist Jean Piaget. Acceptance of his theory coincides with the current dominant environmentalist explanation of intellectual development. Allen Ornstein and Harry Miller provide the following excerpt from Piaget's work.[4]

Many school programs center around individual ability.

Piaget described four stages of intellectual development, which are:

1. *Sensimotor stage (approximately the first two years).* The child progresses from reflex operations, in which surrounding schema are undifferentiated, to complex sensimotor actions, in which there is a progressive organization of the schema. The child comes to realize that objects have permanence; they can be found again. The child begins to establish simple relations among similar objects.

2. *Preoperational stage (approximately ages two to seven).* In this stage, objects and events begin to take on symbolic meaning for the child: a chair is for sitting; birthday parties are a time for celebration; school is a place to learn. At the latter part of this period, the child becomes aware of the concept of number and amount. The child shows an increased ability to learn more complex concepts from his experiences, but must be provided with concrete or familiar examples from which to extract criteria that define that concept.

3. *Concrete operations stage (approximately ages seven to eleven).* The child begins to organize data into logical relations and gains facility in manipulating data in problem-solving situations; these operations occur, however, only if concrete objects are available or if actual past experiences can be drawn upon. The child is able to make judgments in terms of reversibility and reciprocal relations; for example, left and right are spatial relations; "being a foreigner" is a reciprocal process. Understanding develops of the conversion of a liquid to various shapes a tall, narrow glass may hold the same amount of water as a short, wide one.

4. *Formal operations stage (age eleven onward).* This stage is characterized by the development of formal and abstract thought operations. An adolescent is able to analyze ideas and make spatial and temporal relations. He or she can think logically about abstract data and evaluate data according to acceptable criteria. Instead of being bound to a concrete here and now, an adolescent can formulate hypothesis and deduce possible consequences from them.

Piaget's cognitive stages presuppose a maturation process in the sense that development is seen as a continuum. Although the stages are defined as separate phases, they overlap and are by no means precise or binding at a given age. A child's hereditary capabilities and environmental experiences determine the quality of growth for that child at each cognitive stage, and environmental experiences are affected by the family as well as by teachers and schools. Some controversy exists over whether the stages can be accelerated through appropriate experiences.

■ Many Forms of Intelligence

Researchers have found that intelligence may be defined in many different ways, and that students have many different talents for learning. Psychologist Howard Gardner, for one, believes that there is no single form of intellect. Rather, he believes that people draw from a variety of "core" abilities to learn and to solve problems and to produce products that are important to our society. Dr. Gardner suggests that intelligence comes in at least the following forms:[5]

- *Musical intelligence,* or sensitivity to pitch, melody, rhythm, and tone

- *Linguistic intelligence,* or sensitivity to the meaning and order of words and the varied uses of languages
- *Logical-mathematical* intelligence, or the ability to handle long chains of reasoning and to recognize patterns and order in the world
- *Spatial intelligence,* or the ability to perceive the visual world accurately and to recreate, transform, or modify aspects of that world based on one's perceptions
- *Bodily-kinesthetic intelligence,* or a fine-tuned ability to use the body and to handle objects
- *Interpersonal intelligence,* or the ability to notice and make distinctions among others
- *Intrapersonal intelligence,* or access to one's own "feeling life"

Teachers need to be made aware of the different dimensions of intellect that children bring to the classroom. Dr. Gardner believes that all students have many types of intelligence and that we have simply failed to recognize that intellect is an extremely diverse and complex human quality.

■ Differences in Maturity Levels

Studies of children's behavior as related to school adjustment typically illustrate that approximately 20 percent of students are well adjusted to school, 50 percent have no significant problems, 20 percent are mildly disturbed, and 10 percent are disturbed by school. It would not be surprising to find similar degrees of adjustment for pupils at any level of education. Discussion usually deals with differences such as attention span, muscle coordination, capacity for dealing with self-direction, and many other variations associated with maturation. Consideration is given to characteristics of physical, social, emotional, and mental aspects of development. For example, kindergarteners are extremely active physically; are frequently socially quarrelsome, though quick to forget; tend to express emotions openly; and are skillful with language—liking to talk. Primary grade children are prone to the common illnesses of childhood; tend to become more selective in choosing friends; are sensitive to criticism and need frequent recognition; and have more facility in speech than in writing. Elementary grades mark the time when a physical growth spurt occurs in most girls; the peer group begins to serve as the standard for behavior; pupils are emotionally torn between the group code and adult rules; and pupils often set unrealistically high standards for themselves. For junior high students, secondary sex characteristics become increasingly apparent; best friends may replace parents as confidants; intolerance and opinionated behavior arise; and comprehension of abstract concepts increases. By the senior high grades, most students reach physical maturity; girls remain more mature socially than boys; anguish and revolt are reflected in changeover from childhood to adulthood; and students have a high degree of intellectual efficiency.[6]

Hopefully, these thumbnail sketches serve to illustrate the strong need for prospective teachers to have considerable knowledge about differences in maturity levels of children in order to best recognize and serve the unique needs of each pupil. Too often, however, teacher preparation programs permit sketchy information to serve in meeting this very strong need. Very much *is* known about the physical, social, emotional, and

mental characteristics of children at each age level of development. Likewise, much evidence related to successful teaching illustrates that the best teachers possess such knowledge about their pupils.

■ Differences in Rate of Maturation

We have considered some implications for learning of different maturity levels. It is also important to recognize that among individuals within the same general age group there are wide variations in rate of maturation and development.

Our failure to recognize variations in the rates of development among children, and to recognize the importance of the concept of readiness, can cause us to waste tremendous energy in the educational enterprise, trying to accomplish objectives that are simply not appropriate to a child at that point. The same goals may be reached quickly and easily when the students have developed the kinds of physical and mental maturity necessary for reaching them. Trying to achieve such objectives too early may leave the children with initial negative experiences.

Successful teachers constantly strive to keep up with the expanding body of knowledge about learners' growth and development. In recent years, certain differences in rates of maturation indicate that today's youth do mature early, as indicated, for example, by such dimensions as early biological growth in girls (first appearance of the menses two to five years earlier than in the past), voice changes in boys earlier than in the past (average age just over thirteen years rather than eighteen years), early growth maturity (little if any growth after the age of seventeen or eighteen, rather than twenty-six years), and considerably earlier association with regard to premarital sex, motherhood, and marriage. The greater the extent to which classroom teachers incorporate these deeper understandings of learners with their classroom practices, the greater the probability that classroom teachers will arouse in their learners a profound sense of self-respect and personal integrity.

■ Variations in Societal Demands

The problems and issues with which the schools are confronted represent kinds of societal expectations associated with the function of the schools. When the public is asked to state opinions about the schools, problem lists are generally formulated. Such problem lists reflect those aspects of operations needing remediation as suggested by public opinion. In some cases, segments of society often take up the clamor for solving school problems by bringing direct pressure to bear upon school boards, school administrators, and teachers. The scope of societal demands upon the schools and school personnel is reflected in the nature of the questions asked in a recent Annual Gallup Poll of The Public's Attitudes Toward the Public Schools: Should the school year or day be extended? How much homework? Subjects required? Special areas of instruction? National tests for graduation? Prayer in the schools? Nongraded schools? Problems confronting schools? Discipline? Goals of education? While the institutions of society are typically characterized as being slow to adjust to changes in society, societal demands are, nonetheless, ultimately reflected within the total school program.

Much has been said of the rapidly changing nature of the world around us. The pace of change continues to accelerate, bringing with it an increased desire on the part of society for the schools to accelerate the ways in which adjustments to change are being made. Teachers moving into the profession will encounter societal pressures directly and indirectly. The role teachers play in responding to societal concerns can be of vital importance. It is crucial that the underlying causes and sources of all sorts of school concerns be known by teachers. It is also important that teachers carefully assess the validity of all the demands placed upon them and offer their professional expertise when pressures or criticisms are seemingly unwarranted.

Assorted problems associated with the general welfare of the local, state, and federal community often serve as the basis for new, or renewed, societal demands upon the schools. Governmental crises and criminal activities by local officials in various communities and by state and national figures prompt suggestions that the nation's schools are educating poorly so far as morality, ethics, and honesty are concerned. Economic slowdowns bring about either unemployment or a tightened job market or both with the impact upon the schools subsequently represented in demands for more and better retraining opportunities, career and vocational education, and needs assessments to determine new programs to assist students in entering the economic marketplace. Court decisions dealing with religious concerns, individual rights and privileges, segregation matters, academic freedom and academic choice, and sex bias often alter the processes of school management. Many of these kinds of societal pressures for change in the schools become emotion-laden when transferred to the local community. Much attention is given to localities having difficulty accomplishing local racial integration in the schools, for example, when forces at the local level muster against racial integration. Most of these situations arise when a demand from the national society does not square with the local societal expectation. At the same time, rare attention is given to localities which have little, if any, difficulty accomplishing local racial integration in their schools.

Prospective teachers need to be aware of the emotion-laden views they personally possess as related to the multitude of societal demands upon the schools. How will you serve the school organization as well as the school constituents? What are the principles against which you intend to check your emotions prior to reacting? When, if ever, will the demands of society take precedence over your personal beliefs? It appears relatively simply to assume that modern education must be sensitive to the changing demands today's world places upon our children and their schools. The task is, however, to guarantee that educators actually do more than merely tolerate the fact that changes are necessary to meet the demands of society and the educational needs of children attending school.

■ Differences in Objectives

One of the most significant statements concerning educational objectives was formulated in 1938 by the Educational Policies Commission of the National Education Association. In that study, a large group of educators collaborated in the development of objectives under the list headings "objectives of self-realization," "objectives of human relationships," "objectives of economic efficiency," and "objectives of civic responsibility." Throughout the years since that report, those lists of educational objectives have served as a basis for much of the curriculum thrust within the schools of America. To be sure, many other study groups, as well as individual educators, have extended, modified, or more definitely specified additional lists of educational objectives. Examinations of various publications reveal objectives by organizational structure to be commonplace. Guidelines, objectives, organizational suggestions, and the like have been detailed from nursery school to kindergarten, to elementary school, to secondary school, to junior college, to higher education, to the realm of continuing or adult education. Considerable attention has also been given to the objectives of career, vocational, and technical education within the school structure.

A vital component in programs for the preparation of future teachers is a comprehensive study of educational objectives with particular emphasis on the level which the student aspires to teach. Further, the study of and work with educational objectives is a continuing dimension of the work of teachers. Classroom teachers must constantly strive to develop and refine appropriate instructional objectives that relate directly to the more general objectives of the total educational program. While it is the professional task of the teacher to formulate instructional objectives, their students sometimes feel that preset objectives are not important for satisfying their learning needs. Some teachers, particularly at the upper grade level, involve their students in the formulation of the most appropriate learning objectives for the particular class activity.

Obviously, there are many variations concerning the specification of meaningful learning objectives. Some of these variations include: (a) the objectives of general education versus specialized education; (b) the objectives linked to the development of a reasonable level of literacy over a broad range of fundamentals, contrasted with the conception of developing considerable depth in one field; and (c) objectives associated with social class or other group factors. Failure to recognize that the purposes of schooling may be quite different for different individuals may cause us to draw many unwarranted conclusions about the appropriateness of certain content or teaching procedures. The sensitive teacher cannot assume that all come to school with the same objectives, or that those with purposes and interests different from those of the teacher must be remade in the teacher's image.

Psychology provides vast additional information that ought to be included in any discussion of human variability and learning. A continuing task of the contemporary educational psychologist is to draw from available information that which has greatest significance for the professional educators. Teacher-preparation institutions are charged with the responsibility of providing relevant and meaningful experiences for prospective teachers enrolled in their programs. Certified teachers are assumed to be knowledgeable regarding the determinants of human behavior, including the concept of needs and satisfaction of needs, motives and theories of motivation, and the effects of child-rearing practices on motivation. Teachers should be competent in understanding learners as persons, with special consideration for their self-concepts.

■ Child Growth and Development

Growth and development are inclusive terms, each influenced by both heredity and environment. Whether heredity or environment contributes most to one's level of development is open to speculation and disagreement. Of special interest to teachers is knowing the extent to which the behavior of pupils is the result of their inherited potential and/or the result of environmental influences. The influence of inherited factors upon behavior is not under teacher control, but the influence of environmental factors at least partially is. Teachers most effective in bringing out the potential of their pupils are those who are capable of coordinating the maturational processes with the environmental influences of their classrooms.

Our elementary schools have consistently served virtually all youth of school age. Since 1950, marked changes have occurred in the secondary school population of the United States, modifying the nature of that population. In 1950, seventy-six of every one hundred youth aged 14–17 in the general population were enrolled in school. Today ninety-five of every one hundred youth aged 14–17 are enrolled in school. Students with severe basic skill deficiencies now remain enrolled in the upper grades. Likewise, students with mental retardation and physical handicaps are enrolled in secondary schools. Thus, it is increasingly important that all prospective teachers gain considerable knowledge about the growth and development attributes of all learners. In their study of child growth and development, prospective teachers should explore specific aspects such as physical and motor development, emotional development, social development, and individual differences. Adolescence, once expected to begin at age 12 or 13, now may come at age 10 or 11. By their 16th birthday, most youth

Research Finding

11

Children's understanding of the relationship between being smart and hard work changes as they grow.

When children start school, they think that ability and effort are the same thing; in other words, they believe that if they work hard they will become smart. Thus, younger children who fail believe this is because they didn't try hard enough, not because they have less ability.

Because teachers tend to reward effort in earlier grades, children frequently concentrate on working hard rather than on the quality of their work. As a result, they may not learn how to judge how well they are performing.

Teachers who are alert to these beliefs in youngsters will keep their students motivated and on task. They will also slowly nudge their students toward the realism of judging themselves by performance. For example, teachers will set high expectations and insist that students put forth the effort required to meet the school's academic standards. They will make sure slower learners are rewarded for their progress and abler students are challenged according to their abilities.

Doyle, W. (1983). "Academic Work." *Review of Educational Research*, Vol. 53, No. 2, pp. 159–199.

Haurari, O., and Covington, M. V. (1981). "Reactions to Achievement Behavior From a Teacher and Student Perspective: A Developmental Analysis." *American Educational Research Journal*, Vol. 18, No. 1, pp. 15–28.

Stevenson, H. W., Lee, S., and Stigler, S. W. (February 1986). "Mathematics Achievement of Chinese, Japanese, and American Children." *Science*, Vol. 231, pp. 693–699.

Source: *What Works: Research About Teaching and Learning.* Washington, DC: U.S. Department of Education, 1987, page 37.

achieve a cognitive and physical capability that approximates full adulthood. The most successful teachers are those who strive to keep abreast of both subject matter content and child growth and development content through continuous study coupled with experience.

Social Development

Social development involves the ability to get along with others. It is important for a person to achieve social adequacy while attaining his or her individuality. Schools can make special contributions to the social development of children. Factors influencing one's social development are peer groups, sex drives, friendships, and sense of security. The importance of group activities upon the social development of group members is great. Manifestations of various kinds of behavior can be viewed as part of the process of attaining social adequacy.

The earlier physical maturing of youth has been accompanied by a number of significant social changes as well. These include diminishing family influence and control, a new interpretation of the constitutional rights of youth, greater mobility and affluence, a media-nourished awareness of the broader world, and a growing separation of the adult world from youth. The impact of these major trends upon youth is of considerable consequence. A discrete youth subculture has formed, one set apart in many ways from adult life. While most youth achieve a cognitive and physical capability that approximates full adulthood by age 16, youth are segregated from adults by adult-created institutions. Youth are relatively powerless to live their lives as adults and see themselves as outsiders to the dominant social institutions. Contemporary youth have diminishing support from persons of other ages and from the family unit. The resultant youth subculture is considered to be a product of the larger social environment rather than an independent youth movement.

As the most significant social institution available to all our youth, the schools, including the teachers, must strive to accommodate the social needs of youth. Schools neglecting the important social development needs of learners also contribute to the alienation of the youth subculture from adult institutions.

■ Motivation and Learning

Learning takes place best when the learner is motivated. Thus, an important aspect of the teachers' job is to help provide their pupils with motives to learn what is being taught. In addition to a desire

Individuals are never without motivation: good teachers create it.

to learn all that can be learned about learners, teachers should also desire to learn more and more about motivation and learning.

It may be said that individuals are never without motivation. Each of us continually endeavors to maintain and enhance personal adequacy. We tend to remain motivated toward those activities that provide success rather than failure. It follows that a pupil who does well and likes school will more likely respond to school-related activities than a pupil who does poorly in school. As a consequence of this specific aspect of motivation, considerable speculation and debate exists among educators as to the grading practice in schools, particularly since most grade systems include a failing grade. Some argue that if we wish learners to be continually motivated toward school activities, learning experiences should not permit failure. However, if success consists of reaching a goal, somewhere along the way the determination of whether the goal has been reached must be made by the teacher. Learners must be made aware of their progress toward goals. Hopefully, teachers can provide learning situations in which realistic goals are set for learners at their thresholds of achievement, and motivation encourages each to persist until these goals are successfully reached.

Motivation is a complex phenomenon. Factors influencing motivation and learning, in addition to firsthand experiences, include the learner's perception of these experiences, values ascribed to the experiences, and the self-concepts of the learners. Teacher and student variables, such as personality, and teacher and learner styles are related to motivation and learning.

■ Teacher and Learner Styles

The *best* teacher style or the *best* learner style cannot be generalized. Caution must be taken to avoid the trap of judging a teaching style or a learning style as wrong just because it doesn't match one's own style or one's own belief about a learning style. There is considerable overlap between the personal characteristics of teachers and teaching styles, and between the personal characteristics of learners and learner styles. Research evidence suggests that when it comes to classroom behavior, interaction patterns, and teaching styles, teachers who are superior in encouraging motivation and learning in students seem to exhibit flexibility, to perceive the students' point of view, to experiment, and to personalize their teaching.

In addition to individual differences in personality factors, assessment of motivation must give consideration to student reactions to praise and blame, student reactions to success and failure, and student differences in learning style. In the interests of effective motivation, it is important to identify each student's learning style as quickly as possible. What is important for one student is not important for another; this is one reason why cookbook formulas for good teaching are of so little value, and why teaching is inevitably something of an art when it comes to motivating students and helping them learn.

Thomas R. McDaniel is director of graduate education programs at Converse College, Spartanburg, South Carolina. He suggests that effective teachers use their motivational skills to develop a positive climate that nurtures the educational growth of children. Appendix H entitled "How Good A Motivator Are You?" asks teachers a series of important questions about motivation.

■ Summary

In the last chapter, prospective teachers were urged to approach their first classes with consistent day-to-day methods of instruction to help offset confusion among their pupils. This chapter established the need for teachers to meet individual differences among learners as a starting point. Together, the two seemingly contradictory suggestions frame the greatest challenge to teaching—how does the classroom teacher provide group instruction while meeting the individual needs of the students? Not easily, for sure. But the notion that you can learn how to do this only from experience in the classroom begs the need for understanding about the nature of learners before taking your first teaching position. While group instruction is enhanced by consistent methodology, those within the group learn in different ways at different rates. Teachers need to constantly search out those who need individual attention while fulfilling their learning needs.

Teachers must also realize that intellect, or learning ability, comes in many different forms. Each student has talent which the teacher must discover and develop. To do so requires a keen understanding of the nature of learners.

Point of View

Teachers need to understand a great deal about learners and about learning. Such an understanding enables the teacher to design effective learning experiences. The following point of view provides examples of teaching strategies that are consistent with what we know about the nature of learners. They provide future teachers with practical suggestions on goal setting, communicating expectations, understanding content, following instructional material and accepting responsibility.

Five Tips to Improve Teaching

U.S. Department of Education

Many teachers believe they do a good job and don't see the need to invest time and energy to improve the way they teach. However, most teachers are willing to change when given suggestions on improving teaching skills.

These are conclusions reached by researchers at the Institute for Research on Teaching (IRT) at Michigan State University, who study how teacher behavior influences what youngsters learn and how teaching can be improved. IRT found that how teachers teach is as important to student learning as what they teach.

Established in 1976, IRT was funded by the Department of Education's Office of Educational Research and Improvement (formerly the National Institute of Education) and is now supported by a combination of university, State, and Federal sources.

The institute's studies can be applied to teaching in all types of public and private schools. IRT found five key elements of effective teaching. Good teachers do the following:

1. Set Goals. Finding time and energy to accomplish everything that needs to be done is a challenge all teachers face. Many cope successfully with this problem by setting goals, which keeps instruction on track. Teachers without focused goals are more apt to add topics to their lesson plans. So, their students learn about many topics, but master few.

IRT found that some teachers set questionable goals. For example, a few aim to keep students busy by assigning mindless, repetitive seatwork that does little to help students learn. IRT researchers also found that high school teachers and students often strike tacit "bargains" with each other to make school easier. For instance, students with after-school jobs don't have much time for homework, and some teachers respond by assigning less homework. Unfortunately, such bargains may result in a comfortable but academically compromised environment for students.

Many teachers, confronted with too many goals, will concentrate on just one, or substitute one goal for another. Good teachers can accomplish two or more goals simultaneously. For example, some elementary school teachers help students develop language skills while learning science, and good mathematics instructors teach concepts while helping students master computational skills. Differences in instructional goals help to explain differences in teachers' effectiveness.

2. Communicate Expectations. Good teachers influence student behavior and learning by carefully communicating what is expected and why. Some youngsters view school as a requirement rather than a place to learn. Good teachers explain what students will be studying and how it can be useful. Teachers connect new lessons to past lessons and illustrate how lessons relate to everyday experiences. For example, mathematics teachers explain that knowing how to calculate percentages will help students figure out how much to tip in a restaurant, or how to determine the price of sale items. Good teachers monitor students' work to make sure students understand assignments and can complete the work.

IRT found that good instructors teach students strategies for learning in and out of school. These teachers encourage students to practice these strategies frequently, and to work without constant teacher supervision. Good teachers balance this latitude because they know that too much freedom fosters chaos and too little limits what students can accomplish.

3. Understand Content. Good instructors thoroughly understand the subjects they teach. However, research indicates that many prospective elementary school teachers have limited knowledge of their subject area. Teacher education courses focus on teaching skills rather than subject matter. According to IRT studies, many elementary school teachers are uncomfortable teaching science, and many writing teachers are unprepared and uncertain about teaching writing.

Good teachers know also the misunderstandings students bring to class. For example, science students studying light and vision may believe that they can see an object because light from the sun brightens it. If a teacher does not discuss this misconception during the lesson, it will remain. The teacher must communicate that light from the sun is reflected to the retina, and that students see this reflected light when they ''see'' the object.

4. Closely Follow Instructional Materials. Many teachers believe that good teachers don't follow textbooks. On the contrary, IRT found that teachers who closely follow instructional materials improve, rather than impede, the quality of their teaching. Most teachers are not trained to develop their own materials, nor do they have the time to do so.

Although published materials may have faults, good teachers carefully select materials to fit the curriculum and characteristics of their students. Doing so frees them to spend more time with students.

5. Accept Responsibility. Teachers who believe they are responsible for student achievement are more effective than those who believe students alone are responsible for what is learned and how students behave. IRT found that teachers who successfully deal with problem students think they must help solve students' problems. When a student has trouble learning, both teacher and student must assess the situation and make necessary adjustments.

In one study, IRT researchers found that low-aptitude science students do much better when their teacher accepts responsibility for getting all students to learn science. Many science teachers, however, attribute student success or failure solely to students. Teachers who assume that their students are low achievers do little to encourage those students to learn. Teachers differ in how much responsibility they are willing to accept, but most will take on more if supervisors advise them how best to do so.

Teachers, like almost everyone else, are creatures of habit, often reluctant to change. Nonetheless, IRT found that teachers are receptive to changes based on research results, such as these five tips. However, the changes must make sense to the teachers, and they must be given the opportunity to reflect on their practices.

Even then many revert to old teaching habits despite seeing positive results with their students. Researchers cite several reasons for this:

- Teachers often work alone, away from the view and comments of their peers.
- Busy classroom schedules leave teachers little time to reflect on ways to improve.
- Teacher education courses often give new teachers the impression that the only way to figure out what works best for them is through trial-and-error. While struggling to develop their own style, they sometimes forget about professional standards or teaching strategies that have proven successful for other instructors.
- Researchers and reformers often overload teachers by recommending new practices to use without recommending which practices, if any, to eliminate.

Good teaching is difficult. It involves hard work, tough choices, objective evaluations, and a great deal of energy. But classroom teachers must accept responsibility for improving their performance, for no educators exert a greater influence on how much and how well children learn.

For more information on these studies, contact Andrew Porter, Institute for Research on Teaching, Michigan State University, 318 Erickson Hall, East Lansing, Michigan 48824–1034.

Source: "Five Tips to Improve Teaching," *Research in Brief*. Washington, DC: Office of Educational Research and Development, U.S. Department of Education, December 1987.

■ Questions for Discussion

1. Much recent attention has been directed toward the importance of developing positive self-concepts among learners. Some suggest this is much more important than the content being studied. What should be the relation between self-concept of the learner and what is being studied (taught)?

2. What is your opinion regarding the respective influences of the factors of heredity and the factors of environment upon maturation of children?

3. How important is the knowledge of subject matter to a teacher? In what areas should a teacher be most knowledgeable?

4. Historically, educators have claimed that schools ought to give attention to both sound mind and body. Yet, in setting educational priorities, the academic disciplines take precedence. In your opinion, why is it important to stress skill (psychomotor) education as well?

5. What are the various methods that you as a teacher will use to evaluate the progress of your pupils? Do you feel that the various aspects of human differences can be adequately considered in planning for class instruction?

◪ Notes

1. Thomas L. Good, "How Teachers' Expectations Affect Results," *American Education,* December 1982, pp. 25–32.
2. Richard S. Prawat and Judith E. Lanier, *Introduction to Education* (Columbus, Ohio: Charles E. Merrill, 1982), p. 295.
3. Benjamin S. Bloom, "Affective Outcomes of School Learning," *Phi Delta Kappan,* November 1977, p. 197.
4. Allen C. Ornstein and Harry L. Miller, *Looking into Teaching: An Introduction to American Education* (Chicago: Rand McNally, 1980), pp. 408–409.
5. *Education Week,* January 27, 1988, p. 19.
6. Robert F. Biehler, *Psychology Applied to Teaching* (Boston: Houghton Mifflin, 1974), pp. 90–144.

◪ Selected References

Carlson, Neil R. *Physiology of Behavior.* Boston: Allyn & Bacon, 1986.

Eshelman, J. Ross. *The Family: An Introduction.* Boston: Allyn & Bacon, 1985.

Griffin, Jean Latz. "Learning-disabled Children Run Hard to Advance a Single Step." *Chicago Tribune* (October 8, 1984) Sec. 1, p. 6.

Hallahan, D. P., Kauffman, J. M., and Lloyd, J. W. *Introduction to Learning Disabilities.* Englewood Cliffs, N.J.: Prentice-Hall, 1985.

Karmos, Joseph S., and Karmos, Ann H. "A Closer Look at Classroom Boredom." *The Journal of the Association for Teacher Educators* V, nos. 1–2 (Spring–Summer, 1983):49–55.

McDaniel, Thomas R. "A Primer on Motivation: Principles Old and New." *Phi Delta Kappan* (September 1984):46–49.

Orlosky, Donald E., ed. *Introduction to Education.* Columbus, Ohio: Charles E. Merrill, 1982.

Ornstein, Allen C., and Miller, Harry L. *Looking into Teaching, An Introduction to American Education.* Chicago: Rand McNally, 1986.

Seifert, Kelvin L. and Hoffnung, Robert J. *Child and Adolescent Development.* Boston: Houghton Mifflin Co., 1987.

Chapter 13

The Nature of Curriculum

Objectives

After studying this chapter, you should be able to:

■ Identify the various sources and definitions of curriculum.

■ Recognize the relationship between a curriculum and the pluralistic society in the United States.

■ Explore the interrelationships of goals and objectives, instructional strategies, and evaluation as they represent the curriculum.

■ Compare and discuss the similarities and differences among five reports: *A Nation at Risk, James Madison High School, The Forgotten Half, First Lessons,* and *James Madison Elementary School: A Curriculum for American Students.*

■ Recognize the necessity of teacher involvement in reform proposals in order to assure effective implementation of the reform recommendations.

■ Speculate on the likelihood of schools offering formal courses in ethics and values.

■ Explain the rationale for parental choice of schools.

■ Analyze and present arguments both for and against the concepts of educational vouchers and tuition tax credits.

Enrichment Experiences

The following experiences will help you learn more about curriculum and teachers' roles in curriculum affairs, and teacher opinions about the teacher empowerment movement.

■ Visit the learning center or library on your campus to find and read materials directly related to curriculum.

■ Ask nearby school districts for a copy of their curriculum guide, and read the guide.

■ Find and compare copies of two recent reform proposals that are somewhat different in their perspective, for example, *James Madison High School* and *The Forgotten Half.*

■ Interview practicing teachers and parents to elicit their opinions on the recently proposed changes in elementary and secondary education.

■ Interview a practicing teacher about his/her role in curriculum development.

■ Inquire of practicing teachers their opinions about the teacher empowerment movement.

*T*he purposes of this chapter are to provide you with information about the past, present, and proposed curricula of the elementary and secondary schools, along with other curriculum related topics, and to help you gain insights into the curricular aspects of elementary and secondary school education. To achieve those purposes, the following topics are discussed: sources and definitions of curriculum; curriculum in a changing and pluralistic society; the components of any curriculum—goals and objectives, teaching methodology, and evaluation; a review and analysis of five recent educational reform reports; recommendations and reforms in perspective; the teacher and curriculum; character-morality-values-democracy as a part of curriculum; parental choice of school; educational vouchers; tutition tax credits; the relationship of curriculum and economic development; and teacher empowerment. ∎

The expectations of the people at the national, state, and local levels are a major source for the curriculums of our schools. In the early 1980s, the nation's schools were spoken to in strong and sincere terms by a large number of national reports on curriculums and expectations for the schools. The content of those reports and the responses to the reports are discussed later in this chapter.

■ Sources of Curriculum

The primary source of school curriculums is society, with all its expectations. These expectations represent what society desires and values. They also reflect the problems and needs of society. In effect, the expectations of society represent what its members want their society to become for them and their children. Schools, along with families, are major agencies in the transmission of the values of society. Thus, school curriculums emanate from these wishes.

A second source resides within the needs and desires of learners—learners that in our formal system range from the preelementary school child to the mature adult. Much of the stated curriculum for young children is prescribed for them by adults; however, adolescents and particularly mature learners, as a subgroup (students) of society, also have an effect in determining the curriculum.

Expectations are most often translated into course offerings representing a body of knowledge that is referred to as a curriculum. In fact, a standard dictionary definition of curriculum is "all the courses of study offered by an educational institution." School curriculums are more than the courses offered by a particular school. It is a rare school indeed that has formal courses entitled self-worth, self-respect, desire for learning, and respecting others. Yet these characteristics are almost always listed as goals to be attained in school. They are a part of the stated curriculum.

Subject matter is the medium through which the adult mind of the teacher and the immature mind of the learner find communion.

Earl C. Kelley

Education is life, not subject matter.

John Dewey

■ Definitions of Curriculum

There have been many definitions of curriculum over the years. These various definitions have reflected both the thinking of the times and sources of curriculum as discussed previously. Historically the curriculum was thought of as the list of subjects taught in school. This definition reflects the body of knowledge or subject-centered approach. While more recent definitions tend to be broader, subject matter content is still an important part of curriculum. The subject-centered emphasis dominated the educational philosophy of the 1890–1930s period. Since the 1930s, the idea of experience as proposed by John Dewey has steadily gained impetus.

There are a number of definitions of curriculum that include the concept of experiences.[1] They generally include the premises that the curriculum includes educational experiences that are planned to occur in school and for which the school has responsibility, and that they are developed from expectations that a social group has for the learning outcomes of their children. The concept of "experiences" implies an active involvement of the learner with an educational environment, people, and materials, rather than passive receptivity. In addition to reflecting the needs of learners as serving as a source of curriculum, they also relate to the importance of learning theory.

■ Curriculum in a Changing and Pluralistic Society

It should be noted that society changes, and as it does so do the curriculums of schools. Schools' curriculums in colonial America and through the late 1770s were centered on religion with expectations that they would foster and perpetuate the religious beliefs of the community. From that time until the 1860s, the curriculums of our nation's schools were most concerned with producing a literate populace to ensure the preservation of a democratic form of government. The period of the 1860s through the 1920s was a period of economic expansion and growth for the United States. It was during that time that the schools took on a utilitarian approach to provide educated people for filling the large numbers of various jobs that were created. From the 1920s through the present, mass education and equal opportunity for all children have been a central theme. The efforts of the last three decades in the areas of desegregation, rights of women, and the rights of the handicapped are illustrative of the concept of equal educational opportunities. Such equality has not been achieved.

The United States is a pluralistic society consisting of many different subsocieties. This has resulted not only from our multiethnic origin, but also from our emphasis on the protection and enhancement of individual freedoms, as specified in the United States Constitution.

The curriculums resulting during and after the massive immigration to this country (1830–1920) reflected a "Melting Pot" or "Americanization" motive. Elwood Cubberly, a renowned educator and writer, in 1934 called for the nation's schools to adopt a policy of Americanization through which Anglo-Saxon values would replace the allegedly inferior ethnic patterns from countries like Italy, Austria-Hungary, and Russia. He wrote:

> These Southern and Eastern Europeans were of a very different type from the North and West Europeans who preceded them. Largely illiterate, docile, often lacking in initiative, and almost wholly without the Anglo-Saxon conceptions of righteousness, liberty, law, order,

public decency, and government, their coming has served to dilute tremendously our national stock and to weaken and corrupt our political life. . . . Our national life for the past quarter of a century, has been afflicted with a serious call of racial indigestion.[2]

Further,

To assimilate these people into our national life and citizenship is our problem. We must do this, and, we must, if possible, give them the impression of our peculiar institutions and ideals. National safety and welfare alike demand that we not only teach these peoples to use the English language as our common tongue, but that they be educated also in principles and ideals of our form of government. Even under the best of conditions this will require time, and it calls for a constructive national program if effective work is to be done. Social and political institutions of value are the product of long evolution, and they are safe only so long as they are in the keeping of those who have created them or have come to appreciate them. Our religious, political, and social ideals must be preserved from replacement by less noble ideals if our national character is not to be weakened.[3]

Cubberly's position was reflected in the curriculums of schools by a heavy emphasis on English-language instruction, civics, American history, and Anglo-Saxon values. Obviously some "Americanization" took place; ways of speech and ways of dress became largely "Americanized," and an enthusiastic patriotism to the United States developed.[4] Nevertheless, it has become apparent to many scholars "that many individuals and groups will never be able to 'melt' into the American 'pot.' "[5] These groups include blacks, Spanish-Americans, women, Asians, and others. These realities, observed by many persons, verify that the United States is a pluralistic society.

A recent thrust in education related to educating people to live in a pluralistic society is multicultural education. There is little agreement on a precise definition of multicultural education; nevertheless, the following quotation provides some insights into its meaning.

Multicultural education is preparation for the social, political, and economic realities that individuals experience in culturally diverse and complex human encounters. These realities have both national and international dimensions. This preparation provides a process by which an individual develops competencies for perceiving, believing, evaluating and behaving in different cultural settings. Thus multicultural education is viewed as an intervention and an ongoing assessment to help institutions and individuals become more responsive to the human condition, individual cultural integrity, and cultural pluralism in society. . . .

Further,

Multicultural education could include but not be limited to experiences which: (1) Promote analytical and evaluative abilities to confront such issues as participatory democracy, racism and sexism, and the parity of power; (2) Develop skills for values clarification including the study of manifest and latent transmission of values; (3) Examine the dynamics of diverse cultures and the implications for developing teaching strategies; and (4) Examine linguistic variables and diverse learning styles as a basis for the development of appropriate teaching strategies.[6]

While the previous statements were prepared in respect to teacher education, they reflect the spirit and intent of laws recently adopted by many states referring to elementary and secondary education. A recent National Education

Association publication states, "Cultural pluralism, muticultural education, and polycultural education all embrace two common ideas: (1) A state of equal mutual supportive coexistence between ethnocultural groups, and (2) one planet of people of diverse physical and cultural characteristics. Basic to the acceptance of these ideals is the belief that every person respects his or her ethnocultural identity and extends the same respect for the cultures of others."[7] The thrust for multicultural education, although somewhat controversial, could perhaps be the primary thrust of the new future in American education.

■ Goals and Objectives

There are three basic components of any curriculum: goals and objectives, teaching methodology, and evaluation. Goals and objectives, or what it is students are to learn, are fundamental both to teaching methodology and evaluation. Broad goals have been spelled out by a number of national commissions over the years. Broad goals also appear in the philosophy and curricular bulletins of most local school districts.

Illustrative of broad goals prepared by national commissions are those recommended by the White House Conference on Education in 1955. The goals are oriented toward elementary education.

1. The fundamental skills of communication—reading, writing, spelling, as well as other elements of effective oral and written expression; the arithmetical and mathematical skills, including problem solving.
2. Appreciation for our democratic heritage.
3. Civic rights and responsibilities and knowledge of American institutions.
4. Respect and appreciation for human values and for the beliefs of others.
5. Ability to think and evaluate constructively and creatively.
6. Effective work habits and self-discipline.
7. Social competency as a contributing member of his family and community.
8. Ethical behavior based on a sense of moral and spiritual values.
9. Intellectual curiosity and eagerness for lifelong learning.
10. Esthetic appreciation and self-expression in the arts.
11. Physical and mental health.
12. Wise use of time, including constructive leisure pursuits.
13. Understanding of the physical world and man's relation to it as represented through basic knowledge of the sciences.
14. An awareness of our relationships with the world community.[8]

Other commissions over the years that have generated goal statements include: Commission on the Reorganization of Secondary Education, 1918 (Seven Cardinal Principles), and the Educational Policies Commission, 1935–38. Most recently (1977) Harold Shane, under the auspices of the National Education Association, convened a conference to review the Seven Cardinal Principles. The results of this conference confirmed the Seven Cardinal Principles.

Most of the recent reform reports have addressed the importance of educational goals. For example, in 1985, former U.S. Secretary of Education, William Bennett, convened a study group, the Elementary Education Study Group, to assist and advise him in preparing a report about elementary education. The Secretary then wrote *First Lessons: A Report on Elementary Education* (1986) which states curriculum goals for elementary education. *First Lessons* will be discussed later in this chapter. The responsibility for the content in *First Lessons* is clearly that of William Bennett.

For teaching and evaluation purposes, broad goals must be broken down into specific objectives. For illustrative purposes, let us examine three broad goals and develop specific objectives related to them. The following three goals are taken from the report of the 1955 White House Conference on Education:

1. The fundamental skills of communication— reading, writing, spelling, as well as other elements of effective oral and written expression; the arithmetical and mathematical skills, including problem solving.
3. Civic rights and responsibilities and knowledge of American institutions.
11. Physical and mental health.

Specific objectives that might be developed from these sample goals for a first grade class might include:

1a. Count aloud from 1 to 100.
2a. Tell other members of the class two ways in which police officers are important.
3a. Wash hands before eating.

At the secondary level, the same broad objectives might yield the following specific behavioral objectives:

1b. Derive the correct algebraic equation to solve a word problem dealing with time, rate, and distance.
2b. List the steps necessary for a bill to become a law in the United States.
3b. After proper medical clearance, run one quarter mile in two minutes.

Games are important to academic development, and small muscle motor coordination sometimes provides motivation for learning.

Planning is essential to effective teaching.

It should be noted that in this illustration, the objectives are written in performance terms; that is, in terms of behavior that can be observed in the learner. The writing of objectives in this fashion facilitates evaluation.

In many states in recent years, local school districts have been required by the states to develop overall broad goal statements for their schools. Frequently it was mandated that there be community involvement in goal generation, definition, and development. Such mandates clearly recognize the local community prerogative in determining curricula. The goals so developed must then be translated into general objectives and more specific performance objectives to provide a basis for evaluation. Broad goals and general objectives cannot ordinarily be measured directly. Their attainment is supported by logical inference by the achievement of the performance objectives. The development of general objectives and performance objectives is most often a professional prerogative; that is, the prerogative and responsibility of the teaching, administrative, and supervisory staff. The instructional strategies and teaching methodologies are also considered the prerogative of the professional staff.

The previously identified objectives also illustrate different domains of learning. Bloom has identified three domains of objectives—cognitive, affective, and psychomotor.[9] Cognitive objectives are those that are concerned with remembering, recognizing knowledge, and the development of intellectual abilities and skills. Objectives *1a* and *1b* are clearly in this category. Affective objectives are those which are concerned with interests, attitudes, opinions, appreciations, values, and emotional sets. Objective *2a,*

since it may elicit opinions or values, is in the affective domain. Objective *3b* is most clearly psychomotor, involving large muscles.

Thus, the broad objectives of American education can be specifically transformed into specific objectives for children in classrooms.

■ Methodology

Objectives are only one part of the curriculum. They represent the desired goals or outcomes. After a teacher has decided upon the objectives, it then becomes necessary to decide upon a method or means of achieving them. Thus methodology, since it provides the "experiences," is often included in the concept of curriculum.

It is most important at this point in planning that the methodology be appropriate to the attainment of the objective. For example, if an objective for the student is to moderate a small group discussion of four people causing them to arrive at a plan for action on a current social problem, then the teaching method would most certainly include practice discussion sessions. It would probably also include an explanation by the teacher as to how discussions are led. Using other information from learning theory is also important in determining methodology. For example, in the previous illustration involving discussion leadership, the notion of having the students actually lead and participate in discussions rather than merely listen to an instructor tell them how discussions should be led reflects the principle that active participation results in more learning than passive receptivity. Further, if one were to consider motivation as a factor, the topic for discussion would be very important. Since the objective in this case is not specifically aimed at a precise body of content, the topic of discussion could and should be one in which students are interested.

Since methodology, in fact, determines the experiences that students have in achieving objectives, it is an important part of the curriculum.

Evaluation

A third essential part of curriculum is a scheme of evaluation. Teachers, parents, school authorities, and many others need to know what progress students are making. So, in addition to decisions as to what it is students are to learn (objectives), and how they are going to learn (methodology), a curriculum must include a measure of how well students have learned (evaluation). Carefully formulated objectives assist immensely in this task, for it is practically impossible to determine students' achievement if it is not clear what objectives the students are to have achieved. As teachers develop curricula for their students, plans for evaluation which are appropriate for the objective should be included.

Curriculum Recommendations: 1983–1987

Many of the recent reform reports have dealt with school curriculums, and have made recommendations for changes in the curriculum at both the elementary and secondary levels. As a background for the actual reports, the attitudes of the public toward school curriculums are presented first, followed by a discussion of five selected reports. *What Works: Research About Teaching and Learning* (1986) is different from the other four reports. It highlights research findings and their application to teaching and learning, whereas the other four reports make curriculum recommendations. The reports and their authorship are herein presented.

- *A Nation at Risk: The Imperative for Educational Reform* (1983), National Commission on Excellence in Education.
- *What Works: Research About Teaching and Learning* (1986), United States Department of Education.
- *James Madison High School: A Curriculum for American Students* (1988), William J. Bennett, former U.S. Secretary of Education.
- *The Forgotten Half: Non-College-Bound Youth in America* (1988), Interim report by Youth and America's Future: The William T. Grant Foundation Commission on Work, Family and Citizenship.
- *First Lessons: A Report on Elementary Education in America* (1986), William J. Bennett, former U.S. Secretary of Education.

These reports are selected because of their relevance to curriculum and their recentness. Earlier reports, for example, *Academic Preparation for College: What Students Need to Know and Be Able to Do* (1983) by the College Board; and *Educating Americans for the 21st Century* (1983) by the National Science Board Commission on Precollege Education in Mathematics, Science and Technology were also relevant; however, they are similar in their curriculum recommendations to those in *A Nation at Risk,* and to *James Madison High School: A Curriculum for American Students,* and many other reports that essentially emphasized a college preparatory curriculum. *A Nation at Risk* was included because it, as the earliest report, engendered many more reports.

■ **Table 13.1**	Course Requirements for College-Bound Students 1987 Percentages of Responses
Mathematics	94%
English	91%
History/U.S. Government	84%
Science	83%
Computer Training	72%
Career Education	63%
Business Education	59%
Foreign Language	56%
Health Education	54%
Physical Education	45%
Vocational Training	31%
Music	23%
Art	23%

© 1987, Phi Delta Kappan, Inc.

■ **Table 13.2**	Course Requirements for Noncollege-Bound Students 1987 Percentages of Responses
Mathematics	88%
English	85%
Vocational Training	78%
History/U.S. Government	69%
Business Education	65%
Computer Training	61%
Career Education	61%
Science	57%
Health Education	49%
Physical Education	41%
Foreign Language	20%

© 1987, Phi Delta Kappan, Inc.

Public Attitudes Toward the Curriculum   *The 19th Annual Phi Delta Kappa/Gallup Poll of The Public's Attitudes Toward the Public Schools* (1987) provides information about the public's attitudes toward the schools' curriculums. The public was asked three questions about secondary schools. They were:

1. If you were the one to decide, what subjects would you require every high school student who plans to go to college to take?
2. What about those public high school students who do not plan to go to college when they graduate?
3. Which courses would you require them to take?

Tables 13.1 and 13.2 display the public's responses.

The public strongly believes that both college-bound and noncollege-bound students should take mathematics and English. There is a fifteen percentage point difference in the support for History/U.S. Government between the college-bound (84 percent) and the noncollege-bound (69 percent), yet History/U.S. Government ranks fourth for noncollege-bound and third for college-bound students. As expected, vocational training ranks low for the college-bound and is in third place for noncollege-bound. Science ranks fourth for college bound (83 percent) while noncollege-bound students ranked science eighth (57 percent).

It is interesting to note that foreign language ranked eighth (56 percent) for college-bound students. Noncollege-bound students ranked foreign language eleventh (last) (20 percent). Foreign language was not a priority for either the college-bound or noncollege-bound students. The poll did not address how many courses in each of the subjects, for example three years of mathematics, or the depth of the subject such as Practical Mathematics, Business Mathematics, College Algebra, or Pre Calculus.

A Nation at Risk   This report, after building the case that educational achievement had seriously declined, presented five major recommendations. They dealt with (1) the high school curriculum; (2) the necessity for more rigorous and measurable standards and higher expectations for academic performance and student conduct; (3) more time devoted to the five new basics, English, mathematics, science, social studies, and computer science; (4) improve the preparation of teachers and make teaching a more rewarding and respected profession; and (5) that citizens across the nation hold educators and elected officials responsible for providing the leadership necessary to achieve these reforms, and that citizens provide the fiscal support and stability required to bring about the reforms proposed. The discussion that follows is limited to the proposed high school curriculum.

In regard to the content of the high school curriculum, the Report stated:

> We recommend that State and high school graduation requirements be strengthened and that, at a minimum, all students seeking a diploma be required to lay the foundations in the Five New Basics by taking the following curriculum during their 4 years of high school: (a) 4 years of English; (b) 3 years of mathematics; (c) 3 years of science; (d) 3 years of social studies; and (e) one-half year of computer science. For the college bound, 2 years of foreign language in high school are strongly recommended in addition to those taken earlier.[10]

It is important to notice that the curriculum recommendation makes it clear that at a minimum *all* students seeking a diploma be required to take the five new basics as stated. These recommended curriculum requirements, including foreign languages, total 15–½ units of the usual requirements of 18 to 21 units for graduation from high school, leaving little opportunity to take electives. (See Appendix I.)

The Report states that:

> Our recommendations are based on the beliefs that everyone can learn, that everyone is born with an *urge* to learn which can be nurtured, that a solid high school education is within the reach of virtually all, and that life-long learning will equip people with the skills required for new careers and for citizenship.[11]

The Report provides implementing recommendations intended as illustrative descriptions. They are included to clarify what is meant by the essentials of a strong curriculum. For example:

> The teaching of mathematics in high school should equip graduates to: (a) understand geometric and algebraic concepts; (b) understand elementary probability and statistics; (c) apply mathematics in everyday situations; (d) estimate, approximate, measure, and test the accuracy of their calculations. In addition to the traditional sequence of studies available for college bound students, new equally demanding mathematics curricula need to be developed for those who do not plan to continue their formal education immediately.[12]

The curriculum recommendations of *A Nation at Risk* present specific courses supported by illustrative descriptions for *all* students seeking a high school diploma. The illustrative description for mathematics recognizes that not all students will go to college, yet calls for an equally demanding mathematics curricula. There is a brief mention of fine and performing arts and vocational education. It states:

> The high school curriculum should also provide students with programs requiring rigorous effort in subjects that advance students' personal, educational, and occupational goals, such as the fine and performing arts and vocational education. These areas complement the New Basics, and they should demand the same level of performance as the Basics.[13]

The Nation at Risk report asserted that everyone can learn. That is true. It is also true that the capacity to learn is different among individuals—some learn quickly, others learn slowly. Students also have different interests. Some are interested and motivated by the academic basics; others have mechanical or artistic interests and talents and are motivated by such studies. Yes, the basics are important, and should be mastered, but perhaps with recognition of the differences among individuals.

Dr. Terrel H. Bell was the U.S. Secretary of Education when *A Nation at Risk* was written and published. The following quotation taken from an article written by Dr. Bell in 1988 provides an assessment of progress in education since *A Nation at Risk* was released (1983). The article is adapted from his book, *The Thirteenth Man: A Reagan Cabinet Memoir,* New York: Free Press, 1988.[14]

The years since 1983, when the National Commission on Excellence in Education released *A Nation at Risk,* have brought some heartening changes in U.S. education. But we should also be deeply concerned about continuing serious deficiences.

Since the start of the school reform movement almost five years ago, the slide in college entrance examination scores has stopped, and scores in some states have even made substantial gains. High school graduation requirements have been increased dramatically, and there is somewhat more emphasis on mathematics and science. Standards for teacher education and teacher certification are more rigorous, and at least 30 states have taken steps to build career ladders that use the salary structure to reward teachers for distinguished performance. Many states have mandated competency testing both for students and for entry-level teachers. Increasingly, public funding is fostering the use of computers and other electronic technology to teach the basic skills. The content of textbooks and supplementary teaching materials is improving. Such changes are enabling us to educate 60% to 70% of American young people more effectively today than in previous decades.

But we have made no progress in reaching, motivating, and teaching the 30% to 40% who either drop out before graduation or gain their high school diplomas with marginal skills. Many of these young people come from low-income families; huge numbers of them reside in urban ghettos; many of them are blacks or Hispanics. These young people grow up with little motivation, hope, or acquaintance with success. The waste of so many young people is a blight on America's future. Education can change this situation—but, to do so, education itself must change.

. . . For the next President (January 1989) and for candidates seeking public office at every level—federal, state, and local—I present here my program for initiating change in American education. There should be no higher priority for the new Administration. We must launch a nationwide movement as grand in scale as the Marshall Plan, which helped to rebuild Europe at the end of World War II. Our new President must rally support for reshaping education so that the dropout rate falls below 5%, illiteracy is wiped out, and every graduate—regardless of race, ethnic background, or level of parental income—is competent, employable, and adaptable when he or she leaves high school. The Administration's goal should be to develop the most productive, efficient, and cost-effective system of education in the world.

To reach that goal will require reordered priorities and sacrifices on the part of all Americans. With the support of Congress, the next President will have to galvanize the states and local communities to unified action aimed at restructuring and renewing teaching and learning in both the home and the school.

Dr. Bell then continues to describe a curriculum. Essentially what he describes is very similar to the curriculum described in *A Nation at Risk*. He does, however, recognize the need to educate the disadvantaged.

With rare exceptions, all students—regardless of race, ethnic background, economic circumstances, or handicapping condition—must complete the curriculum outlined above. Therefore, we must attend to the needs of those youngsters for whom equal opportunity has proved more an ideal than a reality.

Fortunately, we have had 20 years of experience with three educational programs that were developed to cope with these problems: Head Start for preschoolers, Title I (now Chapter 1) of the Elementary and Secondary Education Act, and the Job Corps. These programs, in effect since 1965, have been partially funded and occasionally mismanaged; nonetheless, they have taught us what works and what doesn't.[15] (From Terrell H. Bell, "Parting Words of the 13th Man," *Phi Delta Kappan,* 400–401. Copyright © 1988 Phi Delta Kappa, Bloomington, IN. Reprinted by permission of the author.)

James Madison High School: A Curriculum for American Students[16]

Former U.S. Secretary of Education, William J. Bennett, in 1987 proposed a curriculum for a mythical high school, James Madison High School. Bennett emphasizes as he did in *First Lessons* that his proposed curriculum is not a statement of federal policy. The Department of Education is prohibited by statute from exercising direction, supervision, or control over the curriculum or program of instruction of any school or school system. Further, the Tenth Amendment to the U.S. Constitution has been interpreted as granting the responsibility for public education to the states.

Figure 13.1 displays the curriculum that Secretary Bennett has recommended for *all* high school students. His recommendations are very similar to those of *A Nation at Risk*. They differ in that Bennett specifically required two years of foreign language, while *A Nation at Risk* strongly recommends two years of foreign language for college-bound students; and the Bennett proposal also is more specific in terms of courses offered.

Subject	1st Year	2nd Year	3rd Year	4th Year
English	Introduction to Literature	American Literature	British Literature	Introduction to World Literature
Social Studies	Western Civilization	American History	Principles of American Democracy (1 *sem.*) and American Democracy and the World (1 *sem.*)	
Mathematics	Three Years Required From Among the Following Courses: Algebra I, Plane & Solid Geometry, Algebra II & Trigonometry, Statistics & Probability (1 *sem.*), Precalculus (1 *sem.*), and Calculus AB or BC			
Science	Three Years Required From Among the Following Courses: Astronomy/Geology, Biology, Chemistry, and Physics or Principles of Technology			
Foreign Language	Two Years Required in a Single Language From Among Offerings Determined by Local Jurisdictions			
Physical Education/ Health	Physical Education/ Health 9	Physical Education/ Health 10		
Fine Arts	Art History (1 *sem.*) Music History (1 *sem.*)		ELECTIVES	

■ **Figure 13.1**

A four-year plan

James Madison High School: A Curriculum for American Students by William Bennett, U.S. Secretary of Education.

For example, Bennett proposes Western Civilization and American History; *A Nation at Risk* refers to social studies in an overall descriptive fashion.

Secretary Bennett expressed that there is a common ground that virtually all our schools can reach, and that most Americans agree about where that common ground is—about what our students should learn.[17]

> We want our students—whatever their plans for the future—to take from high school a shared body of knowledge and skills, a common language of ideas, a common moral and intellectual discipline. We want them to know math and science, history and literature. We want them to know how to think for themselves, to respond to important questions, to solve problems, to pursue an argument, to defend a point of view, to understand its opposite, and to weigh the alternatives. We want them to develop, through example and experience, those habits of mind and traits of character properly prized by our society. And we want them to be prepared for entry into the community of responsible adults.[18]

Former Secretary Bennett espoused high aspirations and high expectations for students. He did, however, recognize that there are individual differences in students.

> American students vary in ability, interest in learning, temperament, career aspirations, upbringing, family background, economic status, and racial and ethnic heritage. . . . There are below average students and gifted students, there are students who speak English as a second language (or not at all), and there are students with learning disabilities and handicaps of varying kind and severity.[19]

Critics may claim that too few of our students are currently equipped to handle the curricular material described here in the time and form suggested. I believe otherwise. I think most Americans could handle the classes in James Madison High School; again I have seen students of all backgrounds do it.[20]

The Secretary recognized that vocational programs could be taken as electives. He noted that assuming that schools offer six classes per day, the James Madison program leaves 12 semester units—a fourth of a student's four-year high school career.

There were critics of Secretary Bennett's curriculum proposal. In general they felt that it was not realistic for many of today's students. "In the view of the president of the American Vocational Association, the proposal fails to meet the needs of more than 80 percent of students who never earn a college diploma."[21]

The next report to be discussed presents a different perspective, but one that needs to be given serious consideration. It deals with the noncollege-bound students.

The Forgotten Half: Non-College-Bound Youth in America. This report is different from the other reports described in this chapter in that it deals with noncollege-bound students; in effect, those students who leave high school with or without a diploma and enter the workforce. The report asserts "that a college degree is not the only way to develop the talents of tomorrow's workers—and for some, it is far from the best way."[22]

The report notes that jobs in manufacturing have dropped dramatically in the last few years. Fields such as transportation, utilities, government, and agriculture have in the past offered steady employment to millions of young adults, but that is no longer the case. Our current technological economy requires advanced skills—which many of the noncollege-bound do not have. Nevertheless the report suggests strongly that (1) these young adults can become productive citizens, and (2) education can be a way to their success, particularly if schools offer varied learning experiences that take advantage of students' abilities, rather than ignore those young people who do not fit the conventional or proper mold. The report recommends ways to bridge the gap from school to work.[23] In summary, the report states that "we are shortchanging too many of our young people—and in the process, we are damaging our nation's future." Ten goals are proposed to help remedy the situation. Those ten goals will require the sustained attention of parents, employers, trade unions, educators, churches, youth-serving agencies, community leaders, and local, state and national authorities in order to assure success.[24]

If the goals of *The Forgotten Half* are implemented and are effective, this report may have the greatest positive impact of all the reports. Furthermore, if the goals are achieved, the effects of that success will strengthen the productivity of our economy. The Point of View article at the end of this chapter provides more information about the dilemma and potential of noncollege-bound students.

First Lessons: A Report on Elementary Education in America. As was the case with *James Madison High School: A Curriculum for American Students, First Lessons* was authored by the former U.S. Secretary of Education William J. Bennett (1986). He did, however, have an advisory group, the Elementary Education Study Group, to assist him in the preparation of the Report. The final Report emanated from opinions of the advisory group, staff research, and studies by public and private agencies. Secretary Bennett emphasized that the Report is not a statement of federal policy; it is a statement of his views on matters, principally the business of state, local, and private authorities to decide.[25]

In *First Lessons,* the Secretary wrote of the Explicit Curriculum and the Implicit Curriculum. The Explicit Curriculum includes the academic offerings of elementary schools including Reading, Writing, Mathematics, Science, Social Studies, The Arts, Foreign Languages, Health and Physical Education, Computers, and Libraries. Each of these subjects is discussed, and recommendations are made for each subject area. The Implicit Curriculum refers to the development of character and morality. It is noted that "values are 'caught' more than 'taught.' " Character and morality are developed in the early years of a child's life, primarily through the family, by what is formally taught and what is learned by observing adult behavior. Children in school also learn about character and morality in school through formal instruction, and by observing the behavior of the school's adult population—primarily the teachers. That is why schools seek out teachers of good character to serve as role models for their students.

An illustration of one interpretation of the Implicit Curriculum is provided in the following quotation:

> Since a primary goal of American elementary education is the development of democratic citizenship, an essential part of the implicit curriculum is each school's interpretation of its responsibility to provide civic education—not only in textbooks and lectures, but through saluting the flag, singing the national anthem,

The object of teaching a child is to enable him to get along without his teacher.

Elbert Hubbard

and other rituals of our national life. Parents might look for more subtle displays of burgeoning democracy as well: Does the school draw on the diversity of its students in celebrating our pluralistic heritage? Does it provide trips to the courts, the mayor's office, the town hall? Does it pause to honor the men and women who fought in foreign wars, and explain what they were fighting for? These are all ways in which schools can build citizenship on a daily basis.[26]

In the introduction of *First Lessons,* the Secretary states that "After studying elementary schools, visiting them, discussing them and consulting with some of the country's leading educators, I conclude that American elementary education is not menaced by a 'rising tide of mediocrity.' (From *A Nation at Risk.*) It is, overall in pretty good shape."[27]

Elementary education nevertheless can be improved; and it will be. It is imperative that elementary education be super—because that is where children start—they need a good start. In that way, they are far more important than secondary schools.

The Secretary set forth the following observations and recommendations in regard to elementary education.

1. The principal goals of elementary education are to build for every child a strong foundation for further education, for democratic citizenship, and for eventual entry into responsible adulthood.
2. Parents have the central role in children's education and must be empowered to play it successfully.
3. Children do not just "grow up." They must be raised by the community of adults—all adults. The community should accept as its

solemn responsibility—as a covenant—the nurture, care, and education of the coming generation.
4. Teachers should be enabled to become professionals. Certification should depend on demonstrated knowledge and skills, not on paper credentials.
5. The principalship should be deregulated so that accomplished people from many fields may become elementary school principals.
6. In order to provide for more teaching and more learning, elementary schools will need more learning time.
7. The chronological lockstep by which children ordinarily enter and progress through school should be loosened to provide for differences in children's abilities.
8. In specific curriculum areas:

   • Every elementary school can and must teach all its students to read.
   • Children should learn that writing is more than filling in blanks. Writing must be part of the whole curriculum, not just language arts.
   • Elementary schools need to teach science, and their science programs should include "hands-on," experimental activities in addition to texts and lectures.
   • Mathematics should extend beyond simple computation and should emphasize problem solving.
   • The social studies curriculum should be transformed. Schools should teach children not only the basic lessons and habits of life in democratic societies, but also impart to them substantial instruction in history, geography, and civics, beginning at the earliest ages.
   • The arts and instruction in the arts should be integral parts of every elementary school.

- Children should gain a basic grasp of the uses and limitations of computers.
- Elementary curricula should include health and physical education.
- Every school should have a library, and every child should have and use a public library card.[28]

Secretary of Education William J. Bennett, in his last days in office, came forth with a second report on elementary education: *James Madison Elementary School: A Curriculum for American Students* (1988). It is in effect an expansion of the proposals in *First Lesson* (1986). The *James Madison Elementary School* promotes the early exposure of children to good literature, intensive instruction in the basic subjects, and foreign language instruction beginning no later than fourth grade. It also presents guidelines for K–8 subject areas by grade level.[29]

The Secretary's comments, general observations, and recommendations dealing with elementary education are timely, appropriate, well stated, and practical. The points he makes can be achieved. It is interesting that *First Lessons* is the first report on elementary education since 1953. Why all the focus on high schools when elementary schools are so very important? Satisfaction or neglect?

■ Report Recommendations and Reforms in Perspective

Many of the reform reports have made recommendations about what ought to be taught to students, how teacher education should be changed, and how teaching should be restructured. Examples of such recommendations include more stringent and more rigorous courses and high school graduation requirements, teacher testing, and the concepts of career ladders and differentiated staffing—instructor, professional teacher, and career professional teachers. Many of these recommendations and changes were made without including teachers on their committees or consulting with teachers. In other words, teachers were excluded, while other persons outside the teaching profession made decisions that teachers would eventually be expected to implement. Local school districts and their board members were also somewhat excluded. Both research findings and conventional wisdom in education and the corporate sectors strongly indicate that if effective change is to be implemented, the people who are expected to implement the change (classroom teachers) should be involved from the beginning.

The national reports have drawn much attention to education and its relationship to our society and our economic development. The attention drawn to education and the call for excellence are extremely important factors with respect to the drive for the improvement of education. Some of the reforms proposed and mandated by the states are, in fact, mechanistic and quick-fix in nature. Requiring more courses, for example, does not assure that more learning will occur. Nevertheless, the task forces and proposers are sincere in their desire for the improvement of education for all students. They clearly recognize the importance of a strong educational system for the United States.

Even so, the mandates of reform must be implemented for improvement to occur. It is reasonable to say that the level of implementation will vary for a number of reasons; the acceptance of the reform proposals by those who must implement them—local school boards and administrators and, of utmost importance, classroom teachers. If teachers can accept the concept of excellence, are given some freedom to implement

Teachers are responsible for implementing the curriculum they have a hand in creating.

the proposed reforms, and will set higher expectations for students, the effort for educational reform will have a general overall positive effect on student achievement.

■ The Teacher and Curriculum

While national commissions and community groups write goals, academic specialists analyze content, and other experts theorize about curriculum, it is the teacher on the front line who actually makes the curriculum. Each day as teachers interact with students, they produce and present curriculum. Even without advance planning, as has been advocated, teachers in doing whatever they do with students are in a sense implementing a curriculum.

The role of teachers in formally planning curriculums is becoming increasingly important. Teachers today are asking for greater participation in educational decision making. Perhaps the most important role they can play in decision making is in cooperatively building curricula. Teachers are experts in providing particular information about curriculums from their experiences in working with students. They are also very often academic specialists. They should participate actively in determining objectives, methodology, and evaluation techniques. Once these facets of curriculum have been decided for a school system or a school, the teachers must then put their individual talents into action in implementing the curriculum. Resourceful teachers at this point develop their own style of teaching as they bring their own uniqueness to the task of teaching.

It is not unusual for professional educators or laypersons to debate whether teaching is an art or a science. It is both, and both are essential for superior instruction to occur. Planning—setting objectives, developing instructional strategies, and evaluating performance—is predominately a scientific activity. The act of teaching, however, which involves the orchestration of the plan as teachers interact with students projecting their personalities and using their style, approaches an art.

■ Organizing for Instruction

The next few paragraphs provide a brief description of five ways that students can be organized for discussion. The topics being presented are individualized instruction, graded and nongraded programs, flexible scheduling, and grouping.

Individualized Instruction   One problem of instruction that has been mentioned in a number of places in this text is that of finding ways to individualize instruction. We know that students are different—they differ in intellectual capacity, interests, rate of achievement, and many other ways. This knowledge indicates that students should be treated and taught as individuals as much as is possible. At the same time, the United States is committed to universal education, and to accomplish this goal we have tended to group students. Elsewhere in this book it was pointed out that historically the most common grouping pattern has been by chronological age. We have also usually assumed that one teacher can instruct thirty youngsters that are within defined limits of normality. Under these circumstances, try as a teacher may, it is extremely difficult to teach specifically to individuals. In a general way it can be said that teachers tend to teach to what they perceive to be a composite average. Of course, there is no such individual as the "average." The problem of individualizing instruction in mass education within the limits of the public's willingness to pay still plagues our educational system.

Graded Programs   Most schools in the United States are graded schools. They organize pupils by age. For example, generally children of age six enter the first grade and become first graders—children entering the second grade become second graders, and lastly they become twelfth graders. Standards, goals, and objectives are established for each grade. While some efforts can be made toward individualized instruction, it is more likely that the children will be taught in small groups by ability and achievement. With a small number of children in the class, there is a greater likelihood for individualized instruction.

Nongraded Programs   An organizational plan that seems to have particular merit for individualizing instruction is that of the nongraded school. Such schools and their programs require a determination of the threshold of achievement of individual learners, and as with most other innovative techniques they require a definite change in the teacher's behavior. Teachers must devote more of their energies to guiding individual learners and acting as resource persons.

The nongraded school operates under the assumption that each child should progress through school at his or her own unique rate of development. The nongraded school, when functioning as it should, is a form of continuous progress education. The pupils are organized within the school to facilitate their individual development. For example, in an elementary school operating under the nongraded plan, what were originally the kindergarten, grades one, two, three, and four are likely to be called the primary school, while grades five, six, seven, and eight are likely to be called the middle school. In this sense, they are open schools. However, this arrangement, in and of itself, does not make a nongraded school. The distinctiveness of the nongraded school lies in the fact that youngsters progress on the basis of achieving specified learning skills, regardless of whether or not those skills are typically thought of as being affixed to a particular grade. In a sense, instead of grouping children by chronological age, they are grouped by their achievement of a specific skill. The skills are arranged sequentially in order of difficulty. Ideally, there is much flexibility among this grouping. For example, the child who learns the elementary skills of reading is moved into another group appropriate to that child's reading development or perhaps is given more independent study time. It is also possible that a youngster could be placed at an advanced level in attainment of reading skills and at the same time be placed at a lower level in arithmetic reasoning. Nongraded schools, when functioning ideally, permit flexibility. There should be less failure in the traditional sense because grade level standards have been removed. Further, the child who learns rapidly should have greater opportunity to do so because specific arrangements are made for that child to progress as rapidly as he or she can without being locked into a graded grouping in which it is likely that instruction will be aimed at the "average" child. The nongraded plan attempts through grouping by developmental achievement skills, along with flexibility and the opportunity for movement between groups, to provide greater avenues for individualization. It has potential to accomplish this task. Much of its potential, however, resides in skills of teachers and administrators to assure that it does in fact promote individual development. There is a persistent danger that nongraded schools based on developmental achievement grouping can become just as rigid as the traditional graded organization. While most nongraded schools are at the elementary school level, the plan is also used at the high school level.

Flexible Scheduling   Flexible scheduling is based upon organizing the school day with shorter time periods. Typically school periods are forty-five to sixty minutes; in flexible scheduling, the day is composed of twenty- to thirty-minute modules. The shorter modular type of programming permits greater flexibility. Students' programs could consist of some sessions being as short as twenty minutes and other sessions of various additive combinations of twenty minutes, depending upon the learning activity. Used together with a combination of special resources available for independent study, flexible scheduling has possibilities for individualizing instruction. In and of itself, however, it does not guarantee individualization. It only creates opportunities that staff members need to capitalize on. At the very least, through encouraging independent study, they encourage the development of students toward accepting greater responsibility for their own progress.

Ability Grouping   Grouping is the practice of assigning students to a group or class by intelligence tests, achievement tests, reading level, grades, teacher evaluation, or any combination of the aforementioned. It is intended through grouping that the teacher can provide more adequately for individual differences. Elementary schools are most likely to group students by subject within the classroom. Secondary schools tend to group by subject, also, but by complete classrooms. For example, in mathematics at the high school level, the following courses might be offered, presented from the least rigorous to the most rigorous: Fundamental Mathematics Skills, Applied Mathematics, Business Mathematics, Modified Algebra, Algebra, Geometry, Geometry Plane/Solid, Intermediate Algebra, Trigonometry/Introduction to College Algebra,

Accelerated Algebra/Analytical Geometry, Advanced Placement Calculus. It is evident that classes are grouped for slow learners, average learners, and the academically talented. Although ability grouping has been defended as a way to help increase learners' achievement levels, this defense is only weakly substantiated by research findings.

Some of the drawbacks of ability grouping are:

• Students who are labeled as low ability usually perform poorly because of the teacher's low expectations of them.

• Problems associated with social class and minority group differences are usually increased with ability grouping.

• Ability grouping tends to reinforce unfavorable self-concepts among children placed in low ability groups.

• Although academically talented students achieve better in high ability groups, low ability students tend to perform poorly in low ability groups.

■ Significant Federal and State Curriculum Mandates

Two acts of Congress, the Bilingual Education Act (1968) and Public Law 94–142 (1975) prescribed curriculum requirements for elementary and secondary schools. Many states have passed legislation requiring multicultural education at the elementary and secondary levels. Many colleges and universities also require coursework and experiences in multicultural education, particularly in their teacher education programs.

Least Restrictive Environment, Public Law 94–142   The Education for All Handicapped Children Act, Public Law 94–142, was passed by Congress in 1975 to be implemented in 1978. The legislation is referred to colloquially as mainstreaming. A major thrust of the Act is to provide equal educational opportunities for the handicapped. Important features of the Act are:

- All handicapped learners between the ages of three and eighteen are to be provided with a free public education.
- Each handicapped child is to have an individualized program, developed jointly by a school official, a teacher, parents or guardian, and if possible by the learner herself or himself.
- Handicapped children are not to be grouped separately—unless severely handicapped, in which case separate facilities and programs would be deemed more appropriate.
- Tests for identification and placement are to be free of racial and cultural biases.
- School districts are to maintain continuous efforts at identifying handicapped children.
- School districts are to establish priorities for providing educational programs.
- Placements of the handicapped require parental approval.
- Private schools are also covered by the Act.
- Retraining and inservice training of all personnel are required.
- Special federal grants are available for school building modification.
- State departments of education are to be designated as the responsible state agency for all programs for handicapped.[30]

The provision for an individualized program is of particular importance to teachers. The complete version of Public Law 94–142 dealing with individualized instruction reads:

> For each handicapped child there will be an "individualized educational program"—a written statement jointly developed by a qualified school official, by the child's teacher and parents or guardian, and if possible by the child himself. This written statement will include an analysis of the child's present achievement level, a listing of both short-range and annual goals, an identification of specific services that will be provided toward meeting those goals and an indication of the extent to which the child will be able to participate in regular school programs, a notation of when these services will be provided and how long they will last, and a schedule for checking on the progress being achieved under the plan and for making any revisions in it that may seem called for.[31]

As this legislation is implemented, it is anticipated that individualized instruction will increase not only in special education but in all educational settings. Since this legislation also requires parental participation, it is also anticipated that more definitive and more specific parental participation will increase in all educational settings.

A second previously mentioned provision of the Act, dealing with the least restrictive environment or "mainstreaming" in its complete version reads:

> Handicapped and nonhandicapped children will be educated together to the extent appropriate, and the former will be placed in special classes or separate schools only when the nature of the

Research Finding

12

Handicapped high school students who seek jobs after graduation are more likely to find them when schools prepare them for careers and private sector businesses provide on-the-job training.

Many individuals with disabilities, especially those handicapped youth who do not attend college, are chronically unemployed. Programs and services to help them get jobs are fragmented. There is little coordination between employment agencies and schools or programs that offer compensatory, social, or vocational help.

Successful school-to-work transition programs have been developed that improve coordination between school staffs, state agencies, and community employers. Under these programs, special education teachers help students explore career possibilities and develop job-seeking skills and work ethics.

Vocational educators cooperate with special education teachers to adapt their instruction to the needs of the students.

Such programs find jobs for students by offering prospective employers incentives such as pre-screened employees, on-the-job assistance with trainees, and most importantly, wage stipends. Employment and rehabilitation staff provide expertise on a referral basis. Additional resources are needed to cover the schools' excess cost of developing jobs and offering training stipends.

"Findings on Youth Employment: Lessons from MDRC Research." (1984). New York: Manpower Development Research Corporation.

Hahn, A., and Lernam, R. (1985). *What Works in Youth Employment Policy?* Washington, DC: Committee on New American Realities.

McCormick, W. (1986). "Work-Ability Today, an Evaluation Perspective." Sacramento, CA: California State Department of Education.

Source: *What Works: Research About Teaching and Learning.* Washington, DC: U.S. Department of Education, 1987, page 76.

severity of the handicap is such that education in regular classes, even if they are provided supplementary aids and services cannot be achieved satisfactorily.

It is these two provisions of the Act that have caused some teachers to become discouraged. Such teachers feel that the conditions under which they work are so difficult already—for example classes of over thirty students—that to try to give

the necessary attention to individualized instruction for handicapped children in their regular classrooms is an added burden which is doomed to failure for both the students and the teacher. Other teachers in more desirable teaching conditions, and who have had some preparation for teaching the handicapped, perceive the Act as reasonable and proper, and find the added tasks challenging and rewarding. It is clear that pre-service and inservice training designed to help teachers function effectively in "mainstreamed" classes is needed. It is also clear that unless proper working conditions with support services are available, some teachers will not be effective in "mainstreamed" classes.

Multicultural Education

The concept of multicultural education has been defined and discussed earlier in this textbook, and its relationship to a pluralistic society was explained earlier in this chapter. The task of implementing the concepts of multicultural education into teacher education and into the curricula of elementary, secondary, and higher education is beginning to be accomplished. Eleven cognitive and eight affective competencies appropriate for teacher preparation programs have been developed.[32] The cognitive competencies are:

Knowledge

- Acquire a knowledge of the cultural experience in both contemporary and historical setting of any two ethnic, racial, or cultural groups.
- Demonstrate a basic knowledge of the contributions of minority groups in America to our society.
- Assess relevance and feasibility of existing models that afford groups a way of gaining inclusion into today's society.

Application

- Identify current biases and deficiencies in existing curriculum, and in both commercial and teacher-prepared materials of instruction.
- Recognize potential linguistic and cultural biases of existing assessment instruments and procedures when prescribing a program of testing for the learner.

- Acquire a thorough knowledge of the philosophy and theory concerning bilingual education and its application.
- Critique an educational environment to the extent of the measurable evidence of the environment representing a multicultural approach to education.
- Acquire the skills for effective participation and utilization of the community.
- Design, develop, and implement an instructional module using strategies and materials to produce a module or unit that is multicultural, multiethnic, and multiracial.

Rationale

- Develop a rationale or model for the development and implementation of a curriculum reflective of cultural pluralism within the K–12 school and be able to defend it on a psychological, sociological, and cultural basis.

Each of the competencies in the original source are accompanied by a statement of rationale and instructional objectives.[33] Another volume provides enabling activities.[34] Students seeking more information should refer to original sources. The eight affective competencies are:

- Developing an awareness in the learners of the value of cultural diversity.
- Assisting the learners to maintain and extend identification with and pride in the mother culture.
- Assisting and preparing the learners to interact successfully in a cross-cultural setting.

- Assisting all to respond positively to the diversity of behavior involved in cross-cultural school environments.
- Recognizing both the similarities and differences between Anglo-American and other cultures, and both the potential conflicts and opportunities they may create for students.
- Recognizing and accepting the language variety of the home, and a standard variety as valid systems of communication, each with its own legitimate functions.
- Recognizing and accepting different patterns of child development within and between cultures in order to formulate realistic objectives.
- Recognizing and accepting differences in social structure, including familial organization and patterns of authority and their significance for the educational environment.

As classroom teachers become competent in multicultural education, the goals of multicultural education are likely to become a part of curriculums and therefore be accomplished in the many classrooms throughout the nation. It is pertinent to note that multicultural education is still somewhat controversial; some perceive it as divisive and destructive of American culture, while others perceive it not only as very appropriate, but also as necessary for the survival of society.

Bilingual-Bicultural Education

The Bilingual Education Act, Title VII of the Elementary and Secondary Education Act, was enacted in 1968. The major purpose of the Act was to help with the special educational needs of growing numbers of American children whose first language is not English. Further impetus to the implementation of bilingual education was the *Lau v. Nichols* decision of the U.S. Supreme Court in 1974. That decision mandated that school districts provide all non-English speaking students with special language instruction to equalize their educational opportunities.

Today approximately 25 percent of the United States population speaks a language other than English as a native tongue. Spanish speaking people represent the largest group, followed by Asian immigrants whose numbers are increasing dramatically. Over 30 percent of the Native Americans speak a native language as their first language.

Bilingual-bicultural education helps learners to strengthen their identity by including their historical, literary, and cultural traditions in the regular curriculum. An important benefit of bilingual-bicultural education is that it enhances the self-concept of the learner, resulting in better academic achievement.

Bilingual-bicultural education is thought of in two basic ways. One view is that it should be transitional, that is, the student should be converted to the English language as quickly as possible. A second view is referred to as maintenance. The advocates of the maintenance viewpoint feel that students should learn English, but maintain and foster their native tongue at the same time. Teaching English as a second language (ESL) is considered viable from both perspectives. Most persons agree with the concept that instruction in the native tongue is worthwhile and necessary for a period of time while the student learns English. The major disagreement centers around the maintenance approach in the schools—that is providing instruction in both languages throughout the person's formal education. Many of the persons objecting to the maintenance approach, however, do feel that it is a valuable asset to know and speak two languages. Objectors point out that language is the major vehicle of culture, and the fostering of languages other than English can be destructive nationally rather than enhancing or enriching a nation. The debate will undoubtedly continue.

The projections of demographic data indicate that the numbers of Asians and Spanish-speaking persons will continue to increase in the future. The schools must be prepared for such students and provide them with an equal opportunity to education, and at the same time provide a mainstream approach so as not to foster what could become a strong ethnic separateness.

■ Character–Morality–Values–Democracy

In the last two or three years, there has been a resurgence of writing about the importance of character development, morals, and values as they relate to the public schools; and to the teaching of citizenship and democracy. The main messages of the articles written were that (1) the schools have failed to teach the morals and values of our democratic society; and (2) that we have let, and in some instances urged, students to develop their own morals and values whatever they may be. Furthermore, some of the articles implied that we have not indoctrinated our students with selected morals and values.

The following quotes express the opinions of one group that has called on the schools to do a better job of teaching democratic values.[35]

> The American Federation of Teachers sponsored a project with the Educational Excellence Network, a coalition of educators devoted to improving American schooling, and Freedom House, a national organization that monitors civil liberties around the world.

The group called for a restructured curriculum enabling schools to purposely impart to their students the learning necessary for an informed reasoned allegiance to the ideals of a free society.

The group produced a document titled *Education for Democracy: Guidelines for Strengthening the Teaching of Democratic Values.*

The signers of the document said they reject the notion that values are "arbitrary" and that teachers in their instruction "must strive to be value free."[36] The group differentiated between the kind of education for which they are calling, "and propaganda" and "indoctrination." Diane Ravitch, Chairperson of the Educational Excellence Network, cosponsor of the project, was quoted as saying, "The idea behind this proposal is that history should be taught with objectivity, but not with neutrality."[37]

The group made the following recommendations:[38]

- A more "substantial, engaging and demanding" social studies curriculum that includes the history of the United States and democratic civilization, and the in-depth study of world geography and at least one non-Western society.
- School curricula with history and geography at their core.
- More history, chronologically taught, with the central theme being "the dramatic struggle" of people to obtain their freedom.
- More attention to world studies, particularly the "realistic and unsentimental" study of both democratic and nondemocratic nations.
- Broader and deeper instruction in the humanities, particularly in literature, biography and ideas.

It is important to note that values are taught in the schools. It is also a fact, however, that children have values when they enter school—values that they learned from their parents and other adults prior to entering school. Nevertheless, values are taught in school, formally and informally. They usually reflect the values of the neighborhood or community. Formal values may appear in documents that spell out the rules and regulations for student conduct. Informally, teachers indicate and communicate values. Children soon learn what teachers believe is right and what is wrong, from their behavior and comments.

The 19th Annual Phi Delta Kappa/Gallup Poll of the Public's Attitudes Toward the Public Schools (1987) asked four questions about character education. The questions and responses to the questions are as follows:

Question. It has been proposed that the public schools include courses on "character education" to help students develop personal values and ethical behavior. Do you think that courses on values and ethical behavior should be taught in the public schools, or do you think that this should be left to the students' parents and the churches?

Answers. Forty-three percent said, yes, the schools should teach values and ethics; 36 percent replied no, the teaching of values and ethics should be left to parents and churches.

Question. Do you think it would be possible or not possible to develop subject matter for a character education course that would be acceptable to most of the people in this community?

Answers. Sixty-two percent said it was possible; 23 percent said it was not possible; and 15 percent said, "Don't know."

Question. If courses about values and ethical behavior were required in the local public schools, who do you think should have the most to say about the content of the courses? The federal government in Washington, the state government, the local school board, the school administrators, the teachers, or the parents?

Answers. Parents, 42 percent; local school board, 24 percent; teachers, 14 percent; school administrators, 10 percent; state government, 9 percent; federal government, 5 percent; and "Don't know," 12 percent.

Question. If students or their parents objected to what was taught in these classes, do you think the students should be excused from these classes or not?

Answers. Fifty-two percent said, "Yes, excused"; 37 percent said, "No, not excused"; 11 percent said, "Don't know."[39]

With only 43 percent of the respondents of the survey indicating that the schools should teach values and ethics; and with 42 percent indicating that the parents should have the most to say about the content and value and ethics courses; and with 52 percent indicating that if students or parents object to what is being taught in the values and ethics courses the students should be excused from the courses, *it appears that there is not a strong commitment from the public for the teaching of values and ethics in the public schools.* Of course, any school district whose constituencies desire to have instruction in values and ethics is free to do so. As was stated earlier, however, values and ethics are being taught informally and formally in schools, but perhaps not in prescribed courses.

◙ Parental Choice of School

Parental choice of schools has been available for many years in this nation through the vehicle of either private or parochial education. Private and parochial schools preceded public schools. Parents who were dissatisfied with public schools could send their children to private schools or organize their own private schools at their own expenses. Most often, private schools were formed for religious reasons.

In the late sixties and early seventies, there was a movement for parental choice different from the private school alternative. Parents began seeking alternative education programs within the public schools. The effect of parental pressure along with pressure from some educators brought about the establishment of some alternative programs within a school, and also opened the opportunity to attend other schools within the school district with some limitations.

Parental choice of schools in its broadest interpretation implies that parents may choose any school, public or private, either within or outside the school district. Parental choice has been most popular in public schools within the school district. In large school districts, there is a clear movement for creating magnet schools—schools that frequently are specialized in such areas as mathematics and science, the performing arts, and the humanities. Such schools offer a complete program, but emphasize their specialization in their curriculum. Students make application to attend magnet schools. Magnet schools are most often for gifted and talented schools. At least three states are using public funds to provide residential high schools for the gifted and talented: North Carolina School for Mathematics and Science; Louisiana School for Mathematics, Science and the Arts; and the Illinois Mathematics and Science Academy. Students must file applications for admission to each of these schools. Each of these schools strives to have the demographics of the state reflected in the student body.

Parental choice in the public schools, however, is not limited to gifted schools. For example, Los Angeles County, California, offers more than one hundred choices to parents including magnet schools, off-campus vocational training, and second-chance programs for those who have left high school. In the Cambridge, Massachusetts, schools all parents indicate three choices among the eleven elementary schools in the district, receiving assignments that maintain racial and language balances.[40]

According to Mary Ann Raywid, schools of choice succeed because of four factors.[41]

- Schools of choice offer a different curricular emphasis or instructional style from traditional "one-best-system" schooling.
- Cohesiveness is a second factor. The sense of shared values among students, parents, teachers, and administrators contributes greatly to the satisfaction with the choice.
- There is autonomy. Teachers and principals in the schools of choice usually enjoy more freedom in selecting peers, resources, and programs.
- Schools of choice generally tend to be smaller or to be units within larger schools. These foster collegiality—also may cost more than traditional schools.

Parental choice for education in public schools in their own school district has suffered little criticism. However, the concept of educational vouchers had been extremely controversial.

Educational Vouchers Educational vouchers were first proposed in 1970. Under a voucher system, parents of all school-age children in a community are given vouchers roughly representing their children's share of the educational budget. A child then uses this voucher to attend any school he or she chooses, public or private, secular or parochial. The voucher plan tries to introduce the element of competition into public education; students choose the best school in the area, and the weaker schools, in theory, are forced to improve or close.

The use of vouchers provided by public funds and used for private education provoke the greatest controversy. They are viewed by their critics as an inappropriate, if not an illegal diversion of public funds. Some see such a diversion as undermining public education.

The Gallup Poll has monitored the public attitudes toward educational vouchers since 1970. The highest percentage of support for vouchers was 51 percent in 1983. The lowest percentage of support was 38 percent in 1971. In the 1987 poll, 44 percent indicated that they favor the use of educational vouchers, while 41 percent indicated that they opposed the vouchers. Fifteen percent responded, "Don't know."[42]

Tuition Tax Credits Another method of parental choice is the use of tuition tax credits. Federal tuition tax credits can be defined as tax rebates to parents who pay private school tuition for their children. Such legislation has been sponsored in every session of the U.S. Congress for nearly two decades. The issue is still very much alive and will continue to be so. A recent booklet on the topic of tuition tax credits noted the following.

> Tuition tax credit legislation, as currently proposed (1985), would not bring about an end to the public schools, as we sometimes hear; nor would its enactment infuse the current school scene with diversity and choice for all, as we are also told. . . . However, tuition tax credits could command a sizable share of what the federal government spends on elementary and secondary education, thus modifying the existing federal role in financing education. Tax credits could also pay a healthy portion of tuition expenses for students attending private schools, especially for those attending less expensive schools.[43]

In the summer of 1983, the U.S. Supreme Court gave proponents of tuition tax credits (deductions) hope by upholding a Minnesota statute, *Mueller v. Allen* (1983). The Minnesota law covered deductions (tax credits) not only for parents who send their children to private schools, but also for those parents who send their children to public schools. The Court ruled 5–4 that the statute was constitutional. Justice Rehnquist's majority opinion noted that (1) the statute had a secular purpose in that parents were assisted in helping defray the costs of educating their children, (2) its effect neither advanced nor inhibited religion because the service was available to children in both public and nonpublic schools, and (3) it did not foster excessive entanglement of church and state. The decision was a narrow one, yet this case is likely to be studied carefully by legislators for its possible bearing on other proposed statutes.

In 1987, Iowa passed legislation for a tuition tax plan similar to the plan that has been implemented in Minnesota. The Iowa law has been challenged by taxpayers who are being represented by the Americans United for Separation of Church and State. They contend that the law violates both the First and Fourteenth Amendments to the U.S. Constitution.

■ Economic Development

One of the reasons, and perhaps the primary reason for the attention given to education through the publication of many national reports, was the need to improve economic development for the United States. We are not nearly as competitive in the international trade markets as we once were. Our educational system in our increasingly technological society needs to prepare students that have the knowledge and skills to be effective leaders and workers in the business and industrial sectors of our economy. Businesses and industries need a well-educated work force, and they rely on the schools to provide that work force. The relationship between a well-educated population and a healthy economy has been well documented.

Strong, solid, and rigorous school curriculums are needed and being developed. Curriculum questions such as—What shall be taught? How shall what is taught be taught? and How can the curriculum be effectively evaluated?—are being addressed. An appropriate and rigorous curriculum taught by excellent teachers will result in students' becoming effective leaders, employers, and employees ready to meet the challenge of improving our economic status in the world.

■ Summary

This chapter began with a discussion of the sources of curriculum which are essentially the expectations of society for the schools and the needs of learners. The role of curriculum in a pluralistic society was addressed, recognizing the need for multicultural education which is discussed in detail in this chapter. The basic components of a curriculum are goals and objectives, that is "what is to be taught," and how it shall be taught (methodology); and the evaluation of the curriculum, that is, "how well students have learned."

Five national reports dealing with the curriculum were presented and summarized. *A Nation at Risk* and *James Madison High School: A Curriculum for American Students* were similar in content. Both of these reports proposed high school curriculums that are quite similar to those curriculums for college-bound students in many high schools today. In essence, they advocate that *all* students take the curriculum that college-bound students take. Both curriculum proposals allow for a somewhat limited vocational education program. Both reports also recognize that remedial education will be needed. Former Secretary Bennett (1987) states in the *James Madison High School* report that "I think most Americans could handle the classes in the James Madison High School; again I have seen students of all backgrounds do it."

The Forgotten Half: Non-College-Bound Youth in America addresses the status of the noncollege-bound students; their dilemma, their potential, and the contributions they could make to our economy. It recommends ten goals that can help the noncollege-bound students enrich their lives and increase their productivity in our society and its economy.

First Lessons: A Report on Elementary Education in America is the first report on elementary education since 1953. The report commends American elementary education.

Recommendations are made for each of the standard elementary subjects. There is an emphasis on the Implicit Curriculum which refers to the development of character and morality. It is noted that values are "caught" more than "taught." Within the Implicit Curriculum, an emphasis is also placed on democratic citizenship.

A perspective on the likelihood of educational reforms being implemented was presented in this chapter. Two important observations were made: (1) teachers were usually not participants in the development of the reform reports, and (2) both research findings and conventional wisdom, in education and the corporate sectors, strongly indicate that, if effective change is to be implemented, the people who are expected to implement the change (classroom teachers) should be involved from the beginning.

Character, morality, values, and democracy were addressed. The public responses to the Gallup Poll (1987), however, did not indicate strong support for the teaching of values and ethics in the public schools.

Parental choice of schools is a growing movement in education. There is little controversy when parental choice is used within a public school or within a public school district. Controversy escalates when public funds are used to support parental choice students in private or parochial schools.

Classroom teachers play a very important role in designing curriculum at the local school district level. In some instances, a few selected teachers have had the opportunity to exert their influence on curriculums at the state and national levels. It is important that you, a prospective teacher, recognize the involvement that teachers have in curriculum development—a process that includes establishing objectives, recommending methodology and ways of evaluating the success of your students and the effectiveness of the curriculum. You will receive instruction in your methods classes should you decide to become a teacher.

Point of View

Chapter 13 provided information about four recent reports: *A Nation at Risk, James Madison High School, The Forgotten Half,* and *First Lessons. The Forgotten Half* differed from the other reports in that it dealt with the noncollege-bound students. The Point of View article for this chapter is *The Forgotten Half: Non-College-Bound Youth in America* by The William T. Grant Foundation Commission on Work, Family and Citizenship. It is supplemental to the information provided in the text. *The Forgotten Half* addresses the status of the noncollege-bound students, their plight, their potential for personal success, and for the contributions they can make to the nation's economy.

The Forgotten Half: Non-College-Bound Youth in America

The William T. Grant Foundation Commission on Work, Family and Citizenship

A college degree is not the only way to develop the talents of tomorrow's workers—and for some, it is far from the best way. There are many opportunities outside the college classroom to develop skills and talents; there are many ways to contribute to a stronger America and to lead a successful personal and family life that do not require a college degree.

The Forgotten Half: Non-College Youth in America, an interim report released on January 20 by Youth and America's Future: the William T. Grant Foundation Commission on Work, Family and Citizenship, calls attention to the approximately 20 million Americans between the ages of 16 and 24 who are not likely to embark on a college education. These young people finish their formal education when they leave high school, with or without a diploma. Yet, like their college-bound peers, they aspire to succeed—to find a niche in the workplace that will enable them to make a living, rear a family, and earn respect. *The Forgotten Half* documents both the good news about their personal accomplishments and the bad news about the economy they face.

The non-college-bound confront high hurdles in their search for rewarding careers. Lacking college degrees, they are increasingly locked out of most high-paid occupations. At the same time, stable jobs that pay well but do not require advanced training are rapidly disappearing.

Between 1979 and 1985 the U.S. suffered a net loss of 1.7 million jobs in manufacturing. At the same time, our quickly changing economy has produced millions of new jobs in the retail and service sectors; wages for these jobs, however, typically stand at only half the level of wages for jobs in manufacturing. Fields such as transportation, communications, utilities, government, and agriculture once offered steady employment to millions of young adults, but that is no longer the case.

Never easy, the plight of the "forgotten half" has become alarming. A highly competitive economy that rests on technology can offer prosperity to those with advanced skills, but those with less education must scramble for jobs that are neither steady nor well-paid. In the future, the U.S. population may be divided not by race or geography, but by education.

Young people who do not attend college need help in moving from high school to a career—help that is often not available. College-bound young people in the U.S. enjoy the benefits of a postsecondary education system that costs an annual $112 billion; after graduation, they are also the beneficiaries of the bulk of the $210 billion per year invested by U.S. businesses to further train and educate their employees. Taxpayers, private donors, and parents gladly pay their share of these costs, which they view as an investment in the future. But there is no such investment in the future of the non-college-bound. For the most part, these young people are left to make it on their own.

■ A Distorted Image

The William T. Grant Foundation Commission on Work, Family and Citizenship has concluded that many of the non-college-bound *are* making it—often by working more than one job, living with parents, delaying marriage and family, and searching for extra training that can advance their careers. These young people are anything but losers, carefree youth without a thought for tomorrow, a generation on the skids.

The commission believes that the media portrait of a "troubled and irresponsible" younger generation is largely a distortion. Indeed, government statistics show the reverse.

- From 1973 to 1983 the annual dropout rate nationwide fell by almost one-fifth, from 6.3% to 5.2%. A survey of young adults between the ages of 25 and 29 in 1986 showed that 86% of them had earned a high school diploma or its equivalent, twice the percentage that had done so in 1940.

- In 1986, 22% of all 25- to 29-year-olds had completed at least four years of college, nearly double the percentage in 1963 and quadruple the percentage in 1940.

- In 1985 the birthrate for young women between the ages of 20 and 24 was less than half what it was in 1960. In 1960, 258 of every 1,000 women in that age group had a child, whereas only 107 of every 1,000 women in that age group had a child in 1985. For girls between the ages of 15 and 19, the birthrate fell from 89 per 1,000 in 1960 to 50.9 per 1,000 in 1985, a drop of 43%.

• The proportion of Americans between the ages of 18 and 25 who said that they had used marijuana in the past month fell from 35% in 1979 to 22% in 1985. Among 12- to 17-year-olds, the percentage of marijuana users within the past month fell from 16.7% in 1979 to 12.3% in 1985.

In the commission's view, the portrayal of American young people as deeply troubled is not only misleading, but harmful. Young people desperately need opportunities to get started in responsible careers. Instead, they are often saddled with an image that suggests they are uninterested and unwilling to assume the responsibilities of adulthood. We ought to correct the record, for the sake of both fairness and accuracy. Complaining about the state of the younger generation is all too common, while a genuine commitment to aiding non-college-bound young people is all too rare.

■ Declining Economic Fortunes

Although many young people without college educations do succeed, the commission is concerned that a large percentage of them are finding it harder than ever to swim against the economic tide. They are seeking jobs they cannot find. The work they do find is often part-time, and they earn too little to support themselves or a family. They are floundering in their efforts to find a place in the society. Some are losing hope that they have much of a future. Recent economic data explain, in part, why this is so.

• In 1986 males between the ages of 20 and 24 who had high school diplomas and were employed earned 28% less in constant dollars than a comparable group in 1973. The income decline was 24% for white males and 44% for black males.

• High school dropouts have suffered an even larger income decline. In 1986 dropouts between the ages of 20 and 24 earned 42% less in constant dollars than a comparable group in 1973.

• In 1984, 12% of all males between the ages of 20 and 24 said that they had no income, up from 7.3% in 1973.

• In 1973, 60% of all employed young males earned incomes high enough to support a three-person family above the poverty level, but by 1985 only 43.7% earned incomes that high.

• The proportion of males under age 24 who were not in college and who were working full-time dropped from 73% in 1974 to 49% in 1986. Similarly, the proportion of young females who were not in college and who were working fulltime fell from 57% in 1968 to 42% in 1986.

• Of the 3.1 million households headed by youths under age 25 in 1985, 30% had incomes below the poverty level–nearly double the percentage in the early 1970s. (Given this fact, it is not surprising that the marriage rate among all 20- to 24-year-olds fell 46% between 1974 and 1985–and fell a full 62% among blacks.)

The members of the commission believe that the American people should set as conscious policy goals the improvement of both employment opportunities and earning levels for all workers, especially those who lack a college education. We offer a series of recommendations and suggestions that can be implemented *immediately,* ranging from a somewhat different approach to school reform to an expanded investment in programs that help young people move into the world of work. We also outline a series of measures to upgrade the U.S. workforce. We support investments in human resources as the most basic and enduring strategy for creating prosperity.

The Forgotten Half explores ways in which a wide range of community institutions, acting in concert with the schools, can provide a more nurturing and responsive preparation for young people who choose paths to adult self-sufficiency other than college. Our report focuses primarily on the non-college-bound, but many of our conclusions and recommendations apply to all young Americans.

■ A Better First Chance

Too often, any discussion of the problems of the young leads quickly to criticisms of the schools for failing to do their job. Most such attacks are unfair and unwarranted. Students may work hard through 12 grades, master the basic skills, compile adequate records, and graduate in good standing—but they are still likely to encounter problems in their efforts to embark on productive careers. The primary problems are the economy and the career paths that are open to the young. Education can help, but it is no magic cure-all for massive changes in the labor market.

The commission disagrees with the direction taken by some of the recommendations put forward by current school reformers. Generally speaking, the recent reports on school reform have focused on the college-bound. These reports have urged that public school curricula and practice be standardized, in order to better prepare the college-bound for higher education. However, for young people who have not fared well in school, "more of the same" may well result in less learning.

Research has confirmed what teachers have long recognized as fact: children learn in different ways. Some children, who do not absorb much from books and lectures, perform far better when they are allowed to work at their own pace or to learn through hands-on activities. The education system rewards students who learn well through conventional paper-and-pencil tasks, but the system should not penalize young people who learn best in other ways. They may have the skills and abilities to become highly productive adults, but they need help getting started. Schools need to offer varied learning experiences that take advantage of students' abilities, rather than ignore those young people who do not fit "the proper mold."

Research has also confirmed the high cost of failure in school. Compared with peers whose reading and mathematics test scores fall in the top half, young people whose scores fall in the bottom fifth are 8.8 times more likely to leave school without a diploma, 8.6 times more likely to have a child out of wedlock, five times more likely to have an income below the poverty line, and 2.2 times more likely to have been arrested during the previous year. Though it does not *guarantee* success, mastery of basic skills clearly correlates with success in later life.

Therefore, the commission believes that society should invest heavily in efforts to strengthen the schools, to raise the level of basic learning, and to set such concrete goals as reducing statewide dropout rates to 10% or less by the year 2000. Some programs that have proved their worth, such as Chapter 1 of the Education Consolidation and Improvement Act, should be expanded to serve all eligible students, including those in the high schools and in summer programs. The commission also recommends that a more varied approach be employed with all students to head off early failure. Young people's learning experiences should be challenging and substantive—but how, where, and with whom they learn should depend on what works best with each student.

States and communities should establish concrete goals related to school completion, youth employment, community service, and parental involvement. These goals should be publicly announced and annually assessed by means of community/school "report cards." Specific guidelines should be developed to direct resources to those schools that fall seriously short of meeting these goals, rather than leaving them to fail.

■ Bridging the Gap from School to Work

For the college-bound student bent on obtaining a degree, the education system provides a ladder from school to career. But this ladder is the exception, not the rule. Most young people—especially the non-college-bound—must enter the world of work with little assistance. This is neither right nor fair. These young people need some assistance, and educators should form alliances with employers and community leaders to give them opportunities to reach beyond the school walls. By moving education into the community, educators tap rich learning possibilities and give young people the exposure and confidence they need to make it in the job market.

State officials should also be more flexible about allowing people over age 18 to return to high school. We should encourage "dropping in," as well as trying to prevent dropping out. Closer collaboration between secondary schools and community colleges, for example, would provide alternative settings for older individuals who wish to return to school but who would be unlikely to function well in the usual high school classroom.

A number of school-to-work programs have been tested nationwide. In general, these programs have increased student achievement and turned out graduates who are mature, responsible, and highly motivated. No single such program is best, but research and experience have convinced members of the commission that many of these programs yield positive outcomes. Thousands of young people who might otherwise drop out and face a troubled future can be salvaged by programs that give them an opportunity to get started in a productive job. Several approaches are worth considering, including the following.

- *Monitored work experience.* This category includes cooperative education, apprenticeships, internships, pre-employment training, and youth-operated enterprises. Each such effort gives students opportunities to gain work experience, to be exposed to adult supervisors and models in the workplace, and to relate their academic learning to the world of work.

- *Community and neighborhood service.* Young people need experience not only as workers, but also as citizens. Service programs expose them to the adult world and teach them the obligations of citizens in building a more caring, compassionate, and competent society. As an element of learning, community service is as important as schooling and work.

- *Redirected vocational education.* The evidence indicates that, with a few exceptions, vocational education does not prepare young people well for *specific* jobs. But its hands-on approach offers students a valuable and effective way to acquire the basic skills and general abilities they will need to be successful in a wide range of endeavors.

- *Incentives.* Low motivation and low expectations for success in the workplace limit students' educational achievement. Recent experiments guaranteeing post-secondary and continuing education, employment, or training to students who do well seem to motivate young people to work hard in school. Such guarantees are much more likely to be successful if the young people also have access to mentors and other adults who can give them personal attention and encouragement.

- *Career information and counseling.* Such services, offered in the schools or through community agencies, can make young people aware of job opportunities and career options and can expose them to adult role models.

• *School volunteers.* Tutoring is the most common form of volunteer activity in the schools. However, adult volunteers can also serve as friends and mentors who expand students' career horizons and help them master the dilemmas and stresses of life. Young people themselves volunteer as tutors, and research indicates that peer tutoring is highly effective for both learner and tutor.

Improving education, elevating skill levels, and providing hands-on experiences are not cure-alls for the problems of the non-college-bound, but they will help. The members of the Commission on Work, Family and Citizenship agree with those who say that America needs to "work smarter" and raise productivity in order to be competitive with other nations. But we believe that something equally important is also at stake. We must address the needs of all our young people, in order to retain their confidence in the American dream.

Most young people understand that doing well in school does not guarantee immediate rewards in the workplace. But if young people have a responsibility to prepare themselves well for the demands of work and adulthood in the 21st century (and we believe that they do), then policy makers, employers, and community leaders have a corresponding obligation: to concern themselves not just with the quantity, but with the *quality* of employment opportunities for young adults. The 50% of American young people who do not go on to college have a right to be able to compete for jobs that are adequate in number, that offer reasonable wages, that provide health insurance and other essential benefits, that offer career advancement in return for diligence and competence, and that provide continuing educational opportunities and retraining benefits for employees who are displaced by technological change.

■ An Added Chance

For most young adults who lack a high school diploma, more hours of traditional schooling in traditional settings will not be the answer. However, they may need other kinds of help. The commission recommends an array of "added chance" opportunities for young people who are out of school and out of work. They include:

• *Intensive training in academic skills.* This component should be added to all employment training programs that do not currently include it.

• *Job Corps.* This intensive residential intervention program has been rigorously evaluated and continuously fine-tuned. Although the program is not for everyone, evaluations have shown that Job Corps graduates have higher earnings, remain employed longer, and more often go on to full-time study. The Job Corps provides society a net return of $1.46 for every tax dollar invested.

• *State and local youth corps.* Fourteen states and 12 cities currently operate year-round youth corps that incorporate various elements of the Job Corps experience. Other states and communities operate summer youth corps programs. An evaluation of the California Conservation Corps found that the work of participants generates a positive economic return even when the value of probable changes in their future lives is not included in the calculation.

• *Nonresidential pre-employment training.* Several national organizations offer pre-employment training and remediation in the basic skills. These efforts deserve encouragement and support.

• *The Job Training Partnership Act (JTPA).* The potential of programs under the JTPA for serving at-risk young people has not been adequately realized; only 5% of eligible youths are currently being served. Moreover, these programs tend to direct their efforts to the young people who are easiest to reach, teach, and place quickly in jobs. With certain changes in management practices, however, these programs could become much more effective in reaching those young people who are hardest to serve.

- *The armed forces.* Although only 9% of all recruits lack high school diplomas, demographic changes now under way are likely to increase that proportion dramatically. Armed forces programs designed to upgrade the academic and work skills of members should be expanded, in order to guarantee that no member will return to civilian life without both a general equivalency diploma and marketable job skills.

■ Equal Access to Lifelong Learning

This nation's fast-changing economy has helped spur the creation of a variety of education and training programs for adults. Whether labeled "lifelong learning" or "recurrent education," these programs are giving adults opportunities to improve their skills and enrich their lives.

As beneficial as these programs are, however, they have largely by-passed those groups that could benefit the most from additional training: underemployed blue-collar workers and the unemployed. Instead, most such programs—and employer-based training, as well—have been directed to adults with some college education. The commission believes that this imbalance needs to be remedied.

Various proposals for correcting this imbalance have been offered. The commission recommends that a serious national study of such proposals be undertaken, aimed at developing an effective and equitable lifelong learning system for all U.S. citizens, including the non-college-bound.

■ Increased Investments in Success

There is no way that the forgotten half of American youth, especially those most at risk, can be adequately served at no extra cost. The commission recognizes the existence of huge government deficits and a high level of private indebtedness; nonetheless, it concludes that this nation cannot afford *not* to invest more resources in its children and young adults. A larger investment in education and training will pay rich dividends in terms of a more productive economy, higher individual earnings, and lower costs for social services for the poor.

Substantial evidence from research shows that public investments do pay off. For example, health and nutrition programs yield healthier mothers and children and reduced medical costs. Head Start and Chapter 1 yield gains in educational attainment. Unfortunately, such programs reach only a fraction of those who are eligible for them, and the benefits often end before young people have consolidated their gains and made them permanent.

Public opinion polls indicate that, despite budget deficits, Americans are willing to spend more on programs for young people. More than 30 states have recently increased taxes in order to maintain or increase social services, including a broad range of programs for the young. But federal spending for such programs, when adjusted for inflation, has declined by 25% or more. All levels of government must do more.

In particular, though, the commission recommends that the federal government increase its current investment in children and youth by at least $5 billion in each of the next 10 years. This expenditure should be covered through some combination of the following methods: a general increase in the tax rates, the elimination of existing tax preferences, the realignment of priorities regarding military and domestic spending, or a new dedicated tax for children and youth (i.e., a surcharge of some specified percentage on the personal income tax).

However the funds are raised, they should be spent in accordance with the following principles: 1) they should be spent primarily for the benefit of at-risk youths; 2) they should supplement (not supplant) prior congressional appropriations; 3) they should be made available with long-term assurances over a period of at least 10 years; 4) the allocations of funds among programs should remain relatively constant from year to year to encourage state and local planning and effective implementation; and 5) the funds should be used to attract matching grants from state, local, and private agencies. The commission does not recommend new top-down legislative mandates or rigidly prescribed look-alike programs. Local leadership must be free to innovate and to refine programs and practices to meet local needs.

Several programs that are already in place seem to be achieving good results. The results would be even better if these programs were more widely available, better coordinated, and more comprehensive. Therefore, the commission urges that additional funds be spread among underfunded programs that have proved their worth. The allocations should be determined by Congress.

Simply as an illustration, the additional funding might be used as follows.

- If we were to add $1.5 billion to the Head Start budget, an additional 600,000 children could be served. (The program currently serves 450,000 children, and about 81% of all eligible 3- to 5-year-olds remain unserved.)
- If we were to add $1.5 billion to the Chapter 1 budget, an additional 2.5 million students could be served. (The program currently serves about five million children, only about half of those who are eligible to receive this remedial help.)
- The Job Corps now maintains 40,500 year-long training slots. Adding $300 million to the Job Corps budget could support some 30 to 50

new Job Corps centers and almost 19,000 additional year-long training slots.
- If we were to add $1.5 billion to the Job Training Partnership Act budget, the JTPA programs could serve up to 500,000 additional young people. These programs currently serve about 463,000 young adults, approximately 5% of those who are eligible.
- A fund of $200 million would enable states and localities to expand several programs aimed at helping to smooth the transition from school to work, such as community and neighborhood service, cooperative education, apprenticeships, high school work-study programs, and youth-operated enterprises.

The commission stresses that the federal government has an important role in meeting the needs of young people. Even more significant steps must be taken by state and local governments and by private agencies. But families, employers, and communities play the most important role of all in helping young people grow into self-sufficient and responsible citizens.

At all levels, we encourage approaches that do things *with*—not *to* or *for*—young people. To succeed, youth must have expanded options that enable and empower them to do more for themselves, their families, and their communities.

■ A Note of Urgency

To sum things up, we are shortchanging too many of our young people—and, in the process, we are damaging our nation's future. To remedy this situation will require sustained attention to the 10 goals that follow by parents, employers, trade unions, educators, churches, youth-serving agencies, community leaders, and local, state, and national authorities.

1. We must help Americans understand the needs of youth in today's society and teach Americans to deal with young people as a resource, not as a problem.

2. We must offer to more young people, substantially earlier in their working lives, responsible and better-paid jobs with clear paths of promotion.

3. We must make schools and other agencies of learning more flexible, both in the ways they teach and in their organizational patterns, and at the same time preserve a challenging core of common learning.

4. We must design and install in most communities an improved system of transition from school to work, especially for the non-college-bound.

5. We must take advantage of the extensive knowledge we now have of model programs that motivate young people and encourage school success.

6. We must develop widespread opportunities for added-chance learning for school dropouts—in particular, by shifting the emphasis of programs under the Job Training Partnership Act to those young people who are most disadvantaged.

7. We must plan and launch a system of lifelong learning that, unlike present arrangements, is fair to young people who do not attend college.

8. We must expand opportunities for young people to serve their communities, with sponsorship from local, state, and private sources.

9. We must emphasize the need of young people for supportive adult relationships during the teenage years, since contemporary changes in the economy and in the family have tended to reduce such opportunities.

10. Finally, we must enlist the balanced participation of all potential sources of public and private funding to accomplish the goals above—in particular, by adding (through appropriate tax provisions) at least $5 billion annually in each of the next 10 years to the funding levels of successful federal programs.

In another context, David Hamburg, president of the Carnegie Corporation of New York, stated well our own conviction about these 10 recommendations. "We'll never know as much as we'd like, since evaluations are difficult and can direct resources away from the strategies themselves," Hamburg said, "but we know enough to act, and we can't afford not to act."

The Forgotten Half recommends to communities, families, employers, and the three levels of government concrete actions that would better serve American youth. These actions would also smooth America's passage through the critical final years of this century and send it, confident and strong, into the next century.

From The William T. Grant Foundation Commission on Work, Family and Citizenship, "The Forgotten Half: Non-College-Bound Youth in America," *Phi Delta Kappan*, 409–414, February 1988. Copyright © 1988 Phi Delta Kappa, Bloomington, IN. Reprinted by permission.

■ Questions for Discussion

1. How should national goals or objectives for education be developed? What individuals or groups should be involved? Why?

2. What are the three basic components of any curriculum as presented in this chapter? Why are they equally important?

3. What should be the role of the teacher in curriculum development?

4. How has the curriculum been affected by our pluralistic society?

5. What are the pros and cons of educational vouchers and tuition tax credits? Are you in favor of these concepts? Why?

■ Notes

1. Students may wish to read materials by such authors as John Dewey, George Beauchamp, B. Othaniel Smith, Arthur Lewis, Alice Miel, Glen Haas, J. Galen Saylor, William Ragan, J. Minor Gwynn, and William Alexander to gain more knowledge about experiences as related to curriculum.

2. Elwood P. Cubberly, *Public Education in the United States* (Boston: Houghton Mifflin, 1934), pp. 485–86.

3. Elwood P. Cubberly, *An Introduction to Education* (Boston: Houghton Mifflin, 1925), pp. 26–27.

4. See Horace M. Kallen, *Culture and Democracy in the United States* (New York: Boni and Liveright, 1924); and Horace M. Kalien, *Cultural Pluralism and the American Idea* (Philadelphia: University of Pennsylvania Press, 1956).

5. Madelon Stent, William R. Hazard, and Harry N. Rivlin, *Cultural Pluralism in Education.* Copyright 1973 by Fordham University. (Englewood Cliffs, N.J.: Prentice-Hall), p. vii.

6. National Council for the Accreditation of Teacher Education, *Standards for Accreditation of Teacher Education* (Washington, D.C.: National Council for Accreditation of Teacher Education, 1977), p. 4.

7. Robert L. Williams, *Cross-Cultural Education: Teaching Toward a Planetary Perspective* (Washington, D.C.: National Education Association, 1977), p. 10.

8. Committee for the White House Conference on Education, *A Report to the President* (Washington, D.C.: U.S. Government Printing Office, April 1956), pp. 91–92.

9. Benjamin S. Bloom, ed., *Taxonomy of Education Objectives* (New York: Longmans, Green, 1956), pp. 6–8.

10. National Commission on Excellence in Education, *A Nation at Risk: The Imperative for Educational Reform* (Washington, D.C.: Superintendent of Documents, U.S. Government Printing Office, 1983), p. 24.

11. Ibid.

12. Ibid., p. 25.

13. Ibid., p. 26.

14. Terrell H. Bell, "Parting Words of the 13th Man," *Phi Delta Kappan,* Vol. 69, No. 6 (February 1988), pp. 400–401.

15. Ibid., p. 403.

16. Excerpted from the "Text of Secretary Bennett's *James Madison High School,*" *Education Week,* Vol. VII, Numbers 15 and 16 (January 13, 1988), pp. 27–30.

17. Ibid., p. 27.

18. Ibid.

19. Ibid.

20. Ibid., p. 28.

21. Robert Rothman, "Plan Earns Qualified Praise," *Education Week,* Vol. VII, Numbers 15 and 16 (January 1988), p. 26.

22. William T. Grant Foundation Commission on Work, Family and Citizenship, "The Forgotten Half: Non-College-Bound Youth in America," *Phi Delta Kappan,* Vol. 69, No. 6 (February 1988), p. 410.

23. Ibid., pp. 411–412.

24. Ibid., p. 414.

25. William J. Bennett, *First Lessons: A Report on Elementary Education in America* (Washington, D.C.: U.S. Department of Education), 1986, p. 4.

26. Ibid., p. 39.

27. Ibid., p. 1.

28. Ibid., p. 2.

29. Deborah L. Gold, "Bennett Presents Model Plan for K–8 Curriculum." *Education Week,* Vol. VIII, No. 1 (September 7, 1988), pp. 1, 38.

30. Leroy V. Goodman, "A Bill of Rights for the Handicapped," *American Education* 12, no. 6, (July 1976): p. 6–7.

31. Ibid., p. 6.

32. H. Prentice Baptiste, Jr., Mira L. Baptiste, and Donna M. Gollnick, eds., *Multicultural Teacher Education: Preparing Educators to Provide Educational Equity,* vol. 1 (Washington, D.C.: American Association of Colleges for Teacher Education, 1980), pp. 44–72.

33. Ibid.

34. H. P. Baptiste, Jr., and M. Baptiste, *Developing the Multicultural Process in Classroom Instruction: Competencies for Teachers,* vol. 1 (Washington, D.C.: University Press of America, 1979).

35. Blake Rodman, "Diverse Group Urges Instruction in Democratic Values," *Education Week,* Vol. VI, No. 35, (May 27, 1987), p. 5.

36. Ibid., p. 5.

37. Ibid.

38. Ibid.

39. Alec Gallup and David Clark, "The 19th Annual Phi Delta Kappa/Gallup Poll of Public Attitudes Toward the Public Schools," *Phi Delta Kappan,* Vol. 69, No. 1 (September 1987), pp. 23–24.

40. Anne Lewis, "Public Schools Offer Vast Choices," *The School Administrator* (Arlington, VA: American Association of School Administrators, 1987), pp. 8, 10.

41. Ibid., pp. 10–11.

42. Gallup and Clark, p. 20.

43. James S. Catterall, *Tuition Tax Credits: Fact and Fiction* (Bloomington, IN: Phi Delta Kappa Educational Foundation, 1983), p. 8.

■ Selected References

Bell, Terrell. "Parting Words of the 13th Man," *Phi Delta Kappan* Vol. 69, no. 6 (February 1988):400–407.

Bennett, William J. *First Lessons: A Report on Elementary Education in America* (Washington, D.C.: U.S. Department of Education), 1986.

Catterall, James S. *Tuition Tax Credits: Facts and Fiction* (Bloomington, IN: Phi Delta Kappan Foundation), 1983.

Kibler, Robert J., et al. *Objectives for Instruction and Evaluation,* 2nd ed. Boston: Allyn and Bacon, 1981.

Nathan, Joe. "Results and Future Prospects of State Efforts to Increase Choice Among Schools," *Phi Delta Kappan* Vol. 69, no. 6 (June 1987):746–752.

Newmann, Fred M. "Can Depth Replace Coverage in the High School Curriculum," *Phi Delta Kappan* Vol. 69, no. 6 (January 1988):345–348.

Ravitch, Diane. *The Troubled Crusade: American Education, 1945–1980.* New York: Basic Books, 1983.

Rothman, Robert. "Bennett Offers High Schools' 'Ideal' Content," *Education Week* Vol. VII, nos. 15, 16 (January 13, 1988):1, 26–30.

Rubin, Louis J. *Artistry in Teaching.* New York: Random House, 1985.

Sizer, Theodore R. *Horace's Compromise: The Dilemma of an American High School.* Boston: Houghton Mifflin, 1984.

Chapter 14

Instructional Resources

Objectives

After studying this chapter, you should be able to:

- Chart a systematic approach to instructional technology, illustrating the elements of planning by teachers.

- Describe the use of media available for instructional purposes.

- Illustrate the various types of software and hardware utilized by teachers in the classroom.

- Discuss the learning resource center in relation to instruction and technology.

- Identify the role of the teacher in utilizing the learning resource center.

- Illustrate media center space relationships in new schools.

- Provide data indicating the influence of corporations as related to educational technology.

- Understand the importance of television in education.

- Include suggestions and opinionnaires for evaluating media programs.

- Explain the use of community resources and outdoor resources as part of the total learning environments.

Enrichment Experiences

The following activities will help you learn more about some of the important topics discussed in this chapter:

- Using the lists of learning center software and hardware given in this chapter, visit an elementary school and a high school for the purpose of evaluating the kinds of software and hardware available to the students. Determine the reasons for inadequacies you discover.

- Interview the personnel of the instructional technology staff of a school system. Obtain information about the kinds of services offered and the extent of their use in the classes.

- Select a desirable field trip for your teaching field in your community. Visit the location selected and develop the plans needed for the class visit.

- After reading several articles on the topic, prepare a paper that discusses the use of commercially prepared technological instructional systems (reading programs, computer-assisted instruction, Westinghouse PLAN, etc.).

- Visit a local travel agency to obtain various materials advertising foreign countries. Arrange these materials in a display for use in elementary and high school classroom instruction situations.

- Read additional literature about the use of television as an instructional tool.

This chapter will introduce you to the wide variety of instructional resources now available for teachers to use in the classroom. These resources include software such as books, printed materials, video tapes, slides, movies, filmstrips, audio tapes, and overhead transparencies. Some of the newer forms of instructional software include computer software and laser videodiscs. Educational hardware refers to the wide variety of machines that teachers can utilize. This chapter also discusses the school library, the learning resource center concept, and other ways that schools are organized to help teachers and students utilize technology. ■

Schools have undergone a great deal of change since the end of World War II. Extensive building programs and experiments with modular scheduling, team teaching, and educational television were brought about in response to the increasing numbers of students during the 1950s. The suddenly changing world of education was spurred by the launching of the Russian satellite Sputnik in 1957. Following Sputnik, the American public demanded improvements in school curriculums. The federal government enacted the National Defense Education Act of 1958, which expanded federal financial aid to education for programs to improve instruction. This act also provided funds to develop audiovisual media services and facilities. Modifications to this act culminated in several federal programs being enacted by the Eighty-ninth Congress. Federal research funds were granted for educational media research and for library research. Big businesses jumped into the competition for this new source of federal money for education and the pace quickened in the development of many kinds of instructional resources.

Title II of the Elementary and Secondary Education Act (ESEA) of 1965 provided federal funds for purchasing prepared materials for the schools. The funding formula of Title II enabled schools to add films, books, journals, learning kits, and other prepared materials which most schools would not otherwise have been able to purchase.

The growth of knowledge and the increase in the financial bases of the schools provided not only an additional stimulus to the growth of educational media, but also provided one of the greatest challenges to teaching. Teachers have more and more come to understand that learning is an active rather than a passive process. A contemporary view of the teacher's primary task is that of facilitator, planner, and director of varied active learning experiences. Teachers also serve as diagnosticians who must demonstrate their competencies for organizing instructional material and techniques geared to the achievement of teaching-learning objectives. Figure 14.1, called "the systematic approach of instructional technology," illustrates the elements of instructional planning which all teachers must carefully consider. This chapter emphasizes the materials and equipment (5), physical facilities (6), and evaluation and improvement (7) conditions of instructional technology as presented in the chart.

■ Use of Media

Educational media are the tools of the professional teacher. Educational media include printed, audio, visual, and real materials. Certainly, texts, graphs, pictures, newspapers, magazines, encyclopedias are educational media. Other important media include films, filmstrips, film loops,

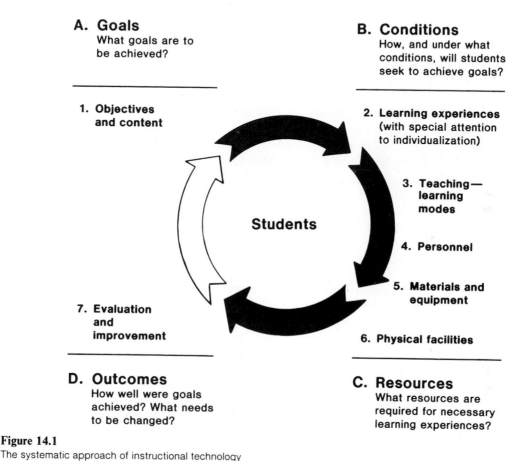

A. Goals
What goals are to
be achieved?

B. Conditions
How, and under what
conditions, will students
seek to achieve goals?

1. **Objectives
and content**

2. **Learning experiences**
(with special attention
to individualization)

3. **Teaching—
learning
modes**

4. **Personnel**

5. **Materials and
equipment**

Students

7. **Evaluation
and
improvement**

6. **Physical facilities**

D. Outcomes
How well were goals
achieved? What needs
to be changed?

C. Resources
What resources are
required for necessary
learning experiences?

■ **Figure 14.1**

The systematic approach of instructional technology

From James W. Brown, Richard B. Lewis, and Fred F. Harcleroad, *A-V Instruction: Technology, Media, and Methods.* Copyright © 1977 McGraw-Hill Publishing Company, New York, NY. Reprinted by permission.

slides, overhead and opaque projectors, commercial and educational television, records, audio tapes, cassette television tapes, the radio, and computer programs. Other things such as animal pets, insects, models of real things such as skeletons and machinery, simulation devices such as driver trainers and communication kits, as well as computers, desktop calculators, and other electronic devices are also important pieces of ware. The media list is ever-increasing to accompany the ever-increasing knowledge growth. Future teachers will be more and more media-minded as they assume their teaching tasks.

In the invention of the motion picture, I intended it—conceived it—as a contribution to education. I am disappointed that it has been turned into an entertainment toy.

Thomas Edison

Software

Software is the body of content materials that have generally been associated with the teacher. Software includes textbooks, paper and pencil, learning materials, workbooks, encyclopedias, newspapers, magazines, graphs, charts, posters, maps, globes, and various kinds of programmed materials. The kinds of materials found in typical school libraries are generally considered as software. Many software products, such as encyclopedias, book-of-the-month publications, and school-oriented papers and magazines, have been manufactured specifically for sale to the home. Software materials are very important to the teaching-learning process and continue to undergo changes in form and patterns of use. With recent attention being given to the so-called back-to-basics movement, printed test and measurement instruments, competency-based materials, and individualized instruction packets are additions to available software.

Title II of the Elementary and Secondary Education Act of 1965 provided millions of dollars to the states to improve educational quality through grants for the acquisition of school library resources. The three categories of materials eligible for acquisition under Title II included software and hardware of various kinds. The categories were school library resources (including audiovisual materials), textbooks, and other printed and published instructional materials. Most states allocated all or most of their Title II funds for school library resources, or for a combination of school library resources and other instructional materials. The expenditure of the original Title II appropriations firmed up the trend among schools to capitalize on the availability of new software and hardware in instruction.

Hardware

Only recently have we begun to make applications of technology and the products of technology to improve education. Such hardware products of technology include all kinds of mechanical and electronic devices that aid or supplement the software products. In many schools, movie projectors, filmstrip and slide projectors, record players, tape recorders, opaque projectors, overhead projectors, reading machines, computers, and other devices of an audiovisual nature are stored in a central location so that use of the equipment may be coordinated for the entire faculty. While much equipment usage takes place in learning centers in some schools, the classroom teacher most frequently uses the normal classroom as the laboratory where instructional hardware is used. Many schools employ a director of audiovisual education who is responsible for the maintenance of equipment and for the coordination of teacher use of equipment. The concept of audiovisual (AV) programs to enhance instruction is considered the forerunner for the thrust in the applications of technology to education.

Availability of federal, state, and local dollars for instructional materials and equipment provided impetus for the development of new businesses aimed at the instruction market. Likewise, reputable established businesses also brought into or joined in the production of instructional technology materials and equipment. After-the-fact evaluative efforts have in some instances revealed that not all of the very expensive technologically refined instructional systems have produced results originally hoped for. In some cases large sums of money were invested in equipment now considered obsolete. For example, some of the first videotape equipment was not only unwieldy in size, but was also very expensive. Newer electronic equipment is not only much easier to use, but is also less expensive. The application of microcomputers to classroom use is an exciting and cost efficient development. Computer power that was either too expensive or impractical a few years ago is now widely available and easy to use. Early claims for the use of computers in the classroom may not be living up to advance publicity. The next chapter is devoted entirely to the use of computers in education.

From all this rapid activity, there is now apparent a clamor for carefully evaluating the many materials and assorted equipment for the purpose of providing sharper tools for better learning.

■ The School Library

Most schools have a school library that houses books available for use by all classes and all students. In some schools, rather than have a central library, books particularly suited to a subject or grade level have been placed into each classroom. School officials disagree about the best way to house books and other print material in a way that will make them conveniently available to students. However, nearly all educators agree that books and various other types of print material are extremely valuable instructional resources and must be made available to students at all levels and in all subjects.

Figure 14.2 shows the number of books held by public school libraries, according to school size.

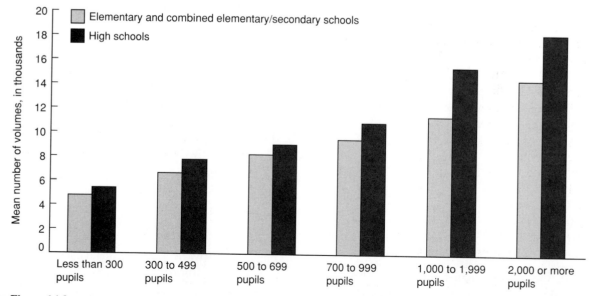

■ Figure 14.2

Volumes held by public school libraries, by size of school and level of education: Fall 1985

Source: U.S. Department of Education, Center for Education Statistics, "National Survey of Public and Private School Libraries and Media Centers, 1985."

Research Finding

13

The use of libraries enhances reading skills and encourages independent learning.

Research has shown that participating in library programs reinforces children's skills and interest in reading. Summer reading programs offered by public libraries, for example, reinforce reading skills learned during the school year. Library programs for preschool children encourage children's interest in learning to read. Both types of programs provide many opportunities for reading, listening, and viewing materials.

Public and school libraries can enhance reading instruction by offering literature-based activities that stress the enjoyment of reading as well as reading skills. Hearing stories and participating in such activities help young children want to learn to read. These programs help children become more aware of the iterary and cultural heritage that is necessary to help them understand much of what they will read and hear as they grow up.

Use of both public and school libraries encourages students to go beyond their textbooks to locate, explore, evaluate and use ideas and information that enhance classroom instruction.

Heyns, B. (1978). *Summer Learning and the Effects of Schooling.* New York: Academic Press.

Loertscher, D., et al. (1986). *Research Report: School Library Media Services in 209 Schools Identified as Exemplary by the U.S. Department of Education.* Unpublished report sponsored by the U.S. Department of Education, Washington, D.C.

Perry, K. (Summer, 1980). "Research in Children's Services in Public Libraries: A Group Project in North Carolina." *Public Libraries.* Vol. 19, pp. 58–60.

Source: *What Works: Research About Teaching and Learning.* Washington, DC: U.S. Department of Education, 1987, page 60.

As one might expect, this figure shows that larger schools tend to have more books in their libraries than do small schools and that high schools tend to have more books than elementary schools.

■ Learning Resource Centers

Existing public school libraries have been criticized severely by various study groups. In 1961, the National Committee for Support of the Public Schools reported that (a) more than 10 million children go to public schools having no libraries, and (b) more than half of all public schools have no library. Such criticism has generated renewed interest in the directions school libraries ought to be taking in order to meet the needs of today's pupils. The development of new instructional technology remains strong, with particular emphasis on software. The traditional concept of the public school library has matured into a concept of a total learning resource center, in which the various mediaware are arranged in a common setting wherein space is provided and specifically allocated for individual and small group usage.

Equipment	Educational Media for Learning	
Record players, tape recorders, radios	Textbooks	Stereographics
Slide and flimstrip projectors and viewers	Supplementary books	Maps, globes
Overhead projectors	Reference books, encyclopedias	Graphs, charts, diagrams
Motion-picture projectors and viewers	Magazines, newspapers	Posters
Television receivers	Documents, clippings	Cartoons
Video-tape recorders, players, viewers	Duplicated materials	Puppets
Teaching machines	Programmed materials	Models, mockups
Computer terminals and print and image	(self-instruction)	Collections, specimens
reproducers	Motion-picture films	Flannel-board materials
Electronic laboratories: audio/video/access	Television programs	Magnetic-board materials
and interaction devices	Radio programs	Chalkboard materials
Telephone with or without other media	Recordings (tape and disk)	Construction materials
accessories	Flat pictures	Drawing materials
Microimage sytems—microfilm, microcard,	Drawings and paintings	Display materials
microfiche	Slides and transparencies	Multi-media kits
Copying equipment and duplicators	Filmstrips	
Cameras—still and motion	Microfilms, microcards	

■ **Figure 14.3**

Learning resource center equipment

From James W. Brown, Richard B. Lewis, and Fred F. Harcleroad, *A-V Instruction: Technology, Media, and Methods*, 4th ed. Copyright © 1977 McGraw-Hill Publishing Company, New York, NY. Reprinted by permission.

Individual study carrels have their own lighting controls and electrical outlets. Small groups can have access to specific resource centers such as math, science, and computer centers. Comfortable furniture, small study desks, and carpeting have replaced obsolete furnishings in these modern learning resource centers. The learning resource center concept demands a high level of utilization necessitating flexible schedule arrangements to permit students time to use the center.

The creation of a learning resource center is not an attempt to do away with the school library. Instead, it attempts to utilize the typical materials of the library and supplement them with additional software and hardware instructional media now available to the teacher. As children become involved in the learning process at different rates of growth, they have a need to pursue learning on an individual basis and also in small group activities. The teacher may now free the learner to go to a center where materials are provided for individual and small group learning. The center should be equipped with such equipment for learning (hardware), and educational media for learning (software), as shown in figure 14.3.

Well-developed learning resource centers allow students access to all media that teachers have access to. In addition, computer terminals permit students to utilize data bases stored by the computers. Interlibrary loans expand the number of print materials available to students everywhere. Availability of the newest learning materials and equipment is not only limited by the financial conditions of respective public school districts, but also by the lack of creativity and courage by the responsible teachers, administrators, and board members of those districts.

But whatever they call it, and wherever they put it, public schools everywhere are going to have to find space for reducing, retaining, reproducing and displaying the incredible mountain of information that new technology now makes available. Sooner than we think, a public school without such facilities will be about as educationally effective as a log without Mark Hopkins there on the end.

Aaron Cohodes

Teacher and the Resource Center

From the preceding general description it appears that the teaching task has been greatly simplified. On the contrary, the teacher must now come face to face with issues in the curriculum that have usually been reserved for administrators, supervisors, and the like. The learning resource center is little more than an administratively planned learning area, and as such its purpose is no different than that of the classroom. Although it holds promise in its potential for individualized learning, it must for the greater part be planned and developed by teachers. It should be supplied with materials that teachers have selected and developed through their experiences with children. Many of the hastily developed program series that were sold by commercial publishers anxious to "get on the bandwagon" proved to be too limiting in application. Increasing numbers of teachers clamor for greater selectivity in making more incisive the thrust and use of prepared materials. Similarly, as professional groups and other agencies increase their dealings with new technology, greater demand is made for specialized materials for the various areas of instruction (driver education, medical programs, technical trades, and the academic disciplines). The production of these materials has added a new dimension to the publishing enterprise.

This type of industrial movement has placed an ever greater responsibility on the teacher working in curriculum. Among the many splendid products on the market today there also may be found hastily developed and poorly researched materials that purport to provide teachers with "the answer" to learning problems. As a result, teachers have the special task of discarding these inferior or worthless programs and adapting those which are useful to the specific situation encountered by each. Of a more highly critical nature, teachers should, in addition to the culling of manufactured materials that may be used for the learning process, continue to develop their own new materials in light of their experience with the learners.

Media Center Space Relationships

The impact that the media center (resource center) concept has had on the planning for a middle school is reflected in figure 14.4. This sketch by Perkins & Will, Chicago (one of the nation's most renowned firms of architects, engineers, planners, and interior designers of school buildings), was from a study for a new middle school in California in which the media center is proposed as the hub of the new building. The South Woodbridge Middle School media center was proposed to be physically and visually at the center of the two-story academic building. The media center is at a midlevel with a ramp going up a half level to the "generalized learning areas," and a ramp going down a half level to the "specialized learning areas." The generalized learning areas are clustered in groups of four to encourage the schools-within-a-school concept. Considering current attention to microcomputers and other electronic equipment designed for classroom instruction, this model places the primary emphasis on software.

St. Charles (Illinois) High School is a relatively new school built to include the latest in instructional media resources. As with the Irvine, California, middle school model (Figure 14.4), the St. Charles High School resource center (Figure 14.5), which serves 2,400 students in

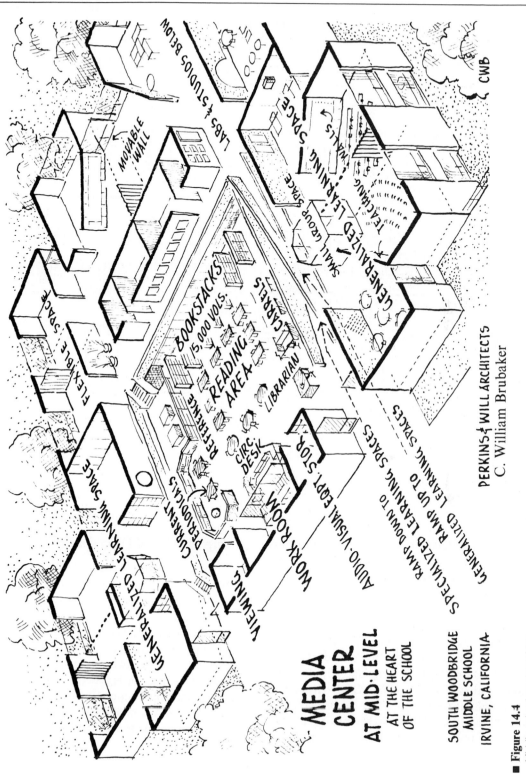

Figure 14.4
Middle school model (1981)

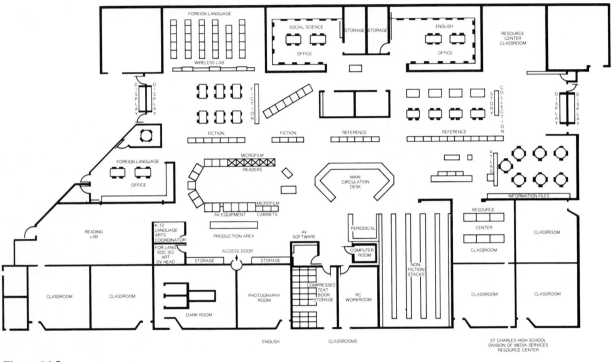

■ Figure 14.5
High school resource center

grades 9–12, places the main focus on print materials. The collection includes 22,000 volumes of books, 125 magazine titles, 1,700 audiovisual items, and 1,200 information files. Special features of this 15,300-square-foot resource center space includes darkroom and graphic arts production areas, foreign language laboratory, compressed textbook storage area, a local history collection, and foreign language, English, and social studies teacher's offices. Of particular note is the small size of the computer room. This school district has the financial resources to upgrade computer resources and is now considering ways to do so.

■ Corporations and Educational Technology

Large sums of money have been invested by private business and by federal acts during the past few years for modifying, adapting, and producing hardware for specific classroom use. The effect of this emphasis has been the expanding and upgrading of the audiovisual program concept. The impact of software and hardware development has brought to focus the systems approach to instruction. In effect, the systems approach to instruction brings together the audiovisual program, the school library, and school personnel.

Recently, the nation has witnessed vast mergers of publishing companies, research bureaus, and manufacturers. Seeing a growing need for all kinds of educational software and hardware, it appears that these corporations have struck a bonanza. American businesses operate on the profit motive and market research indicates new profit margins in instructional materials. Capitalizing on a national concern for increased educational output, these corporations now have the capacity to research, develop, produce, and market an endless variety of educational software and hardware which may be used in the learning process. The knowledge explosion, increasing rates of mobility, the quest for more knowledge in a shorter time, the complex pressures of providing individualized educational opportunity for all citizens, and the educational establishment's seeming inability to direct educational change effectively have all contributed to the birth of these corporations.

■ Instructional Television

Television has now become one of the major teaching aids available in most school districts. The hardware necessary to incorporate television into school programming is relatively economical. A VCR recorder/playback is available for $200, a color monitor is available for $300, and videotapes are one of the cheapest forms of media available to schools. This means that it is no more expensive for a school to acquire what is necessary to utilize television in the classroom than it is to buy one new 16mm movie projector. Furthermore, a new 16mm movie sells for hundreds of dollars whereas a new videotape can be purchased for about fifty dollars.

Furthermore, television programs can be viewed live in the classrooms or these programs can be videotaped for later use. Keeping in mind the wealth of television programs now on the airwaves, teachers should be able to capitalize on television as a very valuable and timely instructional aid.

Excellent lightweight economical video cameras are also now within the price range of most school districts. A video camera can be obtained for approximately $1,000 which will allow teachers and students to create their own videotapes right in the school. This video production opens up an entire new mode of learning to students. An example, for instance, might be a speech class where, as the students are delivering their speeches, they can be videotaped for playback later. The students will learn a great deal about improving their speaking technique by watching themselves on the videotape. Yet another example might be in a science classroom where a video camera can zoom in on an experiment and enlarge the view on television sets so that all of the students in the science room can readily see what is taking place. One last example of the potential use of videotaping equipment in the schools might be related to physical education wherein the teacher is attempting to help students learn psychomotor skills. By videotaping each student practicing a given skill and then allowing the students to see themselves in action, students are likely to be able to develop the skills more quickly. In fact, every creative teacher, no matter what subject or grade level they are teaching, could profitably utilize videotapes as an effective teaching aid. All teachers need to become proficient with the use of television equipment if they are to utilize the latest technology in their classrooms.

Videodiscs and TV monitors in classrooms are effective teaching aids.

■ Laser Videodiscs

Videodiscs represent an exciting new teaching aid. They are relatively cheap, they are very durable, they play as easily as a phonograph record, and they store an absolutely amazing amount of video content. This technology is relatively new and is unfamiliar to many educators at this time. Media specialists predict that videodiscs will eventually become the number one form of media in our school systems. It is very likely that they will replace nearly all forms of movie films, slides, and other forms of video. A videodisc can be used to replace virtually all moving and still forms of visuals. All the teacher needs to utilize this exciting new form of media is a videodisc player and a television monitor. The videodisc players are relatively inexpensive, ranging from $200 to $1500. As they become more commonly used, it is anticipated that they will become more economical.

There are already several thousand educational videodiscs available on the market. It is anticipated that this number will increase very rapidly. The average videodisc cost is only approximately $25 to $35 which is much more economical than the typical 16mm film for other media formats. School systems and teachers should become familiar with this exciting new teaching aid and make plans for incorporating it into the resources made available in their school districts.

■ Evaluating Media Programs

Most school systems have joined the new technology swing in support of instruction for several reasons. In some communities where funds were plentiful, the purchase and utilization of media programs were quickly accomplished as the contemporary thing to do. Federal funds enabled other communities to make expenditures for media programs that were formerly too expensive. The best schools approached the tasks related to the development of media programs on the basis of explicitly stated goals and objectives as related to desired instructional outcomes. Whatever the compelling forces in the development of the various school media programs, media personnel through their professional organization (Association for Educational Communications and Technology) called for the development of instruments that could be used by school personnel in evaluating media programs. Following two years of diligent committee work, the Association for Educational Communications and Technology (AECT) published a draft edition booklet devised especially for field testing.[1] Evaluation instruments are organized into seven sections to provide for the evaluation of those facets of the overall school district related to the media program: School System Profile and Budget, Services, Personnel, Physical Facilities, Collection, Student and Teacher Opinionnaires, and Summary Narrative.

Of particular importance to the prospective teacher are the Student and Teacher Opinionnaires. The rationale for the Student Opinionnaire suggests:

> Students are set forth as the chief reason for the existence of media programs in today's schools. The effectiveness of a media program is, therefore, not just indicated by the materials and equipment available, the dollars spent, and the number of persons employed, but also by the reactions of the clientele served. Are the students using the media center? To what extent? How do they rate the services rendered? The student opinionnaire is included in this instrument to gain answers to questions such as these and to other questions.[2]

A student opinionnaire designed to help evaluate media can be completed simply by placing a check mark in the appropriate box of the five-part scale indicated at the top of the opinionnaire. A composite tabulation of the responses of students would provide invaluable information to the teacher who strives to best utilize the available media materials.

In the evaluation of the media program, a teacher opinionnaire is central to the total evaluation process. The rationale for the teacher instrument stresses the role of the teacher as the architect and facilitator of learning:

> Although the student is always the chief recipient of the media center services, the teacher remains as the architect and facilitator of learning. Are teachers using the media center? What are their opinions concerning the sevices provided? How do they perceive the administrative support of the program? Teachers' reactions to the types, quantity and quality of media center services are needed to properly assess the contributions of the media center to the total instructional program.[3]

The teacher opinionnaire is completed in the same fashion as the student opinionnaire by the mere placing of a check mark in the appropriate box following each statement. Whether or not the beginning teacher, or the experienced teacher for that matter, has had explicit preparation in the

Community resources may be used to supplement the learning activities of schools.

utilization of media programs in support of classroom practice, each teacher would find considerable direction from the careful analysis of the specific items of the student and teacher opinionnaires.

■ Community Resources

More than three-fourths of our population now live either in the central city areas or in the suburbs of those areas. Improved transportation facilities have expanded the availability of community resources for school use. Students now have increased opportunities to learn about many things in their own communities. Many school boards, school administrators, and creative teachers are finding different ways to utilize community resources to supplement the learning activities of the schools.

Considerable education planning is a prerequisite to the proper utilization of community resources. Educators ought to carefully develop community resource guides for the purpose of identifying and describing available educational resources, including community resource persons. Proper utilization of community resources for educational field trips requires preliminary planning that considers certain educational criteria for field trips. Finding and using resource persons, either at their place of work or in the classroom, also requires careful planning for coordinating the contributions of the resource person with the sequence of work students are doing in the classroom.

Obviously, the scope of available community resources is prescribed to a large measure by the nature of the community. However, every school community, large or small, has community resources at its disposal.

■ Outdoor Education

The concept of outdoor education has gained considerable acceptance during the last few years. Programs of outdoor education are increasing in popularity at all levels of the school organization. The simple essence of the outdoor education concept deals with activity and study in an outdoor setting. In some areas, the community resources of agencies such as Boy Scouts and Girl Scouts, YMCA and YWCA, churches, private clubs, and service organizations are utilized in providing outdoor facilities for educational programs sponsored by the local schools. With continued acceptance of the concept, the trend has been toward the development of especially designed and planned outdoor education facilities that are maintained as cooperative ventures among several school districts. In this fashion, the cooperating districts would have at their disposal the services of professionally trained outdoor education personnel hired on a full-time basis. Classroom teachers involved in outdoor education programs would then typically accompany their students on the overnight expeditions to the outdoor education facility.

Many teacher-preparation programs have built into their programs professional laboratory experiences with children in an outdoor setting. For example, the Lorado Taft Campus in Oregon, Illinois, is the outdoor education extension of Northern Illinois University, which is located in DeKalb, Illinois, approximately forty miles away. The elementary teacher-preparation program of the university requires periods of several days to be spent at the outdoor education facility by both junior and senior students. Other teacher education programs that require senior year experiences at the outdoor education facility are in special education, women's physical education,

and industry and technology. The university also offers a master's degree program in Outdoor Education, which leads to the supervision and administration endorsements required by Illinois state law for directors of outdoor education facilities.

Another reason for the growing acceptance rate for outdoor education is its successful implementation in other nations. The international influence of outdoor education is apparent in the field study centers of Great Britain, the country schools in Germany, and the schools of the snow in the French Alps. Australia and Japan are leaders in the outdoor education movement in their part of the world. One of the noticeable program trends, especially on the international scene, is the rapid development of so-called outward bound schools. Such schools usually pit the physical prowess of the participants against the elements of nature. Thus, emphasis on physical survival and adventure experiences are basic to these programs.

■ Summary

This chapter has reviewed some of the important topics related to instructional resources including the general use of educational media in our schools; the distinction between software which is generally printed material and supplies, and hardware which usually refers to pieces of equipment used in our schools; the importance of school libraries; the evolving learning resource center concept; the interest of private enterprise in marketing their products to educators; instructional television; laser videodiscs; how educators can evaluate media programs; the use of community resources by teachers; and the important emerging field of outdoor education.

People preparing for educational careers should obviously seize the opportunity to become familiar with the wide range of instructional resources that are now available for use in our schools. If teachers are to maximize learning for their students, they must not only know about the existence of these resources but also be proficient in their use.

Point of View

■

Laser videodiscs represent one of the newest forms of technology available for use in the classroom. The following article by Royal Van Horn explains the potential that this new device has for educational use. Mr. Van Horn believes that laser videodiscs hold great potential for education. He points out that they are economic and easy to use. He strongly recommends that educators should become familiar with this new, exciting instructional device.

Laser Videodiscs in Education: Endless Possibilities

Royal Van Horn

When something as exciting and revolutionary as laser videodisc technology comes along, it's hard to believe that so many teachers, administrators, and librarians could totally ignore it. Perhaps educators have been too busy "computerizing" schools to pay attention to this technology. Perhaps they don't know that the discs are 10 to 20 times cheaper than film and that they last virtually forever. Perhaps they believe laser videodiscs are an untried or experimental technology. Or maybe they think there are too few good discs available. Whatever the explanation, the response of most educators has definitely been shortsighted.

Laser videodisc technology was first made available to the public in 1978 by MCA DiscoVision. Today, some of the world's largest electronics firms—Sony, Hitachi, Pioneer, and Philips—market videodisc players that range in price from $250 to $1,500.[1]

About 2,500 prerecorded videodiscs are currently available on a variety of topics, and the number is increasing daily.[2] Most major film producers, including Walt Disney, produce and distribute discs, and a number of firms even specialize in educational discs.[3] Moreover, the average disc costs only $30, half the price of a prerecorded videotape and one-tenth the price of a 16mm film. Videodiscs are as easy to play as phonograph records, and, because nothing touches the playing surface of the disc except a beam of light, they should last indefinitely.

Considering all these pluses, it is difficult to explain why educators have not embraced this technology. Perhaps they have simply not considered the many applications of videodiscs.

■ Film Libraries

Film libraries should immediately become videodisc libraries. This is perhaps the most obvious and beneficial application of videodisc technology. Film is an archaic medium with sprocket holes that tear and leaders that break. Projectors for 16mm films are mechanical contraptions with belts, pulleys, and gears. This makes them highly unreliable. Projectors often "lose their loop," and the film must be periodically cleaned and lubricated. Moreover, 16mm films typically range in price from $250 to more than $700, and their life expectancy under heavy use is short. Clearly film is an outdated medium.

Videodiscs, on the other hand, are easy to play, never need rewinding or maintenance, and do not wear out. The total cost of a videodisc player and monitor is roughly equal to the price of a 16mm projector. Because videodisc players are not mechanical, they typically operate more than 4,000 hours before they need repair.

The biggest difference between films and videodiscs, however, is the cost of the media. The average cost of a videodisc is about 10% that of the average film. By converting to videodiscs, a school could increase the number of titles in its library tenfold. Titles that once were available only on film are rapidly becoming available on discs, and some titles are available only on discs.

Using prerecorded videodiscs in schools is just as legal as using 16mm films. Many companies that rent and sell educational films would like educators to believe otherwise. But this "hoax" must not be allowed to continue. The following excerpt from the federal copyright statutes is clear.

Notwithstanding the provisions of section 106, the following are not infringements of copyright:
(1) perfomance or display of a work by instructors or pupils in the course of face-to-face teaching activities of a nonprofit educational institution, unless, in the case of a motion picture or other audiovisual work, the performance, or the display of individual images, is given by means of a copy that was not lawfully made under this title, and that the person responsible for the performance knew or had reason to believe was not lawfully made. . . .[4]

■ School Libraries

Since most videodiscs cost little more than library books (and usually less than filmstrips), a school library can develop a sizable collection of titles. For $1,000 (about the cost of a typical microcomputer), a school could purchase one $300 player and $600 worth of discs. At $30 each, this amount would buy 20 titles. A nice "starter collection" of discs for an elementary school might include titles such as *The First National Kidisc, Fun and Games, Picture Postcards from Space, Beauty and the Beast, Charlotte's Web, Home Planetarium, Maze Mania, Alice in Wonderland, The Living Desert, Pinocchio, Dumbo, The Incredible Storydisc, Gardening at Home, The History Disquiz, 20,000 Leagues Under the Sea, Jack and the Bean Stalk, Mousercise, The Sword in the Stone, The Nutcracker,* and *Snow White.*

When the library's collection of discs is large enough, students could be allowed to check them out for overnight use. The possibility of redefining homework to include "videowork" is certainly intriguing. The school could even lend a disc player to students who did not have access to one at home.

■ Video Glossaries

There are a growing number of discs that can be classified as "video glossaries." Such discs contain large collections of still pictures or "slides." One side of a videodisc can hold 54,000 pictures, and a good disc player can access and display any one of these pictures in two seconds. One simply enters the number of a picture, and two seconds later it appears on the television screen. For a modest cost, a school could easily put together a collection of over a million such pictures. Here are a few examples of video glossaries: *National Gallery of Art,* 1,645 images; *Van Gogh: A Portrait in Two Parts,* 600 images; *BioScience* disc, 6,000 images; *National Air & Space Museum Archival Discs,* 50,000 images per disc; the *Louvre* disc, 1,500 images; *Space Discs,* approximately 10,000 images per disc; *Space Archive* discs, approximately 1,500 images per disc; the *Vancouver* disc, 21,000 images.

Thus video glossary discs could render a library's "vertical file" outdated. Moreover, these purchases would represent a considerable savings over other media, since 35mm slides cost anywhere from $2 to $3 apiece.

■ Discs in Classrooms

The discs mentioned above have many obvious classroom applications, but several specific discs deserve mention. The *KnowledgeDisc* from Grolier and Activenture is the first disc-based encyclopedia. It contains 32,000 entries with more than nine million words—the equivalent of a 20-volume encyclopedia on a single disc. Children seem to enjoy using this alternative to printed encyclopedias.

The *BioScience* disc, with its 6,000 still images of plants and animals classified taxonomically, belongs in every biology/life science classroom. A teacher need only write the frame numbers of the pictures to be used on the daily lesson plan. Nearly all the visuals a teacher would ever need are on this disc and its companion, *Life Cycles*.

History teachers would enjoy using the *History Disquiz*. It contains 45 historically significant newsreel film clips and several thousand "trivia" questions about them. At $9.98 that's less than 25 cents per film clip.

Teachers of earth and space science, as well as others, would find the 12 or so *Space Discs* invaluable. These discs are like having instant access to the visual libraries of NASA and the Jet Propulsion Laboratory.

Often the availability of a single videodisc can justify the purchase of a player and monitor for use in a single course. The *BioScience* disc is a good example. If purchased as 35mm slides, this disc's collection of images could cost as much as $20,000. Even though it costs $500, this disc is easy to justify at roughly nine cents an image.

Never before in the history of education have we had such great potential to alter conventional methods. Businesses have their data processing, scholars have their references, and now educators can have their disc numbers and frame numbers. Here is a brief description of how this change could revolutionize education.

Imagine a U.S. history classroom in the secondary school equipped with a videodisc player that is connected to a conventional 25-inch television set. The following are a few of the discs available for use in that classroom: nine *Victory at Sea* discs (26 episodes of this classic documentary); six *Vietnam* discs (a more recent PBS documentary); five *World at War* discs (a classic documentary series); one *Statue of Liberty* disc (covering its early days to the present); four *America & the World Since World War II* discs (from an ABC news special covering 1945 through 1985); one *History Disquiz* (covering various subjects); one *Vancouver* disc (21,000 archival photos, from 1872–1983); and three *National Air and Space Museum* discs (150,000 photos).

Each lesson plan for this history course would have such numbers as No. 8, 16232, 23344–31000 written all over it. The numbers tell the teacher to use disc number eight, still picture number 16232, and the motion sequence from frame 23344 to frame 31000. By using the wireless infrared remote controller that comes with the disc player, the teacher could stand at the back of the room and start and stop the disc player at will.

Still pictures and motion sequences from various discs have been carefully chosen to make history come alive. When immigrants are discussed, the *Vancouver* discs and the *Statue of Liberty* discs are used. The subject of war—its causes, famous battles, personalities, and the like—could be illustrated from the perspective of three major documentary series. The archival discs make comparisons over the last 100 years a simple process. And, always close at hand, the teacher has a list of the frame numbers of still pictures and motion sequences depicting several hundred historically significant individuals. For example, Martin Luther King's famous "We shall overcome" speech can be found on the *History Disquiz* disc, starting at frame number 7753 and ending at frame number 9097.

Although the application I have described is fictitious, the discs are not. All the discs in this example are currently available, and many sell for as little as $10 each. It is even possible to create a database on a microcomputer that cross-references course topics and disc contents. Then, simply typing "King, Martin" will cause the classroom microcomputer to list all still frames and motion sequences in the classroom collection of discs that include information on Rev. King.

■ CAVI

Many uses for videodiscs are standalone applications. That is, they require only a videodisc player and a monitor. But a videodisc player can also be used as a "computer peripheral." Most schools already own microcomputers; connecting one to a disc player is a simple matter. When that connection is made, a new world of instruction, known as computer-assisted videodisc instruction (CAVI), is created. This new medium combines slides, television, and stereo with computer programming.

To fully comprehend the potential of CAVI, it is necessary to let the mind wander. Imagine creating a videodisc that contained all the slides, spoken explanations, sounds, and motion sequences necessary to illustrate every word and concept in the second-grade reading program. Suppose it took 10,000 pictures, ninety-six 15-second film clips, 45 minutes of spoken explanations, and 15 minutes of music. All of this and more will fit on one side of one videodisc.

Next, imagine that a computer program is written that presents the second-grade reading program on the computer screen. Every time a student has trouble with a new word or concept, pressing the help button on the keyboard immediately causes the videodisc player to access the appropriate explanation from the disc and display it on the screen. The explanation might be any of the still pictures, a short film clip, or an oral explanation. While the disc player was providing these materials, the computer could be analyzing the student's performance, looking for errors in the student's work, or recording performance data. All diagnostic and summative testing, as well as all record keeping, could be done by the computer.

Other examples of CAVI might include using either the *Louvre* disc or the *National Gallery of Art* disc in an art appreciation or art history program. The amount of visual material on either of these two discs is immense. The 45 newsreel film clips on the *History Disquiz* disc could provide the visuals for an excellent CAVI program on recent U.S. history. The possibilities are endless.

The potential of computer-assisted videodisc instruction has not gone unnoticed by industry and the military. IBM and Wang, to cite but two examples, make extensive use of this medium for in-house training programs. The military is investing heavily in this technology and has found it a convenient, cost-effective way to build simulators. Consider an interesting example. To allow a tank gunner to fire just one live round of ammunition costs about $7,000. A computer-videodisc simulator allows unlimited target practice. Gunners become much better marksmen when bullets don't cost $7,000 each. It has been said that, within two years, all military training programs will be produced on videodiscs.

Several dozen excellent CAVI programs are commercially available, and educators with even a small amount of programming experience are beginning to create their own CAVI programs. It is much easier to command the disc player to show a visual than it is to write a computer program that creates one from scratch. For example, to show a portion of video from a computer program written in BASIC, all a teacher needs to do is type: PRINT D$; "VIDEO 3200,3750." This line commands the disc player to play from frame 3200 to frame 3750—about 18 seconds of video.

■ Image Processing

As if videodisc technology and CAVI weren't enough for educators to learn to use productively, a whole new world called "image processing" is opening up. Image processing promises to be to education what data processing is to business.

As I discussed above, a videodisc player can be used in a stand-alone fashion or as a computer peripheral. It can also be used as a computer "input device." To use a videodisc player as a computer input device, a "video capture board" is needed. (This device is also called a "video digitizer" or a "frame grabber.") Whatever it is called, a video capture board is simply a device that changes the output of the videodisc player (that is, a picture) into a digital signal that can be stored in a computer's memory. Once a videodisc picture has been "digitized" and resides in a microcomputer's memory, the picture can be processed. Video capture boards and associated software are available from about $400.[5] Data processing implies manipulating data; image processing implies manipulating images. Once an image resides in computer memory it can be stored on a diskette, displayed on a monitor, printed, or processed—that is, changed. Images can be enlarged, reduced, captioned, inverted left to right, placed next to other images, overlaid with graphics, colored, sectioned, or added to other images. Practically anything one wants to do to an image can be done.

Image processing doesn't sound all that revolutionary until one realizes that 20 videodiscs contain more than a million images. Educators who are now using videodisc technology will soon begin to experiment with this new application, but it is too early to foresee the many creative applications that they will find for image processing.

■ Some Misconceptions

Misconceptions abound regarding laser videodisc technology. Many educators wonder why they should buy videodisc players when they can't be used to record. Why not simply invest in videotapes and a portable recorder?

There are three things that could be done with videotape recorders. First, schools could produce their own programs. But most schools are not equipped to do so, and it is much more difficult and expensive than it might seem. (Experts say it costs between $3,000 and $9,000 per finished minute to produce high-quality video.) Second, broadcast programming could be recorded off the air, but there are many legal problems associated with doing this. Third, schools could purchase prerecorded videotapes. However, videotapes cost more than videodiscs, they wear every time they are used, and they are a linear medium. Finding a particular portion of video on a tape is difficult, but on discs, thanks to frame numbers, it's nearly instantaneous.

Videodiscs also have much higher video and audio fidelity than videotapes. This difference is often not perceptible when a small monitor or home television set is used. But when a large classroom-size monitor or projection television set is used, the difference is immediately apparent. Since educators will often want a large number of people to see the same program, videodiscs are the clear choice.

Many people claim that there are not enough good educational discs available to justify buying disc players. Today there are about 150 discs available that have been produced especially for education, and the number is increasing by one or two a week. In addition, there are about 100 medical videodiscs that have applications in health, life science, and biology classes. Many of the 2,500 popularly available discs also have educational value. For example, the *Nutcracker* wasn't designed to be an educational disc, but many schools could use it as such.

Disc players are often perceived as exotic machines that would be difficult to maintain or to have repaired. The word "laser" adds to this high-tech mystique. The two disc players that I have used for the last five years have yet to need repair, even though they frequently ride in the baggage compartments of airplanes. Most disc players have a 5,000-hour "mean time before failure" and are easy to get repaired once broken. Many manufacturers even inscribe a toll-free telephone number on their players to make finding the nearest repair facility more convenient.

Videodiscs could be called "records that play television." Like records, they are inexpensive and easy to use. Unlike records, they can contain as many as 54,000 slides or 30 minutes of television, and they last almost forever. Educators at all levels need to become familiar with this new technology, and several excellent vehicles exist for doing this, including regularly scheduled conferences and symposia sponsored by the Nebraska Videodisc Design/Production Group and the Society for Applied Learning Technology.[6]

Perhaps the technology is still "too new" for educators to embrace it enthusiastically. But purchasing a player and a few discs to evaluate its potential would seem the wise course. In the near future, a consortium of schools could be formed to promote applications of videodisc technology. Produced in mass, discs could be sold for as little as $5 to $10 each, and players could be purchased for as little as $200. Isn't it about time that videodiscs came to school?

1. Videodisc players on the low end of this range are often new but "out of production." Frequently, they do not come with remote controllers. Some cannot be linked to a microcomputer. Players at the upper end of this range are newer models with vary fast "frame search" times (less than two seconds). Often these top-of-the-line players have internal microprocessors and serial interfaces for convenient connection to computers. The average player probably costs about $500.

2. Laser videodiscs mentioned in this article are available from the following sources: The Instant Replay, 479 Winter St., Waltham, MA 02154-1216; Pioneer Video, 200 W. Grand Ave., Montvale, NJ 07045; and VideoDiscovery, P.O. Box 85877, Seattle, WA 98145-1878. (The Instant Replay's 1986 catalog lists 2,200 discs.)

3. Directories of educational videodiscs are available from: The Minnesota Educational Computing Consortium, 3490 Lexington Ave. N., St. Paul, MN 55126; Systems Impact, Inc., 2084 N. 1200 E. Logan, UT 84321: and Ztek Co., 1330 S. Third St., Louisville, KY 40201.

4. *United States Code, 1982 Edition, Title 17. Copyrights* Section 110(1), p. 37.

5. The following companies advertise inexpensive video digitizer boards: Commodore Computers: Quadram, Inc.: Chorus Data Systems; and AST Research.

6. Addresses for these organizations are: Nebraska Videodisc Design Production Group, KUON TV. University of Nebraska, P.O. Box 83111, Lincoln, NE 68501: and Society for Applied Learning Technology, 50 Culpeper St., Warrenton, VA 22186.

From: Royal Van Horn, "Laser Videodiscs in Education: Endless Possibilities," *Phi Delta Kappan* 696–700, May 1987. Copyright © 1987 Phi Delta Kappa, Bloomington, IN. Reprinted by permission of the author.

■ Questions for Discussion

1. How could uses of new educational media aid in solving some of the school problems arising from the great range of abilities and varied backgrounds among students?

2. Discuss the educational value of television in the classroom. Can schools afford to utilize new television technology such as laser videodiscs?

3. Do you believe that school districts should spend additional money to send students outside the school building for outdoor education experiences? If outdoor education trips require overnight lodging, is it reasonable to require classroom teachers to accompany their classes?

4. How would you use educational television and commercial television as teaching resources? Overhead projectors?

5. List the changes in school-building construction that have been prompted by new instructional technology. How do you plan to use the learning resource center in your teaching?

■ Notes

1. *Evaluating Media Programs: District and School.* Publications Department, Association for Educational Communications and Technology, 1201 16th Street, NW, Washington, D.C. 20036, 80 pp.

2. Ibid., p. 69.

3. Ibid., p. 71.

■ Selected References

Dick, Walter and Carey, Lou. *The Systematic Design of Instruction*. Glenview, IL: Scott Foresman & Co., 1985.

The Equipment Directory of Audio-Visual Computer and Video Products. 30th ed. Fairfax, VA: NAVA, The International Communications Industries Association, 1984–85.

Heinich, Robert; Molenda, Michael; and Russell, James S. *Instructional Media*. New York: Macmillan Publishers, 1986.

Henderson, Robert P. "View from the Corporate Sector." *American Education* (August-September 1982):35–37.

Humphrey, Darrell. "Computers in the Media Center of Tomorrow." *Audiovisual Instruction* (November 1977):24–26.

Locatis, Craig N. and Atkinson, Francis D. *Media and Technology for Education and Training*. Columbus: Charles E. Merrill, 1984.

Watt, Dan. "Teaching Math and Science." *Popular Computing* (November 1984):53–54.

Chapter 15

Use of Computers in the Classroom

Objectives

After studying this chapter, you should be able to:

- Understand the concept of computer-based instruction.

- Discuss a variety of computer applications in educational settings.

- Become familiar with the corporations that produce and sell computer hardware.

- Become familiar with the wide range of instructional software now available for use in our schools.

- Explore creative and fun ways that students can engage in computer learning projects.

- Develop a basic understanding of the word processing capability of computers.

- Explore the potential use of data bases for educators.

- Understand spreadsheets and their potential application in educational settings.

- Decide how much computer programming capability you should have.

- Understand the limitations of computers as instructional tools.

Enrichment Experiences

The following activities will help you learn more about some of the important topics discussed in this chapter:

- Improve your computer understanding and skills.

- Visit a repository of computer software (a learning center, library, or computer lab) and see what educational software they have available for you to examine.

- Write to a half dozen computer software producing companies and ask them to send you their catalogs showing what educational software they sell.

- Visit a nearby school system and find out how they would utilize computers if they had unlimited resources.

- Write to a number of computer hardware companies and ask them to send you brochures showing the equipment that they sell to schools. An alternative may be to visit some local sales representatives to obtain the same information.

- Plan your remaining college program so that you can enroll in several computer-related courses.

This chapter will help you better understand that computers are rapidly becoming as commonplace in our society as are television sets and microwave ovens. The typical student coming into our public schools today has been exposed to a considerable amount of technology in the form of toys, games, and other electronic gadgets. Schools are finding increasingly that students have a computer awareness by the time they enter our high schools. Schools are also discovering that computers are one of the most useful teaching devices ever created.

If you are considering a teaching career, it is imperative that you become familiar with the potential that computers hold for the classroom. This chapter will point out that computers are essential in many ways for future teachers. It will also suggest that you should become proficient in utilizing computers in a variety of ways as an educator. This chapter even suggests that those teachers who possess basic computer programming skills will be in a position to utilize computers more extensively than teachers who have only a computer awareness ■

■ Computer-Based Instruction (CBI)

Stuart D. Milner, an education specialist at the National Training Center of the Internal Revenue Service in Arlington, Virginia, specifies two application functions of computer-based instruction (CBI).

Direct instructional use is called computer-assisted instruction (CAI). This includes such usage modes as drill and practice, tutorials, simulation/gaming, inquiry/dialogue, information retrieval, and problem solving. Instructional management use is called computer-managed instruction (CMI). This includes such instructional support functions as testing, prescribing, record keeping, scheduling, monitoring, and time and resource management.[1]

The rapid recent development of the microcomputer has changed our entire outlook on computer use in education. Many teacher preparation programs now require graduates to be able to apply and manage the microcomputer for instruction. Microcomputers include the same functional components as larger computer systems but cost less and are easier to use. Prospective teachers are urged to carefully examine computer materials available from the many electronics stores. While the listing of each and every company involved in producing computer programs is extensive, many of these materials have limited applications for computer-assisted instruction in the public schools. Yet, the very fact that so many reputable business enterprises engage in the manufacture and marketing of educational systems practically ensures that technology utilization has become a permanent dimension of educating children. As purchase prices become more reasonable, utilization of educational technology in the public schools should increase. Since school budgets often provide less than 1 percent for media and other instructional materials, supplementary support programs are

A microcomputer is easy to use both at home and at school.

necessary to greatly increase school expenditures for media. Regarding computers in the schools, however, increasing numbers of our schools are purchasing them.

A recent National School Boards Association study shows that while over 90 percent of U.S. school districts have purchased computers, fewer than 15 percent have guidelines for using them. And only 40 percent of the districts have used the expensive technology to develop new courses or streamline old ones.

■ Computers in Educational Settings

Figure 15.1 lists some of the uses of computers for teaching and learning, administration, and support services. As computers become more and more available for student use, consideration must be given to the organization of those computer resources. Depending upon the educational feature to be served, school personnel should consider whether the computer resources be located in a computer laboratory, the media center, or the

Teaching and Learning	Administration	Support Services
Drill and practice	Personnel records	Guidance records
Testing	Payroll records	Students' records
Tutorials	Payroll preparation	Vocational information
Word processing	Word processing	College information
Computer-managed instruction	Attendance records	Test score files
(CMI)	School calendar planning	Food services records
Computer programming	Long-term planning	Library search and retrieval
Computer literacy instruction	Statistical analysis	Library loan records
Low-incidence courses	Budget planning	
Instructional simulations	Fire inspection records	
Educational games	Bus scheduling	
Class demonstrations	Mailing lists	
Music writing	Class scheduling	
Homebound instruction	Files maintenance	
Problem solving	Accounts (payable and receivable)	
Special education programming	Staff assignments	
Special tutoring		

■ **Figure 15.1**

Use of computers in educational settings

From William J. Bramble and Emanuel J. Mason, with Paul Berg, *Computers in School*. Copyright © 1985 McGraw-Hill Publishing Company, New York, NY. Reprinted by permission.

classroom. Figure 15.2 presents advantages and/ or limitations of these locations for several features intended to be served by computer resources.

When one assesses the speed with which the electronics industries developed microcomputers, it is not farfetched to envision the age of the world as classroom when the space satellite potential is similarly developed.

■ Use of Educational Computers: A Status Report

It has already been mentioned that schools use computers as an instructional aid more and more each year. A recent survey[2] of the use of computers in our schools reveals just how extensively schools now rely upon this excellent teaching device.

One amazing statistic that grew out of this survey is that the use of microcomputers increased 18 percent in just one year between 1986 and 1987. Of course, as would be expected, some states, depending upon the funds made available, did not increase computer use at all during this particular year. Other states made a special effort to increase computer assisted instruction. For instance, Maryland increased the number of microcomputers in that state by 128 percent.

This same study revealed a 44 percent increase in the number of school districts throughout the United States that now have a computer coordinator. Schools that decide to move heavily into computer utilization evidently feel that it is important for them to have a well-trained coordinator to assist teachers in this effort.

Feature	Computer Laboratory	Media Center	Classroom
Large-group activities	Labs are designed for large-scale activities.	This depends on the media center. Some can accommodate classes.	Large-group activities are limited.
Integration with other media	Computer labs emphasize computers at the expense of integration.	Media centers tend to integrate media.	Computers in classrooms are integrated with other activities.
Efficiency in terms of cost and computer utilization	Labs can be most efficient in medium to large schools.	Use of computers can be spread to all staff members and students at moderate cost.	Classroom computers tend to be used less than two hours per day.
Immediate availability to teachers	Computer utilization must be coordinated with other staff needs.	Computer must be scheduled through media center coordinator.	Computer is always available.
Amount of technical support available to user	Labs are usually run by a trained specialist.	Media center personnel usually have technical training.	Teachers may be on their own.
Flexibility of computer utilization	Lab resources can be used flexibly, and can be checked out to classrooms.	Depending on arrangement, can be very flexible.	Usually limited to individuals and small groups.
Encouragement of cooperative staff effort to achieve identical curriculum objectives	Computer labs can focus staff energies on specific computer application.	Media center approach may focus staff attention on identified priorities in education computing.	Teachers tend to pursue their own objectives.
Cost	Large schools can achieve economy of scale with a lab.	Media center approach uses existing facility and staff.	Placing computers in a classroom is usually the most expensive option.

■ **Figure 15.2**

Organization of computer resources

From William J. Bramble and Emanuel J. Mason, with Paul Berg, *Computers in School.* Copyright © 1985 McGraw-Hill Publishing Company, New York, NY. Reprinted by permission.

This survey also examined the increase in both hardware and software budgets throughout the United States from 1986 to 1987. Many states are spending considerably more money on computers and their related software each year. Unfortunately, some schools spent less money on computer assisted instruction in 1987 than they did in 1986. This serves as a reminder that schools must work very hard at raising the funds necessary to make educational progress. Respondents to this particular survey were asked what factors caused them to increase computer budgets for both hardware and software. The people responding to this survey indicated five main reasons:

1. An effort to integrate computers into the curriculum had become a standard practice within the schools.
2. There was new legislation in their particular state providing additional money for use of computers in the schools.
3. Private industries and other nonpublic sources of money were made available to them to improve their computer utilization.
4. They felt that better computer hardware and software products were now available to the point at which their school district decided to spend considerably more money for such materials.
5. Sufficient numbers of the teachers in their particular school district were now sufficiently knowledgeable about computers to utilize them well in their classrooms.

It is encouraging to realize that our schools are increasingly capable of utilizing this high-tech teaching aid in a sophisticated way to improve education.

This same recent survey found the following additional and encouraging factors:

1. Many states have significantly increased their budgets for computer education, some by as much as 25 percent.
2. Seventeen states have initiated projects whereby they will develop their own state-wide instructional software.
3. Approximately 30 states have initiated curriculum projects which will incorporate commercially developed software.
4. Special long-distance learning projects which utilize computers have been developed in 35 states.
5. Approximately 37 states now have state-wide regional software preview centers where teachers and administrators can go to examine various software packages.
6. Systems for distributing software electronically to all schools have been developed in 20 states.
7. Thirty-two states have developed electronic bulletin board networks for teachers and administrators in all school districts.
8. And finally, 21 states are currently developing systems for collecting educational data statewide and making it available to all school districts.

■ Students Per Microcomputer

Another recent study by Quality Education Data[3] located in Denver, Colorado, points out that schools are acquiring sufficient numbers of microcomputers so that each student now has greater access to this teaching device than ever

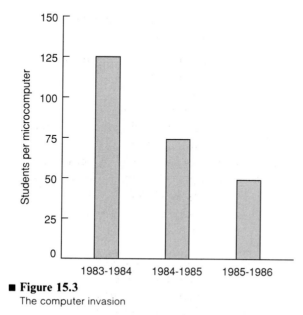

■ Figure 15.3
The computer invasion

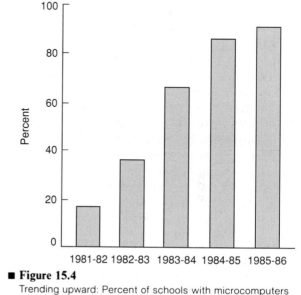

■ Figure 15.4
Trending upward: Percent of schools with microcomputers

before. Figure 15.3 shows that in 1983 approximately 125 students had to share a computer in the typical school in the United States. In 1984, this figure dropped to approximately 75 students per computer. In 1985–86, approximately 50 students shared each computer in the typical school.

Of course, the number of students per microcomputer varies considerably from state to state and from school to school. For instance, in Alaska, only 17 students shared each computer, whereas, in Hawaii, 86 students shared each computer. These data show that while more microcomputers are being made available per student each year, we are still a long way from the ideal of making computers readily accessible to all students in our classrooms.

■ More Schools Using More Computers

In 1981, only 16.5 percent of all the schools had at least one microcomputer. Figure 15.4 shows that this number has increased dramatically since that time, to the point at which in 1985–86 over 90 percent of our schools had at least one microcomputer. The early predictions that there would be limited use for computers in American classrooms have proved to be incorrect.

Even though many of our schools have at least one microcomputer, this does not mean that computers are used extensively in American classrooms. In fact, many of our teachers do not have the skills to utilize microcomputers as of yet.

These teachers must develop these skills in the near future. Another problem which prohibits the extensive use of microcomputers in classrooms is that many schools do not have an adequate number of computers and frequently do not have the best software that is now available. Schools do not have sufficient financial resources to buy all of the hardware and software that they need. Also, until recently, there was not sufficient good software available for school use. Fortunately, there is now an increasing amount of excellent software programming designed for classroom use.

High Tech Toys

Increasingly, students come to our schools having been exposed to a great deal of high technology. For instance, many of the toys in recent years that have been sold in great quantity involve high technology. Examples would be dolls which have been programmed in a way that causes them to move in coordination with their speech. Other examples would be the many educational games that have been programmed to teach children the alphabet, to count, geographical facts, etc. The amazing thing is that technology has been able to produce such high-tech toys in mass quantities at a relatively affordable price.

Computers in the Home

A surprising number of students now come from homes which have personal computers. Even though the use of these computers in homes is often restricted to games, nevertheless, the students become familiar with high-tech equipment.

Increasingly, children are utilizing quite sophisticated hardware in their homes to accomplish sophisticated tasks. Examples would include word processing for older children, mathematic computation, and rather sophisticated learning games. Ironically, it is not uncommon for children to come from homes which have computers and go into schools which do not have computers. The point is that increasingly our students are going to come to school quite familiar with high-technology hardware and will be able to quite naturally utilize such equipment in our schools as it becomes more readily available.

Training Teachers to Utilize Computers

Many states are working hard to provide in-service training in an effort to help teachers learn enough about computers to utilize them in the classroom. Fourteen states now require all students in teacher training programs to take a course related to computer use. Even if the state does not mandate it, most of the 1,200-plus teacher training programs in the United States at least expose their students to computer literacy experiences. The authors of this book highly recommend that all students preparing for a career in teaching not only become computer literate but also seriously study software packages that are available in their particular discipline and generally learn all they can about computers prior to becoming a teacher.

Use of Computers in the Classroom

Computer technology has reached the point where it is now essential that schools make use of this wonderful new teaching device if they are to maximize learning opportunities for students.

Ideally, every student in the United States should have ready access to computers in all academic subjects and at all grade levels. Fortunately, more and more schools are finding a way to make this technology available to their students. Unfortunately, due to the costs, it is probably the case that not a single school in the United States as of yet has all of the computer hardware and software that it should have. And most unfortunately of all, there are still a great many schools that have absolutely no computer availability to their students.

People preparing for teaching careers today absolutely must become familiar with computers and their applications in the educational setting, because computers are destined to play an ever increasingly important role in schools.

■ Computer Hardware

There is an amazing variety of computer hardware now available for potential use in the classroom. There are literally dozens of companies that manufacture microcomputers and related hardware which range in price from several hundred to thousands of dollars. It is anticipated that there will be even more companies manufacturing computer hardware and related products designed for use in the classrooms in the future.

The following list presents a few of the companies that have targeted computer hardware products for sales to school systems throughout the United States:

- Apple Computer, Inc.
  20525 Mariani Avenue
  Cupertino, CA 95014
  (408) 996–1010

- AT&T Co.
  Communications Group
  295 N. Maple Ave.
  Basking Ridge, NJ 07920
  (201) 221–8851

- Digital Equipment Corp.
  146 Main St.
  Maynard, MA 01754
  (617) 897–5111

- Hewlett-Packard
  Palo Alto, CA 94300

- IBM Corporation
  Old Orchard Road
  Armonk, NY 10504
  (914) 765–1900

- Kaypro Corporation
  533 Stevens Avenue
  Solana Beach, CA 92075

- Panasonic Computer Products
  Two Panasonic Way 76–0
  Secaucus, NJ 07094

- Tandy Corporation/Radio Shack
  Dept. 88-A-530
  300 One Tandy Center
  Fort Worth, TX 76102

- Texas Instruments, Inc.
  Data Systems Group
  P.O. Box 809063, DSG-163
  Dallas, TX 75380
  (800) 527–3500

- Unisys Corp.
  1 Burroughs Place
  Detroit, MI 48232
  (313) 972–7000

- Zenith Data Systems
  Glenview, IL 60025

Most schools have a difficult time deciding which type of computers they should purchase. It is difficult to generalize about the way that schools should arrive at this decision. Obviously, if schools had unlimited resources, which they never do, it would be relatively easy for educators to purchase computer hardware by simply buying the best that was available without regard to price. Unfortunately, schools are constantly trying to get the most economical computer equipment which will still get the job done.

Probably the best advice that can be given to individual teachers or school administrators regarding purchasing computer hardware is to examine a variety of computers, and related hardware such as printers, before making a decision. Fortunately, computer manufacturing representatives are very eager to talk to educators about their products, so they are readily available.

Computer hardware gets better and less expensive each year, so it is anticipated that educators will have more and more affordable computer hardware at their disposal as time goes by.

■ Computer Helps for the Teacher

Many of the companies that manufacture computer hardware for educational use also provide excellent help for the teacher who is getting started utilizing computers in the classroom. Of course, teachers must start by first becoming familiar with the computer itself before they can utilize such equipment with their students.

As an example of the materials that have been prepared by computer manufacturers for teachers, the following information is provided in a booklet prepared by Apple Computer Incorporated intended to be used by teachers. This booklet is entitled "The Apple Guide to Personal Computers in Education."[4]

Computers In the Classroom

In rural elementary schools and university science labs, in inner-city high schools and suburban community colleges, in vocational schools and special education centers, personal computers are transforming the learning process. Instead of wondering whether to buy computers, educators are wondering how to get them—and what kind, how many, and what software programs are appropriate.

With personal computers in the classroom, students have a greater desire to learn. The brightest can be stretched to their limits. Slower students can be gently encouraged. The learning-disabled and physically-disabled can participate at their own pace. And teachers have more time to teach, and to direct personal attention where it is most needed.

Computers themselves have also become a focus of attention. Many school districts have set the goal of 100 percent computer literacy for their students. They know that the ability to understand and use computers will soon be an important vocational requirement.

What Can Computers Do?

Personal computers for education are used everywhere from the kindergarten classroom to the superintendent's office, to the university language lab. For example, the color graphics capabilities of the Apple IIe make it perfect for teaching very young children how to distinguish colors and shapes. Sound effects are included in many programs to make them even livelier. Young grade-school students may use the computer for math or spelling lessons. Older students can learn about geography and history. Others may study foreign languages. In the upper grades, computers can be used to simulate experiments—or even to control and monitor them. And at colleges and universities, personal computers are performing professional-level educational and scientific tasks. Meanwhile, at all these levels, teachers and administrators are using Apple computers to monitor student performance, plan budgets, prepare reports, create computer-assisted lessons, and schedule classes. No wonder many schools are buying Apples by the bushel to meet the demand!

A Checklist for Evaluating Software

Since software determines what your computer will do, the quality of the software will determine how well it does it. Computer programs should be carefully chosen for their educational value and ease of use. If at all possible, try out the program in an educational setting before purchase. Carefully decide beforehand what kind of program you're looking for: drill, tutorial, simulation, etc. This checklist will help you evaluate courseware.

Is the program appropriate for the intended subject and grade level in:

[ ]Contents?
[ ]Teaching methods?
[ ]Feedback given (both for right and wrong answers)?
[ ]Use of graphics and sound?
[ ]Legibility and amount of text?
[ ]Number of students who can use it simultaneously?

In operation, does the program:
[ ]Give clear directions?
[ ]Recognize and offer corrective advice for incorrect input (e.g. entering letters instead of numbers)?
[ ]Give the student, rather than the computer, control over the learning process?
[ ]Keep a record of student performance on each lesson?

As a teacher:
[ ]Can you change the content of the program (e.g. add new vocabulary)?
[ ]Does the package contain clearly-written teacher's and users' manuals?
[ ]Is a back-up copy of the program disk provided (or can you make one)?

Any particular program may not meet all these criteria, but by careful comparison, you can get the best value for your students and your school's budget. (© Apple Computer, Inc. Used with permission.)

This is simply an example of the wealth of material available to educators that will help them to first become familiar with computers and then to utilize them as effective instructional aids in the classroom. Appendix K provides a listing of professional organizations for educators who are interested in learning more about computers.

■ Instructional Software

When computers first appeared in classrooms, the typical teacher complaint about them was that there was not sufficient instructional software available so that students could learn directly from the computer. Fortunately, this complaint is no longer valid, because a flood of academic software has been created and made available to schools. There is now instructional software available for virtually all subjects and all student levels. To be sure, not all of this software is excellent. Also, educational software is still relatively expensive.

The following few examples of academic software serve to show the variety now available:

- AppleWorks (Apple Computer, Inc.)
- Author's Assistant (Conduit)
  Bank Street Writer (Scholastic Software & Targeted Learning, Inc.)
- CompareRite (JURISOF, Inc.)
- Crossword Magic (L & S Computerware)
- DB Master (StoneEdge Technologies)
- Drug Alert (Mindscape, Inc.)
- E-Z Pilot (Teck Associates)
- Electric Webster (Cornucopia Software)
- The Electronic Spreadsheet (Minnesota Educational Computing Corporation)
- ESL Picture Grammar (Gessler Software)
- Facemaker (Spinnaker Software Corp.)
- The Factory (Sunburst Communications)
- Friendly Filter (Grolier Electronic Publishing)
- Grammar Gremlins (Davidson & Associates)
- Grammatic (Digital Marketing)
- Homeword (Sierra On-Line, Inc.)
- The Incredible Laboratory (Sunburst Communications)

- Introduction to Alternative Current, Current, Voltage and Power and Magnetism and Electromagnetism (Bergwell Educational Software, Inc.)
- Jazz (Lotus Development Corporation)
- Keep off the Grass (Kingo's Service Corporation)
- Lotus 1-2-3 (Lotus Development Corporation)
- Magic Slate (Sunburst Communications)
- Master Gradebook (Southern Micro Systems)
- Mathematics Courseware Series (Mindscape, Inc.)
- Newsworks (Newsweek)
- Notebook (Window, Inc.)
- One World (Active Learning Systems)
- Oregon Trail (Minnesota Educational Computing Corporation)
- The Other Side (Tom Snyder Productions)
- Populate (Clearinghouse for Academic Software)
- The Print Shop (Broderbund)
- Programmer's Aid (Minnesota Educational Computing Corporation)
- "Punctuation" + Style (Oasis Systems)
- Quickfile (Apple Computer, Inc.)
- Raise the Flags (Apple Computer, Inc.)
- Readability (Micro Power and Light Company)
- Reading Comprehension (Houghton Mifflin Company, Educational Software Division)
- Search Series (McGraw-Hill)
- Sensible Speller (Sensible Software, Inc.)
- Skills Bank (Softwriters Development Corporation)

- Sound Ideas (Houghton Mifflin Company, Educational Software Division)
- The Source (Source Telecomputing Corporation)
- Spelling Speechware (Houghton Mifflin Company, Educational Software Division)
- Stickybear ABC (Weekly Reader Family Software)
- Story Maker (Scholastic Software & Targeted Learning, Inc.)
- Symphony (Lotus Development Corporation)
- Talking Text Writer (Scholastic Software)
- Tribbles (Conduit)
- True BASIC (Addison-Wesley)
- VisiCalc (Visicorp)
- //Write (Random House Media)
- Writer's Helper (Conduit)
- Writing to Read (IBM)

Appendix J contains a partial list of software producers. More educational software becomes available each year. The main problem for teachers is to find the time to examine and evaluate educational software.

■ Computer Learning Projects for Students

A creative teacher will find many ways to utilize the computer in the classroom. A recent issue of *Electronic Learning,* an excellent publication for educators, lists the following creative ways that teachers might use the computer for learning projects:[5]

1. Go to the library and read about reptiles. Use a data base software program like *Friendly Filer* (published by Grolier) or *pfs:file* (Software Publishing) to create a "Creepy Creatures" data file that stores amazing scientific facts about your favorite reptiles.

2. Interview 10 different families who use computers. How does each family use computers? How much time does each family spend per day on the computer? Which family member uses the computer the most? Tally the results of your survey and use a graphics software program such as *Print Shop* (Broderbund) to make a mathematical chart or graph of your findings.

3. With the help of puzzle-making software like *Crosswork Magic* (Mindscape) or *Super Wordfind* (Hartley), create a crossword or word-search puzzle that is made up of your current spelling words.

4. Use an electronic spreadsheet such as *EduCalc* (Grolier) to project the profits of a cake sale. Your spreadsheet template might be organized like this:

	A	B
1	BAKING EXPENSES	
2	CAKE PRICE	
3	ESTIMATED SALES	
4	INCOME	
5	PROFIT	

5. Boot up any word processing software and create a *story chain.* To begin the story chain, one person writes a single sentence. A second person then adds a second sentence that relates to the first one. Participants add to the chain until the story resolves itself. (The unique contribution that a word processing program makes to a story chain is that it lets writers add their sentences anywhere in the story! Two good word processing programs for this activity are Scholastic's *Bank Street Writer III* and Spinnaker's *KidWriter.*)

6. Imagine you are a fly on the wall of your bedroom. Use any Logo language program or a drawing program like *Delta Drawing* (Spinnaker) to draw a detailed map of what you see.

7. You don't need a fancy science laboratory to perform exciting lab experiments. Boot up one of the many laboratory simulation programs available and get to work! Dissect a frog with *Operation Frog* (Scholastic), or solve as many as 50 chemistry experiments with *Chem Lab* (Simon & Schuster).

8. Use a data-base program to set up data files on historical, geographic, and trivial facts about each of our 50 states. Fields for each state file could include: name of state, capital, population, terrain, location, nickname, state flower, and postal abbreviation.

9. Use word processing software to write an 8- to 10-line story. Then use the MOVE function of your word processing software to scramble the order of the sentences. Challenge a friend to unscramble the story. (Note: Younger children can scramble and unscramble the words in one sentence instead of scrambling and unscrambling several sentences in a story.)

10. Set aside one day as Family Appreciation Day. Use a graphics software program like *Certificate Maker* (published by Springboard), *Print Shop* (Broderbund), or *Principal's Assistant* (Mindscape) to create a unique award certificate for each family member. For example, Mother might deserve the "Most Understanding" award; while sister Sue might be worthy of a "Great Athlete" certificate. (From "Take These Computer Challenges! 10 Learning Projects for Children," *Electronic Learning Magazine,* 24, October 1987. Copyright © 1987 Scholastic, Inc., New York, NY. Reprinted by permission.)

■ Computers and Fine Art

At first blush, one may think that computers would have relatively little use in the fine arts. That is not the case. Many of the newest instruments in music, for instance, are actually computers and employ the same high technology as do standard computers, but utilize them to create a wide variety of sounds. Not only are some instruments now adaptations of computer technology, but computers can be effectively used to teach students the basics about music. The fact that approximately two million digital keyboards are now sold in the United States each year is proof of the potential use of high technology in the field of music.

Computer graphics has emerged as an important new art form. It is now possible for artists to generate a work of art simply by programming a computer. Furthermore, as is the case in all academic fields, computer assisted instruction can be effectively used to teach didactic content to art students.

As a generalization, it can be said that computer technology is as applicable to the fine arts as it is in other academic fields. All it takes is a knowledgeable, creative, and determined teacher.

■ Word Processing

One of the major uses of the computer is for "word processing." Word processing involves utilizing the capabilities of a computer to do what traditionally has been done on a typewriter—plus much more. Word processing programs not only allow the user to prepare written material, but to edit, revise, format, correct, and print it. All microcomputers lend themselves especially well to word processing. In fact, many school systems no longer purchase typewriters for use in classrooms (or for their secretaries) but rather purchase microcomputers that can do everything a typewriter did, plus more—and do it better and faster. Increasingly, business education classes such as typewriting, employ microcomputers in place of typewriters. Each student in a typing class would have his/her own microcomputer station. The student would use the microcomputer as a word processor to learn how to do what has traditionally been done on a typewriter. Since the vast majority of secretaries now utilize word processors, it makes more sense to teach these skills in the high schools than to continue to teach traditional typewriting skills.

Many English teachers increasingly utilize word processors to help teach their students writing skills. Word processing allows people to edit and rearrange sentences and paragraphs quickly. There are a number of creative software packages that have been designed to do precisely that. Other teachers have found that word processors are useful in teaching poetry and in conducting research activities on the part of the student.

Teachers themselves have found that utilizing word processors rather than a typewriter is convenient, saves time, and allows a great deal of flexibility. Increasingly, teachers simply have a microcomputer with a word processing program at their disposal, either purchased by the school or themselves, to do more quickly and better what has traditionally been done on a typewriter.

■ Data Bases

We live in an information age when we are confronted with masses of data that are very hard to record, manage, analyze, summarize, and share in understandable form. Computers were especially designed to assist in this process. They have the capability of storing, analyzing, and presenting in understandable forms enormous amounts of information. The software programs that have been designed to accomplish this task are generally referred to as data base programs. These programs range from very simple programs designed for use by young children to extremely complex programs designed, for instance, to handle massive amounts of data such as that stored by our Internal Revenue Service.

School administrators, of course, have many obvious uses for data bases. They are useful to keep track of school budgets, student files, class schedules, and virtually any of the other jobs that must be done to run a school system. Teachers might utilize data base programs to keep track of whatever administrative data they must maintain. Examples might be class attendance, grades, student records, schedules, etc.

There are an increasing number of instructional programs that are data base in nature. Such programs are useful to teach mathematics, geography, history, or any other subjects that involve a fair amount of data. Some advocates believe that data bases could be usefully employed by just about all teachers at all grade levels and in all subjects as a useful teaching device. Of course, a teacher must first become familiar with computers and their applications to be able to do so. Some teachers are even creating their own data base programs.

■ Table 15.1 An Example of a Spreadsheet

Team	Peeps	Requested Food	Cost per Person	Local	Available
USA	10	Hamburgers	$5.10	Yes	May, June
France	7	Bouillabaisse	$1.50	Yes	May, June
England	6	Fish and chips	·$5.40	No	May, June
Germany	8	Brezen	$1.10	Yes	May, June
Austria	5	Wiener schnitzel	$4.25	Yes	May, June
New Zealand	6	Kiwis	$2.70	No	January
Australia	8	Barbequed shrimp	$6.10	Yes	August, September
India	6	Samosas	$2.05	No	May, June
Sweden	5	Knackebrod	$1.95	Yes	May, June
Denmark	6	Polse	$4.60	Yes	May, June

■ Spreadsheets

A spreadsheet is a chart which presents data contained in a data base. The nature of the spreadsheet can be determined by the user. Table 15.1 shows one type of spreadsheet that might be useful to a teacher.

One amazing feature of a computer is the speed with which it can create a spreadsheet. Once a data base is established, by varying the spreadsheet commands, the user can "in the flick of an eye" have a great deal of information immediately calculated and displayed in creative formats on the terminal. First-time computer users are always absolutely amazed at the speed with which a computer can manipulate data and display it in spreadsheet format.

One can immediately see the usefulness of spreadsheets in the educational setting. Teachers can utilize them in their administrative work, and students can use them advantageously as a learning device, in practically all subjects.

■ Desktop Publishing

A relatively new type of program, commonly referred to as "desktop publishing" now makes it very easy to compose and lay out composition by using a personal computer. This program is particularly useful to integrate text and graphics material, doing newsletters, student newspapers, announcements, etc. The program can produce justified right-hand margins and generally produces a professional looking camera-ready copy. Figure 15.5 shows an example product from a desktop publishing program.

The College Connector

Academic Tid Bits
From Here & There

Did you know...

... that beginning August 28, 1989, the G.P.A. for admission to teacher education programs will be 2.5?

... that study booklets are available in Gabel 146 for each area for the State of Illinois Certification Tests?

... that NIU students who took the Illinois State Certification Tests were very successful in passing the tests?

... that registration forms for the Pre-Professional Skills Tests are available in the Office of Testing Services and in Gabel 146?

... that freshmen in teacher preparation programs need to know about the changes in general education certification requirements which go into effect in July of 1992? If you're a freshman, see your advisor about this change.

Advisor Joins Staff

Elementary Education majors have most delightedly and gratefully welcomed Ms. Deborah Kapelski as a full-time academic advisor. On July first she joined Ms. Deborah Brotcke as academic advisor to the more 0 undergraduates in Elementary Education

Someone YOU Should Know!

Have you met Betsy Smith? If not, you'd better look real fast for she is really a woman on the run. Her job in the Office of Clinical Education is that of Coordinator of Clinical Education for all elementary education majors. Sounds interesting! " Coordinating" means that Betsy is responsible for all placements for the first and second pre-student teaching experiences and also for all student teaching placements. Besides this, she is very involved with the Australian students before, after and during their stay in DeKalb, leads the Welcome Committee in pitching a tent and greeting the alumni on Homecoming Day and works with the Committee on International Education Week. Betsy also works with International Programs to assist those students who wish to have a teaching experience in Australia, Costa Rica, England and Spain. She has been seen supervising students in London and visiting Spain and Costa Rica to make arrangements with host schools. Oh yes, in her spare time she studies and attends classes to complete a doctorate in educational psychology.

Betsy is always open to student concerns and works closely with Dr. Michael Henniger, Dr. Pamela Farris, and Dr. Jim Johnson to provide excellent opportunities for NIU student teachers.

Preserving Our Educational Heritage:
Blackwell History of Education
Research Collection

■ **Figure 15.5**
An example of a newsletter prepared with a desktop publishing program.

■ Should Teachers Be Programmers?

A debate exists within teacher education circles as to whether or not it is necessary for teachers to learn how to write computer programs. Generally speaking, experts feel that teachers need not become proficient at programming in order to utilize computers for themselves and their students. For instance, many of the newer computers are "user friendly" and do not require the user to know a great deal about programming, or in fact, even how a computer works. Teachers can simply utilize existing programs, rather than create their own, to accomplish a great deal in the classroom.

On the other hand, experts agree that the more a teacher knows about computers and programming, the better. If a teacher knows how to program at least basic language, he/she will undoubtedly have a much better understanding of the computer and its educational capability. Such a teacher is also more likely to utilize computers in more sophisticated ways as an instructional device.

There is also considerable debate about which programming skills a teacher should possess. Many people feel that if a teacher is to acquire programming skills, they should perhaps concentrate on "Logo" and "BASIC." Logo is a programming language that has been developed primarily by Seymour Papert, while working at the Artificial Intelligence Laboratory at the Massachusetts Institute of Technology. Logo incorporates much of the philosophy of the famous Swiss psychologist, Jean Piaget. In fact, Papert studied with Piaget at one time in his life and very likely was influenced by Piaget's philosophy. Logo utilizes many basic words that a computer can understand. Originally, Logo was used with early main frame computers that needed a primitive language. The main advantage of studying Logo is that it enables the learner to understand a good deal about the basic operation of a computer. In fact, there are many more convenient languages now available that make it easier to use a computer; however, Logo enables the user to understand how computers work and what they are basically capable of doing. Some experts even advocate that the public school students be taught Logo because it is such a basic opportunity to discover learning.

Teacher education students would be well advised to learn Logo as part of their college training. While they may not end up teaching their students to use Logo, it will nevertheless help them with their own computer education.

Other experts believe that all teachers would profit greatly from learning yet another computer programming skill called BASIC. BASIC stands for Beginners All Purpose Symbolic Instruction Code. BASIC was created in the mid-1960s especially for teachers and the field of education. Its creators were interested in facilitating learning as opposed to performing highly sophisticated data processing functions. The computer language employed in BASIC is relatively simple and is an interactive language. Interactive computer languages enable the user and the computer to talk or to interact with one another. This is obviously a very convenient feature for an educative computer language. While BASIC has a number of disadvantages and in many ways is not as sophisticated as more recently developed languages, it is relatively easy to learn and can be taught to younger students.

Learning a language involves a great deal of time and dedication. Such time would be well spent for teachers who are willing to learn such skills. It is highly recommended that college students preparing for careers as teachers work such courses into their college program.

■ Educational Potential and Limitations of Microcomputers

Decker Walker suggests that microcomputers, if used properly, represent a very valuable educational resource, but that they have distinct limitations. Writing in the *Phi Delta Kappan*,[6] Walker lists seven contributions that microcomputers can make to education:

1. More active learning.
2. More varied sensory and conceptual modes.
3. Less mental drudgery.

4. Learning nearer the speed of thought.

5. Learning better tailored to individuals.

6. More independent learning.

7. Better aids to abstraction.

He also points out that microcomputers, like all teaching aids, have limitations. Some of these limitations are:

1. Supplementation of education rather than substitution for it.

2. Difficulty in use.

3. Rapid change and lack of standardization.

4. Scarcity of good programs.

5. Lack of understanding about computer use in education.

6. Favoring of formalism over judgment.

7. Inability to solve current school problems.

(From Decker F. Walker, "Reflections on Educational Potential and Limitations of Microcomputers," *Phi Delta Kappan 65,* 2:103–197, October 1983. Copyright © 1983 Phi Delta Kappa, Bloomington, IN. Reprinted by permission of the author.)

One could add to this list of limitations the fact that most schools cannot afford to buy state of the art computer hardware or an adequate amount of the software. Teachers need to be aware of the fact that computers have limitations in the classroom and that they do not, by any means, solve all of a teacher's problems. Computers are, however, an excellent teaching device when properly used.

■ Electronic Schoolhouses

Our very best schools will soon resemble electronic facilities in which high technology will be utilized in a wide variety of ways to improve learning opportunities for students. We have now reached the point at which electronic information can be freely, quickly, and rather economically distributed throughout the world. It is quite conceivable that schools will eventually be able to access a world-wide information distribution system that will put virtually all knowledge and information at their fingertips. Some people think that such a system would, in fact, be more economical to schools than is the current system for providing information to students by purchasing books, magazines, and other print materials along with movies, slides, and videotapes. It is not inconceivable that, at some point in the future, schools will receive virtually all of their instructional materials via the airways and through computers.

In the electronic schoolhouse of the future, each student would ideally have his/her own terminal and monitor to use throughout the school day. High-speed computers would make available to each student all the learning materials needed. Clearly, the teachers working in such an electronic school would need to be experts on high-tech instruction.

■ Will Computers Replace Teachers?

Some people have wondered if there might come a day when computers will virtually replace teachers in the classroom. Some people have even suggested that this might be a good idea. However, when one analyzes what a computer can do, one quickly comes to the realization that they do not have the ability to replace teachers. Teachers will always be needed to make decisions about what students need to learn and how best to teach students. At the very most, computers will be able to do some of the things very well that historically teachers have tried to do all by themselves.

Computers will simply become another excellent teaching device that teachers may use in their complex job of teaching children. In fact, computers hold the promise of becoming by far the best single teaching aid that has ever been available to teachers. Computers in sufficient numbers can present each student with a unique set of learning opportunities paced to an individual student's needs. There is simply no way that teachers working with 30 students at a time could do this by themselves.

Teachers should not worry about being replaced by computers but rather view the computer as an excellent teaching device that still must be used only when and how the teacher decides it is useful.

■ Summary

This chapter has attempted to show the many ways that computers can be useful in our schools. Topics discussed in this chapter included computer-based instruction (CBI), computers in educational settings, a survey of how extensively schools now use computers, students per microcomputer, high-tech toys, computers in the home, computer training for teachers, inservice computer helps available for teachers, instructional software, example computer learning projects for students, use of computers in the fine arts, word processing, data bases, spreadsheets, desktop publishing, teachers as programmers, the educational potential and limitations of microcomputers, electronic schoolhouses, and the issue of whether or not computers will eventually replace the teacher. It should be obvious to all concerned that contemporary schools should be utilizing computers extensively by this time. Computer technology has reached the stage at which it is extremely useful and economically feasible for all our schools and our teachers today.

Teachers must learn to use computers in a variety of ways if they are to provide their students with the best learning devices available. College students preparing for educational careers should make sure that they not only become computer literate but that they learn all they can about computers, including programming, as part of their college career.

Point of View

Microcomputers have been gradually used in education for some time now. The following point of view article by William C. Bozeman and Jess E. House reflects on the use of microcomputers in education the past ten years and speculates about their use in the next decade. They suggest that computers have not yet made a very large impact on our schools. They also make four major recommendations concerning the future educational use of computers.

Microcomputers in Education: The Second Decade

William C. Bozeman and Jess E. House

Ten years have passed since the first micro-computer was placed into use in an American classroom, and the application of larger computers as instructional delivery systems is now in its third decade. Time and the acquisition of an additional one million microcomputers for education have not served, however, to settle debates raised among both researchers and practitioners regarding the effectiveness of this technological innovation. Indeed, time has served to fuel these debates. The question posed in such discussions is usually some variation on the same theme: "What difference has computing made in our educational process?" or "Has instruction been enhanced through the use of computers in our schools?'' This article will not resolve this issue. It will, however, offer a brief summary of what has been learned, thoughts regarding mistakes that have been made, and recommendations for addressing future questions. The position we take is based upon two beliefs: first, that educators erred in the *implementation process;* and, second, that the *evaluation processes* and paradigms used to assess *effectiveness* have not always been appropriate.

National spending for microcomputers for instruction continues unabated. State departments of education reported expenditures in 1985/86 of an estimated $550 million for computer hardware, with an additional $130 million for software, and higher levels of spending are expected to be reported for 1986/87 when those figures become available. Despite the current trend of increasing expenditures, debates regarding the effectiveness of computer-based instruction (CBI) are likely to become more than academic as educators consider competing demands for allocation of scarce fiscal resources. While state-level computing directors appear confident that ''no backlash [is] in sight,'' others have warned of the ''start of a great backlash of reaction against computers in education.'' As competition for funds increases, decision-makers at all levels of education can be expected to subject the case for continued acquisition of technology to closer scrutiny.

■ Effectiveness of Computer-Based Instruction

Roblyer captures the essence of the debate regarding the effectiveness of computer-based instruction when she asks, ''How much do computers actually improve instructional methods and, consequently, student achievement?'' The question assumes even greater significance when visits to so many schools using computers for instruction reveal dissatisfaction or disagreement among the faculty and administration concerning their real benefits. There is an increasing likelihood that convincing answers to questions of

effectiveness are going to be demanded by decision-makers before they approve additional expenditures.

For purposes of discussion, CBI refers to a curricular program in which there is interaction between the student and the computer. Delivery of instruction is provided in the form of drill-and-practice, tutorials, simulations, games or problem-solving. The instructional sequence and format may be supplemented by some form of management system.

In addition to effectiveness (i.e., learning outcomes), issues related to student attitudes, time savings, instructional efficiency, system costs and learning retention are subjects of debate. To a great extent, the current controversy is fueled by earlier forecasts of a technological revolution and by unfulfilled promises of a great change in the way our nation's schools provide instruction and in the way children learn. As a memorable example, Suppes opined that ''in a few years, millions of schoolchildren will have access to what Phillip of Macedonia's son Alexander enjoyed as a royal prerogative: the personal services of a tutor as well-informed and responsive as Aristotle.''

■ The Research Base

Absence of information is not the major problem: the literature is replete with research concerning CBI effectiveness. Unfortunately, as is the case with much educational research, findings are inconclusive and often contradictory. A number of studies have reviewed and synthesized previous research and findings related to CBI. For example, as far back as 1975, Edwards et al. concluded that traditional instruction supplemented with computer-assisted instruction (CAI) generally led to higher performance levels and that some time savings were achieved. A research review by Thomas supported earlier findings; CAI utilization typically increased achievement as compared with traditional teaching methods. Burns and Bozeman presented a meta-analysis of research studies of computer-assisted mathematics instructional effectiveness. This report further supported the earlier conclusions; mathematics instructional programs supplemented with CAI were more effective in fostering student achievement. Another meta-analysis synthesized the findings of 51 CAI studies. This study provided additional evidence for the position that computers can enhance the effectiveness of instruction, reduce the time required for learning and produce positive attitudes toward computing.

■ Questions Regarding the Research

Reading these and many other studies might lead one to conclude that all is well in the realm of instructional computing. On the average, students fare better if they have access to a CBI program. However, these research efforts can be faulted for methodological problems and a failure to provide conclusive evidence to resolve the question of the effectiveness of CBI. For example, while acknowledging that large-scale surveys of teachers and principals produced only limited evidence about the effectiveness of CBI, Becker reviewed the body of CBI effectiveness research studies and pronounced the evidence very scanty. Obviously, more needs to be learned, and a different research approach is in order. Herein resides a critical deficiency in the CBI research base.

Part of the CBI effectiveness research problem stems from the fact that CBI is not always CBI. While hardware choices have been narrowed to three or four alternatives, the software used in CBI can be selected from as many as 10,000 packages produced by 700 educational software publishers. Different patterns of organization for computer use, and the extreme range in both teacher understanding of CBI and the ends to which CBI may be applied, also serve to confuse the issue. These factors may, as Becker notes, "profoundly affect the direction and size of effects on student

achievement." Details of the specific nature of CBI and the particular context in which CBI was applied are often conspicuously absent in the research literature.

In a study by Mathinos and Woodward, data relative to CBI usage at one school were collected though an extensive questionnaire, lengthy interviews with teachers and administrators, classroom observations and weekly logs kept by teachers and computer lab aides. The researchers found sharp discrepancies between questionnaire responses and evidence gathered through the other measures. As an example, teachers reported that students used computers an average of 8.5 hours per week, but an analysis of weekly logs and firsthand observations indicated that the typical class used the computer for only 45 minutes per week.

Data from the teacher interviews suggested time as the salient issue for them: time for student use, time for software evaluation and curriculum planning, and time for teacher-development activities. The researchers concluded that the school, while appearing to be making exemplary progress in CBI, was a place "where computers are being used only minimally and without apparent focus or educational rationales," where teachers were "overwhelmed, uninspired and frustrated."

■ CBI Implementation

The findings of Mathinos and Woodward illustrate the value of alternative research designs that probe beneath the surface of student-computer ratios and statistical effect sizes to reveal the contextual and programmatic differences in CBI implementation attempts. Case-study research provides the thick descriptions that allow decision-makers in other settings to determine the merit of a particular form of CBI. Further, the case study can be used to conduct a process evaluation that is appropriate as a record of *implementation,* an important area of difficulty and one which can have a significant impact on effectiveness.

Consider the steps or phrases generally employed during the introduction of CBI. First, there is usually some recognition, determination or perception of need. Often this need is stimulated by community influence (or pressure), availability of resources (e.g., a grant or gift), administrative mandate, board policy or program evaluation. Hage and Aiken describe this phase as the *evaluation stage*.

After the general decision has been made to implement some type of CBI, the school or district will likely review courses of action, select hardware, appoint or hire someone to coordinate the efforts, and develop specific recommendations. This *initiation stage,* therefore, is concerned with the choice of a solution and the search for resources required for the program. During this phase, critical planning that may lead to the ultimate success or failure of the implementation should occur but seldom takes place.

The *implementation phase* is the actual attempt to integrate the innovation into the organization. Resistance and disequilibrium are greatest at this time because of conflicts, the realities associated with the new program and the discontinuity between the new program and the existing organizational structure. This stage may offer some educators their first experience with instructional computing. The hallmarks of this phase are occasional workshops and inservice programs for faculty.

The *routination stage* follows implementation. This phase comes after the initial trial and leads to the decision to retain or reject the new program. As the faculty enter the routination stage, they will begin supplementing and supplanting their traditional instructional approaches with CBI. Larger schools and districts may have a media specialist to assist the teachers in the selection of software. By and large, however, the faculty are on their own at this point. A few teachers will realize substantial benefits, primarily through their own diligence and perseverance, but many others will either avoid involvement altogether or become disenchanted in a short time and then find ways to avoid the technology. Whereas the boundaries of the first three stages are generally discernible, computer integration, if not accepted, may just gradually fade away.

Many schools do not undertake long-range planning or provide inservice opportunities, adequate hardware and software, or support personnel. Most CBI advocates would argue that remedying these shortcomings would almost ensure the successful integration of CBI into the instructional life of a school. This may not be true.

The argument that planning and support will ensure successful computer integration was questioned in an investigation of the status of CBI in an elementary school that provided these requisites. The district was in the last year of a five-year district computing plan, and extensive CBI inservice programs were offered to faculty. The school had a 28:1 student-to-computer ratio, a well-stocked software library, a computer coordinator and a computer laboratory aide with considerable expertise. Yet the district essentially failed to achieve satisfactory integration of computers into the curriculum.

While much has been published about computers and education, there has been little reported on the problems of implementing CBI. Not enough is known about how local conditions contribute to the specific nature of CBI projects. And additional research, if it is simply more of the same, will not provide decision-makers with the rationale for continued investment in CBI.

■ Implementation Evaluation

Educators asking what difference CBI makes are naturally concerned with effectiveness. But it is essential to first know how, and the extent to which, the program was actually implemented. Program implementation may be examined by gathering detailed, descriptive evidence about what the CBI program is doing. The importance of implementation evaluation prompted Tornatzky and Johnson to issue this warning:

One faulty assumption of naive evaluation practice is that the conceptual, on-paper description of a program corresponds to what actually is being evaluated in the field setting. . . . An evaluator should never assume that a program has been implemented as advertised when beginning to design an evaluation.

The aim of such process evaluation is to examine how the outcome is produced rather than looking at the product itself. Process evaluations allow decision-makers to understand the dynamics of program operations; they also reveal areas in which programs can be improved, as well as highlight strengths, and isolate the critical elements that have contributed to program successes and failures. This form of qualitative evaluation research holds the potential for answering the question that, predictably, will be heard with increasing frequency: "What difference does it make?"

■ Should Educators Be Discouraged?

Our review of the first decade of the use of microcomputers in the classroom reveals that mistakes have been made and that promises have been left unfulfilled. Should educators be disheartened and bow in deference to the critics of CBI? We think not. Should we be concerned? Most definitely. CBI will likely be in great jeopardy in the near future as expenditures for other programs gain favor. As a strategy, our recommendations are straightforward.

1. Different evaluation paradigms for CBI must be explored. Strategies which examine qualitative aspects of CBI may provide much richer analyses of the strengths and weaknesses of the programs.

2. Implementation processes must be taken more seriously by administrators than in the past. Resources without appropriate faculty development will be of little value.

3. Intelligent integration of CBI into existing curricula is critical, as few programs will rely upon CBI as the primary delivery system in the near future.

4. Process evaluation must be considered in CBI programs. To wait for a "no significant difference" conclusion may lead to an unwarranted and premature death for the program.

Let us conclude on a positive note. Computers are being enjoyed by thousands of students nationally. For many individuals, computing has been their most exciting educational experience. Hopefully, instructional microcomputing's second decade will allow even more people to experience this technology, and, who knows, maybe Suppes' prediction of the Aristotelian tutor will come true.

From William C. Bozeman and Jess E. House, "Microcomputers in Education: The Second Decade," *The Technological Horizons in Education Journal*, 15(6), February 1988. Copyright © 1988 William W. Warnshius, Santa Ana, CA. Used by permission from T.H.E. Journal.

■ Questions for Discussion

1. In what ways can microcomputers be beneficially used by teachers?
2. Should teachers be willing to purchase their own personal computer? Why or why not?
3. What are some of the possible applications of word processing in your particular academic area? Data bases? Spreadsheets? Desktop Publishing?
4. Should teachers be programmers? Why or why not? If yes, to what degree?
5. What are the limitations and disadvantages of computers as instructional devices?

■ Notes

1. Stuart D. Milner, "How to Make the Right Decision about Microcomputers," *Instructional Innovator,* (September 1980), p. 13.
2. "Educational Technology 1987: A Report on EL's Seventh Annual Survey of the States," *Electronic Learning* (October 1987), pp. 39–44.
3. From a study by Quality Education Data, Denver, CO. *NEA Today* (March 1987), p. 7.
4. *The Apple Guide to Personal Computers in Education* (Cupertino, CA, 1983) pp. 6, 15, 16.
5. "Take These Computer Challenges! 10 Learning Projects for Children," *Electronic Learning* (October 1987), p. 24.
6. Walker, Decker F. "Reflections on Educational Potential and Limitations of Microcomputers," *Phi Delta Kappan* 65, No. 2 (October 1983), pp. 103–107.

■ Selected References

Babbie, H. *Apple Logo for Teachers.* Peterborough, NH: Byte/McGraw-Hill, 1982.

Bitter, G. *Computers in Today's World.* New York: John Wiley and Sons, 1984.

Bitter, G., and Camuse, R. *Using a Microcomputer in the Classroom.* Reston, VA: Reston Publishing Co., 1984.

Bramble, W., and Mason, E. *Computers in Schools.* New York: McGraw-Hill, 1985.

Coburn, P., Kelman, P., Roberts, N., Snyder, T. F. F., Watt, D. H., and Weiner, C. *Practical Guide to Computers in Education.* Reading, MA: Addison-Wesley, 1982.

Dennis, J. R., and Kansky, R. J. *Instructional Computing: An Action Guide for Educators.* Glenview, IL: Scott, Foresman, 1984.

Flake, J., McClintock, C., and Turner, S. *Fundamentals of Computer Education.* Belmont, CA: Wadsworth, 1985.

Hallenbeck, M. J., and Boetel, D. F. *Teacher Friendly.* Belmont, CA: David S. Lake Publishers, 1985.

Hofmeister, A. *Microcomputer Applications in the Classroom.* New York: Holt, Rinehart, and Winston, 1984.

Panticl, M., and Petersen, B. *Kids, Teachers, and Computers.* Englewood Cliffs, NJ: Prentice-Hall, 1984.

Riedesel, C., and Clements, D. *Coping with Computers in the Elementary and Middle Schools.* Englewood Cliffs, NJ: Prentice-Hall, 1985.

Salisbury, D. F. "How to Decide When and Where to Use Microcomputers for Instruction." *Educational Technology,* March 1984, pp. 22–24.

Shelley, G., and Cashman, T. *Introduction to Computers and Data Processing.* Brea, CA: Anaheim Publishing, 1980.

Stronge, J., Bell, S., and Keane, D. "School Computers—Success Often Depends on Location." *Electronic Education,* April 1986, pp. 12–13, 22.

"What is Computer Literacy?" In S. J. Taffee, ed. *Computers in Education 85/86.* Guilford, CT: The Dushkin Publishing Group, 1985, p. 224.

Wright, E., and Forcier, R. *The Computer: A Tool for the Teacher.* Belmont, CA: Wadsworth, 1985.

The Organization and Governance of Public Education in the United States

This section of the book is devoted to ways in which schools in the United States are organized, governed, and financed. Each of these functions of the educational enterprise has evolved as the nation has developed. Patterns of organization, governance, and finance reflect rather directly the needs and expectations of society.

The patterns of organization for public education in the early days of the nation were not complicated. Our society was basically an agrarian one with a widely scattered population. Men and women as pioneers were concerned with conquering the frontier. One-room schools for grades 1 through 8 were built in the rural areas, while the multigraded common school developed in towns and cities. Private universities were also established in the very early days. As the frontier was developed, and as the nation began to change to an industrial and urban way of life, the needs of the nation changed and so did its patterns for the organization of education. Today we have public education from nursery school level through the university, along with many other forms of adult education.

The governance of education in the United States is both unique and complicated. It is unique because of its decentralization. Local people in the United States have more of a say about education than do local people in most other nations of the world. It is complicated because it involves at least three and sometimes four levels of government. The legal responsibility for education in the United States rests with state government, while the actual operation of schools is delegated to local government; at the same time, the federal government shows an interest in the enterprise. Again, as our society has changed from agrarian to industrial, and now to an information society, and as our population has become increasingly mobile, the patterns of governance of education have changed. The trend has been toward greater direct control of education at the state and federal levels, particularly in the areas of human and civil rights.

In the last two decades, greater attention has been placed on student and teacher rights. A new type of governance referred to as school-based management has emerged. It allows for greater teacher participation and empowerment at the local school level. New patterns of governance continue to emerge.

The financing of education has changed from an almost completely local effort to a point where, in most states, the local contribution is currently about 45 percent. The state and federal government make up the remainder of the costs. Property tax provides most of the revenue at the local level; sales and income taxes at the state level; and federal income tax at the federal level. State contributions to school financing have tended to equalize the amount of money spent per pupil in a state. Federal monies have been directed toward specific projects.

As society changes, the methods of organizing, governing, and financing education are also likely to change. It should be remembered that institutions are created to serve society, and therefore should be changed by society when necessary and desirable. Institutions also have the responsibility of looking to the future and providing information to their constituencies as to the probable, possible, and preferable directions society may face and/or create for the future.

Chapter 16

Organization for Learning

Objectives

After studying this chapter, you should be able to:

- Relate the purposes and goals of the various levels of education to the structure provided at each level.

- Present the rationales for the growing emphasis on early childhood and adult education.

- Appraise the success of secondary schools.

- Contrast the recommendations for high school curriculums in the recent reform reports with the curriculums of the current comprehensive high schools.

- Recognize the extent and importance of special education.

- Explain the recent concern about the importance of gifted education to our society.

- Describe the important role of adult, secondary, and postsecondary schools in vocational education.

- List the differences between independent and public schools.

- Describe the extent of and rationale for home instruction.

- Explain the reasons for the "miseducation" of young children.

Enrichment Experiences

The following experiences will help you gain insight into the goals and functions of the various levels of education and expand your knowledge regarding independent schools and home instruction.

- Visit a nursery school to observe the specifics as to how developmental goals are being accomplished.

- Interview an adult educator to learn more about the purposes and programs of postsecondary education.

- Interview a vocational educator to learn more about the purposes and programs of vocational education.

- Visit and observe a self-contained special education class. Specifically focus on the differences in the teaching methodology as contrasted to that in a regular classroom.

- Invite an independent (private) school educator to your class to discuss the differences between independent and public schools.

- Interview advocates of home instruction to find out what they think are the benefits of home instruction.

No other people ever demanded so much of education as have the Americans. None other was ever served so well by its schools and educators.

Henry Steele Commager

*T**he major purpose of this chapter is to help you understand the various levels of education and the goals to be achieved at each level. The levels discussed are preprimary (nursery schools, kindergarten, early childhood), elementary, secondary, and higher education (two-year community colleges, four-year colleges, and universities). Also included as related topics are special education, gifted education, vocational education, independent (private) schools, and home instruction ■*

As indicated earlier in this textbook, formal programs of education evolve from the needs and expectations of societies and individuals. As our colonial settlements grew and developed, the colonists recognized that some of their desires for the education of their children could be better met by organizing children in groups and assigning specific adults from the communities to serve as teachers. Thus began the formal organizational patterns for education in the United States. They began with a basic idea of efficiency; it was felt that one adult could teach a group of children, and in so doing permit other adults to pursue other important duties. As the population began to grow and people began to cluster in communities, other principles of organization emerged—for example, the grouping of children by age so that one teacher could concentrate his or her efforts in teaching specific content in the most appropriate way to a particular age group. Later the principalship and superintendency emerged as

specialties needed to effectively conduct the educational program in an organized fashion. While there is still disagreement regarding the *best* organization for learning, particularly for the individual child, it is nevertheless quite clear that American education was organized on at least two basic principles: (1) division of labor—that is, let some adults teach while others engage in other productive work; and (2) classification of students by age or common developmental levels. Organization for learning in the United States, while it has become increasingly refined, still reflects these two basic principles.

■ Purposes and Programs

Today four general divisions of vertical progression in educational organization are clearly recognized: preprimary, elementary, secondary, and higher education. Within these levels many subdivisions exist. Figure 16.1 illustrates the overall status of educational organization as it exists today.

At each of the levels, certain goals and purposes are expected to be accomplished. A sequential program is envisioned based primarily on developing maturity and content complexity. One pertinent general observation that can be made about content is that, as the vertical progression proceeds from preprimary to higher education, the overall educational programs contain less general education and become increasingly specialized. Figure 16.2 illustrates this idea.

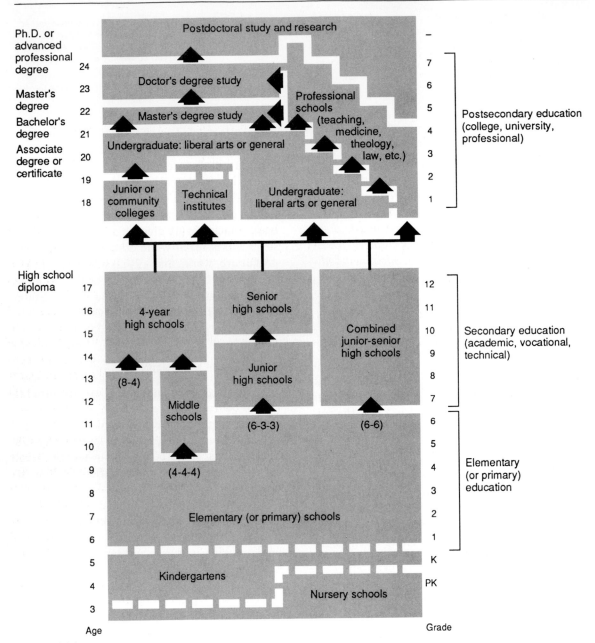

■ Figure 16.1

The structure of education in the United States

Source: Thomas D. Snyder, *Digest of Education Statistics, 1987.* Washington, DC: Center for Educational Statistics, 1987. (Available from the U.S. Government Printing Office, Washington, DC 20402.)

. . .If our schools are to serve as positive agencies for the maintenance of a "free" society, they must be concerned today with "society" as well as with the "child," with "subject matter" as well as with "method," with "product" as well as with human "freedom," and with social and moral "ends" as well as with classroom "procedures" and "educational means". . .

John L. Childs

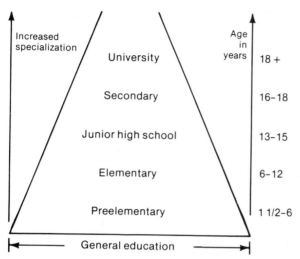

■ **Figure 16.2**
The decrease in time allotted to general education as related to vertical progression

General education is that portion which concerns itself with the development of basic skills and common understandings. These include:

1. Communication arts: speech, language usage, reading, writing, listening, discussing, and spelling.
2. Computational skills and quantitative thinking: arithmetic, reasoning, and problem solving.
3. Social and group living: history, geography, government, community living, human relations, citizenship, value building, character building, and sensitivity to problems of group living.
4. Science: understanding of scientific phenomena and natural law, the use of methods of science in problem solving, understanding the world.
5. Aesthetic development: music, art, and handicrafts.
6. Health: knowledge of the body, nutrition, and health habits.
7. Recreation: play, physical education, and handicrafts.[1]

Specialized education represents that part of the program, generally elective, wherein an individual student pursues a specialty. For example, Johnny Jones and his parents may decide at the end of the eighth grade that the only general education that Johnny will take in the future is that which is required by law, and that his program of secondary education will be vocational with his eventual goal that of becoming an automotive mechanic. At the same time, Ray Noble and his parents may decide that Ray will continue on to higher education and therefore take a specific college preparatory curriculum in high school. Ray may eventually decide to become a lawyer and then will specialize further at the university level. Ann Smith may decide to pursue the college preparatory curriculum in secondary school and, if she so desires and is financially able, could pursue liberal arts in higher education, and in so doing specialize almost completely in general education. It is significant to note that the choice of specialization in the United States is with that of the individual student and her or his parents, and not that of the government or society. To be sure, various state laws do prescribe general education requirements, and societal and economic conditions do often limit the available occupational choices, but basically the choice is the individual's, limited only by her or his particular talents, ambitions, and financial circumstances. In general, today, elementary and secondary education is assured for all regardless of their individual financial resources. Higher education in the form of tax-supported community colleges has increased its availability to all. The trend in the United States today is toward making more and more education available for academically able students.

The remainder of this chapter presents brief descriptions of the organization and purposes of each of the major levels of education.

Preprimary—Early Childhood

Basically, early childhood education consists of two divisions: nursery school and kindergarten. Nursery schools generally include children from the ages of eighteen months to four years, whereas kindergartens generally accept children between the ages of four to six years.

The first nursery school in the United States was opened in 1826, in the model community established by Robert Owen in New Harmony, Indiana; however, it was not until 1919 that the first public nursery school was established. The concept of nursery school education has gained acceptance slowly. Public nursery schools seem to have achieved their greatest impetus in the depression era. More recently, in the 1960s and 1970s through the war on poverty, public nursery school education was stimulated.

The latest data available indicate that the proportion of three- to five-year-old children enrolled in preprimary education rose from 27.1 percent in 1965 to 54.6 percent in 1985 (see fig. 16.3). In 1965, 4.9 percent of the three-year-olds were enrolled in schools as were 16.1 percent of the four-year-olds and 60.6 percent of the five-year-olds. In 1985, two decades later, 28.8 percent of the three-year-olds were enrolled in

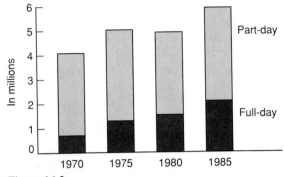

■ **Figure 16.3**

Enrollment of 3- to 5-year-olds in preprimary programs, by attendance status: 1970–1985

Source: U.S. Department of Education, National Center for Education Statistics, *Preprimary Enrollment*; and U.S. Department of Commerce, Bureau of the Census, "Current Population Survey," unpublished data.

schools, as were 49.1 percent of the four-year-olds and 86.5 percent of the five-year-olds. Those dramatic increases are due to the large percentage of working mothers with children. At the kindergarten level, approximately six times as many children are enrolled in public schools as are enrolled in private schools. At the three-year-old and four-year-old levels, approximately 33 percent are enrolled in public schools and 67 percent in private schools. At the five-year-old level, 44 percent are enrolled in public schools and 56 percent in private schools. The trend toward increased enrollments of preprimary children in school is expected to continue in the future.

■ Early Childhood Education

Just as there is a need for day-care, there is a need for early childhood education, particularly for "at risk" children. Children raised in poverty in families that lack stability with parents who have little or no education are "at risk" for failure in school.

Early childhood education can increase the likelihood of success for "at risk" children.

In 1965, The Elementary and Secondary Education Act (ESEA) was passed by the U.S. Congress to help economically disadvantaged children. A disadvantaged child was defined as a child from a family below the government's official poverty level—a specified level of income. One of the projects funded through ESEA was Project Head Start, which provided regular school programs for three- four- and five-year-olds. Head Start was a forerunner to the development of early childhood education. Evaluations of the Head Start programs in the early 1970s revealed that achievement of the Head Start children was not significantly different from the achievement of the children in a control group. However, evaluations of compensatory programs for the disadvantaged children done by the Department of Education and released in 1987 indicated that students receiving compensatory education showed larger increases in standardized test scores than comparable students who did not receive compensatory education. Overall it appears compensatory programs sponsored under Chapter I have provided reasonably effective programs. Chapter 1 of the Education and Improvement Act (1981) is the latest term used for compensatory programs for disadvantaged students.

Support for early childhood education has increased dramatically in the last few years. One reason for the support is the need for child care brought about by the high percentage of working mothers who need child-care services. A second reason is that research findings are providing more evidence that high quality early childhood programs "have both short and long term positive effects on low-income youngsters."[2] Quality in early childhood programs calls for parental involvement, programmatic leadership by supervisors and directors, competent and genuinely enthusiastic teachers, an articulated curriculum of proven effectiveness, a sound in-service training program, and the feedback provided by program evaluation.[3] It is important to note that programs must be designed for preschool children, recognizing their stages of development. They should not be kindergarten programs simply pushed downward. They also require a delicate balance of informal and formal instruction and learning experiences. The National Association for the Education of Young Children, an influential leadership group in shaping early childhood education, has prepared high quality standards for early childhood education.

There are a number of other reasons why there is an increased emphasis on early childhood education. Evidence strongly suggests that it is during the first four or five years of life that many personal behaviors, that is, language, attitudes, and values, begin to take on the form they will retain for a lifetime. Further, rich and wholesome learning environments tend to help children not only socially but academically in the future. It seems only reasonable therefore that investments made in early childhood education should reduce the need for remedial and compensatory programs later in life. It could also help foster a less divisive society in the future, yet one where cultural differences would be appreciated and respected. Life-styles, politics, and economics also have affected the increase in early childhood education. Over half of the states have some form of early childhood education. States with the largest number of preschoolers in poverty are the ones most likely to have state-funded preschool programs. The eight states with the largest numbers of poor preschoolers accounted for 48 percent of the nation's impoverished preschoolers in 1986—all eight states have state-funded early childhood programs.[4]

In a recent article, the following observations were made:[5]

> As more and more federal, state, and local policymakers begin to realize that there is a constituency—motivated by solid research data—that supports early childhood programs, public funding for such programs should grow. But those who are responsible for directing the debate and shaping the programs must have continuing access to pertinent information from research and experience. As they plan and implement new programs, governors, state and national legislators, local policymakers, and educators must consider all the options. The important questions that they must answer include the following:
>
> • Which children should be served?
> • For what part of the day should early childhood programs operate?
> • How much money should be invested in programs?
> • Through what structures should the money be channeled?

Various options directed toward answering those very important and pertinent questions can be found in the Point of View article at the end of this chapter.

Kindergarten

Kindergartens have received greater public acceptance than nursery schools. The first permanent public school kindergarten in the United States was established as a part of the St. Louis, Missouri, public school system in 1873. Since then, public school kindergartens have grown slowly but steadily. In 1940, approximately 661,000 pupils were enrolled in kindergarten. Currently there are approximately 2.8 million five-year-olds enrolled in kindergarten. Kindergarten enrollees are largely in public schools.

Kindergartens and nursery schools have similar goals. Major efforts are made to: (1) develop physical skills, (2) develop skills in interpersonal relationships, (3) enhance the development of a positive self-concept, (4) develop both oral and written language skills, and (5) enhance intellectual concept development. In addition to these developmental tasks, which incidentally are applicable at all levels of education, the preprimary curriculum content includes mathematics, science, social science, humanities, health, and physical education. The uniqueness of preprimary education resides in the selection of appropriate content and materials, and the use of appropriate methodology for very young children. Preprimary programs are extremely flexible; the key principle is in learning by doing— that is, in gaining enriching academic and social experiences without the encumbrance of performing specific tasks and in so doing, learning to work and play effectively with others.

Elementary

The elementary schools have been the backbone of American education. Historically they are referred to as common schools, and traditionally, under the graded organization system, they contained grades 1–8. As was indicated earlier in this text, elementary schools were organized in the colonies. The "Old Deluder Act," passed in Massachusetts, required towns to establish and maintain schools. While Massachusetts had the first compulsory school attendance law in 1852, Pennsylvania, in 1834, became the first state to provide a program of free public schools. The phrase "public schools" as used in the early days of the nation is practically synonymous with the term "elementary schools" today. Horace Mann, known as the "father of the common schools," was most influential in spreading the concept of the importance of a common school education for all citizens of a democracy. An elementary school education was at one time considered to be the terminus in formal education in America. Now it is more truly only the end of one of our most basic steps.

The traditional elementary school organization contained grades one through eight. This traditional organizational structure consisted of three levels: (1) *primary,* containing grades one through three, (2) *intermediate,* containing grades four through six, and (3) *upper,* containing grades seven and eight. After the completion of the traditional eight grades in the elementary school, the student entered a four-year high school. This traditional plan (8–4) dominated the organizational scene up to and through the early twentieth century. In fact, 94 percent of the public secondary schools were four-year high schools in 1920.

Modifications have been made in this plan. In 1910, the first junior high schools were established. They included the upper grades of the elementary schools, and, in some instances, if legal district organization permitted, they included the first year of the four-year high school. This was the beginning of the 6–3–3 plan. By 1958 only 25 percent of the public secondary schools were of the traditional four-year high school variety. Twenty percent of the schools were two- or three-year junior high schools. By 1966, 31 percent of the schools were traditional four-year schools, while 30 percent were of the two- or three-year junior high school variety. The trend seems to be returning to a four-year high school, with a two- or three-year feeder school. There is a decided decline in the high schools made up of five or six years. Under the 6–3–3 plan, elementary education is thought of as including only the first six grades.

Another modification of a more recent vintage is the grouping of grades five through eight and referring to that grouping as a middle school. With this arrangement, the ninth grade is considered as a part of a four-year senior high school. A school system using the middle school organization is referred to as having the 4–4–4 plan. In addition to the 8–4, 6–3–3, and 4–4–4, other plans are used including 6–6, 7–2–3, and 8–2–2. There are a number of reasons for these various plans, some directly related to the goals of instruction, others being only tangential. Let us briefly examine the goals of elementary education as they relate to the organizational patterns.

The goals of the elementary schools, particularly through grade six, are the goals of general education stated earlier in this chapter. Many of these goals are related to coursework and can be sequentially developed. In arithmetic, for example, children count before they add, and add before they multiply. This reasoning is sound and the graded organization is in part based on this rationale. However, other goals of general education such as those dealing with interpersonal relationships, group living, and socialization are more closely related to the personal-social needs of learners. It is from these personal-social needs, resulting from learners' developing maturity, that different organizational patterns have emerged. It reflects an effort again to group students, again by age, but based on developmental personal-social needs of the members of an age group rather than the purely academic content-oriented function of the school.

Junior High School

The junior high school student is a young adolescent. Thirteen-year-old seventh or eighth graders in terms of personal and social development have significantly different needs than preadolescent ten- or eleven-year-olds. This fact suggests a separate organization for these youngsters with somewhat different goals and procedures. Most junior high schools recognizing these differences provide exploratory education. The student is introduced to a variety of specialized educational areas. He or she may be given the opportunity to explore coursework in business, agriculture, home economics, and various trades, plus being given counseling regarding his interests and abilities for further academic pursuits. The junior high school is looked upon organizationally as including the group of youngsters between childhood or preadolescence and the recognized adolescent of the senior high school. Tangentially, many junior high schools came into existence to facilitate school building housing problems. In very practical terms, many junior high schools are converted senior high school buildings. As such, new high schools could be constructed, the old high school put to good use, and pupil housing pressures reduced at the elementary school level. Unfortunately, this type of growth has admittedly produced at times a distinct junior high building and a distinct organizational structure, but *not* a distinct or unique educational program for young adolescents.

Middle Schools

The middle school represents a recent effort to bridge the gap between childhood and adolescence. The junior high school, while designed for this purpose, has tended to become high school oriented. Perhaps the knowledge explosion and the concomitant increased knowledge expectations for younger children, along with increasing social maturity at a lower chronological age, have in part precipitated this development. Nevertheless, many educators feel that today a fifth or sixth through eighth grade grouping can more suitably meet the needs of the ten- to fourteen-year-old population than can either the elementary or junior high school grouping.

The number of middle schools in the United States has increased dramatically. In 1967, there were only 599 middle schools identified in the United States. By 1969, there were 2,298. It has been estimated that in 1980 there were over 5,000 middle schools throughout the nation, based on grade organization and stated program philosophy.[6]

Many junior high schools have drifted away from the unique rationale that brought about their creation. The middle school represents yet another effort to create educational experiences most appropriate for the preadolescent age groupings. Educationally, if it functions as it should, the middle school provides a gradual transition from teacher-directed study to responsible independence, and greater flexibility and opportunity for various instructional methodologies. It also encourages the development of programs designed specifically for preadolescents. Socially and physically it groups youngsters of similar levels of maturity together. Administratively it permits a four-year sequence in high schools, may fit into an overall building pattern, and many facilitate plans for social and academic integration. A combination of these factors brought about the middle school. The middle school has potential, yet it may not be a panacea for the education of preadolescents.

It is important to point out again that organizational patterns are related to goals, but they are also related to physical facilities, and to social problems in the case of the middle school. It is further pertinent to note that in order to achieve efficiency in educating the masses, the American education system has attempted to group pupils by age and by developmental characteristics. While these efforts have resulted in admirable accomplishments, the public schools still have not resolved organizationally the nagging persistent problem of individualizing instruction. Each student is a unique individual who develops and learns at his or her own rate. Can a plan of universal education designed to serve the masses of elementary school children be organized to suit each and every individual? Can each student be made to feel important? Can the individual expectations of each student be met? These are some of the challenges facing educators today, not only at the elementary school level, but at all levels.

Secondary

Secondary education began in the early colonies with the establishment of the first Latin Grammar School in Boston in 1635. Its purposes reflected the expectations of the people. It was to prepare students for college—colleges in those days were predominantly concerned with preparing clergymen, and clergymen could in turn help the people achieve their goal of salvation. The Latin Grammar School was eventually replaced by the tuition academy, the first of which was established by Ben Franklin in Philadelphia. Franklin is credited with broadening the base of secondary education. His academy included students who did not intend to go on to college as well as those who did. He recognized that our developing nation needed men trained in commerce and surveying, for example, as well as in theology and the classics. The concept of the academy grew and flourished, reaching its greatest heights in the middle of the nineteenth century. It met in part the societal needs of a developing nation. It was semipublic in nature, and was supported chiefly by tuition and donations. The academies were gradually replaced by the free public high school, the first of which was established in Boston in 1821. This high school, called the English Classical High School, was for boys only—a high school for girls was established in Boston in 1826. The first coeducational high school was established in Chicago in 1856. Perhaps the biggest boost to free public secondary education, however, was the decision of the Supreme Court of Michigan in 1872, which established the legality of communities to tax themselves for the support of public high schools. The American secondary school has, over a span of three centuries, developed from a privately supported college preparatory institution for a few elite to a publicly supported comprehensive institution available to most American youth.

Approximately 98 percent of all youth ages 14 to 17 are enrolled in secondary schools. No other nation in the world can match this record. While the record is admirable, American secondary education still does not live up to the ideal expectations held for it. There is still a high school dropout rate of about 27 percent.

Secondary education includes the broad spectrum in the graded classification of grades 7–14. The lower portion of the spectrum includes the junior high while the higher portion is represented by community colleges. The middle portion, including either grades 9–12 or grades 10–12 describes the senior high school. Let us consider briefly the contemporary senior high school.

The ideal senior high school is a comprehensive school. Comprehensive means that (1) its curricular offerings present a balance of general and specialized education along with sufficient guidance services and elective courses as to enable a student to pursue a program of his or her choice, and (2) its pupil population is diverse, representing different cultures and socioeconomic groups. If its program is functioning effectively, students should become increasingly different in their achievement levels; that is, the attainments of higher ability students should become increasingly superior by comparison to the attainments of the less able students. This principle should be equally applicable in the college preparatory, vocational, and general curricula students. The comprehensive high school should also permit one to elect courses of one's choice in any of the curricula. In other words, a college preparatory student would not be prohibited from taking a beginning course in typewriting. While students should ideally become increasingly different in their pursuits of specialized education, the comprehensive high school also should cause them to become increasingly alike in such things as their social insight, their attitudinal commitments toward democratic principles, and their empathy for others. Further, students should be prepared to live in a culturally pluralistic society, respecting the differences of cultural groups. Are

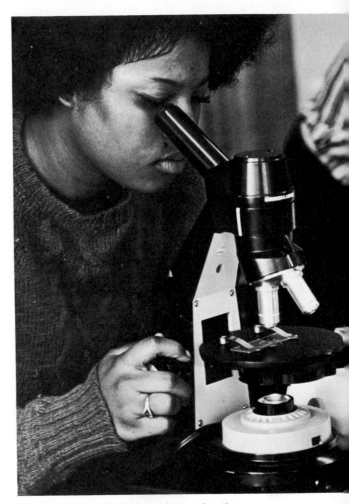

Modern equipment facilitates science education.

our high schools accomplishing these goals? Can we have effective comprehensive high schools in this country when demographically, for example, the poor live with the poor, the rich with the rich, and the black with the black? Can students learn to live with others when they only interact with their own kind in schools? Is the comprehensive high school a realistically attainable organizational goal? Can a high school in a rural area with a total pupil population of less than four hundred pupils be comprehensive? The answers to these questions are being sought—they constitute part of the task of secondary education in America.

Recent educational reform reports, namely, *A Nation at Risk* and *James Madison High School: A Curriculum for American Schools* have proposed high school curriculums with course requirements for graduation for all high school students that are more rigorous than the graduation requirements in many comprehensive high schools today (see chapter 13). For example, the average high school student in 1982 took a total of 21 Carnegie units or 42 semester units. Of these units, 11.5 units were in the "new basics" (English, mathematics, science, social studies, computer science, and foreign languages), and 9.5 units were in electives including business, trade and industry, home economics, arts, and personal development.

A Nation at Risk recommended 13.5 units in the "new basics" be required as a minimum for *all* students seeking a diploma. Assuming the average total requirements in 1982 of 21 units, that leaves 7.5 units for electives, not including 2 units of foreign languages for the college-bound students. The *James Madison High School* proposal required 18 units, 36 semester units, including the "basics," foreign languages, physical education, and fine arts. Assuming six classes per day per year, 24 units or 48 semester units, that leaves 6 units for electives.

The average high school in 1982 allowed for about 45 percent for electives. *A Nation at Risk,* including the basics and foreign languages, allowed for about 26 percent for electives; and the *James Madison High School* proposal, excluding the required physical education courses

which are required in most high schools, allowed for about 33 percent electives. The trend is clearly toward less time for students to take electives, which is somewhat contradictory of the comprehensive high school. The electives that are "at risk" are primarily vocational in nature and/or chosen by noncollege-bound students. It should be noted that the decisions in respect to curriculum are the responsibility of the states and local school districts. They clearly have the power to accept or reject the recommendations or proposals by the federal government or individuals.

■ Special Education

Special education students range from young children to adults. Under PL94-142, the All Handicapped Children Act, it specifies that a free public education will be made available to all handicapped children from age 3 to 21. The number of handicapped students receiving special education under PL94-142 rose from 9.1 percent of all students in 1978 to 11 percent in 1984. Types of handicapped students include specific learning disabled, speech or language impaired, mentally retarded, seriously emotionally disturbed, hard of hearing and deaf, orthopedically handicapped, other health impaired, visually handicapped, multihandicapped, and deaf-blind. Eleven percent of total public school enrollment are specific learning disabled, the highest percentage of all the handicapped conditions; followed by speech and language impaired, 4.7 percent; mentally retarded, 2.9 percent; seriously emotionally disturbed, 1.8 percent; and hard of hearing, 1.0 percent. All other handicapped conditions were below .2 percent.

The All Handicapped Children Act (Public Law 94–142) has dramatically improved the educational opportunities for the handicapped.

As was mentioned earlier in this text, Public Law 94–142, the All Handicapped Children Act has dramatically improved the educational opportunities for the handicapped. The Act specifies that a free public education will be made available to all handicapped children between the ages of 3 and 18 by no later than September, 1978, and all those between 3 and 21 by September, 1980. They will be provided with an "individualized educational program" as mentioned earlier and will be educated with nonhandicapped children to the maximum extent appropriate. In other words, they will be "mainstreamed." Advocates of mainstreaming offer the following reasons for its support: handicapped children do a

■ Table 16.1.   Participation of Public Elementary and Secondary School Students in Selected Special Education Programs, by Race/Ethnicity: 1978 and 1984.

Type of Program	Participants as Percent of Specific Racial/Ethnic Group					
	Total*	White	Black	Hispanic	Asian/Pacific Islander	American Indian/ Alaskan Native
Specific learning disabled						
1978	2.3	2.3	2.2	2.6	1.3	3.5
1984	4.2	4.2	4.5	4.5	1.6	5.2
Educable mentally retarded						
1978	1.4	1.1	3.4	1.0	.4	1.7
1984	1.3	1.0	3.1	1.2	.3	1.4
Trainable mentally retarded						
1978	.2	.2	.4	.2	.2	.2
1984	.2	.2	.4	.3	.2	.3
Seriously emotionally disturbed						
1978	.3	.3	.5	.3	.1	.3
1984	.6	.6	.8	.4	.1	.5
Speech impaired						
1978	2.0	2.0	1.9	1.8	1.8	1.8
1984	2.5	2.7	2.4	2.0	1.7	2.5
Gifted and talented						
1978	1.9	2.1	1.3	1.5	4.6	8
1984	4.2	4.7	2.2	2.1	8.3	2.0

*The percentages of total enrollment are based on enrollment in U.S. public schools, kindergarten through 12th grade.

Source: U.S. Department of Education, Office for Civil Rights, Elementary and Secondary School Civil Rights Survey, 1978 and 1984, unpublished tabulations.

better job of achieving, both academically and socially, when their isolation ends; a regular school setting does a better job of helping handicapped children adjust to and cope with the real world when they grow up than that of a segregated setting; and exposure to handicapped children will help normal children understand individual differences in people and help diminish the stereotyping of the handicapped.[7]

The physical facilities of many institutions are being modified to accommodate the handicapped (table 16.1). It is most appropriate that the United States enhance the opportunities and benefits for the handicapped and also gain the benefits that they can provide to our society and economy.

■ Gifted Education

About one-half of the states have mandated programs for gifted and talented students, and nineteen states certify gifted education teachers.[8] There is not a clear definition of the term gifted and talented. In general, it includes those individuals who stand out above the vast majority of

Research Finding

14

Advancing gifted students at a faster pace results in their achieving more than similarly gifted students who are taught at a normal rate.

Advocates of accelerating the education of gifted and talented students believe that this practice furnishes the extra challenge these students need to realize their full potential. Critics believe acceleration may result in emotional and social stress if a child is unable to get along with older students. Some, concerned about those who remain behind, characterize acceleration as unfair or undemocratic.

Acceleration does not damage students' attitudes about school subjects. Nor do accelerated students necessarily become drudges or bookworms; they ordinarily

continue to participate in extracurricular activities. Such students often become more sure about their occupational goals.

Accelerated students perform as well as talented but older students in the same grade. Despite being younger, accelerated students are able to capitalize on their abilities and achieve beyond the level available to them had they remained in the lower grade.

Cohn, S. J., George, W. C., and Stanley, J. C. (Eds.) (1979). "Educational Acceleration of Intellectually Talented Youths: Prolonged Discussion by a Varied Group of Professionals." In W. C. George, S. J. Cohn, and J. C. Stanley (Eds.), *Educating the Gifted: Acceleration and Enrichment*, (pp. 183–238). Baltimore: Johns Hopkins University Press.

Getzels, J. W., and Dillon, J. T. (1973). "The Nature of Giftedness and the Education of the Gifted." In R. M. W. Travers (Ed.), *Second Handbook of Research on Teaching*, (pp. 689–731). Chicago: Rand McNally.

Goldberg, M. (1958). "Recent Research on the Talented." *Teachers' College Record*, Vol. 60, No. 3, pp. 150–163.

Source: *What Works: Research About Teaching and Learning.* Washington, DC: U.S. Department of Education, 1987, page 78.

people with their intellect and creativity. Over the years, those students that were selected as gifted and talented students were selected primarily by their high scores on paper and pencil intelligence and achievement tests. That process, unfortunately, eliminated many creative people whose talents are not measured with the typical paper and pencil tests. In recent years, however, gifted programs have become more flexible in the

screening for admission to gifted programs. Intelligence is being conceived more broadly. Some gifted programs enroll any student who applies. More research is needed in order to more effectively identify talented students and to provide effective instruction for them.

Federal support for gifted education has declined over the last few years. It may, however, come back because of the nation's need for highly talented people to improve our status in the world

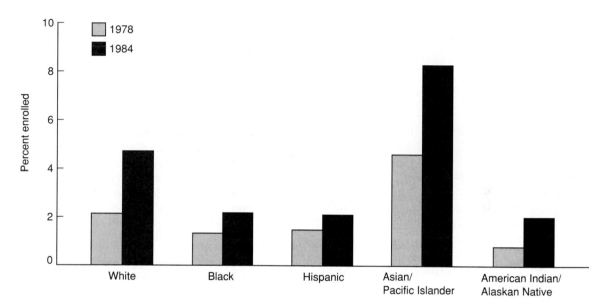

■ Figure 16.4

Percent of students in classes for the gifted and talented,
by race/ethnicity: 1978 and 1984

Source: Office for Civil Rights, Elementary and Secondary School Civil Rights
Survey, 1978 and 1984, unpublished tabulations and Joyce D. Stern and
Marjorie O. Chandler, Center for Educational Statistics. *The Condition of
Education: A Statistical Report* 1987 edition. Washington, DC: Office of
Educational Research and Improvement, U.S. Department of Education, U.S.
Government Printing Office.

economy. We have lost our lead in technology, science, industry, and commerce to other developed nations in the world.

Former U.S. Secretary of Education, Terrel Bell, has urged that:

> a massive effort at the national level be undertaken to identify gifted students and provide services for them. . . . Probably the most neglected group today are gifted and talented young people. . . . These students have as much right (as handicapped and disadvantaged recipients of federal aid) to developing to full fruition their capacities, . . .

assistance to the gifted may be the most urgent unfinished business in education today. . . .
Once the identification process is complete, schools should be required to develop tailored educational plans to serve such students, similar to those for handicapped pupils.[9]

Former Secretary Bell's plea may fall on deaf ears; nevertheless, the trend for gifted education is becoming stronger (see fig. 16.4). Three examples of efforts that states are making in providing gifted education to students selected statewide to study in a single residential location are: North Carolina School for Science and

Mathematics, Illinois Mathematics and Science Academy, and the Louisiana School for Mathematics, Science and Arts. Governor Charles Robb of Virginia has proposed the establishment of five regional high schools throughout the state, four devoted to science and technology and a fifth to the arts.

Community Colleges

The community college has emerged on the American scene in the last seventy years. The Joliet Junior College, established in Joliet, Illinois in 1901, has the distinction of being the oldest extant public junior college; that is, of the public junior colleges founded in the late 1800s and early 1900s, the Joliet Junior College survived and continues to operate as a community college today. It is interesting to note that it was originally conceived as an extension of the high school and therefore considered a part of secondary education and not higher education.

Perhaps it is most accurate to state that for some students the community college is truly an extension of secondary school; for others it is truly higher education, for they often transfer to four-year colleges or universities and graduate; for others it is terminal in specialized education and not an extension of high school, for they pursue goals not related to their previous secondary school experience. The community colleges as they are now organized and operated do have characteristics in common with both high schools and universities. This is as it should be, particularly if community colleges are truly going to become unique educational organizations dedicated to their purposes.

These purposes are, in a general way, to provide:

- Occupational education of post-high-school level
- General education for all categories of its students
- Transfer or preprofessional education
- Part-time education
- Community service

The community college, in meeting its purposes that reflect both individual and societal needs, has emerged as a unique and growing segment of American education. From meager beginnings in the early twentieth century, the number of junior colleges has grown currently to about 1,190 institutions which enroll nearly four million students.

The community college provides for "at home" post-high-school education. Students who cannot financially afford to pursue higher education elsewhere can start in the community college. Others, not seeking higher education, as such, can acquire necessary occupational skills. If an institution is truly a community college, it is responsive to the needs of the members of the community, and provides services for the people of the community. As such it fulfills the expectations of the people for education, expectations that either cannot or may not be met by other institutions. Therein may reside the reason for its uniqueness and success.

Higher Education

Higher education, the capstone of American education, began in the early colonies with the establishment of Harvard College in 1636. It is significant to note that higher education began as

*Colleges aren't strictly for geniuses.
We can't afford to slam the door of
opportunity in the faces of C-level
high school seniors, who will help
make our country's future. We must
fight for our average students.*

Arthur S. Fleming

a private endeavor. Today, approximately 63 percent of the 3,300 institutions of higher education are still under private control. Nevertheless, almost two-thirds of the students in higher education are enrolled in public institutions. The Morrill Act, in 1862, signed into law by President Lincoln was a tremendous boost to public higher education. This Act provided 30,000 acres to each state for each representative and senator then in Congress, or when a state was admitted, for the "endowment, maintenance and support of at least one college where the leading object shall be, without excluding other scientific and classical studies and including military tactics, to teach such branches of learning as are related to agriculture and mechanic arts."

The organization of higher education is such that it facilitates the accomplishment of its purposes. Great responsibilities are placed upon the independent judgment of the students as they pursue their elected course of study; freedoms are provided for professors as they conduct their research; and both philanthropic and public monies are provided to sponsor research in the public interest.

The diversity of institutions both in kind and control contributes to meeting the purposes of higher education. The kinds of institutions include community colleges, technical colleges, liberal arts colleges, municipal colleges and universities, land grant colleges and universities, and graduate and professional schools. Control differences include local, state, federal, sectarian, and nonsectarian private. This diversity permits a wide offering of specialized courses befitting the needs of individuals and society, and at the same time assures academic freedom and responsibility through an almost automatic system of checks and balances.

There are slightly over 3,300 higher education institutions in the United States enrolling over 12 million students. One major change in the past thirty years has been the dramatic reduction of men's and women's colleges. In 1945 schools enrolling only one sex constituted 30 percent of almost all the institutions; today they constitute only 9 percent.

Adult Education

Adult education in its broadest sense includes any learning activity engaged in by adults to provide them with better living opportunities. In a more restricted sense, it refers to programs of education formally organized for people beyond the compulsory school age. These programs are offered by colleges and universities, employers and unions, private specialty schools, armed forces and other governmental agencies, and public elementary and secondary schools. They may be oriented toward a degree or a certificate, or toward specific occupational or life skills. A report by the Carnegie Commission on Higher Education has proposed the following definitions that clarify adult education beyond high school.

> *Postsecondary education* as all education beyond high school.
>
> *Higher education* as oriented toward academic degrees or broad educational certificates. It takes place on college or university campuses or through campus-substitute institutions such as the "open university" with its "external degrees."
>
> *Further education* as oriented toward more specific occupational or life skills rather than academic degrees. It takes place in many noncampus environments—industry, trade unions, the military, proprietary vocational schools, among others.[10]

Adult education, of course, does include persons who have not completed high school. There are many purposes for adult education. Among them are the attaining of literacy and basic education skills by adults whose schooling for one reason or another was incomplete, and for non-English-speaking U.S. citizens; updating occupational and vocational skills in order to keep pace with industrial and technological changes; to gain a better understanding of increasingly complex social, economic, and political institutions; finding ways of utilizing increased leisure time; and adjusting to problems of aging and retirement. One need only read the advertisements in newspapers and magazines, or examine the offerings of the many community colleges, to recognize some of the specific purposes of adult education. More than 18 million persons participated in adult education activities in 1986. Occupational training represents the study area in which most participants enroll, yet the fastest growing area in percentage is the study area of social life and recreation, followed by personal and family living.

While a number of both general and specific recommendations were made in the Carnegie report *Toward a Learning Society,* the central messages of the report were:

- That postsecondary education should be concerned comparatively less with the welfare of a minority of the young and more with that of a majority of all ages.
- That more and better channels for all of youth should be created into life and work and service; for the one-half that do not now go to college, as well as for the one-half that do go.

- That age should be welcomed along with youth into the facilities for education; that continuing education, like libraries and museums, should be open to all ages; that the educational barriers separating the age groups should be removed.
- That education should help create an easier flow of life for all persons from one endeavor to another; that it be a more universal tool of leverage on the processes of life; that, in particular, the walls between work and education and leisure be torn down.
- That postsecondary education take more forms; but that academic programs remain at the center of attention with the highest prestige and the greatest support.
- That higher education concentrate on academic programs, leaving the quasiacademic and the nonacademic programs largely to others; that it continue as the great source of scholarship and the preeminent leader in terms of high standards of effort.
- That new policies reflecting these goals be developed on financing, accreditation, and coordination.
- That the "learning society" can be a better society.[11]

The recommendations are powerful ones. They reflect the concept of continuing education, that is, learning throughout life. The adult education now under way is only a beginning toward continuing education. Continuing education has been defined as "a way of life—namely that of a single, vital, genetic, developmental continuity."[12] It embraces the notion that education is qualitative as well as quantitative—that it can lead to a quality life for all, that education is more than increasing one's storehouse of knowledge.

The declining birthrate combined with the trend for increased longevity has resulted in increases in the percentages of older adults (sixty-five and older) and middle-aged adults (fifty to sixty-four). In the next decade, those persons born during the baby boom following World War II will be moving into the young-middle age adult category (thirty-five to forty-nine) increasing the percentage of our population in that category. The percentage increases in children and teenagers will continue to be smaller than those in the under thirty-five category. These population tendencies, along with the economic and social factors previously mentioned, point up the compelling need for adult education programs. Societal conditions seem right for the implementation of the concept of continuous education—developmental in nature, for all who desire more education with freedom and easy access. "Drop-ins" should be welcome.

While adult education took on many forms early in our history, the beginning of the modern era of the organized movement occurred in 1926 with the formation of the American Association for Adult Education. This organization later merged with the Department of Adult Education of the National Education Association to form the Adult Education Association of the U.S.A. Much of the inspiration and support to organize adult education came from the Carnegie Corporation and its president, Frederick P. Keppel.

■ Vocational Education

Vocational education has been a part of secondary and postsecondary education for many years. The federal Smith-Hughes Act of 1917 stimulated the development of vocational education. High schools built in the late 1920s and early 1930s were generally equipped with appropriate space for agriculture, home economics, and industrial arts. In the last few years, vocational education, while continuing some of the curriculum of the past (including preparation in printing and the various trades), has become more electronically oriented. More sophisticated high-technology kinds of vocational training are appropriate for the future. High schools, area vocational centers, secondary-level adult programs, and community colleges account for virtually all vocational enrollments.

■ Private Education

Private education preceded public education in the United States. It has been available for many years as an alternative to the public schools. Private schools today are increasingly being referred to as independent schools. The National Association of Independent Schools (NAIS), located in Boston, Massachusetts, provides many publications for their membership. The following quotation which describes independent schools and compares them to public schools is taken from a NAIS publication.[13]

What Are Independent Schools?

"Private school" is probably a more familiar term than "independent school," which most people now seem to prefer. An independent school is a nonprofit institution governed by a board of trustees that depends almost entirely on private funds—tuition, gifts, grants—for its financial support.

Most independent schools are accredited by their regional accrediting group and state department of education. All must meet state and local health and safety standards as well as the mandatory school attendance laws.

Unlike public schools, independent schools are not involved in or part of large, formal systems. They do, however, share many informal contacts among themselves and with public schools. The vast majority offer programs that prepare students for college.

Independent schools vary greatly in purpose, organization, and size, and they serve students from all racial, religious, economic, and cultural backgrounds. Some are progressive and innovative, some are conservative and traditional. They are both large and small, day and boarding, single-sex and coeducational. Independent schools have been an integral part of our nation's educational resources since colonial times.

Since each school is free to determine and practice its own philosophy of education, spirit and environment vary from school to school, even though they may display similar organizational structures and educational programs. This diversity among schools is one of their most distinctive characteristics.

How Do Independent Schools Differ from Public Schools?

While all schools have students as their primary concern, they differ substantially in their interpretation of objectives and approaches. Here are some of the basic differences between independent and public schools.

Governance

Independent schools. Each school is incorporated as a nonprofit, tax-exempt corporation and governed by a board of trustees that selects its own members, determines the school's philosophy, selects the chief administrative officer, and bears ultimate responsibility for the school's resources and finances. The chief administrator responsible for the day-to-day operation of the school may be called the headmaster, headmistress, president, or principal. The head's duties are comparable to those of a public school superintendent.

Public schools. Each state determines the number and size of local school districts as well as the rules and regulations that govern the operation of schools and their personnel. Local districts select a committee or board of local citizens to supervise the operation of their schools.

Finances

Independent schools. Tuition is the primary source of support. Additional sources of income are gifts and grants from parents, graduates, foundations, and corporations. Independent schools receive no direct public funds.

Public schools. State and local taxes are the primary sources of funds. The federal government also provides grants for special programs and services.

Curriculum

Independent schools. Each school designs its own curriculum. The majority offer college preparatory programs. Independent schools may provide instruction in areas that are not appropriate for or permitted in public schools, such as religion.

Public schools. The curriculum is determined by the state department of education and the local district's central office. The curriculum must include offerings that are appropriate to the needs of all children in the district.

Student Selection

Independent schools. Each independent school selects those students who it believes will gain most from its educational program. Boarding schools have the special opportunity to serve students from all parts of the country as well as those from foreign countries.

Public schools. For the most part, where students live determines the school to which they are assigned.

Faculty
Independent schools. Each school develops its own criteria for selecting and evaluating teachers. Certification is not required in most states.

Public schools. Each state department of education establishes standards for teachers, and local districts may add to these requirements as they see fit. State certification is required.

Catholic schools served approximately 3.6 million students in 9,900 schools throughout the United States. They have the largest enrollment of all the private schools. In fact, the category of "other religious schools" served only 1.5 million students. Total enrollment in private schools was about 5.6 million in 1985–86. The vast majority (81 percent) of private schools were affiliated with an organized religious group or reported a religious orientation in operation and curriculum. Eighty-six percent of all private school students attended schools with a religious orientation, while 14 percent were enrolled in nonsectarian schools.[14] Over the past ten years, there has been a slight increase in the proportion of students in private elementary and secondary schools from 10 percent to 12 percent.[15]

The Council for American Private Education (CAPE), a coalition of fourteen private school organizations, is planning a two-year study to examine major issues facing private schools. The major problems facing education, according to a CAPE task force are: financial instability, an "elitist" image, demographic shifts in the population, changing societal values, and the lack of lobbying efforts at the state level.[16]

One goal prepared by the task force would be to prepare an annual report card featuring data on the quality, programs and activities of private education. In addition to statistical information on private school enrollment, dropouts, and student achievement, it might also include data on the degree to which private schools reduce the need for education outlays by state and local governments and the number of jobs created by such schools.[17]

Other goals of the project include:[18]

- The development of a statement on prekindergarten education in private schools.
- Increasing links between public and private schools, perhaps with the aim of reducing the number of high school dropouts. The issue of tuition vouchers and other means of fostering parental choice in education would also be studied.
- The fostering of greater private school involvement in the training of teachers both for the public and private schools.
- The creation of a media campaign to counter the "elitist" image of private education.

In a later meeting, CAPE focused on the need to recruit minority teachers. A second major issue discussed at the meeting was accreditation of private schools.[19]

The role of private education in the United States was and still is an important one. We had private nursery schools, kindergartens, elementary schools, secondary schools, and colleges before any of the aforementioned were available in the public domain.

■ Home Instruction

Home instruction was legally authorized by a case in Indiana (State v. Peterman, 1904). The court specified that a school is a place where education is imparted to the young, therefore a home can be a school if a qualified teacher is engaged in instruction as prescribed by the state. The states control home instruction, and the instruction generally must be equivalent to what a public school provides. Such intruction must be carried out in good faith and not practiced as a subterfuge to avoid sending children to school.

> The world of home instruction today is small, but vigorous and diverse. Home schoolers appear to share at least one thing; the firm belief that parents can and should be deeply involved in the education and development of their own children. Otherwise, reasons for undertaking home schooling are as varied as the families and children involved.[20]

It has been estimated that the "actual number of children in home instruction seems to have grown from about 15,000 in the early seventies to well over 120,000 today—and perhaps as many as 200,000."[21] The estimates are based in part upon reports from organizations that supply curriculum materials for home instruction.[22]

As was indicated in the former paragraph, there has been a decided increase in parental requests to provide instruction in their homes for their children. Legal cases related to home instruction have been reported originating in Minnesota, Massachusetts, Maine, Virginia, Iowa, North Carolina, Illinois, and Washington, D.C.

Many legal cases are based upon discontent with the public schools, mentioning that public schools are full of "drugs, sex, and Godlessness"; others claim that public schools are ineffective in dealing with gifted or handicapped children.

Every state now permits home instruction in some form. Some states have stricter guidelines and regulations than other states. The enforcement of state regulations also varies among the states.

■ Summary

The major purpose of this chapter was to introduce the prospective teacher to the various levels of education and the goals to be achieved at each level. Also included as related topics were special education, gifted education, vocational education, private education, and home instruction.

A strong emphasis was placed on preprimary education because of its increasing importance and relatively rapid growth. Preprimary education is designed to provide children a good start not only toward education but also toward life. Research has indicated that with children "at risk," generally those raised in poverty in families that lack stability with parents who have little or no education, that high quality early childhood programs have both short- and long-term positive effects on low-income youngsters. One long-term positive effect might be to reduce the number of people in the permanent underclass. Growth of the early childhood programs stems primarily from the demand for child care, brought about by the high percentage of working mothers with children.

Elementary schools traditionally consisted of three levels: primary, grades 1–3; intermediate, grades 4–6; and upper, grades 7–8. Over the years, junior high schools, generally grades 7–8, and middle schools, grades 4–8 or 5–8, have emerged.

The purposes of a comprehensive high school were described. They were contrasted with the recommended reforms for high school curriculums presented in *A Nation at Risk* and *James Madison High School: A Curriculum for American Schools*. The curriculums recommended in those reports when contrasted with the curriculum in the average high school in 1982 (latest data) indicate a trend toward less time for students to take electives.

There is some evidence that gifted education will grow as our society recognizes how important it is to nurture and provide programs for gifted and talented students.

One unique purpose of public community colleges is to provide community services. In recent years, however, public universities have taken on a somewhat similar function; working with businesses and research laboratories essentially to help in economic development for the nation.

Adult education has been defined in its broadest context as any learning activity engaged in by adults to provide them with better living opportunities. The programs offered range from teaching reading to illiterates to sponsoring programs designed to update the skills of medical doctors. As our society becomes more technical in its nature, the need for retraining and updating of the work force will increase.

Major changes in vocational education have taken place in the last few years. Vocational education has become more electronically oriented. Sophisticated high-technology kinds of vocational training are replacing traditional vocational education programs.

Private education is described and contrasted with public education. Pressed somewhat by the public educational reform movement, private educators are seeking to improve their "elitist" image. They are fostering linkages with public schools, increasing their recruitment of minority teachers, and considering different ways to deal with private school accreditation.

Home instruction is legal and growing. Every state permits home instruction in some form. Some states have stricter guidelines and regulations for home instruction than other states. The states control home instruction and generally expect that the instruction be equivalent to that which a public school provides.

The information provided in this chapter may provide insight in helping you decide which level in the educational hierarchy you would like to teach. It is also helpful to prospective teachers to have a perspective of the complete educational enterprise.

Point of View

In the last few years, early childhood education has received a great deal of attention and has grown dramatically. There is some research evidence that indicates that high quality early childhood programs can have a positive effect on the achievement of at-risk children, helping them to be prepared for entry into the first grade. One of many aspects of high quality early childhood programs is that the curriculum and teaching methodology are specifically designed for the developmental levels of preprimary children that are typically three, four, and five years old. Unfortunately, some early childhood programs appear to be downward extensions of the first grade—taught in a formal way. The article, "The 'Miseducation' of Young Children" authored by David Elkind describes what is happening in early childhood education and what should be happening in early childhood education.

The 'Miseducation' of Young Children

David Elkind

What is happening in the United States today is truly astonishing. In a society that prides itself on its preference for facts over hearsay, on its openness to research, and on its respect for "expert" opinion, parents, educators, administrators, and legislators are ignoring the facts, the research, and the expert opinion about how young children learn and how best to teach them.

All across the country, educational programs intended for school-aged children are being appropriated for the education of young children. In some states . . . educational administrators are advocating that children enter school at age 4. Many kindergarten programs have become full-day kindergartens, and nursery-school programs have become pre-kindergartens. Moreover, many of these kindergartens have introduced curricula, including work papers, once reserved for 1st-grade children. And in books addressed to parents a number of writers are encouraging parents to teach infants and young children reading, math, and science.

When we instruct children in academic subjects, or in swimming, gymnastics, or ballet, at too early an age, we miseducate them; we put them at risk for short-term stress and long-term personality damage for no useful purpose. There is no evidence that such early instruction has lasting benefits, and considerable evidence that it can do lasting harm.

Why, then, are we engaging in such unhealthy practices on so vast a scale? Like all social phenomena, the contemporary miseducation of large numbers of infants and young children derives from the coming together of multiple and complex social forces that both generate and justify these practices. One thing is sure: miseducation does not grow out of established knowledge about what is good pedagogy for infants and young children. Rather, the reasons must be sought in the changing values, size, structure, and style of American families, in the residue of the 1960's efforts to ensure equality of education for all groups, and in the new status, competitive, and computer pressures experienced by parents and educators in the 1980's.

While miseducation has always been with us— we have always had pushy parents—today it has become a societal norm. If we do not wake up to the potential danger of these harmful practices, we may do serious damage to a large segment of the next generation. . . .

. . . [T]he social revolutions of the 1960's effectively transformed our conception of out-of-home programs and of children's readiness to cope with and profit from such programs. The statistics tell the tale. In 1966, only 60 percent of 5-year-olds attended kindergarten, while in 1985, 82 percent of 5-year-olds were attending public, private, or church-sponsored kindergarten programs. Only 25 states provided aid for public kindergartens in 1965; by 1985, all 50 states were providing some form of public support for kindergarten and, increasingly, for pre-kindergarten programs as well.

The proliferation of educational programs for young children is not limited to 5-year-olds. The number of nursery schools has increased a thousandfold since 1965, and the number of licensed day-care centers has grown 234 percent between 1978 and 1985. In 1985, some 2.5 million children (39 percent) attended pre-kindergarten programs compared with only 700,000 (11 percent) in 1965. Never before in our history have so many of our infants and young children been enrolled for extended periods in regular out-of-home programs. . . .

No authority in the field of child psychology, pediatrics, or child psychiatry advocates the formal instruction, in any domain, of infants and young children. In fact, the weight of solid professional opinion opposes it and advocates providing young children with a rich and stimulating environment that is, at the same time, warm, loving, and supportive of the child's own learning priorities and pacing. It is within this supportive, nonpressured environment that infants and young children acquire a solid sense of security, positive self-esteem, and a long-term enthusiasm for learning. . . .

The boom in early-childhood education is, it very much appears, becoming a boom in miseducation. The extent of miseducation of young children has recently elicited a joint statement of concern by a group of national organizations involved in elementary and early-childhood education. These organizations include the Association for Childhood Education International, Association for Supervision and Curriculum Development, International Reading Association, National Association for the Education of Young Children, National Association of Elementary School Principals, and National Council of Teachers of English. Some of the concerns mentioned in the joint statement were as follows:

- Many pre-1st-grade children are subjected to rigid formal pre-reading programs with inappropriate expectations and experiences for their level of development.
- Little attention is given to individual development and individual learning styles.
- The pressures of accelerated programs do not allow children to be risk takers as they experiment with language and internalize concepts about how language operates.
- Too much attention is focused upon isolated skill development or abstract parts of the reading process, rather than upon the integration of oral language, writing, and listening with reading.
- Too little attention is placed upon reading for pleasure; therefore children do not associate reading with enjoyment.

Each of these concerns is centered on one or another facet of miseducation, the many ways we can place children at risk for learning problems to no purpose. The potential dangers of the miseducation practices described above far outweigh any potential gains.

It is not only the schools that are introducing formal instruction to young children; parents are doing so as well. Parents have been barraged with commercial programs and books which promise them that if they follow certain procedures they can not only teach infants and young children reading and math, but also make their offspring brighter and raise their I.Q.—in a phrase, make them "superkids." . . .

Nothing new is offered in these books. . . . The authors are merely extending well-known learning principles downward to infants and young children or formalizing procedures parents use spontaneously when they interact with their offspring. There is absolutely no evidence that such teaching gives children any lasting advantage in reading or that it has any effect on a child's brightness. There is evidence, however, that too early formal instruction can do harm.

The miseducation of infants and young children is not limited to unwarranted efforts to teach them academics; it has extended to all facets of young children's development. The idea that young children can benefit from a program of formal instruction has spread to sports and to exercise, to music and gymnastics, to ballet, beauty contests, and karate. Done well, with a sensitivity to children's physical and intellectual limitations and to their psychological vulnerability, such programs need not necessarily be harmful. Nonetheless, because such programs put infants and young children in inappropriate learning situations, they also put them at risk of physical and/or psychological damage—and this despite the fact that such programs have no proven long-term benefit for youngsters. . . .

[The] study of gifted and talented people who were successful adults gives no support to the idea that early formal instruction creates intellectual giftedness or creative talent. Rather, what is consistent in these autobiographical statements [prepared by mathematicians under 40 who had won Sloan Foundation Fellowships] is that the parents of people who have attained eminence were careful not to impose their own priorities on their children but, instead, to follow each child's lead. In this regard, and in their concern with having their children be well-rounded persons, these parents are exponents of healthy, child-centered early-childhood education.

A recent study of the MacArthur Fellows reinforces [these] findings. . . .

These findings point up the fallacy of early instruction as a way of producing children who will attain eminence. Miseducation, in fact, reverses the natural order of development. With gifted and talented individuals, as with children in general, the most important thing is an excitement about and enthusiasm for learning. Skills are easily learned when the motivation is there. Miseducation, by focusing upon skills to the detriment of motivation, pays an enormous price for teaching infants and young children what amounts to a few tricks. An ounce of motivation is worth a pound of skills anytime.

Another popular argument for early instruction is that children now are intellectually more able at earlier ages because of the modern technology with which they are surrounded. . . .

Actually, this argument has two parts, one having to do with the direct impact of technology itself and the other with the indirect effect of the information conveyed by that technology.

In response to the first half of the argument, there is no evidence that early exposure to a technology in any way accelerates mental development. The overall direct effect of technology on human nature is to extend and amplify but not alter our biological capacities. . . .

Eyeglasses do not improve our visual system any more than a hearing aid enhances our auditory system. In the same way, a computer does not increase our ability to remember any more than using a lever makes us stronger. . . .

Now for the second part of the argument. If technology does not directly improve our sensory or motor capacities, doesn't it do so indirectly through the information it provides? Doesn't this information improve our brains and make us more sophisticated and knowledgeable than if we did not have the technology?

To be sure, there is a point here. Children today do indeed have access to more information than did children of earlier generations. Yet many years ago John Dewey wrote that learning is the "representation of experience," by which he meant that experience, raw information, does not teach in and of itself. It is only when we talk about and reflect upon the experience or information we receive that we learn from it. . . .

For children really to profit from the barrage of information to which they are exposed, they must also be given the time and opportunity to reflect upon that experience. Yet parents today are spending less time talking with their children than in the past. . . .

It is all too easy for us as adults to forget just how inexperienced infants and young children really are and how much they have to learn about the world that we have already conceptualized and now take for granted. . . .

Infants and young children are not just sitting twiddling their thumbs, waiting for their parents to teach them to read and do math. They are expending a vast amount of time and effort in exploring and understanding their immediate world.

Healthy education supports and encourages this spontaneous learning. Early instruction miseducates, not because it attempts to teach, but because it attempts to teach the wrong things at the wrong time. When we ignore what the child has to learn and instead impose what we want to teach, we put infants and young children at risk for no purpose.

■ Questions for Discussion

1. What are the major reasons that early childhood education is considered extremely important?
2. What are the major reasons that adult education has grown so rapidly?
3. Why is vocational education important?
4. What are the reasons for the increase in home instruction? Do you think it is a legitimate option under the compulsory education law? Why? Why not?
5. Do you think that gifted programs should have a high priority in the public schools? Why? Why not?

■ Notes

1. Galen J. Saylor and William M. Alexander, *Curriculum Planning* (New York: Holt, Rinehart and Winston, 1954), p. 356.
2. Lawrence J. Schweinhart and David Weikert, "Evidence that Good Early Childhood Programs Work," *Phi Delta Kappan,* Vol. 66, No. 8 (April 1985), p. 545.
3. Lawrence J. Schweinhart, et al., "The Promise of Early Childhood Education," *Phi Delta Kappan,* Vol. 66, No. 8 (April 1985), p. 545.
4. Lawrence J. Schweinhart and Jeffrey Koshel, "Policy Options for Preschool Programs," *High/ Scope Early Childhood Policy Papers* published in collaboration with the National Governor's Association (Washington, D.C.: 1985), pp. 27–29.
5. Lawrence J. Schweinhart, Jeffrey Koshel, and Anne Bridgman, "Policy Options for Preschool Programs," *Phi Delta Kappan,* Vol. 68, No. 7 (March 1987), pp. 524–525.
6. Sylvester Kohut, Jr., *The Middle School: A Bridge between Elementary and Secondary Schools* (Washington, D.C.: National Education Association, 1980), p. 7.
7. Marjorie Watson, *Mainstreaming with Special Emphasis on the Mentally Retarded* (Washington, D.C.: National Education Association, 1977), p. 7.
8. Robert Rothman, "Former E. D. Secretary Urges More Federal Aid for Brightest Children," *Education Week,* Vol. VII, No. 2 (September 16, 1987), p. 8.
9. Ibid.
10. Carnegie Commission on Higher Education, *Toward a Learning Society* (New York: McGraw-Hill, 1973), p. 15.
11. Ibid.
12. Maxwell H. Goldberg, "Continuous Education as a Way of Life," *Adult Education* 16 (Autumn 1965), p. 6.
13. Bobette Reed and William L. Dandridge, *Minority Leaders for Independent Schools* (Boston: National Association of Independent Schools), publication date not listed.

14. Thomas D. Snyder, *Digest of Education Statistics 1987* (Washington, D.C.: Office of Educational Research and Improvement, Department of Education, 1987), p. 3.

15. Office of Educational Research and Improvement, "Bulletin OERI" (Washington, D.C.: U.S. Department of Education, Center for Education Statistics), March 1987, p. 11.

16. Kirsten Goldberg, "2-Year Study of Private Schools Planned," *Education Week,* Vol. VI, No. 26 (March 25, 1987), p. 6.

17. Ibid.

18. Ibid.

19. Kirsten Goldberg, "College Aid for Minority Teachers Part of CAPE's Agenda," *Education Week,* Vol. VII, No. 9 (November 4, 1987), p. 10.

20. Patricia M. Lines, "An Overview of Home Instruction," *Phi Delta Kappan,* Vol. 68, No. 7 (March 1987), p. 510.

21. Ibid.

22. Ibid.

■ Selected References

Broudy, Harry S. *Truth and Credibility: The Citizen's Dilemma.* New York: Longman, 1981.

Brubaker, Dale L. *Curriculum Planning: The Dynamics of Theory and Practice.* Glenview, IL: Scott, Foresman, 1982.

Coleman, James S. "Quality and Equality in American Education: Public and Catholic Schools." *Phi Delta Kappan* 63 (November 1981):159–164.

Giroux, Henry A. and Purpee, David. *The Hidden Curriculum and Moral Education.* Berkeley, CA: McCutchan, 1983.

Kohut, Sylvester, Jr. *The Middle School: A Bridge between Elementary and Secondary Schools.* Washington, DC: National Education Association, 1980.

Kozol, Jonathan. *Illiterate America.* New York: Doubleday Anchor Press, 1985.

Lightfoot, Sara Lawrence. *The Good High School: Portraits of Character and Culture.* New York: Basic Books, 1982.

Reich, Robert B. *The Next American Frontier.* New York: Times Books, 1983.

Rich, John Martin. *Innovations in Education: Reformers and Their Critics.* Newton, MA: Allyn and Bacon, 1988.

Thomas, Donald. "Gifted and Talented Children: The Neglected Majority." *National Association of Secondary School Principals Bulletin* 60 (October 1976):21–24.

Chapter 17

The Governance of American Education

Objectives

After studying this chapter, you should be able to:

- Present the roles and interrelationships of federal, state, and local governments in American education.

- Describe the federal role in education, the state's function and the roles of various state controlling bodies, and the governance and operations of local school districts.

- Relate specific court cases under the First Amendment to the separation of church and state and to student rights.

- Relate specific court cases under the Fourteenth Amendment to school segregation and desegregation.

- Point out the role of Congress in the area of civil and human rights, particularly in respect to the privacy of educational records and the rights of women.

- Identify the impact of the increased role of the federal judiciary, federal and state legislation, and teacher power in the operation of local school districts.

- Explain the concept of school-based management.

- Explain what changes must be made in or for teachers to gain greater empowerment.

Enrichment Experiences

The following experiences will help you understand how the law affects education, how local school boards and state boards of education function, and how teachers feel about participatory management.

- Ask a librarian on your campus if the library subscribes to the *Phi Delta Kappan* journal. If so, read the short articles that deal with the law and education that appear in each issue.

- Read the amendments to the Constitution of the United States. The first ten amendments are frequently referred to as the Bill of Rights. The First, Tenth, and Fourteenth amendments have direct relevance to education.

- Visit local school board meetings and report your observations to the class.

- Ask a State Department of Education person to attend your class to discuss the state role and function in education.

- Interview an official of a local school district. Ask the official about his/her responsibilities and the major issues currently facing the school district.

- Interview officers from a local teachers' association to seek out their opinions on school-based management.

The powers not delegated to the United States by the Constitution, nor prohibited by it to the States, are reserved to the States respectively, or to the people.

Tenth Amendment United States Constitution

The major purpose of this chapter is to help you understand the governance roles of the federal and state agencies and local school districts. The topics discussed include: the roles and interrelationships of the federal, state, and local governments in American education; court decisions related to the First Amendment to the U.S. Constitution dealing with the separation of church and state and student rights; court decisions related to the Fourteenth Amendment to the U.S. Constitution dealing with segregation, desegregation, and resegregation; teacher rights, role of the Congress in civil and human rights, particularly in respect to the privacy of education records and the rights of women; education as a function of the state and the roles of the various governance bodies; the governance and operations of local school districts; school-based management; erosion of local control and teacher power. ■

The educational system of the United States is unique among the nations of the world. In terms of governance, its most distinctive feature is decentralization. In other words, local governments have decision-making powers in terms of operating local school systems. Education in the United States is a legal function of state government; however, much of the authority of the separate states has been delegated to local government—more specifically, to local boards of education. The federal government also plays a role which can perhaps best be described as one

of an interested party. As the educational system in the United States has developed, the roles of the different levels of government have changed. While education still basically remains a local operation, the participation of state and federal governments has increased. The remainder of this chapter examines the current roles of the various levels of government as they relate to the control and operation of education today in the United States.

■ Federal Government

The federal government has become involved in education in four different, yet related, ways: (1) the application of the United States Constitution, (2) the function and operation of the Department of Education and the National Institute of Education, (3) the direct operation of educational programs by various agencies of the federal government, and (4) the provision of federal aid in its various forms.

United States Constitution

The United States Constitution is the basic law of the land, and as such has had its effects on education. While no specific mention of education is made in the Constitution, the Tenth Amendment has been interpreted as implying that education is a function of the respective states. This interpretation resulted in the development of fifty different state systems of education. Further, it reinforced the type of educational decentralization that had begun to develop in colonial America. While the fifty states are markedly similar in their patterns of education, differences do exist. Examples of differences that exist include: (1) requirements for teacher certification,

Congress shall make no law respecting an establishment of religion or prohibiting the free exercises thereof; or abridge the freedom of speech or of the press; or the right of the people peaceably to assemble and to petition the government for redress of grievances.

First Amendment United States Constitution

(2) graduation requirements, (3) regulations for compulsory attendance, and (4) provisions for teacher pension plans.

The First and Fourteenth Amendments have also had a definite impact on the administration of education in the United States. The First Amendment insures freedom of speech, religion, the press, and the right of petition. The Fourteenth Amendment provides for the protection of specified privileges of citizens. Based upon these amendments, the Supreme Court of the United States has made many decisions that have influenced the course of education in the United States.

Court Decisions: First Amendment

Court decisions based upon the First Amendment have been particularly influential in clarifying the relationship between religion and education. There have been a number of these decisions, and basically they can be classified into three groups: (1) those having to do with the rights of parents to educate their children in private schools, (2) those having to do with the use of public funds to support private education, and (3) those having to do with the teaching or practice of religion in the public schools.

An important case influential in determining the rights of parents to provide education for their children was the Oregon case. Briefly, in 1922 the legislature of Oregon passed a law requiring all children to attend public schools. The United States Supreme Court ruled that the law was unconstitutional (*Pierce* v. *Society of Sisters,* 1925). The reasoning of the Court was that such a law denied to parents the rights to control the education of their children. This decision of the Supreme Court in addition to establishing that private schools have a right to exist, and that

pupils may meet the requirements of compulsory education by attending private schools, also established that a state may regulate all schools, public and private, and require the teaching of specific subjects. The Oregon decision reinforced a historical tradition of private and sectarian education in the United States and gave further impetus to the development of private schools. Thus, two systems of education, public and private, developed in the United States.

Cases having to do with the use of public funds to support private education are numerous. Prominent among them are the *Cochran* and the *Everson* cases. In *Cochran* v. *Louisiana State Board of Education,* 1930, the United States Supreme Court held that a Louisiana textbook statute that provided for furnishing textbooks purchased with tax-raised funds to private school pupils was valid. The ruling was technically based on the Fourteenth Amendment.

More recently, the United States Supreme Court supported a New York law providing for the free loan of public school books to students in private schools (*Board of Education of Central School District No. 1, Towns of Grenbush et al.* v. *Allen,* 1968).

> The majority opinion stated "The law merely makes available to all children the benefits of a general program to lend school books free of charge. Books are furnished at the request of the pupil and ownership remains, at least technically, in the state. Thus no funds or books are furnished to parochial schools, and the financial benefit is to parents and children, not to schools."

In *Everson* v. *Board of Education,* 1947, the United States Supreme Court held that tax-raised funds in a New Jersey school district could be used

No State shall make or enforce any law which shall abrogate the privileges or immunities of citizens of the United States; nor shall any state deprive any person of life, liberty, or property without due process of law; nor deny to any person within its jurisdiction the equal protection of the laws.

Fourteenth Amendment United States Constitution

to reimburse parents for bus fares expended to transport their children to church schools. The decision of the Court in the *Everson* case was based on a five-to-four vote. These decisions permitting the use of public funds to provide transportation and textbooks for students attending private schools were based in the main on *child benefit theory,* the rationale being that the aid benefited the children and not the school or religion. Child benefit theory, while seemingly becoming an established phenomenon at the federal level, has not been unanimously accepted by the states.

Since the *Everson* v. *Board of Education* decision, the highest courts in a number of states, under provisions in their own constitutions, have struck down enactments authorizing free busing of children attending denominational schools. Other state supreme courts have upheld enactments providing for the use of public funds for the transportation of students to denominational schools.

Two recent cases both originating in Missouri tend to further define the use of public funds for free transportation of parochial school students, and the loaning of textbooks free of charge to parochial school students. In 1975, the United States Supreme Court affirmed a federal district court decision in Missouri (*Luetkemeyer* v. *Kaufman*), noting that although a state may provide free transportation to parochial school students, principles of equal protection do not require a state to do so merely because such services are provided to public school pupils. In 1974, the Missouri Supreme Court held that it was a violation of the state constitution for the state to loan

textbooks free of charge to parochial school students. The U.S. Supreme Court denied review of the case, thereby preserving the state court decision. "Thus, although a state *may* lend textbooks to parochial school students, the Court declined to *compel* a state to do so if it is supplying free books to public school pupils."[1]

The matter of the use of public funds for private education is far from settled. Rising costs have made it increasingly difficult for nonpublic schools to survive.

Since 1968 many states have introduced legislation providing for a variety of forms of direct aid to nonpublic schools. Legislation originating in Pennsylvania and Rhode Island eventually was ruled upon by the United States Supreme Court. The Court ruled in both the Pennsylvania case (*Lemon* v. *Kurtzman,* 1971) and the Rhode Island case (*DiCenso* v. *Robinson,* 1971) that the respective laws were unconstitutional. The majority opinion stated: "We conclude that the cumulative impact of the entire relationships arising under the statutes in each State involves excessive entanglements between government and religion." Entanglements were anticipated in accomplishing the necessary state supervision to ensure that state aid would support only secular education in nonpublic schools.

After denying other proposals to aid nonpublic school pupils in Pennsylvania and New York, the United States Supreme Court in 1975 (*Wolman* v. *Walter*) did approve parts of a legislative proposal originating in Ohio. The parts approved as being constitutional included providing nonpublic school pupils with books, standardizing testing and scoring, diagnostic services, and therapeutic and remedial services. Proposals for instructional materials and field trip services were ruled unconstitutional. Perhaps the very carefully drafted Ohio legislation will serve as a model for other states. In general, the Ohio law in the opinion of the Supreme Court avoided excessive entanglements between government and education.

A case before the U.S. Supreme Court in 1985 (*Agiluar* v. *Felton*) provided more insight into the concept of excessive entanglement between government and education. Federal funds were used to send public school teachers into parochial school classrooms to provide remedial or enrichment instruction, aimed mainly at educationally deprived children from poor neighborhoods. Instruction took place during the regular school day in classrooms from which religious symbols had been temporarily removed. The Supreme Court held that excessive entanglement resulted from the need to ensure that classes were free of religious content "requiring a permanent and pervasive *state* presence in the sectarian schools receiving aid."

The matter of the practice of sectarian religion in public schools has been brought before the United States Supreme Court many times. In 1963, the Court ruled that the reading of the Bible and the recitation of the Lord's Prayer are religious ceremonies and if done in public schools are in violation of the First and Fourteenth Amendments to the Constitution. The decision resulted from the appeals of two lower court decisions, one from Pennsylvania, *Schempp* v. *School District of Abington Township,* and the other from Maryland, *Murray* v. *Curlett.* These earlier decisions had held that reading the Bible and saying the Lord's Prayer were not illegal. In *People of the State of Illinois ex rel. McCollum* v. *Board of Education of School District No. 71, Champaign, Illinois,* 1948, the Supreme Court ruled

that release time for religious instruction, with voluntary pupil participation, but conducted on public school property, was a violation of the separation of church and state. In 1952 in *Zorach* v. *Clausen,* the Court upheld a New York statute which provided for release time for religious instruction off the school premises.

More recently, the courts have heard cases dealing with creationism, a religious topic. The U.S. Supreme Court in *Edwards* v. *Aguilard* (1987) ruled that a Louisiana law that mandated balanced treatment for the theories of evolution and creation in the public schools violated the First Amendment's prohibition on government establishment of religion. The Court held that the state legislature's primary intent in enacting the law in 1981 was clearly to advance the religious viewpoint that a supernatural being created humankind, and not to advance the cause of academic freedom, as the state maintained.

A few months later, two federal circuit courts heard cases dealing with textbooks. One case began in Tennessee, *Mozert* v. *Hawkins County Board of Education* (1987); the other originated in Alabama, *Smith* v. *Board of School Commissioners of Mobile County* (1987).

The *Mozert* v. *Hawkins County Board of Education* started from a 1983 decision by the Board when they adopted a Holt, Rinehart and Winston reading series for use in grades one through eight. Shortly thereafter, seven fundamentalist Christian families filed suit against the Board, charging that the books promoted values that were offensive to their religious beliefs. The offensive values included feminism, religious tolerance, and situational ethics.

The case was first heard by U.S. District Judge Thomas G. Hull and he ruled that the children's First Amendment right to free exercise of religion was violated by exposure to the books. In stating the complaint, he said:

> The plaintiffs believe that, after reading the entire Holt series, a child might adopt the views of a feminist, a humanist, a pacifist, an anti-Christian, a vegetarian, or an advocate of a "one-world government." Plaintiffs sincerely believe that the repetitive affirmation of these philosophical viewpoints is repulsive to the Christian faith—so repulsive that they must not allow their children to be exposed to the Holt series. This is their religious belief.

The Judge ordered school officials to allow students whose religious beliefs are offended by the Holt series to opt out of reading instruction only.

A three-judge panel of the Sixth Circuit Court voted unanimously to *reject* Judge Hull's opinion. Chief Judge Lively said:

> The plaintiffs did not produce a single student or teacher to testify that any student was ever required to affirm his or her belief or disbelief in any idea or practice mentioned in the various stories and passages contained in the Holt series.

The second case, *Smith* v. *Board of School Commissioners of Mobile County* (1987) emanated from U.S. District Judge W. Brevard Hand's ruling that secular humanism was being taught in the county's schools in violation of the First Amendment. In his ruling, Judge Hand held that secular humanism was in fact a religion, and that the forty-four textbooks used by the county district were imbued with humanistic religious assumptions in their discussions of human relationships.

In its ruling, the U.S. Court of Appeals for the Eleventh Circuit did not address the question of whether secular humanism was a religion for First Amendment purposes. The court said that secular humanism was not being promoted in the challenged textbooks. The three judge panel of the U.S. Court of Appeals for the Eleventh Circuit voted unanimously to overturn Judge Brevard Hand's ruling that secular humanism was being taught in the Mobile County's schools in violation of the First Amendment's establishment clause.

A case involving the wearing of religious clothing as a teacher in a public school was heard by the Oregon Supreme Court. The teacher was dismissed after she refused to discontinue wearing Sikh religious clothing—a turban and white robes—to her sixth and eighth grade classes. Oregon state law forbids public school teachers from wearing religious clothing while they are teaching.

In *Cooper* v. *Eugene School District No. 4J* (1986) the Oregon Supreme Court noted that the law might indeed infringe upon the First Amendment right of teachers to free exercise of religion. The Court added, however, that the burden placed on such teachers was necessitated by the greater First Amendment responsibility of public schools to not give the appearance of endorsing specific religions.

The U.S. Supreme Court voted to dismiss the appeal for lack of a substantial federal question. Therefore, the decision of the Oregon State Supreme Court remains intact.

The rights assured under the First Amendment have been tested in their relationships to education in areas other than religion. A landmark decision in the area of student rights was made by the United States Supreme Court in

1969 (*Tinker* v. *Des Moines Independent Community School District*). The *Tinker* case centered around a school board's prevention of the wearing of black armbands by students protesting the hostilities in Vietnam. The Court in its majority opinion stated:

> . . . the wearing of armbands in the circumstances of this case was entirely divorced from actually or potentially disruptive conduct by those participating in it. It was closely akin to "pure speech" which, we have repeatedly held, is entitled to comprehensive protection under the First Amendment. . . .
>
> It can hardly be argued that either students or teachers shed their constitutional rights to freedom at the schoolhouse gate.

The *Tinker* case has and will undoubtedly affect the age-old doctrine of *in loco parentis*. The in loco parentis doctrine functioned under the traditional notion that schools and teachers could exercise total control over students because they acted as parent substitutes and out of concern for student welfare. Undoubtedly, the Court's opinion in the *Tinker* case will have an effect on the operation of schools in the United States.

Early in 1988, the U.S. Supreme Court in *Hazelwood School District* v. *Kuhlmeir* ruled that administrators have broad authority to control student expression in school newspapers, theatrical productions, and other forums that are part of the curriculum. In reaching that decision, the Court determined that the *Spectrum,* the school newspaper of the Hazelwood District was not a public forum. The Hazelwood school officials did not "evince" either "by policy or by practice" any intent to open the pages of *Spectrum* to "indiscriminate use by its student reporters and editors, or by the student body generally." Instead, they

"reserve(d) the forum for its intended purpose(s)" as a supervised learning experience for journalism students. Accordingly, school officials were entitled to regulate the contents of the *Spectrum* in any reasonable manner. The Court stated that it is this standard rather than our decision in *Tinker* that governs this case.

Another recent case dealing with student rights dealt with a violation of the Education for All Handicapped Children Act, PL 94–142. That law requires public school officials to keep disruptive or violent handicapped students in their current classrooms pending the hearings on their behavior. In the decision made in *Honig* v. *Roe* (1988), the U.S. Supreme Court upheld lower court rulings that San Francisco school district officials violated the Act in 1980 when they indefinitely suspended and then attempted to expel two emotionally disturbed students who the officials claimed were dangerous.

The Act authorizes officials to suspend dangerous handicapped children for a maximum of ten days. Longer suspensions or expulsions are permissible only if the child's parents consent to the action taken, or if the officials can convince a federal district judge that the child poses a danger to himself or herself or to others.

Associate Judge William J. Brennan writing for the majority of the Court said, "We think it clear . . . that Congress very much meant to strip schools of the *unilateral* authority they had traditionally employed to exclude disabled students, particularly emotionally disturbed students, from school. In so doing, Congress did not leave school administrators powerless to deal with dangerous students."

*Busing is one means to achieve desegregation, but most
often it is controversial.*

■ Court Decisions: Fourteenth Amendment

A most pertinent illustration of the use of the
Fourteenth Amendment was the United States
Supreme Court decision in *Brown* v. *Board of
Education of Topeka,* 1954. The impact of this
landmark decision repudiating the separate but
equal doctrine is still being felt and reacted to.
The judicial pronouncement in this case had legislative power added to it by the Civil Rights Act
of 1964.

A number of cases directly related to the
Brown decision have arisen. Most notable in
recent years are those dealing with metropolitan
desegregation (Richmond, Virginia; Wilmington, Delaware; Louisville, Kentucky; and

Detroit, Michigan). The metropolitan desegregation case arising in Richmond was heard by the
United States Supreme Court in 1973. With a 4–
4 tie vote, with Justice Powell disqualifying himself, the Court upheld a U.S. Court of Appeals
for the Fourth Circuit reversal of the metropolitan plan. In general, the metropolitan plan would
have called for the consolidation of the Richmond, Virginia, schools with the suburban Hen-
ries and Chesterfield County school systems.
Richmond schools were approximately 70 percent black, while the suburban schools were approximately 90 percent white.

In 1974, the United States Supreme Court
in *Milliken* v. *Bradley,* in a 5–4 vote overturned
lower court orders requiring the cross-busing of
children between the Detroit city school system

and fifty-three suburban school districts. In effect, the Supreme Court said: "Before the boundaries of separate and autonomous school districts may be set aside . . . it must first be shown that there has been a constitutional violation within one district that produces a significant segregation effect in another district. . . ." In 1975, metro desegregation orders were upheld in both Wilmington, Delaware, and Louisville, Kentucky. *In both instances it was determined, in effect, that school reorganization or interdistrict actions had the effect of maintaining segregation.*

While many districts are busing to bring about desegregation, the Norfolk, Virginia, board of education recently requested that it be permitted to stop busing students in grades kindergarten through grade 6. Since 1971, the Norfolk school district had been under a court order requiring a mandatory crosstown busing program.

In 1983, the Norfolk school board reverted to the neighborhood school plan. It gerrymandered attendance zones to provide for maximum integration. In junior high schools, the maximum black/white ratio was 72/28, and the minimum was 56/44. Twelve elementary schools would be 70 percent or more black, compared with four elementary schools in the same category under the busing plan. The new plan, that is neighborhood schools, provided for majority-minority transfers whereby any student assigned to a school where his or her race made up 70 percent or more of the student body could transfer to a school where his or her race made up less than 50 percent of the students. Students choosing such a plan were entitled to free transportation.

The federal district court upheld Norfolk's plan. It noted that the city was no longer operating a *de jure* dual system, that is a system that legally permitted racial segregation in public schools. The court found that the plaintiffs had not established that the neighborhood plan was based on discriminatory intent.

The court of appeals in *Riddick* v. *School Board of City of Norfolk* (1986) affirmed the opinion of the federal district court. That affirmation (1) signals a return to the neighborhood school system, and (2) holds that, once a school district converts from a dual (segregated) school system to a unitary (integrated) system, there is no affirmative duty to desegregate further.

Two recent developments related to court ordered desegregation are: the removal of judicial control of school districts; and the question of how the cost of court ordered remedies for desegregation can be shared, if at all.

In 1974, U.S. District Judge W. Arthur Garrity ordered the Boston school district to implement mandatory busing as a remedy for segregation. In the fall of 1987, a federal district appeals court struck down strict court-ordered racial guidelines for student assignments that the city's school had been required to maintain indefinitely. The ruling returns the control of the student assignment process to the Boston School Community for the first time since 1974. Also in the fall of 1987, U.S. District Judge Richard P. Matsch handed down an order that indicated that the Denver board had made a sufficient commitment to remedy racial isolation in its schools warranting his gradual withdrawal of control over the district.

Ordinarily, local school districts are expected to pay the costs of desegregation. In some instances, however, federal courts have ordered states to pay various percentages of the local district's desegregation costs. In Ohio, for example, the state is required to fund 50 percent of the school district's desegregation expenses. However, a three judge panel of the U.S. Court of Appeals for the Sixth Circuit ruled that the sovereign immunity clause of the U.S. Constitution Eleventh Amendment restricts the power of federal courts to order states to help pay for the desegregation of school districts. Judge David Nelson, writing for the three judge panel stated:

> While the federal court system clearly has the power to prohibit segregation . . . in no way does it follow that the judiciary has any corresponding authority to dictate the specific financial arrangements under which the costs of integrating the schools shall be handled.

The decision is binding only within the Sixth Circuit—Kentucky, Michigan, Ohio, and Tennessee. It is likely that this decision of the Sixth Circuit will be appealed eventually to the U.S. Supreme Court because of the dramatic effect it would have in implementing desegregation.

In addition to the First, Tenth, and Fourteenth Amendments to the United States Constitution, the Preamble to the Constitution has also had its effect on the development of education in the United States. The phrase "promote the general welfare," known as the *general welfare clause,* has been the basis for much of the federal support of education. The general welfare clause permits the infusion of federal monies into education as seen fit by the Congress.

■ Teacher Rights

Teachers have the same rights as other citizens. The Fourteenth Amendment provides for substantive due process (e.g., protection against the deprivation of constitutional rights such as freedom of expression) and procedural due process (procedural protection against unjustified deprivation of substantive rights). Most court cases related to teachers evolve from either liberty or property interests. Liberty rights are created by the Constitution itself; property interests are found in some form of legal entitlement such as tenure or certification.

■ Teacher Certification

The primary purpose of teacher certification is to make certain that there are qualified and competent teachers in the public schools. All states have established requirements for teacher certification. Certifying agencies may not arbitrarily refuse to issue a certificate to a qualified candidate. A teaching certificate is a license or a privilege granted to practice a profession—it is not a right. Teacher certification is a property interest that cannot be revoked without constitutional due process.

■ Teacher Employment Contracts

Usually, boards of education have the statutory authority to employ teachers. This authority includes the power to enter into contracts and to fix terms of employment and compensation. A contract usually contains the following elements: the identification of the teacher and the board of education, a statement of the legal capacity of each party to enter into contract, a definition of the assignment specified, a statement of the salary and how it is to be paid, and a provision for signature by the teacher and by the legally authorized agent of the board. A teacher may not enter into legal contract without having a valid teaching certificate issued by the state. Teachers are responsible for making certain that they are legally qualified to enter into contractual agreements. Furthermore, they are responsible for carrying out the terms of the contract and abiding by them. In turn, under the contract, they can legally expect proper treatment from an employer.

■ Discrimination

School districts are prohibited from use of discriminatory practices in hiring, dismissal, promotion, and demotion of school personnel. Most discrimination cases against the school are brought on charges of discrimination on the basis of sex, race, religion, age, and/or a handicap. The burden falls on the defendant (schools) to show that a legitimate nondiscriminatory reason existed for the personnel decision.

Burkey v. *Marshall County Board of Education* (1981) was a decision regarding pay equity. It ruled that the Marshall County school board's policy of paying the female coach of the girls' basketball team half the salary of the male coach of the boys' basketball team violated the Equal Pay Act, Title VII of the Civil Rights Act of 1964, and the U.S. Constitution. The Court also ruled that the board's policy of hiring only male teachers as coaches of boys' sports constituted illegal sex discrimination.

■ Teacher Tenure

Teacher tenure legislation exists in most states. Tenure provides job security for teachers by preventing their dismissal without cause and by requiring that due process be provided. Tenure statutes generally include detailed specifications necessary for attaining tenure and for dismissing teachers who have tenure.

Although due process has been applicable for years to tenure teachers, nontenured teachers do not, for the most part, enjoy the same rights. Nontenured teachers may also have due process rights if spelled out in state statutes; or they may be nonrenewed without any reason being given in those states not providing for due process. If a nontenured teacher is dismissed (as distinguished from nonrenewed) before the expiration of the contract, the teacher is then entitled to due process.

In 1972, the U.S. Supreme Court helped to clarify the difference in the rights of tenured and nontenured teachers. In *Board of Regents* v. *Roth* (1972), the Court held that nontenured teachers were assured of no rights that were not specified in the state statutes. Also in 1972, the Court ruled in *Perry* v. *Sindermann* that a nontenured teacher in the Texas system of community colleges was entitled to due process because the language of the institution's policy manual was such that an unofficial tenure system was in effect. Guidelines in the policy manual provided that a faculty member with seven years of employment in the system acquired tenure and could be dismissed only for cause.

Whether a teacher is tenured or not, that person cannot be dismissed for exercise of a right guaranteed by the federal Constitution. A school board cannot dismiss a teacher, for example, for engaging in civil rights activities outside school, speaking on matters of public concern, belonging to a given church, or running for a public office. These rights are guaranteed to all citizens including teachers.

■ Academic Freedom

Academic freedom has been a vital concern of educators for many years. It means the freedom to control what one will teach and to teach the truth as one discovers it, without fear of penalty. Federal judges have generally recognized certain academic protections in the college classrooms while exhibiting reluctance to recognize rights for elementary and secondary school teachers. Unlike college students, public school pupils are subject to compulsory attendance laws and are viewed as having impressionable minds. Thus there are more restraints on academic freedom on public school teachers than on those who teach in higher education.

A landmark case that dealt with academic freedom at the high school level was *Pickering* v. *Board of Education* (1968). Pickering was a teacher in Illinois who, in a letter published by a local newspaper, was critical of the school board and the superintendent for the way they handled past proposals to raise and use new revenues for the schools. The board of education terminated Pickering's employment, whereupon he brought suit under the First and Fourteenth Amendments. The U.S. Supreme Court upheld Pickering's claim. In its opinion, it stated:

> To the extent that the Illinois Supreme Court's opinion may be read to suggest that teachers may constitutionally be compelled to relinquish the First Amendment rights they would otherwise enjoy as citizens to comment on matters of public interest in connection with the operation of the public schools in which they work, it proceeds on a premise that has been unequivocally rejected in numerous prior decisions of this Court.

The Court held that the problem was how to arrive at a balance between the interests of the teacher, who as a citizen comments on matters of public concern, and the interests of the state, which as an employer promotes the efficiency of its public services through its employees. It is indeed a delicate balance.

Generally, teachers have been supported in their rights to dress in their preferred manner, criticize the policies of their local school boards, wear symbols representing stated causes, participate in unpopular movements, and live unconventional life-styles. But where the exercise of those rights can be shown to have a direct bearing on the teacher's effectiveness, respect, or discipline, these rights may have to be curtailed.

■ Right to Bargain Collectively

Many states already have collective bargaining agreements; undoubtedly, more statutes will be enacted. The details of the statutes and the proposals vary, but generally they include the right of public employees to organize and bargain collectively, to determine the bargaining agent (in the case of teachers usually an AFT or an NEA affiliate), to describe the scope of negotiation, and to provide an impasse procedure. Today, approximately 75 percent of the nation's teachers are covered by collective bargaining agreements.

■ Right to Strike

Courts have ruled on the legality of strikes. The Supreme Court of Connecticut (*Norwalk Teachers' Association* v. *Board of Education,* 1951) and the Supreme Court of New Hampshire (*City of Manchester* v. *Manchester*

Teachers' Guild, 1957) ruled that teachers may not strike. The court opinion in Connecticut stated:

> Under our system, the government is established by and run for all the people, not for the benefit of any person or group. The profit motive, inherent in the principle of free enterprise, is absent. It should be the aim of every employee of the government to do his or her part to make it function as efficiently and economically as possible. The drastic remedy or the organized strike to enforce the demands of unions of government employees is in direct contravention of this principle.

Judges have generally held that public employees do not have the right to strike. A state district court in Minnesota deviated from this view when it said that to hold that a public employee has no right to strike is a personal belief that looks for legality on some tenuous theory of sovereignty or supremacy of government. The court upheld the right to strike as rooted in the freedom of men and women and was to be denied except by clear, unequivocal language in a constitution, statute, ordinance, rule, or contract.

At least seven states—Alaska, Hawaii, Montana, New Hampshire, Oregon, Pennsylvania, and Vermont—permit strikes in their bargaining statutes. At least twenty states have statutes that prohibit strikes.

Recently the U.S. Supreme Court, by a six to three vote, ruled that boards of education can discharge teachers who are striking illegally. Ramifications of this decision, involving a Wisconsin public school, are potentially far-reaching. The Court viewed discharge as a policy matter rather than an issue for adjudication: "What choice among the alternative responses to the teacher's strike will best serve the interests of the school system, the interests of parents and children who depend on the system, and the interests of the citizens whose taxes support it?" The Court said that the state law in question gave the board the power to employ and dismiss teachers as part of the balance it had struck in municipal labor relations (*Hortonville Joint School District No. 1 v. Hortonville Education Association,* 1976).

One can argue that strikes are unlawful when a statute is violated, that the courts in their decisions have questioned the right of public employees to strike, and that some teachers consider strikes to be unprofessional. The question before teachers seems to be whether the strike is a justifiable and reasonable means—after all other ways have been exhausted—of declaring abominable educational working conditions and trying to remedy them.

In summary, the United States Constitution, while it has been intepreted as delegating the function of education to the states, does contain within it protection for the rights of individuals, which must not be violated in the operation of education by states and local districts.

Federal Legislation

In addition to court decisions, federal legislation has decided effects on local school districts. In the last five years, the Buckley Amendment, Title IX, and Public Law 94–142 have had significant impacts. Public Law 94–142, Education for All Handicapped Children Act, has been discussed elsewhere.

We the people of the United States in order to form a more perfect Union, establish justice, insure domestic tranquility, provide for the common defense, promote the general welfare, and secure the blessings of liberty to ourselves and our posterity, do ordain and establish the Constitution for the United States of America.

Preamble, United States Constitution

Buckley Amendment—Privacy of Educational Records

The Buckley Amendment has been federal law since 1974. In essence, it precisely defines who may or may not see individual student records. The Act sets forth the following requirements: (1) allow all parents, even those not having custody of their children, access to each educational record that a school district keeps on their child, (2) establish a district policy on how parents can go about seeing specific records, (3) inform all parents what rights they have under the Amendment, how they can act on these rights according to school policy, and where they can see a copy of the policy, and (4) seek parental permission in writing before disclosing any personally identifiable record on a child to individuals other than professional personnel employed in the district.[2] The Amendment has caused school districts and their teachers and administrators to recognize and implement appropriate procedures in the disclosure of pupil records.

Title IX

The Education Amendments of 1972 make sex discrimination, once a philosophical or moral issue, a legal issue as well. The key provision in Title IX reads: "No person in the United States shall, on the basis of sex, be excluded from participation in, be denied benefits of, or be subjected to discrimination under any educational program or activity receiving federal financial assistance."[3] Any educational institution, public or private, that receives federal monies by way of grant, loan, or contract (other than a contract of insurance of guaranty) is required to comply with

Title IX. Schools at all levels are covered, from preschools to graduate schools. Most public schools at all levels, and many private schools receive federal assistance. Title IX covers virtually all areas of student life: admissions, financial aid, health services, sports, testing, differential rules, and the like.[4] The implementation of Title IX, while still evolving, is having decided impacts on education.

Federal Agency Involvement in Education

The creation of the United States Office of Education represented a formalized federal effort in education. It was originally established in 1867 as the Federal Department of Education. In 1953, after several changes of names, its title officially became the United States Office of Education, and it became part of the Department of Health, Education, and Welfare with a secretary in the President's cabinet.

In October 1979, the Department of Education was created. The Department took on the functions of the U.S. Office of Education. The Office collected and published information about all phases of education in the United States, engaged in conducting and disseminating educational research, provided leadership, and administered much of the federal funding for education. From a meager and mild beginning, the Office of Education, particularly in the last few years, had grown to become a powerful and influential agency.

The new Department of Education was created in a context of political controversy and is still somewhat shaky. Those who favored the creation of the new department felt that education was too important to be lost in the gigantic Department of Health, Education, and Welfare.

*Religion, morality, and knowledge
being necessary to good government
and happiness of mankind, schools
and the means of education shall
forever be encouraged.*

Northwest Ordinance, 1787

Opponents took the position that a national Department of Education would result in more federal control and standardization. Most educational groups, however, supported the creation of the department. In addition to the U.S. Office of Education, the new department will have the National Institute of Education, National Center for Educational Statistics, Civil Rights Office (education activities), and the National Science Foundation within its jurisdiction. Shirley Hufstedler, a judge, was named as the first secretary of the department, but within a year of her appointment she was replaced by Terrel Bell, who resigned his position in December, 1984. His successor, William J. Bennett, resigned in the fall of 1988. In September, Lauro F. Cavazos was appointed Secretary of Education.

Federally Operated Schools

The federal government has accepted responsibility for and directly operates some educational institutions. The Congress provides funds for the operation of the school system of the District of Columbia. The Department of the Interior is responsible for the education of children of National Park Employees, and for outlying possessions (Samoa), and trust territories (Caroline and Marshall Islands). The Bureau of Indian Affairs finances and manages schools on Indian reservations. The Department of Defense is responsible for the four military academies, and also operates a school system for children of military personnel wherever they may be located. Further, the education given in the various training programs of the military services has made a tremendous contribution to the overall educational effort in our nation.

■ **Table 17.1**   Selected Federal Acts That Have Provided Funds for Education.

1785	Ordinance of 1785
1787	Northwest Ordinance
1862	Morrill Land Grant Act
1887	Hatch Act
1914	Smith-Lever Agriculture Extension Act
1917	Smith-Hughes Vocational Act
1930	Civilian Conservation Corps
1933	Public Works Administration
1935	National Youth Administration
1935	Works Program Administration
1940	Vocational Education for National Defense Act
1941	Lanham Act
1944	G.I. Bill of Rights
1946	National School Lunch Act
1950	National Science Foundation
1954	Cooperative Research Program
1958	National Defense Education Act
1963	Manpower Development and Training Act
1964	Economic Opportunity Act
1965	Elementary and Secondary Education Act
—	Amendments of ESEA
1981	Omnibus Budget Reconciliation Act (Block Grants)
1984	Education for Economic Security Act

Source: 1984 Education for Economic Security Act.

Federal Financial Support

Federal funding represents a fourth way in which the federal government has become involved in education. Table 17.1 lists some selected illustrative federal acts that have, either directly or indirectly, provided support for education.

The list of federal acts presented in Table 17.1, while by no means exhaustive, is illustrative. Some general observations can be made from an examination of the list. It is apparent that federal funding for education is not a new phenomenon. The 1785 and 1787 Northwest Ordinance Acts encouraged the establishment of education in the Northwest Territory. The Ordinance of 1785 required the reservation of the sixteenth section of each township for the maintenance of schools. Federal funding since this early beginning has increased steadily. It is also apparent that the funding has been categorical—that is, for a specific purpose. Each of the acts listed had or has a purpose. Let it suffice for purposes of illustration to point out that (1) the Morrill Acts and the Hatch Act encouraged expanded agricultural, mechanical, and scientific education in institutions of higher education; (2) the Smith-Lever and Smith-Hughes Acts encouraged vocational education in secondary schools; (3) the CCC, PWA, NYA, and WPA, while in the main designed to alleviate the economic depression of the 1930s, provided incidental aid to education and youth; (4) the NDEA Act specifically affirmed the feelings of Congress toward the importance of education for national defense; and (5) the ESEA provided many thrusts, including efforts to meet the needs of children of poverty and to encourage research. The ESEA was somewhat unique in federal funding legislation in that it came as close to general aid as any federal legislation ever has, and it further provided the means whereby federal tax funds could be made available to private and church-related schools. In a sense it represented an infusion of the judicial child benefit theory attitudes into legislation. ESEA has been regularly extended with amendments since 1965. The major purpose of the Education for Economic Security Act is to improve education in mathematics and science.

A fourth observation that can be made is that federal funding originates and is administered through a number of federal agencies. For example, in addition to the former Department of Health, Education, and Welfare, funds are administered through the new Department of Education, and the Departments of Agriculture, Defense, Housing and Urban Development, Labor, and Interior; and through agencies such as the Office of Economic Opportunity, Veteran's Administration, and the Peace Corps.

Federal Influence: Direct and Subtle

The federal government is an influential agent in American education. Its influence has been felt directly in terms of protecting individual rights as provided in the Constitution, attaining equality of opportunity for all, promoting general welfare in terms of domestic social and economic problems and national defense, and operating specific educational agencies. Its subtle effect is most strongly exerted through the financial incentives offered to stimulate specific programs.

State Government

Public education in the United States is a state function. States have recognized this function in their respective constitutions and have established laws directing the way in which it shall be conducted. Most states, the exception being Wisconsin, have established state boards of education. The executive duties of administering education at the state level are primarily the responsibility of a state department or office of public instruction. These departments in the various states are headed by a chief executive officer, frequently called the state superintendent of public instruction or the chief state school officer.

Let us briefly examine how each of these segments of control and operation at the state level influence education.

State Constitutions

The constitutional provisions of the states for education, while differing slightly in their precise wording, are markedly similar in their intent. An illustrative example is a statement in Section 2, Article VIII, of the Constitution of the State of Michigan. It reads, "The Legislature shall maintain and support a system of free public elementary and secondary schools as defined by law. Each school district shall provide for the education of its pupils without discrimination as to religion, creed, race, color, or national origin." The various state constitutions are interpreted by state courts and legal counsel as conflicts arise. The decisions of state courts may be appealed to the United States Supreme Court. The United States Supreme Court will usually hear the case if in their judgment it is in the domain of the United States Constitution or federal law.

State Legislatures

The enabling legislation to conduct the educational enterprise is prepared by state legislatures. This legislation is usually classified and bound in a volume referred to as the *school code*. Legislation is both mandatory and permissive, and therefore directs and guides local school boards in their task of operating schools. The greater the tendency to enact permissive legislation, the greater the amount of control delegated to the local boards of education. State legislation is concerned with many aspects of education—for example, district organizational patterns, teacher certification and tenure regulations, financing of schools, and attendance laws.

State legislatures, because of their important position in education, are the subject of much lobbying. In the realm of education, the laws that are formulated deal with children and money, both of which are precious to most citizens. Influential lobbying groups may include: taxpayers' federations; patriotic groups; labor, business, and professional organizations; humane societies; and the various organizations concerned directly with education, such as state teachers' associations, school administrator associations, and school board associations.

State Boards of Education

State boards of education concerned with elementary and secondary education are now in operation with forty-nine of the fifty states, with Wisconsin as the exception: however, Wisconsin does have a state board for vocational education, since this is a federal requirement to be eligible to receive funds for these activities.

Historically, the prototype of the modern-day style of state boards of education was the board established in Massachusetts in 1837. It was the first state board with an appointed secretary—in the person of Horace Mann. Henry Barnard, another pioneer educator, became the first secretary of the Connecticut State Board of Education, and later, after serving in the same capacity in Rhode Island, became the first United States Commissioner of Education.

The duties of state boards of education vary; however, in general, they serve in a policymaking capacity. Policies are formulated and rules and regulations are adopted as are necessary to carry out the responsibilities assigned to state boards by the respective state constitutions and statutes.

They submit annual reports, hear appeals resulting from their own rules and regulations, and determine the extent of their own power in accordance with the law. State boards are also regulatory, that is, they establish and enforce standards in such areas as certification of teachers and accreditation of schools. Other duties may be considered as advisory. Such duties may include considering the educational needs of the state, and making recommendations to the governor and the legislature.

Membership on state boards is attained in three ways: election by the people or their representatives, appointment by the governor, or ex officio by virtue of other office held. Table 17.2 provides this information for each state.

It is interesting to note the differences among states as to their preference in methods of selection. Iowa, New York, and Washington are somewhat unique in their elective procedures. In Iowa, conventions of delegates from areas within the state send nominations to the governor, on the basis of which the governor makes the appointment; in New York, the Board of Regents is elected by the legislature; and in Washington, the state board is elected by members of boards of directors of local school districts. Needless to say, there are advantages and disadvantages to both the elective and the appointive procedures in selecting state school board members. The appointive procedure is considered by its proponents to be more efficient in that it is more likely to establish a harmonious relationship with the governor and that it facilitates the placement of highly qualified persons who would not for various reasons seek election. The proponents of the elective procedures cite the "grass-roots" control feature, and the lesser likelihood of political manipulation. In either case, once members are selected, they usually have staggered terms to avoid a complete change in membership at any one time; they also usually serve without pay, but with reimbursement for their expenses. Both of these provisions serve as safeguards against political patronage.

Chief State School Officers

The chief state school officer occupies an important position in the administration of education within each respective state. Usually this individual is the executive head of the state department of education, and as such, through the administrative staff of the office, provides leadership and supervisory service in addition to the customary clerical and regulatory functions of state departments of education. The chief state school officer presents interpretations of educational needs to the governor, state board of education, and legislature, and frequently influences legislation, both directly and indirectly. While the provision for the state school officer's duties vary from state to state, the duties are specifically delineated by a combination of the respective state constitution and school code. Chief state school officers are likely to receive direction from the state board of education.

Information as to how chief state school officers are selected is also presented in table 17.2. Currently, nineteen state officers are elected by the people or their representatives, twenty-seven are appointed by state boards of education, and four are appointed by the governor. The trend has been away from election and toward appointment, specifically appointment by the state board of education. Arguments advanced in favor of

State	Members of state boards of education			Chief state school officers		
	Elected by people or represent. of people	Appointed by governor	Ex officio	Elected by popular vote	Appointed by state board of education	Appointed by governor
Alabama	x				x	
Alaska		x			x	
Arizona		x		x		
Arkansas		x			x	
California		x		x		
Colorado	x				x	
Connecticut		x			x	
Delaware		x			x	
Florida			x	x		
Georgia		x		x		
Hawaii	x				x	
Idaho		x		x		
Illinois		x			x	
Indiana		x		x		
Iowa	x				x	
Kansas	x				x	
Kentucky		x		x		
Louisiana	x			x		
Maine		x			x	
Maryland		x			x	
Massachusetts		x			x	
Michigan	x				x	
Minnesota		x			x	
Mississippi			x	x		
Missouri		x			x	
Montana		x		x		
Nebraska	x				x	
Nevada	x				x	
New Hampshire		x			x	
New Jersey		x				x
New Mexico	x				x	
New York	x				x	
North Carolina		x		x		
North Dakota		x		x		
Ohio	x				x	
Oklahoma		x		x		
Oregon		x		x		
Pennsylvania		x				x
Rhode Island		x			x	
South Carolina	x			x		
South Dakota		x		x		
Tennessee		x				x
Texas	x				x	
Utah	x				x	
Vermont		x			x	
Virginia		x				x
Washington	x			x		
West Virginia		x			x	
Wisconsin	(No state board)			x		
Wyoming		x		x		
Total	16	31	2	19	27	4

These teachers are engaged in curriculum planning.

appointment include the notion that policy-making should be clearly differentiated from policy execution; that educational leadership should not depend so heavily on one elected official; and that a greater likelihood exists of recruiting and retaining qualified career personnel. Opponents to the appointment procedure claim that, in the main, the official selected under this system would not be responsible to the people. A major objection raised to gubernatorial appointment is the danger of involvement in partisan politics. It is important to note that an elected state school officer is legally a state "official," while an appointed officer is an "employee." As a result of this difference, the working relationship of an

elected official with the state board of education is not likely to be as clear and cleanly defined as it is in instances where the chief state school officer is appointed by the state board of education and therefore clearly an employee.

State Departments of Education

The state departments of education, under the direction of the chief state school officer, carry out the activities of state government in education. Their activities have been classified into five categories: operational, regulatory, service, developmental, and public support and cooperation.[5] Until recent years, their activities have been largely operational and regulatory. Operational activities are those that have to do with the direct operation of schools such as those for the deaf or blind; regulatory activities center around the enforcement of state regulations for schools, such as making certain that only properly certified teachers are employed, and that buildings are safe. The service function has to do with helping local school districts. It includes the sharing of the knowledge and expertise of the state by providing consultant service, research information, or legal advice. Most states have improved their service activities in the past few years. Developmental activities have to do with planning in order to improve the state departments themselves so that they may further develop their capabilities. Public support and cooperation activities involve communicating effectively with the people of the state, the legislature and governor, and other governmental bodies.

While the traditional roles of state departments have emphasized the operational and regulatory functions, the problems of education today indicate that the state departments of education should play a stronger leadership role.

Intermediate Units

The intermediate unit of school organization is that unit between the state department of education and local school districts. Historically, the intermediate unit served a liaison function. In rural areas, with a preponderance of small schools, it also served a direct educational function such as providing guidance or special education services.

The basic purpose of the intermediate unit today is to provide two or more local districts with educational services that they cannot efficiently and economically provide individually. Recently, great strides have been made in this regard, particularly in the providing of special education and vocational-technical education. Area "vo-tech" schools have been aided by relatively high infusions of federal monies. Other examples of services that intermediate units can provide include audiovisual libraries, centralized purchasing, in-service training for teachers and other personnel, health services, instructional materials, laboratories, legal services, and consultant services.

Local School Districts

The agency of governance in education most visible to both citizens and teachers is the local school district. The school district is controlled by a governing board made up of citizens residing in the geographical area that makes up the district.

Local school districts, while similar in their major purpose—the education of children—are widely different in their characteristics. There are currently about 15,500 school districts in the United States enrolling approximately 45 million students in public and private elementary and secondary schools. These districts differ in many ways: geographical size; enrollment; geographical location (urban, suburban, rural); socioeconomic composition; heterogeneity and homogeneity; wealth; type of organization (K–8, 9–12, K–12); and in many other ways. Most of the school districts in the United States are small in terms of enrollment. It has been estimated that 27 percent of the districts enroll less than 300 pupils, and that this total enrollment makes up only about 1.4 percent of the total national enrollment. Yet, only about 1.0 percent of the districts have enrollments greater than 25,000, but these districts enroll about 26 percent of the total national enrollment. The trend in school district organization has been to reduce the number of districts in an effort to obtain a more effective and efficient organization. The number of districts has been reduced from over 100,000 in 1945 to the current 15,500. Such school reorganization is a slow but inevitable process. Along with consolidation the trend has been to establish more districts that include both elementary and secondary education (K–12).

While the "putting together" or consolidation of smaller districts is being encouraged, problems have become apparent in very large city systems such as New York, Chicago, and Los Angeles that can be partly attributed to their immense enrollments. Communications in such districts can become distant and distorted. Patrons in such systems often express strong feelings that their districts are not responsive. They are calling for decentralization to enable them to gain some control over their neighborhood schools. Experimental efforts toward decentralization are being made in such large urban areas as Los Angeles, Chicago, and Miami to meet these desires.

Local Control

Local control becomes a reality through the governing boards of local districts. They may make decisions within the power delegated to them by the state. Some of their powers include those to raise monies; obtain sites; build buildings; provide curricula; employ teachers and other personnel; and admit and assign pupils to schools. Local school boards must conform to mandatory statutes, and operate within powers delegated to them. It is within their power to enact local policies for education providing those policies do not violate existing state laws. Board members are local people. Ninety-five percent of them throughout the United States are elected by popular vote, most frequently in special elections on a nonpartisan basis; the remaining 5 percent are appointed. Appointed boards occur most often in school districts enrolling over 25,000 pupils.

Local control is a characteristic that can be either advantageous or disadvantageous. The local school district, represented in person by board members, often provides the closest relationship that many citizens have with a local form of government. The administration of local schools concerns people deeply, dealing directly as it does with their children. Schools also frequently represent the agency that collects the largest amount of local tax monies. Further, education is viewed by more and more citizens as the most practical way to resolve social and economic problems, particularly at the grass root level. There is little doubt that local control permits citizens to have their say in providing school programs that will be responsive to their local desires and needs. Conversely, local control also permits wide variances in educational opportunity. Local control historically has been conservative and provincial, each district's concern being for its own welfare without a strong regard for state or national problems. It can be argued, for example, that one factor, the mobility of our population, is sufficient reason to support greater centralization. Further, national domestic problems and our national defense require that national policies and programs be implemented in local schools. Actions taken by many states in response to the national reports have also affected local control. Illustrations of those actions are state mandates specifying graduation requirements and testing at various levels.

■ School-Based Management: School Control and Teacher Empowerment

School-based management is a relatively new concept in which authority is given by a school district to a school or schools within the district empowering the school(s) to decide, for example, how they spend money, allocate staff, and organize instruction. The concept has come about in part because of educational reform recommendations urging greater participation and empowerment of teachers in governance particularly at the local school level, and because of the strong demands of parents to have more to say about the education of their children. Two objectives of school-based management are to reduce district regulatory control of schools, and to empower teachers with the opportunity to participate in making decisions for the operation of the local school.

Dade County School District (Florida), which includes the city of Miami, is a leader in developing school-based management. Thirty-two of its 280 schools are involved in implementing school-based management. Each school involved in school-based management must meet two requirements: principals and teachers must devise ways to run the school together and whatever changes they make must have a measurable benefit for students.[6]

> Both the school board and the union have agreed to waive district regulations and contract provisions that stand in the way of educational change. The school board, for example, has suspended requirements regarding maximum class size, the length of the school day, the number of minutes per subject, and when report cards should be handed out. The union has

enabled teachers in specific schools to give up their planning periods, work longer hours for no additional pay, and evaluate their peers.[7]

The Chicago School Reform Act, which went into effect on July 1, 1989, made the following changes on how the Chicago schools are run.

- Local School Councils, to consist of six parents, two community members, two school employees and the principal, will control the local school budget. The councils will have authority to hire and fire the principal; create a school improvement plan with teachers and the principal; and request waivers from the Chicago Teachers Union and the Chicago Board of Education to develop experimental programs.

- The present Chicago Board of Education will be disbanded and the mayor will appoint a 15-member board by May 15, 1989, from nominations made by a commission of parents and community members.

- The Chicago School Reform Oversight Authority, to consist of four mayoral and three gubernatorial appointees, will oversee the board's improvement plan and have the authority to dismiss and discipline school board staff. The authority, with a maximum $500,000-a-year budget from state funds, will monitor administrative spending.

- Central bureaucracy spending must be cut by 25 percent the first year, saving about $46 million to be reallocated to local schools. At least 50 percent of the cuts must come from administrative positions.

- The general superintendent, to be chosen from a national search, will have a three-year performance contract and will negotiate union contracts, formerly a responsibility of the school board. The current superintendent, Manford Byrd Jr., whose contract runs out in 1989, will be eligible to apply for the position.

• Money for programs for low-income children, involving a $100-million-a-year state reallocation, must follow those children to their schools.

• Teachers hired to fill new or vacant positions will be chosen according to merit, not seniority. Principals will be able to remove teachers from a classroom 45 days after giving notice of unsatisfactory performance.

• Principals, who will lose tenured job protection, will be employed under performance contracts controlled by the local school council. The principals will oversee the chief engineers and lunchroom managers of their schools.[8]

The Rochester, New York, School District has implemented school-based management along with other types of educational reform activities. (See appendix L.)

School-based management is being considered widely, yet only a few schools have reported that they have implemented the concept. It is anticipated that more school districts will become involved in school-based management. It has promise for success. Time will tell if it turns out to be a cure or a curse.

Local Schools

Schools can be the subject of much community controversy. This can originate over sex education, a change in attendance center boundaries, closing a neighborhood school, textbooks, methods of discipline, or losing too many athletic contests. It may be stirred up because more emphasis is put on athletics than on music or art, or not enough emphasis on basic subjects. Sometimes the dismissal or transfer of a principal or teacher

brings out very strong feelings. Controversy may even result from the enforcement of a federal or state mandate that the local citizens don't agree with. The focus of the controversy is usually the members of the board of education—the elected representatives of the people.

Members of boards of education cannot avoid politics as many of them would wish to do. Their election or reelection depends on how well the people feel they are representing them, and how successful the schools are in educating their children. Board membership is frequently a thankless task at best. Yet, many board members enjoy their service, and many of them do a great job in providing direction for local schools—the essence of local control.

Erosion of Local Control

It is obvious that local boards of education do not have the control they once had. Court decisions and federal legislation cited earlier have been a significant factor in this loss of local control. Since 1981, with the passage of the Omnibus Budget Reconciliation Act (block grants) more power has been given to the states, particularly in fiscal affairs, by the federal government. Another major factor has been the increasing power of teachers and their associations. A third thrust, parent power, has just recently been exerted. Parents want a much stronger voice in education, particularly in relation to school programs and high taxes. Their apparent immediate target is the local district board of education.

Teacher Power

There was a time in our history when, for all practical purposes, teachers had little or no influence in determining the conditions of their employment, let alone enough power to influence educational policies. In recent years, however,

Research Finding

15

Successful principals establish policies that create an orderly environment and support effective instruction.

Effective principals have a vision of what a good school is and systematically strive to bring that vision to life in their schools. School improvement is their constant theme. They scrutinize existing practices to assure that all activities and procedures contribute to the quality of the time available for learning. They make sure teachers participate actively in this process. Effective principals, for example, make opportunities available for faculty to improve their own teaching and classroom management skills.

Good school leaders protect the school day for teaching and learning. They do this by keeping teachers, administrative chores and classroom interruptions to a minimum.

Effective principals visibly and actively support learning. Their practices create an orderly environment. Good principals make sure teachers have the necessary materials and the kind of assistance they need to teach well.

Effective principals also build morale in their teachers. They help teachers create a climate of achievement by encouraging new ideas; they also encourage teachers to help formulate school teaching policies and select textbooks. They try to develop community support for the school, its faculty, and its goals.

In summary, effective principals are experts at making sure time is available to learn, and at ensuring that teachers and students make the best use of that time.

Bird, T., and Little, J. W. (1985). *Instructional Leadership in Eight Secondary Schools.* Final Report to the U.S. Department of Education. National Institute of Education, Boulder, CO: Center for Action Research, ERIC Document No. ED 263694.

Bossert, S. (May 1985). "Effective Elementary Schools." In R. Kyle (Ed.), *Reading for Excellence: An Effective Schools Sourcebook* (pp. 45–49). Washington, DC: U.S. Government Printing Office.

Carnine, D. R., Gersten, R., and Green, S. (December 1982). "The Principal as Instructional Leader: A Second Look." *Educational Leadership,* Vol. 40, No. 3, pp. 47–50.

Source: *What Works: Research About Teaching and Learning.* Washington, DC: U.S. Department of Education, 1987, page 64.

teachers have begun to exert their power through their professional organizations. Local teacher groups are affiliated with national organizations, namely the National Education Association or the American Federation of Teachers. The topic of professional organizations and their roles in teacher power was considered in an earlier chapter. Let it suffice to say at this point that today teachers do have power.

Teacher power is manifested at the local district level by the use of a local organization to press for collective bargaining. While the term *collective bargaining* has been defined in many ways, in terms of power it means a formalization of access procedures to the legally defined school power structure. Physically it results in a written document, called an *agreement,* which most frequently spells out conditions of employment. The question of what is and what is not negotiable has not yet been clearly defined. It ranges from the broad definition of everything that affects a teacher, including curriculum, textbooks, in-service training, student teaching programs and many other items, to a narrow limitation considering just salaries. In some states, the legislature has clearly defined the subject matter for negotiation while, in other states, the issue is still wide open. Teacher groups have been extremely powerful in lobbying for and against various negotiation bills at the state level.

The power that teachers have gained they have gained through organization. Their ultimate weapon has been a work stoppage or strike, which incidentally is not considered under the traditional judicial view as being legal. Nevertheless, the number of teacher strikes has steadily increased.

Teachers have asked for, and in some cases demanded, a share in educational decision making. In some cases, these requests have been formalized, and in a sense legitimatized as a part of a negotiations agreement. In general, teachers have expressed disagreement and resistance to the traditional flow of authority for decision making from the top down. They have been asking to be heard as citizens and as responsible, trained professionals. The recommendations of educational reform, if implemented, would give teachers at the local school level more power in decision making, as was indicated in the discussion about school-based management. Their voices are being heard today and will be heard more tomorrow.

As they speak, they should be constantly aware of their responsibilities—responsibilities that they have as citizens and educators for the destinies of children and our society. If their actions and their use of power are perceived by many citizens as being irresponsible, which they are in some instances, it is likely that the power of the general public will be exerted as a counterthrust, as it has been in some instances. The ultimate power for education in a democratic nation resides in the people.

Federal-State-Local Interrelationships

The federal-state-local relationships of the past evolved as our country grew and developed. As our nation changed from basically a sparsely populated and agrarian society to an urban industrialized society which now has become increasingly an information society, the nature of the federal-state-local relationship has changed. While the states have been and still are the major source of legal control, the federal government has increased its influential and legal roles, particularly in efforts to assure constitutional rights and to respond to both foreign and domestic issues. The federal government's response to domestic problems that relate to education, such as poverty and segregation, and its tendency to attack such problems quite directly, rather than channel its efforts through state agencies, has at least in part caused state school officials to organize to have their views heard. The Omnibus Budget Reconciliation Act (Block Grants) (1981) did, in fact, result in federal funds being given to the states rather than to local school districts, and therefore providing the states with greater discretion in the way they could use the funds.

New federal-state-local relationships are emerging. Each level of government tends to look at the purposes of education from its own perspective: local school districts see their immediate local needs; states, the welfare of the state and its overall constituency; the federal government, its concern with equality, national security, and national domestic problems. While it is difficult to predict what the future relationships will be, it is clear that educational purposes and problems that are not resolved at the local level are likely to be taken on by another level of government. The problems that we face seem to be of a magnitude that make state and federal involvement necessary to resolve them. A new federal-state-local educational partnership is necessary and is emerging to forge solutions to problems of and related to education.

■ Summary

The purpose of this chapter was to introduce you to the governance roles of the federal and state agencies and the local school districts. The first topic discussed was the role of the federal government.

The federal government has become involved in education in four different ways: (1) the application of the United States Constitution to education, (2) the functions and operations of the Department of Education, (3) the direct operation of educational programs by various agencies of the federal government, and (4) the provision of federal aid in its various forms. Of these four, the one that affects education the most is the application of the U.S. Constitution to education. Education is not mentioned in the U.S. Constitution. The Tenth Amendment has been interpreted as implying that education is a function of the respective states. The First Amendment which insures freedom of speech, religion, the press and the right of petition has been frequently applied to education, as has the Fourteenth Amendment providing for the protection of specified privileges and rights of citizens.

Court decisions based upon the First Amendment have frequently had to do with the relationships between religion and education. Essentially there are three issues related to religion and education: (1) those having to do with the rights of parents to educate their children in public schools; (2) those having to do with the use of public funds to support private education; and (3) those having to do with the teaching or practice of religion in the public schools. Cases and court decisions in regard to those issues were presented and discussed. A second application of the First Amendment deals with the freedom of expression. The cases selected for that topic specifically deal with the students' rights of expression—their freedoms of speech, writing, and others.

A most pertinent illustration of the use of the Fourteenth Amendment was the United States Supreme Court decision in *Brown* v. *Board of Education of Topeka* (1954). The impact of this landmark decision repudiating the separate but equal doctrine is still being felt and reacted to. Desegregation was discussed along with busing.

All state constitutions have provisions for education. The role of state legislature is to prepare enabling legislation to conduct the educational programs in their respective states. State boards of education are the administrative agencies that implement and regulate the laws and rules adopted by the legislatures. The chief state school officers, elected or appointed, are expected to provide leadership and supervision in addition to the customary clerical and regulatory functions of state departments of education. They are expected to make recommendations for educational needs to their respective governors, state boards of education, and legislatures. They are expected to influence educational legislation.

Local school districts are the agencies of control in education most visible to the citizens in the district. Boards of education are the policy makers at the local level. They make decisions within the power delegated to them by the state. It is within their power to enact local policies for education providing those policies do not violate existing state laws.

School-based management is a relatively new and growing concept in which authority is given by the school district to a *school* or *schools* within the district, empowering the school(s) to decide, for example, how they spend money, allocate staff, and organize instruction. It greatly increases teacher participation and empowerment in decision making in the local schools.

This chapter has provided an overview of the governance of public education at the elementary and secondary levels. As such, it will help you understand the governance roles at the federal, state, and local schools, and how those roles are related to each other. It is likely that the empowerment of the teachers in *local school* governance will increase in the next few years.

Point of View

One of the topics discussed briefly in chapter 17 was teacher empowerment which was recommended in many educational reform proposals. Teacher empowerment, if implemented, would give teachers greater participation in making decisions for the operation and governance of a local school. It is closely related to the concept of school-based management which was also discussed in chapter 17.

The point of view article for this chapter, "A Blueprint for Empowering Teachers" by Gene Maeroff provides more information about teacher empowerment. This article points out that "Empowerment becomes inevitable when teachers have so much to offer and are so sure about what they know that they can no longer be shut out of the policy-making process."

A Blueprint for Empowering Teachers
Gene Maeroff

BONNIE DAVIS, a social studies teacher in a St. Louis suburb, recalled the day that her principal, whom she had always addressed as "Doctor" (even though they were about the same age), invited her to call him by his first name. That day came after Davis, who had been teaching at the school for many years, had gained confidence through participation in a summer program and had finally started asserting herself professionally. "I think he saw me in a new way," Davis said of her principal.

Teachers throughout the nation need to be seen "in a new way." That change in perception can be the beginning of empowerment. And the empowerment of teachers is essential if the schools are to improve. As long as teachers are not adequately valued by themselves and by others, they are not apt to perform with the necessary assurance and authority to do the job as well as they can.

If teachers can be lifted in three key areas—each of which complements the others—they will be able to flex muscles that have been allowed to atrophy. Those three areas involve their status, their knowledge, and their access to decision making.

- Boosting the status of teachers is fundamental because, simply put, those who have lost the will are not likely to find the way. The ability to look at themselves and at their colleagues through new eyes can liberate teachers from self-imposed shackles.

- As Francis Bacon noted long ago, "Knowledge itself is power." Making teachers more knowledgeable is an obvious step in enhancing their power. Part of the reason why teachers do not exert more authority is that they are not sufficiently educated and informed to do so. Clearly, a teacher not versed in history must depend on others to supply a curriculum for a history course. A teacher intimidated by mathematics is not likely to be able to critique a math textbook. Teachers whose academic and pedagogical backgrounds are shaky must repeatedly defer to the judgments of supervisors, who are the presumed experts.

- Finally, allowing teachers access to the lofty towers of power requires the building of psychological ladders that they may climb to escape their isolation and to gain an overview that teachers do not ordinarily attain. It also requires connecting teachers with one another and with principals, building collegiality and a process of shared decision making that has been all too rare in the schools.

More than many other occupations, teaching is practiced in isolation—an isolation that is crushing at times. Collegiality is nonexistent for many teachers, unless hurried lunches over plastic trays in unkempt lunchrooms are viewed as exercises in colleagueship (rather than as the complaint sessions they are more likely to be). Knowledge is the currency in which a teacher deals; yet the teacher's own knowledge is allowed to become stale and devalued, as though ideas were not the lifeblood of the occupation. The circumstances of teaching (and the relatively meager salaries) cause teachers not to respect themselves, much less each other. As long as teachers occupy so lowly a niche, they are not apt to gain access to decision making.

There will be no empowerment while teachers feel small and insignificant because they are doing a job that they think is not adequately appreciated by those outside the schools. In *Horace's Compromise*, Theodore Sizer cited three elements that our culture uses to signal respect: autonomy, money, and recognition.[1] Sizable salary increases for teachers, such as those negotiated last year in Rochester, New York, are not likely to become widespread for a long, long time, but in the interim a great deal can be done about autonomy and recognition. However, the situation that currently

exists for many teachers, especially in problem-plagued urban school districts, produces not empowerment, but impotence.

Teachers are so unaccustomed to gaining power that those in Seattle, for example, could not believe that they were really being given authority to revise the curriculum, through a special, foundation-sponsored program. According to Jim Grob, the director of that program, even after the teachers got involved, "they were waiting for the other shoe to drop," waiting for the moment when Grob would tell them what ideas he wanted them to rubber-stamp. "It took them a couple of weeks to believe that they would have power," Grob said. "They had been around long enough to know that that doesn't ordinarily happen."

A vehicle for pursuing empowerment is already in place. It is an old and familiar part of every teacher's life: inservice education. But a thorough overhaul is needed if inservice education is to fulfill its potential for prying open the door to empowerment. At its best, operating in a manner that has been all too infrequent in the past, inservice education can break down isolation and build networks, bolster confidence, increase knowledge of subject matter and of pedagogy, provide the kind of learning that fires enthusiasm, and involve teachers in the kinds of projects that provide access to decision making.

National programs, including those in Seattle and St. Louis, sponsored in recent years by the Rockefeller Foundation (for teachers of the humanities) and by the Ford Foundation (for teachers of mathematics) provide models for such inservice education. The Carnegie Corporation began a somewhat similar program for teachers of science. Elements of empowerment have also been woven into the programs of the National Endowment for the Humanities, the National Science Foundation, and other educational projects for schoolteachers—including some of the better teacher centers across the U.S. None of these efforts has delivered a guaranteed ticket to empowerment, but together they provide the pieces from which a blueprint for empowerment can be constructed.

In the programs that were most successful, teachers were paid to spend time learning in intensive summer sessions, and their learning was reinforced by activities throughout the school year for which they were given released time. The content of the summer sessions was often intellectually challenging, and the teacher participants dug into their fields with a relish that many did not realize they possessed. The settings were sometimes plush and prestigious, the sessions included such amenities as dinners and field trips, and the teacher participants were brought into contact with professors and businesspeople. Teachers helped to set the agenda for their own learning by stating their needs. The goal was to get teachers accustomed to acting and being perceived as professionals.

A concentrated summer session, perhaps even including overnight stays at a university or some other locale, was important at the beginning, because it put the teachers in a place unencumbered by negative associations. Furthermore, by spending unusually long periods together in circumstances different from those at school, the teachers bonded in ways that gave promise of enhancing their relationships throughout the school year. The best inservice education programs produced teachers who cared about their work and who were engaged by the content of their disciplines.

Professionals usually have a sense of authority about what they do, and they are recognized as experts in their fields. They feel good about themselves and are respected by others. Similarly, the empowerment of teachers has more to do with individual deportment than with the ability to boss others. This is not the strutting, order-issuing sort of empowerment. Rather, it is the power to exercise one's craft with quiet confidence and to help shape the way the job is done. Empowerment becomes inevitable when teachers have so much to offer and are so sure about what they know that they can no longer be shut out of the policymaking process.

Empowerment can mean running the show, but many teachers say that they do not want responsibility for all the decisions in their schools. What they desire is that their voices be heard and heeded. They yearn for dignity. They want their needs and opinions reflected in the policies of the school and of the district; they want influence. Empowering teachers need not mean that principals cease to be in charge, but it should mean that principals engage in more consultation and collaboration. This philosophy is guiding an experiment in the public schools of Dade County, Florida, where attempts are being made to redraw traditional lines of authority so that teachers can assume more responsibility for instructional policies without disrupting the role of the principal.

Schools everywhere can take a first step in this direction by relieving teachers of the burden of clerical and noninstructional duties and transferring those duties to paraprofessionals. Schedules would be changed to allow teachers more freedom to leave their schools during the day for conferences devoted to subject matter or pedagogy. Teachers would have easier access to telephones and copying machines, and secretarial help would be more readily available to them. Dining rooms and lounges for teachers would be pleasant and attractive. Teachers would no longer be infantilized by administrators. Teachers would have more opportunities to plan together, teach together, and observe each other.

In fact, restructuring the teacher's schedule is vital if teachers are to have time to be involved in curriculum planning, textbook selection, the training of new teachers, and other policy matters. "Bells are always ringing, and you're running back and forth," Shahdia Khan, an English teacher in Seattle, said of the usual schedule. "You get a half-hour for lunch, and there's no time to interact professionally with your colleagues."

If school districts are serious about inservice education, they ought to incorporate it into the regular working day (with released time from classes), as well as schedule it during the summer and other free times (with appropriate compensation). To be truly empowering, inservice education must in no way smack of being an add-on. Genuine prestige must be associated with it. Using retreats for educational purposes should become a regular practice. Teachers should have to compete for admission to some of the programs. Both symbolically and literally, inservice education must be moved out of dingy classrooms and into the kinds of settings that signal to everyone that the activity is valued. Teachers who are adept at what they do must take on more of the teaching responsibility for inservice education.

The trappings of the settings can help uplift teachers, as was discovered in Philadelphia in connection with the Collaboratives for Humanities and Arts Teaching (CHART), sponsored by the Rockefeller Foundation in that city and in St. Louis, Seattle, and elsewhere. In Philadelphia, CHART sessions met in such stately places as the Rosenbach Museum and Library, a brownstone on one of the city's most exclusive streets; the Historical Society of Pennsylvania, a research facility used by scholars and filled with portraits of the city's founding fathers; the Independence Hall complex, with its 18th-century flavor; the Atwater Kent Museum, a building of imposing columns that contains artifacts of the city's history; the Philadelphia Museum of Art, a Parthenon-like structure with a sweeping view of the city; and the University Museum of the University of Pennsylvania, one of the world's great archeological museums, right in the middle of an Ivy League

campus. Obviously, such places are not going to be used every time teachers gather for an inservice education session, but it is possible to use settings of this kind at least part of the time.

Ideally, programs should include cadres of teachers from each participating school. This is important if teachers are to have a support structure when they return to the classroom. Too many teachers tell of returning from wonderful institutes, brimming with knowledge and inspiration, only to find that their colleagues scorn them. Initially, there must be groups of at least four or five teachers from the same faculty, so that—like a fifth column—they may then work together from within the school to seek changes and to win adherents among their colleagues.

Teachers have more chance of gaining access to the mechanisms of power if they operate as a network of like-minded agents of change. New knowledge and fresh applications are most likely to take hold in a school in which a group of teachers are similarly enthusiastic about those ideas and bond together. They can turn to one another for the support and encouragement that is so often missing from teachers' professional lives.

Teachers stride toward empowerment when they improve their instructional techniques, when they deepen their knowledge of their disciplines, when they adopt an interdisciplinary perspective, and when they learn where to go and what to do to fill the gaps in their knowledge. The more that teachers' knowledge makes them indispensable to their schools and their school systems, the more power they will gain over decisions involving teaching and learning.

Teachers are hungry for stimulating educational experiences. If they did not care about learning, they would not have contemplated careers in the classroom. But they end up divorced from scholarship and devoid of time and incentives to continue to learn.

Janis Nathan, a teacher for 16 years in the Los Angeles public schools, worked with colleagues through CHART to develop an interdisciplinary team-teaching approach in the humanities. Of that experience, she said:

It is easy to become single-minded. Because of my experience in the program, I now look at a book from at least five separate perspectives. I didn't do that before. I am not thrilled about giving up my summer, but there is so much meat here. It works on my creative juices, and that lifts my morale. The possibilities have increased for me. Ordinarily, a lot of teaching gets repetitive without teachers meaning it to.

In New York City, Bob Levanthal, another CHART participant, recalled that his college preparation to become a history teacher was largely devoted to learning about Europe and the U.S. After the New York State Board of Regents mandated that schools do more to teach about Africa, Asia, and Latin America, Leventhal realized that his education had left him unprepared to comply with what was being asked of him. "It can be terrifying to walk into a classroom and have to teach something you've never taught before," he said. "As a teacher you are supposed to have insights and interpretations that go beyond simply having read the book the night before the kids did." What he learned through his involvement in CHART helped Leventhal feel more confident about the assignment and pointed the way toward the kind of professional renewal that should be more widely available to all teachers.

But teachers who are being asked to change must be persuaded that there are rewards to be reaped—even if the rewards are solely intrinsic ones. Otherwise, why should they put themselves on the spot? Some teachers in St. Paul, Minnesota, for instance, admitted that they did not give essay tests because they thought that the scoring of such tests took too much time. Through their participation in writing workshops held in conjunction with CHART, these teachers eventually learned that they did not have to feel guilty about not marking every mechanical error in a paper, that they could promote the development of their students' writing and thinking skills without getting bogged down in minutiae. "That might empower them by giving them a better perspective on what to expect of themselves as social studies teachers," said Carole Snyder, the English supervisor for the school system.

In their many calls for higher student achievement, school reformers sometimes forget that changing students depends to a large extent on changing teachers. If teachers continue to do the same old things, it is unlikely that student performance will improve.

An evaluation report to the Ford Foundation on the Urban Mathematics Collaborative it sponsored pointed out that, for many of the teacher participants, the application of new ideas within the traditional classroom structure was not obvious. The report stated:

In working toward change, teachers are unsure of how to use external resources. For too long, materials have simply been given to teachers without giving them an opportunity to reflect, think, or argue about what needs to be done. Now, the situation has changed, but most teachers are unaware of how to ask for and use external resources.[2]

Teachers who are knowledgeable are less apt to stand back, especially at a time when schools are in ferment and the mood is receptive to change. Teachers must be given seats at the tables where important decisions are made. Where they are not already represented on committees that select the principals for their schools, teachers should be placed on those committees—a step no less radical than allowing professors to serve on presidential search committees for their campuses. Allowing teachers some voice in the selection of principals could help to build "a better relationship between the two by creating some mutual interdependence," according to Sandra Feldman, president of the United Federation of Teachers in New York City.[3]

The pursuit of empowerment need not be guerrilla warfare. Teachers and administrators do not have to snipe at each other like members of rival gangs feuding over disputed terrain. The more that is done to build support for teachers among administrators, the better. Inservice education that leads to released time, joint planning periods, and interdisciplinary teaching, for example, requires the cooperation of principals. Although the first order of business is to link teachers into networks, there is an accompanying need to win the backing of supervisors at both the building and the district levels. Administrators must learn that empowering teachers is in administrators' own best interest— and, more important, in the best interest of students.

Any campaign to empower teachers will be aided by parallel efforts to strengthen the ability of principals and other supervisors to do their own jobs better. A lack of confidence in their ability to lead assuredly breeds the kind of insecurity among principals that makes some of them feel threatened by the prospect of empowering teachers.

On the other hand, the ablest principals are less concerned with being bosses than with seeing their schools succeed. They are more like symphony conductors who give leadership to a blend of individual artists than like train conductors who officiously manage all comings and goings. The report of the National Commission on Excellence in Educational Administration (a group headed by Daniel Griffiths, the former dean of education at New York University) underscores the need for better training of school principals.[4]

Ideally, collegiality will lead teachers and administrators to work as partners and to share power. No longer should teachers have to become principals to influence policy. The Carnegie Forum Task Force on Teaching as a Profession recommended that schools create a professional environment for teachers by giving them the discretion and autonomy that professionals in other fields enjoy. "This does not mean no one is in charge," the task force added, "but it does mean that people practicing their profession decide what is to be done and how it is to be done within the constraints imposed by the larger goals of the organization."[5]

The history of CHART in Los Angeles provides a textbook example of how implementation can be carried out in a way that gives administrators a stake in the outcome at each step of the process. Los Angeles administrators admitted that they fell into line and backed CHART because they perceived that their bosses supported the project. Word filtered down from level to level, with the administrator above always wanting to know that the one below was committed to the venture.

"I had always thought that, if you want to do something good, you should close your door and keep quiet about it," said Neil Anstead, a Los Angeles teacher who was instrumental in the spread of interdisciplinary programs in the district. "But administrators are not so bad—and, if you take the time to involve them in what you are doing, they can be good."

It is equally essential to capture the support of teacher unions for teacher empowerment programs by involving union leaders in the planning and by making it clear that the aim of teacher empowerment is not to undermine collective bargaining. Unless unions are willing to be flexible, there is not likely to be the room for maneuvering that empowerment demands. The rigid enforcement of contract provisions is more suitable to the assembly line than to the classroom, where success often depends on improvisation. Like others who sell their talents for a living, teachers should not have to give away services. But there must be leeway for redefining the role of teachers in ways that will allow them to be more professional. Meanwhile, if they are serious about empowering teachers, the unions must ultimately become partners with school systems in ridding schools of tenured teachers whose level of incompetence is such that empowering them would be like letting children drive cars.

But school systems cannot be counted on to initiate programs aimed at empowering teachers. For this reason, most of the previously discussed ventures sponsored by the Rockefeller and Ford Foundations were carried out through an agency akin to a public education fund. School systems are not evil entities, but various constraints make them less likely to be able to serve as teacher advocates in the fashion of an independent agency. The agencies that sponsor such ventures can only hope that participating school systems will eventually institutionalize the principles of empowerment embodied in these programs.

The autonomy of such an agency as a public education fund allows it to function as an intermediary, sidestepping bureaucratic impediments and making sure from the outset that money is spent for its intended purpose. The outside agency has its own integrity, and it is under the aegis of a board of community leaders. Such an agency is thus in a position to stand up for a single program. Without such advocacy, the $1 million to $2 million to be spent on a given project could readily be absorbed into a district budget that is 10 to 100 times as large.

Altogether too much money has already been invested in projects in which the investment falls through the cracks, like the dime that a child drops through a grating on a sidewalk—leaving no evidence of its ever having existed. The steps on salary schedules are supposed to reward teachers for experience in the classroom and for continuing education outside the classroom. It is time to give

new meaning to this process and to renew the teaching force in ways that persuade both the best veterans and the most promising prospects that teaching can be a lifelong career. There is no better way of doing this than by giving teachers the power to do their jobs as well as they can—and then expecting that students will learn to the full extent that circumstances permit.

1. Theodore R. Sizer, *Horace's Compromise: The Dilemma of the American High School* (Boston: Houghton Mifflin, 1984), p. 183.

2. Thomas A. Romberg and Allan Pitman, *Annual Report to the Ford Foundation: The Urban Mathematics Collaborative Projects* (Madison: University of Wisconsin, 1985), p. 15.

3. Sandra Feldman, ''On Principals and School Reform,'' *New York Teacher Bulletin*, 7 December 1987, p. 7–A.

4. National Commission on Excellence in Educational Administration. *Leaders for America's Schools* (Tempe, Ariz.: University Council for Educational Administration, 1987).

5. Carnegie Task Force on Teaching as a Profession, *A Nation Prepared: Teachers for the 21st Century* (New York: Carnegie Forum on Education and the Economy, 1986), p. 39.

Gene I. Maeroff, Senior Fellow. Carnegie Foundation for the Advancement of Teaching, Princeton, NJ.

■ Questions for Discussion

1. How has the interpretation of the United States Constitution affected the operations of public schools?

2. Can education in the United States continue to be effective by continuing its long-time tradition of local control? Provide a rationale for your answer.

3. How have local boards of education had their traditional powers reduced?

4. Do you think that school-based management is a practical and viable solution for local school governance? Why? Why not?

5. How can teachers best be prepared for the implementation of teacher empowerment?

■ Notes

1. Thomas J. Flygare, "State Aid to Public Schools: Diminished Alternative," *Phi Delta Kappan* 57, no. 3 (November 1975):204.

2. Lucy Knight, "Facts About Mr. Buckley's Amendment," *American Education* 13, no. 5 (June 1977):6.

3. Bernice Sandler, "Title IX: Antisexism's Big Legal Stick," *American Education* 13, no. 5 (June 1977):6.

4. Ibid.

5. Ronald F. Campbell, Gerald E. Stroufe, and Donald H. Layton, *Strengthening State Departments of Education* (Chicago: University of Chicago Press, 1967), p. 10.

6. Lynn Olson, excerpted from "The Sky's the Limit: Dade Ventures Self-Governance," *Education Week* Vol. VII, No. 13, (December 2, 1987), pp. 1, 18.

7. Ibid., p. 18.

8. *Chicago Tribune*, Section 1 (Monday, July 4, 1988), p. 10.

■ Selected References

Bakalis, Michael J. "Power and Purpose in American Education," *Phi Delta Kappan* 65, no. 1 (September 1983):7–13.

Bjorklun, Eugene C. "Secular Humanism," *The Educational Forum* 52, no. 3 (Spring 1988):211–221.

"De Jure," *Phi Delta Kappan*. (A regular feature in each issue of *Phi Delta Kappan* providing timely and pertinent information about school law cases.)

Fischer, Louis; Schimmel, David; and Kelly, Cynthia. *Teachers and the Law*. New York: Longman Inc., 1987.

Guthrie, James W. "School-Based Management: The Next Needed School Reform," *Phi Delta Kappan* 68, no. 4 (December 1986):305–309.

Hoy, Wayne K., and Miskel, Cecil. *Educational Administration: Theory, Research, and Practice*. New York: Random House, 1985.

Hudgins, H. C. Jr., and Vacca, Richard S. *Law and Education: Contemporary Issues and Court Decisions*. Charlottesville, VA: The Michie Company, 1985.

McCarthy, Martha M. *A Delicate Balance: Church, State and the Schools*. Bloomington, IN: Phi Delta Kappa, 1983.

Ravitch, Diane. *The Troubled Crusade: American Education: 1945–1980*. New York. Basic Books, 1983.

Valente, William D. *Law in the Schools*. Columbus, OH: Charles E. Merrill, 1980.

Chapter 18

Financing the Educational Enterprise

Objectives

After studying this chapter, you should be able to:

■ Identify the magnitude of the educational enterprise in terms of the people involved.

■ Analyze the concept of education as an investment in individuals, social development, and the economy.

■ Explain the separate sources of public school revenue, their advantages and disadvantages, and their systematic relationship to one another.

■ Identify the two major goals necessary to improve school financing.

■ Present the relationship between school finance and the concept of equality of opportunity.

■ Explain the need and importance of state aid.

■ List reasons for the current call for accountability and suggest proposals for responsive action.

■ Describe the fiscal and political issues surrounding state aid.

Enrichment Experiences

The following experiences will help you understand the complex issues related to achieving a tax system in which taxpayers are called upon to support education in proportion to their ability to pay (equity) and making an adequate education available to all students (equal opportunity).

■ Ask a local school superintendent or business manager to come to your class to explain the local budgeting process and the local school district budget.

■ Interview a local school district official to discuss the problems of financing the schools with local property taxes.

■ Invite a county or township tax assessment official to your class to discuss the assessing process in your area.

■ Study and evaluate the plan for state support of education in your state.

■ Ask a regional superintendent of schools to explain to your class the relationship between the relative wealth of school districts and fiscal equity.

■ Invite a member of your State Senate or a member of your House of Representatives to speak to your class about state aid to education.

The major purposes of this chapter are to help you (1) understand and analyze the sources of revenue (money) for school districts, (2) recognize the differences of financial capability among states and among school districts within a state, and (3) explain how states provide money to poor local school districts in an effort to help them provide an adequate education for their students. Topics included are: education as a national investment; sources of school revenue; school finance and equality of opportunity; state aid; wealth differences among states; recommendations for establishing equality in financing education; accountability; and expectations and expenses. ■

Education in the United States is big business. Currently, about 45 million pupils are enrolled in public and private elementary and secondary schools, and 2.6 million teachers are employed to instruct these students. Nearly one out of four persons in the nation directly participates in the education process.[1] Projections for 1990 indicate approximately 46.6 million students and 2.7 million teachers.[2] It is also pertinent to note that in many small to medium-sized communities education is the biggest business in town.

■ Education as a National Investment

As a nation, our investment in education has been a sizable amount. Figure 18.1 illustrates the nation's effort to support education by comparing educational expenditures with gross national product (GNP). Gross national product, calculated by the Bureau of Economic Analysis, U.S.

Department of Commerce, represents the total national output of goods and services at market prices. It measures this output in terms of the expenditures by which the goods and services are acquired. The expenditures comprise purchases of goods and services by consumers and government, gross private domestic investment, and net exports of goods and services. GNP provides one measuring stick of our national investment in education. With some fluctuations, educational expenditures as a percentage of GNP have steadily risen from 4.8 percent in 1959 to 7.5 percent in 1970. It remained relatively steady until 1977 when it dropped to 6.9 percent. Its lowest percentage between 1959 and 1985 was 6.5 percent in 1981. (See figure 18.1.)

While it approaches the impossible to estimate what proportion of the wealth of a nation *should* be allocated for education, it does seem clear that we in the United States are limited more by our willingness to pay than by our ability to pay. In other words, our task as a nation seems to be to delineate a hierarchy of values—that is, to clearly spell out and place in rank order what we desire or what "ought to be." Once this is done, we must commit monies to convert our words into action.

Social development, closely intertwined with economic development, is also related to education. A basic premise undergirding our form of government is that informed citizens are necessary to our national survival. The skills (such as literacy) necessary to be an informed citizen and the skills necessary for problem solving are enhanced through education. The values of society, or the ways of life that we cherish, are transmitted in part through our educational system.

Education is an investment, not a cost. It is an investment in free men, it is an investment in social welfare, in better living standards, in better health, in less crime. It is an investment in higher production, increased income, and greater efficiency in agriculture, industry, and government. It is an investment in a bulwark against garbled information, half-truths, and untruths, against ignorance and intolerance. It is an investment in human talent, human relations, democracy, and peace.

President's Commission on Higher Education

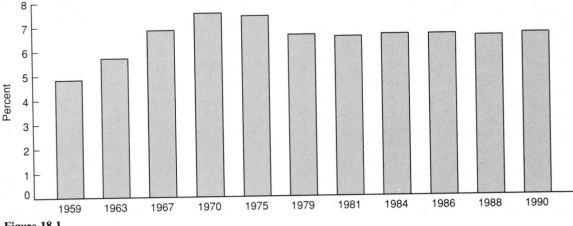

■ Figure 18.1

Total expenditures for education as a percentage of Gross National Product: United States 1959–1990

Source: Data from Thomas D. Snyder, *Digest of Education Statistics 1987.* Washington, DC: Center for Education Statistics, 1987, page 24. Author's projections for 1986, 1988, and 1990.

Investment in education is an investment in society, both economically and socially. Education in a sense is the servant of society. Americans must continue to use education to foster the achievement of their ideals.

■ Sources of School Revenue

The monies used to finance the public educational enterprise today come largely from taxation, but this has not always been the case. In colonial America, monies for schools were often obtained from lotteries and charitable contributions. Churches of the various denominations financed education for some. It was not unusual in the very early days of our nation for the patrons of the schools to provide services such as supplying wood, making building repairs, or boarding teachers in lieu of money.

Public support for education in this nation in terms of taxes was secured only after a long, hard battle. However, the concept that education should be a public responsibility dates back to our early heritage. The Massachusetts laws of 1642, 1647, and 1648 referred to earlier in this text illustrate the New England attitude that at least common school education should be a public rather than a private responsibility. In the early 1800s, the movement for free public schools gained impetus. Pennsylvania in 1834 became the first state to adopt free elementary education. In 1872, the village of Kalamazoo, Michigan, voted to establish a public high school to be supported by taxation. A lawsuit was filed to test the legality of using taxation to provide a high school.

There are obviously two educations.
One should teach us how to make a
living and the other how to live.

James Truslow Adams

Expenditures for school libraries are investments in America's future.

The opinion of the State Supreme Court of Michigan was that the action was legal and constitutional. By the end of the nineteenth century, public schools were financed almost completely by local funds derived from local taxation.

Important to the rise of public financial support for education (taxes) was the belief that education benefited the public as well as the individual or the family. Today money to support education comes from a variety of taxes collected by local, state, and federal governments. These governments in turn distribute taxes to local school districts to operate their schools. The three major kinds of taxes used to provide revenue for schools are property taxes, sales or use taxes, and income taxes. In general, local governments use the property tax, state governments rely upon the sales tax and the income tax, and the federal government relies heavily upon the income tax.

It is important to note the percentage of support for public elementary and secondary schools contributed by each level of government. In 1919–20, about 83.0 percent of school revenues came from local governmental sources, 16.5 percent from state sources, and about .3 percent from federal sources. Over the years, this has changed, with a marked increase in state support up to 1978, and most recently, in 1981, a decrease in federal support. Table 18.1 illustrates the percentage of revenue received from the three sources since 1919.

While table 18.1 provides data from an overall national viewpoint, an examination of the data from selected individual states reveals wide variations from the national statistics. It should be remembered that education is a function of the state and therefore variability is to be expected.

■ **Table 18.1.**   Percentage of Revenue Received from Federal, State, and Local Sources for Public Elementary and Secondary Schools

School year	Percentage of revenue		
	Federal	State	Local
1919–20	.3	16.5	83.2
1929–30	.4	16.9	82.7
1939–40	1.8	30.3	68.0
1949–50	2.9	39.8	57.3
1955–56	4.6	39.5	55.9
1957–58	4.0	39.4	56.6
1959–60	4.4	39.1	56.5
1961–62	4.3	38.7	56.9
1963–64	4.4	39.3	56.3
1965–66	7.9	39.1	53.0
1967–68	8.8	38.5	52.7
1969–70	8.0	39.9	52.1
1975–76	8.9	44.6	46.5
1978–79	9.8	45.6	44.6
1980–81	9.2	47.4	43.4
1981–82	7.4	47.6	45.0
1983–84	6.8	47.8	45.4
1984–85	6.5	48.8	44.7

Source: Thomas D. Snyder, *Digest of Education Statistics 1987*. Washington, DC: Center for Education Statistics, page 107 U.S. Government Printing Office.

Table 18.2 illustrates the estimated percentages of revenue by governmental source for public elementary and secondary schools for selected states. The states are arranged in the table in a descending order in terms of local support. The average percentages in the United States for the same period are estimated to be: local 44.7, state 48.8, and federal 6.5.

The variation in state financial support illustrated in table 18.2 represents primarily a variation in general state aid. That is, state monies are provided to supplement the local education effort, and for the most part are not "earmarked" or "tagged" for special purposes or programs. The variation in federal support in the main is a reflection of *categorical aid*—that is, specific aid for a specific purpose or to resolve a unique problem. For example, the Smith-Hughes Act provided a stimulus for vocational education; the National Defense Education Act of 1958 emphasized the enhancement of science, mathematics, foreign languages, and counseling services; the Elementary and Secondary Act of 1965 had as one important feature the provision of monies to assist school districts in providing programs for children of poverty. Other federal aid programs are designed to aid school districts that are affected by federally induced population impaction such as may occur near a military installation or major federal research installation. Both state and federal aid are aimed at enhancing equality of opportunity, which is to be considered later in this chapter.

The whole people must take upon themselves the education of the whole people and must be willing to bear the expense of it.

John Adams

■ Table 18.2. Percentage of Revenue by Governmental Source for Public Elementary and Secondary Schools, for Selected States (1984–85)

State	Percentage of revenue		
	Local	State	Federal
New Hampshire	90.4	5.0	4.9
Nebraska	68.1	25.1	6.8
Illinois	59.2	36.4	4.5
Missouri	54.3	38.5	7.2
Florida	38.0	54.4	7.6
North Carolina	26.2	64.6	9.2
Mississippi	24.3	59.3	16.5
Alabama	21.8	65.8	12.4
Alaska	20.3	71.5	8.2
Hawaii	0.1	89.0	10.9

Source: Thomas D. Snyder, *Digest of Education Statistics 1987*. Washington, DC: Center for Education Statistics, page 108, U.S. Government Printing Office.

The various categorical grants provided directly to school districts have been consolidated into block grants, providing greater freedom to the states in deciding how they wish to spend the money (Omnibus Budget Reconciliation Act of 1981).

As was mentioned earlier, local support for schools comes predominantly from the property tax. The property tax is one of the oldest forms of taxation, based on the premise that a measure of a man's property was a measure of his wealth. Property is most often considered in two categories, real estate and personal. Personal property may include such things as automobiles, furniture, machinery, livestock, jewelry, and less tangible items as stocks and bonds. The property tax was particularly appropriate for an agrarian economy.

The property tax, as with most forms of taxation, has both distinct advantages and disadvantages. Its major advantage is that it provides a regular and stable form of income. While it is perhaps not as sensitive to economic changes as the sales and income taxes, neither is it absolutely rigid. The stability of the property tax will likely cause it to continue to be the mainstay of local public school support.

A major disadvantage of the property tax has to do with establishing equality of assessment. In other words, parcels of property of equal value should be assessed at the same value. This is extremely difficult to accomplish. Wide variations exist among school districts and states. Studies have indicated variation in assessment of residential property from 5.9 percent of sale value in one state to 66.2 percent in another. Inequality of assessment causes the property tax to be an unfair tax.

The property tax is most generally thought of as a proportionate tax, that is, one that taxes according to ability to pay. However, inequality of assessment and the trend in an urban economy for wealth to be less related to real estate than it was in an agrarian economy have caused the tax to become somewhat regressive. Regressive taxes are those such as sales and use taxes that have a relatively greater impact on lower income groups.

State support for schools comes mainly from the sales tax and income tax. Sales and income taxes are lucrative sources of state revenue, and both taxes are relatively easy to administer. The sales tax is collected bit by bit by the vendor, who is responsible for record keeping and remitting the tax to the state. The state income tax can be withheld from wages, hence facilitating collections. The sales tax is considered a *regressive tax* because all persons pay the sales tax at the same rate; therefore, persons in low income groups pay nearly as much tax for essentials as do those in high income groups. The income tax is clearly a *progressive tax* because it is scaled to the ability of the taxpayer to pay. Both state sales and income taxes are direct and certain, they are responsive to changes in the economy, and they can be regulated by a state legislature, which is responsible for raising the money. It is interesting to note that on a nationwide basis approximately 55 percent of all state revenue has come from sales taxes and 29 percent from income taxes. The remainder has come from licenses and miscellaneous taxes.

Federal support for schools comes from monies raised primarily from personal and corporate income taxes.

■ School Finance and Equality of Opportunity

The opportunity for equal education is related to the financial ability of specific areas to pay for education. While wealth is not the only factor related to equality of opportunity, as was pointed out by the *Brown* decision, it certainly is an important one.

Children are educated in local school districts, which by and large still produce nationwide about 45 percent of the monies used for education. These monies are raised primarily with the property tax, and therefore are dependent upon the real estate wealth of the district. Wealthy districts, therefore, can provide more monies for education than poor districts with the same tax effort.

Suppose, for example, that the total assessed valuation, that is, the value of all the property as determined by a tax assessor of a district, is $90 million, and the district has 1,000 pupils. This hypothetical district would then have an assessed valuation of $90,000 per pupil. A tax rate of $2.00 per $100 of assessed valuation would produce $1,800 per pupil. By the same token, if a neighboring district had an assessed valuation of $30 million and had 1,000 pupils, it would have $30,000 of assessed valuation per pupil, which at the same rate of $2.00 per $100 of assessed valuation would produce only $600 per pupil. With the same tax rate, or the same effort, one of these districts could spend $1,800 per pupil while the other could spend only $600 per pupil. In general, this results in children in wealthy districts being provided greater opportunities for education than children in poor districts.

Great differences can exist in wealth per pupil from school district to school district. Industrial developments can increase valuations in some districts, while at the same time neighboring districts may be largely residential with little valuation and large numbers of pupils.

A number of court cases have arisen in respect to inequality of education as a function of the wealth of school districts. The *Serrano* case is illustrative. In *Serrano* v. *Priest,* the California Supreme Court was called upon to determine whether or not the California public school financing system, with its substantial dependence on local property taxes, violated the Fourteenth Amendment. In a 6–1 decision on August 30, 1971, the Court held that heavy reliance on unequal local property taxes "makes the quality of a child's education a function of the wealth of his parents and neighbors." Furthermore, the Court declared, "Districts with small tax bases simply cannot levy taxes at a rate sufficient to produce the revenue that more affluent districts produce with a minimum effort." The data presented in the *Serrano* case revealed that the Baldwin Park school district spent $577 per pupil, while the Beverly Hills school district spent $1,232. Yet, the tax rate of $5.48 in Baldwin Park was more than double the rate of $2.38 in Beverly Hills. The discrepancies are a result of the difference in wealth between the two districts. Beverly Hills had $50,885 of assessed valuation per child, while Baldwin Park had only $3,706 valuation per child—a ratio of thirteen to one. Suits similar to *Serrano* were filed in at least twenty-two states.

The United States Supreme Court consented to hear an appeal of the *Rodriguez* case, which originated in Texas and was similar to *Serrano*. In *Rodriguez,* the U.S. Supreme Court, in 1973 in a 5–4 decision, reversed the lower court and thus reaffirmed the local property tax as a basis for school financing. Justice Potter Stewart voting with the majority admitted that "the method of financing public schools . . . can be fairly described as chaotic and unjust." He did not, though, find it unconstitutional. The majority opinion written by Justice Lewis F. Powell stated that "we cannot say that such disparities are the product of a system that is so irrational as to be invidiously discriminatory." The opinion also noted that: the poor are not necessarily concentrated in the poorest districts; states must initiate fundamental reform in taxation and education; and the extent to which quality of education varies with expenditures is inconclusive. Justice Thurgood Marshall in the dissenting opinion charged that the ruling "is a retreat from our historic commitment to equality of educational opportunity." A number of commissions have made recommendations to improve the financing of schools. States have also attempted to alter their methods of financing schools. A brief description of state aid prior to *Rodriguez* provides a basis for understanding the problem today.

■ State Aid—Historically

States have recognized the disparaging differences in wealth among local districts, and through state aid programs, have attempted to provide financial equalization for educational purposes. This makes good sense, particularly since the state has the primary responsibility for education.

State aid can be classified by its use as being either general or categorical. General aid may be used by the recipient school district as it desires. Categorical aid is earmarked for specific purposes. Examples of categorical aid include monies for special education, driver education, vocational education, or transportation. Categorical aid is sometimes used as an incentive to encourage programs that are perceived as being needed.

General aid usually represents the states' efforts to equalize opportunity. The underlying premise is that each child, regardless of his or her place of residence or the wealth of the particular school district in which he or she lives, is entitled to receive essential basic educational opportunities. General aid is usually administered through some type of foundation program. The foundation concept involves the establishment of a per pupil dollar value, which represents the desired foundation education in a state. The usual connotation of the word *foundation* is basic or minimum. Therefore, the foundation level is usually less than the actual per pupil expenditures. A state, in establishing a foundation level, is in effect assuring that the amount of the per pupil foundation level will be expended for education for each pupil in the state. Foundation programs do encourage equality of opportunity from a financial viewpoint; however, *it is important to observe that they assure equalization only to a prescribed level.* Districts can and do vary greatly in their expenditure per pupil.

The actual monies used to achieve the foundation level expenditures come from both state and local sources. Most often a minimum local district tax rate is established, and the money this tax rate produces is subtracted from the foundation level with the remainder being paid by the state. The local tax rate will produce more money in a wealthy district than it will in a poor district. This concept is also a part of the equalization principle. Figure 18.2 presents a graphic representation of equalization and the foundation principle. *It is important to note, however, that local districts can, and frequently do, spend more than the foundation level.*

■ Wealth Differences among States

Differences in wealth exist among states just as they do among school districts within states. Since assessment practices differ from state to state, it is difficult to use assessed valuation per pupil as

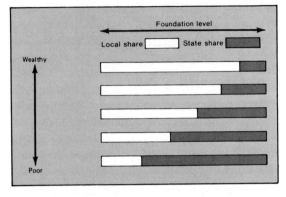

■ Figure 18.2
The principle of equalization as related to the foundation level

an index to compare the wealth of states. A more accurate index is personal income per capita. States with per capita income greater than $17,000 include Alaska and the Federal District of Columbia, Connecticut, and New Jersey, while Utah, Arkansas, West Virginia, and Mississippi have per capita personal incomes of less than $10,500. Average per capita income in the United States is $13,867.[3]

Expenditures per pupil vary widely, partly because of the differences in wealth among districts and states. The average current annual expenditure per pupil in the United States is $3,449. Alaska, New Jersey, New York, and Wyoming, along with the Federal District of Columbia, all spend in excess of $4,500 per pupil, while Arkansas, Kentucky, Mississippi, Tennessee, and Utah all spend less than $2,400 per pupil.[4]

As indicated previously in this chapter, federal aid has increased over the years. However, as discussed earlier in this book, the aid has been primarily categorical. The Elementary and Secondary Education Act of 1965 with its subsequent amendments and with its emphasis on improving educational opportunities for children of poverty, while categorical, comes as close to general aid as any federal aid ever has.

■ Recommendations for Establishing Equality in Financing Education

It is clear that differences in wealth among school districts can and often do result in vastly different expenditures per pupil. It is also clear that wealthy school districts, using the same effort (tax rate) as that of poor districts, can provide more monies for education. Two of the overall goals of a variety of proposals to improve school financing therefore are: to achieve equal or nearly equal expenditures per pupil, and at the same time to equalize the effort that school districts must expend to equalize expenditures. These goals cannot be accomplished without states providing a larger portion of the support of education at the local level.

As indicated earlier, the foundation-equalization approach was an initial effort in this respect. The major difficulties with the foundation-equalization approach were and still are (1) foundation levels established were not sufficient to overcome gross inequities, and (2) local school districts were given "local leeway" (freedom) to exceed the foundation-equalization level. Attempts made in the past few years (post-*Serrano*) to establish equality have emanated from the basic foundation-equalization model. The crucial elements of this model are (1) the foundation-equalization level established, (2) the degree of local tax effort required, and (3) the amount of local leeway permitted. One approach suggested is to limit the amount of local leeway. Basically, this approach reduces the discrepancy

in per pupil expenditures. A second approach provides no local leeway, thereby producing equalized per pupil expenditures with state monies supplementing the local tax yield to the equalization level. The same end result could be realized with full state funding, a position some authorities have taken.

A third approach involves equalized percentage grants and is referred to as *power equalization*. It is designed to satisfy fiscal equality and at the same time permit local school districts to use higher than state-established tax rates. School districts are permitted, usually within limits, to establish their own level of expenditure beyond the required state minimum. The level of expenditure selected results in a state-designated local tax rate. In this approach, the state guarantees equal levels of expenditure for equal tax effort and in that respect may meet the equal-protection clause of the Constitution. The plan does, however, result in unequal expenditures per pupil brought about by variations in effort and not wealth. The problem of equal educational opportunity based on equal per pupil expenditures will not easily be solved.

Other issues that are likely to make the financing of schools difficult in the years ahead are the fear of inflation, taxpayer revolt, increasing enrollments, and mandatory programs. Inflation has not been a factor in the last few years, as it has stabilized around 4 to 5 percent a year. However, the fear of increasing inflation in the future still remains in the minds of many people. They know that if inflation increases school expenditures will increase and higher tax rates are likely to be the result. The likelihood of those circumstances engenders taxpayer revolt, such as efforts to legislatively limit taxing power. Increasing enrollments will result in increasing school expenditures. State and federal mandates, including educational reform mandates, frequently have not been funded by the states, leaving the local school districts with the challenge of raising more revenue with the local property tax.

■ Accountability

Earlier in this book reference was made to the expressed dissatisfaction with the educational accomplishments of public school pupils. In a sense, the educational expectations of individuals and society were not being met. Questions were being raised about the notion that increased spending brings about better education. The term *cost-effectiveness* was being used in respect to education. The roots of accountability rest in unmet expectations and increased costs as they relate to education. The call for research and data to determine the relationship between dollars expended for education and benefits accrued to individuals and society represents the thrust of accountability.

To be accountable means to be responsible. In schools, this requires (1) explicit results that represent achievements, and (2) the dollar costs of these achievements. The end product should be a report of the costs of programs in terms of the accomplishments of the programs.

A danger that lurks in the implementation of an accountability system is the chance that goals that do not lend themselves to objective measurement will be dropped. This must be avoided. A great effort must be made to measure *all* goals as best they can be measured.

Education is an investment in society.

■ Expectations and Expenses

Early in this chapter, it was said that our expenditures for education were limited more by our willingness to pay than our ability to pay. They also seem to be limited by our inability to demonstrate definitively the value of education. Do we have the willingness to support our expectations for education? What are our national priorities? As a nation compared to other nations in the world we are wealthy. We do have pockets of poverty, and parts of our nation are more able than others to support education. If, as a *nation,* we believe that education is important, and that education can help us achieve our national goals and professed ideals, then we must effectively muster and utilize our financial resources accordingly.

■ Summary

The major purposes of this chapter were to help you (1) understand and analyze the sources of revenue (money) for school districts, (2) to recognize the differences of financial capability among states and among school districts within a state, and (3) explain how states provide money to poor local school districts in an effort to help them provide an adequate education for their students.

The three major kinds of taxes used to provide revenue for schools are property taxes, sales or use taxes, and income taxes. The major advantage of the property tax is that it provides a regular and stable form of income. Its stability will likely cause it to continue to be the mainstay of local public school support. A major disadvantage of the property tax is the inequality of the assessment of the various properties. The property tax is most generally thought of as a proportionate tax, that is, one that taxes according to ability to pay. However, inequality of assessment and the trend in an urban economy for wealth to be less related to real estate than it was in an agrarian economy have caused the tax to become somewhat regressive. Regressive taxes are those such as sales and use taxes that have a relatively greater import on lower income groups.

Sales and income taxes are lucrative sources of revenue for the states, and both taxes are easy to administer. The sales tax is collected by the vendor, who is responsible for record keeping and remitting the tax to the respective state. The state income tax is withheld from wages, hence facilitating collections.

As was indicated earlier, the sales tax is a regressive tax, causing low income people to pay as much tax for essentials as do high income people. The income tax is clearly a progressive tax because it is scaled to the ability of the taxpayer to pay. Both sales and income taxes are direct and certain, responsive to the economy, and they can be regulated by the state legislature which is responsible for raising the money. Federal support for schools comes primarily from personal and corporate income taxes.

There are large differences among the levels of wealth in local school districts within a state. Local school districts are highly dependent upon property taxes to raise money locally. Poor districts with high tax rates raise less local income than rich districts with lower tax rates. Clearly, poor districts are at a disadvantage, and as a result their students are less likely to receive an education equal to that provided by a rich district. *Serrano v. Priest* (1971) is an illustration of the aforementioned circumstances.

In recognition of the differences of wealth among local school districts, and correspondingly therefore, the fiscal inequalities among educational programs, the states have provided money (state aid) to help the school districts that are poor to offer stronger educational programs. Unfortunately, seldom does state aid bring the level of expenditures of the poor districts up to that of the rich districts. The trends, nevertheless, are toward the states paying an increasingly higher percentage of revenue for schools, and local school districts paying an increasingly lower percentage of school revenue. Those trends may or may not help in the efforts to provide equality of education. State legislatures have the challenge to bring about equity in taxation—that is, a tax system in which taxpayers are called upon to support education in proportion to their ability to pay—and making an adequate education equally available to all students.

As was indicated earlier in this book, teacher organizations have become powerful and successful in shaping legislation throughout the country. They have supported legislation over the years to try to bring about equality of education. As a prospective teacher, you should be familiar with the fundamental issues of school finance. School finance is a basic and major factor in the education profession.

Point of View

Historically the main source of funding for local school districts was the local property tax. Over the last few years, the states have increased their financial contributions to local school districts with revenue raised from sales and income taxes, thus reducing the tax load of local school districts. A major purpose of the increased state funding was to reduce the effects of the inequities of the property tax as a local source of funds—the amount of money produced by the same tax rate varies dramatically dependent upon the wealth of the local school districts—poor districts receive less money than rich districts assessing the same tax rate. The intent of state aid is to equalize opportunity for students from a fiscal aspect.

State aid has been helpful to local school districts. Over the years, it has also been political and controversial. The point of view article, "Staking a Claim" by William Montague describes the difficulty of developing a "fair" state aid formula and the political hazards faced by state senators and representatives should they vote for a state aid formula that does not favor their own political district. Political pressure can dominate a state's state aid policy.

Staking a Claim

William Montague

Alta, Utah—Even as school-funding issues are becoming increasingly technical and complex, politicians—and politics—are playing a larger and more aggressive role in the highly sensitive job of allocating state tax dollars for education.

This seeming paradox was a topic of considerable discussion among the 30 or so legislative fiscal analysts who gathered at this mountain resort late last month for an intensive two-day seminar on school-finance policy.

Faced with a baffling array of complicated decisions—the average state may have six or seven different aid formulas, each based on dozens of variable factors—state legislators are expanding their staffs, developing their own information sources, and staking out a more active part in formulating policy and putting it into practice.

To an increasing degree, seminar participants said, legislative leaders are unwilling to defer to the forces—powerful governors, influential lobbyists, and massive state education agencies—that have traditionally dominated the policymaking arena.

And in an era of tight budgets and taxpayer resentment, these experts noted, political leaders are growing louder in their demands for more accountability and better results for the money they spend—a trend reinforced by the educational excellence movement.

The reasons for this evolution in the balance of power are both institutional and political, according to John Augenblick, a noted school-finance consultant who addressed the conference. As legislatures have become more professsional in recent years, he said, they have become more capable of asserting their control over the power of the purse.

And politically, he added, nearly every state senator or representative has become keenly aware that even a minor change in a school-funding formula can have a dramatic impact on his or her home district.

"They know that school finance is the most highly political aspect of a state's operations," Mr. Augenblick told seminar participants. "Enormous political pressures can be brought to bear whenever anyone talks about reform. It can be a terrible experience."

■ Core Concerns

Such pressures can often dominate a state's education policy, Mr. Augenblick and other experts noted. While many reform theorists now downplay the relationship between funding and school quality, financial issues remain the core concern of most legislatures, Mr. Augenblick said.

"It's not the only game in town, as it may have been in the 1970's," he said, "but it's still crucial."

A state's finance system, he explained, can provide a powerful set of incentives for local districts to enact desired reforms.

It also provides the basic framework for debating nearly every policy issue that comes before a legislature.

To cope with these complex issues, seminar participants said, legislative leaders have come to rely heavily on their personal and committee staff members. A growing number of legislatures have established centralized fiscal offices to provide nonpartisan research and advice.

The importance of such specialists was reflected in the seminar itself, which was sponsored by the National Conference of State Legislatures. The annual event is specifically designed to give staff members a chance to compare notes and identify current trends.

"Too often state policymakers are operating in a vacuum," said John Myers, N.C.S.L.'S director of education programs and a former Kansas state representative.

"Staff people need to know what's going on in other states, what's working and what's not working."

Such information, participants noted, has become even more vital in the wake of the last two decades' desegregation and equalization reforms, many of which were forced on unwilling politicians by the courts.

"The legislatures have learned that once the courts [intervene in education disputes], it can be a long time before they get out," said Kent McQuire, a senior policy analyst with the Education Commission of the States.

Before such incursions happen, he said, political leaders need to "grab the bull by the horns and try to solve problems themselves."

■ An Imperfect World

But in the imperfect world of partisan politics, crafting workable solutions requires legislators and their staff members to strike a delicate balance between reform objectives and practical realities, Mr. Augenblick said.

He cited the example of Vermont, where a recent effort to equalize school aid succeeded only after a bargain was struck with lawmakers from Burlington, which has the state's wealthiest and most urban school district.

"In a situation like that, you can talk all you want about equity and theoretical goals, but in the end you are going to deal with [powerful] delegations. And that means making deals," Mr. Augenblick said.

Participants from several states reported similar political maneuvers as their legislatures grapple with difficult funding questions. For example:

- Suburban districts in Indiana are already lobbying to recoup some of the financial losses they suffered this year in that state's sweeping reform bill, according to Teresa Bailey, a budget analyst with the state's Legislative Services Agency.

- In Minnesota, Republicans repealed the state's controversial "recapture" system after they took control of the House of Representatives in 1984, noted William Marx, a House fiscal expert. The law tended to redistribute property-tax revenues from suburban Republican strongholds to poorer, more marginal districts. The Democrats, having recently regained control of the lower house, are considering whether to reinstate the provision.

- In one New England state where finance changes are under consideration, a staff analyst said, the chairman of the Senate education committee, who represents a wealthy suburban district, is keeping a weather eye on his constituency.

  "He has said he is willing to look at reforms, but it's clear to everyone that he is not going to come out the loser in all this," she said.

■ Home-District Worries

Ironically, the development of more modern information systems has tended to reinforce the home-district worries of legislators, a trend that Mr. Augenblick dubbed "printout-itis."

Using sophisticated computer applications, legislative analysts can now keep close track of exactly how much money any given district stands to win or lose from a proposed reform, and how those changes will affect various programs or student populations within a district.

According to a New Jersey analyst, staff researchers in that state's legislature even prepare printouts that compare changes in state funding levels with the results of district tax-levy elections.

This, he said, allows House and Senate members to judge how voters will respond to the need to raise more revenue locally.

"You are going to find a lot of people who only look at . . . how much money their district is going to get," said Mr. Augenblick. "Once that tendency gets started in a legislature, it can be almost incurable."

As a result, he said, legislators may adopt a policy of first determining what the best result is for their district, and then developing an argument that seeks to justify that result on the grounds of equity or efficiency.

Such strategies have their counterparts at the local level, according to one legislative analyst.

Taxpayers from wealthy districts in his state, he said, often cite the gap between what they pay out in taxes and what they get back from the state in aid.

Such "pseudo-fairness" arguments, this analyst said, have proven highly persuasive with some legislators.

"To a certain extent that is just the way the world works," commented Mr. Augenblick. "But we would hope to see a more informed debate on these issues."

And to a large extent, he said, the public has seen a more enlightened approach. Despite the limitations of electoral politics, he argued, the nation's legislatures have compiled a generally good record of responding to demands for meaningful reform.

In some cases, he said, canny legislative leaders have short-circuited regional interests by putting major reforms to a statewide vote of the people, as Wyoming did in 1983 when it successfully revamped its funding system.

But more frequently, he said, change is made possible by a small group of committed legislators who are willing to put a state's general welfare above the immediate demands of their own districts.

"There are statesmen who will do that," said Mr. Augenblick. "Their districts may lose from [the reforms], but they have the capacity to take a longer view of the world. Combine that with expert knowledge, and you have a very potent force."

From William Montague, "Staking a Claim," *Education Week*, Vol. VII, No. 6, pp. 1, 12, October 14, 1987. Copyright © 1987 Editorial Projects in Education, Washington, DC.

■ Questions for Discussion

1. What are the three main kinds of taxes used to produce revenue for schools? Discuss each of these in terms of their productivity and fairness.

2. How would you defend the support of education through taxation?

3. What essentially is the meaning of a "foundation" plan?

4. What factors in our society have caused the change in the educational support level provided by the three levels of government?

5. What are the issues that are likely to make the financing of schools difficult in the years ahead? Which of the issues do you think will have the greatest impact on school financing? Why?

■ Notes

1. Thomas D. Snyder, *Digest of Education Statistics 1987*. Washington, D.C.: Center for Education Statistics, 1987, pp. 1, 9, 10.

2. Ibid., pp. 9–10.

3. National Education Association, *Rankings of the States 1987*. Washington, D.C.: National Education Association, 1987, p. 27.

4. Thomas D. Snyder, p. 113.

■ Selected References

Guthrie, James. "School Based Management: The Most Needed Education Reform." *Phi Delta Kappan* 68 no. 4 (December 1986):305–309.

Hoy, Wayne K., and Miskel, Cecil. *Educational Administration: Theory, Research, and Practice.* New York: Random House, 1985.

Hunt, James B. "Education for Economic Growth." *Phi Delta Kappan* 65, no. 8 (April 1984):538–541.

Johns, Roe L.; Alexander, Kern; and Morphet, Edgar. *The Economics and Financing of Public Education,* Englewood Cliffs, New Jersey: Prentice-Hall 1983.

Long, David. "Rodriguez: The State Courts Respond." *Phi Delta Kappan* 64, no. 7 (March 1983):481–484.

Monahan, William G.; and Hengst, Herbert R. *Contemporary Educational Administration.* New York: Macmillan, 1984.

Odden, Allan. "Sources of Funding for Educational Reform." *Phi Delta Kappan* 67, no. 5 (January 1986):335–340.

Persell, Caroline H. *Education and Inequality.* New York: The Free Press, 1977.

Rich, John Martin. *Innovations in Education: Reformers and Their Critics.* Needham Heights, MA: Allyn and Bacon, 1988.

Sherman, Joel D. "Financing the Future." *Community Education Journal* X, no. 4 (July 1983):5–6.

Appendix A

The Fourteen Competencies of the
Virginia Beginning Teacher Assistance Program
Revised: April 1988

1. Academic Learning Time

The competent teacher knows that learning is directly related to the amount of time learners are actively engaged in planned learning activities. The one relationship most clearly established by process product research is the relationship between academic engaged time and learner's achievement gains.

The beginning teacher demonstrates knowledge of this competency by:

Planning for the efficient use of class time

Minimizing the amount of time spent on procedural matters

Using non-punitive technique for maintaining learner involvement in assigned tasks

Maintaining continuous focus on the lesson topic

2. Accountability

The competent teacher knows the importance of holding learners responsible for completing assigned tasks. It is important for the teacher to make sure that every student actually undergoes the learning experiences planned for him or her.

Holding the learner personally responsible for completing assigned learner tasks is also important because it gives learners practice in assuming and discharging personal responsibilities.

The beginning teacher demonstrates knowledge of this competency by:

Planning just what tasks each learner is supposed to complete

Making clear to the learners what they are expected to accomplish

Clearly establishing consequences of not completing an assigned task

Checking to see whether learners work on their tasks

3. Clarity of Structure

The competent teacher knows that learning is facilitated if the lesson is presented in a clear systematic sequence consistent with the objectives of instruction. Learning is a conscious activity of the learner which proceeds (according to research in human learning) most efficiently when the learner is aware of the relationship of each part of the activity to the other parts and to the whole.

The beginning teacher demonstrates knowledge of this competency by:

> Preparing outlines, reviews, and summaries, beforehand
>
> Beginning the lesson or unit with a statement of purpose, outline, etc.
>
> Making interrelations among parts of the lesson clear to learners
>
> Ending the lesson or unit with a summary or review

4. Individual Differences

The competent teacher knows that learners progress at different speeds, learn in different ways, and respond to different kinds of motivation. Few generalizations about learning are better established than this one. Research indicates that teaching strategies should be adapted to these differences if all learners are to achieve at their full potential.

The beginning teacher demonstrates knowledge of this competency by:

> Planning ways of dealing with individual differences in learner's abilities, cultural background, handicaps
>
> Defining different objectives for different learners
>
> Providing alternate ways for different learners to achieve common objectives
>
> Providing for learners with special problems (such as hearing or visual impairment, severe learning differences)
>
> Providing for learners with unusual talents or abilities
>
> Arranging the classroom for easy access for physically handicapped learners

5. Evaluation

The competent teacher knows that learner progress is facilitated by instructional objectives which are known to the learners and which coincide with the objectives of evaluation. Important information about learner status can be obtained informally while teaching can be used in making tactical teaching decisions. Additionally, formal assessment of the learner's progress is important in making instructional decisions, grading, and promotional decisions. Competence in matching given instructional objectives with informal and formal evaluation contributes to the soundness of the teacher's decisions during the course of instruction.

The beginning teacher demonstrates knowledge of this competency by:

> Planning evaluation (formal and informal) whenever he or she plans instruction
>
> Designing formal evaluation procedures that are both relevant and fair
>
> Asking questions, observing learners' work, and checking learners' understanding regularly during instruction to evaluate progress
>
> Informing learners about how their performance will be evaluated

6. Consistent Rules

The competent teacher knows that rules for classroom behavior must be clear and consistent, and that learners must understand and accept the rules and the consequences of violating them. When rules are unclear or applied inconsistently, classroom management is difficult; when rules are clear and consistently applied, the classroom seems almost to manage itself.

The beginning teacher demonstrates knowledge of this competency if:

It is seldom necessary to restate rules of conduct

Disruptive pupil behaviors are infrequent

When disruptive behaviors occur, the teacher deals with them in a non-punitive manner

7. Affective Climate

The competent teacher knows that learning occurs more readily in a classroom environment which is non-punitive and accepting. Research indicates that achievement gains are related positively to an affective environment which is non-punitive, i.e., relatively free from hostility and threats.

The beginning teacher demonstrates knowledge of this competency by:

Acting relaxed, good-humored, and accepting learner behavior

Avoiding hostility and punitiveness

8. Learner Self-Concept

The competent teacher knows that a learner's achievement may be enhanced by improving his self-concept, and that his self-concept is enhanced if the teacher's expectations are high and if the teacher shows appreciation of the learner's personal worth.

The beginning teacher demonstrates knowledge of this competency by:

Planning lessons that relate to learner's background and interests

Encouraging learners to do better

Praising correct performance of difficult tasks or correct answers to a difficult question

Helping learners develop appreciation of their own cultural heritage

Helping learners develop feelings of personal worth

Showing courtesy to and concern for learners

9. Meaningfulness

The competent teacher knows that learning is facilitated when content is related to learner's interests, common experiences, or to information with which they are familiar. Although the importance of meaningfulness in learning has been formally established by research in human learning done in psychological laboratories, practicing teachers have recognized its importance for many years.

The beginning teacher demonstrates knowledge of this competency by:

Planning ways of relating instruction to interests and previous knowledge of learners

Pointing out relationships between lesson or unit content and things learners already know

Pointing out relationships between lesson or unit content and outside or "real world" interests of learners

Asking questions of learners that require them to identify relationships between what they are learning and something they already know

Planning activities that require learners to identify relationships between what they are learning and something that is important to them outside the classroom

Relating instruction to the cultural backgrounds of learners

10. Planning

The competent teacher knows the importance of deliberate and varied planning activities. Instructional planning should reflect the teacher's knowledge that: (1) learning activities should match the instructional objectives; (2) learning is facilitated when ideas are communicated in more ways than one and when two or more sensory modes are employed; (3) the current literature on the teaching profession should be regularly consulted; and (4) learners' scores on standardized tests contain important and useful information about the class as a group and about individual learners.

Planning activities should reflect the teacher's knowledge of instructional objectives and activities, multiple instructional modes, the current professional literature, and the interpretation of test data facilitate instruction and learner progress.

The beginning teacher demonstrates knowledge of this competency by:

Using test data in defining objectives or choosing learner activities, content, materials or media

Using relevant professional literature in defining objectives or choosing learning activities, content, materials or media

Defining objectives that move learners toward long-term goals

Defining objectives on the basis of differing needs of groups and individuals

Defining objectives in measurable terms

Using information about test reliability, validity, and test norms

Using objectives as a basis for planning learning activities

Planning different activities for learners with different abilities, interests, and cultural backgrounds

Planning alternative ways for learners to achieve the same objectives

Planning for the use of different media

11. Questioning Skills

The competent teacher knows how to phrase different kinds of questions, that different types of questions are most effective in promoting different types of learning, and which type to use for which purpose. Asking questions is a major professional teaching tool and the skillful use of questions has been extensively studied and researched.

The beginning teacher demonstrates knowledge of questioning skills by:

Questioning skills during drill or practice sessions:

Asking questions that test learners' ability to recall or apply material learned previously

Avoiding difficult questions, higher order questions, and questions that call for original answers

Questioning skills during a recitation:

Asking questions that test students' knowledge or comprehension of a topic being studied

Giving feedback on student answers and voluntary comments

Answering students' questions

Questioning skills during a discussion:

Asking open-ended questions that call for student opinions, beliefs, etc.

Giving positive feedback to students' answers and voluntary comments

Accepting student answers and voluntary comments

Avoiding questions that test students' knowledge or comprehension

12. Reinforcement

The competent teacher demonstrates awareness that the skillful use of reinforcement is an effective means of encouraging and discouraging particular behaviors. Establishment of the importance of reinforcement in modifying human behavior and clarification of principles governing its use has been one of the principal achievements of research in learning.

The beginning teacher demonstrates knowledge of this competency by:

Giving positive rather than negative feedback

Not using punishment to motivate learners

Calling attention to desirable behaviors

Using positive feedback to cue learners to behavioral expectations

13. Close Supervision

The competent teacher knows that more is learned during individual and small group activities if the learners are monitored. Research indicates that learning is facilitated during activities when they are monitored rather closely, presumably because this increases the amount of learner engagement. Close supervision also provides opportunities for the teacher to assist and encourage learners.

This competency is demonstrated only when learners are working independently or in small groups. The beginning teacher demonstrates knowledge of this competency by:

Monitoring activity of all learners

Helping learners who have difficulties

14. Awareness

The competent teacher knows that effective classroom management depends on knowing what is occurring in the classroom and that the learners perceive the teacher knows what is going on. The teacher who is aware of what is going on in the classroom is likely to increase learner participation in learning activities and reduce disruptions.

This competency is demonstrated when the teacher is working with the class as a whole. The beginning teacher demonstrates knowledge of this competency by:

Maintaining constant awareness of level of interest and attention of learners

Making learners aware of teacher awareness

From *BTAP Competencies and Indicators.* Reprinted by permission of the Virginia Department of Education, Richmond, VA.

Appendix B

Teacher Supply and Demand by Field and Region

Region / Field	Alaska	Hawaii	North-west	West	Rocky Mtns.	Great Plains/ Midwest	South Central	South-east	Great Lakes	Mid-Atlantic	North-east
Agriculture	—	3.00	4.00	2.57	3.00	3.08	3.00	3.00	4.00	4.00	3.00
Art	2.00	2.00	1.86	1.81	2.08	2.17	2.40	2.53	2.26	2.00	2.50
Bilingual Ed.	3.00	2.00	4.29	4.74	4.50	4.24	4.63	3.45	4.27	3.58	4.14
Business	4.00	4.00	3.50	3.46	2.90	2.74	2.76	2.90	3.39	3.82	3.75
Computer Science	3.00	4.00	4.14	4.25	4.44	4.00	4.39	4.28	4.27	4.21	4.29
Counselor-Elem.	3.00	5.00	3.57	2.25	2.95	3.42	3.14	2.95	3.23	2.60	3.14
Counselor-Sec.	3.00	5.00	3.63	2.45	3.05	3.15	2.86	2.90	3.43	2.94	2.78
Data Processing	3.00	3.00	3.67	3.67	3.88	3.96	3.69	4.07	3.97	4.56	4.67
Driver Ed.	3.00	1.00	1.75	2.50	2.00	2.21	2.71	2.69	2.67	2.33	3.00
Elementary-Primary	3.00	1.00	2.38	3.58	3.00	2.29	3.58	2.79	2.30	2.61	2.85
Elementary-Intermediate	3.00	1.00	2.25	3.58	3.18	2.38	3.54	2.96	2.44	2.61	3.00
English	2.00	4.00	3.00	3.84	3.25	3.17	3.33	2.79	3.23	3.38	3.36
Health Education	4.00	2.00	1.63	2.29	1.60	1.59	2.29	2.13	1.90	1.77	2.63
Home Economics	2.00	1.00	2.25	2.25	2.38	2.31	2.38	2.31	2.73	3.50	3.00
Industrial Arts	2.00	5.00	3.50	2.83	3.20	2.78	3.55	3.67	3.09	4.33	5.00
Journalism	3.00	2.00	2.14	3.06	3.11	3.00	2.80	2.93	3.10	2.40	4.00
Language, Mod.-French	3.00	4.00	3.00	2.92	3.20	3.26	3.16	3.83	3.61	3.11	3.60
Language, Mod.-German	3.00	3.00	3.00	2.79	3.45	3.30	2.83	3.80	3.57	2.83	3.25
Language, Mod.-Spanish	3.00	4.00	3.57	3.96	3.73	3.43	3.22	3.95	3.88	3.21	3.50
Library Science	4.00	3.00	3.60	3.54	3.78	2.84	3.62	3.60	3.50	3.33	3.00
Mathematics	3.00	5.00	4.13	4.84	4.58	4.24	4.75	4.64	4.65	4.48	4.70
Music-Instrumental	4.00	1.00	4.21	3.27	3.91	3.29	2.86	2.68	3.21	2.61	3.13
Music-Vocal	4.00	1.00	3.71	2.71	3.55	3.18	2.59	2.62	3.04	2.44	3.13
Physical Education	2.00	1.00	1.17	1.86	1.67	1.25	2.24	1.86	1.48	1.60	1.43
Psychologist (school)	4.00	—	3.60	2.84	3.17	3.75	3.20	3.50	3.69	3.36	3.25
Science-Biology	2.00	5.00	2.63	4.19	3.00	3.58	3.78	4.12	3.37	3.93	3.60
Science-Chemistry	2.00	5.00	3.63	4.48	4.17	4.25	4.39	4.56	4.52	4.31	4.70
Science-Earth	3.00	5.00	3.00	4.08	3.45	3.72	4.22	4.08	3.71	4.08	3.89
Science-General	3.00	5.00	3.00	4.17	3.25	3.64	4.05	4.04	3.82	3.92	3.89
Science-Physics	2.00	5.00	3.50	4.57	4.46	4.24	4.41	4.56	4.62	4.44	4.67
Social Sciences	3.00	1.00	1.86	2.28	1.91	1.91	2.27	1.71	2.18	2.50	2.56
Social Worker (school)	—	—	2.50	3.00	2.38	2.82	2.67	2.83	3.06	2.60	2.50
Speech	3.00	1.00	2.43	2.92	3.09	2.39	2.64	3.00	2.70	2.70	4.00
Spec.-Deaf Education	3.00	4.00	3.50	3.50	4.43	3.67	4.00	4.00	3.52	3.50	3.40
Spec.-ED/PSA	3.00	4.00	4.14	4.20	4.67	4.13	4.17	4.29	4.37	3.79	3.89
Spec.-Gifted	3.00	3.00	3.29	3.43	4.00	4.12	4.13	4.28	3.94	3.55	3.71
Spec.-LD	3.00	4.00	3.86	4.30	4.78	4.15	4.30	4.50	4.31	3.77	3.88
Spec.-MR	3.00	4.00	4.00	4.29	4.67	3.85	4.26	4.27	4.00	3.68	3.94
Spec.-Multi. Handi.	3.00	4.00	4.00	4.40	4.67	4.21	4.25	4.47	4.28	3.94	3.94
Spec.-Reading	3.00	3.00	3.17	3.06	3.89	3.44	3.91	4.00	3.36	3.20	3.00
Speech Path./Audio.	3.00	—	3.50	3.67	4.44	4.22	3.71	4.27	4.26	4.00	4.33
COMPOSITE	2.95	3.16	3.15	3.44	3.43	3.18	3.45	3.49	3.42	3.34	3.47

KEY: 5 = Considerable, 4 = Some Shortage, 3 = Balanced, 2 = Some Surplus, 1 = Considerable Surplus

From *Tenth Annual Teacher Supply/Demand Survey*, January 1986. Copyright © 1986 Association for School, College and University Staffing, Addison, IL.

Appendix C

Objectives of the AFT

Article II

Objects

Section 1. To obtain exclusive bargaining rights, including the right to strike, for teachers and other educational workers, public employees, health care employees and other workers.

Section 2. To bring local and state federations of teachers and other workers into relations of mutual assistance and cooperation.

Section 3. To obtain for teachers and other workers all of the rights to which they are entitled in a free society.

Section 4. To improve standards for teachers, educational workers and other workers, by promoting better preparation, encouraging relevant in-service training, and securing the working conditions essential to the best performance of professional service.

Section 5. To improve the standards for registered nurses, allied health professionals and other health-care employees by advancing economic status, promoting better preparation in basic education programs, encouraging and promoting continuing education, securing working conditions essential to the best performance of services and the most effective delivery of health care.

Section 6. To improve standards for public employees by working for the passage and strengthening of collective bargaining and civil service legislation in the states, promoting continuing education for state employees, and securing working conditions conducive to the best performance and delivery of public service.

Section 7. To encourage the hiring and retention of competent teachers and other educational workers, the maintenance of modern well-equipped schools, and the promotion of such educational programs and conditions in American schools, as will enable their students to equip themselves better to take their places in the economic, social, and political life of the community.

Section 8. To promote the welfare of children by providing progressively better educational opportunities for all, regardless of race, color, creed, sex, and social, political or economic status.

Section 9. To promote the welfare of the health-care consumer by promoting progressively better access to and utilization of health-care resources in this country.

Section 10. To fight all forms of bias due to race, creed, sex, social, political or economic status, or national origin.

Section 11. To support and promote the ideals of democracy as envisioned in the Constitution of the United States of America, its Bill of Rights and other Amendments, to work for passage and retention of just laws which will improve the educational climate for students, teachers and other workers in education, and to encourage them to exercise their proper rights and responsibilities under these laws.

Section 12. To encourage locals to organize chapters of retired members within their jurisdiction.

From *Constitution of the American Federation of Teachers, Article II, 1986*, pages 1–2. Used by permission of the American Federation of Teachers, Washington, DC.

Appendix D

Goals and Resolutions of the NEA

Foreword

The Constitution of the National Education Association indicates that the goals of the Association shall be the 10 goals stated in the Preamble. These goals are, therefore, regularly set forth in a statement of resolutions adopted by the Representative Assembly.

Resolutions are formal expressions of opinion, intent, belief, or position of the Association. They shall set forth general concepts in clear, concise language, shall be broad in nature, shall state the positions of the Association positively and without ambiguity, and shall be consistent with the goals of the Association as stated in the Preamble of the Constitution.

Preamble

The Preamble of the Constitution of the National Education Association of the United States states:

We, the members of the National Education Association of the United States, in order that the Association may serve as the national voice for education, advance the cause of education for all individuals, promote the health and welfare of children and/or students, promote professional excellence among educators, gain recognition of the basic importance of the teacher in the learning process and other employees in the educational effort, protect the rights of educational employees and advance their interests and welfare, secure professional autonomy, unite educational employees for effective citizenship, promote and protect human and civil rights, and obtain for its members the benefits of an independent, united education profession, do hereby adopt this Constitution.

A. Serve as the National Voice for Education

Educational Opportunity for All
  Public Education
Public Education/National Defense
Excellence in Education
Understanding and Support of Public
  Education
Effective School Climate
U.S. Department of Education
U.S. Federal Schools
Federal Financial Support for Education
Improving Neglected Schools

Deleterious Programs
Tuition Tax Credits
Voucher Plans
Tax Reform
Educational/Economic Stability of States
National Health Insurance
Media
Media Utilization
Rural Education
Urban Development
Community Education
School Boards
Public School Buildings
Arbor Day Preservation of Our Heritage

Environmental Education
Energy Programs
Hazardous Materials
Radiation and Chemical Pollution
Nuclear Power Plants
Organizations of Other Nations

B. Advance the Cause of Education for All Individuals

Instructional Excellence
Higher Education Research and Study Grants
Evaluation and Promotion in Higher Education
Need-Based Funding in Higher Education
Foreign Language Education
American Indian/Alaska Native Education
Chicano-Hispano Education
Asian and Pacific Islander Education
Black American Education
Career Education
Youth and Adult Training Programs
Sexism in Education
Energy Education
Nonviolence in Schools
Educational Bureaucracy
Business Support for Public Education
Technology in the Educational Process
Labor Movement Education
Metric System
Basic Financial Support of Public Education
Funding for Education Legislation
Federal Impact Aid
Financial Crisis

C. Promote the Health and Welfare of Children and/or Students

Student Rights and Responsibilities
Homework
Early Childhood Development and Kindergarten
Middle School and Junior High Programs
High School Equivalency Testing
Standardized Testing of Students
Higher Education
Credit Hour Evaluation
Student Health and Personnel Services
School Counseling Services
Student Sexual Orientation

Student Stress
Programs Before and After School
Athletic Programs
Extracurricular Participation
Time To Learn
Extracurricular Funding
Transfer of Student Records
Discipline
Multicultural/Global Education
Vocational Education
Driver Education
Fine Arts Education
Conflict Resolution Education
Law-Related Education
Family Life Education
Alternative Programs for At Risk and/or Special Needs Students
Discriminatory Academic Tracking
Gifted, Talented, and Creative Students
Educational Programs for Limited English Proficiency Students
Education for All Handicapped Students
Education for Homeless Children
Homebound Instruction
Home Schooling
Correspondence Programs
Communication Between the Hearing and the Hearing Impaired
Left-Handed Students
Education of Migrants
Education of Refugee Children and Children of Undocumented Aliens
School Transportation
AIDS Education
AIDS/HIV Testing of Students
Admission of Students with AIDS
Substance Abuse
Alcohol Advertising
International Drug Trade
Drug and Alcohol Testing of Students
Lifesaving Techniques
Youth Camp Safety
Family Stability
Family Stability for Children
Adolescent Pregnancy and Parenting
Protection of Handicapped Infants
Day Care

Child Support Payments
Family Violence
Abduction of Children
Child Abuse, Neglect, and Exploitation
Missing Children
Extremist Groups
Youth and Gang-Related Activity
Juvenile Offender Education
State Juvenile Codes

D. Promote Professional Excellence Among Educators

A Licensed Educator in Every Professional Position
Teacher Evaluation
Competency Testing and Evaluation
Administrator Training and Evaluation
Class Size
Time To Teach
Teacher Preparation Programs: Entry
Teacher Preparation Programs: Content and Evaluation
Teacher Preparation Programs: Student Teaching
Teacher Preparation Programs: Professional Participation
Participation in Professional Associations
Professional Development
Professional Development Resource Centers
Mentor Programs
Neurological Disorder Awareness
Teacher Exchange Programs
Intern Programs
Mandated Standards for Educational Programs
Impact of Federal and State Legislative Mandates
School Libraries/Media Centers
School Nurses

E. Gain Recognition of the Basic Importance of the Teacher in the Learning Process and Other Employees in the Educational Effort

Selection of Materials and Teaching Techniques
Development of Materials

Instructional Materials and Teaching Techniques Challenges
Cultural Diversity in Instructional Materials and Activities
Religious Heritage in Instructional Materials
Academic and Professional Freedom
Evaluation of Student Learning

F. Protect the Rights of Educational Employees and Advance Their Interests and Welfare

Collective Bargaining Rights
Collective Bargaining and Grievance Procedures
Pay Equity/Comparable Worth
Salaries and Benefits
Economic Welfare
Uniform Compensation
Unemployment/Disability Compensation
Strikes
Differentiated Staffing
Job Sharing
Summer Schools, Extended School Year, and Year-Round Schools
Education in Correctional and Rehabilitation Agencies
Employment in Federal Schools Overseas
Educators and Active Duty Service
Misuse of Part-Time Faculty
Substitute Teachers
Noninstructional Aides and Auxiliary Personnel
Noninstructional Support Staff
Personnel Policies and Procedures
Nondiscriminatory Personnel Policies/ Affirmative Action
Continuing Employment and Fair Dismissal Practices
Employee Rights Pending Court Action
Reduction in Force
Mandated Retraining
Retirement
Social Security
Protection of Retirement System Assets and Earned Benefits
Acountability and Assessment
Protection of School Personnel
Protection of Educational Employee Advocates

Physical Environment for Education
Right to Privacy
Privileged Communications
Recording Devices in Schools
Access to Copyrighted Materials for
  Educational Use
Tax Deductions for Professional Expenses
Save Harmless/Teacher Liability
Transportation Liability Insurance
Health Examinations
Drug and Alcohol Testing
AIDS/HIV Testing of Educational Employees
Employees with AIDS
Stress on School Personnel
Medication and Medical Services in Schools

G. Secure Professional Autonomy

Accreditation of Teacher Preparation
  Institutions
Certification
Professional Standards Boards
Licensure

H. Unite Educational Employees for Effective Citizenship

The Education Employee as a Citizen
U.S. Constitutional Convention
The Right To Know
The Right To Vote
Statehood for the District of Columbia

I. Promote and Protect Human and Civil Rights

Human Relations in the School
Integration in the Public Schools
Institutional Discrimination
Ethnic-Minority Educators
Black Higher Education Institutions
Sectarian Practices in the School Program
The Holocaust
Civil Rights
Martin Luther King Day
Fair Housing
Protection of Senior Citizens
Care of the Mentally Ill
Federal Support for Public Welfare
Equal Opportunity for Women

Sexual Harrassment
Family Planning
Sexual Assault
Victims of a Crime
Invasion of Privacy
Military Veterans
Highway Safety
Control of Guns and Other Deadly Weapons
Violence Against and Exploitation of Asian/
  Pacific Islanders
Immigration
Internment/Containment Policies
The Right To Organize
Migrant Workers
English as the Official Language
Accessibility for the Handicapped
World Peace
Peaceful Resolution of Conflicts
World Court
Nuclear Freeze/Reduction
Teaching About Nuclear War
Human Rights
Elimination of Racial, Ethnic, and Religious
  Discrimination
World Hunger

J. Obtain for Its Members the Benefits of an Independent, United Education Profession

Strong Professional Associations
Supporting Locals in Jeopardy
Appointments by the President of the United
  States
Membership Participation in the Association
Minority Participation in the Association
Retired Member Participation
Promotion of Teaching as a Career Choice
Universal Teacher Rights

Foreword: Source: *NEA Handbook 1988–89*. Resolutions of the National Education Association, Washington, DC: National Education Association. Used by permission.

Preamble: Source: *NEA Handbook 1988–89*. Constitution of the National Education Association of the United States. Washington, DC: National Education Association. Used by permission.

List of Resolutions: Source: *NEA Handbook 1988–89*. Resolutions of the National Education Association. Washington, DC: National Education Association. Used by permission.

Appendix E

AIDS: Sorting Out Truth from Myths

Question	Answer
What is AIDS?	A fatal disease that cripples the immune system, leaving the victim susceptible to illnesses the body can usually fight off, such as pneumonia, meningitis and a cancer called Kaposi's sarcoma.
What causes AIDS? What are the symptoms?	AIDS is caused by a virus usually known as human immunodeficiency virus, or HIV. Symptoms of full-blown AIDS include a persistent cough, fever and difficulty in breathing. Multiple purplish blotches and bumps on the skin may indicate Kaposi's sarcoma, a cancer associated with AIDS. The virus can also cause brain damage.
How is AIDS diagnosed?	By the appearance of pneumonia and other persistent infections, by tests that show damage to the immune system and by a positive test for antibodies to the AIDS virus.
How can you get AIDS?	Mostly by having sex with an infected person or by sharing needles and syringes used to inject drugs. The virus, present in blood, semen and vaginal secretions, can be transmitted from one homosexual partner to another and during sexual intercourse both from a man to a woman and from a woman to a man.
Who runs the greatest risk?	Of the more than 29,000 U.S. cases, 65 percent have been homosexual or bisexual men, 25 percent intravenous drug users, 4 percent heterosexuals and 3 percent persons who received blood or blood products, a third of whom have been people with hemophilia or other blood disorders. How 3 percent more caught the disease hasn't been determined. There have been about 400 cases in children.
What is the risk for heterosexuals?	The greater the number of sexual partners, the greater the risk. The chances of infection from one encounter are between 1 in 1,000 and 1 in 10.
Can AIDS be transmitted from an infected woman to her unborn child?	Yes—about a third of the babies born to mothers with AIDS are infected. Most will develop the disease and die.
Can you get AIDS by shaking hands, hugging, social kissing, crying, coughing or sneezing? By French kissing? By eating food prepared by someone with AIDS? By an insect bite?	No known cases have been transmitted in any of these ways.
Can you get AIDS by piercing your ears?	Possibly, though as yet no one has. If you plan to get your ears pierced, to have acupuncture treatments or to be tattooed, insist on a sterile needle.

Question	Answer
Is it dangerous to sit next to someone who has AIDS or who is infected with the virus?	No.
Can AIDS be transmitted by someone who is infected but doesn't show symptoms?	Yes. This is mainly how the AIDS virus is transmitted.
What's the difference between being infected with the AIDS virus and having AIDS?	People infected with the virus can have a wide range of symptoms—from none to mild to severe. At least a fourth to a half of those infected will develop AIDS within four to 10 years. Many experts think the percentage will be much higher.
How can anyone be absolutely certain his or her sex partner is safe?	You can't. But experts believe that couples who have had a totally monogamous relationship for the past decade are safe. A negative blood test, of course, would be near-certain evidence of safety.
How can I avoid catching AIDS?	If you test positive for the AIDS antibody, shoot drugs or engage in other activities that increase the chances of catching AIDS, inform your sex partner, and use a condom if you have sex. If your partner tests positive, or if you think he or she has been exposed to AIDS because of past sexual practices or through the use of intravenous drugs, a condom should be used. If you or your partner is in a high-risk group, avoid oral contact with the genitals or rectum, as well as sexual activities that might cut or tear the skin or the tissues of the penis, vagina or rectum. Avoid sex with prostitutes. Many are addicted to drugs and often get AIDS by sharing contaminated needles with other addicts.
What are some of the diseases that affect AIDS victims?	Almost all AIDS victims get a parasitic infection of the lungs called *Pneumocystis carinii* pneumonia, a cancer called Kaposi's sarcoma or both. Other ailments include unusually severe yeast infections, herpes and parasites.
Who should be tested for AIDS?	Gay men and intravenous drug users. Their sex partners. Anyone who has had several sex partners, if their sexual history is unknown, during any one of the last five years.
How accurate is the blood test?	It is very accurate, but not infallible. A more sophisticated and expensive test called the Western Blot is used to confirm borderline cases.
What should I do if I test positive?	See a physician immediately for a medical evaluation. Use a condom during sex. Do not donate blood, body organs, other tissue or sperm. Do not share toothbrushes, razors or other implements that could become contaminated with blood.
Is banked blood safe?	Yes. It is tested and discarded if contaminated. In addition, people in high-risk groups have been asked not to donate blood.

Appendix F

Significant Dates in Black-American History

1619	The first Negroes to be brought to the American colonies arrived in Virginia as indentured servants.
1688	Quakers in Germantown, Pa., issued the first formal antislavery protest in the Western Hemisphere.
1775	The Pennsylvania Abolition Society, the first antislavery society in America, was founded.
1787	Congress barred the extension of slavery into the Northwest Territory.
1807	British Parliament abolished the slave trade. Congress barred the importation of new slaves into U.S. territory.
1827	The first Negro newspaper, *Freedom's Journal,* began publication in New York City.
1830	The U.S. Census Bureau reported that 3,777 Negro heads of families owned slaves.
1847	Frederick Douglass, a former slave and a lecturer with the Massachusetts Antislavery Society, began publishing *North Star,* an abolitionist newspaper.
1849	Harriet Tubman escaped from slavery in Maryland. She became one of the most venturesome conductors on the Underground Railroad, leading over 300 slaves to freedom. Benjamin Roberts filed the first school integration suit on behalf of his daughter. The Massachusetts Supreme Court rejected the suit and established a "separate but equal" precedent.
1854	James A. Healy was ordained a priest in Notre Dame cathedral, Paris. He later became America's first Negro Roman Catholic bishop. The first Negro College, Lincoln University, was founded as Ashmun Institute in Oxford, Pa.
1865	By the end of the Civil War, some 186,000 Negroes had served with the Union forces. The Thirteenth Amendment, freeing all slaves, was passed by Congress. The Freedman's Bureau was organized to aid and protect newly freed blacks in the South.
1867	Morehouse College, Atlanta, Ga., and Howard University, Washington, D.C., were founded.
1875	Congress passed a civil rights act prohibiting discrimination in such public accommodations as hotels and theaters.
1881	Tennessee passed a "Jim Crow" law instituting segregated railroad travel that set a trend among other states in the South.
1896	The National Association of Colored Women was organized in Washington, D.C.; Mary Church Terrell served as its first president.
1910	The National Association for the Advancement of Colored People (NAACP) was founded in New York.
1911	The National Urban League was founded. It was originally made up of two groups—the Committee for Improving the Industrial Conditions of Negroes and the League for the Protection of Colored Women.

1917	Ten thousand Negroes marched down Fifth Avenue in New York to protest the many lynchings in the South. The parade was led by W. E. B. DuBois. Race riots broke out in East St. Louis, Illinois.
1942	The Congress of Racial Equality (CORE), an action oriented civil rights group, was founded by James Farmer in Chicago.
1947	Statistics amassed by Tuskegee Institute indicated that in the period 1882–1947 3,426 Negroes were lynched in the United States. Of these, 1,217 were lynched in the 1890–1900 decade.
1951	Ralph J. Bunche, who won a Nobel Peace Prize in 1950, was appointed Under-Secretary of the United Nations, the highest ranking American employed by the international body.
1954	In "Brown v. Board of Education of Topeka" the U.S Supreme Court held that segregation in public education denied equal protection of the laws.
1955	A bus boycott in Montgomery, Ala., was led by Dr. Martin Luther King, Jr., after Rosa Parks was arrested for refusing to give up her seat to a white man.
1961	CORE began "Freedom Rides" that rolled through the South, protesting segregation.
1962	James Meredith desegregated the University of Mississippi, after President Kennedy dispatched troops and riots killed two persons.
1963	August 28: The March on Washington in which more than 200,000 Americans from all walks of life converged on the nation's capital constituted one of the largest single protests in American history. The marchers gathered on the steps of the Lincoln Memorial to dramatize discontent with the Negro's plight.
1964	Three young civil-rights workers—Michael Schwerner, Andrew Goodman, and James E. Chaney—were murdered in Mississippi.
1968	April 4: While standing on the balcony of a Memphis motel, Dr. Martin Luther King, Jr., was shot and killed by a sniper.
1972	The busing of children, both black and white, from one neighborhood school district to another became an important political issue. The Nixon administration supported and signed into law a bill which prohibited busing solely to achieve racial integration.
1977	The TV dramatization of Alex Haley's book *Roots* was seen by the largest audience ever. The story chronicled the black author's family history from mid-eighteenth-century African beginnings.
1978	U.S. Supreme Court ruled that the University of California Medical School at Davis must admit Allan P. Bakke, a 38-year-old white engineer, as the school's minority-admissions plan was inflexible and racially biased. The justices ruled, however, that race could be considered as a university admission factor. Black leaders expressed concern regarding the decision.

Permission: Hammond Incorporated, Maplewood, NJ.

Appendix G

History of Education—Highlights

about 4000	B.C.	Written language developed
about 2000	B.C.	First schools
479–338	B.C.	Period of Greek Brilliance
445–431	B.C.	Greek Age of Pericles
303	B.C.	Few private Greek teachers set up schools in Rome
167	B.C.	First Greek library in Rome
0		Christ born
31–476	A.D.	Empire of Rome
476	A.D.	Fall of Rome in the West
800	A.D.	Charlemagne crowned Emperor
1100		Turning point in mediaeval history, civilization saved
1150		Universities of Paris and Bologna
1209		Cambridge founded
1295		Voyage of Marco Polo
1384		Order of Brethren of the Common Life founded
1400		Thirty-eight universities; 108 by 1600
1423		Printing invented
1456		First book printed
1500		250 Latin Grammar Schools in England
1517		Luther nails theses to cathedral door, beginning of Reformation
1519–1521		Magellan first circumnavigates the globe
1534		Founding of Jesuits
1536		Sturm established his Gymnasium in Germany, setting the type of the classical secondary school
1601		English Poor Law, established principle of tax-supported schools
1618		Holland had compulsory school law
1620		Plymouth Colony, Massachusetts, settled
1635		Boston Latin Grammar School founded
1636		Harvard founded, first college in North America
1642		Massachusetts law of 1642, compelled inspection
1647		Massachusetts law of 1647, compelled establishment of schools
1662		First newspaper in England
1672		First teacher-training class, Father Demia, France
1684		Brothers of the Christian Schools founded
1685		First normal school, de la Salle, Rheims, France
1697		First teacher-training in Germany, Francke's Seminary, Halle
1751		Benjamin Franklin established first academy in the United States
1762		*Emile* of Rousseau published
1775–1789		Revolution, United States
1785, 1787		Northwest Ordinances
1789		Adoption of Constitution, United States
1798		Lancaster discovered Monitorial plan of education
1804		Pestalozzi's Institute of Yverdon established
1806		First Lancastrian School in New York

1819	Dartmouth College Decision
1821	First American High School established in Boston
1821	Troy Seminary for Women, E. Willard, first higher education for women, United States
1823	Hall, First Normal School in the United States, Concord, Vermont
1826	Froebel's *The Education of Man*
1827	Massachusetts Law compelled high schools
1837	Massachusetts had first state board, H. Mann first secretary
1839	First public normal school, United States, Lexington, Massachusetts
1852	First compulsory school law, Massachusetts
1855	First kindergarten in United States, German, Mrs. Schurz
1857	Founding of the National Teachers' Association (National Education Association)
1861–1865	Civil War
1861	Oswego Normal School (Sheldon)
1862	Morrill Land-Grant College Act; College of Engineering, military science, agriculture in each state
1868	Herbartian Society founded
1872	Kalamazoo Decision, made high schools legal
1873	First public kindergarten established in St. Louis
1874	Kalamazoo Decision established rights to devote tax money to high schools
1881	Booker T. Washington established Tuskegee Institute
1888	Teachers College, Columbia founded
1890	Second Morrill Act
1892	Committee of Ten established
1902	First junior college established in Joliet, Illinois
1909–1910	First junior high schools established at Berkeley, California and Columbus, Ohio
1914	Smith-Lever Act
1917	Smith-Hughes Act, encouraged agriculture, industry, and home economics education in the United States
1918	Cardinal Principles of Secondary Education
1920	Compulsory education in all states
1932–1940	Eight Year Study of thirty high schools was completed by the Progressive Education Association. Reported favorably on the work of the modern school
1937	George-Dean Act
1944	G.I. Bill of Rights for World War II veterans
1945	UNESCO established
1950	National Science Foundation Act
1952	G.I. Bill's educational benefits extended to Korean veterans
1952	U.S. Supreme Court ruling on released time for religious instruction
1954	U.S. Supreme Court decision required eventual racial integration of public schools
1958	National Defense Education Act
1961	Peace Corps established
1962	U.S. Supreme Court ruling on prayers in public schools
1963	U.S. Supreme Court ruling on Bible reading in public schools
1964	Civil Rights Act (Public Law 88–352)
1965	Elementary-Secondary Education Act (Public Law 89–10)
1965	Higher Education Act
1966	G.I. Bill's educational benefits extended to Southeast Asia War Veterans
1967	Education Professions Development Act
1968	Handicapped Children's Early Education Assistance Act
1972	Indian Education Act passed, designed to help native Americans to help themselves
1972	Title IX Education Amendment outlawing discrimination on the basis of sex
1975	Education for All Handicapped Children: Public Law 94–142 implemented
1978	Supreme Court rules against reverse discrimination in *Bakke* case

Appendix H

How Good a Motivator Are You?

Check your motivational practices by rating yourself on the questions below. Add your totals in each column. Score yourself as follows: 90–100, excellent; 80–90, good; 70–80, fair; below 70, poor.

	Usually (4 points)	Sometimes (2 points)	Never (0 points)
1. I believe my students are competent and trustworthy.			
2. I avoid labeling students.			
3. I avoid sarcasm, put-downs, and ridicule of students.			
4. I send explicit invitations to succeed.			
5. I listen to what my students really say.			
6. I let students know they are missed.			
7. I make good use of student experts in the class.			
8. I use heterogeneous groups to build interdependence.			
9. I teach leadership and communication skills.			
10. I avoid overemphasis on competition, rewards, and winning.			
11. I help groups evaluate their effectiveness in group *process*.			
12. I give equal time, attention, and support to low-ability students.			
13. I communicate high expectations to my students.			
14. I focus on future success rather than past failures.			

	Usually (4 points)	Sometimes (2 points)	Never (0 points)
15. I look for what is positive in student work and behavior.			
16. I set and communicate clear goals for instruction.			
17. I use well-designed, thought-provoking questions to stimulate readiness.			
18. I use objects as "focusing events" to stimulate interest.			
19. I use brainstorming to stimulate interest before beginning a lesson.			
20. I use set induction activities that connect a present experience to a lesson concept.			
21. I ask low-risk, open-ended questions.			
22. I wait three to five seconds after asking a divergent question.			
23. I suspend judgment and redirect a question to get multiple responses.			
24. I paraphrase and clarify responses instead of judging and praising.			
25. I personalize learning.			

Appendix I

State-Required Carnegie Units by Subject: 1958–1986

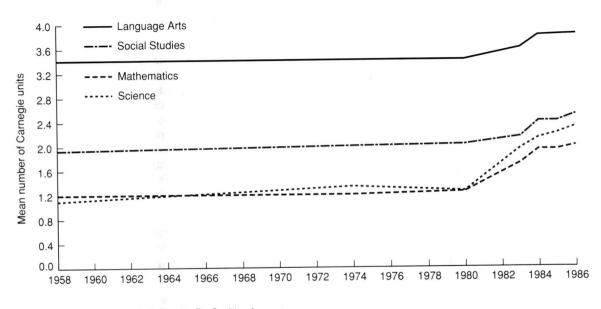

Source: Joyce D. Stern and Marjorie O. Chandler. *The Condition of
Education 1987 Edition.* Washington, DC: U.S. Department of Education,
1987, page 87.

Appendix J

Alphabetical Listing of Software Producers

Active Learning Systems
P.O. Box 1984
Midland, MI 48640
800–423–0818

Addison-Wesley
One Jacob Way
Reading, MA 01867
617–944–3700

Apple Computer, Inc.
20525 Mariani Avenue
Cupertino, CA 95014
408–996–1010

Ashton-Tate
20101 Hamilton Avenue
Torrance, CA 90502
213–329–8000

Broderbund
17 Paul Drive
San Rafael, CA 94903
415–479–1170

Comal User's Group, U.S.A., Ltd.
6041 Monona Drive
Madison, WI 53716
608–222–4432

CompuServe Information Services
P.O. Box 20212
5000 Arlington Centre Boulevard
Columbus, OH 43220
614–457–8600

Conduit
The University of Iowa
Oakdale Campus
Iowa City, IA 52242
319–353–5789

Cornucopia Software
1625 Beverly Place
Borkoloy, CA 94707
415–524–8098

DCH Educational Software
DC Heath and Company
125 Spring Street
Lexington, MA 02173
800–235–3565

Digital Marketing
2363 Boulevard Circle
Walnut Creek, CA 94595
415–497–1000

Gessler Software
900 Broadway
New York, NY 10003
212–673–3113

Grolier Electronic Publishing, Inc.
Sherman Turnpike
Danbury, CT 06816
203–797–3500

IBM
Contact local IBM marketing office for information

L & S Computerware
1589 Fraser Drive
Sunnyvale, CA 94086
408–738–3416

Lotus Development Corporation
55 Cambridge Parkway
Cambridge, MA 02142
617–577–8500

McGraw-Hill
School Division
1221 Avenue of the Americas
New York, NY 10020
212–512–2000

Micro Power and Light Company
12820 Hillcrest Road, #219
Dallas, TX 75230
214–239–6620

Microsoft
10700 Northrup Way, Box 97200
Bellevue, WA 98009
206–828–8080

Mindscape, Inc.
3444 Dundee Road
Northbrook, IL 60062
312–480–7667

Minnesota Educational Computing Corporation
3490 Lexington Avenue North
St. Paul, MN 55126
612–481–3500

Newsweek
P.O. Box 414
Livingston, NJ 07039
800–526–2595

Oasis Systems
2765 Reynolds Way
San Diego, CA 92103
714–291–9489

Scholastic Software & Targeted Learning, Inc.
730 Broadway
New York, NY 10003
212–505–3000

Science Research Associates (SRA)
155 N. Wacker Drive
Chicago, IL 60607
312–984–7000

Sensible Software, Inc.
210 South Woodward, Suite 229
Birmingham, MI 48011
313–258–5566

Sierra On-Line, Inc.
P.O. Box 485
Coarse Gold, CA 93614
209–683–6858

Simpac Educational Systems
1105 North Main Street, Suite 11-C
Gainesville, FL 32601
904-376-2049

Software Publishing Corporation
P.O. Box 7210
1901 Landings Drive
Mountain View, CA 94039
415-962-8910

Sorcim Corporation
2195 Fortune Drive
San Jose, CA 95131
408-942-1727

Source Telecomputing Corporation
1616 Anderson Road
McLean, VA 22102
800-336-3330

Spinnaker Software Corp.
One Kendall Square
Cambridge, MA 02139
617-494-1200

StoneEdge Technology
P.O. Box 455
Spring House, PA 19477
215-641-1825

Sunburst Communications
39 Washington Avenue
Pleasantville, NY 10570
914-769-5030

Teck Associates
P.O. Box 8732
White Bear Lake, MN 55110
612-429-5570

Tom Snyder Productions
123 Mt. Auburn Street
Cambridge, MA 02138
617-876-4433

Visicorp
2895 Zanker Road
San Jose, CA 95134
408-946-9000

Weekly Reader Family Software
245 Long Hill Road
Middletown, CT 06457
203-638-2400

Window, Inc.
469 Pleasant Street
Watertown, MA 02171
617-923-9147

Appendix K

Professional Organizations for Computer Educators

American Educational Research Association (AREA)
1230 Seventeenth Street, NW
Washington, DC 20036

Association for Computers in Mathematics and Science Teaching
P.O. Box 4
Austin, TX 78765

Association for Computing Machinery (ACM)
1133 Avenue of The Americas
New York, NY 10036

Association for the Development of Computer-Based Instructional Systems (ADCIS) Computer Center
Western Washington University
Bellingham, WA 98225

Association for Educational Communications and Technology (AECT)
1126 Sixteenth Street NW
Washington, DC 20036

Association for Educational Data Systems (AEDS)
1201 Sixteenth Street NW
Washington, DC 20036

Educational Products Information Exchange (EPIE) Institute
P.O. Box 839
Water Mill, NY 11976

International Council for Computers in Education (ICCE)
University of Oregon
1787 Agate Street
Eugene, OR 97403–1923

Microcomputer Software and Information for Teachers (MicroSIFT)
Northwest Regional Educational Laboratory
300 S. 6th Avenue
Portland, OR 97204

National Council of Teachers of Mathematics (NCTM)
1906 Association Drive
Reston, VA 22091

National Science Teachers Association (NSTA)
1742 Connecticut Avenue NW
Washington, DC 20009

Society for Applied Learning Technology (SALT)
50 Culpepper Street
Warrenton, VA 22186

Softswap
San Mateo County Office of Education
333 Main Street
Redwood City, CA 94063

Technical Education Research Center (TERC)
8 Eliot Street
Cambridge, MA 02138

Appendix L

A New Model for School Leadership

A new model for school leadership

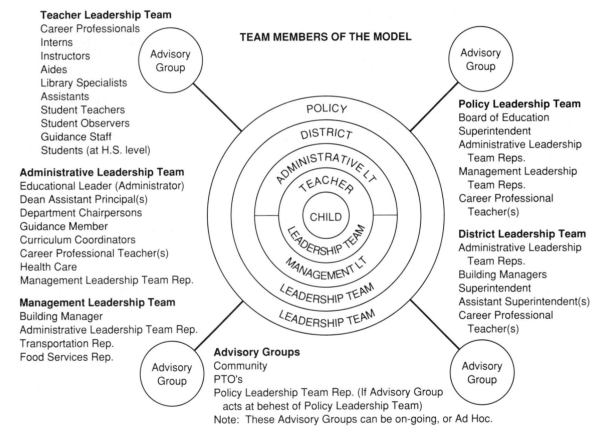

TEAM MEMBERS OF THE MODEL

Teacher Leadership Team
Career Professionals
Interns
Instructors
Aides
Library Specialists
Assistants
Student Teachers
Student Observers
Guidance Staff
Students (at H.S. level)

Administrative Leadership Team
Educational Leader (Administrator)
Dean Assistant Principal(s)
Department Chairpersons
Guidance Member
Curriculum Coordinators
Career Professional Teacher(s)
Health Care
Management Leadership Team Rep.

Management Leadership Team
Building Manager
Administrative Leadership Team Rep.
Transportation Rep.
Food Services Rep.

Policy Leadership Team
Board of Education
Superintendent
Administrative Leadership
  Team Reps.
Management Leadership
  Team Reps.
Career Professional
  Teacher(s)

District Leadership Team
Administrative Leadership
  Team Reps.
Building Managers
Superintendent
Assistant Superintendent(s)
Career Professional
  Teacher(s)

Advisory Groups
Community
PTO's
Policy Leadership Team Rep. (If Advisory Group
  acts at behest of Policy Leadership Team)
Note: These Advisory Groups can be on-going, or Ad Hoc.

Circles in diagram (from outer to inner): POLICY, DISTRICT, ADMINISTRATIVE LT, TEACHER, CHILD, LEADERSHIP TEAM, MANAGEMENT LT, LEADERSHIP TEAM, LEADERSHIP TEAM

Advisory Group (x4)

Glossary

ability grouping Organizing pupils into homogeneous groups according to intellectual ability for instruction

academic freedom The opportunity for a teacher to teach without coercion, censorship, or other restrictive interferences

academic program A program of studies designed primarily to prepare students for college

academic support A category of educational expenditures including library, galleries, audio/visual services, academic computing support, ancillary support, academic administration, personnel development, and course and curriculum development

academy An early American secondary school which stressed practical subjects

accountability Holding schools and teachers responsible for what students learn

accreditation Recognition given to an educational institution that has met accepted standards applied to it by an outside agency

achievement test An examination that measures the extent to which a person has acquired certain information or mastered certain skills, usually as a result of specific instruction

aesthetics Refers to the nature of beauty and judgments about it

affective domain Attitudinal and emotional areas of learning, such as values and feelings

alternative education Unconventional educational experiences for students not adequately served through regular classes; such alternatives include schools without walls, magnet schools, street academies, free schools, and second-chance schools

American Federation of Teachers (AFT) A national organization of teachers primarily concerned with improving educational conditions and protecting teachers' rights

anecdotal record A brief, written report of an individual's exceptional behavior

aptitude The ability to profit from training or instruction of a specified kind

articulation The relationship existing between the different elements of the educational program—the different curricular offerings, the school's program and out-of-school educational activities, and the successive levels of the educational system

associate degree A degree granted for the successful completion of a subbaccalaureate program of studies, usually requiring at least 2 years (or equivalent) of full-time college-level study; includes degrees granted in a cooperative or work/study program

attendance area An administrative unit consisting of the territory from which children may legally attend a given school building

audiovisual material Any device by means of which the learning process may be encouraged or carried on through the sense of hearing and/or the sense of sight

average daily attendance (ADA) The aggregate days attendance of a given school during a reporting period divided by the number of days school is in session during this period. Only days on which the pupils are under the guidance and direction of teachers should be considered as days in session. The average daily attendance for groups of schools having varying lengths of terms is the sum of the average daily attendances obtained for the individual schools.

bachelor's degree   A degree granted for the successful completion of a baccalaureate program of studies, usually requiring at least 4 years (or equivalent) of full-time college-level study; includes degrees granted in a cooperative or work/study program

back to basics   A broad, largely grass roots movement evolving out of a concern for declining test scores and student incompetence in math and reading

BASIC   Beginners All-purpose Symbolic Instruction Code. A high-level language used extensively on microcomputers

basic administrative unit   The local school district, the unit for the operation of elementary and secondary schools or for contracting for school services

behavioral objective   Precise statement of what the learner must do to demonstrate mastery at the end of a prescribed learning task

bilingual education   Educational programs in which both English-speaking and non-English-speaking students participate in a bicultural curriculum using both languages

binary   Any system that is composed of only two alternate states, such as 0 and 1 or on and off, etc.

bit   Binary digit. The smallest unit of information meaningful to a computer, usually represented as 0 or 1. Multiple bits form a byte.

board of education   Constituted at the state and local levels, these agencies are responsible for formulating educational policy. The members are sometimes appointed, but more frequently they are elected at the local level.

boot/boot up   The process of starting up a computer so that it is ready for normal operation

branch   The process within a program of skipping to a nonsequential step or selecting among alternate nonsequential steps

buffer   A storage area or device that can temporarily hold data being transferred from one part of the computer system to another, from one computer to another, or from a computer to a peripheral device

busing   A method for remedying segregation by transporting students to schools that have been racially or ethnically unbalanced

byte   A series of bits, usually seven or eight, that is used to code numbers, letters, and special characters

capital outlay   An expenditure that results in the acquisition of fixed assets or additions to fixed assets, which are presumed to have benefits for more than one year. It is an expenditure for land or existing buildings, improvements of grounds, construction of buildings, additions to buildings, remodeling of buildings, or initial, additional, and replacement of equipment.

career education   The totality of educational experience through which one learns about occupational opportunities and about work

Carnegie unit   A standard of measurement that represents one credit for the completion of a 1-year course

categorial aid   Financial aid to local school districts from state or federal agencies for specific, limited purposes only

certification   The act, on the part of a state department of education, of granting official authorization to a person to accept employment in keeping with the provisions of the credential

Chapter 1 programs   Federally funded programs at the preelementary school level designed to provide learning opportunities for those children who have not had access to environments and experiences conducive to academic achievement

Chief State School Officer   Usually the executive head of a state department of education

child advocacy movement   A movement dedicated to defining, protecting, and ensuring the rights of children

child-centered instruction   Instruction that is designed for the interests, abilities, and needs of individual students

chip   A small piece of semiconducting material (such as silicon) upon which electrical circuits are etched

class size The membership of a class at a given date

classroom environment The physical structure, emotional climate, aesthetic characteristics, and learning resources of a school classroom

classroom teacher A staff member assigned the professional activities of instructing students in classroom situations, for which the daily student attendance figures for the school system are kept

COBOL Common Business Oriented Language. A high-level language typically used in business

collective bargaining A procedure, usually specified by written agreement, for resolving disagreements on salaries, hours, and conditions of employment between employers and employees through negotiations

command An instruction to a computer system to perform a specific task

common school A school open to the general public and providing similar education to all classes

competency The demonstrated ability to perform specified acts at a particular level of skill or accuracy

competency-based certification The general process by which the state (or agency or organization authorized by the state) provides a credential to an individual. Processes may require individuals to demonstrate a mastery of minimum or essential generic and specialization competencies and other related criteria adopted by

the board through a comprehensive written examination and through other procedures that may be prescribed by the board of educational examiners.

competency-based education Learning based upon highly specialized concepts, skills, and attitudes related directly to some endeavor

comprehensive high school A secondary school which attempts to cater to the needs of all students by offering more than one course of specialization in its program

compulsory education School attendance which is required by law on the theory that it is for the benefit of the commonwealth to educate all the people

computer An electronic device consisting of interrelated components that can accept, process, and display data under program control

computer-assisted instruction (CAI) Direct two-way teaching/ learning communication between a student and programmed instructional material stored in a computer

computer literacy Term used to describe the knowledge and skills necessary to function adequately in an environment utilizing computer and information technology

computer network Connected computers that have the ability to exchange information

computer program A series of commands that tells a computer to do a specific thing or series of things

computer science A group of instructional programs that describes computer and information sciences, including computer programming, data processing, and information systems

consolidation The act of forming an enlarged school by uniting smaller schools in order to provide better school facilities and increased educational opportunities

content Subject matter

continuing education An extension of opportunities for study and training following completion or withdrawal from full-time high school and/or college programs

cultural bias Accepting one's own cultural values as valid for all

cultural pluralism A way of describing a society made up of many different cultural groups coming together to form a unified whole

curriculum All educational experiences under supervision of the school

dame school A low-level primary school in the colonial and early national periods usually conducted by an untrained woman in her own home

data A general term meaning any and all information, facts, numbers, letters, and symbols which can be acted on or produced by a computer

data base Information stored in an organized system of electronically accessible files

day-care center A place or institution charged with caring for children

decentralization A process whereby some higher central source of responsibility and authority assigns certain responsibilities and authority to subordinate positions

de facto segregation The segregation of students resulting from circumstances such as housing patterns rather than from school policy or law

de jure segregation The segregation of students on the basis of law, school policy, or a practice designed to accomplish such separation

desegregation The process of correcting past practices of racial or any other form of illegal segregation

differentiated staffing Education personnel, selected, educated, and deployed so as to make optimum use of their abilities, interests, preparation, and commitments; it gives them greater opportunity and autonomy in guiding their own professional growth.

disk or diskette A round piece of magnetic coated material, either rigid metal or flexible (floppy) plastic, used to store data with greater density, speed, and reliability than is available on cassettes

disk drive A computer peripheral that can write data to and read data from a removable diskette

display A method of representing computer information in visual form. The most common ways of representing computer information are via CRTs and printed paper.

DOS Any Disk Operating System. Also part of the name of specific systems such as MS-DOS or DOS 3.3

downtime Any period of time when the computer is not available or not working

due process The procedural requirements that must be followed in such areas as student and teacher discipline and placement in special education programs. It exists to safeguard individuals from arbitrary, capricious, or unreasonable policies, practices, or actions.

early childhood education Any systematic effort to teach a child before the normal period of schooling begins

eclecticism Drawing elements from several educational philosophies or methods

educable child A child of borderline or moderately severe mental retardation who is capable of achieving only a limited degree of proficiency in basic learnings, and who usually must be instructed in a special class

educational attainment The highest grade or regular school attended and completed

educational technology Scientific application of knowledge of educational institutions for purposes of instruction or institutional management

educational television (ETV) Educational programs in the broadest sense—cultural, informative, and instructive—that are usually telecast by stations outside the school system and received on standard television sets by the general public

elementary school Grades 1–6 inclusive; grades 1–8 inclusive in some school systems

enrollment The total number of students registered in a given school unit at a given time, generally in the fall of a year

equal educational opportunity Giving every student the educational opportunity to fully develop whatever talents, interests, and abilities she or he may have without regard to race, color, national origin, sex, handicap, or economic status

essentialism The doctrine that there is an indispensable, common core of culture (knowledge, skills, attitudes, ideals, etc.) that should be taught systematically to all, with rigorous standards of achievement

evaluation Testing and measurement to determine the effectiveness, quality, and progress of learning and instruction

exceptional learner One who deviates from the normal intellectually, physically, socially, or emotionally in growth and development so markedly that she or he cannot receive maximum educational benefits without modifications in the regular school program

existentialism A philosophy that emphasizes the ability of an individual to determine the course and nature of her or his own life

expenditures per pupil Charges incurred for a particular period of time divided by a student unit of measure, such as average daily attendance or average daily membership

expulsion Permanent withdrawal of a student's privilege to attend a certain school or class

file A group of related records, such as an inventory

flexible scheduling A technique for organizing time more effectively in schools to meet the needs of instruction by dividing the day into uniform time modules which can be combined to fit the task at hand

FORTRAN Formula Translator. A high-level language particularly suited to mathematical and scientific applications

full potential The talents, skills, and abilities an individual can acquire and/or develop if provided with the proper learning experiences and environments

general education Those learnings which should be the common possession of all educated persons

gifted learner The term most frequently applied to those with exceptional intellectual ability, but may also refer to learners with outstanding ability in athletics, leadership, music, creativity, and so forth

graded school system A division of schools into groups of students according to the curriculum or the ages of pupils as in the six elementary grades

handicapped learner One who is mentally retarded, hard of hearing, deaf, speech-impaired, visually handicapped, seriously disturbed emotionally, physically handicapped, or otherwise health-impaired

hard copy Printed output from a computer system

hard disk A rigid magnetic disk that is capable of retaining very large quantities of information

hardware Mechanical and electronic devices that aid in classroom instruction

heterogeneous grouping A group or class consisting of students who show normal variation in ability or performance

high school graduate A person who received formal recognition from the school authorities for completing the prescribed high school course of study; excluded equivalency certificates

homogeneous grouping The classification of pupils for the purpose of forming instructional groups having a relatively high degree of similarity in regard to certain factors that affect learning.

hornbook A single printed page containing the alphabet, syllables, a prayer, and other simple words, and which was used in colonial times as the beginner's first book or preprimer. Hornbooks were attached to a wooden paddle for ease in carrying, and were covered with a thin sheet of transparent horn for protection

independent school A nonpublic institution governed by a board of trustees that depends almost entirely on private funds—tuition, gifts, and grants

individualized education program (IEP) The mechanism through which a handicapped child's special needs are identified; goals, objectives, and services are outlined; and methods for evaluating progress are delineated

input/output Called I/O for short, this is a general term for (1) the external equipment (such as a modem or printer) connected to a computer and (2) the two-way exchange of information that goes on between the computer and that equipment

in-service education Continuing education for teachers who are actually teaching, or who are in service

instructional materials center (IMC) An area where students can withdraw books, newspapers, pamphlets, and magazines, and have access to sound tapes, slides, and films; spaces are usually provided for the learner to use these materials

instructional staff   Number of positions during the school year. In local schools includes all public elementary and secondary (junior and senior high) day-school positions (or full-time equivalents) that are in the nature of teaching or in the improvement of the teaching-learning situation. Includes supervisors of instruction, principals, teachers, guidance personnel, librarians, psychological personnel, and other instructional staff.

instructional technology   The application of scientific method and knowledge to teaching and learning either with or without machines, and which is commonly responsive to the learning needs of individual students

instructional television (ITV) Lessons telecast specifically for educational institutions and received usually only by special arrangements and on special equipment

integrated software   A single program that can perform more than one major application and can transfer information among the applications

integration (racial)   The process of mixing students of different races in schools to overcome segregation

interest centers   Usually associated with an open classroom, such centers provide for independent student activities related to a specific subject

international education   The study of educational, social, political, and economic forces in international relations with special emphasis on the role and potentialities of educational forces; also included programs to further the development of nations

joystick   An input device that allows the user to control the movement of the cursor on the screen by the hand movement of a stick or level

junior high school   A separately organized and administered secondary school intermediate between the elementary and senior high schools, usually including grades 7, 8, and 9 (in a 6-3-3 plan) or grades 7 and 8 (in a 6-2-4 plan).

keyboard   An input device that allows alphanumeric input to a computer by striking keys

kindergarten   A term coined by Froebel who began the first schools for children aged, four, five, and six years

land-grant college   A college maintained to carry out the purposes of the first Morrill Act of 1862, and supplementary legislation granting public lands to states for the establishment of colleges that provide practical education, such as agriculture and mechanic arts

laser printer   A nonimpact printer that uses laser technology to produce high quality text and graphic output

Latin Grammar School   A classical secondary school with a curriculum consisting largely of Latin and Greek, the purpose of which was preparation for college

learning   A change of behavior as a result of experience

learning resources center   A specially designed space containing a wide range of supplies and equipment for the use of individual students and small groups pursuing independent study

least restrictive environment The program best suited to meet a handicapped child's special needs while remaining as close as possible to the regular educational program

logo   A computer language that is based on the teaching of the Swiss psychologist Jean Piaget and emphasizes learning by discovery in a computer-based learning environment

mainstreaming   A plan by which exceptional children receive education in the regular classroom as much of the time as possible

memory   The capacity of a computer to store information temporarily or permanently in the form of patterns of binary 1s and 0s

mentally handicapped student   A student whose mental powers lack maturity or are deficient in such measure as to be a hindrance to normal achievement

mental retardation   Below average intellectual functioning

menu   A list of commands that most ready-made programs will display on request

merit pay   Teacher pay based on evaluation of classroom teaching. Additional remuneration for outstanding teachers

methodology   Procedure used to teach the content or discipline

microcomputer   Small computer often used for teaching and learning, administration, and support services in the school

microteaching   A clinical approach to teacher training in which the teacher candidate teaches a small group of students for a brief time while concentrating on a specific teaching skill

middle school   A type of two-to-four year school organization containing various combinations of the middle grades (commonly grades 5 to 8), and serving as an intermediate unit between the elementary school and the high school

minicourse   A short, self-contained instructional sequence

minimum competency testing Exit level tests designed to ascertain whether students have achieved basic levels of performance in such areas as reading, writing, and computation

modem   An input/output device that transfers information, enabling a computer to send and receive data over a telephone line

motivation   Impetus that causes one to act

mouse   A hand-held input device that is moved on a flat surface to position the screen cursor

multicultural education Education for cultural understanding and accceptance

multi-purpose high school Features comprehensive, diversified offerings to meet the needs of all the students regardless of their special interests, aptitudes, and capacities

national assessment   A massive national testing program which helps ascertain the effectiveness of American education and how well it is retained

National Council for the Accreditation of Teacher Education (NCATE)   An organization that evaluates teacher education programs in many colleges and universities, and grants accreditation if appropriate

National Education Association (NEA)   The largest organization of educators, the NEA is concerned with the overall improvement of education, and of the conditions of educators

nongraded school   A type of school organization in which grade lines are eliminated for a sequence of two or more years

nonverbal communication   The act of transmitting and/or receiving messages through any means not having to do with oral or written language, such as eye contact, facial expressions, or body language

normal school   Historically, the first American institution devoted exclusively to teacher training

nursery school   A school that offers supervised educational experiences for prekindergarten children, giving them opportunities to express themselves and develop relationships within their peer group

objective   Purpose or goal

open classroom   A modern educational innovation in which self-contained classrooms are replaced with an open plan with individualized instruction and freedom for the child to move about the school

open enrollment   The practice of permitting students to attend the school of their choice within their school system

open space school   A school building without interior walls

outdoor education   Activity and study in an outdoor setting

output   Information sent from the computer after processing to any peripheral device

overachievement   Performing above the level normally expected on the basis of ability measures

paraprofessional   One who serves as an aide, assisting the teacher in the classroom

parochial school   An institution operated and controlled by a religious denomination

pedagogy   The scientific study of education

perennialism   Educational philosophy emphasizing constancy and unchanging truths

performance-based education Learning designed to produce actual accomplishment as distinguished from knowing

philosophy of education Principles that guide professional educators in decision making

pragmatism   A philosophy that maintains that the value and truth of ideas are tested by their practical consequences

printer   A device that produces a computer printout

private school or institution   A school or institution which is controlled by an individual or agency other than a state, a subdivision of a state, or the federal government, which is usually supported primarily by other than public funds, and the operation of whose program rests with other than publicly elected or appointed officials

program   (1) A set of instructions that tell the computer to do something; (2) To prepare the set of instructions

programmer   A person who writes computer programs

progressive education   An educational philosophy emphasizing democracy, the importance of creative and meaningful activity, the real needs of students, and the relationship between school and community

progressive tax   A tax frequently scaled to the ability of the taxpayer to pay; the income tax is a progressive tax

progressivism   Educational philosophy in which learning focuses on the experiences of the child while she or he is acquiring the content of the curriculum

property tax   A tax based on the value of property, both real estate and personal

psychomotor domain   Motor skill area of learning

psychomotor learning   The acquisition of muscular development directly related to mental processes

PTA   Parent Teacher Association; officially the National Congress of Parents and Teachers

Public Law 94–142   A federal law mandating equal educational opportunity for handicapped persons

pupil-teacher ratio   The enrollment of pupils at a given period of time, divided by the full-time equivalent number of classroom teachers serving these pupils during the same period

racial bias   The degree to which an individual's beliefs and behavior are prejudiced on the basis of race

racial discrimination   Any action that limits or denies a person or group of persons opportunities, privileges, roles, or rewards on the basis of race

racism   The collection of attitudes, beliefs, and behavior that results from the assumption that one race is superior to other races

RAM   Random Access Memory. Memory chips that can be both written to and read from by the computer.

regressive tax   A tax that affects low income groups disproportionately; the sales tax is a regressive tax

reorganization   The act of legally changing the designation of a school district; changing the geographical areas of a school district or incorporating a part or all of a school district with an adjoining district

scanning   The process of transferring information from a printed page directly to a computer system

school-based management   A relatively new concept in which authority is given by a school district to a school or schools within the district empowering the school(s) to decide, for example, how they spend money, allocate staff and organize instruction providing teachers with the opportunity to participate in making decisions for the operations of the local school—a local council made up of a principal, teachers, and in some instances parents, is the governance unit for the local school

school district   An educational agency at the local level that exists primarily to operate public schools or to contract for public school services. This term is used synonymously with the terms *local basic administrative unit* and *local education agency.*

school finance Ways in which monies are raised and allocated to schools

school superintendent The chief administrator of a school system, responsible for implementing and enforcing the school board's policies, rules, and regulations, as well as the state and federal requirements

secondary school Junior and senior high school; usually grades 7–12 inclusive

self-contained classroom A form of classroom organization in which the same teacher conducts all or nearly all the instruction in all or most subjects in the same classroom for all or most of the school day

self-instructional device A term used to include instructional materials that can be used by the student to induce learning without necessarily requiring additional human instructional assistance, including computers, programmed textbooks, and other devices

self-perception/self-concept Whom does the individual perceive himself or herself to be?

separate but equal A legal doctrine that holds that equality of treatment is accorded when the races are provided substantially equal facilities, even though those facilities are separate.

sexism The collection of attitudes, beliefs, and behavior that results from the assumption that one sex is superior to the other

software Programs that are used to direct a computer to perform specified tasks

special education A school program designed for the child who is exceptional, that is, either gifted or below normal in ability

spreadsheet An electronic tabular workspace that can be used to enter and manipulate data

state aid Funding provided to local school districts out of tax revenue raised by the state; frequently used in an effort to provide equality of opportunity within a state

subject-centered school or curriculum A curriculum organization in which learning activities and content are planned around subject fields of knowledge, such as history and science

supervisory staff Principals, assistant principals, and supervisors of instruction (does not include superintendents or assistant superintendents).

teacher aide A lay person who assists teachers with clerical work, library duties, housekeeping duties, noninstructional supervision, and other nonprofessional tasks.

Teacher Corps A federally funded program that gives teachers and student teachers opportunities to work with disadvantaged children in their homes and communities while attending courses and seminars on the special problems they encounter

teacher production Related to the number of new teachers prepared by colleges and universities

teacher shortage The number of teaching positions vacant, abolished, or withdrawn because a candidate was sought and not found, courses were eliminated because of budget cuts or administrative decisions not to offer courses in a given field, a teacher was laid off, or a position was filled by a temporary substitute

teaching center Combination library, workshop, and laboratory with rich resources to help teachers solve problems and grow professionally

team teaching A plan by which several teachers, organized into a team with a leader, provide the instruction for a larger group of children than would usually be found in a self-contained classroom

technical education A program of vocational instruction that ordinarily includes the study of the sciences and mathematics underlying a technology, as well as the methods, skills, and materials commonly used and the services performed in the technology. Technical education prepares individuals for positions—such as draftsman or lab technician—in the occupational area between the skilled craftsman and the professional person

tenure A system of school employment in which educators, after having served a probationary period, retain their positions indefinitely unless dismissed for legally specified reasons through clearly established procedures

terminal An input/output device usually consisting of a keyboard for entering information and a screen for displaying output

total expenditures Includes all current expenditures, capital outlay, and interest on the school debt

tracking The method of placing students according to their ability level in homogeneous classes or learning experiences

ungraded school Synonymous with nongraded school

values Principles that guide an individual in terms of personal decision making

values clarification A model, comprised of various strategies, that encourages students to express and clarify their values on different topics

videodisc A round plastic platter that can retain data and audio and video material in digital form

vocational education Training which is intended to prepare the student for a particular job or to give a basic skill needed in several vocations

voucher plan A means of financing schooling whereby funds are allocated to students' parents who then purchase education for their children in any public or private school

word processing The application of computers to the creating, manipulating, storing, and printing of written material

work-study program Program that combines part-time classroom study with gainful employment in industry or in the community

Credits

Chapter 1

Fig. 1.1 These data were collected as part of the annual survey of teachers conducted by Louis Harris and Associates, Inc., for Metropolitan Life Insurance Company. Reprinted by permission.

Chapter 2

Fig. 2.1 Source: Division of Teacher Education, Kentucky Department of Education. *Kentucky Teacher Preparation and Certification Handbook.* (Frankfort, KY: Superintendent of Public Instruction, 1976), 37. **Fig. 2.2** From Charles W. Case, Judith Lanier, and Cecil G. Miskel, "The Holmes Group Report: Impetus for Gaining Professional Status for Teachers," *Journal of Teacher Education,* 41, July/August 1986. Copyright © 1986 American Association for Teacher Education, Washington, DC. Reprinted by permission. **Excerpt, page 38** From *A Nation Prepared: Teachers for the 21st Century.* Copyright © 1986 Carnegie Forum on Education and the Economy, Washington, DC. **Excerpt, page 39** National Governors' Association. **Excerpt, page 40** National Governors' Association. **Excerpt, page 41** Reprinted with permission of the Education Commission of the States, *The Next Wave,* 1987.

Chapter 3

Excerpt, page 71 From "Discipline vs. Self-Discipline: What's the Difference?" *Self-Discipline: Helping Students Succeed,* 4–5. Copyright © American Association of School Administrators, Arlington, VA. Reprinted by permission. **Fig. 3.5** From National Center for the Study of Corporal Punishment and Alternatives in the Schools-Temple University, Philadelphia, PA. Reprinted by permission.

Chapter 4

Fig. 4.1 Lieberman, Ann. (February 1986). "Collaborative Work." *Educational Leadership* 43, (February 1986), 4–8. Reprinted with permission of the Association for Supervision and Curriculum Development. Copyright © by ASCD. All rights reserved. Interaction Observation Form designed by Georgea M. Sparks, Janet Kiersted, and Mae Gundlach.

Chapter 5

Fig. 5.5 From *NEA Today,* September 1987, 7. Copyright © 1987 National Education Association, Washington, DC. Reprinted by permission.

Chapter 6

Excerpt, pages 129–130 From *NEA Research/Gallup Opinion Polls. Public and K–12 Teacher Members,* 1986, 6–7. Copyright © 1986 National Education Association, Washington, DC. Reprinted by permission. **Fig. 6.2** From *Survey and Analysis of Salary Trends, 1987.* Used by permission of the American Federation of Teachers, AFL-CIO, Washington, DC. **Fig. 6.3** From National Education Association, "Attitudes Toward the Profession," *Status of the American Public School Teacher 1985–86,* 1987, 59. Copyright © 1987 National Education Association, Washington, DC. Reprinted by permission.

Chapter 7

Fig. 7.1 Source: *NEA Handbook 1987–88.* Washington, DC: National Education Association. Used by permission. **Fig. 7.2** From AFL-CIO Constitution, July 1986, page 23. Copyright © 1986 American Federation of Teachers, Washington, DC. Reprinted by permission. **Fig. 7.3** American Federation of Teachers AFL-CIO, Washington, DC. Reprinted by permission.

Chapter 9

Fig. 9.5 From Barbara Bates, "Sex Bias in Language: An Issue Worth Talking About," *Thresholds in Education,* pp. 28–29, February 1978. Copyright © 1978 Thresholds in Education Foundation, Dekalb, IL. Reprinted by permission. **Fig. 9.6** From "Suicidal Students," *NEA Today,* page 5, January/February 1985. Copyright © 1985 National Education Association, Washington, DC. Reprinted by permission. **Excerpt, page 216** From *Why School Health,* 1987, 4–6, 9. Copyright © 1987 American Association of School Administrators, Arlington, VA. Reprinted by permission. **Excerpt, page 216** From Robert D. Allers, "Children from Single-Parent Homes," *Today's Education, 1982–1983 Annual,* 68–70. Copyright © 1983 National Education Association, Washington, DC. Reprinted by permission. **Fig. 9.9** Reprinted with permission from *Education Week.* Volume VII, Number 9, November 4, 1987.

Chapter 10

Fig. 10.2 From E. P. Cubberley, *The History of Education* (Boston: Houghton Mifflin Company, 1920), p. 699. Copyright Board of Trustees of Leland Stanford Junior University. Stanford, California. Used by permission.

Chapter 14

Figs. 14.1 and 14.3 From James W. Brown, Richard B. Lewis, and Fred F. Harcleroad, *A–V Instruction: Technology, Media, and Methods.* Copyright © 1977 McGraw-Hill Publishing Company, New York, NY. Reprinted by permission.

Chapter 15

Figs. 15.1 and 15.2 From William J. Bramble and Emanuel J. Mason, with Paul Berg, *Computers in School.* Copyright © 1985 McGraw-Hill Publishing Company, New York, NY. Reprinted by permission. **Fig. 15.3** From *NEA Today,* 7, March 1987. Copyright © 1987 National Education Association, Washington, DC. Reprinted by permission. **Fig. 15.4** From *Today's Education, 1986–1987,* 19, 1987. Copyright © 1987 National Education Association, Washington, DC. Reprinted by permission. **Fig. 15.5** *The College Connector* by James H. Johnson. Reprinted by permission.

Chapter 16

Excerpt, pages 397–399 From Bobette Reed and William L. Dandridge, *Minority Leaders for Independent Schools.* Copyright © National Association of Independent Schools, Boston, MA. Reprinted by permission.

Illustrations by Precision Graphics

Figs. 1.1, 2.1, 2.2, 3.2, 3.3, 3.4, 3.5, 3.6, 4.1, 5.2, 5.3, 5.4, 5.5, 6.1, 6.2, 6.3, 7.2, 8.1, 9.1, 9.3, 9.4, 9.5, 9.6, 9.7, 9.9, 10.1, 13.1, 14.2, 14.3, 15.1, 15.2, 15.3, 15.4, 16.3, 16.4, 18.1, p. 478, p. 482.

Photo Credits

Part Opener 1: © James Shaffer; **page 14:** © Jeff Thiebauth/Lightwave; **page 18:** © Robert Kalman/The Image Works; **page 32:** © Gail B. Int Veldt; **page 44:** © Laimute E. Druskie; **page 79:** © Oscar Palmquist/Lightwave; **page 87:** © Elizabeth Crews/The Image Works; **page 93, Part Opener 2:** © David M. Grossman; **page 112:** © James Ballard; **page 119:** © Carolyn A. McKeone; **page 138:** © Elizabeth Crews/The Image Works; **page 140:** © Jean-Claude Lejeune; **page 150:** © Chicago Teachers' Union; **page 152:** © National Education Association; **Part Opener 3:** © James Shaffer; **page 174:** © David Strickler; **page 185:** © National Education Association; **page 202:** © David M. Grossman; **page 220:** © James Ballard; **pages 228, 229, 230, 231, 232, 234, 236, 238, 239, 245 (both):** courtesy of History of Education Research Center, Northern Illinois University, DeKalb, Illinois; **page 257:** © David M. Grossman; **page 258:** © David Strickler; **Part Opener 4:** © Carolyn A. McKeone; **page 275:** © Jean-Claude Lejeune; **page 282:** © Hildegard Adler; **page 293:** © Jean-Claude Lejeune; **page 305:** © James Ballard; **page 340:** © James Shaffer; **page 342:** © Hildegard Adler; **page 353:** © David M. Grossman; **Part Opener 5:** © Oscar Palmquist/Lightwave; **page 388:** © Jean-Claude Lejeune; **page 390:** © Bob Daemmrich/The Image Works; **page 414:** © UPI/Bettmann Newsphotos; **page 426:** © Carolyn A. McKeone; **page 445:** © Mark Antman/The Image Works; **page 452:** © Gail B. Int Veldt.

Index